Sexual Harassment Law

Sexual Harassment Law

History, Cases, and Practice

SECOND EDITION

Jennifer Ann Drobac

SAMUEL R. ROSEN PROFESSOR OF LAW, INDIANA UNIVERSITY,
ROBERT H. McKINNEY SCHOOL OF LAW

Carrie N. Baker

PROFESSOR OF THE STUDY OF WOMEN & GENDER
SMITH COLLEGE

Rigel C. Oliveri

ISABELLE WADE AND PAUL C. LYDA PROFESSOR OF LAW
UNIVERSITY OF MISSOURI SCHOOL OF LAW

CAROLINA ACADEMIC PRESS
Durham, North Carolina

ISBN 978-1-5310-0936-6
eISBN 978-1-5310-0937-3
LCCN 2019950630

Carolina Academic Press
700 Kent Street
Durham, North Carolina 27701
Telephone (919) 489-7486
Fax (919) 493-5668
E-mail: cap@cap-press.com
www.cap-press.com

To the people who help to prevent and prosecute sex-based harassment and for all the brave survivors who have announced #MeToo.
Jennifer Ann Drobac

To my students. You give me hope for the future.
Carrie N. Baker

To Griffin and Shennie: The future is yours. May it be better.
Rigel C. Oliveri

Contents

Table of Cases

Preface

SEXUAL HARASSMENT LAW: HISTORY, CASES & PRACTICE is the second edition of Professor Jennifer Ann Drobac's SEXUAL HARASSMENT LAW: HISTORY, CASES & THEORY. That book was the first comprehensive textbook to explore sex-based harassment law for a full-semester law school course. For this second edition, Professors Carrie N. Baker and Rigel C. Oliveri join Professor Drobac. Together, we bring our unique scholarly talents, professional experiences, and shared dedication to civil rights to create a textbook accessible to college students, graduate students, and others.

This new edition traces the development of American law, practice strategies, and legal reasoning concerning sexual harassment in employment, education, housing, prisons, and the military, updated with recent cases. This edition also explores the #MeToo movement, which has made sexual harassment a much-discussed topic everywhere. In its discussion of statutory law, case law, and legal reasoning, this edition acknowledges the usefulness of traditional legal analysis of sex-based oppression. It also, however, recognizes the experiences, perspectives, and creativity of parties and lawyers involved in sexual harassment litigation and remediation. It considers how the law successfully curbs abuses or how and why it fails to address sex-based abuses of power.

In addition to careful analysis of relevant law, this book also examines topics such as street harassment, online harassment, press coverage, extralegal responses to misconduct, and mandatory arbitration, among others. Ethics hypotheticals at the end of each chapter incorporate the study of professional responsibility into this examination of sexual harassment law.

This book is divided into 10 chapters. Chapter 1 examines the legal and theoretical developments of sexual harassment law in the 1970s and 1980s. It covers the early interpretation of the 1964 Civil Rights Act and the initial rejection of the notion that Title VII prohibits sexual harassment. It follows the shifting tide that resulted in the understanding that sexual harassment constitutes discrimination "because . . . of sex." It credits, in part, early feminist activists and scholars who facilitated that shift and the necessary recognition of the plight of many female workers. Chapter 2 introduces the concept of intersectionality—how gender, race, class, and other aspects of identity intersect to shape people's experience of sexual harassment— through the examination of the Anita Hill/Clarence Thomas hearings in 1991. It also reviews contemporary examples of the intersectionality of sex-based oppression, such as immigrant farmworker women and low-wage restaurant workers.

Delving into law and practice, Chapters 3 and 4 explore each element of the plaintiff's prima facie case. Chapter 5 explains liability damages. These chapters demonstrate how courts have interpreted the law narrowly to deny relief to many harassed individuals. Chapter 6 surveys sexual harassment law in the educational context under Title IX of the 1972 Educational Amendments to the Civil Rights Act, which courts have interpreted even more narrowly than Title VII. Chapter 7 addresses sexual harassment law in housing under the Fair Housing Act and Chapter 8 covers sexual harassment in the highly regimented environments of prisons and the military.

Introducing new topics, Chapter 9 examines street harassment and online harassment. Chapter 9 reconsiders traditional defenses, analyzing defendants' assertion of First Amendment free speech protection and the exploitation of plaintiffs' sexual history. This Chapter also highlights how media coverage of sexual harassment cases can influence the course of litigation. Finally, Chapter 10 explores the rise of the #MeToo movement and calls for reform of sexual harassment law to expand coverage, close loopholes, and make the law more effective.

We offer this textbook because we believe that sexual harassment law merits full semester coverage. The pervasiveness of sexual harassment, as well as the many substantive law fields that influence its redress, prompts in-depth analysis. This edition reflects the evolution of the study of sexual harassment law. Because we also see a continuing need for ethics education, in this edition we place an ethics hypothetical at the end of each chapter. These hypos are based on real experiences from our years of sexual harassment law practice. We have also retained selected theoretical excerpts and quotes that provide a variety of different perspectives regarding sexual harassment and the legal response to it. This book necessarily reflects our philosophy that one cannot separate the "law" from legal theory or from practical application. Only an integrated approach to legal problems produces the most effective tool for managing our society and personal relations. Thus, we incorporate legal theory and practice considerations into every chapter. We debated calling this book *Sex-Based Harassment: History, Cases, and Practice* because sexual harassment law was originally a common law creation from the sex-based discrimination prohibition in Title VII. In the end, we chose to stay with the more common appellation to avoid confusion and because sexual harassment law has evolved to become a substantive legal field in its own right, distinct and distinguishable from other types of antidiscrimination law.

We thank the many contributors to both editions of this textbook. For this edition in particular, we want to thank the Indiana University McKinney Law Library Faculty: Professors Miriam A. Murphy, Susan David deMaine, and Benjamin J. Keele. We are also grateful for the excellent research assistance we received from Kristen Coffey, Jessica Dickinson, Alexia Lopez, Deborah P. Morton, Nick Moscalick, and

Emma Seymour. Finally, we thank Julie C. Ardelean and Rachel Renee Mitchell for their careful editorial work and Emma Seymour for her help on the index.

In the edited cases, articles, and other materials, ellipses indicate omitted footnotes and citations. We omitted most footnotes and citations. When we retained footnotes from original sources, original footnote numbering was preserved.

Finally, we invite comments and suggestions regarding this book. You can reach us through Professor Jennifer Drobac, Indiana University Robert H. McKinney School of Law, 530 W. New York St., Indianapolis, IN 46202-3225, (317) 278-4777, jdrobac@iu.edu.

JENNIFER ANN DROBAC
Indianapolis, Indiana

CARRIE N. BAKER
Northampton, Massachusetts

RIGEL C. OLIVERI
Columbia, Missouri

Acknowledgments

Burstyn, Linda, *The Weinstein Effect*, Ms. Magazine, Spring 2018, pages 21–25. Reprinted with permission from *Ms.* magazine, © 2018.

Chamallas, Martha, *The New Gender Panic: Reflections on Sex Scandals and the Military*, 83 Minn. L. Rev. 305 (1998). Reprinted with the permission of the author.

Grossman, Joanna, *The Culture of Compliance: The Triumph of Form Over Substance in Sexual Harassment Law*, 26 Harv. Women's L.J. 3, 2003. Reprinted with the permission of the author.

Mazur, Diane, *Women, Responsibility, and the Military*, 74 Notre Dame L. Rev. 1 (1998). Volume 74, Number 1, Notre Dame Law Review (October 1998) pages 1-45. Reprinted with permission. © by Notre Dame Law Review, University of Notre Dame.

Oppenheimer, David Benjamin, *Exacerbating the Exasperating: Title VII Liability of Employers for Sexual Harassment Committed by Their Supervisors*, 81 Cornell L. Rev. 66, 81-88, 124-129 (1995). Reprinted with the permission of the author.

Raghu, Maya and Joanna Suriani, *#MeTooWhatNext: Strengthening Workplace Sexual Harassment Protections and Accountability*, National Women's Law Center, December 21, 2017. Reprinted with the permission of the National Women's Law Center.

Robertson, James, *Cruel & Unusual Punishment in U.S. Prisons*, 36 Am. Crim. L. Rev. 1 (1999). Reprinted with the permission of the author, © 1999.

Rogers, Paul, *2 Agencies Investigating ex SCO Chief*, San Jose Merc. News, February 12, 1993. Reprinted with the permission of the *San Jose Mercury News* and the author.

Rogers, Paul, *Another Worker Targets Michels An Ex-aide Charges Him with Sexual Harassment*, San Jose Merc. News, December 16, 1992. Reprinted with the permission of the *San Jose Mercury News* and the author.

Rogers, Paul, *Software Firm Founder Accused of Harassment*, San Jose Merc. News, December 5, 1992. Reprinted with the permission of the *San Jose Mercury News* and the author.

About the Authors

Jennifer Ann Drobac, M.A., J.D., J.S.D.
Professor Drobac is the Samuel R. Rosen Professor of Law at the Indiana University Robert H. McKinney School of Law. She holds her doctoral (J.S.D.) and J.D. degrees from Stanford Law School and Master's and Bachelor's degrees in History from Stanford University.

Her scholarly work has been published in a variety of law reviews and journals. In 2005, she finished the first edition of this textbook, *Sexual Harassment Law: History, Cases and Theory* (Carolina Academic Press, 2005). In 2016, she offered her second book *Sexual Exploitation of Teenagers: Adolescent Development, Discrimination, and Consent Law* (University of Chicago Press, 2016) (rated "Essential," the highest rating by *Choice*, a publication of the Association of College and Research Libraries). She is currently working on another monograph project, *The Myth of Consent*, under contract for publication with Cambridge University Press (anticipated 2020). This book will analyze the neuroscientific and psychosocial aspects of decision making by vulnerable adults and offer legal solutions for reform.

Since the beginning of October 2017, Professor Drobac has given more than 120 interviews to media outlets concerning sexual harassment, #MeToo, and a number of high-profile cases. Her comments have appeared in *The Washington Post*, *The New York Times*, *Vox*, and *MarketWatch*, to name just a few.

From 1992 to 2001, she practiced law in California, focusing on sexual harassment law litigation, and from 1997 to 2000, she served as a lecturer at Stanford Law School. Following law school, she clerked for the Honorable Barefoot Sanders, U.S. District Court for the Northern District of Texas.

Carrie N. Baker, J.D., Ph.D.
Professor Baker is a Professor and the Director of the Program for the Study of Women and Gender at Smith College in Northampton, Massachusetts. Baker has a Bachelor of Arts degree in philosophy from Yale University, a Juris Doctor degree from Emory University School of Law, and Master of Arts and Doctor of Philosophy degrees from Emory University's Institute of Women's Studies. She was editor-in-chief of the *Emory Law Journal* while in law school and later served as a law clerk to United States District Court Judge Marvin H. Shoob in Atlanta, Georgia.

Baker's research and teaching centers on gender, law, public policy, and feminist social movements, with a focus on sexual harassment, sex trafficking, and reproductive rights and justice. Her first book, *The Women's Movement Against Sexual Harassment* (Cambridge University Press, 2008), won the National Women's Studies Association 2008 Sara A. Whaley book prize. This book examines how a diverse grassroots social movement created public policy on sexual harassment in the 1970s and 1980s. Baker's second book, *Fighting the US Youth Sex Trade: Gender, Race and Politics* (Cambridge University Press, 2018), tells the story of activism against youth involvement in the sex trade in the United States between 1970 and 2015. Baker has published articles in a range of journals, including the *Journal of Women, Politics, and Policy*; the *Journal of Women's History*; the *Journal of Human Trafficking*; the *Journal of Law and Inequality*, and *Emory Law Journal*. Baker is a regular writer for *Ms.* magazine and serves on the editorial board of the journal *Meridians: feminism, race, transnationalism*.

Rigel C. Oliveri, J.D.
Professor Oliveri is the Isabelle Wade and Paul C. Lyda Professor of Law at the University of Missouri. She holds a Bachelor of Arts in Political and Social Thought from the University of Virginia and a Juris Doctor degree from Stanford Law School, where she was elected to the Order of the Coif.

Professor Oliveri is a nationally recognized expert on fair housing law. Her scholarship focuses on housing discrimination, residential segregation, zoning and property rights, and sexual harassment. Her published work has appeared in a number of law reviews, journals, and books. She was recently featured in a national program put on by the Department of Housing and Urban Development on sexual harassment in housing. She currently serves as a Commissioner for the Columbia, Missouri, Public Housing Authority.

Following law school, Oliveri served as a law clerk to the Honorable Stephanie K. Seymour on the United States Court of Appeals for the Tenth Circuit. Prior to joining the Missouri Law faculty, she served as a trial attorney with the U.S. Department of Justice through the Honors Graduate Program. She practiced in the Civil Rights Division, Housing and Civil Enforcement Section, where she litigated and tried a number of significant cases involving housing discrimination and sexual harassment in housing. In 2003 she was awarded a Special Commendation from the Attorney General for outstanding service.

Sexual Harassment Law

Chapter 1

The Early History and Development of U.S. Sexual Harassment Law

1. Introduction

On a rainy Sunday afternoon in May 1975, close to 300 women gathered at a community center in Ithaca, New York. They shared their stories of sexual coercion and abuse on the job—behavior many had experienced but few had ever mentioned. "Speak outs," as they were called at the time, were a common technique used in the women's movement to raise awareness about silenced issues, such as illegal and unsafe abortion, rape, and domestic violence. When sharing their stories in public, women realized they were not alone. Many women had these experiences, and they realized these issues were not just a personal problem but were political, created by economic and political conditions that were related to the systemic oppression of women. With this insight, feminists analyzed their experiences to identify the ideological and institutional factors that undergirded these issues. They also developed strategies to resist gendered violence and abuse. To make their experiences more visible, women gave names to the issues they raised, coining new terms like "wife battering," "date rape," and "sexual harassment."

The month before the May speak out, Lin Farley, Karen Sauvigné, Susan Meyer, and other feminist activists gathered to brainstorm about what to put on the poster advertising the event. They considered several alternatives—"sexual coercion on the job," "workplace sexual abuse," and "sexual intimidation." The term "sexual harassment" gained support because it encompassed the broad range of behaviors in the workplace that concerned these women. The concept of sexual harassment included demands for sex in exchange for jobs, promotions, and raises, as well as the sexist and sexual comments, touching, and grabbing women experienced so often in the workplace.

At the speak out, women told their gut-wrenching stories of retaliatory terminations when they refused to comply with bosses' sexual demands. They recounted the stress of constant barrages of sexualized behaviors that eroded their concentration on their work. A survey of the attendees found that 7 out of 10 of the 155 respondents had experienced sexual harassment.[1] A *New York Times* reporter

---

1. Carrie N. Baker, The Women's Movement against Sexual Harassment 33 (2008).

covered the speak out, publishing the first national news story on sexual harassment in August 1975.[2]

The organizers of the speak out then formed an organization, Working Women United (WWU), which endeavored to raise awareness about sexual harassment and organize women to resist. WWU eventually became a national clearinghouse for information on the issue, collecting and circulating legal briefs filed in cases across the country. WWU created a legal referral network to help women find attorneys to file lawsuits. Another important early group, Alliance Against Sexual Coercion (AASC), located in Cambridge, Massachusetts, developed some of the earliest theoretical analysis of the issue. AASC connected sexually harassing behavior to systemic inequalities between men and women and between employers and employees. Around the same time, women across the country began to bring legal cases alleging that sexual coercion in the workplace violated Title VII of the Civil Rights Act (CRA) of 1964. These events began a decade-long process that would eventually lead the United States Supreme Court to recognize sexual harassment as a federal civil rights violation.[3]

This chapter describes the activism and court decisions that led to *Meritor Savings Bank v. Vinson* (1986),[4] the first Supreme Court sexual harassment case. It also defines some basic terms—sex, sexuality, gender, and gender identity. Relying on these terms, Chapter 1 introduces sexual harassment in the workplace and in educational contexts and the laws that address both.

A. Defining Sex

An understanding of "sex" is key to understanding laws against sex-based harassment. People use the word "sex" to refer to multiple concepts—biological sex, gender, sexual orientation, or sexual activity. Biological sex relates not only to one's chromosomes, but also to one's hormones and physical characteristics—breasts, penis, and vagina. In American society, we tend to think of biological sex as binary. A person is either male or female. Typically, males have XY chromosomes, elevated levels of testosterone, and a penis. Females usually have XX chromosomes, elevated levels of estrogen and progesterone, breasts, and a vagina. Newborns are assigned a sex, based on the appearance of their external genitalia at the time of birth, often without consideration of their chromosomes and/or internal genitalia.

In fact, a fair amount of sex diversity exists among human beings (and other animals). For example, a significant number of people are born intersex. The Intersex Society of America defines intersex:

---

2. Enid Nemy, *Women Begin to Speak Out Against Sexual Harassment at Work*, N.Y. Times (Aug. 19, 1975).
3. Baker, *supra* note 1, at 27–48.
4. 477 U.S. 57 (1986).

"Intersex" is a general term used for a variety of conditions in which a person is born with a reproductive or sexual anatomy that doesn't seem to fit the typical definitions of female or male. For example, a person might be born appearing to be female on the outside, but having mostly male-typical anatomy on the inside. Or a person may be born with genitals that seem to be in-between the usual male and female types—for example, a girl may be born with a noticeably large clitoris, or lacking a vaginal opening, or a boy may be born with a notably small penis, or with a scrotum that is divided so that it has formed more like labia. Or a person may be born with mosaic genetics, so that some of her cells have XX chromosomes and some of them have XY.[5]

Until recently, doctors customarily operated on the bodies of children born visibly intersex to make them conform to male or female norms.[6]

More generally, male- and female-identified people engage in behavior that enhances physical characteristics assumed to be ideal for their respective sex. For example, some women seek female breast enhancements and some men consume steroids for more muscular bodies. While we think of biological sex as fixed and natural, environmental factors may play a role in how physical characteristics manifest.[7]

Gender is related to sex but is distinct. Gender can refer to both gender expression and gender identity. Gender expression occurs through the normative social behaviors associated with one's assigned sex. American society encourages males and females to exhibit masculine and feminine gendered behaviors, respectively. Gender manifests in how people walk, sit, and talk. Gender expression happens through gender roles (e.g., breadwinner versus homemaker) and activities (e.g., football player versus ballerina). Children learn the gendered behaviors associated with their assigned sex by observing adults and older siblings, watching media depictions of males and females, and playing with gendered toys adults give them. Gender nonconforming people exhibit variances from these gender norms.

In addition to gender expression, people also have gender identities. Gender identity is one's internal sense of gender, which does not necessarily align with one's assigned sex. Gender identities include male, female, and non-binary. Gender nonbinary people do not identify as either male or female. Cisgender people have a gender identity that aligns with their assigned sex, while transgender people do not.

---

5. *What is Intersex?*, Intersex Society of North America, http://www.isna.org/faq/what_is _intersex.

6. In 2016, the Board of Trustees of the American Medical Association issued a report stating that doctors should defer medical or surgical intervention on intersex children until the child is able to participate in the decision-making process. Patrice M. Harris, Am. Med. Ass'n, Report of the Board of Trustees, Supporting Autonomy for Patients with Differences of Sex Development (2016).

7. Judith Lorber, Paradoxes of Gender 37–54 (1994).

The third aspect of sex is sexuality, which includes sexual orientation and sexual behaviors. Traditional norms assign heterosexuality to males and females. Specifically, society expects that people will be sexually attracted to people of the "opposite" sex. However, gay men and lesbian women find people of the same sex appealing. Many people identify as bisexual, meaning they find both sexes attractive. Recent research reveals that one-quarter of people now identify as bisexual.[8] Some people identify as asexual, meaning they have no sexual feelings or desires. Others identify as pansexual, meaning they are not limited in sexual choice with regard to biological sex, gender, or gender identity.[9] People use "queer" as an umbrella term to refer to non-cisgender and/or non-heterosexual people. Sexual behaviors include more than penetrative vaginal-penile, anal, and oral sex. Sexual activity also encompasses solo self-pleasuring and various group activities. For example, sexts are a sexual activity for people who do not even occupy the same physical space. A person's sexual behaviors do not always align with their sexual orientation. For example, someone might identify as heterosexual but engage in sexual behaviors with people of the same sex.

Many people assume that biological sex, gender expression, and gender identity align, along with sexual orientation and behaviors. Thus, traditional norms hold that males are masculine, identify as men, are attracted to females, and engage in sexual behavior with females only. Meanwhile, traditional norms define females as feminine, self-identifying as women, attracted to males, and engaging in sexual behaviors only with males. People often conflate biological sex with gender. For example, if someone asks students what sex their teacher is, the students might assume they are being asked about the teacher's biological sex. Their response will typically be female or male. However, they probably do not know their instructor's chromosomes, hormone levels, internal morphology, or even external morphology. Their answer will be based on how they perceive their teacher's gender assignment—informed by what the teacher wears, whether and how the teacher accessorizes, and how the teacher walks. But nontraditional expressions of gender abound—"butch" women, effeminate men, androgynous persons, and more. Sex, gender expression, gender identity, sexual orientation, and sexual behaviors exist along continuums, and these attributes and behaviors do not necessarily align. An individual may fall at any point along these continuums in any combination. For example, someone's biological sex may be female, their gender identity transgender, their gender expression masculine, and their sexual orientation bisexual. That said, he may engage in sexual behavior with women only. These concepts are important to understanding sexual harassment as a form of sex-based discrimination.

---

8. Jaime Ballard, *More Young Americans Now Identify as Bisexual*, YouGov (June 18, 2018).

9. Jennifer Ann Drobac, Sexual Exploitation of Teenagers: Adolescent Development, Discrimination, and Consent Law 126–27 (2016).

B. Defining Sexual Harassment

Nothing in the U.S. Constitution or the U.S. Code specifically defines, or for that matter even explicitly prohibits, sexual harassment in civilian contexts.[10] But courts have ruled that sexual harassment violates Title VII of the Civil Rights Act of 1964, which prohibits sex discrimination in employment, and other civil rights statutes.

The original draft of Title VII addressed race discrimination and not sex discrimination. In the final hours of debate on the House floor, when the passage of the bill appeared imminent, conservative Representative Howard W. Smith (R-VA), who opposed the bill, proposed adding "sex" as a prohibited ground for discrimination. Smith expressed concern that white women would be disadvantaged in comparison to African Americans if the bill did not include a prohibition of sex discrimination.

Liberal male members of the House spoke against the amendment, which they feared would endanger the underlying legislation. However, several female supporters of women's rights spoke in favor of Smith's proposal. The amendment passed, as did the bill, without Smith's support. The Senate approved the bill with little discussion of the sex provision.

As a result, limited history of congressional intent exists as to the meaning of "sex" to guide jurists. The law, which applies to employers with 15 or more employees, states:

It shall be an unlawful employment practice for an employer—

1) to fail or refuse to hire or to discharge any individual, or otherwise to discriminate against any individual with respect to his compensation, terms, conditions, or privileges of employment, because of such individual's race, color, religion, sex, or national origin; or

2) to limit, segregate, or classify his employees or applicants for employment in any way which would deprive or tend to deprive any individual of employment opportunities or otherwise adversely affect his status as an employee, because of such individual's race, color, religion, sex, or national origin.[11]

In the early 1970s, women began filing lawsuits arguing that sexual harassment was sex discrimination in violation of Title VII.

In developing a definition of sexual harassment, courts turned to the Equal Employment Opportunity Commission (EEOC), the agency charged with Title VII's enforcement. In 1980, the EEOC defined sexual harassment as "unwelcome sexual advances, requests for sexual favors, and other verbal or physical conduct of a sexual nature."[12] A supervisor harasses a subordinate employee when he makes compliance

---

10. The Uniform Code of Military Justice defines sexual harassment in the same way that the EEOC has defined it. *See* 10 U.S.C. § 1561(e) (2012).

11. 42 U.S.C. § 2000e-2 (2012).

12. 29 C.F.R. § 1604.11 (a) (2013).

with sexual demands a term or condition of employment or the basis for employment decisions involving that individual. But workplace sexual harassment also includes when supervisors, co-workers, or even employees engage in unwelcome sexual or sex-based behavior toward another when this behavior unreasonably interferes with a worker's job performance or creates an intimidating, hostile, or offensive work environment.[13] Under Title VII and most state fair employment practice statutes (FEPS), the conduct must be either severe or pervasive to qualify as actionable sexual harassment for which the target can file a lawsuit.[14] A jury or judge decides what conduct qualifies as severe or pervasive in light of the totality of the circumstances. Chapter 3 reviews the specific elements of the prima facie case for sexual harassment. Chapter 4 explains the evolving standards of employer liability for all types of sex-based harassment.[15]

Similar to Title VII, courts have ruled that sexual harassment in educational contexts violates Title IX of the Education Amendments of 1972,[16] which prohibits sex discrimination in federally funded schools. The U.S. Department of Education Office for Civil Rights (OCR) states, "Sexual harassment is unwelcome conduct of a sexual nature[,] . . . unwelcome sexual advances, requests for sexual favors, and other verbal, nonverbal, or physical conduct of a sexual nature."[17] The definition continues, "Sexual harassment of a student can deny or limit, on the basis of sex, the student's ability to participate in or to receive benefits, services, or opportunities in the school's program."[18]

Note the similarity between the OCR definition and that from the EEOC. Both require that the conduct be unwelcome and sexual. These definitions are narrow and do not highlight nonsexual forms of abuse. For example, they do not explain that gender animosity may motivate some forms of hostile, sex-based harassment. Both Titles VII and IX, however, prohibit this form of behavior. One important distinction between these laws is that the Supreme Court requires harassment to be "severe and pervasive" under Title IX, but only "severe or pervasive" under Title VII.[19]

C. Prevalence and Impact of Sexual Harassment

How common is sexual harassment? Studies have widely divergent results depending on how researchers have chosen respondents and what questions they asked. When researchers used a randomly representative sample (called a "probability sample") and asked employees if they have experienced "sexual harassment," which

---

13. *Id.*

14. *See, e.g.,* Meritor Sav. Bank v. Vinson, 477 U.S. 57, 67 (1986).

15. *See also* 29 C.F.R. § 1604.11(a) (2013).

16. 20 U.S.C. §§ 1681–1688 (2013).

17. Revised Sexual Harassment Guidance: Harassment of Students by School Employees, Other Students, or Third Parties, 66 Fed. Reg. 5512–01 (2001).

18. *Id.*

19. *See infra* Chapters 3, 6.

they did not define, approximately 25% reported experiencing "sexual harassment."[20] When researchers asked employees the same question in surveys using convenience samples (not randomly representative, e.g., respondents from one organization), and sexual harassment was similarly not defined, 50% of women reported they had been sexually harassed.[21] When researchers asked employees selected from probability samples whether they had experienced one or more specific sexually based behaviors, such as unwanted sexual attention or sexual coercion, 40% of women responded affirmatively.[22] When researchers asked these questions using convenience samples, 75% of respondents reported that they had. These studies show that many people do not call unwelcome, sex-based behaviors sexual harassment, even if they find these behaviors offensive.[23]

Researchers have also studied sexist or crude behavior—sometimes called "gender harassment"—in the workplace. These behaviors may include "sexually crude terminology or displays (for example, calling a female colleague a derogatory sexual word or posting pornography) and sexist comments (such as telling anti-female jokes or making comments that women do not belong in management)."[24] Almost 60% of women reported having experienced gender harassment in surveys using probability samples.[25]

Most research on sexual harassment focuses only on women, but the federal government's Merit Systems Protection Board surveyed all federal employees in 1980, 1987, and 1994. It asked whether respondents had experienced unwanted sexual attention or sexual coercion. Forty-two percent of women and 15% of men responded in the affirmative in 1981, as did 42% of women and 14% of men in 1988, and 44% of women and 19% of men in 1994.[26] Surveys of LGBT workers also show high rates of sexual harassment. Using probability samples, researchers found that 35% of LGBT workers reported harassment in one study.[27] In another study, 58% of LGBT people reported that they heard derogatory comments about sexual orientation and gender identity in their workplaces. Research on transgender people reveals particularly high rates of harassment.[28]

---

20. CHAI R. FELDBLUM & VICTORIA A. LIPNIC, U.S. EQUAL EMP. OPPORTUNITY COMM'N, SELECT TASK FORCE ON THE STUDY OF HARASSMENT IN THE WORKPLACE: REPORT OF CO-CHAIRS 8 (June 2016).

21. *Id.*

22. *Id.* at 8–9.

23. *Id.* at 9.

24. *Id.*

25. *Id.* at 9–10.

26. *Id.* at 10.

27. *Id.*

28. *Id.* at 10–11. The report also discussed current research on harassment based on race, ethnicity, disability, age, and religion, as well as "intersectional harassment," meaning harassment based on two or more protected characteristics. *Id.* at 11–14.

Research has shown that sex-based harassment has significant negative psychological, physical, and financial effects. Workplace sexual harassment undermines women's workplace authority, reduces them to sexual objects, and reinforces sexist stereotypes about appropriate gender behavior.[29] Sexual harassment can result in anger, harm to self-esteem and self-worth, reduced job satisfaction, increased absenteeism and work withdrawal, and a deterioration of co-worker relationships.[30]

The psychological effects of sexual harassment include depression, anxiety, stress, and even Post Traumatic Stress Disorder (PTSD), including flashbacks and panic attacks. These symptoms can lead to substance abuse problems and attempted suicide.[31] The physical effects include high blood pressure, stomach problems, headaches, and other stress-related ailments. The stress can impact cardiovascular function, autoimmune diseases, and metabolic function. Physical effects can include hair loss, hives, loss of appetite, weight gain or loss, nausea, sleeplessness, lethargy, inability to concentrate, neck pain, and muscle aches.

Many women who experience sexual harassment in their twenties and early thirties suffer financially during this formative career stage. Lost promotions, abandoned jobs, and other consequences can depress lifelong earnings. Moreover, sexual harassment affects not only directly targeted women but also other women in the hostile environment.[32] Sexual harassment in other contexts, such as education and housing, produces similar effects. We explore these effects in greater detail throughout this book.

2. Early Cases

Plaintiffs who brought lawsuits in the mid-1970s filed before the EEOC issued sexual harassment guidance. They argued that sexual harassment was sex discrimination in violation of Title VII. That strategy would eventually prevail, but courts did not immediately accept the argument. Moreover, courts posed many other questions. What did the language "conditions, or privileges of employment" mean? Are sexual demands a discriminatory condition of employment? Are working conditions free from sexual demands a privilege of employment? In addition, Title VII holds employers responsible for sexual harassment but does not apply directly to supervisory employees or co-workers. Should the law hold employers responsible

---

29. *Id.* at 333.

30. Heather McLaughlin, Christopher Uggen & Amy Blackstone, *Sexual Harassment, Workplace Authority, and the Paradox of Power*, 77 Am. Soc. Rev. 625, 634–35 (2012).

31. Jason N. Houle et al., *The Impact of Sexual Harassment on Depressive Symptoms During the Early Occupational Career*, 1 Soc'y & Mental Health 89 (2011); Margaret S. Stockdale, T.K. Logan & Rebecca Weston, *Sexual Harassment and Posttraumatic Stress Disorder: Damages Beyond Prior Abuse*, 33 Law & Human Behavior 405 (2009).

32. Heather McLaughlin, Christopher Uggen & Amy Blackstone, *The Economic and Career Effects of Sexual Harassment on Working Women*, 31 Gender & Soc'y 333, 352 (2017).

for the behaviors of supervisory employees? Courts struggled with these questions and more in the 1970s and 1980s.

Six cases filed between 1971 and 1975 led the legal effort against sexual harassment and set the framework for the development of the law.[33] All six cases involved male supervisors who made sexual demands of subordinate female employees. When the women refused the advances, the supervisors terminated, demoted, or professionally isolated the women. This form of sexual harassment later came to be known as "quid pro quo" sexual harassment.

A. Private Matters, Not Workplace Discrimination

Five of the six district courts to hear these cases ruled that Title VII did not cover sexual harassment. The district court judges who decided these early cases focused on whether the alleged conduct was workplace discrimination or a private matter. The plaintiffs argued that sexual coercion in the workplace was an economic issue that impaired women's participation in the workplace. The defendants contended that the conduct was personal conduct in violation of corporate policy, so that employers were not responsible. In all but one of the cases, the judges ruled that sexual workplace misconduct was a private matter, neither related to employment nor based on sex. They concluded that employers were not liable for this behavior under Title VII.

For example, in *Barnes v. Train* (1974), Judge John Lewis Smith ruled against Paulette Barnes. Barnes alleged she experienced harassment when she was a 28-year-old mother of three working as an administrative assistant in the Office of Equal Opportunity of the Environmental Protection Agency (EPA). Barnes alleged that, within a week of starting her job in July 1971, the male director of her office, Norris Snydor, "began a campaign to extract sexual favors" from her by repeatedly inviting her out for social activities after hours, making sexual remarks to her, and suggesting that he would promote her if she had a sexual affair with him. Barnes resisted, telling Sydnor that she wanted their relationship to be strictly professional and her employment status to be based on her work performance. Barnes alleged that Snydor then began a "conscious campaign" to belittle and harass her and to strip her of her job duties. Snydor allegedly denied her a promised promotion, abolished her job, and reassigned her to a position of lesser responsibility. Her former position, she alleged,

---

33. *See, e.g.,* Barnes v. Train, 13 Fair Empl. Prac. Cas. (BNA) 123 (D.D.C. 1974), *rev'd sub nom.* Barnes v. Costle, 561 F. 2d 983 (D.C. Cir. 1977); Corne v. Bausch & Lomb, Inc., 390 F. Supp. 161 (D. Ariz. 1975), *vacated and remanded,* 562 F.2d 55 (9th Cir. 1977); Garber v. Saxon Bus. Products, Inc., 14 Empl. Prac. Dec. ¶7586 (E.D. Va. 1976), *rev'd and remanded,* 552 F.2d 1032 (4th Cir. 1977); Williams v. Saxbe, 413 F. Supp. 654 (D.D.C. 1976), *rev'd in part and vacated in part sub nom.* Williams v. Bell, 587 F.2d 1240 (D.C. Cir. 1978); Miller v. Bank of Am., 418 F. Supp. 233 (N.D. Cal. 1976), *rev'd,* 600 F.2d 211 (9th Cir. 1979); Tomkins v. Pub. Serv. Elec. & Gas Co., 422 F. Supp. 553 (D.N.J. 1976), *rev'd,* 568 F.2d 1044 (3d Cir. 1977). See BAKER, *supra* note 1, at 16–17, for detailed descriptions of the facts of these cases.

was subsequently reinstated and filled by a white woman at a much higher salary level. In ruling against Barnes, Judge Smith explained:

> The substance of plaintiff's complaint is that she was discriminated against, not because she was a woman, but because she refused to engage in a sexual affair with her supervisor. This is a controversy underpinned by the subtleties of an inharmonious personal relationship. Regardless of how inexcusable the conduct of plaintiff's supervisor might have been, it does not evidence an arbitrary barrier to continued employment based on plaintiff's sex.[34]

The notion that sexual harassment resulted from discordant personal relationships was common.[35] Courts also concluded that because the offensive behavior resulted not from a discriminatory employer policy but from the personal sexual desires of a supervisor, Title VII provided no relief.

The following early cases reveal how courts initially failed to connect offensive conduct with the fact that only women, not men, had complained. With few exceptions, only women suffered—economically and emotionally—from this "natural sex phenomenon," as some courts described the behavior. Courts eventually interpreted Title VII to provide federal protection from sexually abusive workplace behavior. By the end of the 1970s, some states had passed laws explicitly prohibiting workplace sexual harassment.[36] However, the path to this outcome was not smooth.

Corne v. Bausch & Lomb, Inc.
390 F. Supp. 161 (D. Ariz. 1975)[37]

FREY, District Judge.

Plaintiffs Jane Corne and Geneva DeVane filed the present complaint alleging a violation of civil rights based on sex discrimination.

. . . .

. . . [The complaint alleged that plaintiffs] were repeatedly subjected to verbal and physical sexual advances from defendant Price; defendant Price's illegal activities were directed not only to plaintiffs but also to other female employees and thus constituted a condition of employment that discriminates by sex in violation of Title VII; cooperation with defendant Price's illegal activities resulted in favored employment that discriminates by sex in violation of Title VII; immediately before the filing of the complaint with the E.E.O.C., defendant Price's activities directed to plaintiffs became so onerous that plaintiffs were forced to resign.

---

34. *Barnes*, 13 Fair Emp. Prac. Cas. at 123.

35. *See, e.g., Corne*, 390 F. Supp. at 163–64; *Tomkins*, 422 F. Supp. at 556–57.

36. *See, e.g.*, WIS. STAT. § 111.32(5)(g)(4) (1979); 1980 Mich. Legis. Serv. 626 (West); 1980 Conn. Legis. Serv. 634 (West).

37. This case was later vacated and remanded. Corne v. Bausch & Lomb, Inc., 562 F.2d 55 (9th Cir. 1977).

. . . .

Assuming that all allegations in the complaint are true, plaintiffs have failed to state a claim for relief under Title VII of the Civil Rights Act.

. . . .

. . . In the present case, Mr. Price's conduct appears to be nothing more than a personal proclivity, peculiarity or mannerism. By his alleged sexual advances, Mr. Price was satisfying a personal urge. Certainly no employer policy is here involved; rather than the company being benefited in any way by the conduct of Price, it is obvious it can only be damaged by the very nature of the acts complained of.

Nothing in the complaint alleges nor can it be construed that the conduct complained of was company directed policy which deprived women of employment opportunities. A reasonably intelligent reading of the statute demonstrates it can only mean that an unlawful employment practice must be discrimination on the part of the employer, Bausch and Lomb. Further, there is nothing in the Act which could reasonably be construed to have it apply to 'verbal and physical sexual advances' by another employee, even though he be in a supervisory capacity where such complained of acts or conduct had no relationship to the nature of the employment.

It would be ludicrous to hold that the sort of activity involved here was contemplated by the Act because to do so would mean that if the conduct complained of was directed equally to males there would be no basis for suit. Also, an outgrowth of holding such activity to be actionable under Title VII would be a potential federal lawsuit every time any employee made amorous or sexually oriented advances toward another. The only sure way an employer could avoid such charges would be to have employees who were asexual.

. . . .

It is ordered that defendants' Motions to Dismiss, are granted and the complaint, is dismissed.

Tomkins v. Public Service Electric & Gas Co.
422 F. Supp. 553 (D.N.J. 1976)[38]

STERN, District Judge.

Plaintiff Adrienne Tomkins was formerly employed by defendant Public Service Electric and Gas Company (hereinafter PSE&G). She was fired by PSE&G under circumstances which are presently in dispute. . . . The gravamen of plaintiff's complaint is that she was subjected to sexual harassment by her male supervisor. She further alleges that the company retaliated against her when she protested the

---

38. This case was reversed on appeal. Tomkins v. Public Service Electric & Gas Co., 568 F.2d 1044 (3d Cir. 1977).

supervisor's actions. Plaintiff seeks to proceed under the authority of Title VII of the Civil Rights Act of 1964.

. . . .

Plaintiff was hired as an office worker at the company's Newark offices in 1971. Her progress through the lower grades of office employment was normal until she was assigned to the defendant supervisor. Plaintiff at this time was approaching eligibility for a promotion to a secretarial position. The complaint alleges that the supervisor requested that plaintiff take lunch with him outside the office premises, purportedly to discuss her prospects with the firm. Plaintiff contends that the supervisor used the opportunity to make sexual advances to her. She charges that she was detained by the supervisor against her will through economic threats and physical force.[39]

Plaintiff alleges that she complained to the company about the lunchtime incident. She sought a transfer and accepted a less desirable position in the company. She contends that her complaints about the conduct of the supervisor resulted in retaliation against her in the form of disciplinary layoffs and threats of demotion and salary cuts. Some 15 months after the incident which provoked her complaints, plaintiff was fired by PSE&G. In sum, plaintiff claims that her superior's sexual advances coupled with his threats of reprisals, and the company's subsequent retaliation and ultimate termination of her services because of her complaints, constitute violations of Title VII.

. . . .

Each defendant contends that the allegations of the complaint state no cause of action under this provision, and that the complaint must therefore be dismissed.

Title VII has presented the federal courts with numerous difficult issues of construction and application. This lawsuit raises two issues: whether sexual harassment of a female employee by a male supervisor constitutes sex discrimination within the meaning of Title VII; and whether the conduct of an employer after a complaint of such harassment can amount to sex discrimination within the meaning of Title VII.

In company with three of the four district courts that have considered the issue, this Court holds that *sexual* harassment and *sexually* motivated assault do not constitute sex discrimination under Title VII.

Title VII was enacted in order to remove those artificial barriers to full employment which are based upon unjust and long-encrusted prejudice. Its aim is to make

---

39. Tomkins alleged that her supervisor gave her an ultimatum to engage in an affair with him or lose her job. She reported that he said, "I can't walk around the office with a hard-on all the time" and "This is the only way we can have a working relationship." When Plaintiff refused, her supervisor grabbed her arm and said, "You're not going anywhere. You're going with me to the 13th floor" of the hotel. He also warned, "Don't go to anyone for help because I have something on all of them, all the way to the top, and they're not going to do anything to help you." He then forcibly held her and kissed her. Baker, *supra* note 1, at 17.

careers open to talents irrespective of race or sex. It is not intended to provide a federal tort remedy for what amounts to physical attack motivated by sexual desire on the part of a supervisor and which happened to occur in a corporate corridor rather than a back alley. In this instance the supervisor was male and the employee was female. But no immutable principle of psychology compels this alignment of parties. The gender lines might as easily have been reversed, or even not crossed at all. While sexual desire animated the parties, or at least one of them, the gender of each is incidental to the claim of abuse. Similarly, the pleadings in this case aver that the supervisor's advances were spurned. Had they been accepted, however, and plaintiff thereby preferred, could co-workers be heard to complain in federal court as well? It is clear that such a claim is simply without the scope of the Act. The abuse of authority by supervisors of either sex for personal purposes is an unhappy and recurrent feature of our social experience. Such conduct is frequently illegal under the penal statutes of the relevant jurisdiction. Such conduct might well give rise to a civil action in tort. It is not, however, sex discrimination within the meaning of Title VII even when the purpose is sexual. EEOC urges that a contrary decision would not open the floodgates to litigation. The Commission argues that only sexual advances from a superior to a subordinate under the cloak of the superior's authority would be actionable under Title VII, and then only if such a practice contributed to an employment-related decision. But plaintiff's theory rests on the proposition, with which this Court concurs, that the power inherent in a position of authority is necessarily coercive. And, as the representative of the EEOC candidly conceded in oral argument, every sexual advance made by a supervisor would be made under the apparent cloak of that authority. Any subordinate knows that the boss is the boss whether a file folder or a dinner is at issue. Finally, the Court recalls Judge Williams' observation in *Miller*: "The attraction of males to females and females to males is a natural sex phenomenon and it is probable that this attraction plays at least a subtle part in most personnel decisions." This natural sexual attraction can be subtle. If the plaintiff's view were to prevail, no superior could, prudently, attempt to open a social dialogue with any subordinate of either sex. An invitation to dinner could become an invitation to a federal lawsuit if a once harmonious relationship turned sour at some later time. And if an inebriated approach by a supervisor to a subordinate at the office Christmas party could form the basis of a federal lawsuit for sex discrimination if a promotion or a raise is later denied to the subordinate, we would need 4,000 federal trial judges instead of some 400.

The second issue tendered by plaintiff's complaint concerns the conduct of the employing company subsequent to her complaint about the supervisor. When a female employee registers a complaint of sexual abuse and the company chooses to fire her rather than investigate, the corporate response may constitute discrimination based on sex. In brief, it may reflect a conscious choice to favor the male employee over the female complainant on the ground that a male's services are more valuable than a female's. Such a preferential practice may violate the Act even though the grievance procedures do not by their terms implicate characteristics peculiar to either gender. It matters not whether the basis for the discriminatory treatment is a previous sexual assault or a matter related to salary or promotion. When a female employee registers a complaint and the grievance is not only not adequately processed, but the complainant is persecuted for having the temerity to advance it at all, the Act is violated to the extent that such a corporate posture is sex-based. If a company decides that, whatever the merits of the underlying controversy, the female will be terminated because she is female, that is sex discrimination. Plaintiff must be permitted her day in Court on this issue. Accordingly, PSE&G's motion to dismiss must be denied.

. . . .

Notes and Discussion

1. *Corne v. Bausch & Lomb, Inc.* What statements in Judge Frey's opinion draw one's attention and why? In *Corne*, Judge Frey stated that "Mr. Price was satisfying a personal urge." How did Judge Frey know Price's motivation? Aside from a "personal urge," what else might have motivated Price? Judge Frey stated that the "complained of acts or conduct had no relationship to the nature of employment." Was he correct? Judge Frey warned that finding for plaintiff would lead to "a potential federal lawsuit every time any employee made amorous or sexually oriented advances toward another." Is this true? Was Judge Frey correct that the only way for employers to "avoid such charges would be to have employees who were asexual"?

2. *Tomkins v. Public Service Electric & Gas Co.* In *Tomkins*, one of the reasons given by Judge Stern for denying Tomkins's claim is that it might allow employees to bring a claim if a supervisor favored a co-worker for complying with his sexual demands. Should co-workers have a sex discrimination claim if a boss gives a promotion to a romantic partner? Does it matter if the co-worker is a male or a female? Judge Stern stated, "sexual desire animated the parties, or at least one of them." In light of the fact that Tomkins stated that her supervisor's sexual advances were unwelcome, why might Judge Stern have said that? What did Judge Stern suggest when he said, an "invitation to dinner could become an invitation to a federal lawsuit if a once harmonious relationship turned sour at some later time"? Is this likely? If some number of women were to falsely claim sexual harassment, would that be a reason not to prohibit it?

3. *Miller v. Bank of America* The facts of these early cases reveal not only sexist but also racist atmospheres that many women faced in the early 1970s. For example, Margaret Miller, a machine operator, alleged that her white male boss showed up uninvited at her home with a bottle of wine in hand and said, "I've never felt this way about a black chick before." He then promised he would get her "off the machines" if she would have sex with him. When she refused his advances, he fired her.[40]

Relying on *Corne*, Judge Stuart A. Wein dismissed Miller's complaint. He opined, "The attraction of males to females and females to males is a natural sex

---

40. Catharine A. MacKinnon, Sexual Harassment of Working Women 35 (1979).

phenomenon and it is probable that this attraction plays at least a subtle part in most personnel decisions."[41] In a footnote, he also rejected the race discrimination claim. He wrote, "This is not a race discrimination case. While the complaint is couched in terms of both race and sex discrimination, plaintiff's counsel, during argument before the Court, conceded that the case should stand or fall on the issue of sex discrimination."[42] Judge Wein failed to perceive job discrimination of any kind. Is Judge Wein correct? Is this also a race discrimination case?

4. "[B]ecause of . . . sex. . . ." What does this phrase mean in Title VII? What did the legislature mean by "sex"? What are alternate ways of defining the word "sex"?

5. Personal Proclivity What reasoning supports the contention that the alleged perpetrator's behavior is nothing but a "personal proclivity" and therefore unrelated to discrimination? Might Judge Frey have found discrimination if a white supervisor had spit at an African-American clerk due to a personal "peculiarity or mannerism"? How would Judge Stern distinguish a "physical attack motivated by sexual desire" of a woman and a physical attack motivated by personal revulsion of a Muslim? Do the facts support or negate Judge Stern's assertion that "the gender of each [party] is incidental to the claim of abuse" in a sexual harassment case? Judge Stern quoted the judge in *Miller,* stating that the "attraction of males to females and females to males is a natural sex phenomenon and it is probable that this attraction plays at least a subtle part in most personnel decisions." Is this true? If so, what is the best way to ensure fair treatment in the workplace, especially if women are much more likely than men to be in subordinate positions there? By saying that heterosexual desire is a "natural phenomenon," were these judges saying that sexual harassment in the workplace is inevitable? That it is acceptable? Were they arguing that "boys will be boys"? Should "nature" be a defense to sexual harassment?

6. A Tort Claim? Judge Stern announced that Title VII was "not intended to provide a federal tort remedy for what amounts to a physical attack motivated by sexual desire on the part of a supervisor and which happened to occur in a corporate corridor rather than a back alley." Are sexual harassment cases more appropriately addressed as regular tort claims (e.g., intentional infliction of emotional distress, battery, or assault) rather than as civil rights claims? In 1979, Catharine MacKinnon argued:

> [T]ort is conceptually inadequate to the problem of sexual harassment to the extent that it rips injuries to women's sexuality out of the context of women's social circumstances as a whole. . . . [T]he tort approach misses the nexus between women's sexuality and women's employment, the system of reciprocal sanctions which, to women as a gender, become cumulative. . . .
>
> Unsituated in a recognition of the context that keeps women secondary and powerless, sexual injuries appear as incidental or deviant aberrations

---

41. *Miller,* 418 F. Supp. at 236.
42. *Miller,* 418 F. Supp. at 234 n.1.

which arise in one-to-one relationships gone wrong. The essential purpose of tort law . . . is to compensate individuals one at a time for mischief which befalls them as a consequence of the one-time ineptitude or nastiness of other individuals. . . . [Sexual harassment] is a group-defined injury which occurs to many different individuals regardless of unique qualities or circumstances, in ways that connect with other deprivations of the same individuals, among all of whom a single characteristic — female sex — is shared. Such an injury is *in essence* a group injury. The context which makes the impact of gender cumulative — in fact, the context that makes it injurious — is lost when sexual harassment is approached as an individual injury, however wide the net of damages is cast. Tort law compensates individuals for injuries while spreading their costs and perhaps setting examples for foresightful perpetrators; the purpose of discrimination law is to change the society so that this kind of injury need not and does not recur. Tort law considers individual and compensable something which is fundamentally social and should be eliminated.[43]

Are MacKinnon's arguments persuasive? Why or why not?

7. Employer Policy Was Judge Frey correct that a "reasonably intelligent reading of the statute demonstrates it can only mean that an unlawful employment practice must be discrimination on the part of the employer"? If so, how could later decisions justify relief under Title VII when the alleged harasser was only a supervisor and not the principal employer? In *Tomkins*, the court adopted the plaintiff's theory, "that the power inherent in a position of authority is necessarily coercive." The court declined, however, to assign liability for abusive conduct to the employer who delegated that authority. Why?

8. The Floodgates Does the prohibition of sexual harassment under Title VII ban a supervisor's "attempt to open a social dialogue with any subordinate of either sex"? Judge Stern feared that workplace rudeness might become a federal offense necessitating "4,000 federal trial judges instead of some 400." In the *Miller* case, Judge Wein warned that "it is conceivable under plaintiff's theory that flirtations of the smallest order would give rise to liability."[44] Were these concerns realistic? If so, how could courts prevent such a drastic result and still protect targets of abuse? If Title VII prohibits sexual harassment as sex discrimination and sexual harassment is pervasive, does it matter how many judges the bench needs to deal with the problem? Why or why not?

9. Retaliation Title VII states:

> It shall be an unlawful employment practice for an employer to discriminate against any of his employees or applicants for employment, for an employment agency, or joint labor-management committee controlling

---

43. MacKinnon, *supra* note 40, at 171–72.
44. *Miller*, 418 F. Supp. at 236.

apprenticeship or other training or retraining, including on-the-job training programs, to discriminate against any individual, or for a labor organization to discriminate against any member thereof or applicant for membership, because he has opposed any practice made an unlawful employment practice by this subchapter, or because he has made a charge, testified, assisted, or participated in any manner in an investigation, proceeding, or hearing under this subchapter.[45]

In *Tomkins,* Judge Stern declined to dismiss Tomkins's retaliation claim. When the underlying conduct does *not* constitute harassment actionable under Title VII, does an employee's termination for a complaint still constitute sex discrimination? Or might an employer be justified in terminating an individual who "cries wolf"?

10. **Protest and Termination** PSE&G fired Tomkins 15 months after she complained. If her termination had been the only form of retaliation, would she have had trouble establishing a causal connection between the complaint and the retaliation? How much of a delay should defeat the retaliation charge?

B. African-American Women Led the Way

Because legal opinions rarely mention the race of the parties, few Americans realize that African-American women pioneered legal change regarding sexual harassment and sex discrimination law.[46] Three of the six plaintiffs in the early cases — including Paulette Barnes, Margaret Miller, and Diane Williams — were African-American women. Another African-American woman, Mechelle Vinson, would later win the first Supreme Court case on sexual harassment. African-American women brought every major precedent-setting sexual harassment case in these early years. The next chapter will explore why this was the case.

On appeal, these women, as well as Tomkins, Corne, and DeVane, turned to civil rights and feminist attorneys who were familiar with Title VII sex and race discrimination law. Legal precedent already established that racial harassment violated Title VII.[47] No such precedent existed for sexual harassment. Feminist attorneys drew parallels to racial harassment. They argued that a male employer who fires a woman for refusing his sexual advances had discriminated against her because of sex and, therefore, violated Title VII. These lawyers also filed race discrimination claims for their African-American clients. Supervisors had replaced Barnes and Miller with white women. Williams sued for harassment by a white man.

While district court judges ruled against Barnes, Miller, Corne, DeVane, and Tomkins, not every court that considered the question of sexual harassment denied relief. The same year that Judge Stern decided *Tomkins,* Judge Charles Richey authored

---

45. 42 U.S.C. § 2000e-3(a) (2012).
46. *See* BAKER, *supra* note 1.
47. Rogers v. EEOC, 454 F.2d 234 (5th Cir. 1971).

Williams v. Saxbe (1976), the first decision to hold that sexual harassment violates Title VII. Judge Richey had a distinctly different approach to sexual harassment than Judge Stern.

Diane Williams was a young African-American woman working as a public information specialist with the Justice Department's Community Relations Service (CRS), which mediated racial tensions in troubled communities. Williams alleged that her African-American male supervisor, Harvey Brinson, who was married with four children, attempted to date her but that she repeatedly refused. Williams alleged that many married male supervisors dated the single female employees at CRS. Brinson, said Williams, had a "notorious reputation for dating his staff members."[48] According to Williams, women who acquiesced to such requests received better work assignments and promotions from male supervisors at CRS. Williams alleged that because she resisted Brinson's advances, he "began a process of fault finding" against her. He criticized her work habits in general and her attitude toward him in particular. He subjected her to "oral and written attacks both professional and personal" and threatened her with transfer or termination. Eventually in September 1972, Brinson fired Williams, allegedly for poor performance.

Williams v. Saxbe
413 F. Supp. 654 (D.D.C. 1976)[49]

CHARLES R. RICHEY, District Judge.

. . . [T]he motion to dismiss presents the issue of whether the retaliatory actions of a male supervisor, taken because a female employee declined his sexual advances, constitutes sex discrimination within the definitional parameters of Title VII. . . .

. . . .

[The defendant argues that] . . . "Plaintiff was allegedly denied employment enhancement not because she was a woman, but rather because she decided not to furnish the sexual consideration claimed to have been demanded. Therefore, plaintiff is in no different class from other employees, regardless of their gender or sexual orientation, who are made subject to such carnal demands."

While defendants' argument is appealing, it obfuscates the fact that, taking the facts of the plaintiff's complaint as true, the conduct of the plaintiff's supervisor created an artificial barrier to employment which was placed before one gender and not the other, despite the fact that both genders were similarly situated. . . .

The fact that "Congress intended to strike at the entire spectrum of disparate treatment of men and women resulting from sex stereotypes," does not mean that only a "sex stereotype" can give rise to sex discrimination within Title VII. The

---

48. Affidavit of Diane Rennay Williams at 36, Williams v. Bell, 587 F.2d 1240 (D.C. Cir. 1978).
49. On appeal, this case was reversed in part and vacated in part. Williams v. Bell, 587 F.2d 1240 (D.C. Cir. 1978).

statute prohibits "*any* discrimination based on . . . sex. . . ." [Emphasis added.] On its face, the statute clearly does not limit discrimination to sex stereotypes. . . .

. . . .

Defendants' argument must be rejected because a finding of sex discrimination under s 2000e-16(a) does not require that the discriminatory policy or practice depend upon a characteristic peculiar to one of the genders. That a rule, regulation, practice, or policy is applied on the basis of gender is alone sufficient for a finding of sex discrimination. . . .

. . . .

Notes and Discussion

1. Sex Stereotypes The defendant in *Williams* argued that sex stereotypes were "irrelevant to the description of the alleged class." Judge Richey noted that Title VII "does not limit discrimination to sex stereotypes" and ruled on alternative grounds. Do sex stereotypes play a role in sexual harassment? If so, how? Use sex stereotyping theory to make an argument that sexual harassment violates Title VII. Why do you think Judge Richey did not use this argument?

2. A Bisexuality Defense? Footnote 6 of Judge Richey's opinion in the *Williams* case addresses the possibility of a supervisor who makes sexual advances toward both male and female employees:

> This court also rejects any argument that this cannot be sex discrimination because the application of the rule would depend upon the sexual preference of the supervisor, as opposed to some other reason. But the reason for the discrimination under Title VII is not necessary to a finding of discrimination. . . .
>
> It is also notable that since the statute prohibits discrimination against men as well as women, a finding of discrimination could be made where a female supervisor imposed the criteria of the instant case upon only the male employees in her office. So could a finding of discrimination be made if the supervisor were a homosexual. And, the fact that a finding of discrimination could not be made if the supervisor were a bisexual and applied this criteria to both genders should not lead to a conclusion that sex discrimination could not occur in other situations outlined above.[50]

Editorialists across the country condemned the *Williams* decision, often focusing on Judge Richey's comment about bisexuality in footnote 6. Do you find Judge Richey's reasoning persuasive?

Scathing criticism in the media condemned Judge Richey's decision for making "office hanky panky" a federal civil rights violation.[51] While Judge Richey's opinion was courageous for his time, other courts would soon follow.

---

50. *Williams*, 413 F. Supp. at 659 n.6.
51. BAKER, *supra* note 1, at 122–24.

3. The Tide Turns: *Barnes v. Costle*

In the late 1970s, appellate courts reversed or vacated all of the lower court decisions that had dismissed Title VII sexual harassment claims. Why the shift?

First, women who organized against sexual harassment had been working hard to raise public awareness of sexual harassment. After the Ithaca speak out, feminists knew that they had to have evidence of the impact of sexual harassment on working women in order to convince judges and the public that sexual harassment was a serious issue. Therefore, they prioritized research into the issue, surveying women about their experiences and the impact on their health and work. In 1975, WWU published results from their first survey on sexual harassment, which showed that sexual harassment was widespread and negatively impacted women's workforce participation.[52] This and other research showed that sexual harassment disproportionately harmed women. Litigators cited these studies in the early appellate briefs.

Across the country, other feminist activists and organizations secured media coverage to raise awareness, filed more lawsuits, and petitioned legislatures and Congress to address the problem. For example, founders of WWU moved to New York City in June of 1977 and changed the name of their organization to Working Women United Institute (WWUI) (and later to Working Women's Institute). On October 22, 1977, women celebrated the organization's rebirth in New York City with a speak out cosponsored by *Ms.* magazine. Approximately 200 women, including feminist icons Gloria Steinem and Robin Morgan, attended the four-hour event at the Community Church of New York on the Lower East Side. *Ms.* published a cover story on sexual harassment in its November 1977 issue. Karen Sauvigné and Susan Meyer, WWUI's founders, began to appear regularly on television and radio shows, including *Good Morning America*, the *Phil Donahue Show*, and the *Mike Douglas Show*. Sauvigné and Meyer gave public talks and conducted workshops and trainings for communities, corporations, and schools. Alliance Against Sexual Coercion in Cambridge, Massachusetts, also continued its work to understand and raise awareness about sexual harassment, and provided services to women experiencing harassment.

A second important factor in jurisprudential change was the increased involvement of feminist attorneys and organizations who supported appeals of the lower court dismissals. The Women's Legal Defense Fund in Washington, D.C., referred the *Barnes* appeal to feminist attorney Linda Singer. Another feminist attorney, Mary Dunlap, Founder of Equal Rights Advocates in San Francisco, took over the appeal in *Miller*. Heather Sigworth, a founding member of the Tucson chapter of the National Organization for Women, led the appeal in *Corne*.

Third, amicus curiae briefs, filed in several of the early successful appeals, also contributed to the change. Black Women Organized for Political Action in Washington, D.C., filed a brief in the *Williams* case and the Mexican American Legal

---

52. *Id.* at 32–34.

Defense and Education Fund filed briefs in *Miller* and *Tomkins*. Equal Rights Advocates filed a brief in *Tomkins*. These briefs cited the research of Working Women United concerning the extent and severity of sexual harassment on women in the workplace in order to convince judges that sexual harassment was not "just a personal problem," but was in fact an arbitrary barrier to workplace participation and advancement in violation of Title VII.[53]

The first appellate court to rule that sexual harassment was sex discrimination in violation of Title VII was the District of Columbia Circuit Court of Appeals in the *Barnes* case. Judge Spottswood Robinson III authored the court's opinion. Before serving on the bench, Robinson had been a civil rights attorney with the NAACP and had worked on the famous case of *Brown v. Board of Education*.[54] Compare Judge Richey's reasoning in *Williams* to that of Judge Robinson in the *Barnes* case.

Barnes v. Costle

561 F.2d 983 (D.C. Cir. 1977)

SPOTTSWOOD W. ROBINSON, III, Circuit Judge:

. . . .

By adoption of Title VII of the Civil Rights Act of 1964, Congress made it an unlawful employment practice . . . "to . . . discriminate against any individual with respect to his . . . terms, conditions, or privileges of employment, because of such individual's . . . sex. . . ." Unfortunately, the early history of that legislation lends no assistance to endeavors to define the scope of this prohibition more precisely, if indeed any elucidation were needed. It was offered as an addition to other proscriptions by opponents in a last-minute attempt to block the bill which became the Act, and the bill, with the amendment barring sex-discrimination, then quickly passed. Thus, for an eight-year period following its original enactment, there was no legislative history to refine the congressional language.

When, however, the 1964 Act was amended by the Equal Employment Opportunity Act of 1972, there was considerable discussion on the topic. Not surprisingly, it then became evident that Congress was deeply concerned about employment discrimination founded on gender, and intended to combat it as vigorously as any other type of forbidden discrimination. The report of the House Committee on Education and Labor declared in ringing tones that the statute eight years after passage still had much to accomplish in order to elevate the status of women in employment:

> Numerous studies have shown that women are placed in the less challenging, the less responsible and the less remunerative positions on the basis of their sex alone.

---

53. *Id.* at 49–50.
54. 347 U.S. 483 (1954).

Such blatantly disparate treatment is particularly objectionable in view of the fact that Title VII has specifically prohibited sex discrimination since its enactment in 1964.

The Committee emphasized that women's employment rights are not "judicial divertissements," and that "[d]iscrimination against women is no less serious than other forms of prohibited employment practices and is to be accorded the same degree of social concern given to any type of unlawful discrimination." The report of the Senate Committee on Labor and Public Welfare reveals a similar commitment to eradication of sex discrimination:

> While some have looked at the entire issue of women's rights as a frivolous divertissement, this Committee believes that discrimination against women is no less serious than other prohibited forms of discrimination, and that it is to be accorded the same degree of concern given to any type of similarly unlawful conduct. As a further point, recent studies have shown that there is a close correlation between discrimination based on sex and racial discrimination, and that both possess similar characteristics.

Not unexpectedly, then, during the thirteen years since enactment of Title VII it has become firmly established that the Act invalidates all "artificial, arbitrary and unnecessary barriers to employment when the barriers operate invidiously to discriminate on the basis of . . . impermissible classification[s]." Title VII has been invoked to strike down a wide variety of impediments to equal employment opportunity between the sexes, including insufficiently validated tests, discriminatory seniority systems, weight-lifting requirements, and height and weight standards solely for those of one gender. Congress could hardly have been more explicit in its command that there be no sex-based discrimination "against any individual with respect to his . . . terms, conditions, or privileges of employment. . . ."

. . . .

The question [here] is whether the discrimination, in the circumstances described by appellant, was as a matter of law "based on . . . sex. . . ."

. . . .

It is much too late in the day to contend that Title VII does not outlaw terms of employment for women which differ appreciably from those set for men, and which are not genuinely and reasonably related to performance on the job.

The District Court felt, however, that appellant's suit amounted to no more than a claim "that she was discriminated against, not because she was a woman, but because she refused to engage in a sexual affair with her supervisor." . . . To say, then, that she was targeted in her employment simply because she declined the invitation is to ignore the asserted fact that she was invited only because she was a woman subordinate to the inviter in the hierarchy of agency personnel. Put another way, she became the target of her superior's sexual desires because she was a woman, and was asked to bow to his demands as the price for holding her job. The circumstance imparting high visibility to the role of gender in the affair is that no male employee was susceptible to such an approach by appellant's supervisor. Thus gender cannot be eliminated from the formulation which appellant advocates, and that formulation advances a prima facie case of sex discrimination within the purview of Title VII.

It is clear that the statutory embargo on sex discrimination in employment is not confined to differentials founded wholly upon an employee's gender. On the contrary, it is enough that gender is a factor contributing to the discrimination in a substantial way. That this was the intent of Congress is readily apparent from a small but highly significant facet of the legislative history of Title VII. . . .

. . . .

Notes and Discussion

1. Sex Stereotypes Judge Robinson in *Barnes* argued that "but for her womanhood . . . [Barnes's] participation in sexual activity never would have been solicited." Does this comment relate to sex stereotypes? Why did Judge Robinson not address sex stereotypes in his opinion?

2. Legislative History In *Barnes*, Judge Robinson discussed extensively the legislative history of a 1972 amendment to Title VII, in which Congress engaged in a much more fulsome discussion of sex discrimination than it had in 1964. How did the court use this legislative history to reach its decision? Why did Judge Robinson rely on legislative history?

3. Inharmonious Personal Relationships In response to the lower court's reference to the case as "underpinned by the subtleties of an inharmonious personal relationship," Judge Robinson expressed concern about "implications to which it is susceptible." What are the implications of the lower court's view? About what was Judge Robinson concerned?

4. Analogies to Racial Harassment In their appellate briefs, an important strategy that plaintiffs' attorneys used to frame sexual harassment as sex discrimination was to analogize sexual harassment to racial harassment. They argued that if Title VII prohibited harassment based on race, national origin, and religion, it should also bar harassment based on sex. These plaintiffs cited *Rogers v. E.E.O.C.,* other cases, and EEOC decisions confirming that employers had a duty to maintain an atmosphere free of racial intimidation and insult. How is sexual harassment similar to or different from racial harassment? Why do you think the courts did not address the parties' racial harassment analogy arguments?

5. Judicial Perspective How might Judge Robinson's African-American identity and his background as a civil rights attorney have influenced his understanding of the issue and his view of Paulette Barnes's claims?

4. Early Sexual Harassment Legal Theory

In the fall of 1976, the Alliance Against Sexual Coercion published its first position paper, written by founders Freada Klein and Lynn Wehrli. Wehrli had just completed an in-depth theoretical study of sexual harassment as a master's thesis at MIT, titled *Sexual Harassment at the Workplace: A Feminist Analysis and Strategy for Social Change*. In her thesis, Wehrli developed what she called a "dominance" theory of sexual harassment. She argued that sexual harassment in the workplace is both an expression and a perpetuation of the unequal power relationships between men and women, and between employers and employees. Wehrli argued that the extent to which men exercise their dominance through sexual harassment depends on social conditions, personal choices, and threats to dominance. Social conditions include differences in socialization of males and females, males' greater access to instruments of power, the absence of sanctions, high unemployment, and women's historically marginal position in the labor market. Threats to dominance include an active feminist movement and the increasing entrance of women into traditionally male-dominated fields. In the face of these threats, explained Wehrli, men are more likely to actively reassert their dominance by sexually harassing women. Wehrli suggested that dominance takes a sexual form because of the predominant view of women as sexual objects and the strong cultural associations between dominance, masculinity, and sexual prowess.[55] Professor Catharine MacKinnon later cited Wehrli's thesis in her influential 1979 book *Sexual Harassment of Working Women*.

A. Catharine MacKinnon's *Sexual Harassment of Working Women*

Similar to Wehrli's dominance theory, MacKinnon developed an "inequality approach" for why sexual harassment was sex discrimination in violation of Title VII. MacKinnon first began researching sexual harassment as a graduate student in political science at Yale in the mid-1970s. Her father, Judge George MacKinnon, served on the United States Court of Appeals for the District of Columbia and wrote a concurring opinion in *Barnes v. Costle*, issued just a few months after his daughter graduated from Yale Law School in 1977. According to MacKinnon, she shared a draft of her sexual harassment research with the law clerks in her father's chambers. She also shared her work with Nadine Taub, who quoted MacKinnon in her *Tomkins* appellate brief.[56]

---

55. Lynn Wehrli, *Sexual Harassment at the Workplace: A Feminist Analysis and Strategy for Social Change* (1976) (unpublished M.A. thesis, Massachusetts Institute of Technology); *see also* Freada Klein & Lynn Wehrli, *Sexual Coercion on the Job?*, Sister Courage 6 (Oct. 1976).

56. Anna-Maria Marshall, *Closing the Gaps: Plaintiffs in Pivotal Sexual Harassment Cases*, 23 Law & Soc. Inquiry 761, 786–87 (1998); Elvia R. Arriola, *"What's the Big Deal?" Women in the New York City Construction Industry and Sexual Harassment Law, 1970–1985*, 22 Colum. Hum. Rts. L. Rev. 21, 42–44 (1990).

In *Sexual Harassment of Working Women*, MacKinnon distinguishes between two types of sexual harassment: "quid pro quo" sexual harassment (a phrase she coins) and what she calls "condition of work" harassment (later called hostile work environment harassment). She defines quid pro quo harassment as a situation where a "woman must comply sexually or forfeit an employment benefit." The second category, condition of work sexual harassment, includes less direct sexual behavior where the woman is "never promised or denied anything explicitly connected with her job" but that makes her work environment unbearable.[57]

MacKinnon's most important contribution, however, is her legal argument for why sexual harassment constitutes sex discrimination. She distinguishes two prevailing theories of sex discrimination, the differences approach and the inequality approach, and then argues that sexual harassment is sex discrimination under both theories. She explains the two theories as follows:

> The first approach envisions the sexes as socially as well as biologically *different* from one another, but calls impermissible or "arbitrary" those distinctions or classifications that are found preconceived and/or inaccurate. The second approach understands the sexes to be not simply socially differentiated but socially *unequal*. In this broader view, all practices which subordinate women to men are prohibited. The differences approach, in its sensitivity to disparity and similarity, can be a useful corrective to sexism; both women and men can be damaged by sexism, although usually it is women who are. The inequality approach, by contrast, sees women's situation as a structural problem of enforced inferiority that needs to be radically altered.[58]

The differences approach seeks to achieve equality by applying "the formula that 'similarly situated' persons should be treated the same, meaning that persons in relevantly similar circumstances should be treated relevantly similarly." The less commonly applied sex inequality theory understands that sex discrimination is the systematic domination of women by men. This theoretical perspective examines "whether the policy or practice in question integrally contributes to the maintenance of an underclass or a deprived position because of gender status."

While both of these approaches provide a remedy for sex discrimination, the differences approach is weaker, argues MacKinnon. She reasons that critics can manipulate an analysis to obscure the social reality of power differentials between men and women. She explains:

> Implicit in the distinction in approach are different conceptions of reasonable comparability: must women and men be able to be compared on the variable in question? Further, exactly what the variable in question is defined to be is decided by the approach which is taken. Under the differences

---

57. MACKINNON, *supra* note 40, at 32, 40.
58. *Id.* at 4–5.

approach, if the context is defined so that the sexes cannot be reasonably compared, discrimination cannot be seen to be sex-based. By contrast, the inequality approach comprehends that women and men may, due to sex or sexism, present noncomparabilities. In this view, lack of comparability is not a permissible basis for socially perpetuating women's disadvantages.[59]

MacKinnon gives the example of pregnancy. Cisgender men and women are not comparable because only women experience pregnancy. Under the differences approach, therefore, if a policy harms pregnant people, the policy does not discriminate. MacKinnon cites the 1976 Supreme Court case of *General Electric v. Gilbert*,[60] which held that an employer's disability plan that excluded pregnancy does not discriminate against women. Under the inequality approach, however, MacKinnon concludes this policy is discriminatory because it disadvantages women and perpetuates women's subordination to men.

MacKinnon argues that sexual harassment is sex discrimination under both theories, but that the differences theory is inadequate. Under the differences approach, sexual harassment constitutes sex discrimination because men and women are comparable with regard to sexual harassment (both sexes can be sexually harassed) but the sexes are not treated the same (women are harassed more). MacKinnon argues that this approach is inadequate because it presumes equality (comparability) to measure disparity. Moreover, it ignores that the sexes are in fact substantially unequal. In contrast, the inequality approach highlights that sexual harassment expresses and reinforces women's social inequality to men. According to MacKinnon, "under the inequality approach, sexual harassment is seen to disadvantage women as a gender, within the social context in which women's sexuality and material survival have been constructed and joined, to women's detriment."[61] Thus, under both approaches, sexual harassment is sex discrimination. However, the differences approach obscures the unequal relations of power between men and women that make women more vulnerable to sexual harassment than men.

MacKinnon also argues that sexual harassment is more than an individual injury. She emphasizes it as a group-based discrimination that harms all women by reinforcing women's subordinate status in the workplace. She suggests that sex segregation in the workplace, male control of hiring and firing, and male control of women in other spheres of life make women systematically vulnerable to sexual harassment. MacKinnon writes:

> Intimate violation of women by men is sufficiently pervasive in American society as to be invisible. Contained by internalized and structural forms of power, it has been nearly inaudible. Conjoined with men's control over women's material survival, as in the home or on the job, or over

59. *Id.* at 5.
60. 429 U.S. 125, 161–62 (1976).
61. MacKinnon, *supra* note 40, at 6.

women's learning and educational advancement in school, it has become institutionalized. Women employed in the paid labor force, typically hired "as women," dependent upon their income and lacking job alternatives, are particularly vulnerable to intimate violation in the form of sexual abuse at work. In addition to being victims of the practice, working women have been subject to the social failure to recognize sexual harassment as an abuse at all. Tacitly, it has been both acceptable and taboo; acceptable for men to do, taboo for women to confront, even to themselves.[62]

Building on Wehrli's dominance theory, MacKinnon believes that unequal power between men and women is critical to understanding sexual harassment—how it happens, its impact, its interconnections, and why it continues. She notes:

> Sexual harassment, most broadly defined, refers to the unwanted imposition of sexual requirements in the context of a relationship of unequal power. Central to the concept is the use of power derived from one social sphere to lever benefits or impose deprivations in another. . . .
>
> . . . .
>
> Typically, employers, husbands, judges, and the victims themselves have understood and dismissed such incidents [of sexual harassment] as trivial, isolated, and "personal," or as universal "natural" or "biological" behaviors. This book interprets sexual harassment in the context of women's work and sex roles, in which women as a group are seen to occupy a structurally inferior as well as distinct place. Sexual harassment is argued to derive its meaning and detrimental impact upon women not from personality or biology, but from this *social* context. The defining dimensions of this social context are employer-employee relations (given the women's position in the labor force) and the relationship between the sexes in American society as a whole, of which sexual relations are one expression.[63]

MacKinnon explicitly links women's subordinate position in the workplace to sexual harassment. She reasons:

> Work is critical to women's survival and independence. Sexual harassment exemplifies and promotes employment practices which disadvantage women in work (especially occupational segregation) and sexual practices which intimately degrade and objectify women. In this broader perspective, sexual harassment at work undercuts a woman's potential for social equality in two interpenetrated ways: by using her employment position to coerce her sexually, while using her sexual position to coerce her economically. Legal recognition that sexual harassment is sex discrimination in employment would help women break the bond between material survival and sexual

---

62. *Id.* at 1.
63. *Id.* at 1–2.

exploitation. It would support and legitimize women's economic equality and sexual self-determination at a point at which the two are linked.[64]

MacKinnon's ground-breaking work set the stage for future developments in sexual harassment law and legal theory.

Notes and Discussion

1. The Differences and Inequality Approaches What do you think are the strengths and weaknesses of the differences approach and the inequality approach to sex discrimination described by MacKinnon? How are the two approaches distinctive? Which is more effective for arguing that Title VII should prohibit sexual harassment? Which theory was used by Judge Richey in the *Williams* case? What about in the *Barnes* and *Tomkins* appellate decisions?

2. Framing and Impermissible Classifications The differences approach suggests that how one frames the comparison of women and men affects whether the comparison produces a difference that one might call arbitrary. If one frames a comparison using pregnancy, men and women compare differently. If one makes another comparison using a broader framework—health care needs—women and men appear similar. Specifically, both men and women need health care. Thus, the framing of the comparison changes the possible results. Is this a strength or a weakness of this approach?

When reframing influences, whether one distinguishes women and men necessarily affects the discovery of arbitrary or impermissible classifications. Consider whether an employer's refusal to hire workers with children involves impermissible classifications. Framed in that manner, the ban creates no distinct sex classifications because both men and women have children. But what if you reframe the interdiction to prevent the hire of primary caregivers? On its face, that ban looks gender neutral, but we know that women provide more child care, on average, than men. Thus, the reframing creates an impermissible sex classification in its application. Are there other examples of how framing might change the results of a comparative analysis?

3. Framing and the Inequality Approach Does framing also influence the methodology of the inequality approach? The inequality approach assumes a framework in which men subordinate women—a fairly expansive framework. If one broadens the frame even more, however, one might see men sexually harassing men, especially effeminate men or transgender men. How might MacKinnon have dealt with this picture using an inequality approach? With respect to gay men and lesbians, MacKinnon concluded that "the vulnerability of gays is analogous to that of women."[65] Does her theory of subordination extend to effeminate, heterosexual men and to masculine, heterosexual women? If not, should it?

---

64. *Id.* at 7.
65. *Id.* at 204.

4. Social Context/Social Meaning MacKinnon suggests that sexual harassment disadvantages "women as a gender, within the social context in which women's sexuality and material survival have been constructed and joined, to women's detriment."[66] If men and women were truly equal in our society, would men still sexually harass women? If yes, would sexual harassment still constitute sex discrimination under MacKinnon's analysis? Are there any problems with relying on social context to define sexual harassment? See *infra* Chapter 3 (Justice Scalia's appeal to "common sense and social context" in *Oncale v. Sundowner Offshore Serv's, Inc.*). Should *social meaning* dictate the definition of sex generally? Why or why not?

MacKinnon suggests that if a perpetrator harasses both men and women, such behavior would not constitute sex discrimination. Is that always true? Might the social context of "equal opportunity" harassment exacerbate the subordinating or demeaning nature of the harassment directed at women? See, e.g., *Swinton v. Potomac Corp.*, 270 F.3d 794, 807 (9th Cir. 2001) (rejecting the equal opportunity harasser defense in a race harassment case); *Steiner v. Showboat Operating Co.*, 25 F.3d 1459, 1464 (9th Cir. 1994) (holding that the reasonable woman might be affected differently from the reasonable man); but see *Holman v. Indiana*, 211 F.3d 399, 402 (7th Cir. 2000) (affirming that the equal opportunity harasser escapes Title VII purview); *Colston v. Cleveland Public Library*, No. 12-4103 (6th Cir. 2013) (same).

Even if the social context does not influence the behavior, what if male and female targets interpret the behavior differently? Might that difference influence the determination of whether the conduct is sex discrimination? Should the "eyes of the beholder" matter?

5. Sexuality and Gender Later in the book, MacKinnon discusses sexuality and gender:

> [T]he sexuality of women vis-à-vis men could be considered an aspect of "gender *per se*." Discrimination "because of sexuality" would be merged with, and subsumed under, discrimination "because of sex." This could be more or less a social or a biological conception, depending upon the understanding of the determinants of sexuality and gender. . . .
>
> . . . .
>
> The "sexuality, not gender" analysis . . . was expressed in its most extended form by the government on behalf of the defendants in *Barnes* and *Williams*. "The impetus for the creation of the class must be distinguished from the primary variable which describes the class." In their attempt to distinguish sexual treatment from gender, neither specifies what the "impetus for the creation of the class" is supposed to be. The implication is that it is the sex drive, or something to do with sexuality. In fact, it is the male supervisor's *sexist behavior* which "creates the class." Women are

---

66. *Id.* at 6.

sexually harassed *because they are women*, in the full social meaning of the term. Sexual harassment is a clear social manifestation of male privilege incarnated in the male sex role that supports coercive sexuality reinforced by male power over the job. It is not incumbent upon the victims to explain why a given male chooses to express his sexism in this way, or with them. They need not connect his "impetus" for "creating the class" with its defining variable—their femaleness—to make out a case of sex discrimination. The male supervisor's behavior makes this connection itself by demanding sexual favors of women. In doing so, he "creates the class" and defines its primary variable according to his sexual preferences. In such cases, the distinction between "the creation of the class" and "the primary variable which describes the class" is nothing but the distinction between male and female.[67]

MacKinnon asks whether sexuality is "a source, form, and sphere of social inequality or whether it is merely a sphere onto which other forms of unequal power . . . are displaced and imposed. . . ."[68] Which is it? Does it matter in the workplace whether sexuality is a source of inequality or a convenient forum for imposed subordination? Is sexuality a status or a practice? Should it be protected under Title VII? Are there any "practices" associated with a particular race or creed that enjoy protection by antidiscrimination laws? Is sexuality unique to each sex? If so, how? If not, should it still enjoy Title VII protection?

Is it true, as MacKinnon asserts, that our culture interrelates heterosexuality and gender, or "social conceptions of maleness and femaleness"? If so, how? Is an attack upon sexuality "an attack upon womanhood"? What if the perpetrator directs the attack against gay male sexuality? Is that still an attack upon womanhood or is that an attack against manhood? If it is an attack against manhood, is it distinctly discrimination because of sex? If our culture interrelates heterosexuality and gender, is it possible to disassociate the two?[69] If courts fail to deconstruct the interconnection, do they treat discrimination because of sexuality the same as discrimination because of sex? Or do courts fail to perceive their own heterosexist bias and treat sexuality discrimination, especially minority sexuality discrimination, differently from sex discrimination?

Is it accurate, as MacKinnon suggests, that sexual harassment constitutes sex discrimination in the workplace? When MacKinnon explains that men sexually harass women "*because they are women*," she speaks in terms of female sexuality. Is it correct that only female sexuality and its abuse justify the identification of sexual harassment as sex discrimination? If not, are there other factors that might explain sexual harassment and confirm it as a subset of sex discrimination?

---

67. *Id.* at 183, 191–92.
68. *Id.* at 59.
69. *See infra* Chapter 2.

6. Impetus for the Creation of the Class/Motivation MacKinnon de-emphasizes the importance of "sex drive" and emphasizes, instead, "sexist behavior." Should courts focus on the behavior as MacKinnon suggests? Does the perpetrator's motivation matter? If it does, can anything other than (non-bisexual) sexual desire or gender animus support a claim of sexual harassment as sex discrimination? Should proving the perpetrator's intent or motivation be part of the plaintiff's prima facie case?

B. Nadine Taub's *Keeping Women in Their Place: Stereotyping Per Se as a Form of Employment Discrimination*

Another important legal theorist of sexual harassment was Nadine Taub. In 1980, Taub published *Keeping Women in Their Place: Stereotyping Per Se as a Form of Employment Discrimination*,[70] in which she proposes an expansion of discrimination theory. In her article, Taub argues that sexually harassing behavior is based on sex stereotyped views of women. Taub explains:

> Sexual references, as well as explicit demands for sexual cooperation, convey the message that a woman is a sexual object before she is a contributing worker, and whether it is consciously undertaken or not, such behavior serves to reinforce woman's sexual role. Indeed, such behavior is probably the quintessential expression of stereotypic role expectations. Like other expressions of stereotypic expectations occurring at the workplace, it is dysfunctional in two respects. Whether or not perceived as flattering by women, sexual advances remind women of a socially-imposed incongruity between their role as worker and as woman. By thus arousing role conflict in women, advances interfere with their performance. By underscoring their sexual identity in the eyes of male supervisors, sexual advances make it less likely that women will be viewed as persons capable of performing a demanding task, and consequently, less likely that they will have the opportunity to try to do so.[71]

Sexual stereotypes, suggests Taub, are based on, but also perpetuate, views of women as primarily sexual objects rather than workers.

Taub argues that sexual harassment does not fit into traditional concepts of discrimination, which require a showing of hostile motive, differential treatment, or disparate impact. She notes that "because those making sexual demands and allusions are often merely acting out the roles they have been taught by society, unaware of the hostile nature of their conduct, the notion of old-time evil motive, equivalent to racial animus, seems inappropriate."[72] Furthermore, proof that men and women experience unequal treatment may not exist for sex-segregated jobs if there are no

---

70. 21 B.C. L. Rev. 345 (1980).
71. *Id.* at 361.
72. *Id.*

similarly situated males. Finally, because of the individual nature of sexual harassment, rarely will it indicate a neutral company policy with a disparate impact. However, Taub acknowledges that corporate tolerance of harassing behavior might amount to a policy.

By 1980, when Taub published this article, there was strong precedent for Title VII's prohibition of quid pro quo sexual harassment, but no court had yet ruled that Title VII prohibited hostile environment sexual harassment by supervisors or peers. In her article, Taub provides a theoretical foundation from which courts could expand their sexual harassment jurisprudence to encompass this broader range of behavior and to hold employers responsible for addressing it. Taub clarifies what a plaintiff must show to prove a case of hostile environment sexual harassment. She explores the kind of behavior that creates discriminatory "terms and conditions of employment" under Title VII.

Taub criticizes courts' inequality approach to sexual harassment. In both *Barnes* and *Tomkins*, the courts held that plaintiffs need only show that "but for the plaintiff's gender the solicitation would not have occurred." In this way, the courts employed a "symmetrical analysis" by focusing on the sexuality of the harasser and the hypothetical female harasser of male employees. But symmetrical analysis ignores the "asymmetrical social reality of the sexual harassment phenomenon," thereby underestimating its dimensions and its seriousness. She notes:

> [S]exual allusions are so rarely directed by women at men, and because it is so difficult to envision them as interfering with a man's ability to function on the job, a legal analysis that insists on symmetry is unlikely to recognize the detrimental effect that such conduct, when directed by men at women, has on equal opportunity in employment.[73]

Taub concludes that "such conduct harms women workers in particular." She emphasizes that women are more likely than men to be in subordinate positions in the workplace, and therefore subject to the sexual demands of their supervisors.

She also argues that women are more vulnerable to sexual coercion by their bosses because "males in our society have the exclusive right to initiate sexual interaction with others."[74] This behavior is "uniquely disturbing to women" because "it is a reminder, a badge or incident of a servile status, which women are striving to leave behind. . . . [S]exual allusions, whether 'friendly' or hostile, emphasize that the female is a body, not a person capable of working."[75] According to Taub, "sexual advances—even those that stop short of actually coercing sexual cooperation—invoke woman's historically inferior position, her socialization as sex object, and her inability to be seen as a capable worker."[76] Therefore, under the sex stereotyping

---

73. *Id.* at 367.
74. *Id.*
75. *Id.* at 368.
76. *Id.* at 371.

theory, "it would be sufficient to show that the adverse employment decision was based on an expectation that women should conform to a certain pattern of behavior whether or not that expectation was based on hostility, and whether or not there is a similarly situated male who received different treatment." She concludes that "[t]he recognition of discrimination as adverse decisions based on stereotypes *per se* means focusing on the effects of acts, not on the intent of the actor."[77]

Notes and Discussion

1. Sex Stereotypes and Sexual Harassment Is Taub correct that sexual harassment is the "quintessential expression of stereotypic role expectations"? Taub argues that sexual harassment is based on sex stereotypes of women as sexual objects and reinforces "women's sexual role." Is that true? What is "women's sexual role"? Taub wrote her article in 1980. Has society's view of "women's sexual role" changed since Taub wrote her article?

2. Traditional Discrimination What three traditional discrimination concepts does Taub describe? Why does she conclude that sexual harassment does not fit neatly within those traditional frameworks? What does she propose instead? Does Taub suggest that the bisexual harasser who targets both men and women does not discriminate on the basis of sex? Would such an assertion be consistent with her notion of the subordinated position women hold in society and in the workplace in particular? Explain.

3. Defining Sexual Harassment and Employer Liability Taub argues that sex stereotyping theory can help define the scope of conduct to be proscribed and the extent of employer liability. Is she correct that sexual harassment is based on sex stereotyped attitudes that disadvantage women in the workplace? What behavior should be prohibited? What does this mean for employers' responsibility to address sexually harassing behavior?

4. MacKinnon or Taub? Compare MacKinnon's inequality approach to Taub's sex stereotyping theory. Which approach do you find more useful to support the argument that sexual harassment is sex discrimination and why?

5. Hostile Work Environment Harassment

While office workers brought some of the earliest sexual harassment cases, blue-collar women in male-dominated occupations, such as construction and coal mining, also organized around the issue in the 1970s. As women broke into these traditionally male fields, they experienced tremendous hostility from men. Sometimes this hostility took the form of sexualized behavior—dirty jokes, sexual graffiti, pornography posted on walls, repeated propositioning, and sexual assault. But

---

77. *Id.* at 418.

often men expressed their hostility to women through nonsexualized behavior such as social isolation, work sabotage, verbal abuse, and physical violence. Groups such as Wider Opportunities for Women in Washington, D.C., and the Coal Employment Project in Oak Ridge, Tennessee, organized support for women, filed lawsuits, and pressed the federal government to address the issues of discrimination and harassment. These activists broadened the response beyond supervisor quid pro quo sexual harassment. They targeted all forms of hostile environment sex-based harassment by both bosses and co-workers.[78]

In response to a lawsuit filed by female construction workers, the Department of Labor adopted the first federal regulations concerning sexual harassment in 1978. Those regulations required employers to ensure a working environment free of harassment, intimidation, and coercion. They also mandated that contractors assign two or more women to each construction project, if possible.[79]

Courts also began to hear hostile environment sexual harassment cases, including the case of another pioneering African-American plaintiff named Sandra Bundy. Bundy was a Vocational Rehabilitation Specialist with the District of Columbia Department of Corrections. She experienced harassment from both supervisors and co-workers. Despite a finding that "improper sexual advances to female employees [was] standard operating procedure, a fact of life, a normal condition of employment" at the Department of Corrections, the federal district court judge ruled against Bundy. He concluded that she experienced no "tangible economic harm"— namely, she was not fired. Publicity from Bundy's trial, as well as news from several other cases brought by D.C. city employees, caught the attention of Congressman James M. Hanley.

Hanley, a Democrat from New York and Chair of the House Subcommittee on Investigations of the Post Office and Civil Service Committee, initiated an investigation into sexual harassment in the federal government.[80] In October and November 1979, Hanley held congressional hearings. A number of women's rights advocates, union representatives, heads of government agencies, and even survivors, such as Dianne Williams, testified.[81] Hanley directed the heads of three federal agencies to address the issue of sexual harassment.

First, he directed the Merit Systems Protection Board to conduct a survey of sexual harassment in the federal workplace. In September 1980, the Board published its survey of 23,000 federal employees, revealing that 42% of women and 15% of men reported experiencing sexual harassment in the previous two years. Second, he requested the Office of Personnel Management to develop a model policy and procedures to address sexual harassment for use throughout the federal workplace.

---

78. BAKER, *supra* note 1, at 67–81.

79. 41 C.F.R. §§ 60-40 (1978); 29 C.F.R. § 30 (1978).

80. BAKER, *supra* note 1, at 111–15.

81. Sexual Harassment in the Federal Government: Hearings before the Subcommittee on Investigations of the Committee on Post Office and Civil Service, 96th Cong. (1979).

This protocol would serve as a model program for state and local governments as well as private employers.

Finally, Hanley asked EEOC Chair Eleanor Holmes Norton to develop sexual harassment guidelines. Intended to facilitate the processing of complaints within the EEOC, this guidance would also serve private employers covered by Title VII. Hanley's subcommittee issued a report in April 1980 concluding that sexual harassment was widespread in the federal government and an "extremely serious matter."[82]

Hanley's third directive had a lasting influence on the development of sexual harassment law. Under the direction of Norton, an African-American woman who had been an active leader in the civil rights movement, the EEOC promulgated the first set of guidelines to advise courts. Norton had addressed sexual harassment years earlier as the Chair of New York City's Human Rights Commission when Working Women United founder Lin Farley had testified before the Commission about the issue. Informed by experience, Norton led the EEOC to adopt expansive guidelines that prohibited both quid pro quo and hostile environment sexual harassment. The EEOC finalized its sexual harassment guidelines in November 1980, shortly after Ronald Reagan's landslide victory. Consider how the EEOC defined sexual harassment and employer responsibility.

EEOC Guidelines on Sexual Harassment
29 C.F.R. 1604.11 (1980)

§ 1604.11 Sexual harassment.

(a) Harassment on the basis of sex is a violation of Sec. 703 of Title VII. Unwelcome sexual advances, requests for sexual favors, and other verbal or physical conduct of a sexual nature constitute sexual harassment when

    (1) submission to such conduct is made either explicitly or implicitly a term or condition of an individual's employment,

    (2) submission to or rejection of such conduct by an individual is used as the basis for employment decisions affecting such individual, or

    (3) such conduct has the purpose or effect of unreasonably interfering with an individual's work performance or creating an intimidating, hostile, or offensive working environment.

(b) In determining whether alleged conduct constitutes sexual harassment, the Commission will look at the record as a whole and at the totality of the circumstances, such as the nature of the sexual advances and the context in which the alleged incidents occurred. The determination of the legality of a particular action will be made from the facts, on a case by case basis.

---

82. Staff of H. Subcomm. on Investigations of the Comm. on Post Office & Civil Service, 96th Cong., Sexual Harassment in the Federal Government 22 (Comm. Print Apr. 30,1980).

As soon as Reagan arrived in office, his administration promptly attempted to rescind the EEOC sexual harassment guidelines. Vigorous opposition by the women's movement blocked this attempt. Reagan eventually replaced Eleanor Holmes Norton with a new Chair of the EEOC—Clarence Thomas.

Notes and Discussion

1. Hostile Environment Sexual Harassment The district court in *Williams* and the appellate courts of *Barnes* and *Tomkins* had already recognized the first two types of harassment described in the guidelines. No court, however, had found liability for hostile work environment harassment, which constituted the third type described in the EEOC guidelines. MacKinnon describes condition of work sexual harassment as follows:

> In the quid pro quo, the woman must comply sexually or forfeit an employment opportunity. . . . In sexual harassment as a condition of work, the exchange of sex for employment opportunities is less direct.
>
> . . . .
>
> . . . [A woman] may be constantly felt or pinched, visually undressed and stared at, surreptitiously kissed, commented upon, manipulated into being found alone, and generally taken advantage of at work—but never promised or denied anything explicitly connected with her job. . . . Never knowing if it will ever stop or if escalation is imminent, a woman can put up with it or leave. Most women hardly choose to be confronted by "the choice of putting up with being man handled, or being out of work." Most women are coerced into tolerance.
>
> . . . .
>
> Sexual harassment as a working condition often does not require a decisive yes or no to further involvement. The threat of loss of work explicit in the quid pro quo may be only implicit without being any less coercive. . . .
>
> . . . .
>
> . . . At the point of resistance the quid pro quo that was implicit all long in the working condition—the "tolerate it or leave" in her mind becomes "now that you don't tolerate it, you're leaving" from the boss—is forced into the open, and the two categories converge.[83]

Does the EEOC definition capture the full range of behavior envisioned by MacKinnon in this passage? Is the definition too narrow? Too broad? Do the guidelines cover nonsexual, sexist harassment?

2. Unwelcomeness The EEOC guidelines target "unwelcome sexual conduct." How might complainants prove such behavior? Must they express that the behavior is

---

83. MacKinnon, *supra* note 40, at 32, 40, 44, 46.

unwelcome, and if so, how? What does such a requirement imply about workplace norms?[84]

3. Unreasonable Interference What do the EEOC guidelines mean by "unreasonably interfering with an individual's work performance"? Is there such a thing as reasonable interference with work?[85]

4. Intimidating, Hostile, or Offensive From whose perspective is a working environment determined to be "intimidating, hostile or offensive"? From the plaintiff's, the alleged harasser's, or the employer's? Research shows that men and women react differently to sexual behavior in the workplace. Should gender factor into evaluations of whether behavior is offensive? How offensive must the behavior be to amount to sexual harassment? Must plaintiffs show they were physically or psychologically harmed by the alleged sexual misconduct?[86]

5. Sexual Harassment and Free Speech? What is "verbal conduct"? In the public workplace, might restrictions on "verbal conduct" violate employees' First Amendment rights? What about pornography in the workplace?[87]

The importance of the EEOC guidelines became immediately evident in January 1981. That year, the Court of Appeals for the D.C. Circuit cited them in a groundbreaking decision in favor of Sandra Bundy. Bundy had appealed the district court decision against her to reassert her hostile work environment claim. Judge Spottswood Robinson, who had written the *Barnes* decision, joined Judge J. Skelly Wright, who authored the *Bundy* decision, to reverse the lower court.

Bundy v. Jackson
641 F.2d 934 (D.C. Cir. 1981)

J. SKELLY WRIGHT, Chief Judge:

. . . [A]ppellant asks us to extend *Barnes* by holding that an employer violates Title VII merely by subjecting female employees to sexual harassment, even if the employee's resistance to that harassment does not cause the employer to deprive her of any tangible job benefits.

The District Court in this case made an express finding of fact that in appellant's agency "the making of improper sexual advances to female employees (was) standard operating procedure, a fact of life, a normal condition of employment," and that the director of the agency, to whom she complained of the harassment, failed to investigate her complaints or take them seriously.

. . . .

---

84. *See infra* Chapter 3, 2. Element Two: The Unwelcomeness of Sexual Harassment.

85. *See infra* Chapter 3, 3.B. *The Reasonableness Standard.*

86. *See infra* Chapter 3, 3. Element Four: Conduct That Affects the Terms, Conditions, or Privileges of Employment.

87. *See infra* Chapter 9, 3. The First Amendment Defense.

[One supervisor] casually dismissed Bundy's complaints, telling her that "any man in his right mind would want to rape you," and then proceeding himself to request that she begin a sexual relationship with him in his apartment. Bundy rejected his request.

. . . .

[This case presents] the novel question whether the sexual harassment of the sort Bundy suffered amounted by itself to sex discrimination with respect to the "*terms, conditions, or privileges of employment*." Though no court has as yet so held, we believe that an affirmative answer follows ineluctably from numerous cases finding Title VII violations where an employer created or condoned a substantially discriminatory work environment, regardless of whether the complaining employees lost any tangible job benefits as a result of the discrimination.

Bundy's claim on this score is essentially that "conditions of employment" include the psychological and emotional work environment that the sexually stereotyped insults and demeaning propositions to which she was indisputably subjected and which caused her anxiety and debilitation illegally poisoned that environment. This claim invokes the Title VII principle enunciated by Judge Goldberg in *Rogers v. Equal Employment Opportunity Comm'n.* (1972). The plaintiff in *Rogers*, a Hispanic, did not claim that her employer, a firm of opticians, had deprived her of any tangible job benefit. Rather, she claimed that by giving discriminatory service to its Hispanic clients the firm created a discriminatory and offensive work environment for its Hispanic employees. Granting that the express language of Title VII did not mention this situation, Judge Goldberg stated:

> Congress chose neither to enumerate specific discriminatory practices, nor to elucidate in extenso the parameter of such nefarious activities. Rather, it pursued the path of wisdom by being unconstrictive, knowing that constant change is the order of our day and that the seemingly reasonable practices of the present can easily become the injustices of the morrow. Time was when employment discrimination tended to be viewed as a series of isolated and distinguishable events, manifesting itself, for example, in an employer's practices of hiring, firing, and promoting. But today employment discrimination is a far more complex and pervasive phenomenon, as the nuances and subtleties of discriminatory employment practices are no longer confined to bread and butter issues. As wages and hours of employment take subordinate roles in management-labor relationships, the modern employee makes ever-increasing demands in the nature of intangible fringe benefits. Recognizing the importance of these benefits, we should neither ignore their need for protection, nor blind ourselves to their potential misuse.

The Fifth Circuit then concluded that the employer had indeed violated Title VII. Judge Goldberg explained that "terms, conditions, or privileges of employment"

> is an expansive concept which sweeps within its protective ambit the practice of creating a work environment heavily charged with ethnic or racial

discrimination. . . . One can readily envision working environments so heavily polluted with discrimination as to destroy completely the emotional and psychological stability of minority group workers . . . .

. . . .

The relevance of these "discriminatory environment" cases to sexual harassment is beyond serious dispute. Racial or ethnic discrimination against a company's minority clients may reflect no intent to discriminate directly against the company's minority employees, but in poisoning the atmosphere of employment it violates Title VII. Sexual stereotyping through discriminatory dress requirements may be benign in intent, and may offend women only in a general, atmospheric manner, yet it violates Title VII. Racial slurs, though intentional and directed at individuals, may still be just verbal insults, yet they too may create Title VII liability. How then can sexual harassment, which injects the most demeaning sexual stereotypes into the general work environment and which always represents an intentional assault on an individual's innermost privacy, not be illegal?

Moreover, an important principle articulated in *Rogers v. Equal Employment Opportunity Comm'n, supra*, suggests the special importance of allowing women to sue to prevent sexual harassment without having to prove that they resisted the harassment and that their resistance caused them to lose tangible job benefits. Judge Goldberg noted that even indirect discrimination is illegal because it

> may constitute a subtle scheme designed to create a working environment imbued with discrimination and directed ultimately at minority group employees. As patently discriminatory practices become outlawed, those employers bent on pursuing a general policy declared illegal by Congressional mandate will undoubtedly devise more sophisticated methods to perpetuate discrimination among employees. . . .

Thus, unless we extend the *Barnes* holding, an employer could sexually harass a female employee with impunity by carefully stopping short of firing the employee or taking any other tangible actions against her in response to her resistance, thereby creating the impression the one received by the District Court in this case that the employer did not take the ritual of harassment and resistance "seriously."

Indeed, so long as women remain inferiors in the employment hierarchy, they may have little recourse against harassment beyond the legal recourse Bundy seeks in this case. The law may allow a woman to prove that her resistance to the harassment cost her her [sic] job or some economic benefit, but this will do her no good if the employer never takes such tangible actions against her.

> And this, in turn, means that so long as the sexual situation is constructed with enough coerciveness, subtlety, suddenness, or one-sidedness to negate the effectiveness of the woman's refusal, or so long as her refusals are simply ignored while her job is formally undisturbed, she is not considered to have been sexually harassed.

C. MacKinnon, *Sexual Harassment of Working Women* 46–47 (1979). It may even be pointless to require the employee to prove that she "resisted" the harassment at all. So long as the employer never literally forces sexual relations on the employee, "resistance" may be a meaningless alternative for her. If the employer demands no response to his verbal or physical gestures other than good-natured tolerance, the woman has no means of communicating her rejection. She neither accepts nor rejects the advances; she simply endures them. She might be able to contrive proof of rejection by objecting to the employer's advances in some very visible and dramatic way, but she would do so only at the risk of making her life on the job even more miserable. Id. at 43–47. It hardly helps that the remote prospect of legal relief under *Barnes* remains available if she objects so powerfully that she provokes the employer into firing her.

The employer can thus implicitly and effectively make the employee's endurance of sexual intimidation a "condition" of her employment. The woman then faces a "cruel trilemma." She can endure the harassment. She can attempt to oppose it, with little hope of success, either legal or practical, but with every prospect of making the job even less tolerable for her. Or she can leave her job, with little hope of legal relief and the likely prospect of another job where she will face harassment anew.

Bundy proved that she was the victim of a practice of sexual harassment and a discriminatory work environment permitted by her employer. Her rights under Title VII were therefore violated. We thus reverse the District Court's holding on this issue and remand it to that court so it can fashion appropriate injunctive relief. And on this novel issue, we think it advisable to offer the District Court guidance in framing its decree.

. . . .

Applying [the EEOC] Guidelines to the present case, we believe that the Director of the agency should be ordered to raise affirmatively the subject of sexual harassment with all his employees and inform all employees that sexual harassment violates Title VII of the Civil Rights Act of 1964, the Guidelines of the EEOC, the express orders of the Mayor of the District of Columbia, and the policy of the agency itself. The Director should also establish and publicize a scheme whereby harassed employees may complain to the Director immediately and confidentially. The Director should promptly take all necessary steps to investigate and correct any harassment, including warnings and appropriate discipline directed at the offending party, and should generally develop other means of preventing harassment within the agency.

. . . .

Notes and Discussion

1. Racial Harassment and Sexual Harassment *Bundy* stands as the first decision to find liability when the plaintiff had not necessarily suffered a tangible economic loss during the course of sexually harassing conduct. Reversing the district court, which refused Bundy declaratory and injunctive relief, the appellate court relied on race and national origin discrimination precedents. How are racial and sexual harassment similar? How are they different? Is analogizing sexual harassment to racial harassment an effective legal strategy? What are the advantages and/or drawbacks?

2. Race and Sexual Harassment As in the cases of Diane Williams and Paulette Barnes, the *Bundy* case involved an African-American woman alleging sexual harassment by an African-American man. Is it a coincidence that these three precedent-setting sexual harassment cases all involved African Americans? In the first Supreme Court case on sexual harassment, *Meritor Savings Bank v. Vinson*, 477 U.S. 57 (1986), the plaintiff and alleged harasser were also African Americans. Why might African-American women be disproportionately represented in sexual harassment cases?

Note that Judge Robinson participated in both the *Barnes* and *Bundy* decisions. He also took part in the decisions upholding *Williams* and ruling in favor of the plaintiff in *Vinson* when it was before the D.C. Circuit Court of Appeals. As a result, Judge Robinson was clearly the single most influential federal judge in the development of sexual harassment law. How might have Judge Robinson's race and civil rights background influenced his views on this issue?[88]

3. Sexual Harassment Theory What reasoning does the court use to justify its finding that Title VII prohibits hostile environment sexual harassment? Recognizing the harm of sex role stereotypes, the *Bundy* court held that "sexual stereotyping . . . may be benign intent . . . yet it violates Title VII." Did the theories of Catharine MacKinnon and Nadine Taub influence the *Bundy* decision?

Following *Bundy*, courts remained split concerning the viability of hostile work environment claims. They also could not agree under what circumstances employers should be found liable. A year later the United States Court of Appeals for the Eleventh Circuit issued an opinion that clarified how to prove a hostile environment sexual harassment case under Title VII.

6. Formulation of the Prima Facie Case

In *Henson v. City of Dundee,* the Eleventh Circuit laid out the prima facie elements for a hostile environment sexual harassment case. Four years later, these elements served as the basis for the Supreme Court opinion in *Meritor Savings Bank v. Vinson.*

Henson v. City of Dundee
682 F.2d 897 (11th Cir. 1982)

VANCE, Circuit Judge:

. . . Appellant, Barbara Henson, filed a Title VII action against the City of Dundee, Florida alleging sexual harassment on her job with the police department.

---

88. *See infra* Chapter 2.

At the close of appellant's case, the district court entered judgment for the City of Dundee and this appeal followed.

Henson was hired as a dispatcher in the five-officer Dundee police department on January 14, 1975. . . .

Henson claims that during the two years she worked for the Dundee police department, she and her female co-worker were subjected to sexual harassment by the chief of the Dundee police department, John Sellgren. She alleges that this harassment ultimately led her to resign under duress on January 28, 1977. . . .

At trial, Henson attempted to prove three types of sexual harassment. First, she claimed that Sellgren created a hostile and offensive working environment for women in the police station. She and her former co-worker, Dicks, testified that Sellgren subjected them to numerous harangues of demeaning sexual inquiries and vulgarities throughout the course of the two years during which Henson worked for the police department. Henson stated that in addition to these periodic harangues, Sellgren repeatedly requested that she have sexual relations with him. The district court, however, did not permit Henson's attorney to present evidence that Sellgren had also made sexual advances to Dicks. Henson testified further that she complained of Sellgren's conduct in 1976 to the city manager, Jane Eden, but that Eden took no action to restrain Sellgren.

Henson also claimed that her resignation on January 28, 1977 was tantamount to a constructive discharge based upon sex in violation of Title VII. Specifically, she testified that on January 18, 1977 Sellgren suspended her for two days on the pretext that she had violated an office policy by bringing food into the dispatch room. According to Henson, this policy had not been previously enforced, and she regarded the suspension as a warning by Sellgren that she would be fired if she did not accede to his sexual requests. She therefore claimed that her resignation was involuntary.

Finally, Henson claimed that Sellgren prevented her from attending the local police academy because she refused to have sexual relations with him. She testified that Sellgren made it clear to her that if she agreed to have a relationship with him, he would help her gain the approval of the city manager to attend the academy. Both Henson and Dicks testified that during this period two of the male CETA dispatchers were sent to the police academy. This testimony was corroborated by other witnesses and by the employment records of the two male dispatchers. Additionally, the city manager testified that Henson was qualified to attend the police academy and that she would have permitted Henson to attend if Sellgren had informed her of Henson's interest in the academy.

. . . .

I.

Sexual harassment and work environment

Henson contends that a plaintiff states a claim under Title VII by alleging that sexual harassment perpetrated or condoned by an employer has created a hostile or offensive work environment. . . . We agree that under certain circumstances the creation of an offensive or hostile work environment due to sexual harassment can violate Title VII irrespective of whether the complainant suffers tangible job detriment. We therefore reverse the district court's order as to this claim and remand for a new trial on Henson's work environment claim.

. . . .

Sexual harassment which creates a hostile or offensive environment for members of one sex is every bit the arbitrary barrier to sexual equality at the workplace that racial harassment is to racial equality. Surely, a requirement that a man or woman run a gauntlet of sexual abuse in return for the privilege of being allowed to work and make a living can be as demeaning and disconcerting as the harshest of racial epithets. A pattern of sexual harassment inflicted upon an employee because of her sex is a pattern of behavior that inflicts disparate treatment upon a member of one sex with respect to terms, conditions, or privileges of employment. There is no requirement that an employee subjected to such disparate treatment prove in addition that she has suffered tangible job detriment.

. . . .

. . . Rather, the plaintiff must allege and prove a number of elements in order to establish her claim. These elements include the following:

(1) *The employee belongs to a protected group.* As in other cases of sexual discrimination, this requires a simple stipulation that the employee is a man or a woman.

(2) *The employee was subject to unwelcome sexual harassment.* The E.E.O.C. regulations helpfully define the type of conduct that may constitute sexual harassment: "sexual advances, requests for sexual favors, and other verbal or physical conduct of a sexual nature. . . ." 29 C.F.R. s 1604.11(a) (1981). In order to constitute harassment, this conduct must be unwelcome in the sense that the employee did not solicit or incite it, and in the sense that the employee regarded the conduct as undesirable or offensive.

(3) *The harassment complained of was based upon sex.* The essence of a disparate treatment claim under Title VII is that an employee or applicant is intentionally singled out for adverse treatment on the basis of a prohibited criterion. In proving a claim for a hostile work environment due to sexual harassment, therefore, the plaintiff must show that but for the fact of her sex, she would not have been the object of harassment.

In the typical case in which a male supervisor makes sexual overtures to a female worker, it is obvious that the supervisor did not treat male employees in a similar fashion. It will therefore be a simple matter for the plaintiff to prove that but for her sex, she would not have been subjected to sexual harassment. However, there may be cases in which a supervisor makes sexual overtures to workers of both sexes or where the conduct complained of is equally offensive to male and female workers. In such cases, the sexual harassment would not be based upon sex because men and women are accorded like treatment. Although the plaintiff might have a remedy under state law in such a situation, the plaintiff would have no remedy under Title VII.

(4) *The harassment complained of affected a "term, condition, or privilege" of employment.* The former fifth circuit has held that the state of psychological well being is a term, condition, or privilege of employment within the meaning of Title VII. Rogers v. EEOC, 454 F.2d at 238. The court in *Rogers* made it clear, however, that the "mere utterance of an ethnic or racial epithet which engenders offensive feelings in an employee" does not affect the terms, conditions, or privileges of employment to a sufficiently significant degree to violate Title VII. *Id.* For sexual harassment to state a claim under Title VII, it must be sufficiently pervasive so as to alter the conditions of employment and create an abusive working environment. Whether sexual harassment at the workplace is sufficiently severe and persistent to affect seriously the psychological well being of employees is a question to be determined with regard to the totality of the circumstances.

(5) *Respondeat superior. . . .*[89]

In this case, Henson has made a prima facie showing of all elements necessary to establish a violation of Title VII. Dismissal of her claim was therefore erroneous.

. . . .

II.

Henson asserts two other claims of sexual harassment, that she was constructively discharged from employment because of her sex and that she was denied the opportunity to attend the police academy because she refused Sellgren's sexual importunities. The district court dismissed each claim, largely because it disbelieved crucial portions of Henson's testimony regarding historical facts in the case.

. . . .

B. Constructive Discharge

In *Young v. Southwestern Savings & Loan Association*, 509 F.2d 140, 144 (5th Cir. 1975), the former fifth circuit determined that when "an employee involuntarily resigns in order to escape intolerable and illegal employment requirements" to which he or she is subjected because of race, color, religion, sex, or national origin, the employer has committed a constructive discharge in violation of Title VII. In this case, the judge disbelieved Henson's testimony that she resigned from the Dundee Police Department because of sexual harassment, finding instead that she resigned because the man with whom she had been having an affair was forced to resign from the department. Although the evidence on this point presents close questions of credibility and conflicting inferences, we cannot say that the finding of the district judge was clearly erroneous.

. . . .

---

89. See *infra* Chapter 4 for a discussion of employer liability.

C. Permission to attend the police academy

An employer may not require sexual consideration from an employee as a quid pro quo for job benefits. In order to establish a violation of Title VII on grounds of sexual harassment of this kind, an employee must prove a number of elements, many of which are similar to the proof required to establish the existence of a hostile or offensive work environment:

(1) *The employee belongs to a protected group.*

(2) *The employee was subject to unwelcome sexual harassment.*

(3) *The harassment complained of was based upon sex.*

(4) *The employee's reaction to harassment complained of affected tangible aspects of the employee's compensation, terms, conditions, or privileges of employment.* The acceptance or rejection of the harassment by an employee must be an express or implied condition to the receipt of a job benefit or the cause of a tangible job detriment in order to create liability under this theory of sexual harassment. As in the typical disparate treatment case, the employee must prove that she was deprived of a job benefit which she was otherwise qualified to receive because of the employer's use of a prohibited criterion in making the employment decision.

(5) *Respondeat superior. . . .*[90]

. . . .

In this case, Henson has alleged all of the elements of a *quid pro quo* sexual harassment claim. The district judge, however, did not believe Henson's testimony that Sellgren insisted upon sexual favors as a condition to her attendance at the academy. . . .

. . . .

. . . [T]here is a substantial risk that the district judge based his evaluation of Henson's credibility upon a clearly erroneous view of the availability of corroborating evidence. . . . Here, the district judge's thorough misapprehension of the factual situation surrounding Henson's testimony on the issue of the police academy assignment prevents us from deferring to his credibility finding. We conclude that Henson is entitled to a new trial on her claim for sexual harassment which allegedly prevented her from attending the police academy.

. . . .

Affirmed in Part, Reversed in Part, and Remanded with Instructions.

Notes and Discussion

1. Hostile Work Environment How did the *Henson* majority justify its conclusion that harassment without a tangible economic consequence violates Title VII? What kind of an analogy did it draw to explain its reasoning? Is the analogy relevant? Why or why not?

---

90. See *infra* Chapter 4 for a discussion of employer liability.

Is it fair to say that hostile work environment harassment produces no tangible economic consequences? Imagine that a target pays a psychotherapist to help her deal with sexual harassment. Do the medical bills constitute a tangible economic detriment? What if a target cannot perform her job as well and, therefore, does not qualify for a promotion? Is that a tangible economic detriment? Did the early courts define economic detriment too narrowly? Does the definition of economic detriment reflect a male bias? If so, explain why. See generally, Susan Estrich, *Sex at Work*, 43 Stan. L. Rev. 813, 834 (1991) (arguing the tangible economic effects of hostile environment harassment).

Is the distinction between hostile work environment and quid pro quo harassment really that helpful? Was there a way for courts to address the issue of economic detriment or damage without creating two different categories of sexual harassment? Explain.

2. The Prima Facie Case The *Henson* court was one of the first to enumerate the elements of the prima facie case for sexual harassment. Other courts use slightly different requirements. See, e.g., *Quantock v. Shared Marketing Serv's, Inc.*, 312 F.3d 899, 903 (7th Cir. 2002) (requiring that "(1) she was subjected to unwelcome sexual advances, requests for sexual favors, or other verbal or physical conduct of a sexual nature; (2) the conduct was severe or pervasive enough to create a hostile work environment; (3) the conduct was directed at her because of her sex; and (4) there is a basis for employer liability."); *O'Rourke v. City of Providence*, 235 F.3d 713, 728 (1st Cir. 2001) (identifying six elements including subjective and objective standards).

3. Because of Sex What was the theoretical reasoning, if any, used in *Henson* to justify finding that sexual harassment constituted sex discrimination? If there was a coherent theory, from where might it have come?

The *Henson* court ruled, "In proving a claim for a hostile work environment due to sexual harassment, therefore, the plaintiff must show that but for the fact of her sex, she would not have been the object of harassment. . . ."[91] Presumably if there are no men in the workplace to show that a perpetrator targeted only women, a plaintiff must rely on what Taub described as the "hypothetical similarly situated male" to prove her case. If a court accepts, without proof, the plaintiff's argument that the hypothetical male would not have been sexually harassed, does the court reveal a sex role bias? Does the court necessarily assume that the typical male (harasser) is heterosexual? If not, what justifies its conclusion?

Bundy held that sex stereotyping violates Title VII. Did the *Henson* court rely on a theory of sex stereotyping to explain sexual harassment as sex discrimination? Does a supervisor who makes sexual advances to members of both sexes ever violate Title VII? Why or why not? See, e.g., *Steiner v. Showboat Operating Co.*, 25 F.3d 1459, 1464 (9th Cir. 1994) (holding that a reasonable woman might be affected differently

---

91. Henson v. City of Dundee, 682 F.2d 897, 904 (11th Cir. 1982).

from a reasonable man); *Kopp v. Samaritan Health Sys.*, 13 F.3d 264 (8th Cir. 1993) (allowing that a harasser who abused all employees might have been more abusive to women than men).

If certain sexual behaviors offend both men and women, should that fact preclude a suit for a Title VII violation as the *Henson* court suggested it should? According to the EEOC's *Policy Guidance on Sexual Favoritism*, both men and women may sue for an "atmosphere demeaning to women" if they can establish that the conduct was severe or pervasive enough to create a hostile working environment. 8 Fair Empl. Prac. Man. (BNA), part C at 405:6819-21 (Jan. 2, 1990); see also *Sims v. Montgomery County Comm'n.*, 766 F. Supp. 1052, 1074 (M.D. Ala. 1990) (opining that the harassment against women created a hostile environment for "those male officers who harbor a respect and concern for all their fellow officers, irrespective of sex, and who find offensive to their conscience . . . an environment in which all officers . . . cannot share equally in the opportunities of employment.").

4. Severity and Pervasiveness Did the *Henson* court adequately define what constitutes behavior severe or pervasive enough to affect a "term condition, or privilege" of employment? If not, how could it have improved the definition?

Until 1986, the Supreme Court remained silent on the issue of harassment as sex discrimination. Twenty-two years after the passage of the Civil Rights Act of 1964, however, the Supreme Court confirmed that sexual harassment with an associated, tangible economic impact violates Title VII. The case was brought by yet another brave African-American woman, Mechelle Vinson, against Meritor Savings Bank. The Court also held that Title VII prohibits hostile environment sexual harassment, i.e., harassment without an associated tangible economic affect. The Court left unclear, however, under what circumstances such claims could be successful. Note the areas of contradiction and ambiguity in the Court's opinion.

Meritor Savings Bank, FSB v. Vinson
477 U.S. 57 (1986)

JUSTICE REHNQUIST, J., delivered the opinion of the Court.

. . . .

I

In 1974, respondent Mechelle Vinson met Sidney Taylor, a vice president of what is now petitioner Meritor Savings Bank (bank) and manager of one of its branch offices. When respondent asked whether she might obtain employment at the bank, Taylor gave her an application, which she completed and returned the next day; later that same day Taylor called her to say that she had been hired. With Taylor as her supervisor, respondent started as a teller-trainee, and thereafter was promoted to teller, head teller, and assistant branch manager. She worked at the same branch for four years, and it is undisputed that her advancement there was based on merit alone. In September 1978, respondent notified Taylor that she was taking sick leave for an indefinite period. On November 1, 1978, the bank discharged her for excessive use of that leave.

Respondent brought this action against Taylor and the bank, claiming that during her four years at the bank she had "constantly been subjected to sexual harassment" by Taylor in violation of Title VII. She sought injunctive relief, compensatory and punitive damages against Taylor and the bank, and attorney's fees.

At the 11-day bench trial, the parties presented conflicting testimony about Taylor's behavior during respondent's employment. Respondent testified that during her probationary period as a teller-trainee, Taylor treated her in a fatherly way and made no sexual advances. Shortly thereafter, however, he invited her out to dinner and, during the course of the meal, suggested that they go to a motel to have sexual relations. At first she refused, but out of what she described as fear of losing her job she eventually agreed. According to respondent, Taylor thereafter made repeated demands upon her for sexual favors, usually at the branch, both during and after business hours; she estimated that over the next several years she had intercourse with him some 40 or 50 times. In addition, respondent testified that Taylor fondled her in front of other employees, followed her into the women's restroom when she went there alone, exposed himself to her, and even forcibly raped her on several occasions.[92] These activities ceased after 1977, respondent stated, when she started going with a steady boyfriend.

Respondent also testified that Taylor touched and fondled other women employees of the bank, and she attempted to call witnesses to support this charge. But while some supporting testimony apparently was admitted without objection, the District Court did not allow her "to present wholesale evidence of a pattern and practice relating to sexual advances to other female employees in her case in chief, but advised her that she might well be able to present such evidence in rebuttal to the defendants' cases." *Vinson v. Taylor* . . . 23 FEP Cases 37, 38–39, n. 1 (DC 1980). Respondent did not offer such evidence in rebuttal. Finally, respondent testified that because she was afraid of Taylor she never reported his harassment to any of his supervisors and never attempted to use the bank's complaint procedure.

Taylor denied respondent's allegations of sexual activity, testifying that he never fondled her, never made suggestive remarks to her, never engaged in sexual intercourse with her, and never asked her to do so. He contended instead that respondent made her accusations in response to a business-related dispute. The bank also denied respondent's allegations and asserted that any sexual harassment by Taylor was unknown to the bank and engaged in without its consent or approval.

---

92. Vinson also testified that in May 1976 she required a doctor's attention for serious vaginal bleeding after Taylor brutally raped her. Vinson v. Taylor, 23 Fair Empl. Prac. Cases (BNA) 37 (D.D.C. 1980), *rev'd*, 753 F.2d 141 (D.C. Cir. 1985), *aff'd sub nom.* Meritor Sav. Bank, FBS v. Vinson, 477 U.S. 57 (1986).

The District Court denied relief, but did not resolve the conflicting testimony about the existence of a sexual relationship between respondent and Taylor. It found instead that:

> "[if] [respondent] and Taylor did engage in an intimate or sexual relationship during the time of [respondent's] employment with [the bank], that relationship was a voluntary one having nothing to do with her continued employment at [the bank] or her advancement or promotions at that institution."

Id. . . . 23 FEP Cases, at 42. The court ultimately found that respondent "was not the victim of sexual harassment and was not the victim of sexual discrimination" while employed at the bank.

. . . .

The Court of Appeals for the District of Columbia Circuit reversed. 753 F.2d 141 (1985).

. . . .

II.

. . . .

Respondent argues, and the Court of Appeals held, that unwelcome sexual advances that create an offensive or hostile working environment violate Title VII. Without question, when a supervisor sexually harasses a subordinate because of the subordinate's sex, that supervisor "discriminate[s]" on the basis of sex. Petitioner apparently does not challenge this proposition. It contends instead that in prohibiting discrimination with respect to "compensation, terms, conditions, or privileges" of employment, Congress was concerned with what petitioner describes as "tangible loss" of "an economic character," not "purely psychological aspects of the workplace environment." Brief for Petitioner 30–31, 34. In support of this claim petitioner observes that in both the legislative history of Title VII and this Court's Title VII decisions, the focus has been on tangible, economic barriers erected by discrimination.

We reject petitioner's view. First, the language of Title VII is not limited to "economic" or "tangible" discrimination. The phrase "terms, conditions, or privileges of employment" evinces a congressional intent "'to strike at the entire spectrum of disparate treatment of men and women'" in employment. Los Angeles Dept. of Water and Power v. Manhart, 435 U.S. 702, 707, n. 13 (1978), quoting Sprogis v. United Air Lines, Inc., 444 F.2d 1194, 1198 (CA7 1971). Petitioner has pointed to nothing in the Act to suggest that Congress contemplated the limitation urged here.

Second, in 1980 the EEOC issued Guidelines specifying that "sexual harassment," as there defined, is a form of sex discrimination prohibited by Title VII. . . . The EEOC Guidelines fully support the view that harassment leading to noneconomic injury can violate Title VII.

In defining "sexual harassment," the Guidelines first describe the kinds of workplace conduct that may be actionable under Title VII. These include "[u]nwelcome sexual advances, requests for sexual favors, and other verbal or physical conduct of a sexual nature." 29 CFR § 1604.11(a) (1985). Relevant to the charges at issue in this case, the Guidelines provide that such sexual misconduct constitutes prohibited "sexual harassment," whether or not it is directly linked to the grant or denial of an economic *quid pro quo*, where "such conduct has the purpose or effect of unreasonably interfering with an individual's work performance or creating an intimidating, hostile, or offensive working environment." § 1604.11(a)(3).

In concluding that so-called "hostile environment" (i.e., non *quid pro quo*) harassment violates Title VII, the EEOC drew upon a substantial body of judicial decisions and EEOC precedent holding that Title VII affords employees the right to work in an environment free from discriminatory intimidation, ridicule, and insult. Rogers v. EEOC, 454 F.2d 234 (CA5 1971), *cert. denied*, 406 U.S. 957 (1972), was apparently the first case to recognize a cause of action based upon a discriminatory work environment. In *Rogers*, the Court of Appeals for the Fifth Circuit held that a Hispanic complainant could establish a Title VII violation by demonstrating that her employer created an offensive work environment for employees by giving discriminatory service to its Hispanic clientele. The court explained that an employee's protections under Title VII extend beyond the economic aspects of employment:

> "[T]he phrase 'terms, conditions or privileges of employment' in [Title VII] is an expansive concept which sweeps within its protective ambit the practice of creating a working environment heavily charged with ethnic or racial discrimination. . . . One can readily envision working environments so heavily polluted with discrimination as to destroy completely the emotional and psychological stability of minority group workers . . . ."

454 F.2d, at 238. Courts applied this principle to harassment based on race, religion, and national origin. Nothing in Title VII suggests that a hostile environment based on discriminatory sexual harassment should not be likewise prohibited. The Guidelines thus appropriately drew from, and were fully consistent with, the existing case law.

Since the Guidelines were issued, courts have uniformly held, and we agree, that a plaintiff may establish a violation of Title VII by proving that discrimination based on sex has created a hostile or abusive work environment. As the Court of Appeals for the Eleventh Circuit wrote in *Henson v. Dundee*, 682 F.2d 897, 902 (1982):

> "Sexual harassment which creates a hostile or offensive environment for members of one sex is every bit the arbitrary barrier to sexual equality at the workplace that racial harassment is to racial equality. Surely, a requirement that a man or woman run a gauntlet of sexual abuse in return for the privilege of being allowed to work and make a living can be as demeaning and disconcerting as the harshest of racial epithets."

Of course, as the courts in both *Rogers* and *Henson* recognized, not all workplace conduct that may be described as "harassment" affects a "term, condition, or privilege" of employment within the meaning of Title VII. See Rogers v. EEOC, *supra*, at 238 ("mere utterance of an ethnic or racial epithet which engenders offensive feelings in an employee" would not affect the conditions of employment to sufficiently significant degree to violate Title VII); Henson, 682 F.2d, at 904 (quoting same). For sexual harassment to be actionable, it must be sufficiently severe or pervasive "to alter the conditions of [the victim's] employment and create an abusive working environment." *Ibid.* Respondent's allegations in this case—which include not only pervasive harassment but also criminal conduct of the most serious nature—are plainly sufficient to state a claim for "hostile environment" sexual harassment.

The question remains, however, whether the District Court's ultimate finding that respondent "was not the victim of sexual harassment," effectively disposed of respondent's claim. . . . First, the District Court apparently believed that a claim for sexual harassment will not lie absent an *economic* effect on the complainant's employment. Since it appears that the District Court made its findings without ever considering the "hostile environment" theory of sexual harassment, the Court of Appeals' decision to remand was correct.

Second, the District Court's conclusion that no actionable harassment occurred might have rested on its earlier "finding" that "[i]f [respondent] and Taylor did engage in an intimate or sexual relationship . . . , that relationship was a voluntary one." But the fact that sex-related conduct was "voluntary," in the sense that the complainant was not forced to participate against her will, is not a defense to a sexual harassment suit brought under Title VII. The gravamen of any sexual harassment claim is that the alleged sexual advances were "unwelcome." 29 CFR § 1604.11(a) (1985). While the question whether particular conduct was indeed unwelcome presents difficult problems of proof and turns largely on credibility determinations committed to the trier of fact, the District Court in this case erroneously focused on the "voluntariness" of respondent's participation in the claimed sexual episodes. The correct inquiry is whether respondent by her conduct indicated that the alleged sexual advances were unwelcome, not whether her actual participation in sexual intercourse was voluntary.

Petitioner contends that even if this case must be remanded to the District Court, the Court of Appeals erred in one of the terms of its remand. Specifically, the Court of Appeals stated that testimony about respondent's "dress and personal fantasies," which the District Court apparently admitted into evidence, "had no place in this litigation." *Ibid.* The apparent ground for this conclusion was that respondent's voluntariness *vel non* in submitting to Taylor's advances was immaterial to her sexual harassment claim. While "voluntariness" in the sense of consent is not a defense to such a claim, it does not follow that a complainant's sexually provocative speech or dress is irrelevant as a matter of law in determining whether he or she found particular sexual advances unwelcome. To the contrary, such evidence is obviously relevant. The EEOC Guidelines emphasize that the trier of fact must determine the existence of sexual harassment in light of "the record as a whole" and "the totality of circumstances, such as the nature of the sexual advances and the context in which the alleged incidents occurred." 29 CFR § 1604.11(b) (1985). Respondent's claim that any marginal relevance of the evidence in question was outweighed by the potential for unfair prejudice is the sort of argument properly addressed to the District Court.

. . . .

Notes and Discussion

1. Unwelcomeness The Court held, "The gravamen of any sexual harassment claim is that the alleged sexual advances or conduct were 'unwelcome.'" For the Court, volition and acquiescence do not necessarily equate with welcomeness. The Court acknowledged that the determination of welcomeness "turns largely on a credibility determination[.]" Are there any problems with this evidentiary procedure? Explain. Many scholars have called for the abandonment of the "welcomeness" review. See, e.g., Grace S. Ho, *Not Quite Rights: How the Unwelcomeness Element in Sexual Harassment Law Undermines Title VII's Transformative Potential*, 20 Yale J. Law & Fem. 131 (2008). Are there any potential problems with eliminating this element of the plaintiff's case?

2. The Plaintiff's Conduct The Court rejected the circuit court's view that Vinson's dress and personal fantasies "had no place in this litigation." Why did the Court decide that the plaintiff's behavior might be relevant and admissible? Wendy Pollack, a founding member of Chicago Women in Trades, suggested:

> Fearing a chilling effect on normal heterosexual relations in the workplace, the courts have devised ostensibly neutral rules of evaluation to discredit women. This includes the *Meritor* Court's holding that evidence of Vinson's "sexually provocative speech or dress" is "obviously relevant" in light of the "totality of the circumstances." But in contrast to the Court's apparent suggestion, no manner of speech or dress gives a man a right of sexual access to a woman. Moreover, "a woman does not waive her Title VII rights by her sartorial or whimsical proclivities." If Vinson's speech or dress was inappropriate for the work environment, she should have been told, not raped. However, consideration of the totality of the circumstances according to the Court apparently includes evaluating a woman's success in controlling the "animal nature" of men, from which women must protect themselves.
>
> Scrutinizing a victim's speech or dress, no matter how objective the evaluation, keeps the issue individualized and personal—as just one individual interacting with another. This narrows the scope of inquiry as to the offender's actions, but widens the scope of inquiry regarding the victim's actions. Shifting the focus from the offender's actions to the victim's actions (but not her viewpoint) legitimates sexual harassment by offering the offender an excuse for his behavior. Perhaps the courts should term the

offender's argument in these cases the "unreasonable woman" defense, as it appears to be that it is the victim's conduct, speech, dress, or personality which causes the problem, rather than the harassment.[93]

Many feminists have suggested that a review of the plaintiff's dress and behavior harkens back to the old rape cases in which the target was often put on trial for her behavior. See, e.g., Susan Estrich, *Sex at Work*, 43 Stan. L. Rev. 813, 826–43 (1991) (discussing comparison to rape law and the focus on the conduct of the target); see also Christina A. Bull, Comment, *The Implications of Admitting Evidence of a Sexual Harassment Plaintiff's Speech and Dress in the Aftermath of* Meritor Savings Bank v. Vinson, 41 UCLA L. Rev. 117 (1993). Are these legal theorists correct? Why or why not? What litigation or evidentiary problems relating to the plaintiff's conduct should counsel for both the plaintiff and the defense anticipate?

3. The Prima Facie Case Did *Meritor* clarify the elements of the prima facie case? Following *Meritor*, many courts struggled with determining the legal requirements to state a prima facie case.

4. Severe or Pervasive Conduct The Court ruled that only severe or pervasive conduct would be sufficient to affect a "term, condition, or privilege" of employment. Analogizing to race cases, the Court suggested that the "'mere utterance of an ethnic or racial epithet which engenders offensive feelings in an employee' would not affect the conditions of employment to sufficiently significant degree to violate Title VII." The Court specified that the conduct must "alter the conditions of [the victim's] employment and create an abusive working environment." How can one tell when behavior alters the "conditions" of employment? How many sex-based epithets does it take to create an abusive working environment? How should the target know when conduct crosses the line of what the Court thinks should be tolerated? See generally Richard L. Wiener & Linda E. Hurt, *Social Sexual Conduct at Work: How Do Workers Know When It Is Harassment and When It Is Not?*, 34 Cal. W. L. Rev. 53 (1997).

5. Constructive Knowledge A bank representative testified that the bank had no knowledge of Sidney Taylor's behavior. When courts find pervasive harassment, they will often infer the employer's knowledge of the problem. See, e.g., *Katz v. Dole*, 709 F.2d 251, 255 (4th Cir. 1983) (holding that "harassment was so pervasive that employer awareness may be inferred"). Is such an inference appropriate in *Meritor*? Why or why not? Does it matter that Taylor was a Vice-President of the bank?

6. The Spectrum of Disparate Treatment In rejecting the view that Title VII prohibits only tangible economic barriers based on discrimination, the Court noted Congress's "intent to strike at the entire spectrum of disparate treatment of men and women in employment." Based on the *Meritor* decision, how far does this spectrum extend? Does *Meritor* anticipate the protection of same-sex harassment? How about the protection of effeminate men or masculine women? How about the protection

---

93. Wendy Pollack, *Sexual Harassment: Women's Experience vs. Legal Definitions*, 13 Harv. Women's L.J. 35, 56–57 (1990).

of gay men and lesbians? In defining discrimination based on "sex," does the Court consider only biological sex, but not gender or sexual orientation?

7. Legal Theory Once the Supreme Court granted certiorari in *Meritor*, Catharine MacKinnon wrote the appellate brief.[94] Are either MacKinnon's or Taub's perspectives found within this opinion? If so, where? If not, why not? What legal theory, if any, does *Meritor* use in finding that sexual harassment is sex discrimination?

While feminist activism and early legal cases raised awareness about workplace sexual harassment, it was not until 1991 that the issue reached a mainstream audience when Oklahoma Law School Professor Anita Hill accused Supreme Court nominee Clarence Thomas of sexual harassment. Televised live with around-the-clock commentary, congressional hearings on the accusations brought the issue of sexual harassment into the living rooms and workplaces of men and women around the country. Chapter 2 addresses these events as well as additional issues.

7. Application of Law and Ethics
Hypothetical #1

On her first day at work as an associate attorney at a large Midwest firm, Joan Holladay meets Roger Starling, her supervising partner. Roger specializes in insurance defense work. Joan also meets their secretarial assistant, Peggy Oldham. As Roger introduces Peggy he comments, "Now, I don't want you girls getting chatty at the Keurig, my team has billable hours to maintain." As they leave, Joan overhears Roger say to Peggy, "Get that bitch attorney from the Jones case on the phone and tell her she can take her counteroffer and go fuck herself with it. And use those words!"

Heading to their first meeting, Roger tells Joan, "This is a new client who won't want to deal with a girl. He is the President of Zie Corp. He and the company have been sued for sexual harassment but I'll let you sit in as we may need you to deal with the media. Just let me do all the talking today." Offended but unwilling to confront her supervising partner on the first day, Joan says nothing and follows Roger.

Legal issue: Does any of this behavior constitute sexual harassment?

In the conference room, Roger introduces Clyde. Clyde immediately turns to Joan and says, "Hon, would you get us some coffee?" Again offended, Joan says nothing because she does not want to alienate a big client. When Joan returns, Roger and Clyde have agreed to begin negotiations with plaintiff's counsel.

As they conclude the meeting, Clyde slips his arm around Joan, above her waist, and gives her a little squeeze. "Nice job," he says, "You are quite a 'looker' and will be a valuable asset in our negotiations." Joan inches away from Clyde but again

---

94. Marshall, *supra* note 56, at 787.

says nothing. She thinks that Roger will intercede on her behalf when he interrupts. However, he says, "Sorry, Clyde, this one's my girl!"

Legal issue: Does any of this behavior constitute sexual harassment?

After Clyde leaves, Joan explains to Roger that she felt uncomfortable when Clyde hugged her and asks him how he would like her to handle any future situations like that one. Laughing, Roger closes the office door and then approaches Joan, putting his arm around her shoulders and then sliding his hand slowly down her back. He says, "Joan, I can give you a lot of guidance, show you how it's done, if you'll learn to play my way. Peggy's on my team, we have a lot of fun together; that's why she's still with this firm after 15 years. She's not getting any younger and she knows it, but I reward loyalty."

He continues, "You think I'm the only one who makes his own rules? This is the fast lane, girl. Do you know Brad over in bankruptcy? Those clients who give him a little get a whole lot back. Brad's quite a guy. In fact, with some clients, he doesn't even return their calls until they put out a bit. I'm much more generous than that! So, what do you say? It would be a shame for your career to stall at this stage." Roger's hand has moved all the way down her back and starts stroking her buttocks.

Horrified and sickened, Joan flees his office and takes refuge in the restroom where she finds Peggy. She relays to Peggy all Roger has said. Peggy responds, "You aren't the first one and you won't be the last. Don't bother complaining, though, he'll make sure you never work in this town again. I've seen it happen."

Legal issue: Is this behavior sexual harassment? Are there other legal issues here?

In addition to Title VII and other sexual harassment law, the American Bar Association's Model Rules of Professional Conduct might assist you in evaluating this hypothetical problem. Rule 8.4 specifies:

It is professional misconduct for a lawyer to:

(a) violate or attempt to violate the Rules of Professional Conduct, knowingly assist or induce another to do so, or do so through the acts of another;

(b) commit a criminal act that reflects adversely on the lawyer's honesty, trustworthiness or fitness as a lawyer in other respects;

(c) engage in conduct involving dishonesty, fraud, deceit or misrepresentation;

(d) engage in conduct that is prejudicial to the administration of justice;

(e) state or imply an ability to influence improperly a government agency or official or to achieve results by means that violate the Rules of Professional Conduct or other law;

(f) knowingly assist a judge or judicial officer in conduct that is a violation of applicable rules of judicial conduct or other law; or

(g) engage in conduct that the lawyer knows or reasonably should know is harassment or discrimination on the basis of race, sex, religion, national origin, ethnicity, disability, age, sexual orientation, gender identity, marital status or socioeconomic status in conduct related to the practice of law. . . .[95]

Further Questions

1. Did Roger's behavior toward Peggy violate Rule 8.4?

2. Did Roger's behavior toward Joan violate Rule 8.4?

3. Did Roger's failure to correct Clyde's behavior violate Rule 8.4?

4. Is Brad's behavior sexual harassment and can Joan include it in any claims she might have?

5. Do you think the other partners in Roger's firm have committed an ethics violation if Roger has created a hostile work environment by sexually harassing women?

8. Review

The Prima Facie Cases

Quid Pro Quo Harassment

1. Membership in a protected class;

2. Unwelcome sexual harassment;

3. Based on sex;

4. That affects a *tangible economic* aspect of employment;

5. Respondeat superior.

Hostile Work Environment Harassment

1. Membership in a protected class;

2. Unwelcome sexual harassment;

3. Based on sex;

4. That affects the terms, conditions, or privileges of employment;

5. Respondeat superior.

Introductory Legal Definitions

1. Title VII makes it "an unlawful employment practice for an employer . . . to discriminate against any individual with respect to his compensation, terms, conditions, or privileges of employment, because of such individual's race, color, religion, sex, or national origin." 42 U.S.C. § 2000e-2(a)(1). Generally, **sexual harassment** is "unwelcome sexual advances, . . . verbal or physical conduct of a sexual nature . . . which interferes with work or creates an intimidating or hostile work environment." 29 C.F.R. § 1604.11(a)(EEOC Regulations)(1980).

2. Quid Pro Quo Harassment occurs when submission to or rejection of unwelcome sexual conduct by an individual employee is used as the basis for employment decisions affecting that employee. For example, the employer says, "If you sleep with me, you'll get a pay raise."

---

95. MODEL RULES OF PROF'L CONDUCT R. 8.4 (2016).

3. Hostile Work Environment Harassment occurs when submission to unwelcome sexual conduct is made either explicitly or implicitly a term or condition of an employee's employment. Unwelcome conduct that unreasonably interferes with an individual's job performance *or* creates an intimidating, hostile, or offensive working environment can constitute unlawful sex discrimination, even if it leads to no tangible or economic job consequences.

Chapter 2

Intersectionality

1. The Intersection of Sexism and Racism

In 1991, two events catapulted sexual harassment into the public spotlight. First, at the annual Tailhook convention of U.S. Navy aviators in September, as many as 70 male officers forced at least 25 women to run "the gauntlet" as the men sexually molested the women. One molested female officer, Lieutenant Paula Coughlin, filed formal charges. Second, in October, Oklahoma Law School Professor Anita Hill formally accused Supreme Court nominee Clarence Thomas of sexual harassment.

President George H.W. Bush had nominated Clarence Thomas to fill the seat vacated by the first African American to sit on the United States Supreme Court—Associate Justice Thurgood Marshall. Justice Marshall was an icon of the civil rights movement. Before he ascended to the Supreme Court, Justice Marshall was chief counsel for the NAACP Legal Defense and Educational Fund and the architect of *Brown v. Board of Education*.[1] Once on the Supreme Court, Justice Marshall reliably voted to strengthen civil rights.

In contrast to Marshall, Thomas was an opponent of civil rights. He openly opposed affirmative action, despite being a beneficiary of these programs himself. In 1987, Thomas said such programs "create a narcotic of dependency."[2] Thomas also dealt harshly with sexual harassment complainants. For example, during his tenure as Chair of the Equal Employment Opportunity Commission (EEOC) from 1982–1990, Thomas shifted the Commission's support away from sexual harassment plaintiffs and toward defendant employers.

President Bush's nomination of Thomas to fill Justice Marshall's Supreme Court seat placed African Americans in an excruciating dilemma. They could either support an opponent of civil rights or decline to support an African American for the highest court in the land. If the Senate did not confirm Thomas, an all-white Supreme Court might once again be deciding legal controversies.

After Bush nominated Thomas, the FBI engaged in a routine background and security check. During the investigation, the FBI collected the affidavit of Professor Hill, who had worked for Thomas a decade earlier at the Department of Education's

---

1. 347 U.S. 483 (1954).
2. William M. Welch, *Thomas Presided Over Shift in Policy at EEOC, Records Show*, AP News (July 25, 1991).

Office of Civil Rights (OCR) and at the EEOC. In her affidavit, Hill provided details about Thomas's sexually coercive behavior toward her while she was his employee at the OCR and EEOC.

Despite these revelations, Senate Judiciary Chair Joseph Biden (D-DE) decided not to pursue Hill's allegations. Then someone leaked her affidavit to the media. Female members of Congress stormed Senate chambers demanding hearings on the allegations. Biden relented and in October 1991, the 10 white male members of the Senate Judiciary Committee heard testimony from Anita Hill, Clarence Thomas, and their supporters.

The hearings became a national obsession, and a seriously flawed lesson in sexual harassment law. Senatorial treatment of Hill demonstrated for millions of viewers watching the televised proceedings just how difficult it was to bring and prove charges of sexual harassment. Disincentives for women who complain, discussed for years by feminist legal scholars, became painfully apparent during the Hill/Thomas hearings. Public scrutiny of Hill's credibility, her behavior, and her mental stability justified long-standing feminist concerns about the treatment of sexual harassment complainants. Public opinion polls taken during the proceedings revealed that 58% of those asked believed Thomas over Hill.[3]

In addition to raising the issue of workplace sexual harassment for national discussion, the Hill/Thomas hearings highlighted race relations. Race-related biases and the historical legacy of racial subordination played important roles in the hearings since both Hill and Thomas were African Americans, while the Senate Judiciary Committee was composed entirely of white men. Thomas and his supporters used race as a political tool by invoking the image of a lynching to describe the proceedings. He manipulated the horrific history of lynching in the United States to gain public sympathy and, ironically, discredit Hill.

Feminist, race-conscious scholars noted the long history of sexual harassment and abuse of African-American women by white men in the United States. Hill herself never used this legacy to defend herself against Republican attacks. Even if she had appealed to race, few Americans would have been familiar with this history. In addition, the public failed to empathize with the figure of an ambitious, Yale-educated, African-American, female lawyer. In contrast, people were aware of widespread lynching of African-American men, particularly in the South, and many felt sorry for Thomas, the aggrieved African-American male.[4]

The proceedings also demonstrated the importance of information control, presentation, and media manipulation. People who controlled information and its

3. A year later, a *Wall Street Journal* poll found that national opinion had shifted in favor of Hill (44%) to Thomas (34%). Jill Abramson, *Reversal of Fortune: Image of Anita Hill Brighter in Hindsight*, Wall St. J. (October 5, 1992).

4. Nell Irvin Painter, *Hill, Thomas, and the Use of Racial Stereotype, in* Race-ing Justice, Engendering Power: Essays on Anita Hill, Clarence Thomas, and the Construction of Social Reality 200 (Toni Morrison ed., 1992). Both Hill and Thomas were Republicans.

"spin," most notably those who controlled the news media, wielded the most political power.

Evaluate the opening statements of both Clarence Thomas and Anita Hill and consider whether sexual harassment occurred. Read the witness statements and discussion that follows and look for recurring themes relevant to both sexual harassment and race discrimination cases.

Testimony of Clarence Thomas

Hearings Before the Senate Judiciary Committee, October 11, 1991[5]

Mr. Chairman, Senator Thurmond, members of the committee. As excruciatingly difficult as the last two weeks have been, I welcome the opportunity to clear my name today. No one other than my wife and Senator Danforth, to whom I read this statement at 6:30 a.m. has seen or heard this statement. No handlers, no advisors.

The first I learned of the allegations by Professor Anita Hill was on September 25, 1991, when the FBI came to my home to investigate her allegations. When informed by the FBI agent of the nature of the allegations and the person making them, I was shocked, surprised, hurt and enormously saddened. I have not been the same since that day.

For almost a decade my responsibilities included enforcing the rights of victims of sexual harassment. As a boss, as a friend, and as a human being I was proud that I had never had such an allegation leveled against me, even as I sought to promote women and minorities into non-traditional jobs.

In addition, several of my friends who are women have confided in me about the horror of harassment on the job or elsewhere. I thought I really understood the anguish, the fears, the doubts, the seriousness of the matter. But since September 25th, I have suffered immensely as these very serious charges were leveled against me. I have been racking my brains and eating my insides out trying to think of what I could have said or done to Anita Hill to lead her to allege that I was interested in her in more than a professional way and that I talked with her about pornographic or X-rated films.

Contrary to some press reports, I categorically denied all of the allegations and denied that I ever attempted to date Anita Hill when first interviewed by the FBI. I strongly reaffirm that denial.

Let me describe my relationship with Anita Hill. In 1981, after I went to the Department of Education as an assistant secretary in the office of civil rights, one of my closest friends from both college and law school, Gil Hardy, brought Anita Hill to my attention. As I remember, he indicated that she was dissatisfied with her

---

5. Hearings Before the Senate Committee on the Judiciary, 102d Cong., 1st Sess. pt. 4, 5–10, 27 (1991).

law firm and wanted to work in government. Based primarily, if not solely, on Gil's recommendation, I hired Anita Hill.

During my tenure at the Department of Education, Anita Hill was an attorney advisor who worked directly with me. She worked on special projects, as well as day-to-day matters. As I recall, she was one of two professionals working directly with me at the time. As a result, we worked closely on numerous matters. I recall being pleased with her work product and the professional but cordial relationship which we enjoyed at work. I also recall engaging in discussions about politics and current events.

Upon my nomination to become Chairman of the Equal Employment Opportunity Commission, Anita Hill, to the best of my recollection, assisted me in the nomination and confirmation process. After my confirmation, she and Diane Holt, then my secretary, joined me at EEOC. I do not recall that there was any question or doubt that she would become a special assistant to me at EEOC, although as a career employee she retained the option of remaining at the Department of Education.

At EEOC, our relationship was more distant and our contacts less frequent as a result of the increased size of my personal staff and the dramatic increase and diversity of my day-to-day responsibilities. Upon reflection, I recall that she seemed to have had some difficulty adjusting to this change in her role. In any case, our relationship remained both cordial and professional.

At no time did I become aware, either directly or indirectly, that she felt I had said or done anything to change the cordial nature of our relationship. I detected nothing from her or from my staff, or from Gil Hardy, our mutual friend, with whom I maintained regular contact. I am certain that had any statement or conduct on my part been brought to my attention I would remember it clearly because of the nature and seriousness of such conduct, as well as my adamant opposition to sex discrimination and sexual harassment. But there were no such statements.

In the spring of 1983, Mr. Charles [Kothey] contacted me to speak at the Law School at Oral Roberts University in Tulsa, Oklahoma. Anita Hill, who is from Oklahoma, accompanied me on that trip. It was not unusual that individuals on my staff would travel with me occasionally. Anita Hill accompanied me on that trip primarily because this was an opportunity to combine business and a visit to her home.

As I recall, during our visit at Oral Roberts University, Mr. [Kothey] mentioned to me the possibility of approaching Anita Hill to join the faculty at Oral Roberts University Law School. I encouraged him to do so and noted to him, as I recall, that Anita Hill would do well in teaching. I recommended her highly and she eventually was offered a teaching position.

. . . .

Throughout the time that Anita Hill worked with me I treated her as I treated my other special assistants. I tried to treat them all cordially, professionally, and respectfully and I tried to support them in their endeavors and be interested in and supportive of their success. I had no reason or basis to believe my relationship with Anita Hill was anything but this way until the FBI visited me a little more than two weeks ago.

I find it particularly troubling that she never raised any hint that she was uncomfortable with me. She did not raise or mention it when considering moving with me to EEOC from the Department of Education, and she'd never raised it with me when she left EEOC and was moving on in her life. And, to my fullest knowledge, she did not speak to any other women working with or around me who would feel comfortable enough to raise it with me, especially Diane Holt, to whom she seemed closest on my personal staff. Nor did she raise it with mutual friends such as Linda Jackson and Gil Hardy.

This is a person I have helped at every turn in the road since we met. She seemed to appreciate the continued cordial relationship we had since day one. She sought my advice and counsel, as did virtually all of the members of my personal staff.

During my tenure in the executive branch as a manager, as a policymaker, and as a person, I have adamantly condemned sex harassment. There is no member of this Committee or this Senate who feels stronger about sex harassment than I do. As a manager, I made every effort to take swift and decisive action when sex harassment raised or reared its ugly head. The fact that I feel so very strongly about sex harassment and spoke loudly at EEOC has made these allegations doubly hard on me. I cannot imagine anything that I said or did to Anita Hill that could have been mistaken for sexual harassment.

But with that said, if there is anything that I have said that has been misconstrued by Anita Hill or anyone else to be sexual harassment, then I can say that I am so very sorry and I wish I had known. If I did know, I would have stopped immediately and I would not, as I've done over the past two weeks, have to tear away at myself, trying to think of what I could possibly have done. But I have not said or done the things that Anita Hill has alleged. God has gotten me through the days since September 25th, and he is my judge.

. . . .

During the past two weeks, I lost the belief that if I did my best all would work out. I called upon the strength that helped me get here from Pin Point, and it was all sapped out of me. It was sapped out of me because Anita Hill was a person I considered a friend whom I admired and thought I had treated fairly and with the utmost respect. Perhaps I could have better weathered this if it was from someone else. But here was someone I truly felt I had done my best with. Though I am by no means a perfect person, no means, I have not done what she has alleged, and I still don't know what I could possibly have done to cause her to make these allegations.

When I stood next to the President in Kennebunkport being nominated to the Supreme Court of the United States, that was a high honor; but as I sit here before you 103 days later, that honor has been crushed. From the very beginning, charges were leveled against me from the shadows, charges of drug abuse, anti-Semitism, wife-beating, drug use by family members, that I was a quota appointment, confirmation conversion, and much, much more. And now, this.

. . . .

I'm not going to allow myself to be further humiliated in order to be confirmed. I am here specifically to respond to allegations of sex harassment in the workplace. I am not here to be further humiliated by this committee or anyone else, or to put my private life on display for prurient interests or other reasons. I will not allow this committee or anyone else to probe into my private life. This is not what America is all about. To ask me to do that would be to ask me to go beyond fundamental fairness.

Yesterday I called my mother. She was confined to her bed, unable to work and unable to stop crying. Enough is enough.

Mr. Chairman, in my 43 years on this earth I have been able with the help of others and with the help of God to defy poverty, avoid prison, overcome segregation, bigotry, racism and obtain one of the finest educations available in this country, but I have not been able to overcome this process. This is worse than any obstacle or anything that I have ever faced.

Throughout my life I have been energized by the expectation and the hope that in this country I would be treated fairly in all endeavors. When there was segregation I hoped there would be fairness one day or some day. When there was bigotry and prejudice, I hoped that there would be tolerance and understanding some day.

. . . .

I will not provide the rope for my own lynching or for further humiliation. I am not going to engage in discussions nor will I submit to roving questions of what goes on in the most intimate parts of my private life or the sanctity of my bedroom. These are the most intimate parts of my privacy, and they will remain just that, private.

SEN. BIDEN: Thank you, Judge. You will not be asked to.

Testimony of Anita F. Hill

Hearings Before the Senate Judiciary Committee, October 11, 1991[6]

. . . .

. . . Upon graduation from law school, I became a practicing lawyer with the Washington, DC, firm of Ward, Hardraker, and Ross.

In 1981, I was introduced to now Judge Thomas by a mutual friend. Judge Thomas told me that he was anticipating a political appointment, and he asked if I would be interested in working with him. He was, in fact, appointed as Assistant Secretary of

---

6. *Id.* at 36–40, 54–58, 88–89, 112–13.

Education for Civil Rights. After he had taken that post, he asked if I would become his assistant, and I accepted that position.

In my early period there, I had two major projects. The first was an article I wrote for Judge Thomas' signature on the education of minority students. The second was the organization of a seminar on high-risk students which was abandoned because Judge Thomas transferred to the EEOC where he became the chairman of that office.

During this period at the Department of Education, my working relationship with Judge Thomas was positive. I had a good deal of responsibility and independence. I thought he respected my work and that he trusted my judgment. After approximately three months of working there, he asked me to go out socially with him.

What happened next and telling the world about it are the two most difficult things—experiences of my life. It is only after a great deal of agonizing consideration and sleepless number—a great number of sleepless nights that I am able to talk of these unpleasant matters to anyone but my close friends.

I declined the invitation to go out socially with him and explained to him that I thought it would jeopardize what at the time I considered to be a very good working relationship. I had a normal social life with other men outside of the office. I believed then, as now, that having a social relationship with a person who was supervising my work would be ill-advised. I was very uncomfortable with the idea and told him so.

I thought that by saying no and explaining my reasons my employer would abandon his social suggestions. However, to my regret, in the following few weeks, he continued to ask me out on several occasions. He pressed me to justify my reasons for saying no to him. These incidents took place in his office or mine. They were in the form of private conversations which would not have been overheard by anyone else.

My working relationship became even more strained when Judge Thomas began to use work situations to discuss sex. On these occasions, he would call me into his office for reports on education issues and projects, or he might suggest that, because of the time pressures of his schedule, we go to lunch to a government cafeteria. After a brief discussion of work, he would turn the conversation to a discussion of sexual matters.

His conversations were very vivid. He spoke about acts that he had seen in pornographic films involving such matters as women having sex with animals and films showing group sex or rape scenes. He talked about pornographic materials depicting individuals with large penises or large breasts involved in various sex acts. On several occasions, Thomas told me graphically of his own sexual prowess.

Because I was extremely uncomfortable talking about sex with him at all and particularly in such a graphic way, I told him that I did not want to talk about these subjects. I would also try to change the subject to education matters or to nonsexual personal matters such as his background or his beliefs. My efforts to change the subject were rarely successful.

Throughout the period of these conversations, he also from time to time asked me for social engagements. My reaction to these conversations was to avoid them by eliminating opportunities for us to engage in extended conversations. This was difficult because at the time I was his only assistant at the Office of Education — or Office for Civil Rights.

During the latter part of my time at the Department of Education, the social pressures and any conversation of his offensive behavior ended. I began both to believe and hope that our working relationship could be a proper, cordial, and professional one.

When Judge Thomas was made Chair of the EEOC, I needed to face the question of whether to go with him. I was asked to do so, and I did. The work itself was interesting, and at that time it appeared that the sexual overtures which had so troubled me had ended. I also faced the realistic fact that I had no alternative job. While I might have gone back to private practice, perhaps in my old firm or at another, I was dedicated to civil rights work, and my first choice was to be in that field. Moreover, the Department of Education itself was a dubious venture. President Reagan was seeking to abolish the entire department.

For my first months at the EEOC, where I continued to be an assistant to Judge Thomas, there were no sexual conversations or overtures. However, during the fall and winter of 1982, these began again. The comments were random and ranged from pressing me about why I didn't go out with him to remarks about my personal appearance. I remember him saying that some day I would have to tell him the real reason that I wouldn't go out with him.

He began to show displeasure in his tone and voice and his demeanor and his continued pressure for an explanation. He commented on what I was wearing in terms of whether it made me more or less sexually attractive. The incidents occurred in his inner office at the EEOC.

One of the oddest episodes I remember was an occasion in which Thomas was drinking a Coke in his office. He got up from the table at which we were working, went over to his desk to get the Coke, looked at the can and asked, "Who has pubic hair on my Coke?" On other occasions, he referred to the size of his own penis as being larger than normal, and he also spoke on some occasions of the pleasures he had given to women with oral sex.

At this point, late 1982, I began to feel severe stress on the job. I began to be concerned that Clarence Thomas might take out his anger with me by degrading me or not giving me important assignments. I also thought that he might find an excuse for dismissing me.

In January of 1983, I began looking for another job. I was handicapped because I feared that, if he found out, he might make it difficult for me to find other employment and I might be dismissed from the job I had. Another factor that made my search more difficult was that there was a period—this was during a period of a hiring freeze in the government. In February of 1983, I was hospitalized for five days on an emergency basis for acute stomach pain which I attributed to stress on the job.

Once out of the hospital, I became more committed to find other employment and sought further to minimize my contact with Thomas. This became easier when Allison Duncan became office director, because most of my work was then funneled through her and I had contact with Clarence Thomas mostly in staff meetings.

In the spring of 1983, an opportunity to teach at Oral Roberts University opened up. I participated in a seminar—taught an afternoon session and seminar at Oral Roberts University. The dean of the university saw me teaching and inquired as to whether I would be interested in pursuing a career in teaching, beginning at Oral Roberts University. I agreed to take the job in large part because of my desire to escape the pressures I felt at the EEOC due to Judge Thomas.

When I informed him that I was leaving in July, I recall that his response was that now I would no longer have an excuse for not going out with him. I told him that I still preferred not to do so. At some time after that meeting, he asked if he could take me to dinner at the end of the term. When I declined, he assured me that the dinner was a professional courtesy only and not a social invitation. I reluctantly agreed to accept that invitation, but only if it was at the very end of a working day.

On, as I recall, the last day of my employment at the EEOC in the summer of 1983, I did have dinner with Clarence Thomas. We went directly from work to a restaurant near the office. We talked about the work I had done, both at education and at the EEOC. He told me that he was pleased with all of it except for an article and speech that I had done for him while we were at the Office for Civil Rights. Finally, he made a comment that I will vividly remember. He said that if I ever told anyone of his behavior that it would ruin his career. This was not an apology, nor was it an explanation. That was his last remark about the possibility of our going out or reference to his behavior.

In July of 1983, I left the Washington, DC, area and have had minimal contact with Judge Clarence Thomas since. I am of course aware from the press that some questions have been raised about conversations I had with Judge Clarence Thomas after I left the EEOC. From 1983 until today, I have seen Judge Thomas only twice. On one occasion, I needed to get a reference from him, and on another he made a public appearance in Tulsa.

. . . .

It is only after a great deal of agonizing consideration that I am able to talk of these unpleasant matters to anyone except my closest friends. As I've said before these last few days have been very trying and very hard for me and it hasn't just been the last few days this week. It has actually been over a month now that I have been under the strain of this issue.

Telling the world is the most difficult experience of my life, but it is very close to having to live through the experience that occasioned this meeting. I may have used poor judgment early on in my relationship with this issue. I was aware, however, that telling at any point in my career could adversely affect my future career. And I did not want early on to burn all the bridges to the EEOC.

As I said, I may have used poor judgment. Perhaps I should have taken angry or even militant steps, both when I was in the agency, or after I left it. But I must confess to the world that the course that I took seemed the better as well as the easier approach.

I declined any comment to newspapers, but later when Senate staff asked me about these matters I felt I had a duty to report. I have no personal vendetta against Clarence Thomas. I seek only to provide the committee with information which it may regard as relevant.

It would have been more comfortable to remain silent. I took no initiative to inform anyone. But when I was asked by a representative of this committee to report my experience, I felt that I had to tell the truth. I could not keep silent.

Testimony of Clarence Thomas

Hearings Before the Senate Judiciary Committee, October 12, 1991[7]

Senator, I would like to start by saying unequivocally, uncategorically, that I deny each and every single allegation against me today that suggested in any way that I had conversations of a sexual nature or about pornographic material with Anita Hill, that I ever attempted to date her, that I ever had any personal sexual interest in her, or that I in any way ever harassed her.

Second, and I think a more important point, I think that this today is a travesty. I think that it is disgusting. I think that this hearing should never occur in America. This is a case in which this sleaze, this dirt, was searched for by staffers of members of this committee, was then leaked to the media, and this committee and this body validated it and displayed it at prime time over our entire nation. How would any member on this committee, any person in this room, or any person in this country, would like sleaze said about him or her in this fashion? Or this dirt dredged up and this gossip and these lies displayed in this manner? How would any person like it?

The Supreme Court is not worth it. No job is worth it. I'm not here for that. I'm here for my name, my family, my life and my integrity. I think something is dreadfully wrong with this country when any person, any person in this free country would be subjected to this.

This is not a closed room. There was an FBI investigation. This is not an opportunity to talk about difficult matters privately or in a closed environment. This is a circus. It's a national disgrace. And from my standpoint as a black American, as far

---

7. *Id.* at 157–58, 160–65.

as I'm concerned, it is a high-tech lynching for uppity blacks who in any way deign to think for themselves, to do for themselves, to have different ideas, and it is a message that unless you kow-tow to an old order, this is what will happen to you. You will be lynched, destroyed, caricatured by a committee of the US Senate rather than hung from a tree.

. . . .

SEN. HEFLIN: . . . Now, you, I suppose, have heard Professor Hill, Ms. Hill, Anita F. Hill testify today.

JUDGE THOMAS: No, I haven't.

SEN. HEFLIN: You didn't listen?

JUDGE THOMAS: No, I didn't. I've heard enough lies.

SEN. HEFLIN: You didn't listen to her testimony at all?

JUDGE THOMAS: No, I didn't.

SEN. HEFLIN: On television?

JUDGE THOMAS: No, I didn't. I've heard enough lies. Today is not a day that in my opinion is high among the days in our country. This is a travesty. You spent the entire day destroying what it has taken me 43 years to build, and providing a forum for that.

SEN. HEFLIN: Well, Judge Thomas, you know, we have a responsibility, too. And as far as I'm involved, I had nothing to do with Anita Hill coming here and testifying. We're trying to get to the bottom of this, and if she is lying, then I think you can help us prove that she was lying.

JUDGE THOMAS: Senator, I am incapable of proving the negative. It did not occur.

SEN. HEFLIN: Well, if it did not occur, I think you are in a position, certainly your ability to testify to, in effect, to try to eliminate it from people's minds.

JUDGE THOMAS: Senator, I didn't create it in people's minds. This matter was investigated by the Federal Bureau of Investigation in a confidential way. It was then leaked last weekend to the media. I did not do that. . . .

. . . .

. . . This leaked on me and it is drowning my life, my career and my integrity and you can't give it back to me and this committee can't give it back to me and this Senate can't give it back to me. You have robbed me of something that can never be restored.

SEN. DECONCINI: I know exactly how you feel.

SEN. HEFLIN: Judge Thomas, one of the aspects of this is that she could be living in a fantasy world. I don't know. We're just trying to get to the bottom of all of these facts. But if you didn't listen and didn't see her testify, I think you put yourself in an unusual position. You in effect are defending yourself and basically some of us want to be fair to you, fair to her, but if you didn't listen to what she said today, then that puts it somewhat in a more difficult task to find out what the actual facts are relative to this matter.

JUDGE THOMAS: The facts keep changing, Senator. When the FBI visited me, the statements to this committee and the questions were one thing. The FBI's subsequent questions were another thing, and the statements today as I received summaries of them were another thing. It is not my fault that the facts changed. What I have said to you is categorical; that any allegations that I engaged in any conduct involving sexual activity, pornographic movies, attempted to date her, any allegations, I deny. It is not true. So, the facts can change, but my denial does not. Ms. Hill was treated in a way that all my special assistants were treated: cordial, professional, respectful.

SEN. HEFLIN: Judge, if you are on the bench and you approach a case where you appear to have a closed mind and that you are only right, doesn't it raise issues of judicial temperament?

JUDGE THOMAS: Senator? Senator, there is a big difference between approaching a case objectively and watching yourself being lynched. There is no comparison whatsoever.

SEN. HATCH: If I might add, he has personal knowledge of this as well, and personal justification for anger.

. . . .

SEN. HATCH: . . . [Anita Hill] said to the FBI that you told her about your sexual experiences and preferences, that you asked her what she liked, or if she had ever done the same thing, that you discussed oral sex between men and women, that you discussed viewing films of people having sex with each other and with animals, and that you told her that she should see such films, and that you liked to discuss specific sex acts and the frequency of sex. What about that?

JUDGE THOMAS: Senator, I would not want to—except being required to here—to dignify those allegations with a response. As I have said before, I categorically deny them. To me, I have been pilloried with scurrilous allegations of this nature, I have denied them earlier, and I deny them tonight.

SEN. HATCH: Judge Thomas, today in a news statement, in addition to what she told the FBI, which I have to agree with you is quite a bit, she made a number of other allegations, and what I'd like to do is—some of the most specific were for the first time today in addition to these, which I think almost anybody would say are terrible. Now I'd just like to give you an opportunity, because this is your chance to address her testimony. At any time, did you say to Professor Hill that she could ruin your career if she talked about sexual comments you allegedly made to her?

JUDGE THOMAS: No.

SEN. HATCH: Did you say to her in words or substance that you could ruin her career?

JUDGE THOMAS: No.

SEN. HATCH: Should she ever have been afraid of you and your—and any kind of vindictiveness to ruin her career?

JUDGE THOMAS: Senator, I have made it my business to help my special assistants. I recommended Ms. Hill for her position at Oral Roberts University. I've always spoken highly of her. I had no reason prior to the FBI visiting me a little more than two weeks ago to know that she harbored any ill feelings toward me or any discomfort with me. This is all new to me.

SEN. HATCH: It's new to me, too, because I read the FBI report at least ten or fifteen times. And I didn't see any of these allegations I'm about to go into, including that one. But she seemed to sure have a recollection here today.

Now, did you ever say to Professor Hill in words or substance—and this is embarrassing for me to say in public—but it has to be done, and I'm sure it's not pleasing to you—did you ever say in words or substance something like there is a pubic hair in my Coke?

JUDGE THOMAS: No, Senator.

SEN. HATCH: Did you ever refer to your private parts in conversations with Professor Hill?

JUDGE THOMAS: Absolutely not, Senator.

SEN. HATCH: Did you ever brag to Professor Hill about your sexual prowess?

JUDGE THOMAS: No, Senator.

SEN. HATCH: Did you ever use the term Long Dong Silver in conversation with Professor Hill? Had you—

JUDGE THOMAS: No, Senator.

SEN. HATCH: Did you ever have lunch with Professor Hill at which you talked about sex or pressured her to go out with you?

JUDGE THOMAS: Absolutely not.

SEN. HATCH: Did you ever—

JUDGE THOMAS: I have had no such discussions nor have I ever pressured or asked her to go out with me beyond her work environment.

SEN. HATCH: Did you ever tell Professor Hill that she should see pornographic films?

JUDGE THOMAS: Absolutely not.

SEN. HATCH: Did you ever talk about pornography with Professor Hill?

JUDGE THOMAS: I did not discuss any pornographic material or pornographic preferences or pornographic films with Professor Hill.

SEN. HATCH: So you never even talked or described pornographic materials with her?

JUDGE THOMAS: Absolutely not.

SEN. HATCH: Amongst those or in addition?

JUDGE THOMAS: What I have told you is precisely what I told the FBI on September 25th, when they shocked me with the allegations made by Anita Hill.

SEN. HATCH: Judge Thomas, those were a lot of allegations. Those were a lot of charges: Talking about sexual experiences and preferences, whether she liked it or had ever done the same thing; oral sex, viewing films of people having sex with each other and with animals, that maybe she should see such films, discuss specific acts, talk about pubic hair and Coke, talking about your private parts, bragging about sexual prowess, talking about particular pornographic movies.

Let me ask you something. You have dealt with these problems for a long time. At one time I was the Chairman of reviewing the EEOC and I might add the Department of Education. Now, I am the ranking member today, and I have known you for 11 years. And you're an expert because you are the person who made the arguments to the then Solicitor General Freed that the administration should strongly take a position on sexual harassment cases in the *Meritor Savings Bank v. Vincent* case, and the Supreme Court adopted your position.

Did I misstate that?

JUDGE THOMAS: Senator, what you have said is substantially accurate. The— what I attempted to do in my discussions with the solicitor is to have them be aggressive in that litigation, and EEOC was very instrumental in the success in the *Meritor* case.

. . . .

SEN. HATCH: Now let me ask you something. I described all kinds of what I consider to be gross, awful sexually harassing things. Which, if you take them in cumulation, have to gag anybody.

Now, you've seen a lot of these sexual harassment cases as you've served there at EEOC. What is your opinion with regard to what should have been done with those charges and whether or not you believe that—let's take Professor Hill in this case—should have done something, since she was a Yale Law graduate who taught civil rights law at one point, served in these various agencies, and had to understand that there's an issue of fairness here.

JUDGE THOMAS: Senator, if any of those activities occurred, it would seem to me to clearly suggest or to clearly indicate sexual harassment. And anyone who felt that she was harassed could go to an EEO officer at any agency and have that dealt with confidentially—at Department of Education, if she said it occurred there, or at EEOC. Those are separate tracks at EEOC. I do not get to review those if they involve me, and at the Department of Education there's a separate EEO officer for the whole department. It would have nothing to do with me.

But if I were an individual advising a person who'd been subjected to that treatment, I would advise her to immediately go to the EEO officer.

SEN. HATCH: And the EEO office, then, would bring the parties together or at least would confront the problem head-on, wouldn't it?

JUDGE THOMAS: The EEO officer would provide counseling, and—

SEN. HATCH: Within a short period of time?

JUDGE THOMAS [continuing]: Within a short period of time, as well as, I think, if necessary, actual—an actual charge would [be lodged].

SEN. HATCH: So the charge would be made and the charge would then—the person against whom it was made would have a chance to answer it right then, right up front, in a way that could resolve it and stop this type of activity if it ever really occurred?

JUDGE THOMAS: That's right.

SEN. HATCH: And you just said it never really occurred.

JUDGE THOMAS: It never occurred. That is why there was no charge.

SEN. HATCH: See, one of the problems that has bothered me from the front of this thing, is these are gross. Accumulated, I don't know why anybody would put up with them or why anybody would respect or work with another person who would do that. And if you did that, I don't know why anybody would work with you—

. . . .

JUDGE THOMAS: Senator, my relationship with Anita Hill prior to September 25th, was cordial and professional. And I might add one other thing. If you really want an idea of how I treated women, then ask the majority of the women who worked for me. They're out here. Give her—give them as much time as you have given one person, the only person who has been on my staff who has ever made these sorts of allegations about me.

Notes and Discussion

1. **Media "Spin"** Why did Judge Thomas announce at the beginning of his statement that "no handlers" had seen it? Did that assurance make him more credible? Was it likely he was briefed before preparing his statement? Does it matter? Thomas referred to his understanding of sexual harassment "horrors" and its seriousness. Later, Senator Hatch referred to Thomas's role in *Meritor*. What was the irony of Hatch's reference? Was Thomas's mother relevant to these proceedings? Why did he mention her? When Thomas asked the members of the committee how they would like having such allegations lodged against them, to whom was he really speaking— only the senators? Why did Thomas not listen to Hill's presentation? Is it likely that someone told him what she said? Why or why not?

2. **Sexual Harassment Generally** If Thomas understands sexual harassment as he claims, why does he not understand why Hill might not complain? Or is her failure to speak out before inexplicable and unjustifiable? If what Hill alleged was true, did Thomas's behavior constitute sexual harassment? Why or why not? If so, was it quid

pro quo or hostile environment sexual harassment? Is it plausible that Hill suffered stress-related stomach pain causing her hospitalization?

3. The Relevance of Race Was race relevant in the Hill/Thomas hearings? Why or why not? What stereotypes circulated in the hearings and public commentary? Three times Thomas referred to the proceedings as a lynching. Was this a lynching as he claimed? Explain.

Ten years after Thomas's confirmation, Professor Mark Niles reviewed Thomas's tenure on the Court and commented upon the Hill/Thomas hearings:

> Notwithstanding the difficult position in which he [Thomas] found himself (or placed himself, depending on which of the various stories one believes), I was stunned by Justice Thomas' public and passionate contention that he believed that the attacks upon him were racially motivated. Indeed, he referred to the attacks and the process surrounding them as a "high-tech lynching for uppity blacks" in his statement to the Senate Judiciary Committee.
>
> In retrospect one can only assume that Thomas would have regretted comparing his odyssey, painful as it must have been, to the deaths and brutal mutilations of thousands of other African-Americans over the past 200 years. But even with the rhetoric somewhat toned down, it seemed like an odd and inconsistent charge to be made by Thomas for at least two reasons. First, he had distinguished himself as one of the few African-Americans who demonstrated an almost enthusiastic willingness to reject allegations of discrimination raised by other racial minorities in his position as head of the United States Equal Employment Opportunity Commission ("EEOC") and elsewhere. It is ironic that during Thomas' most serious personal and professional crisis, a man who had built his career on a belief (one can only assume that it was a sincerely held one) that too many of the difficulties that African-Americans have experienced since the civil rights movement have been attributed to racial bias, would fall back on this same explanation to describe his situation. Thomas used the now legendary "race card" in a more profound and significant way than Johnny Cochran or anyone else has ever used it.
>
> Second, Thomas' claim of racial discrimination had such a remarkably weak basis. Thomas' allegation appears to have been that the allegations of sexual harassment were not only erroneous, but were only raised against him because he was a black person who was also a conservative by people who had a particular animus to black conservatives (as opposed, I assume, to black liberals and/or white conservatives). So even if one accepts Thomas' factual assertion—that there was an organized attempt to smear his good name orchestrated by people who wanted to harm him because of the combination of his race and his ideology—as true, it is difficult to see how such an act, as despicable as it may be, would constitute racial discrimination.

Again, according to Thomas, it was his willingness to express his beliefs that resulted in the attacks on him. If another black man had expressed other beliefs, under this theory, he would not have been attacked in the same way. Although one can imagine a subtle and nuanced argument that explains the ways how the intersection of race with other factors such as gender, class, or ideology can lead to a wholly independent experience of discrimination other than the commonplace form of overt racial bias, it is easy to imagine how Thomas and other judicial conservatives would respond to such a textured and subtle legal construction. Suffice it to say, the EEOC under Thomas' leadership was not at the forefront of groundbreaking new causes of action for new kinds of racial discrimination. While on the Court, Justice Thomas has expressed a willingness to support such expansions if they extend to actionable instances of racial discrimination.

> While I am again reluctant to claim knowledge of the motivations of others, the inherent inconsistency of Justice Thomas' beliefs and actions caused me great concern. The inconsistency arose from the willingness of Thomas, who had raised serious and indeed compelling arguments about the negative impact of frivolously using the "race card" and the impact such assertions have on those who genuinely suffer from racial bias, to use that very same "race card" when his place on the highest court was in doubt, and when the allegation rang hollow.[8]

Did Professor Niles make a valid point regarding the inconsistency of Thomas's actions at the EEOC and his lynching claim at the hearing? Did Thomas's argument—that he was targeted for his conservative views—dilute his race discrimination charge, as Niles asserted? Did Thomas use the "race card" frivolously?

Professor Niles cited an article from *The Nation,* discussing how, as head of the EEOC, Thomas initially defended some affirmative action policies. Then in 1984, Thomas opposed all affirmative action and began blocking enforcement of anti-discrimination laws. In fact, he told the Heritage Foundation in 1987 that "I believe firmly that I should have taken a more aggressive stand against affirmative action in earlier years."[9]

4. Credibility Based on their opening statements, who was more credible? Why? What did Anita Hill have to gain by coming forward? Both Hill and Thomas were Republicans. Does this fact undermine the claim that there was a conspiracy against Thomas?

In an *L.A. Times* opinion editorial, Stanford law professor Barbara Babcock drew upon her extensive knowledge of courtroom tactics to analyze the strategies

---

8. Mark C. Niles, *Clarence Thomas: The First Ten Years Looking for Consistency*, 10 Am. U.J. Gender Soc. Pol'y & L. 327, 335–38 (2002).

9. Bruce Shapiro, *Good Reasons for Doubting Thomas*, The Nation (Sept. 23, 1991), at 336.

employed by Thomas in the Senate confirmation hearings.[10] Babcock identified three tactics that Thomas and his defenders used to challenge Hill's credibility: paint Thomas as the real victim, attack the process as flawed, and attack Hill's credibility.

Babcock argued that the hearings were typical for rape and sexual harassment trials in that they focused on the credibility of the two parties, but that these hearings were unusual in several respects. First, according to Babcock, "when the contest comes down to a question of credibility, jurors will tend to believe the witness who appears most like them or who they would like to be—the one who dresses better, whose language is more precise, whose habits appear more proper." But in this regard, Hill and Thomas were "virtually identical."

Second, explained Babcock, the defense will often seek to avoid the credibility issue, and the hard task of proving that someone is lying, by suggesting that one party has made a mistake. However, the testimonies of Hill and Thomas were diametrically opposed—so someone had to have been lying.

Finally, Babcock argued that motive was a central factor in the Hill/Thomas hearings. Thomas's motive to lie was clear—to win a seat on the Supreme Court, but potential motives for Hill to lie were hard to imagine, especially given her stellar background. Typically, defense attorneys will claim that an accuser is a jilted lover or a personal enemy, but there were no facts to support these narratives. Therefore, witnesses claimed that "Hill had fantasized a relationship between the two of them [and] that Hill was a psychopath suffering from some sort of erotomania that would cause her to make up sexual encounters with others." But this tactic clearly conflicted with Hill's appearance and demeanor.

So Thomas and his supporters turned to a second defense—that Thomas was the victim of "a vast conspiracy in which unnamed outside groups used Hill as a dupe." According to Babcock, that argument allowed Thomas's defenders "to center their attack, not on Hill, but on the outside groups[.]" Presumably, jurors were more likely to disfavor those groups. Second, that strategy allowed defenders "to play on the prospective jury's racial sympathies by portraying Thomas as a hardworking conscientious black man under attack, not by a black woman, but by 'slick' lawyers using Hill as a tool."[11] Was Barbara Babcock correct—did the conspiracy theory allow Thomas's supporters to play on "racial sympathies"?

5. Clarence Thomas's Legacy at the EEOC The EEOC, which under the leadership of Eleanor Holmes Norton had supported the development of strong laws against sexual harassment, changed significantly after Ronald Reagan appointed Clarence Thomas as Chair in 1982. For example, under Thomas, the Commission filed a brief in support of the defendant/employer in the first Supreme Court sexual harassment case, *Vinson v. Meritor Savings Bank*. The EEOC argued that hostile environment

---

10. Barbara A. Babcock, Editorial, *Panel's 'Swearing Contest' Emerging as a Classic Battle for Credibility*, L.A. Times (Oct. 13, 1991).

11. *Id.*

sexual harassment was "special" and "distinct" because of "the naturalness, the pervasiveness, and what might be called the legal neutrality of sexual attraction (as contrasted to racial prejudice)." They explained, "[w]hereas racial slurs are intrinsically offensive and presumptively unwelcome, sexual advances and innuendo are ambiguous."[12] The EEOC brief expressed concern that "sexual harassment charges do not become a tool by which one party to a consensual sexual relationship may punish the other."[13] The EEOC arguments implied that women lie about sexual harassment, and it selectively read the record to attack Vinson's credibility.[14] Does Thomas's legacy at the EEOC help explain his behavior during the hearings?

6. Media Coverage Then and Now The Hill/Thomas hearings occurred before widespread use of the World Wide Web. Cable television broadcast the hearings live and gave extended coverage of commentary about the hearings, but media was largely unidirectional, from television news reporters to viewers, or in the case of newspapers, from journalists to readers (except for letters to the editor). Corporations controlled the content and framing of news about the hearings.

With the advent of the World Wide Web in the 1990s, and later social media, how does the circulation of information about sexual harassment differ today? What is the significance of that difference? What role did social media play in the rise of #MeToo protests and what impact did it have on the development of the issue?[15] How might the internet and social media have changed the impact of the Hill/Thomas hearings? How was the media coverage of the Hill/Thomas hearings similar or different from the coverage of Senate Judiciary hearings on Christine Blasey Ford's allegations against Supreme Court nominee Brett Kavanaugh in 2018?

Testimony of Witnesses in Support of Anita Hill:
Ellen M. Wells, John W. Carr, Judge Susan Hoerchner, and Joel Paul

Hearings Before the Senate Judiciary Committee, October 13, 1991[16]

MS. WELLS: Good afternoon, Senators. My name is Ellen M. Wells. I am a project manager at the American Public Welfare Association in Washington, DC. I received a master's degree in public affairs and a juris doctor from the George Washington University.

I met Professor Hill in 1981 at a social gathering and we developed a friendship. I was also acquainted with Judge Thomas during the late 1970's and early 1980's

---

12. Brief for the United States & the Equal Employment Opportunity Commission as Amici Curiae at Part A, Meritor Sav. Bank, FSB v. Vinson, 477 U.S. 57 (1986) (No. 84-1979), 1985 WL 670162, at *13.

13. *Id.* at *15.

14. Carrie N. Baker, The Women's Movement Against Sexual Harassment 164–66 (2008).

15. *See infra* Chapter 10.

16. Hearings Before the Senate Committee on the Judiciary, 102d Cong., 1st Sess. pt. 4, 273–78, 302–05, 323–25 (1991).

as a result of our joint membership in the Black Republican Congressional Staff Association.

. . . .

. . . In the fall of 1982, Professor Hill shared with me in confidence the fact that she considered Judge Thomas's behavior toward her in the office to be inappropriate. Professor Hill did not at that time, nor in subsequent conversations provide exact details about the actions she found inappropriate conduct. She did tell me they were sexual in nature. I should note that I did not ask for details for two reasons: Neither Professor Hill nor I would have been comfortable discussing such matters. Women typically don't talk in sexually explicit terms. Second, she appeared to simply need a sympathetic ear. And as her friend, that is what I tried to provide.

I believed the statements made by my friend, Professor Hill. As she told me of this situation, she appeared to be deeply troubled and very depressed. And later, I remember talking to her by telephone while she was in the hospital, and she explained to me that what she was suffering from [what] appeared to be job related — job-stress related.

I think it is important for me to state that Professor Hill did not contact me in connection with this hearing. In fact, because of the way our lives have been proceeding, I have not seen nor spoken to Professor Anita Hill in two years. I called the law school and left a message of support and willingness to be of assistance if needed. My call jogged her memory of what she had said to me. As a consequence, Professor Hill asked her attorneys to get in touch with me.

Finally, Senators, I would like to say that I am not a party to any effort to derail Judge Thomas's confirmation to the Supreme Court by any interest group or by individuals who may not agree with his political philosophy. I am here as an individual simply as a matter of conscience to tell you what I was told by Anita Hill. And I believe this information relevant to the decision that you are called upon to make.

Thank you.

SEN. BIDEN: Thank you very much. Mr. Carr.

MR. CARR: Mr. Chairman, Senator Thurmond, members of the committee, my name is John William Carr. I reside in the City of New York. I am an attorney by profession and a partner at the law firm of Simpson, Thacher and Bartlett.

I met Anita Hill in the spring of 1981. At the time, we were introduced by a mutual friend while they both were employed at the law firm of Wald, Harkrader and Ross in Washington, DC. I was a student at the time at Harvard University, where I was simultaneously pursuing a law degree at the Harvard Law School and an MBA degree at the Harvard Business School.

During the final semester of the 1982–83 academic year, I developed a social relationship with Anita Hill. I lived in Cambridge, Massachusetts, and she lived in Washington, DC, which made seeing one another very difficult. However, during this particular period we spoke several times at length on the telephone.

During one of these telephone conversations, Anita Hill revealed to me that her supervisor was sexually harassing her. I recall that she did not initially volunteer this information. Rather, during the telephone conversation it quickly became clear to me that she was troubled and upset. In response to my expressions of concern about her feelings, Anita Hill told me that she was upset because her boss was making sexual advances towards her. I recall that she was clearly very disturbed by these advances and that she cried during the telephone call.

I knew that Anita Hill worked for Clarence Thomas at the Equal Employment Opportunity Commission. In this telephone conversation, it was immediately clear to me that she was referring to Judge Thomas. I asked her to tell me what he had done. It is my recollection that she told me that Clarence Thomas had asked her out on dates and showed an unwanted sexual interest in her. She was very uncomfortable talking about these events and said that she did not want to go into any detail about the actions that had so upset her. I do recall, however, that she said these sexual advances had taken place before. It was clear to me at that time that she found this very painful to talk about, and I did not push her to speak of it further.

At this point the conversation turned to how appalling it was that the head of the EEOC would engage in sexual advances towards one of his own employees. I thought it was outrageous and, in a perverse sort of way, ironic that the person in charge of fighting discrimination in the workplace could harass an employee in this way. This portion of the conversation I dominated with my own repeated expressions of outrage. It is because of this outrage and irony that I recall our conversation today.

It was clear that Anita Hill did not want to continue to dwell on these incidents, and the conversation moved to other subjects.

. . . .

SEN. BIDEN: Thank you very much, sir. Judge Hoerchner.

MS. HOERCHNER: Mr. Chairman and members of the committee, my name is Susan Hoerchner. . . . I am a workers compensation judge in California. I have known Anita Hill for about 13 years. We met when she was my editor for a project at Yale Legislative Services when we were first year law students. We soon became friends.

. . . .

When Anita and I graduated from law school, both of us, as it happened, came to Washington for our first jobs. . . . We were both busy with our new jobs so we did not get together with great frequency. What we did do, however, was keep in touch by telephone. Those conversations would often last as much as an hour.

I remember in particular one telephone conversation I had with Anita. I should say before telling you about this conversation that I cannot pin down its date with certainty. I am sure that it was after she started working with Clarence Thomas, because in that conversation she referred to him as her boss, Clarence.

It was clear when we started this conversation that something was badly wrong. Anita sounded very depressed and spoke in a dull monotone. I asked Anita how things were going at work. Instead of a cheery, "Oh, just busy," her usual response, this time she led me to understand that there was a serious problem. She told me that she was being subjected to sexual harassment, to whom [sic] she referred by name. That boss was Clarence Thomas. Anita's use of the words sexual harassment made an impression on me because it was the first time I had heard that term used by a friend in personal conversation.

Anita said that Clarence Thomas had repeatedly asked her out. She told me that she had, of course, refused, but that he wouldn't seem to take no for an answer. He kept pressing her and repeating things like, "I'm your type," and "You know I'm your kind of man but you refuse to admit it."

One thing Anita told me that struck me particularly and that I remember almost verbatim was that Mr. Thomas had said to her, "You know, if you had witnesses, you'd have a perfect case against me." She told me that she was very humiliated and demoralized by Mr. Thomas' behavior, and that it had shaken her faith in her professional ability.

At the end of this conversation, Anita seemed more depressed than when it began. Contrary to my hope, talking things out did not seem to have given her any relief or comfort. After our conversation, I was both saddened and concerned about my friend. Because it had been so painful for Anita to talk about the matter, I did not try to pull information out of her. In subsequent conversations with Anita, I learned that the problem continued, but I do not recall in detail further conversations about this matter.

Mr. Chairman, in conclusion, as a result of the high esteem in which her law school classmates hold her, 65 members—over 65 members of Anita's law school class have been contacted and have signed the following statement: "It has been our privilege to know Anita Hill, professionally and personally, since the late '70s when we were in law school together. The Anita Hill we have known is a person of great integrity and decency. As colleagues, we wish to affirm publicly our admiration and respect for her. She is embroiled now in a most serious and difficult controversy, which we know is causing her great pain. We make no attempt to analyze the issue involved or to prejudge the outcome. We do, however, wish to state emphatically our complete confidence in her sincerity and good faith, our absolute belief in her decency and integrity. In our eyes, it is impossible to imagine any circumstances in which her character could be called into question. We are dismayed that it has been. We know that it could not be by anyone who knows her.

Anita has imperiled her career and her peace of mind to do what she felt was right. We know we are powerless to shield her from those who will seek to hurt her out of ignorance, frustration or expediency in the days ahead, that we will have failed ourselves if we did not at least raise our voices in her behalf. She has our unhesitating and unwavering support."

Thank you, Mr. Chairman.

SEN. BIDEN: Thank you very much. Mr. Paul.

MR. JOEL PAUL: Mr. Chairman, Senator Thurmond, members of the Committee, I am an associate professor of law at the Washington College of Law at American University here in Washington. Before joining the faculty at American University in 1986, I practiced banking and corporate law in California. Presently I teach international business and trade and foreign relations law.

I'm here to give my account of what I was told in the summer of 1987 by Professor Anita Hill —

. . . .

And to give my impressions of Professor Hill's character and credibility.

As soon as I read Professor Hill's allegations in the Washington Post on Monday morning, I realized that I had a duty to come forward and to give my account, because I knew that Professor Hill's allegations were not an Eleventh Hour fabrication, as some have said, but rather a more specific description of events she related to me more than four years ago.

. . . During the course of her research at our school, we had a number of occasions to talk about her interest in the American University and our interest in having her join the faculty.

During one such occasion, over lunch in the university cafeteria, I asked Professor Hill why she had left the EEOC. This was a logical question to ask in the course of discussing with her employment history. Professor Hill responded, reluctantly and with obvious emotion and embarrassment, that she had been sexually harassed by her supervisor at the EEOC. I was shocked and astonished by her statement, which is why I remember the incident so vividly. I do not recall whether she went on to say the name "Clarence Thomas," but if she had said it, the name would not have meant anything to me at that time because I had no idea who Judge Thomas was.

I asked Professor Hill if she had sought any recourse for her situation, and she said no. When I asked her why not, she said that she felt she had no effective recourse in that situation.

I believe that Professor Hill's statement to me was truthful. Professor Hill at that time had no reason to claim sexual harassment as an explanation for leaving the EEOC. Many people leave government jobs for teaching positions. Thus, I concluded then and I still believe that she was telling the truth.

On Monday morning after I read the news of Professor Hill's allegations, I phoned some of my colleagues from my home to ask their advice about what to do with this information that I had. When I arrived at school later that morning, another colleague, Ms. Susan Dunham, on her own initiative came to me, having read the article in the Post —

. . . .

And she reminded me—that is, Ms. Susan Dunham reminded me, of the fact that I had communicated to her the substance of my conversation with Professor Hill shortly after it had occurred in the summer of '87. I then recalled that indeed, right after my lunch conversation with Professor Hill, I went to Ms. Dunham, who had some practical experience in the field of employment discrimination, and I told her of Professor Hill's problems at the EEOC. Ms. Dunham said at that time that this was a case of the fox guarding the hen house. That phrase stuck in my mind. I was pleased that Ms. Dunham independently could confirm my memory of these events. I had at that time and I have now no reason to question the facts as Professor Hill related them to me. I always regarded her as having the highest integrity. I know her to be a deeply religious person.

Moreover, I cannot believe that she could be politically motivated. I know from numerous conversations with her that she served faithfully in the Reagan administration, that she was generally in sync with the goals of that administration, and that she did not disagree with the overall policies of the administration. Indeed, when Judge Robert Bork was nominated to the Supreme Court in the summer of 1987, I remember vividly that Professor Hill supported his nomination and told me that she held him in extremely high esteem as a former teacher of hers at Yale. Her strong support of Judge Bork led to a number of loud lunch-table disagreements between Professor Hill and other colleagues of mine.

Thus, I cannot accept the conclusion that her statements have been motivated by political ideology. . . .

I came forward on my own initiative to recount what I was told by Professor Hill. I have not spoken to Professor Hill since sometime prior to the nomination of Judge Thomas. I have never discussed my testimony or any aspect of these hearings with Professor Hill or any person representing Professor Hill or with any organization or anyone representing any organization.

Mr. Chairman, I am here to help you get to the facts. Thank you.

Testimony of Witnesses in Support of Clarence Thomas: J.C. Alvarez, Nancy E. Fitch, Diane Holt, and Phyllis Berry-Myers

Hearings Before the Senate Judiciary Committee, October 13, 1991[17]

MS. J.C. ALVAREZ: My name is J.C. Alvarez. I'm a business woman from Chicago. I'm a single mom raising a 15-year-old son, running a business. In many ways, I'm just a John Q. Public from Middle America, not unlike a lot of the people watching out there, and not unlike a lot of your constituents.

But the political world is not a world that I'm unfamiliar with. I spent nine years in Washington, DC, a year with Senator Danforth, two years with the Secretary of

17. Hearings Before the Senate Committee on the Judiciary, 102d Cong., 1st Sess. pt. 4, 338–45, 426–27 (1991).

Education, a short stint at the Federal Emergency Management Agency, and four years as special assistant to Clarence Thomas at the EEOC.

. . . .

I know Clarence Thomas and I know Anita Hill. . . . I don't know how else to say it, but I have to tell you that it just blew my mind to see Anita Hill testifying on Friday. Honest to goodness, it was like schizophrenia. That was not the Anita Hill that I knew and worked with at EEOC. On Friday, she played the role of a meek, innocent, shy Baptist girl from the south, who was a victim of this big, bad man. I don't know who she was trying to kid, because the Anita Hill that I knew and worked with was nothing like that.

She was a very hard, tough woman. She was opinionated. She was arrogant. She was a relentless debater. And she was the kind of woman who always made you feel like she was not going to be messed with, like she was not going to take anything from anyone. She was aloof, and she always acted as if she was a little bit superior to everyone, a little holier-than-thou.

I can recall at the time that she had a view of herself and her abilities that did not seem to be based in reality. For example, it was sort of common knowledge around the office that she thought she should have been Clarence's chief legal adviser and that she should have received better assignments. And I distinctly remember what I would hear about her feeling that way or when I'd see her pout in office meetings about assignments that she had gotten, I used to think to myself, "Come on, Anita, let's come down to earth and live in reality." She'd only been out of law school a couple of years and her experience and her ability couldn't begin to compare with some of the others on the staff.

But I also have to say that I was not totally surprised at her wanting these assignments, because she definitely came across as someone [who] was ambitious and watched out for her own advancement. She wasn't really a team player, but more someone who looked out for herself first. You could see the same thing in her relationships with others at the office.

. . . .

You could see that Anita Hill was not a real team player, but more someone who looked out for herself. You could see this even in her relationships with others at the office. She mostly kept to herself although she would occasionally participate in some of the girl talk among the women at the office. And I have to add that I don't recall her being particularly shy or innocent about that either.

You see, Senators, that was the Anita Hill that we all knew and we worked with. And that's why hearing her on Friday was so shocking. No, not shocking, it was so sickening. Trust me! The Anita Hill I knew and worked with was a totally different personality from the Anita Hill I heard on Friday. The Anita Hill I knew before was nobody's victim.

The Clarence Thomas I knew and worked with also was not who Ms. Hill alleges. Everyone who knows Clarence knows that he is a very proud and dignified man.

With his immediate staff, he's very warm and friendly—sort of like a friend or a father. You could talk with him about your problems, go to him for advice, but like a father, he commanded and he demanded respect. He demanded professionalism and performance and he was very strict about that. Because we were friends outside of the office, perhaps in private, I might have called him "Clarence." But in the office, he was Mr. Chairman. You didn't joke around with him, you didn't lose your respect for him, you didn't become too familiar with him, because he would definitely let you know that you had crossed the line. Clarence was meticulous about being sure that he retained a very serious and professional atmosphere within his office without the slightest hint of impropriety and everyone knew it.

We weren't a coffee-klatching group, we didn't have office parties or Christmas parties because Clarence didn't think that it was appropriate for us to give others the impression that we were not serious or professional or perhaps working as hard as everyone else. He wanted to maintain a dignity about his office and his every behavior and action confirmed that.

As his professional colleague, I traveled with him, had lunch and dinner with him, worked with him one on one and with others. Never did he ever lose his respect for me, never did we ever have a type of discussion of the type that Ms. Hill alleges, never was he the slightest bit improper with me. In every situation I have shared with Clarence Thomas he has been the ultimate professional, and he has required it of those around him, in particular, his personal staff.

From the moment they surfaced, I thought long and hard about these allegations. You see, I, too, have experienced sexual harassment in the past. I've been physically accosted by a man in an elevator who I rebuffed. I was trapped in a Xerox room by a man who I refused to date. Obviously, it is an issue I have experienced, I understand, and I take very seriously.

But having lived through it myself, I find Anita Hill's behavior inconsistent with these charges. I can assure you that when I come into town, the last thing I want to do is call either of these two men up and say hello, or see if they want to get together.

To be honest with you, I can hardly remember their names, but I can assure you that I would never try and even maintain a cordial relationship with either one of them.

Women who have really been harassed would agree. If her allegations were true, you put as much distance as you can between yourself and that other person. What's more, you don't follow them to the next job, especially if you're a black, female, Yale Law School graduate. Let's face it. Out in the corporate sector, companies are fighting for women with those kind of credentials. Her behavior just isn't consistent with the behavior of a woman who has been harassed, and it just doesn't make sense.

Senators, I don't know what else to say, to have you understand the crime that has been committed here. It has to make all of us suspicious of her motives. When someone of her legal background comes in here at the 11th hour, after ten years and having had four other opportunities, through congressional hearings, to oppose this man, and alleges such preposterous things.

I have been contacted by, I think, every reporter in the country, looking for dirt. When I present the facts as I experienced them, it's interesting — they don't print it. It's just not as juicy as her amazing allegations.

What is this country coming to, when an innocent man can be ambushed like this, jumped by a gang whose ringleader is one of his own proteges, Anita Hill. . . .

As a mother with a child, I can only begin to imagine how Clarence must feel, being betrayed by one of his own. Nothing would hurt me more. And I guess he described it best in his opening statements on Friday. His words and his emotions are still ringing in all of our ears and all of our hearts.

I have done the best I could, Senators, to be honest in my statement to you. I have presented the situation as it was then, as I lived it, side by side with Clarence and with Anita. You know, I talked with my mom before I came here, and she reminded me that I was always raised to stand up for what I believe. I have seen an innocent man being mugged in broad daylight, and I have not looked the other way. This John Q. Public came here and got involved.

. . . .

MS. FITCH: Mr. Chairman and Senator Thurmond, members of the committee, my name is Dr. Nancy Elizabeth Fitch. I have a BA in English literature and political science from Oakland University, which was part of Michigan State University at the time.

. . . .

And a Master's and PhD in history from the University of Michigan in Ann Arbor. I have taught at Sangamon State University in Illinois; been a social science research analyst for the Congressional Research Service of the Library of Congress; been a special assistant and historian to the then Chairman of the US Equal Employment Opportunity Commission, Clarence Thomas; an assistant professor of history at Lynchburg College in Virginia; and presently assistant professor of African American studies at Temple University in Philadelphia.

From 1982 to 1989, I worked as a special assistant/historian to then Chairman Clarence Thomas of the US Equal Employment Opportunity Commission. I worked for and with him seven years and have known him for nine. I researched the history of African-Americans, people of color, and women, and their relationship to issues including employment, education, and training. These were used for background on speeches, special emphasis programming at the Commission, and for policy position papers.

. . . .

In these nine years, I have known Clarence Thomas to be a person of great integrity, morally upstanding, professional, a decent person and exemplary boss. Those years spent in his employ as a Schedule C employee, a political appointee, were the most rewarding of my work life to that time. My returning to higher education I attribute to his persuading me to return to what I loved, not continuing as a bureaucrat, but returning to teaching.

I would like to say Judge Thomas, besides being a person of great moral character, I found to be a most intelligent man. . . . If these allegations, which I believe to be completely unfounded and vigorously believe unfounded, were true, we would be dealing not only with venality, but with abject stupidity with the person shooting himself in the foot, having given someone else the gun to use at any time. There is no way Clarence Thomas, CT, would callously, venally hurt someone.

A smart man concerned about making a contribution to this country as a public official, recognizing the gravity and weightiness of his responsibilities and public trust, a role model and mentor who would, by his life and work, show the possibilities in America for all citizens given opportunity, well, such a person such as this, Judge Clarence Thomas, would never ever make a parallel career in harassment, ask that it not be revealed, and expect to have and keep his real career. And I know he did no such thing. He is a dignified, reserved, deliberative, conscientious man of great conscience, and I am proud to be at his defense.

. . . .

Thank you.

SEN. BIDEN: All right. Ms. Holt?

MS. HOLT: Mr. Chairman, Senator Thurmond, members of this Committee, my name is Diane Holt. I'm a management analyst in the office of the Chairman of the Equal Employment Opportunity Commission. I have known Clarence Thomas for over 10 years. For 6 of those years I worked very closely with him, cheek to cheek, shoulder to shoulder, as his personal secretary.

My acquaintance with Judge Thomas began in May of 1981 after he had been appointed as Assistant Secretary for Civil Rights at the Department of Education. I had been the personal Secretary to the outgoing Assistant Secretary for several years. Upon Judge Thomas' arrival at the Department he held a meeting with me in which he indicated that he was not committed to bringing his own secretary and had no wish to displace me. Because he was not familiar with my qualifications, he made no guarantees, but gave me an opportunity to prove myself. That is the kind of man he is.

In May of 1982, Judge Thomas asked me to go to the EEOC with him, where I worked as his secretary until September of 1987. I met Professor Hill in the summer of 1981 when she came to work at the Department of Education as attorney advisor to Judge Thomas. After about a year, Judge Thomas was nominated to be Chairman of the EEOC. He asked both Professor Hill and myself to transfer with him.

Both Ms. Hill and I were excited about the prospect of transferring to EEOC. We discussed the greater potential for individual growth at this larger agency. We discussed and expressed excitement that we would be at the right hand of the individual who would run this agency.

When we arrived at the EEOC, because we knew no one else there, Professor Hill and I quickly developed a professional relationship, a professional friendship, often having lunch together.

At no time did Professor Hill intimate, not even in the most subtle of ways, that Judge Thomas was asking her out or subjecting her to the crude, abusive conversations that have been described, nor did I ever discern any discomfort when Professor Hill was in Judge Thomas's presence.

Additionally, I never heard anyone at any time make any reference to any inappropriate conduct in relation to Clarence Thomas. The Clarence Thomas that I know has always been a motivator of staff, always encouraging others to grow professionally. I personally have benefited from that encouragement and that motivation.

In sum, the Chairman Thomas that I have known for 10 years is absolutely incapable of the abuses described by Professor Hill.

SEN. KENNEDY: Thank you very much.

Ms. Myers?

MS. BERRY-MYERS: And you can call me Phyllis Berry since that was my name that I used throughout my professional life, and that's probably what most people are going to refer to me as.

Mr. Chairman, Senator Thurmond and members of the committee, I am Phyllis Berry. I know and have worked with both Clarence Thomas and Anita Hill. I have known Judge Thomas since 1979 and Anita Hill since 1982. Once Clarence Thomas was confirmed as the Chairman of the Equal Employment Opportunity Commission and had assumed his duties there, he asked me to come and work with him at the Commission. I joined his staff as a special assistant in June of 1982. . . .

. . . Clarence Thomas's behavior toward Anita Hill was no more, no less than his behavior toward the rest of his staff. He was respectful, demanding of excellence in our work, cordial, professional, interested in our lives and our career ambitions.

. . . Anita Hill indicated to me that she had been a primary advisor to Clarence Thomas at the Department of Education. However, she seemed to be having a difficult time on his EEOC staff as being considered just one of many, especially on a staff where others were as equally or more talented than she.

. . . Anita Hill often acted as though she had a right to immediate, direct access to the Chairman. Such access was not always immediately available. I felt she was particularly distressed when Allison Duncan became chief of staff and her direct access to the Chairman was even more limited.

. . . .

. . . Anita Hill has asserted that she thought the Department of Education was going to be abolished, and that was one factor in her decision to accept a position with Clarence Thomas at the EEOC. Well, at that same time there was much discussion in Congress about the abolition of EEOC as well. It was seriously suggested that Title VII enforcement functions . . . be redistributed to other agencies of the federal government and that the Commission itself should be abolished. Anyone involved with the confirmation proceedings of Clarence Thomas to the EEOC chairmanship, as Anita Hill was, surely would have been aware of this.

I have known Clarence Thomas in times of his darkest moments and in his shining triumphs. I've had a role in most of his confirmation battles, none of which have ever been easy. In that capacity, I have been privy to the most intimate details of his life. In all that time, never, never has anyone raised allegations such as Anita has. Clarence Thomas, whom I admire and greatly respect, is a fine and decent man. He does not deserve this savaging of his character, of his reputation, of his honor. He does not deserve this.

Notes and Discussion

1. Credibility Did the testimony of the supporting witnesses change the credibility balance? If so, how? How did the first set of witnesses support Hill's allegations? How did the second set of witnesses attempt to undermine Hill's allegations? Did racial or sexual stereotypes play into the testimony of the supporting witnesses? Wells, Carr, Fitch, Holt, and Berry-Meyers are African Americans. Did Hill's failure to file a lawsuit against Thomas in 1981 or 1982 undermine her credibility? Why might she have declined to file a lawsuit? Recall that courts issued the *Bundy* appellate decision in January 1981 and the *Henson* opinion in August 1982.

2. Senate Hearings Were the Senate hearings designed to obtain the truth? Was determining the truth possible? Why or why not? Were the hearings fair? Explain. In addition to Hill, several women submitted testimony that Thomas harassed them as well, but Biden did not allow this testimony and the media did not report on the existence of other complainants.[18] What might have been the impact of this corroborating testimony had Biden allowed these women to testify? Why do you think Biden did not allow their testimony? Why did the press not cover the existence of the other complainants?

3. Confirmation On October 15, 1991, the Senate voted to confirm Thomas. Justice Thomas has participated in every Supreme Court sexual harassment opinion since then, always aligning himself against the plaintiffs.

4. Press Slander of Anita Hill Journalist David Brock infamously described Anita Hill as "a little nutty and a little slutty" in an article for the *American Spectator*. He later published a book, titled *The Real Anita Hill: The Untold Story* (1993), arguing that Anita Hill's testimony was a hoax concocted by Thomas's enemies. Brock later admitted that he had lied about Anita Hill.[19]

---

18. *See* Jill Abramson, *Do You Believe Her Now?* N.Y. Magazine (Feb. 18, 2018).
19. Alex Kuczynski & William Glaberson, *Book Author Says He Lied in His Attacks on Anita Hill in Bid to Aid Justice Thomas*, N.Y. Times (June 27, 2001).

5. Other Contemporaneous Commentary—"Neo-Puritan" Gender Relations?
During the fall of 1991, numerous commentators, in addition to Barbara Babcock, explored the significance of the Thomas hearings. Harvard sociology professor Orlando Patterson believed that the hearings opened a new debate on gender relations. He suggested that they served as a challenge to "the legalistic, neo-Puritan and elitist model of gender relations promoted by the dominant school of American Feminists."[20]

According to Patterson, Thomas operated in a cultural milieu that would have been very familiar to Hill and other Southern working-class women, especially African-American women. Patterson (who is an African-American man) referred to Thomas's behavior toward Hill as a "down-home style of courting." In an *L.A. Daily News* opinion editorial, Patterson defended Thomas as follows:

> I am convinced that Hill perfectly understood the psycho-cultural context in which Thomas allegedly regaled her with his Rabelaisian humor (possibly as a way of affirming their common origins), which is precisely why she never filed a complaint against him.

> Raising the issue 10 years later was . . . disingenuous . . . because she has lifted a verbal style that carries only minor sanction in one subcultural context and thrown it in the overheated cultural arena of mainstream, neo-Puritan America, where it incurs professional extinction.

> If my interpretation is correct Thomas was justified in denying making the remarks, even if he had in fact made them, not only because the deliberate displacement of his remarks made them something else but on the utilitarian moral grounds that any admission would have immediately incurred a self-destructive and grossly unfair punishment.[21]

Is Patterson correct that class and race make a difference in the ability to understand what happened between Thomas and Hill? Is he making an assumption about how a "reasonable woman" in Hill's position should have understood Thomas' conduct? Does the African-American, Southern working-class subculture that Patterson described and that allegedly understands a "down-home style of courting" really exist? If it does, does its existence legitimate Thomas's alleged behavior? If Hill understood this "courting" and should have understood what exposing Thomas would do outside of African-American, Southern working-class subculture, why might Hill have made her complaint?

If Hill's allegations were true, was Thomas justified in denying the behavior as Patterson asserted? Is it true, as Patterson claimed, that Hill suffered no emotional or career damage as a result of Thomas's "coarseness"? Professor Patterson declared the death of the American "culture of slavery." Is it really dead for women? For

---

20. Orlando Patterson, *Lessons of the Thomas Confirmation the Social Ethos: Neo-Puritan Fallacies Cannot Explain Race, Gender Progress*, L.A. DAILY NEWS, Oct. 20, 1991.
21. *Id.*

African-American women? Explain. Legal scholar Kimberlé Crenshaw criticized Patterson's arguments as follows:

> Patterson's argument is enlightening because we see here that sexual ste-reotypes about African Americans not only can be believed by Blacks as well as whites, but that these beliefs might explain why harassers of both races might treat women differently on the basis of race. For example, white harassers may believe that certain behavior is acceptable to Black women because "they" are different, while Black harassers may believe that certain behavior is acceptable because "we" are different. Of course, there are prob-ably significant differences in the way these harassers are perceived by Black women, but the point remains that race shapes Black women's vulnerability to harassment in both instances.
>
> Perhaps most troubling, however, is Patterson's use of a cultural differ-ence to legitimate the unwelcome and often hostile harassment of Black women when it is intraracial. How ironic it is that such an affirmative action defense to sexual harassment would be offered to defend Clarence Thomas, a man who otherwise refuses to recognize the most legitimate of cultural differences. This cultural defense effectively deflects criticisms of sexist atti-tudes and practices that subordinate Black women and other women of color in our communities. The conversation-ending effect of cultural arguments is grounded in the complex politics of race. Many whites, knowing little about other people of color, can do little more than defer to a distinguished spokesman who declares that his group is simply different. Moreover, some whites may be predisposed to accept the claims of difference, especially in matters relating to sexuality. People of color may also be silenced by the cul-tural defense out of our desire to maintain our much needed communal bonds and out of a well-placed fear that minority cultures, generally under assault, must be protected in order to survive. Organized women must begin to grapple with these issues, to find ways of empowering women of different cultural heritages to oppose sexist practices within our community and to oppose racist assaults against our communities.[22]

Was Crenshaw's criticism of Orlando Patterson's adoption of racial stereotypes fair? Crenshaw disputed that cultural differences explained Thomas's behavior as Pat-terson alleged. Was Crenshaw persuasive when she suggested that "people of color may also be silenced by the cultural defense out of our desire to maintain our much needed communal bonds"?

6. Other Contemporaneous Commentary — Political Backlash Another commen-tator, Martha Burke, predicted a female political backlash as a result of the senato-rial "beat[ing]" that Anita Hill endured. In the *L.A. Daily News*, Burke recounted

---

22. Kimberlé Crenshaw, *Race, Gender, and Sexual Harassment*, 65 S. Cal. L. Rev. 1467, 1471–72 (1992).

the events surrounding Hill's testimony. After describing Biden's resistance to holding hearings on Hill's allegations, and the Senate's reluctance to postpone the Thomas confirmation vote for hearings, Burke relayed how Senator Alan Simpson (R-WY) invoked images of violence when he predicted that Hill would be "'injured, destroyed and bloodied'" if she testified against Thomas. Burke reviewed how Republicans trashed Hill's character and attacked her mental stability while Democrats just watched. Burke concluded that Americans had seen the "'good ol' boys club' in action." She proffered:

> Most [female Americans] do not have the luxury of telling the boss off, quitting their jobs or filing expensive and time-consuming lawsuits. They keep quiet, try to avoid the harasser, look for other work and leave without making a scene when they can. They behave professionally and remain outwardly courteous. To do otherwise would invite the same treatment Anita Hill received at the hands of the Judiciary Committee: being labeled a troublemaker, fantasizer, man-chaser, woman scorned, liar.

. . . .

> The confirmation of Clarence Thomas is only the latest in a line of insults to women stretching from previous anti-woman Supreme Court appointments to the erosion of abortion rights and Sen. Alan Simpson's declaring sexual harassment to be "crap."
>
> Women now have the political clout to elect any candidate to any office if they vote together — and vote as women first. They also have the votes to send the good ol' boys home, and they should do just that.[23]

Have American feminists promoted a "neo-Puritan and elitist model of gender relations" as Patterson asserted? Or is the "good ol' boys club" still in action as Burke asserted? In 1991, Patterson asserted that American culture had made great strides vis-à-vis race and gender relations. Were his assertions accurate? Were the hearings good for the advancement of African Americans in the eyes of white Americans? Did Americans see how African-American women exercise power? Or was Burke correct that the hearings were "a testament as to why women don't come forward" about sexual harassment? Was Burke accurate that "[m]ost [women] do not have the luxury of telling the boss off, quitting their jobs, of filing expensive and time-consuming lawsuits"?

Did Burke's backlash materialize? Called "The Year of the Woman," 1992 witnessed a large number of women run successfully for political offices. During the 1992 Presidential election, more women (47%) voted for William Jefferson Clinton than for President George H.W. Bush and H. Ross Perot. As President-elect, Clinton named more women to his Cabinet than any previous President. With Clinton

---

23. Martha Burke, *The Feminist Movement: Women's Backlash Could Devastate Both Parties in '92*, L.A. DAILY NEWS (Oct. 20, 1991).

as President, did women fare any better than under President George H.W. Bush? Explain.

7. Anita Hill after the Hearings In 1995, Anita Hill and Emma Coleman Jordan published an anthology of essays examining the context and consequences of the hearings, *Race, Gender, and Power in America: The Legacy of the Hill-Thomas Hearings* (1995). Hill later published her memoir, *Speaking Truth to Power* (1998), in which she described in detail how her accusations came to light. This book also recounts her experience of testifying before the Senate Judiciary Committee. It also details the subsequent impact of the hearings on her life.

Hill has continued to speak out on sexual harassment. She participated at a 2011 conference at Hunter College, "Sex, Power and Speaking Truth: Anita Hill 20 Years Later." She is a leader of the Time's Up Commission and the Hollywood commission, Sexual Harassment and Advancing Equality in the Workplace. The Hill/Thomas hearings have been portrayed on film in the 2013 documentary *Anita* and the 2016 HBO drama *Confirmation*.

8. The Impact of the Hearings Many people worried that the harsh treatment of Hill during and after the hearings would discourage women from coming forward with their complaints. The opposite occurred. Increased public awareness of sexual harassment led to record numbers of EEOC sexual harassment cases. Women's anger, conveyed through their political efforts, resulted in a record number of new congresswomen in 1992. In 1994, activists achieved a long-time women's movement goal — passage of the Violence Against Women Act (VAWA).

VAWA accomplished many tasks. First, it created new federal crimes against interstate gender-based violence. Second, it provided generous funding for rape crisis centers and domestic violence shelters, which was renewed and expanded for decades. Third, it established a federal civil rights cause of action for gender-based violence (which was later ruled unconstitutional by the Supreme Court in the case of *U.S. v. Morrison*, 529 U.S. 598 (2000), with Thomas in the majority). Finally, the Act created Federal Rule of Evidence 412, which limited defendants' ability to introduce evidence of or cross-examine plaintiffs about their past sexual behavior in civil sexual harassment cases.

Congress renewed and expanded VAWA funding in 2005 and 2013. It allowed the funding to lapse, however, for the first time in February 2019. This lapse occurred shortly after the Senate confirmed Donald Trump's nomination of Brett Kavanaugh to the Supreme Court and after hearings on allegations from Professor Christine Blasey Ford that Kavanaugh had sexually assaulted her when they were in high school. What is the significance of Congress's failure to reauthorize VAWA, especially in light of the #MeToo movement?[24]

9. Scholarly Responses The Hill/Thomas hearings generated an outpouring of commentary and some deep soul searching, particularly among African-American

---

24. See *infra* Chapter 10 for a discussion of the #MeToo movement.

women. Pulitzer and Nobel Prize-winning author Toni Morrison edited an anthology of essays about the hearings, *Race-ing Justice, En-Gendering Power* (1992). This book engaged with a range of issues, including African-American political culture, racial stereotypes, double standards, white feminism, and history. The collection included essays by preeminent scholars, including Patricia Williams, Nell Irvin Painter, Paula Giddings, Cornell West, and Kimberlé Crenshaw.

The collection began with an open letter to Justice Thomas from Judge A. Leon Higginbotham Jr. of the Third Circuit. Higginbotham reminded Thomas that his [Thomas's] life would have been very different but for the work of civil rights activists and organizations that opened doors to education and employment, for him and others, through cases like *Brown v. Board of Education*. He implored Thomas to remember that other people enabled his professional successes. Thomas's appointment to the Supreme Court was the "culmination of years of heartbreaking work by thousands who preceded" him.[25] If Judge Higgenbotham had hopes of convincing Thomas to be more supportive of civil rights than his prior record demonstrated, Higginbotham was likely sorely disappointed.

2. Intersectionality Theory

A. Defining Intersectionality

Just two years before the Hill/Thomas hearings, critical race theory founder Kimberlé Crenshaw coined the term "intersectionality" in her essay *Demarginalizing the Intersection of Race and Sex: A Black Feminist Critique of Antidiscrimination Doctrine, Feminist Theory and Antiracist Politics*.[26] Crenshaw's theory of intersectionality transformed feminist legal theory. She analyzes how the intersections of gender, race, class, and sexuality shape not only individual experiences, but also social institutions such as politics, law, public policy, and the media. These aspects of identity are not "unitary, mutually exclusive entities, but rather . . . reciprocally constructing phenomena" that interact on multiple levels.[27] Because laws and policies usually address only one form of oppression at a time, the intersections of oppressions continue obscured and denied. Similarly, social movements historically focused on singular forms of oppression—racism in the civil rights movement or sexism in the women's movement. Again, advocates ignored or minimized intersecting oppressions experienced

25. A. Leon Higginbotham, Jr., *An Open Letter to Justice Clarence Thomas from a Federal Judicial Colleague*, 140 U. Pa. L. Rev. 1005, 1007 (1991).

26. Kimberlé Crenshaw, *Demarginalizing the Intersections of Race and Sex: A Black Feminist Critique of Antidiscrimination Doctrine, Feminist Theory, and Antiracist Politics*, 1 U. Chi. Legal F. 139 (1989). In 1991, Crenshaw published a second essay in which she developed her theory further. *See* Kimberlé Crenshaw, *Mapping the Margins: Intersectionality, Identity Politics, and Violence against Women of Color*, 43 Stan. L. Rev. 1241 (1991).

27. Patricia Hill Collins, *Intersectionality's Definitional Dilemmas*, 41 Ann. Rev. of Soc. 1–20, 1 (2015).

by women of color. Crenshaw's intersectionality is a dynamic analysis of structures, social processes, ideologies, and representations used to understand the complex, multidimensional power hierarchies in society.

In a 1992 essay, *Race, Gender, and Sexual Harassment*, Crenshaw employs intersectionality theory to analyze the Hill/Thomas hearings, and the vulnerability of African-American women to sexual harassment in particular. "[B]etween a rock and a hard place" is how Crenshaw characterizes the dilemma faced by women who experience sexual harassment: "our choices as women are limited to silently tolerating sexual harassment and other abuses or confronting the further degradation and psychic assault that we are sure to receive if we speak out and resist."[28] Crenshaw argues that this dilemma of sexual harassment is unique for African-American women. She explains:

> African-American women by virtue of our race and gender are situated within at least two systems of subordination: racism and sexism. This dual vulnerability does not simply mean that our burdens are doubled but instead, that the dynamics of racism and sexism intersect in our lives to create experiences that are sometimes unique to us. In other words, our experiences of racism are shaped by our gender, and our experiences of sexism are often shaped by our race.[29]

According to Crenshaw, African-American women experience racialized sexual harassment.

In sexual harassment cases, as in rape cases, courts and commentators focus on the conduct and character of accusers rather than on the behavior of the accused. According to Crenshaw, "the inquiry is animated by myths about women, about assumptions regarding our veracity, about our integrity, and even about our grasp upon reality."[30] For African-American women, however, these biases go much further and have deep historical roots. Crenshaw explains that "forced sexual access to Black women was institutionalized in slavery and was central to its reproduction. Rape and other sexual abuses were justified by the myth that Black women were sexually voracious and indiscriminate. . . . The stereotypes that justified sexual abuse of Black women are still very much a part of our current society." Perpetrators justify this abuse by employing racialized stereotypes of African-American women to blame them for the abusive conduct directed toward them. Abusers target African-American women by merging "racist myths with their vulnerability as women." Crenshaw argues:

> Perhaps it is due to this racialization of sexual harassment that Black women are disproportionate[ly] represented as plaintiffs in [sexual harassment] cases. There is little room to doubt that this behavior is hostile and

---

28. Crenshaw, *Race, Gender, and Sexual Harassment, supra* note 22, at 1467.
29. *Id.* at 1467–68.
30. *Id.* at 1469.

discriminatory. Racism may provide the clarity to see that sexual harassment is not a flattering or misguided social overture but an intentional act
of sexual discrimination that is threatening, and humiliating.

Racist stereotypes also influence perceptions of African-American women's credibility. Crenshaw writes:

> Historically Black women's words were not taken as true. In our own legal
> system, a connection was once drawn between chastity and lack of veracity.
> In other words, a wom[a]n who was likely to have sex was not likely to tell
> the truth. Because Black women were not expected to be chaste, similarly,
> they were unlikely to tell the truth. Judges were known to instruct juries to
> take a Black woman's word with a grain of salt. One judge warned jurors
> that the general presumption of chastity applicable to white women did not
> apply to Black women. Lest we believe that these attitudes are a thing of the
> past, a very recent study of jurors in rape trials revealed that Black women's
> integrity is still very deeply questioned by many people in society.[31]

Furthermore, racist stereotypes influence perceptions of harm resulting from sexual abuse. Crenshaw explains:

> [A]ttitudes of jurors seem to reflect a common belief that Black women are
> different from white women and that sexually abusive behavior directed
> toward them is somehow less objectionable. Said one juror in a case involv-
> ing the rape of a Black pre-teen, "being from that neighborhood she probably
> wasn't a virgin anyway." A recent study found that assailants who assault
> Black women are less likely to receive jail time than those who attack white
> women. Another found that when they are incarcerated, the average sen-
> tence given to Black women's assailants is two years. The average sentence
> given to white women's assailants is ten years.[32]

Therefore, justice is elusive for African-American women. They experience higher
rates of sexual harassment and assault but jurors discount their complaints and
injuries.

Crenshaw criticizes both feminist and anti-racist politics for ignoring how racist
and sexist stereotypes intersect in the experiences of African-American women. She
notes:

> We talk frequently about the way male racism shapes the betrayal of Blacks,
> usually men (as Black male criminals), and the way sexism shapes the por-
> trayal of women, usually white (as sex objects). We talk less frequently about
> the way these representations intersect to create an image of Black women
> as sexual deviants — as a combination of the criminal and the sexual.[33]

---

31. *Id.* at 1470.
32. *Id.* at 1470.
33. *Id.* at 1471.

Crenshaw calls for an intersectional politics that accounts for the ways that multiple systems of oppression interact in the lives of African-American women.

Speaking to the African-American community, Crenshaw decries the reluctance to confront intraracial sexual harassment and assault. Addressing why the Hill/Thomas hearings were so difficult for African Americans, Crenshaw explains:

> [T]he pervasive silence about this issue in the Black community is grounded in fears that speaking about sexual abuse will reinforce negative racial stereotypes about Blacks in general and about Black men in particular. Of course this silence creates a classic double bind. To speak, one risks the censure of one's closest allies. To remain silent renders one continually vulnerable to the kinds of abuses heaped upon people who have no voice. While many Black women are understandably silent out of a belief that our interests are best served by a singular focus on race, many are beginning to see our silences as costly and ultimately counterproductive to the interests of the entire Black community. For example, we are well aware that Black women are disproportionately likely to be the sole economic support for their families. Sexual harassment, whether interracial or intraracial, is thus a race issue for the Black community because it not only places Black women in personal jeopardy, but it also threatens the well-being of the majority of Black families who are dependent on a female wage earner.[34]

As a result, argues Crenshaw, anti-racist organizers must address gender issues as well as racial issues, and the intersections between them.

Similarly, Crenshaw calls on women's rights advocates to address how race and gender intersect in women's experiences. A women's agenda, argues Crenshaw, should center on marginalized women as "a way of combating the divide and conquer strategy that has so successfully pitted women's interests against the interests of people of color." Crenshaw elaborates:

> A central problem that was revealed during the Hearings is that women's issues are often seen by the public as representing the selected concerns of a few well placed, overly influential white women. One of the most troubling manifestations of this attitude is represented by those who claim that any Black woman who raises a gender related issue is simply acting on the white women's agenda and not on that of the Black community. . . . Organized women must affirmatively act to make women's issues relevant to communities of color as well as to working class and poor women. This effort requires that they go beyond the usual practice of incorporating only those aspects of women's lives that appear to be familiar as "gender" while marginalizing those issues that seem to relate solely to class or to race.[35]

---

34. *Id.* at 1472.
35. *Id.* at 1473.

Crenshaw implores feminists to confront some of the "silences about the connections between racism and sexism" in order to have a broader appeal and address the needs of *all* women.

Notes and Discussion

1. Genealogy of Intersectionality While Crenshaw coined the term *intersectionality* and developed the theory in contemporary times, the concept of intersectional oppressions has a long history. In the 1830s, abolitionist and women's rights advocate Maria Stewart lectured about the rights of African-American women. In 1892, Anna Julia Cooper published *A Voice from the South: By a Black Woman of the South*, calling for civil and women's rights. Scholars consider this book to be one of the first articulations of African-American feminism. Lawyer Pauli Murray also explored the intersections of oppressions in her famous 1964 speech "Jim Crow and Jane Crow" in which she explained the impact of segregation on African-American women. A few years later, Frances Beal published the essay, *Double Jeopardy: To Be Black and Female*, examining the position of African-American women at the intersection of racism and sexism. These are just a few of many examples of how African-American women have showcased the intersecting systems of oppression that have shaped their lives.[36]

2. Racism and Sexual Harassment Does racism "provide the clarity to see that sexual harassment is not a flattering or misguided social overture, but an intentional act of sexual discrimination," as Crenshaw suggests?

3. Rape Law Crenshaw uses rape law to explain how "Black women have experienced sexual aggression." Are her comparisons helpful? If so, how? Are Crenshaw's references to criminal incarceration statistics useful? Why or why not?

4. Racial Stereotypes What are the racial stereotypes about African-American women that play a role in sexual harassment cases? How are racial stereotypes still prevalent today? Do other women of color experience racial stereotypes that influence their experience of sexual harassment? Latinas? Asian-American women? What about Native-American women or Arab-American women? Was the criticism of Hill—that she "betrayed" one of her own (see, e.g., Testimony of J.C. Alvarez, *supra*)—a reference to racial disloyalty? What did Crenshaw say about such "disloyalty"?

5. The Politics of the Thomas Nomination In a passage not excerpted, Crenshaw argues that the hearings demonstrated the "efforts to put at odds the constituencies mobilized around gender and race issues."[37] To what is she referring?

6. Cultural Differences There is some evidence that Asian-American women are less likely to report sexual harassment because of cultural differences. Should courts

---

36. *See* Bonnie Thornton Dill & Ruth Enid Zambrana, Emerging Intersections: Race, Class, and Gender in Theory, Policy, and Practice (2009).

37. Crenshaw, *supra* note 22, at 1468.

consider cultural differences when evaluating the reasonableness of an employee's actions in a sexual harassment case?[38]

B. The Discourse of Exit

A critical observation of Crenshaw's theory of intersectionality is that we all exist within hierarchical systems that erect barriers or open doors differentially depending upon our sex, race, class, and other characteristics. Conservative ideologies of individualism often obscure these systems by insisting that individuals control their lives and can always "pull themselves up by their bootstraps." The reality is that we all live within systems of opportunity and disadvantage that shape our lives.

In a 1992 essay, *In Love, Work, and the Confirmation Hearings*, legal scholar Martha R. Mahoney explained how the Senators' questions and the media commentary assumed an "ideology of exit" based on a privileged perspective. That thinking undermined Anita Hill's credibility and ignored the constraints on her life.[39] Mahoney's article addresses how people used Anita Hill's choice, to continue working for Clarence Thomas after he sexually harassed her, against Hill in both the Senate hearings and public discourse. Mahoney clarifies the ideology of exit as follows:

> Exit—the door with the glowing red sign—marks the road not taken that proves we chose our path. Prevailing ideology in both law and popular culture holds that people are independent and autonomous units, free to leave any situation at any time, and that what happens to us is therefore in some measure the product of our choice. When women are harmed in love or work, the idea of exit becomes central to the social and legal dialogue in which our experience is processed, reduced, reconstructed and dismissed. Exit is so powerful an image that it can be used both to dispute the truth of our statements and to keep people from hearing what we say at all. The image of exit hides oppression behind a mask of choice, forces upon us a discourse of victimization that emphasizes individualism and weakness rather than collectivity and strength, and conceals the possibility and necessity of alliance and resistance to oppression.[40]

Mahoney questions the assumption that people can and should always leave an oppressive situation. She identifies the flawed reasoning that if they do not, they are responsible for what happens to them. This blame-the-victim mentality unfairly shifts responsibility for abuse from the perpetrator to his target.

Addressing workplace sexual harassment, as well as intimate partner violence, Mahoney explains:

---

38. *See, e.g.*, Andrew Tae-Hyun Kim, *Culture Matters: Cultural Differences in the Reporting of Employment Discrimination Claims*, 20 WM. & MARY BILL RIGHTS J. 405 (2011).

39. Martha R. Mahoney, *Exit: Power and the Idea of Leaving in Love, Work, and the Confirmation Hearings*, 65 S. CAL. L. REV. 1283 (1992).

40. *Id.* at 1283–84.

Once exit is defined as the appropriate response to abuse, then staying can be treated as evidence that abuse never happened. If abuse is asserted, "failure" to exit must then be explained. When that "failure" becomes the point of inquiry, explanation in law and popular culture tends to emphasize victimization and implicitly deny agency in the person who has been harmed. Denying agency contradicts the self-understanding of most of our society, including many who share characteristics and experiences of oppression with the person who is being harmed. The conservative insistence that we are untrammeled actors plays on this sensibility, merging rejection of victimization with an ideology that denies oppression. The privatization of assaults on women makes it particularly difficult to identify a model of oppression and resistance, rather than one of victimization and inconsistent personal behavior.

Equating exit and agency denies the possibility and legitimacy of resistance against oppression. Since both staying and leaving can be normal acts of resistance, the focus on exit warps inquiry and treats as illegitimate the struggle to make the fundamental areas of life more one's own. To recognize oppression and resistance in the lives of women, we must reject exit as the test of truth or the core of agency. If we emphasize antisubordination in love and work, we will see resistance differently and see different allies as well.[41]

The ideology of exit characterizes toleration of an abusive relationship as merely a form of victimization. Mahoney construes staying and fighting for a job or relationship as a form of agency.

The ideology of exit not only obscures women's varied forms of resistance, but it also undermines women's credibility. Mahoney describes how Hill's refusal to quit her job, and her move with Thomas to the EEOC from the Department of Education, may have been an act of resistance and agency. However, people used Hill's decisions as evidence to impugn her credibility. Mahoney offers:

Failure to exit was raised to dispute the truth of her claims of fact, her account of words spoken by Clarence Thomas (if he really said that, why did she follow him to the EEOC?). Failure to exit was also raised to argue that, if he indeed said those things, his statements could not have been entirely unsought and unwelcome. This position allowed listeners to reconcile absolutely contradictory factual claims with centrist agnosticism or cynicism about truth (maybe they were both telling the truth as they saw it, or, they were both lying in part). Failure to exit was seen as an indication of inconsistency between her actions and her report of her feelings, making suspect her overall credibility (she couldn't be telling the truth, because if she felt the disgust she claimed, she would have left). Finally, failure to exit

---

41. *Id.* at 1285.

was used in a sort of waiver argument to imply at least political oppor-
tunism, if not dishonesty (if it wasn't bad enough to leave or bring charges
then, why bring this up now?).[42]

These victim-blaming attacks undermined Hill's credibility with the white male
Senators as well as the public.

Mahoney contends that most women do not leave abusive situations. She points
out that "the image presented in the confirmation hearings—exit as the normal
prompt response to harassment—is inconsistent with the actions of the majority of
women who neither report harassment nor leave their jobs." Mahoney elaborates:

> Exit is also not the norm for many workers who encounter painful
> choices about work . . . .
>
> So the normal responses to abuse and harassment in love and work
> conflict with the image of exit. Yet exit retains great rhetorical power. . . .
> Failure to exit promptly can affect the way a woman's account—or even
> uncontested facts—are heard, remembered, or weighed. . . .
>
> . . . The ideology of exit implicitly denies inequality in relationships
> by emphasizing mutual freedom to leave. This rhetoric actually *increases
> inequality* by strengthening the position of the abuser, because it makes sus-
> pect the choice most women make—neither leaving nor suing.[43]

There are tremendous costs to women in leaving a job—financial, professional, and
personal. Women may not be able to afford to incur these costs, and they should not
have to leave in order to be free from sexual harassment.

In addition to her exploration of exit, Mahoney focuses on another vital tool used
by women—"voice." Mahoney suggests that efforts to change an abusive situation
or cope within it, rather than leave it, are expressions of "voice." She explains that
"in the context of sexual harassment, voice would include, among other actions,
telling the perpetrator to 'knock it off,' filing complaints through company mechanisms, bringing lawsuits, or taking political action."[44] But, as she notes, the abuse
itself affects exit and voice. "The alternatives for exit—the possibilities of new
jobs—can be shaped by the good will of the harasser. But the public exercise of
'voice' carries a stigma and may also involve traumatic recounting of personal experience, including experience of the abuse itself. The private exercise of voice—the
one that women adopt when they tell the harasser to stop—is invisible at the time
and is hidden in retrospect in the question 'why didn't she leave?'"[45] Senate Judiciary
Committee and media treatment of Hill was evidence itself of the risks of the public
exercise of voice.

---

42. *Id.* at 1286–87.
43. *Id.* at 1289.
44. *Id.* at 1290.
45. *Id.*

Mahoney also analyzes how the assumption that sexually harassed women will and should leave a job denies the necessity and importance of work and workplace relationships in women's lives. She notes that women "have pride in their work, or in their capacity for hard work, for holding on to work, for survival." She reasons that "as a test of facts or authenticity of response, exit makes all these ties invisible and eliminates from our understanding of agency the time and effort required to shape one's life under adverse conditions."[46]

The Thomas hearings focused on the harm of harassment to women, but not on the harm it does to their careers, their sense of themselves as workers, and the sense of dignity and purpose that work gives to people. During the hearings, members of the Senate Judiciary Committee and the media appeared to disregard Anita Hill's repeated description of her strong sense of purpose in her work. Mahoney comments:

> Despite her extraordinary record of achievement, the public and the senators could not perceive in this African-American woman a person with a fine mind—and a finely trained mind—who would seek intellectual challenge and feel committed to using her abilities for worthy ends. To the extent she was heard, work was treated as a question of opportunism or careerism, not idealism or substance.[47]

Mahoney demonstrates how the assumption of exit is built into the very structures of the American capitalist workplace. She theorizes:

> Free exit from employment is not a new myth; it is the fundamental underlying tenet of American capitalism. Our jurisprudence holds firm notions of formal equality and mutuality. The fiction that employees and employers are equally, mutually free to walk out is a time-honored one in American law. Exit uses the question of mobility to cover up the power dynamic in the mutuality principle. By emphasizing the woman's freedom to leave, we actually vest in her employer the freedom to take actions that can force her out of her work life. Asking why she didn't leave masks the employer's power to force exit for which the doctrine of constructive discharge is an apologetic, partial compensation.[48]

In combination with other social hierarchies like sexism, racism, and socioeconomic class, the norms of the capitalist workplace make women highly vulnerable to sexual harassment and abuse. The discourse of exit focuses on the individual. Observers assume that workers are wholly autonomous and mobile. This view obscures the social context of power and control in which sexual harassment occurs.

---

46. *Id.*
47. *Id.* at 1293.
48. *Id.* at 1296–97.

Notes and Discussion

1. Defense Strategies Mahoney outlines several strategies often used to defend against claims of sexual harassment and assault. Are these defense strategies still in use today? Are they more or less effective depending on the race or class of the accuser?

2. Exit and Choice Did Hill's failure to "exit" hurt her credibility with some people? Is the decision to exit the same for a secretary, a grocery clerk, a lawyer, and a neurosurgeon? Explain. Is it harder for an African-American woman to exit than a white woman? Why or why not? Does the ideology of exit deny inequality in relationships as Mahoney asserts? Does exit deny the importance of work and the ties to people at work? What other repercussions does a focus on exit create?

3. Victimization and Agency Why does Mahoney resist a victim-centered approach to sexual harassment? How does she think political conservatives react to a victim-centered approach? What does Mahoney mean by voice and why does she emphasize it? What interferes with voice? Does Mahoney think that women are free agents? If not, why not? Does our culture recognize women's agency? Explain.

4. Ideology of Exit and Inequality How does the ideology of exit and its assumptions of individualism and autonomy function to exacerbate inequality, as Mahoney argues? How does it "strengthen the position of the abuser"? Mahoney reasons that this ideology influences public discourse about child custody cases and women's use of self-defense against batterers. How? Does the ideology function in other contexts?

5. Exit and Intersectionality How does Mahoney's critique of the ideology of exit relate to Crenshaw's concept of intersectionality? Do you see evidence of the confluence of ideas concerning exit and intersections of oppression in this new era of #MeToo?[49]

3. Applying Intersectionality Theory

A. Vulnerability of Farmworkers and Restaurant Workers to Sexual Abuse on the Job

In the 1970s, feminists argued that sexual harassment was a form of economic rape and an abuse of power.[50] Sources of power might include the economic power of employers over employees, the social power of men over women, that of white people over African-American people, or any other power disparity or combination of power disparities. Men who sexually harass and assault women often do so by abusing supervisorial and economic positions of power (e.g., a boss, teacher,

---

49. *See infra* Chapter 10.
50. Baker, *supra* note 14, at 95.

landlord, or police officer). These men take advantage of women's vulnerabilities created by social and economic inequalities.

For example, according to farmworker organizer Monica Ramirez, "undocumented farmworker women are being preyed upon by individuals who believe that these women will not take action against them and they will never experience any kind of accountability because the women are undocumented."[51] Fear of deportation, argues Ramirez, keeps farmworker women from reporting sexual harassment and assault or from suing to enforce their rights. Since the 1990s, scholars, researchers, and activists have deployed Crenshaw's intersectionality theory to analyze intersecting systems of power. Immigration status, age, class, and employment sector dynamics all function to aggravate sexual harassment.

A close look at farmworkers reveals how intersecting systems make particular workers more vulnerable. In 2012, Human Rights Watch published *Cultivating Fear: The Vulnerability of Immigrant Farmworkers in the US to Sexual Violence and Sexual Harassment* about the extensive impact of sexual harassment on immigrant farmworker women.[52] Based on interviews with 160 farmworkers, growers, law enforcement officials, attorneys, service providers, and other agricultural workplace experts in eight states, the study found that many farmworker women faced sexual violence and harassment on the job. The report states:

> Sexual violence and harassment in the agricultural workplace are fostered by a severe imbalance of power between employers and supervisors and their low-wage, immigrant workers. Victims often then face systemic barriers—exacerbated by their status as farmworkers and often as unauthorized workers—to reporting these abuses and bringing perpetrators to justice. . . .
>
> . . . .
>
> . . . [S]exual harassment is a "recurring, day in and day out, significant problem for women farmworkers. . . . It's not a made-up issue, it's real." A 2010 survey of 150 farmworker women in California's Central Valley found that 80 percent had experienced some form of sexual harassment, while a report by the Southern Poverty Law Center found that a majority of their 150 interviewees had also experienced sexual harassment.[53]

Other studies have revealed similarly high rates of sexual harassment of farmworker women.[54]

---

51. Interview with Monica Ramirez (on file with Carrie N. Baker), at 34:20.
52. Human Rights Watch, *Cultivating Fear: The Vulnerability of Immigrant Farmworkers in the US to Sexual Violence and Sexual Harassment* (May 15, 2012), https://www.hrw.org/report/2012/05/15/cultivating-fear-vulnerability-immigrant-farmworkers-us-sexual-violence-and-sexual.
53. *Id.* at 3.
54. Mary Bauer & Monica Ramirez, Injustice on our Plates: Immigrant Women in the U.S. Food Industry (Southern Poverty Law Center, 2010); *see also* Christa Conry, *Forbidden Fruit:*

Multiple factors contribute to farmworker women's vulnerability to sexual harassment and abuse. These factors include a lack of documentation, language barriers, geographic isolation, racist and sexist stereotypes, low wages, and poverty. The Human Rights Watch report notes that perpetrators are foremen, supervisors, farm labor contractors, company owners, and "anyone else who has the power to hire and fire workers as well as confer certain benefits, such as better hours or permission to take breaks. Farmworkers frequently depend on employers for housing and transportation, creating more opportunities for those who seek to take advantage of vulnerable workers."[55] An environment tolerant of abuse enables co-workers to sexually harass and assault women as well. When farmworker women resist the abuse or report incidents to management, they and their family members may "suffer retaliation, getting fewer hours, more abusive treatment, or, worst of all, losing their jobs altogether. Those who live in employer-provided housing can even find themselves homeless. Some farmworkers who had filed sexual harassment lawsuits reported they were 'blackballed' and shut out of jobs at other farms."[56]

The Human Rights Watch report confirms that women farmworkers exist at the intersection of multiple identities and systems that make them vulnerable to sexual harassment and assault. As women of color, they face racism and sexism. As poor women, they are economically vulnerable. As immigrants, they face xenophobia and language barriers. About half of farmworkers are undocumented and their abusers use their fear of deportation as a weapon against them. Even if farmworkers have H-2A temporary agricultural worker visas, those documents restrict workers to one employer. This restriction guarantees that they cannot simply exit an abusive work environment.

Furthermore, many labor laws exclude agricultural workers. For example, farmworkers do not have the right to unionize. Even if labor laws apply, multiple other barriers contribute to the vulnerability of farmworkers, especially undocumented farmworkers. The Human Rights Watch report affirms:

> Unauthorized workers often struggle to find legal representation, since federally funded legal services organizations are prohibited (with some exceptions) from representing unauthorized immigrants. . . .
>
> . . . .
>
> And while police are supposed to vigorously investigate crimes against all victims, regardless of immigration status, the increasing involvement of local police in federal immigration enforcement has fueled immigrants' fear of the police and their desire to avoid contact with the police, even to report crimes. . . .

Sexual Victimization of Migrant Workers in America's Farmlands, 26 HASTINGS WOMEN'S L.J. 121 (2015).

55. HUMAN RIGHTS WATCH, *supra* note 51, at 4.

56. *Id.* at 5.

... Where farmworkers did report the abuses to employers, many supervisors and employers ignored their complaints or retaliated against them, including with threats of deportation.[57]

When farmworkers lose their jobs, they are often not eligible for unemployment insurance or workers' compensation. The report concludes, "[F]armworkers simply cannot afford to lose their jobs, and they often have few options for other employment if farm work is not available." Especially in the current anti-immigrant political climate, this intersection of factors makes farmworker women particularly vulnerable to sexual harassment and assault.

Similar to farmworker women, female servers in restaurants suffer high rates of sexual harassment, in part because restaurant workers earn a sub-minimum wage. Law permits employers to pay less than minimum wage under the assumption that these workers will make up the difference in tips. The federal sub-minimum wage is $2.13 an hour. Furthermore, women make 66% of average tips garnered by male restaurant workers. Women of color earn 40% of that male average. A report by the Restaurant Opportunities Centers (ROC) and Forward Together, *The Glass Floor: Sexual Harassment in the Restaurant Industry*, documents how structural forces construct vulnerability to sexual harassment in the restaurant industry:

> [T]ipped restaurant workers are expected to collect the remainder of their wages from customers' tips, creating an environment in which a majority female workforce must please and curry favor with customers to earn a living. Depending on customers' tips for wages discourages workers who might otherwise stand up for their rights and report unwanted sexual behaviors.
>
> Since women restaurant workers living off tips are forced to rely on customers for their income rather than their employer, these workers must often tolerate inappropriate behavior from customers, co-workers, and management. This dynamic contributes to the restaurant industry's status as the single largest source of sexual harassment claims in the U.S. While seven percent of American women work in the restaurant industry, more than a third (an eye-opening 37%) of all sexual harassment claims to the Equal Employment Opportunity Commission (EEOC) come from the restaurant industry. Even these high levels of complaints to the EEOC may underreport the industry's rate of sexual harassment. Restaurant workers in focus groups gathered through this study noted that sexual harassment is "kitchen talk," a "normalized" part of the work environment and that many restaurant workers are reluctant to publicly acknowledge their experiences with sexual harassment.

. . . .

---

57. *Id.* at 6–7.

Living off tips makes an industry already rife with sexual harassment even more dangerous. Women restaurant workers living off tips in states where the sub-minimum wage for tipped workers is $2.13 per hour (hereinafter called '$2.13 states') are twice as likely to experience sexual harassment as women in states that pay the same minimum wage to all workers. Tipped women workers in $2.13 states reported that they were three times more likely to be told by management to alter their appearance and to wear 'sexier,' more revealing clothing than they were in states where the same minimum wage was paid to all workers. Conversely, tipped women workers in states that have eliminated the sub-minimum wage were less likely to experience sexual harassment.

The high levels of sex harassment experienced by all restaurant workers—and by women and tipped restaurant workers in particular—are even more troubling given that the size of the industry means that many young women in America are introduced to the world of work in a restaurant. A restaurant job is often the first job a young woman obtains, whether she stays in the industry her whole life or moves on to another career. This environment is where many women first learn their worth as workers. Countless young women start out as early as high school working as part-time servers, bussers, hostesses, and dishwashers in casual, family restaurants and fast-food chains that are notorious for low wages, poor sanitary and safety conditions, and sexual harassment. A negative first experience in the restaurant increases the likelihood that women will come to expect sexual harassment in other work environments. In our study, women who had previously worked as tipped workers were 1.6 times as likely to live with harassing behaviors in the workplace as the women who were currently employed as tipped workers.

It is critical to contextualize the concept of 'living with' sexual harassment in the workplace as something different than consent. Our survey and focus group results show that most workers either ignore or put up with harassing behaviors because they fear they will be penalized through loss of income from tips, unfavorable shifts, public humiliation, or even job loss. At the same time, workers are taking steps to address the impact of harassment on their well-being. Seventy-six percent of workers who experienced sexual harassment talked to their families and friends about their experiences, 73% talked to their co-workers, and 44% talked to a supervisor. Eighty-eight percent of workers who experienced sexual harassment reported that they'd be more likely to talk to their supervisor about these experiences if they were part of a group of co-workers.

Together these findings paint a troubling portrait of endemic sexual harassment in the restaurant industry. Widespread harassment, particularly towards women and tipped workers, demonstrates how power is used to exert control over other workers' bodies and livelihoods. Our data

shows that all too often the economic insecurity of living off tips contributes to higher levels of physical insecurity being reported by all restaurant
workers—and particularly women restaurant workers—in a workplace
rife with sexual harassment. In order to reduce the pressures that increase
sexual harassment, we must eliminate the sub-minimum wage for tipped
workers while implementing and strengthening policies to educate workers on their rights and reduce rates of sexual harassment. Legislating one
fair wage, so all workers are ensured a minimum wage sufficient to cover
their basic needs, and eliminating a sub-minimum wage for tipped workers, can give all workers greater personal agency, creating a safer and more
equitable workplace.[58]

Female servers generally come from low-income backgrounds and are disproportionately women of color. The intersection of gender, race, and class makes them
particularly vulnerable to sexual harassment and reduces their access remedies.

The ROC United report explains how gender stereotypes intersect with capitalist imperatives and the sub-minimum wage law to increase female vulnerability to
sexual harassment. The report finds:

Tipped women working in restaurants reported to ROC-United that the
cultural expectation of their work in terms of appearance and behavior is
often 'sexy,' deferential and available, "date ready," as one server in Houston described it. In restaurants, the basic and widespread "philosophy of
service as pleasing customers, indulging them, and giving them what they
want," intersects with a system that demands that customers pay these
workers' wages in tips and creates an environment in which inappropriate
behavior by customers towards service staff becomes commonplace.

The sub-minimum wage system also impacts how managers supervise
tipped employees in the restaurant industry. Studies have shown, for example, that this system can impact a worker's employment; managers interpret
poor tips as signs of poor performance, and may also seek to hire workers
based on a desire to fulfill customer expectations, such as having attractive staff. Customers pay for a sexualized vision of 'good service,' owners
demand it, and co-workers observe and internalize a system that places the
worker in a subservient and vulnerable service role. The sub-minimum
wage system shapes the experience of sexual harassment in the workplace
by restaurant workers in a number of ways:

1. Since tipped workers who earn a sub-minimum wage depend on
   customers to provide their wages, customers can feel entitled to treat
   servers inappropriately. . . .

58. RESTAURANT OPPORTUNITIES CENTERS UNITED & FORWARD TOGETHER, THE GLASS FLOOR:
SEXUAL HARASSMENT IN THE RESTAURANT INDUSTRY 1–4 (2014).

2. The system of workers having to obtain their wages from customers has the effect of blurring boundaries, as it becomes difficult for workers to effectively draw lines between providing good service and tolerating inappropriate behavior from customers.

3. Due to their desire to keep customers happy, management can be unresponsive to, or even indulgent of customer misbehavior. Management also at times encourages sexual harassment from customers and co-workers by requiring employees to flirt and dress suggestively.

4. Women workers are often required or feel the need to dress or act in a sexualized manner in order to secure larger checks and tips from customers. As a result, women's bodies are further commoditized.

5. Women restaurant workers often have to tolerate inappropriate comments and sexual harassment while at work in order to ensure their earnings are not impacted negatively and to maintain job security. . . .

6. Accepting or tolerating sexual harassment in the workplace differs from consent but due to the constraints on workers, few address the harassing behaviors on the job. Instead, workers tend to seek support outside the work environment. Over three quarters of workers who experienced sexual harassment sought support from a friend or family member.[59]

Note how this passage describes the interaction of the structural and ideological factors that influence women's experience of sexual harassment, the sub-minimum wage structure and ideologies of female sexual objectification and subservience.

Another recent study by ROC United, *Take Us Off the Menu*, reveals that young women's experiences of sexual harassment in the restaurant industry increase their lifelong tolerance of harassment. Between one-third and one-half of all Americans first work in the restaurant industry. According to the report, a majority of women who previously worked as tipped workers reported tolerating sexual harassment later in life regardless of what professions they eventually entered. Discouraged from recognizing these formative experiences as sexual harassment, they internalize harassing behavior as a norm for acceptable workplace behavior.[60]

Notes and Discussion

1. Applying Intersectional Theory What intersections exist in the case of farmworker women and tipped workers? What factors create the unequal relationships of power that abusers exploit to harass?

---

59. *Id.* at 7–8.
60. Restaurant Opportunities Centers United, Take Us Off the Menu: The Impact of Sexual Harassment in the Restaurant Industry 3 (2018).

2. Child Labor Agriculture is one of the few fields exempt from child labor laws. How might age interact with sex, race, class, and immigration status to make girls working in agriculture particularly vulnerable to sexual abuse? What about farmworker boys? Do they face different risks?

3. Ideology of Exit How might Mahoney's arguments about the ideology of exit apply to the cases of farmworker women and tipped workers?

4. Male-Dominated Occupations Occupations such as construction, mining, military service, and policing have higher than average rates of sexual harassment. Use Crenshaw's theory of intersectionality to determine what factors might contribute to high rates of sexual harassment in these occupations.

5. Solutions ROC United and Forward Together argue that fair wage laws would reduce restaurant workers' vulnerability to harassment. Is this true? Why or why not? Are there other strategies to address the structural contributors to sexual harassment?

6. Workplace Culture The ROC United report suggests that restaurant workers learn to tolerate sexual harassment. Is there an expectation in the restaurant industry that servers should tolerate harassing comments or behaviors, or even participate in them by "flirting," in order to obtain better tips? If so, does this expectation violate Title VII?

B. Interlocking Systems of Oppression

Structural factors such as immigration law and the sub-minimum wage, as well as ideological factors such as sex and race stereotypes, contribute to high rates of workplace sexual harassment. These factors can intersect in women's lives to prevent them from responding. These intersections, however, are often invisible. Feminist philosopher Marilyn Frye concretizes these intersections using the metaphor of a birdcage. Each wire of the cage represents one form of oppression. Examining each wire of the cage, an observer might wonder why the bird does not just fly around the wire. Only by stepping back and realizing the relationships among the wires of the cage does one see why the bird stays confined. Frye explains:

> The root of the word "oppression" is the element "press." The press of the crowd; pressed into military service; to press a pair of pants; printing press; press the button. Presses are used to mold things or flatten them or reduce them in bulk, sometimes to reduce them by squeezing out the gasses or liquids in them. Something pressed is something caught between or among forces and barriers which are so related to each other that jointly they restrain, restrict or prevent the thing's motion or mobility. Mold. Immobilize. Reduce. . . .

> The mundane experience of the oppressed provides another clue. One of the most characteristic and ubiquitous features of the world as experienced

by oppressed people is the double bind situations in which options are reduced to a very few and all of them expose one to penalty, censure or deprivation. For example, it is often a requirement upon oppressed people that we smile and be cheerful. If we comply, we signal our docility and our acquiescence in our situation. We need not, then, be taken note of. We acquiesce in being made invisible, in our occupying no space. We participate in our own erasure. On the other hand, anything but the sunniest countenance exposes us to being perceived as mean, bitter, angry or dangerous. This means, at the least, that we may be found "difficult" or unpleasant to work with, which is enough to cost one one's livelihood; at worst, being seen as mean, bitter, angry or dangerous has been known to result in rape, arrest, beating and murder. One can only choose to risk one's preferred form and rate of annihilation.

. . . .

Women are caught like this, too, by networks of forces and barriers that expose one to penalty, loss or contempt whether one works outside the home or not, is on welfare or not, bears children or not, raises children or not, marries or not, stays married or not, is heterosexual, lesbian, both or neither. Economic necessity; confinement to racial and/or sexual job ghettos; sexual harassment; sex discrimination; pressures of competing expectations and judgments about women, wives and mothers (in the society at large, in racial and ethnic subcultures and in one's own mind); dependence (full or partial) on husbands, parents or the state; commitment to political ideas; loyalties to racial or ethnic or other "minority" groups; the demands of self-respect and responsibilities to others. Each of these factors exists in complex tension with every other, penalizing or prohibiting all of the apparently available options. And nipping at one's heels, always, is the endless pack of little things. If one dresses one way, one is subject to the assumption that one is advertising one's sexual availability; if one dresses another way, one appears to "not care about oneself" or to be "unfeminine." If one uses "strong language," one invites categorization as a whore or slut; if one does not, one invites categorization as a "lady" — one too delicately constituted to cope with robust speech or the realities to which it presumably refers.

The experience of oppressed people is that the living of one's life is confined and shaped by forces and barriers which are not accidental or occasional and hence avoidable, but are systematically related to each other in such a way as to catch one between and among them and restrict or penalize motion in any direction. It is the experience of being caged in: all avenues, in every direction, are blocked or booby trapped. . . .

Cages. Consider a birdcage. If you look very closely at just one wire in the cage, you cannot see the other wires. If your conception of what is before you is determined by this myopic focus, you could look at that one wire, up and down the length of it, and unable to see why a bird would not just fly around the wire any time it wanted to go somewhere. Furthermore, even if, one day at a time, you myopically inspected each wire, you still could not see why a bird would have trouble going past the wires to get anywhere. There is no physical property of any one wire, nothing that the closest scrutiny could discover, that will reveal how a bird could be inhibited or harmed by it except in the most accidental way. It is only when you step back, stop looking at the wires one by one, microscopically, and take a macroscopic view of the whole cage, that you can see why the bird does not go anywhere; and then you will see it in a moment. It will require no great subtlety of mental powers. It is perfectly obvious that the bird is surrounded by a network of systematically related barriers, no one of which would be the least hindrance to its flight, but which, by their relations to each other, are as confining as the solid walls of a dungeon. . . .

It is now possible to grasp one of the reasons why oppression can be hard to see and recognize: one can study the elements of an oppressive structure with great care and some good will without seeing the structure as a whole, and hence without seeing or being able to understand that one is looking at a cage and that there are people there who are caged, whose motion and mobility are restricted, whose lives are shaped and reduced.

. . . .

As the cageness of the birdcage is a macroscopic phenomenon, the oppressiveness of the situations in which women live our various and different lives is a macroscopic phenomenon. Neither can be seen from a microscopic perspective. But when you look macroscopically you can see it—a network of forces and barriers which are systematically related and which conspire to the immobilization, reduction and molding of women and the lives we live.[61]

Frye's metaphor of the birdcage is useful in understanding both women's experiences of sexual harassment and why they might not report it. Penalties lie in all directions. If targets smile and go along with the abuse, observers assume the targets welcome it. If targets object, they alienate their bosses or co-workers who assume them to be "difficult." If targets report, employers or supervisors retaliate and blackball women in their field of specialty. If targets do not report, then employers will claim that the abuse did not happen, or was not severe.

Much of the public discourse around the Hill/Thomas hearings focused on why she did not leave, why she did not report the behavior, and why she waited 10 years to reveal it. In light of Frye's birdcage metaphor, each option was fraught. Hill chose the option of confronting Thomas directly, and when he did not stop, she eventually left the practice of civil rights law to become a law professor. But that exit was not

---

61. Marilyn Frye, The Politics of Reality: Essays in Feminist Theory 2–7 (1983).

enough for the white men of the Senate Judiciary Committee, the media, and many members of the public.

African-American feminist theorist Patricia Hill Collins elaborates upon the interconnectedness of oppressions. Collins distinguishes "additive models of oppression" from an interlocking system or matrix of domination. She explains:

> Additive models of oppression are firmly rooted in the either/or dichotomous thinking of Eurocentric, masculinist thought. One must be either Black or white in such thought systems—persons of ambiguous racial and ethnic identity constantly battle with questions such as "what are you, anyway?" This emphasis on quantification and categorization occurs in conjunction with the belief that either/or categories must be ranked. The search for certainty of this sort requires that one side of a dichotomy be privileged while its other is denigrated. Privilege becomes defined in relation to its other.

> Replacing additive models of oppression with interlocking ones creates possibilities for new paradigms. The significance of seeing race, class, and gender as interlocking systems of oppression is that such an approach fosters a paradigmatic shift of thinking inclusively about other oppressions, such as age, sexual orientation, religion, and ethnicity. Race, class, and gender represent the three systems of oppression that most heavily affect African-American women. But these systems and the economic, political, and ideological conditions that support them may not be the most fundamental oppressions, and they certainly affect many more groups than Black women. Other people of color, Jews, the poor, white women, and gays and lesbians have all had similar ideological justifications offered for their subordination. All categories of humans labeled Others have been equated to one another, to animals, and to nature.

> Placing African-American women and other excluded groups in the center of analysis opens up possibilities for a both/and conceptual stance, one in which all groups possess varying amounts of penalty and privilege in one historically created system. In this system, for example, white women are penalized by their gender but privileged by their race. Depending on the context, an individual may be an oppressor, a member of an oppressed group, or simultaneously oppressor and oppressed. . . .

> Embracing a both/and conceptual stance moves us from additive, separate systems approaches to oppression and toward what I now see as the more fundamental issue of the social relations of domination. Race, class, and gender constitute axes of oppression that characterize Black women's experiences within a more generalized matrix of domination. Other groups may encounter different dimensions of the matrix, such as sexual

orientation, religion, and age, but the overarching relationship is one of domination and the types of activism it generates.[62]

An additive model of oppression assumes that discrimination against African-American women is similar to the discrimination experienced by African-American men and that experienced by white women. Collins argues, however, that African-American female discrimination is unique. She also calls attention to how these intersections make visible privileged positions, as well as disadvantaged positions.

Collins contends that systems of oppression function at three levels: the institutional, symbolic, and individual levels. The institutional level of oppression is represented through "systemic relationships of domination and subordination structured through social institutions such as schools, businesses, hospitals, the workplace, and government agencies." According to Collins, "even though the workings of the institutional dimension of oppression are often obscured with ideologies claiming equality of opportunity, in actuality, race, class and gender place Asian-American women, Native American men, white men, African-American women, and other groups in distinct institutional niches with varying degrees of penalty and privilege." Examples of institutional-level oppressive systems would be farmworker exemptions from labor laws, restrictive immigration laws paired with high demand for farmworkers, and sub-minimum wage laws.

To explain the institutional dimension of oppression, Collins examines the race, class, and gender dynamics of an antebellum plantation. She states:

> We have a very interesting chain of command on the plantation—the affluent White master as the reigning patriarch, his White wife helpmate to serve him, help him manage his property and bring up his heirs, his faithful servants whose production and reproduction were tied to the requirements of the capitalist political economy, and largely propertyless, working class White men and women watching from afar. In essence, the foundations for the contemporary roles of elite White women, poor Black women, working class White men, and a series of other groups can be seen in stark relief in this fundamental American social institution. While Blacks experienced the most harsh treatment under slavery, and thus made slavery clearly visible as a racist institution, race, class and gender interlocked in structuring slavery's systemic organization of domination and subordination.[63]

Collins suggests the antebellum plantation as a metaphor for the interlocking relations of power in current societal institutions. Even today, Congress is 73% white male, with women and people of color representing a small minority. The leadership of Fortune 500 companies is largely white male, as is the leadership of colleges and universities across the United States. Occupational segregation and low pay in

---

62. Patricia Hill Collins, Black Feminist Thought: Knowledge, Consciousness, and the Politics of Empowerment 225–26 (1990).

63. *Id.* at 31.

female-dominated occupations reflect the devaluation of women's work. Women still do the large majority of unpaid childcare. Ideologies that justify this skewed representation and distribution of power and resources shore up institutional dimensions of oppression.

Collins defines the symbolic dimension of oppression as "widespread, societally-sanctioned ideologies used to justify relations of domination and subordination." She reasons that "central to this process is the use of stereotypical or controlling images of diverse race, class and gender group."[64] Collins invites her readers to compile a list of traits typically associated with masculinity and femininity. She notes that masculinity is associated with aggression, leadership, rationality, strength, and intellect. Femininity is associated with passivity, servitude, emotionality, weakness, and physicality. She explains, however, that this list is not race-neutral. Specifically, she suggests:

> Not only does this list reflect either/or dichotomous thinking and the need to rank both sides of the dichotomy, but ask yourself exactly which men and women you had in mind when compiling these characteristics. This list applies almost exclusively to middle class White men and women. The allegedly "masculine" qualities that you probably listed are only acceptable when exhibited by elite White men, or when used by Black and Hispanic men against each other or against women of color. Aggressive Black and Hispanic men are seen as dangerous, not powerful, and are often penalized when they exhibit any of the allegedly "masculine" characteristics. Working class and poor White men fare slightly better but are also denied the allegedly "masculine" symbols of leadership, intellectual competence, and human rationality. Women of color and working class and poor White women are also not represented on this list, for they have never had the luxury of being "ladies." What appear to be universal categories representing all men and women instead are unmasked as being applicable to only a small group.

It is important to see how the symbolic images applied to different race, class and gender groups interact in maintaining systems of domination and subordination. If I were to ask you to repeat the same assignment, only this time, by making separate lists for Black men, Black women, Hispanic women and Hispanic men, I suspect that your gender symbolism would be quite different. In comparing all of the lists, you might begin to see the interdependence of symbols applied to all groups. For example, the elevated images of White womanhood need devalued images of Black womanhood in order to maintain credibility. While the above exercise reveals the interlocking nature of race, class and gender in structuring the symbolic dimension of oppression, part of its importance lies in demonstrating how

---

64. *Id.* at 32.

race, class and gender pervade a wide range of what appears to be universal language.[65]

Collins notes that these stereotypes serve as controlling images that influence how people perceive and treat different women. These images or stereotypes also influence institutions to reinforce systems of oppression and privilege. The white male senators' treatment of Anita Hill demonstrates how institutional and symbolic systems of oppression can come together to disadvantage women.

Yet another dimension of oppression is at the individual level. On this dimension, Collins comments:

> Whether we benefit or not, we all live within institutions that reproduce race, class and gender oppression. Even if we never have any contact with members of other race, class and gender groups, we all encounter images of these groups and are exposed to the symbolic meanings attached to those images. On this dimension of oppression, our individual biographies vary tremendously. As a result of our institutional and symbolic statuses, all of our choices become political acts. Each of us must come to terms with the multiple ways in which race, class and gender as categories of analysis frame our individual biographies.[66]

Using Frye's birdcage metaphor and Collins's three dimensions of oppression, one can better understand female farmworkers' and restaurant servers' experiences. Their sexual harassment is not just random and individualized. Broader institutional and symbolic factors shape this abuse. Institutional factors, such as immigration law, labor law exemptions, and sub-minimum wage laws place women workers in positions of vulnerability vis-à-vis their employers.

Gender, race, and class ideologies empower harassers and discredit women who report sexual harassment and abuse. Together, these interlocking systems guarantee that women, particularly women of color and poor women, face more harassment and lack access to remedies. Various aspects of sexual harassment law, presented throughout this book, help one to think about how institutional, symbolic, and individual factors influence people's experience of harassment, their responses, defendants' behaviors, and judges' opinions in legal cases.

Notes and Discussion

1. Applying the Birdcage Metaphor What are the "networks of forces and barriers" that constrain farmworker women and tipped restaurant workers? How are these forces "systematically related to each other"? How do different aspects of oppression interrelate to constrain farmworker women and/or tipped restaurant workers?

---

65. *Id.* at 32–33.
66. *Id.* at 34–35.

2. Collins on Oppression What is the difference between additive and interlocking models of oppression? How does this difference relate to Crenshaw's theory of intersectionality and Frye's bird cage metaphor? What does Collins mean by "categories of humans labeled Others"? What does she mean by the "social relations of domination"? How do these concepts relate to sexual harassment? What other structural or symbolic factors might influence the likelihood that a person will experience sexual harassment?

3. Intersections with Age How might young or old people be particularly vulnerable to sexual harassment in the workplace? How might age interact with sex and race to make young girls of color particularly vulnerable?

4. Low-Wage Workers What challenges do low-wage earning women, single mothers, or women living in poverty face with regard to sexual harassment in the workplace? How might college or law school debt influence a recent graduate's ability to respond to sexual harassment in her first job?

5. Other Intersections What other intersections might influence women's experience of sexual harassment?

4. Intersectionality in the Courts

In her 1989 article *Demarginalizing the Intersections of Race and Sex*, Kimberlé Crenshaw documents judicial resistance to concurrent sex and race discrimination claims. She argues that courts disaggregate these claims, even when they arise together in one case. If an employer can show that he did not discriminate against African-American men or white women, then an African-American woman cannot win her case, even if there is evidence that the employer discriminates against her. Crenshaw uses the metaphor of a traffic intersection to illustrate her point. Specifically, courts will consider discrimination coming from only one side or the perpendicular direction but often fail to consider how these multidirectional forces collide at the center.

Many courts have resisted plaintiffs' attempts to introduce evidence of racialized sexual harassment. However, one appellate court acted exceptionally in the 1987 case of *Hicks v. Gates Rubber Company*. While reading the majority and dissenting opinions in *Hicks*, consider how the judicial opinions portray sex and race discrimination. How might an intersectional analysis enable one to see things that might otherwise remain invisible? How could it provide a singular analysis for disaggregated race and sex discrimination, or an additive analysis that considers them both, but not in an intersectional way?

Hicks v. Gates Rubber Co.

833 F.2d 1406 (10th Cir. 1987)

HOLLOWAY, Chief Judge.

. . . .

At trial, Hicks sought to establish that the work environment at Gates during her probationary period was permeated with racial and sexual hostility. Gates' employees testified that an atmosphere existed in which racial slurs and jokes were tolerated. . . .

. . . Hicks also claimed that during her probationary period she was sexually harassed. She recounted an incident during a trip to patrol the hangar where Holec reached over and rubbed her thigh and said, "I think you're going to make it." . . .

. . . .

. . . Gates strenuously disputed Hicks' contention that she had been sexually harassed by Holec, asserting that Hicks had misconstrued an innocent and harmless gesture of encouragement.

. . . In addition, Hicks said that the following day, November 9, Gleason touched her on the buttocks and said "'I'm going to get you yet.'" At about this time, on instructions from the manager of security, Ely, Gleason also began making notations on Hicks' job performance.

. . . .

Not long after receiving the verbal warning, Hicks said that she was again sexually harassed by Gleason. She was taking a break on patrol when Gleason drove up in a go-cart. He stopped and said, "I caught you," or "I got you." He then allegedly grabbed Hicks' breasts and she "fell over, and he got on top of [her]." Gleason denied such acts.

. . . .

[The Court affirmed the lower court's dismissal of the racial harassment claim and the quid pro quo sexual harassment claim. Then it turned to the hostile environment harassment claim, which the lower court had failed to reach. The Court also considered] whether incidents of racial harassment which may, by themselves, be insufficient to support a racially hostile work environment claim can be combined with incidents of sexual harassment to prove a pervasive pattern of discriminatory harassment in violation of Title VII.

. . . .

The . . . question is whether, in determining the pervasiveness of the harassment against a plaintiff, a trial court may aggregate evidence of racial hostility with evidence of sexual hostility. We conclude that such aggregation is permissible.

The purpose of Title VII is "the removal of artificial, arbitrary and unnecessary barriers to employment when the barriers operate invidiously to discriminate on the basis of racial or other impermissible classifications." *Griggs v. Duke Power Co.*, 401 U.S. 424, 431 (1971). Title VII prohibits an employer from discriminating against any individual because of race or because of sex. "The use of the word 'or' evidences Congress' intent to prohibit employment discrimination based on any or all of the listed characteristics." *Jefferies v. Harris Co. Community Action Ass'n*, 615 F.2d 1025, 1032 (5th Cir. 1980).

In *Jefferies*, the plaintiff made claims of race and sex discrimination arising out of the defendant's failure to promote her and its decision to terminate her. When the trial court dismissed her claims of race discrimination and sex discrimination, the plaintiff appealed, arguing that the court had erred in refusing to consider her claim of discrimination based on both race and sex. The Fifth Circuit agreed. Relying on cases that disparate treatment of a sub-class of women would constitute a violation of Title VII, the court concluded that "discrimination against black females [could] exist even in the absence of discrimination against black men or white women." *Jefferies*, 615 F.2d at 1032. We are persuaded that the Jefferies ruling is correct.

Hicks introduced evidence that her supervisor, Gleason, had made serious racial slurs against blacks. Such evidence should be considered on remand to determine whether there was a pervasive discriminatory atmosphere, combining the racial and sexual harassment evidence, so that a hostile work environment harassment claim may have been established by Hicks. Even though we have held that the evidence sufficiently supports the discrete finding that Gates did not maintain a work environment openly hostile to blacks, that evidence on racial treatment should be considered for this combined purpose here with the sexual harassment evidence.

In sum, without expressing any view on the merits of the ultimate determination that should be made on the hostile work environment sexual harassment claim of Hicks, that claim is remanded to the district court for reconsideration.

. . . .

Accordingly, the judgment is reversed and the case is remanded for further proceedings in accord with this opinion.

. . . .

SETH, Circuit Judge, dissenting:

I must respectfully dissent from the majority opinion . . . .

. . . .

[T]he majority agrees with the trial court's finding that the work environment was not openly hostile to black employees. However it directs the trial court on remand to aggregate "racial hostility" and "sexual hostility" in determining the pervasiveness of "the harassment." . . . There are, of course, many cases wherein discrimination is alleged based on both sex and race and many where both have been found to exist. However, it is difficult to see how we could on remand aggregate "racial hostility" where none was found to exist with anything else. Here again the majority would have the trial court evaluate the impact of the overall working conditions arising from whatever cause rather than try the case as a sexual harassment case under *Meritor*.

The case as it now stands is not a combination of statutorily protected characteristics advanced as a subclass as in *Jefferies* nor as a "plus" case.

I would affirm the trial court in all respects.

Notes and Discussion

1. Intersectionality The lower court dismissed Hicks' claim for racial harassment, yet Judge Holloway directed the lower court to consider evidence of racial harassment when considering Hicks' hostile environment sexual harassment claim. Is the dissent right that it makes no sense to direct the lower court to consider evidence of racial harassment if it has already dismissed the racial harassment claim, which the appellate court affirmed? If not, why? How would Crenshaw defend the majority opinion?

2. Complex Bias Courts are more likely to grant summary judgment for employers when cases involve multiple claims (e.g., race and sex).[67] Why do you think that would be the case? How could Crenshaw's intersectionality theory help explain the interconnections of race and sex discrimination?

5. Application of Law and Ethics
Hypothetical #2
(based on a true story)

Steve is the Vice President of Manufacturing and Hiring Manager for CCC, a company that advertises itself on its letterhead as "A Christ-Centered Corporation." Steve goes to see employment attorney Ana. He is concerned that the executive committee of CCC, on which he sits, is discriminating against a well-qualified employee who has applied for a permanent position with the company. He thinks the company will refuse to hire her permanently. Steve wants to know whether conduct at CCC constitutes discrimination or harassment.

Ana learns from Steve that Kim interviewed at CCC for a temporary position in Steve's division. After the first interview, Steve heard from his secretary that several staff members had been gossiping about Kim's gender. People had suggested that she was a "he" because, even though she presented herself as a woman in all respects, she had a distinctively low-pitched voice. Female staff members were worried that they would have to share the restroom with Kim if she were hired for the

---

67. *See* Minna J. Kotkin, *Diversity and Discrimination: A Look at Complex Bias*, 50 Wm. & Mary L. Rev. 1439 (2009).

temporary position. Steve ignored this gossip and took no further action at the time other than to hire Kim.

Legal issue: Is Steve's failure to act discriminatory?

Steve explains that Kim has done a wonderful job over the last few months and that she is clearly the best qualified of all of the candidates for the permanent position. He believes, however, that the executive committee will ignore his recommendation that CCC hire her because the executive committee believes she is a "transvestite," lesbian, and/or transgender. (Kim privately self-identifies as pansexual.)

Ana advises Steve not to discriminate against Kim.

Several months later, Steve brings to Ana's office a box of documents he has been collecting regarding Kim's employment at CCC. Steve explains that most of these documents are from his own file concerning Kim. However, he explains that he found a letter from CCC's legal counsel, Gina, at the photocopier recently. Gina's letter to the President addresses Kim's hire, saying:

> Being in the right morally does not mean that one is in the right legally. In our secular, humanistic society there are many laws which embody secular moral judgments (i.e. gay is OK) while making illegal Christian moral judgments. . . . One possible alternative occurs to me. Give the permanent position to the other person, but keep (or at least offer to keep) Kim as a consultant indefinitely on some commercially reasonable basis. This avoids the permanent employment of Kim while simultaneously decreasing the impression of discrimination and her personal and financial interest in suing.

Legal Issues: Does this letter evidence discrimination? Is this letter protected by the attorney-client privilege?

An e-mail print-out from CCC's President to Steve and the other executive committee members concerning counsel's letter states:

> With Kim as a manager, she will be involved in hiring decisions at least of any people to work for her, and for ANY position at CCC, she will be spreading the word among like-minded friends/acquaintances of hers. And if any of them happen to be homosexuals or AIDS victims or people of other religions . . . then again we will again have a gun to our heads with regard to hiring the person, i.e., since we know we are obviously prejudiced and can refuse to hire the person only if we have a documentable reason not to hire him. . . .

Steve leaves his box of documents at Ana's office for Ana's review.

Legal Issues: Does this email evidence discrimination? Is this email protected by the attorney-client privilege?

If the executive committee fails to hire Kim and she sues for discrimination, Steve wants to know if he and/or the company can be held liable. (See *infra* Chapter 4.)

Theoretical Issue: How could Ana (or Steve or CCC) take an intersectional approach to this situation?

1. Is it necessary for Ana to establish whether Steve has come to see her in his personal or corporate capacity? Why or why not?

2. Are any legal or professional ethical issues raised by what CCC's counsel, Gina, has advised in her letter?

3. Are any legal or professional ethical issues raised by the President's email?

4. Discuss any other issues you believe might merit further research and investigation.

Chapter 3

Refining the Prima Facie Case

Meritor left many questions unanswered which led to inconsistent appellate decisions and prompted vehement responses from feminist legal scholars. It also obscured the required elements of the prima facie case. Lower courts struggled with what harassment "based on sex" meant. Ambiguity also existed concerning the unwelcomeness element, and the sufficient level of offense required to support an actionable lawsuit.

1. Elements One and Three: Membership in a Protected Class/Harassment Based on Sex

A. Definition of Terms as Applied

The requirement that the plaintiff be a member of a protected class and that she prove the harassment was based on sex are closely related. The *Henson* court explained that membership in a protected class requires only a "simple stipulation that the employee is a man or a woman." A person of any sex can claim to be the target of sexual harassment. Harder to prove is that the perpetrator acted *because of* the plaintiff's sex.

In a simple case, neither of these elements poses great difficulty. For example, in *Meritor*, Mechelle Vinson was the direct target of explicitly sexual language and conduct by Sydney Taylor, her male supervisor. Vinson had no trouble demonstrating that she was a member of a protected class, and the court inferred that her sex prompted Taylor's harassment. The inference should be the same if the sexes in that scenario were reversed, which is to say, where a man is sexually harassed by a woman.[1]

The application of law becomes more complicated the further the facts stray from the *Meritor* scenario. How should a court treat nonsexual harassing conduct directed at a woman, allegedly because she is female? What about sexualized work-place behavior that is not directed *at* a particular person, but which one sex finds particularly offensive? Can a person sexually harass another person of the same sex? What if a man claims to be harassed for failing to conform to male gendered

---

1. *See, e.g.*, Gardinella v. General Electric Co., 833 F. Supp. 617 (W.D. Ky. 1993).

stereotypes? What if this man is gay or transgender? Courts have addressed all of these scenarios in recent years.

Courts have not always been careful, however, in defining terms as they applied the law. Chapter 1 highlights the importance of definitional clarity. Imprecise use or understanding of these terms has led to much confusion and inconsistent law. As Professor Mary Anne Case observes, "the concept of gender has been imperfectly disaggregated in the law from sex on the one hand and sexual orientation on the other." She notes:

> Courts toss around the words "gender," "masculine," "feminine," and "sex stereotyping" fairly often in sex discrimination cases. But they do not always use these terms consistently or self-consciously, and they do not always recognize gender issues when such issues are presented. Courts often conflate gender with sex and particularly with sexual orientation, often without acknowledging and sometimes apparently without being aware that they are doing so.[2]

For the cases in this section, pay close attention to the type of discrimination at issue and the terms the courts use. Consider how well these terms match up with what the plaintiff argued and whether they align with the facts of the case.

B. When Is Conduct Based on Sex?

As discussed in Chapter 1, biological markers of sex — sex organs, hormones, and chromosomes — are not usually visible in the workplace. Most people identify sex by gendered behavior and appearance, which may or may not conform to socially accepted notions of masculine or feminine. Therefore, courts have grappled with the extent to which discrimination or harassment based on a failure to conform to gendered stereotypes can constitute discrimination based on "sex."

Although not a harassment case, *Price Waterhouse v. Hopkins* provided foundational doctrine on sex stereotyping as discrimination. Plaintiff Ann Hopkins sued her employer for failing to promote her to partner because of her sex. Although she had performed well by objective standards, the male partners who evaluated her criticized her interpersonal skills. Her evaluations reprimanded her for being "overly aggressive, unduly harsh, difficult to work with and impatient with staff." As the Supreme Court noted, some of the partners had reacted negatively to Hopkins because she was a *woman* with these personality traits. The Court found:

> One partner described her as "macho"; another suggested that she "over-compensated for being a woman"; a third advised her to take "a course at charm school." Several partners criticized her use of profanity; in response, one partner suggested that those partners objected to her swearing only

---

2. Mary Anne Case, *Disaggregating Gender from Sex and Sexual Orientation: The Effeminate Man in the Law and Feminist Jurisprudence*, 105 Yale L.J. 1, 17 (1995).

"because it's a lady using foul language." Another supporter explained that Hopkins "ha[d] matured from a tough-talking somewhat masculine hard-nosed mgr to an authoritative, formidable, but much more appealing lady ptr candidate." But it was the man who, as Judge Gesell found, bore responsibility for explaining to Hopkins the reasons for the Policy Board's decision to place her candidacy on hold who delivered the *coup de grace:* in order to improve her chances for partnership, Thomas Beyer advised, Hopkins should "walk more femininely, talk more femininely, dress more femininely, wear make-up, have her hair styled, and wear jewelry."[3]

The District Judge held that Price Waterhouse had unlawfully discriminated against Hopkins on the basis of sex by consciously giving credence and effect to partners' comments that resulted from sex stereotyping. A plurality of the Supreme Court, in an opinion written by Justice Brennan, agreed:

> In the specific context of sex stereotyping, an employer who acts on the basis of a belief that a woman cannot be aggressive, or that she must not be, has acted on the basis of gender.
>
> Although the parties do not overtly dispute this last proposition, the placement by Price Waterhouse of "sex stereotyping" in quotation marks throughout its brief seems to us an insinuation either that such stereotyping was not present in this case or that it lacks legal relevance. We reject both possibilities. As to the existence of sex stereotyping in this case, we are not inclined to quarrel with the District Court's conclusion that a number of the partners' comments showed sex stereotyping at work. As for the legal relevance of sex stereotyping, we are beyond the day when an employer could evaluate employees by assuming or insisting that they matched the stereotype associated with their group, for "'[i]n forbidding employers to discriminate against individuals because of their sex, Congress intended to strike at the entire spectrum of disparate treatment of men and women resulting from sex stereotypes.'" An employer who objects to aggressiveness in women but whose positions require this trait places women in an intolerable and impermissible catch 22: out of a job if they behave aggressively and out of a job if they do not. Title VII lifts women out of this bind.[4]

Thus, the Court set precedent for the review of sex stereotyping in sexual harassment cases.

Notes and Discussion

1. Sex Stereotyping and Gender "Sex" for the *Price Waterhouse* plurality included gender stereotypes. How does this compare to the manner in which courts treat other prohibited bases for discrimination? Do courts define race narrowly to include

3. 490 U.S. 228, 235 (1989).
4. *Id.* at 250–51.

only skin color? Or do they include stereotypical manifestations of race and racial heritage such as particular dress, hairstyle, food eaten, types of music preferred, symbolic gestures, etc.? What if a harasser abused someone who was not of color because of her corn-rowed hair and rap music? Would a court dismiss such a case as a grooming and music preference issue, not within the purview of Title VII? Similarly, do you think courts would dismiss a religious discrimination case involving a Jew who did not eat pork because Title VII does not cover discrimination on the basis of diet? Alternately, would a court dismiss a religious discrimination case against a Jew because she did not "look" or "act" Jewish? Even if the perpetrators assumed she was Jewish and discriminated against her on that basis?

2. Terminology Does *Price Waterhouse* contribute to the confusion of the terms "sex" and "gender" that Professor Case has noted? Or does it make the point that the two are impossible to disaggregate from a legal standpoint?

3. Demonstrating Stereotypes How can advocates present evidence that particular stereotypes exist and are at work in a particular case? The plaintiff in *Price Waterhouse* used expert testimony from a psychologist to explain how stereotyped thinking manifested itself in the partners' comments. How might a defendant counter such an argument?

4. Differential Effects of Stereotypes Note the dual way in which stereotypes can harm women at work: A woman may be penalized for failing to conform to conventionally female stereotypes (by being aggressive, for example) but also penalized for conforming to such stereotypes (by not being aggressive enough). While men do not encounter the "double-bind," they may be at a greater risk for harassment if they defy stereotyped expectations of masculinity. As Professor Mary Ann Case observes, "The man who exhibits feminine qualities is doubly despised, for manifesting the disfavored qualities and for descending from his masculine gender privilege to do so."[5]

In addition to gender stereotyping, courts have had to determine whether other factual scenarios describe conduct engaged in "because of" sex. Faced with several common forms of sexual harassment, Judge Howell M. Melton decided *Robinson v. Jacksonville Shipyards, Inc.* and gave sex a broader definition. *Robinson* remains one of the most detailed and comprehensive evaluations of a sexual harassment case. The breadth and depth of *Robinson*'s analysis facilitates a thorough understanding of sexual harassment law as it developed in the years after *Meritor*. *Robinson* specifically enumerated three explanations for discrimination "because of . . . sex." Consider how the different types of offensive behavior described in the decision suggest different explanations for the conduct.

---

5. Case, *supra* note 2, at 3.

Robinson v. Jacksonville Shipyards, Inc.

760 F. Supp. 1486 (M.D. Fla. 1991)

MELTON, District Judge.

[Plaintiff Lois Robinson was a female welder employed by Jacksonville Shipyards, Inc. ("JSI"). She was one of a very small number of female skilled craftworkers employed by JSI, which ran several shipyards where workers repaired ships.]

. . . .

The JSI Working Environment

JSI is, in the words of its employees, "a boys club," and "more or less a man's world[.]" Women craftworkers are an extreme rarity. The company's EEO-1 reports from 1980 to 1987 typically show that women form less than 5 percent of the skilled crafts. . . . Leslie Albert, Lawanna Gail Banks, and Robinson each testified that she was the only woman in a crowd of men on occasions when each was sexually harassed at JSI. JSI has never employed a woman as a leaderman, quarterman, assistant foreman, foreman, superintendent, or coordinator. Nor has any woman ever held a position of Vice-President or President of JSI.

Pictures of nude and partially nude women appear throughout the JSI workplace in the form of magazines, plaques on the wall, photographs torn from magazines and affixed to the wall or attached to calendars supplied by advertising tool supply companies ("vendors' advertising calendars"). Two plaques consisting of pictures of naked women, affixed to wood and varnished, were introduced into evidence, and identified by several witnesses as having been on display for years at JSI in the fab shop area under the supervision of defendant Lovett.

Advertising calendars have been delivered for years to JSI by vendors with whom it does business. JSI officials then distribute the advertising calendars among JSI employees with the full knowledge and approval of JSI management. JSI employees are free to post these advertising calendars in the workplace. (It is not a condition of JSI's contracts with the vendors that the advertising calendars be posted.) . . . Generally speaking, these calendars feature women in various stages of undress and in sexually suggestive or submissive poses. . . .

. . . Welding foreman Fred Turner noted it was accepted at the shipyards for vendors to supply calendars of nude women, but he had never known of a vendor distributing a calendar of nude men and, if one did so, he would think the "son of a bitch" was "queer."

. . . .

Management employees from the very top down condoned these displays; often they had their own pictures. McIlwain, for example, has been aware for years of *Playboy-* and *Penthouse*-style pictures showing nude women posted in the workplace; he refused to issue a policy prohibiting the display of such pictures. Both

Brown and Stewart have encountered pictures of nude or partially nude women in the work environment at JSI. Nevertheless, both men have concluded, and agreed with each other, that there is nothing wrong with pictures of naked or partially naked women being posted in the JSI workplace. Ahlwardt kept a "pin-up" himself; Lovett, like some other foremen, had vendors' advertising calendars in his office. Coordinators, who are members of management, and who are responsible for ensuring that government contracts are performed to the satisfaction of the federal government, have had pornographic magazines in the desks of their trailers.

Sexual Harassment of Plaintiff

Robinson credibly testified to the extensive, pervasive posting of pictures depicting nude women, partially nude women, or sexual conduct and to the occurrence of other forms of harassing behavior perpetrated by her male coworkers and supervisors. . . . The Court also recognizes some limitations in Robinson's testimony. She tried to ignore some sexual comments. Her testimony included many episodes of harassment not previously disclosed in her answers to defendants' interrogatories because, as stated in those answers, the frequency with which the incidents occurred over the course of her employment made delineating every one a difficult task. Robinson's demeanor at trial reflected the emotional nature of her recollections. Moreover, the large number of male employees and the often surreptitious nature of the postings and graffiti writings left Robinson incapable of identifying many of her harassers. . . .

Robinson's testimony provides a vivid description of a visual assault on the sensibilities of female workers at JSI that did not relent during working hours. She credibly testified that the pervasiveness of the pictures left her unable to recount every example, but those pictures which she did describe illustrate the extent of this aspect of the work environment at JSI. She testified to seeing in the period prior to April 4, 1984, the three hundredth day prior to the filing of her EEOC charge:

(a) a picture of a woman, breasts and pubic area exposed, inside a drydock area in 1977 or 1978.

(b) a picture of a nude Black woman, pubic area exposed to reveal her labia, seen in the public locker room.

(c) drawings and graffiti on the walls, including a drawing depicting a frontal view of a nude female torso with the words "USDA Choice" written on it, at the Commercial Yard in the late 1970's or early 1980's, in an area where Robinson was assigned to work.

(d) a picture of a woman's pubic area with a meat spatula pressed on it, observed on a wall next to the sheetmetal shop at Mayport in the late 1970's.

(e) centerfold-style pictures in the Mayport Yard toolroom trailer, which Robinson saw daily in the necessary course of her work for over one month in the late 1970s. . . .

(f) pictures of nude or partially nude women in the fab shop lockers at the Commercial Yard in 1978 through 1980.

. . . .

(i) pictures in the shipfitters' shop at the Commercial Yard, in 1983, observed by Robinson while she was walking to the welding shop, including a frontal nude with a shaved pubic area and corseted nude with her breasts and buttocks area exposed. . . .

(j) a picture of a woman with her breasts exposed, on the outside of a shack on a ship in the Commercial Yard. . . .

Robinson's testimony concerning visual harassment in the period commencing April 4, 1984, includes:

(a) a picture of a nude woman with long blonde hair wearing high heels and holding a whip, waved around by a coworker, Freddie Dixon, in 1984, in an enclosed area where Robinson and approximately six men were working. . . .

(b) calendars posted in the pipe shop in the Commercial Yard, in 1983 or 1984, including a picture in which a nude woman was bending over with her buttocks and genitals exposed to view. . . .

(c) a picture of a nude woman with long blond hair sitting in front of a mirror brushing her hair, in a storage area on a ship. . . .

. . . .

(f) pictures in the shipfitters' trailer on board the U.S.S. Saratoga, in January 1985, including one picture of two nude women apparently engaged in lesbian sex. . . .

. . . .

(j) a picture of a nude woman left on the tool box where Robinson returned her tools, in the summer of 1986. The photograph depicted the woman's legs spread apart, knees bent up toward her chest, exposing her breasts and genitals. . . .

(k) pictures seen in the shipfitters' trailer, in 1986, including one of a woman with short blond hair, wearing a dark vest pulled back to expose her breasts. . . .

. . . .

(o) a drawing on a heater control box, approximately one foot square, of a nude woman with fluid coming from her genital area, in 1987, at the Commercial Yard.

. . . .

(q) a dart board with a drawing of a woman's breast with her nipple as the bull's eye, in 1987 or 1988, at the Commercial Yard.

. . . .

(s) pictures of nude and partially nude women posted in the engine room of the *M/V Splay*, in 1988, at the Commercial Yard, including a picture of a nude woman in a kneeling position and a calendar featuring photographs of nude women. . . .

(t) a shirt worn by the shop steward, in December 1988, with a drawing of bare female breasts and the words "DALLAS WHOREHOUSE" written on it.

In January 1985, following a complaint by Robinson concerning a calendar in the shipfitters' trailer, the words "Men Only" were painted on the door to that trailer.

Robinson also testified about comments of a sexual nature she recalled hearing at JSI from coworkers. In some instances these comments were made while she also was in the presence of the pictures of nude or partially nude women. Among the remarks Robinson recalled are: "Hey pussycat, come here and give me a whiff," "The more you lick it, the harder it gets," "I'd like to get in bed with that," "I'd like to have some of that," "Black women taste like sardines," "It doesn't hurt women to have sex right after childbirth," "That one there is mine," "Watch out for Chet. He's Chester the Molester" (referring to a cartoon character in a pornographic magazine who molests little girls), "You rate about an 8 or a 9 on a scale of 10[.]" She recalled one occasion on which a welder told her he wished her shirt would blow over her head so he could look, another occasion on which a fitter told her he wished her shirt was tighter (because he thought it would be sexier), an occasion on which a foreman candidate asked her to "come sit" on his lap, and innumerable occasions on which a coworker or supervisor called her "honey," "dear," "baby," "sugar," "sugar-booger," and "momma" instead of calling her by her name. Robinson additionally related her exposure to joking comments by male coworkers about a woman pipefitter whose initials are "V.D."

Robinson encountered particularly severe verbal harassment from a shipfitter, George Nelson ("Nelson"), while assigned to work with him on a number of different nights in 1986 at the Mayport Yard. Nelson regularly expressed his displeasure at working with Robinson, making such remarks as "women are only fit company for something that howls," and "there's nothing worse than having to work around women." On one occasion, Nelson responded to Robinson's inquiry regarding a work assignment by stating, "I don't know, I don't care where you go. You can go flash the sailors if you want." On other occasions, Nelson ridiculed Robinson in front of the Navy fire watch personnel. When Robinson confronted Nelson over her perception of his behavior as sexual harassment, Nelson denied he was engaging in harassment because he had not propositioned her for sexual favors. Nelson subsequently made Robinson's perception of "harassment" a new subject of ridicule and accused her of "crusading on a rabbit."

On one occasion, George Leach told an offensive joke in Robinson's presence, the subject matter of which concerned "boola-boola," a reference to sodomous rape. . . . Leach later teased Robinson in a threatening fashion by yelling "boola-boola" at her in the parking lot at JSI. Robinson subsequently learned that some shipfitters had dubbed her "boola-boola" as a nickname arising out of these events.

Robinson testified concerning the presence of abusive language written on the walls in her working areas in 1987 and 1988. Among this graffiti were the phrases "lick me you whore dog bitch," "eat me," and "pussy." This first phrase appeared on the wall over a spot where Robinson had left her jacket. The second phrase was freshly painted in Robinson's work area when she observed it. The third phrase appeared during a break after she left her work area to get a drink of water.

. . . .

Sexual Harassment of Other Female Craftworkers

The Court heard testimony from two of Robinson's female coworkers, Lawanna Gail Banks ("Banks") and Leslie Albert ("Albert"), concerning incidents of sexual harassment to which they were subjected, including incidents that did not occur in Robinson's presence. The Court heard this evidence for several reasons. First, as with the incidents outside the time frame of a Title VII complaint involving Robinson, incidents involving other female employees place the conduct at issue in context. The pervasiveness of conduct constituting sexual harassment outside Robinson's presence works to rebut the assertion that the conduct of which Robinson complains is isolated or rare. Second, the issue in this case is the nature of the work environment. This environment is shaped by more than the face-to-face encounters between Robinson and male coworkers and supervisors. The perception that the work environment is hostile can be influenced by the treatment of other persons of a plaintiff's protected class, even if that treatment is learned second-hand. Last, other incidents of sexual harassment are directly relevant to an employer's liability for the acts of employees and to the issue of an appropriate remedy for the sexual harassment perpetrated against Robinson.

Banks and Albert both confirmed the description of the work environment related by Robinson. Each of these other women endured many incidents of sexually harassing behavior. . . .

. . . .

Based on the foregoing, the Court finds that sexually harassing behavior occurred throughout the JSI working environment with both frequency and intensity over the relevant time period. Robinson did not welcome such behavior.

Effect of JSI Work Environment on Women

The foregoing evidence was supplemented with the testimony of various experts. Plaintiff called experts in the fields of sexual stereotyping and sexual harassment; defendants presented expert testimony on the relative offensiveness of pornographic materials to men and women.

. . . .

Conclusions of Law
Title VII

. . . .

Five elements comprise a claim of sexual discrimination based on the existence of a hostile work environment: (1) plaintiff belongs to a protected category; (2)

plaintiff was subject to unwelcome sexual harassment; (3) the harassment complained of was based upon sex; (4) the harassment complained of affected a term, condition or privilege of employment; and (5) *respondeat superior*, that is, defendants knew or should have known of the harassment and failed to take prompt, effective remedial action. [Ed. note: the standard expressed here for employer liability is no longer good law.]

Robinson indisputably belongs to a protected category.

The threshold for determining that sexually harassing conduct is unwelcome is "that the employee did not solicit or incite it, and . . . that the employee regarded the conduct as undesirable or offensive." *Henson*, 682 F.2d at 903 (citations omitted).

The relevant conduct in this case is the posting of pictures of nude and partially nude women in the workplace, the sexually demeaning remarks and jokes made by male workers, and harassment lacking a sexually explicit content such as the "Men Only" sign. The credible testimony of Robinson, corroborated by the observations of her supervisors and coworkers, attests to the offense she took at this behavior. Moreover, not a scintilla of evidence suggests that she solicited or incited the conduct. Robinson did not welcome the conduct of which she complains.

The third element imposes a requirement that Robinson "must show that but for the fact of her sex, she would not have been the object of harassment." This causation requirement encompasses several claims. For example, harassing behavior lacking a sexually explicit content but directed at women and motivated by animus against women satisfies this requirement. Second, sexual behavior directed at women will raise the inference that the harassment is based on their sex. A third category of actionable conduct is behavior that is not directed at a particular individual or group of individuals, but is disproportionately more offensive or demeaning to one sex. This third category describes behavior that creates a barrier to the progress of women in the workplace because it conveys the message that they do not belong, that they are welcome in the workplace only if they will subvert their identities to the sexual stereotypes prevalent in that environment. That Title VII outlaws such conduct is beyond peradventure.

The harassment of which Robinson complains was based upon her sex. The Findings of Fact reflect examples of the three aforementioned types of behavior. She suffered nonsexual harassing behavior from coworkers such as George Leach, who verbally abused or shunned her because she is a female. The "Men Only" sign also illustrates this type of harassment. She suffered incidents of directed sexual behavior both before and after she lodged her complaints about the pictures of nude and partially nude women. The pictures themselves fall into the third category, behavior that did not originate with the intent of offending women in the workplace (because no women worked in the jobs when the behavior began) but clearly has a disproportionately demeaning impact on the women now working at JSI. . . .

. . . .

Notes and Discussion

1. "But for" Theory Judge Melton acknowledged that offensive behavior is actionable when "the harassment complained of was based upon sex[.]" He adopted the "but for" theory to evaluate the facts: but for her sex, Robinson would not have been the target of sexual harassment. Did Judge Melton consider any other underlying theory to find harassment "because of . . . sex"? Explain. Did the men of Jacksonville Shipyards post pictures of nudes in an effort to target Robinson because of her sex? If not, what underlying theory of sexual harassment law justifies a finding of discrimination "because of . . . sex"?

While Judge Melton relied upon the "but for" paradigm, he found within it three types of claims. Sex-specific animus constitutes the first. Would Melton consider this category broad enough to include gender-specific animus, hostility directed towards persons who fail to conform to the traditional gender stereotypes of masculinity and femininity? Why or why not?

The third category Judge Melton described includes behavior, not necessarily directed at one individual, which disproportionately offends or demeans one sex. Does this last category fit neatly within the "but for" theory of sexual harassment? Would the behavior at Jacksonville Shipyards have fallen into this category if the offending photographs had included pictures of nude men? Isn't it possible that men could also be offended by nude pictures of women? Does this opinion foreclose the ability of a man to file a harassment complaint on that basis? Would complaints from men that they found the pictures offensive and that the pictures enforced traditional male stereotypes insulate the behavior from Title VII regulation?

2. Job Segregation The *Robinson* opinion noted that the plaintiff was one of only a very few skilled female craftworkers at her jobsite. Referencing the "Men Only" sign posted at one of the trailers, the court concluded that one of the forms of sexual harassment to which she was subjected consisted of nonsexual treatment motivated by animus against women. Does this conclusion suggest that sexual harassment is a more complex phenomenon than originally described in *Meritor*? Is such harassment just as likely to be based on a need to subordinate and exclude women from male-oriented work spaces as it is to be based on sexual desire?

Consider the observations of Professor Vicki Schultz:

> The prevailing paradigm privileges conduct thought to be motivated by sexual designs—such as sexual advances—as the core sex- or gender-based harassment. Yet much of the gender-based hostility and abuse that women (and some men) endure at work is neither driven by the desire for sexual relations nor even sexual in content.
>
> . . . .
>
> . . . . Indeed, many of the most prevalent forms of harassment are actions that are designed to maintain work—particularly the more highly rewarded

lines of work—as bastions of masculine competence and authority. Every day, in workplaces all over the country, men uphold the image that their jobs demand masculine mastery by acting to undermine their female colleagues' perceived (or sometimes even actual) competence to do the work. The forms of such harassment are wide-ranging. They include characterizing the work as appropriate for men only; denigrating women's performance or ability to master the job; providing patronizing forms of help in performing the job; withholding the training, information, or opportunity to learn to do the job well; engaging in deliberate work sabotage; providing sexist evaluations of women's performance or denying them deserved promotions; isolating women from the social networks that confer a sense of belonging; denying women the perks or privileges that are required for success; assigning women sex-stereotyped service tasks that lie outside their job descriptions (such as cleaning or serving coffee); engaging in taunting, pranks, and other forms of hazing designed to remind women that they are different and out of place; and physically assaulting or threatening to assault the women who dare to fight back. Of course, making a woman the object of sexual attention can also work to undermine her image and self-confidence as a capable worker. Yet, much of the time, harassment assumes a form that has little or nothing to do with sexuality but everything to do with gender.[6]

Does it matter whether harassment is motivated by subordination/exclusion or desire? Which is easier for the law to comprehend? Think about these questions in the context of same-sex harassment, addressed in the next section.

C. Same-Sex Harassment as Discrimination Based on Sex

Another question about when harassment is "based on" a plaintiff's sex arises in the context of same-sex harassment. Although several lower courts had determined that same-sex harassment was not within the purview of Title VII, a unanimous Supreme Court held otherwise.

Oncale v. Sundowner Offshore Services, Inc.
523 U.S. 75 (1998)

Justice SCALIA delivered the opinion of the Court.

This case presents the question whether workplace harassment can violate Title VII's prohibition against "discriminat[ion] ... because of ... sex," 42 U.S.C. § 2000e-2(a)(1), when the harasser and the harassed employee are of the same sex.

I

The District Court having granted summary judgment for respondents, we must assume the facts to be as alleged by petitioner Joseph Oncale. The precise details

---

6. Vicki Schultz, *Reconceptualizing Sexual Harassment*, 107 YALE L.J. 1683, 1686–87 (1998).

are irrelevant to the legal point we must decide, and in the interest of both brevity and dignity we shall describe them only generally. In late October 1991, Oncale was working for respondent Sundowner Offshore Services, Inc., on a Chevron U.S.A., Inc., oil platform in the Gulf of Mexico. He was employed as a roustabout on an eight-man crew which included respondents John Lyons, Danny Pippen, and Brandon Johnson. Lyons, the crane operator, and Pippen, the driller, had supervisory authority. On several occasions, Oncale was forcibly subjected to sex-related, humiliating actions against him by Lyons, Pippen, and Johnson in the presence of the rest of the crew. Pippen and Lyons also physically assaulted Oncale in a sexual manner, and Lyons threatened him with rape.

Oncale's complaints to supervisory personnel produced no remedial action; in fact, the company's Safety Compliance Clerk, Valent Hohen, told Oncale that Lyons and Pippen "picked [on] him all the time too," and called him a name suggesting homosexuality. Oncale eventually quit—asking that his pink slip reflect that he "voluntarily left due to sexual harassment and verbal abuse." When asked at his deposition why he left Sundowner, Oncale stated: "I felt that if I didn't leave my job, that I would be raped or forced to have sex."

Oncale filed a complaint against Sundowner in the United States District Court for the Eastern District of Louisiana, alleging that he was discriminated against in his employment because of his sex. Relying on the Fifth Circuit's decision in *Garcia v. Elf Atochem North America,* the District Court held that "Mr. Oncale, a male, has no cause of action under Title VII for harassment by male co-workers." On appeal, a panel of the Fifth Circuit concluded that *Garcia* was binding Circuit precedent, and affirmed. We granted certiorari.

II

. . . .

Title VII's prohibition of discrimination "because of . . . sex" protects men as well as women . . . , and in the related context of racial discrimination in the workplace we have rejected any conclusive presumption that an employer will not discriminate against members of his own race. . . . If our precedents leave any doubt on the question, we hold today that nothing in Title VII necessarily bars a claim of discrimination "because of . . . sex" merely because the plaintiff and the defendant (or the person charged with acting on behalf of the defendant) are of the same sex.

Courts have had little trouble with that principle in cases . . . where an employee claims to have been passed over for a job or promotion. But when the issue arises in the context of a "hostile environment" sexual harassment claim, the state and federal courts have taken a bewildering variety of stances. Some, like the Fifth Circuit in this case, have held that same-sex sexual harassment claims are never cognizable under Title VII. Other decisions say that such claims are actionable only if the plaintiff can prove that the harasser is homosexual (and thus presumably motivated by sexual desire). Still others suggest that workplace harassment that is sexual in content is always actionable, regardless of the harasser's sex, sexual orientation, or motivations.

We see no justification in the statutory language or our precedents for a categorical rule excluding same-sex harassment claims from the coverage of Title VII. As some courts have observed, male-on-male sexual harassment in the workplace was assuredly not the principal evil Congress was concerned with when it enacted Title VII. But statutory prohibitions often go beyond the principal evil to cover reasonably comparable evils, and it is ultimately the provisions of our laws rather than the principal concerns of our legislators by which we are governed. Title VII prohibits "discrimination . . . because of . . . sex" in the "terms" or "conditions" of employment. Our holding that this includes sexual harassment must extend to sexual harassment of any kind that meets the statutory requirements.

Respondents and their *amici* contend that recognizing liability for same-sex harassment will transform Title VII into a general civility code for the American workplace. But that risk is no greater for same-sex than for opposite-sex harassment, and is adequately met by careful attention to the requirements of the statute. Title VII does not prohibit all verbal or physical harassment in the workplace; it is directed only at "*discrimination* . . . because of . . . sex." We have never held that workplace harassment, even harassment between men and women, is automatically discrimination because of sex merely because the words used have sexual content or connotations. "The critical issue, Title VII's text indicates, is whether members of one sex are exposed to disadvantageous terms or conditions of employment to which members of the other sex are not exposed." *Harris, supra,* at 25 (GINSBURG, J., concurring).

Courts and juries have found the inference of discrimination easy to draw in most male-female sexual harassment situations, because the challenged conduct typically involves explicit or implicit proposals of sexual activity; it is reasonable to assume those proposals would not have been made to someone of the same sex. The same chain of inference would be available to a plaintiff alleging same-sex harassment, if there were credible evidence that the harasser was homosexual. But harassing conduct need not be motivated by sexual desire to support an inference of discrimination on the basis of sex. A trier of fact might reasonably find such discrimination, for example, if a female target is harassed in such sex-specific and derogatory terms by another woman as to make it clear that the harasser is motivated by general hostility to the presence of women in the workplace. A same-sex harassment plaintiff may also, of course, offer direct comparative evidence about how the alleged harasser treated members of both sexes in a mixed-sex workplace. Whatever evidentiary route the plaintiff chooses to follow, he or she must always prove that the conduct at issue was not merely tinged with offensive sexual connotations, but actually constituted "*discrimination* . . . because of . . . sex."

And there is another requirement that prevents Title VII from expanding into a general civility code: As we emphasized in *Meritor* and *Harris,* the statute does not reach genuine but innocuous differences in the ways men and women routinely interact with members of the same sex and of the opposite sex. The prohibition of harassment on the basis of sex requires neither asexuality nor androgyny in the workplace; it forbids only behavior so objectively offensive as to alter the "conditions" of the target's employment. "Conduct that is not severe or pervasive enough to create an objectively hostile or abusive work environment—an environment that a reasonable person would find hostile or abusive—is beyond Title VII's purview." *Harris,* 510 U.S., at 21, citing *Meritor,* 477 U.S., at 67. We have always regarded that requirement as crucial, and as sufficient to ensure that courts and juries do not mistake ordinary socializing in the workplace—such as male-on-male horseplay or intersexual flirtation—for discriminatory "conditions of employment."

We have emphasized, moreover, that the objective severity of harassment should be judged from the perspective of a reasonable person in the plaintiff's position, considering "all the circumstances." *Harris, supra,* at 23. In same-sex (as in all) harassment cases, that inquiry requires careful consideration of the social context in which particular behavior occurs and is experienced by its target. A professional football player's working environment is not severely or pervasively abusive, for example, if the coach smacks him on the buttocks as he heads onto the field—even if the same behavior would reasonably be experienced as abusive by the coach's secretary (male or female) back at the office. The real social impact of workplace behavior often depends on a constellation of surrounding circumstances, expectations, and relationships which are not fully captured by a simple recitation of the words used or the physical acts performed. Common sense, and an appropriate sensitivity to social context, will enable courts and juries to distinguish between simple teasing or roughhousing among members of the same sex, and conduct which a reasonable person in the plaintiff's position would find severely hostile or abusive.

III

Because we conclude that sex discrimination consisting of same-sex sexual harassment is actionable under Title VII, the judgment of the Court of Appeals for the Fifth Circuit is reversed, and the case is remanded for further proceedings consistent with this opinion.

It is so ordered.

Notes and Discussion

1. Same-Sex Harassment and "Sex" Does the unanimous *Oncale* opinion attempt to define sex? Specifically, does Justice Scalia consider that the term "sex" might include anything other than, or in addition to, biological or chromosomal sex? Quoting Justice Ginsburg's concurrence in *Harris,* Scalia focused on "whether members of one sex are exposed to disadvantageous terms or conditions of employment to which members of the other sex are not exposed." Oncale's was a single-sex workplace. Shouldn't that condition make it impossible for Oncale to prove harassment because of sex? What if there had been a woman at Oncale's workplace who was *not* the target of harassment? What if she were?

2. Same-Sex Harassment and Sexual Orientation Recall that *Meritor* held that when perpetrators (presumably men) target women with sexual behavior, one may infer sex-based harassment. Does such an inference reveal a heterosexual bias?

Justice Scalia wrote that an inference of sex harassment could be made in a same-sex harassment case if there were credible evidence that the perpetrator was homosexual. Is this the only way to reach such an inference? Notice that there was no discussion in the *Oncale* opinion about whether the perpetrators of the harassment were gay. Why not? Earlier courts had permitted a male plaintiff to state a claim against a harasser of the same sex only if he could claim that his harasser was homosexual and motivated by actual sexual desire. For example, see *Wrightson v. Pizza Hut of America, Inc.* which held:

> We first addressed the issue of same-sex sexual harassment only recently in *McWilliams v. Fairfax County Board of Supervisors*. There, we held that no Title VII cause of action for "hostile work environment" sexual harassment lies when both the perpetrator and target of the harassment are heterosexuals of the same sex. In *McWilliams,* however, we expressly reserved the question of whether Title VII prohibits same-sex "hostile work environment" harassment where the perpetrator of the harassment is homosexual. Today, we squarely address this issue, and hold that a claim under Title VII for same-sex "hostile work environment" harassment may lie where the perpetrator of the sexual harassment is homosexual.[7]

3. Stereotyping and Same-Sex Harassment Justice Scalia participated in the *Price Waterhouse* decision, joining Justice Kennedy's dissent. Kennedy wrote, "I think it important to stress that Title VII creates no independent cause of action for sex stereotyping. Evidence of use by decision-makers of sex stereotypes is, of course, quite relevant to the question of discriminatory intent. The ultimate question, however, is whether discrimination caused the plaintiff's harm."[8] Was Justice Scalia's position in *Price Waterhouse* concerning gender stereotypes consistent with his opinion in *Oncale*?

Several *Oncale* commentators have wondered vaguely if sex stereotyping motivated the aggressors. See, e.g., Ellen Goodman, *Sexual Harassment Isn't about Sex; It's about Stereotypes*, Boston Globe, December 7, 1997, at C7 (remarking, "Who knows why they went after Oncale. All of these men are heterosexuals. Was it because Oncale, the father of two, was small?"); Morning Edition, NPR Radio Broadcast, March 5, 1998 (noting, "Nobody seems to know why Oncale . . . was singled out for this treatment except that he's a small man—5'4" tall—and perhaps seemed easy to pick on."); but see Mary Judice, *Isolated Incidents*, New Orleans Times-Picayune, January 25, 1998, at F1 (explaining, "With a wiry, 5'4" frame, Oncale says he doesn't think his size has anything to do with the alleged abuse.").

---

7. 99 F.3d 138, 141 (4th Cir. 1996).

8. *Price Waterhouse*, 490 U.S. at 294 (Kennedy, J., dissenting).

3 · REFINING THE PRIMA FACIE CASE

4. An "Equal Opportunity" Harasser? What ramifications would the *Oncale* decision have for a workplace in which both men and women are sexually harassed? If a person targets sexually oriented behavior toward members of both sexes, can that be considered harassment "because of sex"? Most courts would answer this question in the negative. For example, in *Holman v. Indiana*, the court opined:

> In *Oncale*, the Supreme Court reiterated that "Title VII's prohibition of discrimination 'because of . . . sex' protects men as well as women" and it held that this prohibition applies to the same-sex harasser, whether or not that harasser is motivated by sexual desire. In doing so, it underscored that the touchstone of Title VII is, of course, discrimination or disparate treatment. . . .
>
> The Court explicated what it meant by "discrimination" in sexual harassment cases; it is to be determined on a gender-comparative basis: "The **critical issue**, Title VII's text indicates, is whether members of one sex are exposed to disadvantageous terms or conditions of employment *to which members of the other sex are not exposed*." . . . Thus a violation of Title VII only occurs because of sex discrimination. Both before and after *Oncale*, we have noted that because Title VII is premised on eliminating *discrimination*, inappropriate conduct that is inflicted on both sexes, or is inflicted regardless of sex, is outside the statute's ambit. Title VII does not cover the "equal opportunity" or "bisexual" harasser, then, because such a person is not *discriminating* on the basis of sex. He is not treating one sex better (or worse) than the other; he is treating both sexes the same (albeit badly).[9]

5. Reasonableness and Common Sense The *Oncale* Court ruled that the offensiveness of the conduct should be judged "from the perspective of a reasonable person in the plaintiff's position, considering 'all the circumstances.'" Did Scalia indicate a gender-neutral person? Or did the Court determine that the sex of the target dictates the sex of the "reasonable person"? Or is there another interpretation of what the court meant?

The Court also suggests that "[c]ommon sense, and an appropriate sensitivity to social context, will enable courts and juries to distinguish between simple teasing or roughhousing among members of the same sex[.]" Is this assertion true? Professor Jennifer Drobac argues that reliance on these factors actually contributes to "the potential for prevalent, biased community attitudes to insulate discriminatory practices from attack."[10]

6. Facts *Oncale* deliberately refused to engage with the underlying facts of the case. As Justice Scalia states at the outset, "The precise details are irrelevant to the legal point we must decide, and in the interest of both brevity and dignity we shall

---

9. 211 F.3d 399, 402 (7th Cir. 2000).

10. Jennifer A. Drobac, *The* Oncale *Opinion: A Pansexual Response*, 30 MCGEORGE L. REV. 1269, 1270 (1999).

describe them only generally." He then makes only cursory references to the facts that, on multiple occasions "Oncale was forcibly subjected to sex-related, humiliating actions against him . . . in the presence of the rest of the crew." He also notes, briefly, that Oncale was "physically assaulted . . . in a sexual manner" by his co-workers and threatened with rape. The appellate court gave a more complete recitation of the facts:

> Oncale alleges that the harassment included Pippen and Johnson restraining him while Lyons placed his penis on Oncale's neck, on one occasion, and on Oncale's arm, on another occasion; threats of homosexual rape by Lyons and Pippen; and the use of force by Lyons to push a bar of soap into Oncale's anus while Pippen restrained Oncale as he was showering on Sundowner premises.[11]

Scalia's rationale for his reticence was that the issue was purely a legal one: whether same-sex sexual harassment is covered by Title VII. Would more detailed facts have contributed to an understanding of the case? Of the legal issues? Justice Scalia was the author of *Bowers v. Hardwick*,[12] which permitted states to criminalize homosexual sodomy. Does Scalia's refusal to provide these details "in the interest of . . . dignity" in fact betray a degree of homophobia, or at the very least discomfort with the concept of homosexual activity?

7. *Oncale* **Revisited** The appellate court remanded the case for further proceedings consistent with the opinion, but the case settled just days before trial. The parties agreed to keep the terms of the settlement confidential.[13]

D. Sexual Orientation Discrimination as Conduct Based on Sex

Sexual orientation is not among the protected characteristics in Title VII. A number of states have added sexual orientation to their state civil rights statutes, some with respect to only public-sector employers and some with respect to both the public and the private sectors. Those states include California, Connecticut, Hawaii, Massachusetts, Minnesota, New Jersey, New Mexico, New York, Oregon, Pennsylvania, Rhode Island, Vermont, Washington, and Wisconsin. In 1996, Congress defeated by one vote the Employee Non-Discrimination Act (ENDA), legislation that would have added sexual orientation to the list of characteristics recognized under Title VII.

In May 1998, President Clinton added sexual orientation to the list of protected characteristics included in an antidiscrimination order for federal employees. Executive Order 11,478 (as amended).

---

11. 83 F.3d 118, 118–19 (5th Cir. 1996).

12. 478 U.S. 186 (1986).

13. Mary Judice, *LA Offshore Worker Settles Sex Suit: Harassment Case Made History in Supreme Court*, New Orleans Times-Picayune (Oct. 24, 1998), at C1.

On July 15, 2015, the EEOC issued an administrative ruling that Title VII's prohibition of employment discrimination on the basis of sex extends to claims based upon sexual orientation. *Baldwin v. Foxx*, Appeal No. 0120133080. In support of its decision, the EEOC stated that "sexual orientation" is a concept that "cannot be defined or understood without reference to sex." Further, noting that courts have already consistently prohibited "discrimination based on an employee's association with a person of another race," the EEOC stated that sexual orientation discrimination is similarly prohibited "because it is associational discrimination on the basis of sex." Finally, the EEOC concluded that sexual orientation discrimination falls within the ambit of Title VII because "it necessarily involves discrimination based on gender stereotypes[.]"

In July 2016, the EEOC issued a bulletin confirming the agency's protection for members of the LGBTQ community against employment discrimination and retaliation for reporting discrimination. EEOC protections extend to both federal and private sector employees, regardless of any state and local laws that suggest otherwise. The EEOC has not formally reversed its position. However, President Trump's Department of Justice has recently made clear that it does *not* consider sexual orientation discrimination to fall under Title VII's prohibition against sex discrimination.

Nevertheless, a number of plaintiffs have brought cases under Title VII, claiming that they were harassed or discriminated against because of their sexual orientation, but that such discrimination actually constitutes sex discrimination. For decades, courts refused to hear these cases, concluding that "sex discrimination" did not encompass "sexual orientation discrimination." For example, in *Dillon v. Frank*, the Sixth Circuit refused to hear the case of a gay man who alleged that his co-workers called him a "fag," wrote graffiti saying that he "sucks dicks," and physically assaulted him. The court explained:

> The question Dillon poses for us is whether . . . a hostile working environment involving sexual epithets and directed at a person because of perceived sexual behavior (homosexuality) is . . . proscribed by Title VII. In effect, Dillon asks us to define "because of sex" to mean "because of anything relating to being male or female, to sexual roles, or to sexual behavior." Because we believe that only discrimination based on being male or female is prohibited by Title VII, and that the cases proscribing hostile environment sexual harassment are not to the contrary, we affirm the district court [in dismissing the suit].[14]

In a 2017 refusal to hire case, *Hively v. Ivy Tech Community College*, the Seventh Circuit ruled that Title VII prohibits discrimination based on sexual orientation.[15] No court has found, however, sex-based harassment because of a plaintiff's sexual orientation. In the following Ninth Circuit case, a sex-stereotyping theory

14. 952 F.2d 403, No. 90-2290 at *4 (6th Cir. 1992).
15. 830 F.3d 698 (7th Cir. 2017).

succeeded for a man harassed because he was effeminate. The plaintiff relied on the *Price Waterhouse* precedent.

Nichols v. Azteca Restaurant Enterprises, Inc.
256 F.3d 864 (9th Cir. 2001)

GOULD, Circuit Judge:

Antonio Sanchez brought this action against his former employer, Azteca Restaurant Enterprises, Inc. . . . Sanchez claimed that he was verbally harassed by some male co-workers and a supervisor because he was effeminate and did not meet their views of a male stereotype. Sanchez further asserted that he was terminated in retaliation for opposing the harassment. Following a bench trial, the district court entered judgment in favor of Azteca on all claims.

. . . .

I

Azteca operates a chain of restaurants in Washington and Oregon. It employed Sanchez from October 1991 to July 1995. Sanchez at first worked as a host in Azteca's Burien restaurant, and later worked as a food server at the Southcenter restaurant.

Throughout his tenure at Azteca, Sanchez was subjected to a relentless campaign of insults, name-calling, and vulgarities. Male co-workers and a supervisor repeatedly referred to Sanchez in Spanish and English as "she" and "her." Male co-workers mocked Sanchez for walking and carrying his serving tray "like a woman," and taunted him in Spanish and English as, among other things, a "faggot" and a "fucking female whore." The remarks were not stray or isolated. Rather, the abuse occurred at least once a week and often several times a day.

. . . .

. . . Sanchez reported and described the specifics of the harassment to Azteca's human resources director, Arnie Serna. Sanchez made his complaint during a meeting that had been convened to address a fight between Sanchez and a co-worker. Sanchez, Serna, and the Southcenter general manager were present. During the meeting, Sanchez told Serna that he had complained to the Southcenter general manager many times, and expressed concern that the harassment would continue to be ignored.

. . . .

. . . [A] couple of months after his meeting with Serna, Sanchez became involved in a heated argument with an assistant manager, and walked off the job. He was fired for leaving work in the middle of his shift. A month later, Sanchez filed a charge of discrimination with the EEOC. Thereafter, he initiated this lawsuit.

Following a bench trial, the district court concluded that Sanchez had not been subjected to a hostile environment. Stating that it gave "greater credibility to the defense witnesses and their testimony," the court concluded that Sanchez's workplace had been neither objectively nor subjectively hostile, and that the alleged harassment did not take place "because of sex." . . .

. . . .

III

. . . .

. . . We disagree with each of these conclusions and, where applicable, the clearly erroneous findings upon which they are based.

. . . .

C. Because of Sex

Sexual harassment is actionable under Title VII to the extent it occurs "because of" the plaintiff's sex. Sanchez asserts that the verbal abuse at issue was based upon the perception that he is effeminate and, therefore, occurred because of sex. In short, Sanchez contends that he was harassed because he failed to conform to a male stereotype.

Sanchez's theory derives from *Price Waterhouse v. Hopkins*, in which the Supreme Court held that a woman who was denied partnership in an accounting firm because she did not match a sex stereotype had an actionable claim under Title VII. Hopkins, the plaintiff in *Price Waterhouse*, was described by various partners as "macho," in need of "a course in charm school," "a lady using foul language," and someone who had been "a tough-talking somewhat masculine hard-nosed manager." Hopkins was advised that she could improve her partnership chances if she would "walk more femininely, talk more femininely, dress more femininely, wear make-up, have her hair styled, and wear jewelry." Writing for the plurality, Justice Brennan held that "[i]n the specific context of sex stereotyping, an employer who acts on the basis of a belief that a woman cannot be aggressive, or that she must not be, has acted on the basis of gender."

Sanchez contends that the holding in *Price Waterhouse* applies with equal force to a man who is discriminated against for acting too feminine. We agree.

At its essence, the systematic abuse directed at Sanchez reflected a belief that Sanchez did not act as a man should act. Sanchez was attacked for walking and carrying his tray "like a woman"—i.e., for having feminine mannerisms. Sanchez was derided for not having sexual intercourse with a waitress who was his friend. Sanchez's male co-workers and one of his supervisors repeatedly reminded Sanchez that he did not conform to their gender-based stereotypes, referring to him as "she" and "her." And, the most vulgar name-calling directed at Sanchez was cast in female terms. We conclude that this verbal abuse was closely linked to gender.

Price Waterhouse sets a rule that bars discrimination on the basis of sex stereotypes. That rule squarely applies to preclude the harassment here. . . .

Following *Price Waterhouse*, we hold that the verbal abuse at issue occurred because of sex. Because we hold that Sanchez has established each element of his hostile environment claim, we further hold that the conduct of Sanchez's co-workers and supervisor constituted actionable harassment. . . .

. . . .

Notes and Discussion

1. Stereotyping The *Azteca* opinion relies heavily on *Price Waterhouse*'s theory of sex stereotyping as sex discrimination. Will this reasoning apply in most or every case of sexual orientation harassment, on the argument that every gay or lesbian person fails to conform to the heteronormative stereotype? If so, is this merely bootstrapping sexual orientation claims into claims that are supposed to be based on sex?

Professor Francisco Valdes argues that *failing* to recognize such stereotyped discrimination as sex discrimination creates a sexual orientation "loophole." He contends:

> The bottom line of the doctrinal status quo is that courts can and do (re)characterize sex and gender discrimination as sexual orientation discrimination virtually at will. This practice employs sexual orientation to create a loophole for sex and gender biases, which makes it extremely difficult (if not impossible) fully to eradicate those biases. Of course, this loophole is made viable by the continuing legality of sexual orientation biases; the loophole can exist only because discrimination based on sexual orientation remains generally legal. . . . [T]his loophole effectively licenses various acts and strains of conflationary discrimination that are based on sex and on gender, as well as on sexual orientation. Consequently, the conflation contorts the analysis and distorts the results of cases raising actual or perceived sex and/or gender and/or sexual orientation issues.[16]

Is Valdes correct?

2. Association Theory Some courts have recognized another theory under which sexual orientation discrimination can be considered sex discrimination. This theory holds that a homosexual plaintiff is targeted for discrimination or harassment because of the sex of the person with whom s/he associates. The Seventh Circuit's opinion in *Hively v. Ivy Tech Community College* is a good example of such reasoning. The court held:

> It is now accepted that a person who is discriminated against because of the protected characteristic of one with whom she associates is actually being disadvantaged because of her own traits. This line of cases began with *Loving [v. Virginia]*, in which the Supreme Court held that "restricting the freedom to marry solely because of racial classifications violates the central

---

16. Francisco Valdes, *Queers, Sissies, Dykes, and Tomboys: Deconstructing the Conflation of "Sex," "Gender," and "Sexual Orientation" in Euro-American Law and Society*, 83 Cal. L. Rev. 1, 24 (1995).

meaning of the Equal Protection Clause." The Court rejected the argument that miscegenation statutes do not violate equal protection because they "punish equally both the white and the Negro participants in an interracial marriage." When dealing with a statute containing racial classifications, it wrote, "the fact of equal application does not immunize the statute from the very heavy burden of justification" required by the Fourteenth Amendment for lines drawn by race.

. . . .

   . . . The Court in *Loving* recognized that equal application of a law that prohibited conduct only between members of different races did not save it. Changing the race of one partner made a difference in determining the legality of the conduct, and so the law rested on "distinctions drawn according to race," which were unjustifiable and racially discriminatory. So too, here. If we were to change the sex of one partner in a lesbian relationship, the outcome would be different. This reveals that the discrimination rests on distinctions drawn according to sex. . . .[17]

3. Sexualized Workplace Conduct Most people would agree that abusive sexual behavior does not belong in the workplace. Should courts adopt a blanket rule that such conduct is automatically based on sex, regardless of the specific motive of the perpetrator? Would this be consistent with Title VII?

4. Sexual Orientation — A Protected Category? All of the opinions above — even the ones that would deny coverage of sexual orientation — seem to agree that discrimination or harassment based on sexual orientation is wrong. The majority opinion in *Hively*, as well as Judge Posner's concurrence, point out the tremendous changes in law and public attitudes about sexual orientation that have occurred in the last 15 years. What explains Congress's failure to amend Title VII to include it as a protected category or the Supreme Court's failure to address the issue? In light of this situation, what are lower courts to do when faced with harassment that is clearly based on sexual orientation? How do you think the Supreme Court, which affirmed a right of same-sex marriage in 2014, would rule on this issue?

   The Court recently announced that it has accepted two cases on this issue for the term that begins in October 2019. In *Zarda v. Altitude Express, Inc.*, the Second Circuit, sitting en banc, held that a gay man could bring a claim under Title VII alleging that he was fired due to his sexual orientation.[18] In *Bostock v. Clayton County Board of Commissioners*, the Eleventh Circuit upheld the dismissal of a gay man's Title VII claim, holding summarily that "[d]ischarge for homosexuality is *not* prohibited by Title VII."[19]

---

17. 853 F.3d 339, 347–49 (7th Cir. 2017).
18. 883 F.3d 100 (2d Cir. 2018).
19. 723 Fed. Appx. 964 (11th Cir. 2018).

E. Gender Identity and Transgender Discrimination as Conduct Based on Sex

In the years since *Oncale*, courts have had similar disagreements over the issue of whether harassment based on gender identity and trans status constitute discrimination "because of . . . sex," covered under Title VII. Initially, courts took the view that discrimination against trans people was not within the statute's purview. For example, in *Ulane v. Eastern Airlines, Inc.,* the Seventh Circuit ordered the trial court to dismiss a claim brought by a transgender woman who was fired from her job after she transitioned from male to female. Note the disdainful tone the *Ulane* court uses to describe gender identity and the transitioning process. The court stated:

> Other courts have held that the term "sex" as used in the statute is not synonymous with "sexual preference." The district court recognized this, and agreed that homosexuals and transvestites do not enjoy Title VII protection, but distinguished transsexuals as persons who, unlike homosexuals and transvestites, have sexual *identity* problems; the judge agreed that the term "sex" does not comprehend "sexual preference," but held that it does comprehend "sexual identity." The district judge based this holding on his finding that "sex is not a cut-and-dried matter of chromosomes," but is in part a psychological question—a question of self-perception; and in part a social matter—a question of how society perceives the individual. The district judge further supported his broad view of Title VII's coverage by recognizing Title VII as a remedial statute to be liberally construed. He concluded that it is reasonable to hold that the statutory word "sex" literally and scientifically applies to transsexuals even if it does not apply to homosexuals or transvestites. We must disagree.

> Even though Title VII is a remedial statute, and even though some may define "sex" in such a way as to mean an individual's "sexual identity," our responsibility is to interpret this congressional legislation and determine what Congress intended when it decided to outlaw discrimination based on sex. The district judge did recognize that Congress manifested an intention to exclude homosexuals from Title VII coverage. Nonetheless, the judge defended his conclusion that Ulane's broad interpretation of the term "sex" was reasonable and could therefore be applied to the statute by noting that transsexuals are different than homosexuals, and that Congress never considered whether it should include or exclude transsexuals. While we recognize distinctions among homosexuals, transvestites, and transsexuals, we believe that the same reasons for holding that the first two groups do not enjoy Title VII coverage apply with equal force to deny protection for transsexuals.

> . . . .

> The trial judge originally found only that Eastern had discriminated against Ulane under Count II as a transsexual. The judge subsequently

amended his findings to hold that Ulane is also female and has been discriminated against on this basis. Even if we accept the district judge's holding that Ulane is female, he made no factual findings necessary to support his conclusion that Eastern discriminated against her on this basis. All the district judge said was that his previous "findings and conclusions concerning sexual discrimination against the plaintiff by Eastern Airlines, Inc. apply with equal force whether plaintiff be regarded as a transsexual or a female." This is insufficient to support a finding that Ulane was discriminated against because she is *female* since the district judge's previous findings all centered around his conclusion that Eastern did not want "[a] *transsexual* in the cockpit" (emphasis added).

Ulane is entitled to any personal belief about her sexual identity she desires. After the surgery, hormones, appearance changes, and a new Illinois birth certificate and FAA pilot's certificate, it may be that society, as the trial judge found, considers Ulane to be female. But even if one believes that a woman can be so easily created from what remains of a man, that does not decide this case. If Eastern had considered Ulane to be female and had discriminated against her because she was female (*i.e.*, Eastern treated females less favorably than males), then the argument might be made that Title VII applied, . . . but that is not this case. It is clear from the evidence that if Eastern did discriminate against Ulane, it was not because she is female, but because Ulane is a transsexual—a biological male who takes female hormones, cross-dresses, and has surgically altered parts of her body to make it appear to be female.[20]

More recently, courts have taken a different approach, both in tone and analysis, to such discrimination.

The following case, like *Hively*, demonstrates how a modern court disavows precedent and permits a trans plaintiff to pursue a sex-based discrimination claim.

Schroer v. Billington
577 F. Supp. 2d 293 (D.D.C. 2008)

JAMES ROBERTSON, District Judge.

. . . [The Plaintiff, Diane Schroer, applied for a position as a Specialist in Terrorism and Internal Crime with the Congressional Research Service at the Library of Congress. Her extensive and distinguished military service background made her particularly well-qualified for this position. Schroer was working with a licensed clinical social worker to develop a medically appropriate plan for transitioning from male to female at the time she applied. Because she had not yet changed her legal name or begun presenting as a woman, she applied for the position as "David J.

---

20. 742 F.2d 1081, 1084–85, 1087 (7th Cir. 1984).

Schroer," her legal name at the time. She was offered the position. After she accepted it but before she began work, she notified CRS officials about her pending transition. The offer was withdrawn. Schroer sued.]

. . . .

II.

. . . .

A. Sex stereotyping

. . . .

After *Price Waterhouse*, numerous federal courts have concluded that punishing employees for failure to conform to sex stereotypes is actionable sex discrimination under Title VII.

Following this line of cases, the Sixth Circuit has held that discrimination against transsexuals is a form of sex stereotyping prohibited by *Price Waterhouse* itself:

> After *Price Waterhouse*, an employer who discriminates against women because, for instance, they do not wear dresses or makeup, is engaging in sex discrimination that would not occur but for the victim's sex. It follows that employers who discriminate against men because they do wear dresses and makeup, or otherwise act femininely, are also engaging in discrimination, because the discrimination would not occur but for the victim's sex.
>
> . . .
>
> [D]iscrimination against a plaintiff who is transsexual — and therefore fails to act and/or identify with his or her gender — is no different from the discrimination directed against Ann Hopkins in Price Waterhouse, who, in sex-stereotypical terms, did not act like a woman. Sex stereotyping based on a person's gender nonconforming behavior is impermissible discrimination, irrespective of the cause of that behavior.

Smith v. Salem 378 F.3d 566, 574–75 (6th Cir. 2004).

. . . .

Schroer's case indeed rests on direct evidence, and compelling evidence, that the Library's hiring decision was infected by sex stereotypes. . . . [Charlotte] Preece [the decisionmaker] testified that her difficulty comprehending Schroer's decision to undergo a gender transition was heightened because she viewed David Schroer not just as a man, but, in light of her Special Forces background, as a particularly masculine kind of man. Preece's perception of David Schroer as especially masculine made it all the more difficult for her to visualize Diane Schroer as anyone other than a man in a dress. Preece admitted that she believed that others at CRS, as well as Members of Congress and their staffs, would not take Diane Schroer seriously because they, too, would view her as a man in women's clothing.

What makes Schroer's sex stereotyping theory difficult is that, when the plaintiff is transsexual, direct evidence of discrimination based on sex stereotypes may look a great deal like discrimination based on transsexuality itself, a characteristic that, in and of itself, nearly all federal courts have said is unprotected by Title VII. Take Preece's testimony regarding Schroer's credibility before Congress. As characterized by Schroer, the Library's credibility concern was that she "would not be deemed credible by Members of Congress and their staff because people would perceive her to be a woman, and would refuse to believe that she could possibly have the credentials that she had." Plaintiff argues that this is "quintessential sex stereotyping" because Diane Schroer is a woman and does have such a background. But Preece did not testify that she was concerned that Members of Congress would perceive Schroer simply to be a woman. Instead, she testified that "everyone would know that [Schroer] had transitioned from male to female because only a man could have her military experiences."

Ultimately, I do not think that it matters for purposes of Title VII liability whether the Library withdrew its offer of employment because it perceived Schroer to be an insufficiently masculine man, an insufficiently feminine woman, or an inherently gender-nonconforming transsexual. One or more of Preece's comments could be parsed in each of these three ways. While I would therefore conclude that Schroer is entitled to judgment based on a Price Waterhouse-type claim for sex stereotyping, I also conclude that she is entitled to judgment based on the language of the statute itself.

B. Discrimination because of sex

Schroer's second legal theory is that, because gender identity is a component of sex, discrimination on the basis of gender identity is sex discrimination. In support of this contention, Schroer adduced the testimony of Dr. Walter Bockting, a tenured associate professor at the University of Minnesota Medical School who specializes in gender identity disorders. Dr. Bockting testified that it has long been accepted in the relevant scientific community that there are nine factors that constitute a person's sex. One of these factors is gender identity, which Dr. Bockting defined as one's personal sense of being male or female.

The Library adduced the testimony of Dr. Chester Schmidt, a professor of psychiatry at the Johns Hopkins University School of Medicine and also an expert in gender identity disorders. Dr. Schmidt disagreed with Dr. Bockting's view of the prevailing scientific consensus and testified that he and his colleagues regard gender identity as a component of "sexuality" rather than "sex." According to Dr. Schmidt, "sex" is made up of a number of facets, each of which has a determined biologic etiology. Dr. Schmidt does not believe that gender identity has a single, fixed etiology.

The testimony of both experts—on the science of gender identity and the relationship between intersex conditions and transsexuality—was impressive. Resolving the dispute between Dr. Schmidt and Dr. Bockting as to the proper scientific definition of sex, however, is not within this Court's competence. More importantly (because courts render opinions about scientific controversies with some regularity), deciding whether Dr. Bokting or Dr. Schmidt is right turns out to be unnecessary.

The evidence establishes that the Library was enthusiastic about hiring David Schroer—until she disclosed her transsexuality. The Library revoked the offer when it learned that a man named David intended to become, legally, culturally, and physically, a woman named Diane. This was discrimination "because of ... sex."

. . . .

Imagine that an employee is fired because she converts from Christianity to Judaism. Imagine too that her employer testifies that he harbors no bias toward either Christians or Jews but only "converts." That would be a clear case of discrimination "because of religion." No court would take seriously the notion that "converts" are not covered by the statute. Discrimination "because of religion" easily encompasses discrimination because of a change of religion. But in cases where the plaintiff has changed her sex, and faces discrimination because of the decision to stop presenting as a man and to start appearing as a woman, courts have traditionally carved such persons out of the statute by concluding that "transsexuality" is unprotected by Title VII. In other words, courts have allowed their focus on the label "transsexual" to blind them to the statutory language itself.

. . . .

The decisions [such as *Ulane*] holding that Title VII only prohibits discrimination against men because they are men, and discrimination against women because they are women, represent an elevation of "judge-supposed legislative intent over clear statutory text." [Courts which hold] that discrimination based on changing one's sex is not discrimination because of sex . . . essentially reason "that a thing may be within the letter of the statute and yet not within the statute, because not within its spirit, nor within the intention of its makers." This is no longer a tenable approach to statutory construction. Supreme Court decisions [such as *Oncale*] have applied Title VII in ways Congress could not have contemplated. . . .

For Diane Schroer to prevail on the facts of her case, however, it is not necessary to draw sweeping conclusions about the reach of Title VII. Even if the decisions that define the word "sex" in Title VII as referring only to anatomical or chromosomal sex are still good law—after that approach "has been eviscerated by Price Waterhouse,"—the Library's refusal to hire Schroer after being advised that she planned to change her anatomical sex by undergoing sex reassignment surgery was literally discrimination "because of ... sex."

. . . .

Conclusion

In refusing to hire Diane Schroer because her appearance and background did not comport with the decisionmaker's sex stereotypes about how men and women should act and appear, and in response to Schroer's decision to transition, legally, culturally, and physically, from male to female, the Library of Congress violated Title VII's prohibition on sex discrimination.

. . . .

Notes and Discussion

1. Common Meaning Consider the ramifications for this issue in practice. How would a plaintiff's advocate prove that her transgender client was discriminated against because of sex? What would a defense lawyer use to dispute this? Do the courts in the above cases treat the issue as one of fact or one of law?

2. Transitioning Both Schroer and Ulane experienced problems at work when they underwent gender affirmation surgery. Does this lend support to the argument that it was the transition itself, not the plaintiffs' sex, that motivated the employers' discriminatory treatment? How does the *Schroer* court address this question?

3. Transgender Status as "Sex" Is discrimination based on transgender status more easily connected to gender than sex? Or should it be considered per se discrimination, because it directly references the disconnect between a person's biological and identified sex? Professor Michael Vargas characterizes the *Schroer* opinion as embracing the latter view:

> Thus, since her goal was not to transgress stereotypes, but to adopt an entirely new gender and conform to its stereotypes, Price Waterhouse did not apply. . . . [T]his same logic suggests that Schroer should have a claim for sex discrimination per se, since her offer was rescinded solely because of her gender identity, which the court defined as the "real variations" in how biological sex and social concepts of gender, both protected by Title VII already, interact together.[21]

The First Circuit has apparently adopted this approach, recognizing that discrimination against transgender individuals constitutes sex discrimination per se, without the need to rely on a specific allegation or theory of sex stereotyping. In *EEOC v. R.G. & G.R. Funeral Homes, Inc.* (2018), the employer argued that transgender discrimination could not constitute sex discrimination because individuals of any sex could be transgender. In response, the court noted that "[b]ecause an employer cannot discriminate against an employee for being transgender without considering that employee's biological sex, discrimination on the basis of transgender status necessarily entails discrimination on the basis of sex — no matter what sex the employee was born or wishes to be."[22] The Supreme Court has recently accepted the *R.G.* case for its term beginning in October 2019.

4. Reconceptualizing Sexual Harassment Theory As the cases in this section make clear, many forms of harassment may qualify as discrimination "because of . . . sex." Same-sex sexual harassment, related to the plaintiff's sexual orientation, and

---

21. Michael J. Vargas, *Title VII and the Trans-Inclusive Paradigm*, 32 J. Law & Ineq. 169, 191 (2014).

22. 884 F.3d 560, 578 (6th Cir. 2018).

harassment for the failure to conform to gender stereotypes, due to transgender identity, may also constitute sex-based discrimination.

These developments in the application of antidiscrimination law have led some legal scholars to reconceptualize the theoretical underpinnings of sexual harassment law. In particular, commentators grappled with whether and how a broader understanding of gender-based harm could be reconciled with the subordination theory first advanced by Catharine MacKinnon, which describes sexual harassment as predominantly the male impulse to dominate women.

Professor Kathryn Abrams argues for what she calls "an enhanced subordination account (i.e., one that analyzes both sex and gender and encompasses phenomena like the oppression of non-conforming men)."[23] She observes:

> Sexism involves a hierarchy between men and women, but it is rarely concerned simply with the relations between the biological sexes. Most forms of sexism also involve a valuation of masculine norms — those practices or characteristics associated with men — and a devaluation of feminine norms — those practices or characteristics associated with women. Similarly, most forms of sexism involve a confinement of men and women to paradigmatically masculine and feminine roles. This confinement prevents women from partaking of the privilege that may flow from manifesting more socially valued characteristics. It also prevents men from compromising the hierarchy among values by embracing devalued norms. . . .
>
> . . . .
>
> . . . [W]orkers may engage in vigorous disciplinary action against colleagues whose action or self-presentation threatens to undermine the primacy of masculine norms. Men or women who object to these norms or practices may be targeted, as may men who manifest nonmasculine traits.[24]

What does Abrams contribute to the theoretical landscape? How does her account reconcile MacKinnon's original formulation with the more nuanced issues presented by sex stereotyping, sexual orientation, and transgenderism?

2. Element Two: The Unwelcomeness of Sexual Harassment

A. Definition, Purpose, and Critiques

"Welcome harassment" has been described as a contradiction in terms; the word "harassment" itself contains an assumption that it is something undesirable. The

---

23. Kathryn Abrams, *The New Jurisprudence of Sexual Harassment*, 83 Cornell L. Rev. 1169, 1172, 1203 (1998).
24. *Id.* at 1209, 1212.

unwelcomeness requirement is also anomalous as an element of a prima facie case. No other tort requires the plaintiff to put forth evidence from the outset that the harmful conduct being complained of was unwanted.

The unwelcomeness requirement stems from a single word in the EEOC's *Guidelines on Discrimination Because of Sex*, originally promulgated in 1980. Recall that it defines sexual harassment as "[*u*]*nwelcome* sexual advances, requests for sexual favors, and other verbal or physical conduct of a sexual nature constitute sexual harassment. . . ."[25]

In *Henson v. Dundee* the Eleventh Circuit noted that "[i]n order to constitute harassment, this conduct must be unwelcome in the sense that the employee did not solicit or incite it, and in the sense that the employee regarded the conduct as undesirable or offensive." In *Meritor Savings Bank, FSB v. Vinson*, the Supreme Court clarified that "welcome" should not be equated with "voluntary." Recall that the Court specified:

> [T]he fact that sex-related conduct was "voluntary," in the sense that the complainant was not forced to participate against her will, is not a defense to a sexual harassment suit brought under Title VII. The gravamen of any sexual harassment claim is that the alleged sexual advances were "unwelcome." . . . The correct inquiry is whether the respondent by her conduct indicated that the alleged sexual advances were unwelcome, not whether her actual participation in sexual conduct was voluntary.[26]

Thus, one might argue that acquiescence is not consent.

The Court, however, inserted some additional considerations into the analysis. The *Meritor* Court noted:

> While "voluntariness" in the sense of consent is not a defense to such a claim, it does not follow that a complainant's sexually provocative speech or dress is irrelevant as a matter of law in determining whether he or she found particular sexual advances unwelcome. To the contrary, such evidence is obviously relevant.[27]

Since *Meritor*, and because of the Court's lack of guidance, lower courts have grappled with the contours of the unwelcomeness requirement.

Notes and Discussion

1. Purpose Why is there an unwelcomeness requirement? Commentators have generally posited two reasons. The first is that not all conduct of a sexual nature is unwelcome in the workplace. The law was not intended to prohibit consensual workplace relationships or playful banter and mild off-color joking (at least when

---

25. 29 C.F.R. 1604.11 (emphasis added).
26. 477 U.S. 57, 68 (1986).
27. *Id.* at 69.

all parties enjoy and engage in it). Second, a showing of unwelcomeness is necessary to provide notice to the harasser that his conduct is problematic. Do these purposes justify the requirement?

2. Criticism The unwelcomeness requirement has been the subject of significant criticism. In an influential article, Professor Susan Estrich compares the controversy to a similar one in rape cases, regarding consent or its absence. She argues that the unwelcomeness requirement opens the door to "some of the most pernicious doctrines of rape law."[28] She notes:

> On its face, the standard presents at least three serious problems. First, as in rape cases, the focus is on the victim, not on the man: She may be less powerful, and economically dependent, but she still is expected to express unwelcomeness. Unless she does, no burden is placed on him to refrain from abusing his position of power. A doctor may be required, by tort law, to secure affirmative and informed assent *before* he lays his hands on a woman; but a boss may freely touch any woman subordinate, until and unless she expresses, through her conduct, her nonassent. The justification for imposing the notice requirement on the woman, according to one leading commentator, is "[a]s the saying goes, 'even dirty old men need love.'" Perhaps this is so, but why the law should protect this quest—at the expense of the emotional and bodily integrity of the female employee—is not so obvious. At the very least, we might demand that such men look for "love" outside of work, or at least ask for it first.
>
> The second problem with the unwelcomeness standard, as defined by the Supreme Court, is that "conduct" is the yardstick by which we measure assent. The plain implication is that a polite "no" may not suffice. Though it is bad enough to presume consent in the absence of words, it is worse still to presume it notwithstanding a woman's words.
>
> Third, and most pernicious of all, since the focus of inquiry is on the plaintiff, and since the unwelcomeness test must be met by her conduct, should we be surprised if the trial focuses on what the plaintiff wears, how she talks, even who else she sleeps with? Whatever unwelcomeness means, the Court in *Vinson* squarely held that a "complainant's sexually provocative speech or dress" is "obviously relevant" in determining whether she found the particular sexual advances unwelcome.[29]

What are the implications of the determination that a plaintiff's speech and dress are "obviously relevant" to whether sexual harassment was welcome? Does this hold women responsible for harassing behavior?

Professor Henry L. Chambers Jr. observes that the unwelcomeness requirement "also affirmatively protects the putative harasser who did not realize that the

---

28. Susan Estrich, *Sex at Work*, 43 STAN. L. REV. 813, 828 (1991).
29. *Id.*

target of his conduct did not welcome it. Such protection inappropriately validates a putative harasser's mistake even when the harasser's conduct occurs in the workplace—a place Title VII suggests should be free of sex discrimination. . . ."[30] More significant, he argues, is the fact that the unwelcomeness requirement encourages the harasser to argue that he did not breach workplace or societal norms. "Thus, the requirement may allow harassment to pass as unremediable horseplay and may allow the harasser to suggest that his conduct was playful or misunderstood, and thereby brand the plaintiff a dishonest flirt who welcomed the conduct or an inflexible prude."[31]

3. The Plaintiff's Burden Should the law place the burden on harassment survivors to demonstrate that sexual conduct is unwelcome in the workplace? Professor Chambers argues that this expectation actually serves to create the presumption that sex-related workplace conduct is welcome until proven otherwise. He explains:

> When proving the lack of acquiescence becomes the key to recovery, employees become fair targets for gender-motivated conduct until putative harassers are told their conduct is unwelcome. This is problematic because, although sexual advances can be welcome in some contexts, the suggestion that sex-based or gender-motivated conduct in the workplace should be considered welcome until the employee subjected to those advances objects may not be a reasonable one."[32]

Should law place the burden on all employees to refrain from sexual conduct unless there have been affirmative manifestations of consent? Consider these questions in light of *Blake v. MJ Optical, Inc.* (2017):

> [The plaintiff Bobette Blake and Marty Hagge had known each other for 25 years, during which Blake worked for Marty's family business, MJ Optical. Marty eventually became the company's Vice President and Blake's supervisor. The two also maintained a cordial friendship outside of work.] Blake claims that all changed at her husband's funeral in 1999. Marty attended the funeral, as did his father and several other MJ Optical employees. Blake says she was standing outside the funeral home when Marty walked by and "grabbed [her] fanny." When Blake asked "What was that all about?" Marty replied, "I thought you needed it." That was the entirety of the exchange.
>
> However that was not the end of the conduct Blake now cites as the basis for this action. From that point onward, Marty would occasionally touch Blake's buttocks at "[v]arious times during the workday." According to Blake, Marty "would either smack it really hard or grab [her] whole cheek of [her] butt. I mean, it was no love pat." Blake flashed "a dirty look" at least

---

30. Henry L. Chambers Jr., *(Un)Welcome Conduct and the Sexually Hostile Environment*, 53 ALA. L. REV. 733, 784 (2002).
31. *Id.*
32. *Id.* at 765.

once in response to the touching, but she never verbalized her complaint to Marty or anyone else given her belief it "[w]ouldn't have done any good." Marty also began telling Blake she "needed to find a man," which Blake took to mean "that if [she] had sex with a man, that it would make [her] happy." Again, any frustrations Blake had about these recurring comments were not communicated to Marty or anyone else. Blake also recalls one exchange where she was standing in front of Marty's desk when he commented on her breasts, saying "you'd better watch those things because they're going to poke my eyes out" and asking whether her nipples were "the size of nick[el]s or quarters." "[E]mbarrassed" by the interaction, Blake says she "probably turned red" and "went home and bought padded underclothes."

. . . .

. . . After the complained-of conduct began in 1999, Blake continued to work at MJ Optical for almost fifteen years without once telling Marty to stop or complaining to anyone else at MJ Optical.

During those fifteen years, Blake and Marty joked around with one another; they occasionally exchanged "I love yous"; and Blake sometimes touched Marty "between the shoulders." While we are not under any illusion these acts are similar in kind to Marty's unprofessional and boorish behavior, it does nothing to convey the allegedly severe and pervasive conduct was unwelcome. There is no evidence Marty was aware his conduct distressed Blake, either. Quite the opposite—Marty apparently saw his conduct as an attempt "to lighten [the] mood a bit," and Blake recalls Marty would say she "need[ed] to be happy." When Blake finally did go to Marty to complain about how Marty treated her, she did not mention any of the conduct she now claims created a hostile work environment. Other than "a dirty look"—which it is unclear whether anyone even noticed—the first indication Blake gave that she felt discriminated against was when she filed her administrative charge alleging as much. This is too little, too late. Blake cannot show she indicated in a timely manner the complained-of conduct was unwelcome, thus she cannot maintain a claim for hostile work environment.[33]

Why might Blake have kept silent about Marty's treatment of her? Should a female subordinate be required to confront her supervisor? Should some conduct—such as a supervisor "occasionally" grabbing or slapping a woman's buttocks at work—be considered presumptively unwelcome?

How appropriate is it to expect women to confront their harassers in light of the fact that empirical studies have consistently found that most harassment survivors do not tell anyone—even friends or spouses—about what is happening to them?[34]

---

33. 870 F.3d 820, 823, 829–30 (8th Cir. 2017).

34. *See, e.g.,* Louise F. Fitzgerald et al., *Why Didn't She Just Report Him?: The Psychological and Legal Implications of Women's Responses to Sexual Harassment,* 51 J. Soc. Issues 117 (1995);

Should plaintiffs' advocates be prepared to introduce such evidence by expert witnesses in order to educate judges and juries about typical survivor behavior?

4. Is Unwelcomeness Necessary? To succeed on a sexual harassment claim, a plaintiff must prove one of two conditions. First, she can show that she suffered a tangible job detriment, such as a demotion or firing. Alternately, she must prove that she experienced a hostile work environment. The second condition requires that the conduct was severe or pervasive, offensive to her, and offensive to a reasonable person in her situation, such that it constructively altered the terms or conditions of her employment. Is it possible for either of these situations to be considered "welcome" by an employee? Professor Estrich argues:

> Thus the welcomeness inquiry is either utterly gratuitous or gratuitously punitive. It is gratuitous when the environment is not proven objectively to be hostile, because an unwelcome environment which is not objectively hostile does not give rise to liability in any event. It is gratuitously punitive if the environment is found objectively hostile, for in that case the employer can nonetheless escape the burden of addressing the issue, by portraying this particular woman as so base as to be unworthy of respect or decency, and by arguing that she thus welcomed, through her conduct, an environment which a "reasonable" woman would have perceived as hostile. In either case, welcomeness serves as a means to keep the focus on the woman rather than the supervisor; on what she, rather than he, has done wrong; and on whether *she* deserves to be treated with human decency, rather than whether *he* violated the standards of decency and humanity.[35]

Consider this critique in light of *Blake v. MJ Optical*, discussed in the preceding note. Does it make sense to require a showing of unwelcomeness if the harassment is gender-based but nonsexual? Note that harassment based on other protected characteristics such as race or religion does not require a showing of unwelcomeness. What is the difference?

B. Evidentiary Issues in Proving Unwelcomeness

The *Meritor* court's determination that evidence of a plaintiff's "provocative speech or dress" was "obviously relevant" to the issue of welcomeness created great confusion among courts. It also caused innumerable problems for plaintiffs who were more human than perfect. The multiple opinions in *Burns v. McGregor Electronic Industries, Inc.* demonstrate the legal havoc that *Meritor* wrought. For the

---

Cheryl R. Kaiser & Carol T. Miller, *Stop Complaining! The Social Costs of Making Attributions of Discrimination*, 27 Personality & Soc. Psych. Bull. 254 (2001); Theresa M. Beiner, *Sex, Science and Social Knowledge: The Implications of Social Science Research on Imputing Liability to Employers for Sexual Harassment*, 7 Wm. & Mary J. Women & L. 273 (2001).

35. Estrich, *supra* note 28, at 833.

Burns opinions below, evaluate whether they reinforce or dispel concerns raised by Professor Estrich.

Burns v. McGregor Electronic Industries, Inc.

955 F.2d 559 (8th Cir. 1992)

WOLLMAN, Circuit Judge.

. . . .

I.

On August 30, 1985, [Lisa Ann] Burns filed a complaint alleging constructive discharge from her employment with McGregor, a stereo speaker manufacturer employing fifty to seventy-five workers. . . .

McGregor, which is located in McGregor, Iowa, is owned by Paul Oslac, a resident of Chicago, Illinois. Burns testified that during her first period of employment with McGregor, manager-trainee Marla Ludvik often made sexual comments as Burns left the restroom, such as "have you been playing with yourself in there?" Ludvik also made almost daily comments to other workers that she did not think Burns took douches, that she saw Burns riding in Oslac's car, and that Burns was going out with Oslac. Ludvik tried to convince Burns to date male employees. Supervisors Cleo Martin and Eldon Rytilahti heard Ludvik's remarks. Burns complained to Martin and to Mary Jean Standford, then the plant manager, but nothing changed.

The plant consisted of assembly lines in the basement and on the main floor, an office, a laboratory, and a third floor apartment used by Oslac when he visited the plant. Burns testified that Oslac showed her advertisements for pornographic films in *Penthouse* magazine, talked about sex, asked her to watch pornographic movies with him, and made lewd gestures, such as ones imitating masturbation. A former worker, Kim Heisz, saw one of Oslac's gestures. Oslac asked Burns for dates at least once a week. She gave him excuses rather than direct refusals because, she testified, she feared the loss of her job. She stated that his behavior made her angry, upset, and "real nervous," and that sometimes she would cry at work or at home. Burns also testified that there was no one above Oslac to whom she could complain; and that although she received no complaints, her work slowed down and she started dropping assembly parts. She voluntarily left McGregor on August 10, 1981.

Burns returned on September 15, 1981, because, she maintained, she needed the work. The newly-hired plant manager, Virginia Kelley, placed her in a higher-paying quality control job. Burns testified that during this period Oslac visited the plant from 11:00 a.m. Monday until 9:00 a.m. Tuesday of each week and that he spent most of this time with her. He continued to ask for dates and wanted to engage in oral sex so she would "be able to perform [her] work better." When Burns refused a date, Oslac told her, "I'm tired of your fooling around and always turning me down. You must not need your job very bad." Believing that Oslac intended to fire her, she accepted an invitation to dinner at his apartment on the condition that her mother would join them. Burns testified that her mother refused to go, so her father, Daniel Burns, went with her. As the district court found, Oslac appeared shocked when Burns' [sic] father appeared at the dinner with Burns. After the meal, Daniel Burns told Oslac he knew what was going on and for Oslac "to leave the girls alone at work."

Burns further testified that during her second period of employment Ludvik, who was then a supervisor, circulated a petition to have Burns fired because nude photographs of her, taken by her father, appeared in two motorcycle magazines—*Easyrider* and *In the Wind*. One full frontal view of Burns revealed a pelvic tattoo; two photographs highlighted jewelry attached to her pierced nipples. Burns testified that she had willingly allowed her father to do the piercing and photography. She did not take copies of the magazines into the plant. Former employee Deborah Johnson testified that she saw Ludvik showing employees the magazine and the petition. Burns testified that after Oslac learned about the nude photos from Ludvik, he told her, "They're ganging up on you and trying to get rid of you. If you don't go out with me, I might just let them do it." Oslac then asked Burns to pose nude for him in the plant in return for overtime pay.

Burns further testified that she was humiliated by plant gossip that she was Oslac's girlfriend; that supervisor June Volske tried to get her to sit on Oslac's lap, to go out with him, or to go up to his apartment; and that coworker Eugene Ottaway called her vulgar names. She complained to Kelley, who appeared to try to "do something" for a period of time, and to Kelley's successor. Burns testified that her second period of employment was "hostile" and "extremely worse" than the first. She quit again on June 20, 1983.

Burns returned to McGregor for the third time on September 26, 1983, because, she said, Kelley had returned to the plant and because she needed work to support herself, her father, and her brother. When Burns expressed concerns about Oslac's behavior, Kelley assured her that Oslac would no longer enter the plant. Oslac continued to visit Burns, although he did not spend as much time with her as he had previously. According to Burns, he repeatedly asked her to go out, pose nude, and watch pornographic movies. On one occasion when other employees were present, Oslac threw his arm around her, cupped his hand as if to grab her breast, and said, "Well, I see I got you back, lover." He also gave her an *Easyrider* calendar.

Oslac had not visited the plant within the four to six weeks preceding Burns' last day, July 19, 1984. On that day, Burns asked Ottaway to move stacks of speakers, and he refused. Burns reported this to a supervisor, who instructed Ottaway to move the speakers. Ottaway then pushed and shoved the stacks, all the while calling Burns a series of vulgar names similar to those he admitted to having called her on other occasions, and placed the speakers so high she could not reach them. When Burns asked him to make the stacks lower, Ottaway threw the speakers across the room. Burns began crying and tried to get a supervisor to stop Ottaway, but the supervisor did nothing. Burns left work and did not return.

Burns testified that the overall work environment was "hostile and offensive." She testified that during the last six weeks of her third period of employment at McGregor she overheard Ottaway tell a fellow worker that "he should throw [Burns] over the [conveyor] belts" and commit an act of sodomitic intercourse upon her. Called as a witness for McGregor, Ottaway denied making the statement attributed to him by Burns about "throwing her over the belts." He admitted on direct examination, however, that he had called Burns names—"anything nasty." He testified that Burns had responded by calling him similar names. He further testified that during the speaker-throwing incident on July 19, 1984, he was angry at Burns and had "called her every name in the book." Finally, on redirect examination, he testified that he hadn't treated Burns any differently than he had the other women working at the plant.

Coworker Diane Zinkle testified that Eugene Ottaway and other male employees had subjected Burns to continual verbal abuse. She also testified that Burns did not yell or call Ottaway names during the July 19 speaker-throwing incident.

Coworker Mary Ellen White testified by deposition that the general working atmosphere at McGregor was bad and characterized it as the "last resort of anybody that needs a job." While she never saw Oslac ever directly harass Burns, she said that she had seen Oslac touch almost everyone in the plant in improper ways. She had seen Oslac sit under the conveyor belt rubbing the legs of the women at the line and had seen him rubbing the front or the back of female workers with his hands or a newspaper. She overheard Oslac telling dirty jokes on several occasions. She once saw Oslac drop his pants to his knees in front of several female workers. She overheard Oslac say that he wanted to show them a bruise on his leg. Oslac was, according to White, "always" in Burns' testing booth. She said that Ottaway harassed Burns on the line and that Volske "picked" on Burns. She stated that she was subject to constant comments from supervisors at the plant which she considered to be sexually harassing, such as "have you got your period," and "if you didn't have sex all night, you wouldn't be tired." She also heard these sorts of comments directed at Burns and Burns' mother.

Testifying by way of deposition, Oslac denied Burns' allegations. He testified that he had invited Burns and her father to dinner at his apartment because Burns was planning to quit and that he convinced her father to talk her into staying. He claimed that he never talked to Burns at all during her last period of employment. He admitted spending quite a bit of time in her testing booth during her second period of employment, but said that Burns needed a lot of encouragement. He admitted showing several workers a bruise, but said that he pulled his pant leg up to do so and did not drop his pants to his knees. He claimed that the *Easyrider* calendar was given to him by Burns, not the other way around.

On the basis of this and other testimony, the district court indicated that it had some difficulty in determining what actually went on at McGregor because "rumor and gossip ran rampant." The court found that several forces contributed to Burns' decision to quit her job: the general working conditions; gossip about the nude photos (and the resulting treatment by co-employees); unwanted sexual advances by Oslac; and the sexually-charged name-calling during the running dispute with other employees about moving and stacking speakers. The district court found "the primary reason [Burns quit] was the incident on the last day during which she and Eugene Ottaway got into a violent name-calling argument and speakers were knocked about."

The district court found that the sexual harassment that Burns received from her co-workers peaked during the second period of employment and resulted from the publication of the nude photos. The court found that there was little or no sexual harassment directed toward Burns by her co-workers during her third period of employment at McGregor. The court found that "[i]n view of [Burns'] willingness to display her nude body to the public in Easy Riders publications, crude magazines at best, her testimony that she was offended by sexually directed comments and Penthouse or Playboy pictures is not credible." The court stated that it had no doubt that Oslac had made unwelcome sexual advances to Burns during her first two employment periods, but that Burns had exaggerated the severity and pervasiveness of the harassment and its effect upon her. The district court concluded that, in light of the whole record and the totality of the circumstances, Burns had failed to prove "by a preponderance of credible evidence" that the sexual harassment was sufficiently severe or pervasive to alter the conditions of her employment and create an abusive work environment, citing *Meritor Savings Bank v. Vinson.*

. . . .

IV.

. . . .

To prevail in her sexual harassment claim based on "hostile environment", Burns must show that 1) she belongs to a protected group; 2) she was subject to unwelcome sexual harassment; 3) the harassment was based on sex; 4) the harassment affected a term, condition, or privilege of employment; and 5) McGregor knew or should have known of the harassment and failed to take proper remedial action. [Ed. note. This last element has been modified by subsequent Supreme Court decisions.]

. . . .

The second . . . element requires the plaintiff to show that she was subject to unwelcome sexual harassment. The district court had "no doubt" that Oslac made unwelcome sexual advances toward Burns during the first two periods she was employed, but found that there were few opportunities for Oslac to see her during the third period. The court also found that Burns lacked credibility when she testified that she was offended by the pornographic pictures and by the sexual comments.

The threshold for determining that conduct is unwelcome is "that the employee did not solicit or incite it, and the employee regarded the conduct as undesirable or offensive." The district court's finding that Oslac's advances were unwelcome necessarily required the district court to believe Burns' testimony that Oslac's behavior was offensive to her. Thus, the district court's finding that Oslac made unwelcome advances toward Burns and its finding that Burns was not credible when she stated that Oslac's behavior was offensive appear on their face to be internally inconsistent.

There is no evidence in the record that Burns solicited any of the conduct that occurred. However, the gossip, lewd talk, and the petition all occurred after the nude photographs of Burns appeared. These incidents were incited by the nude photographs and must be considered separately from Oslac's conduct. His conduct occurred both before and after Burns appeared in the magazines and did not change in kind or intensity after the appearance of the photos, though his advances tapered off during Burns' third period of employment. Eugene Ottaway's conduct and that of Burns' supervisors must also be analyzed separately from the conduct that occurred after Burns appeared nude. Ludvik, a plant supervisor, made inappropriate sexual and personal remarks and encouraged Burns to go out with Oslac, both before and after the nude pictures appeared. When Burns complained to supervisors about Oslac's behavior, she received either no response or promises that were not kept. Ottaway, according to the record, knew of the nude pictures and harassed Burns about them, but he also called Burns and other employees names of a sexual nature. Burns' complaints to her supervisor about Ottaway's conduct bore no results. The district court should, on remand, take all of this conduct into account as part of the "totality of the circumstances" in determining whether Burns found the conduct unwelcome. "The correct inquiry is whether [the plaintiff] by her conduct indicated that the alleged sexual advances were unwelcome[.]"

Evidence regarding a plaintiff's sexually provocative speech or dress is relevant "in determining whether he or she found particular sexual advances unwelcome." Thus, in making the determination as to whether the conduct directed at Burns was unwelcome, the nude photo evidence, though relating to an activity engaged in by Burns outside of the workplace, may be relevant to explain the context of some of the comments and actions directed by Oslac and coworkers to Burns.

. . . .

Our disposition of this case should not be read as constituting a *de facto* entry of judgment for Burns. That is not our intention, for we would not presume to substitute our view of the evidence for that of the experienced trial judge, who had the benefit of observing the demeanor of at least some of the witnesses whose testimony was received at trial. Rather, we ask the district court to review the evidence in the light of the considerations we have expressed above. What outcome will flow from those additional findings is for the district court to determine in the first instance.

The judgment is reversed, and the case is remanded to the district court for further findings consistent with this opinion.

Notes and Discussion

1. Federal Rule of Evidence (FRE) 412 Federal Rule of Evidence 412, commonly referred to as the "Rape Shield Law," is an evidentiary exclusion rule. The Rule was originally created to protect survivors of sexual crimes from "the invasion of privacy, potential embarrassment and sexual stereotyping that is associated with public disclosure of intimate sexual details and the infusion of sexual innuendo into the factfinding process."[36]

In 1994 the Rule was amended to include survivors of civil sexual offenses, particularly sexual harassment. Today it provides:

> (a) Prohibited Uses. The following evidence is not admissible in a civil or criminal proceeding involving alleged sexual misconduct:
>
> (1) evidence offered to prove that a victim engaged in other sexual behavior; or
>
> (2) evidence offered to prove a victim's sexual predisposition.
>
> (b) Exceptions.
>
> . . . .
>
> (2) Civil Cases. In a civil case, the court may admit evidence offered to prove a victim's sexual behavior or sexual predisposition if its probative value substantially outweighs the danger of harm to any victim and of unfair prejudice to any party. The court may admit evidence of a victim's reputation only if the victim has placed it in controversy.

According to the Advisory Committee, the Rule should be read to bar "evidence relating to the alleged victim's sexual behavior or alleged sexual predisposition, whether offered as substantive evidence of for impeachment, except in designated circumstances in which the probative value of the evidence significantly outweighs possible harm to the victim," and also to bar "evidence that does not directly refer to sexual activities or thoughts but that the proponent believes may have a sexual connotation for the factfinder . . . such as that relating to the alleged victim's mode of dress, speech, or life-style[.]"[37] The burden shifts to the proponent of the particular evidence to prove its admissibility.

How might this rule have applied in *Burns* (which predated the 1994 amendments)? Given that it is the trial court judge who determines whether the exception of (b)(2) applies, would this rule have necessarily changed the outcome? If the nude pictures were not relevant to Burns's allegations, where should courts draw the line concerning a plaintiff's conduct and her alleged offense?

Note that most states do not have a corollary to FRE 412. Also, FRE 412 applies to the admissibility of such evidence, not whether it can be the subject of discovery. Should defense attorneys delve into questions of the plaintiff's background, dress, and behavior in discovery? Does this raise ethical concerns? What can a plaintiff's attorney do to prevent this?

---

36. FED. R. EVID. 412 Advisory Committee's Note to 1994 Amendment.

37. *Id.*

2. Unwelcomeness and Offense The appellate court found an inconsistency between the district court's conclusion that Burns did not welcome Oslac's conduct and its failure to believe that she found Oslac's behavior offensive. What can explain the district court's willingness to make two such contradictory conclusions? Does this lend support to Professor Estrich's opinion above that the unwelcomeness requirement is "gratuitously punitive"?

The district court found that "[i]n view of [Burns'] willingness to display her nude body to the public in Easy Rider publications, crude magazines at best, her testimony that she was offended by sexually directed comments and Penthouse or Playboy pictures is not credible." Professor Wendy Pollack noted two years *before* the first *Burns* appellate decision:

> The overwhelming impression created by hostile work environment sexual harassment cases is that, regardless of the standard applied, women simply are not trusted. This is true for decisions that find for plaintiffs as well as those which find against them. Women are not taken seriously, so the behavior complained of and the injury suffered are not treated as serious. Since the behavior and injury are not taken seriously, the men who engage in sexual harassment are not taken seriously. And if the offenders are not taken seriously, how can women take sexual harassment seriously? This circuitous reasoning belies women's experience of sexual harassment and the reality of male domination and female subordination within the gender hierarchy. The manipulation of the legal doctrine discredits women and their experiences, treating them with suspicion and mistrust.[38]

Is Pollack correct or is *Burns* an exception?

3. Irrelevant Evidence FRE 412 limits the relevance of the plaintiff's sexual behavior to situations where it is probative of whether the harasser had reason to believe his conduct toward her was not unwelcome. Thus, evidence about non-work behavior, or behavior that the harasser was not aware of, should not be admissible. For example, in *Swentek v. USAir* (1987), the court explained:

> We note at the outset that the trial court misconstrued what constitutes unwelcome sexual harassment. It held that Swentek's own past conduct and use of foul language meant that Ludlam's comments were "not unwelcome" even though she told Ludlam to leave her alone. In his oral opinion, the judge determined, not that Swentek welcomed Ludlam's comments in particular, but that she was the kind of person who could not be offended by such comments and therefore welcomed them generally. We think that was error. Plaintiff's use of foul language or sexual innuendo in a consensual setting does not waive "her legal protections against unwelcome harassment."

---

38. Wendy Pollack, *Sexual Harassment: Women's Experience vs. Legal Definitions*, 13 HARV. WOMEN'S L.J. 35, 69 (1990).

The trial judge must determine whether plaintiff welcomed the particular conduct in question from the alleged harasser.

This view is in accord with the Supreme Court's decision in *Vinson*. There, the Court held that evidence of the plaintiff's provocative speech and dress was relevant in determining whether she welcomed sexual advances from her supervisors. Unlike this case, however, the evidence of Vinson's past conduct bore directly on her contact with the alleged harasser. Vinson worked with her supervisor daily, and her dress and conversation were relevant in determining whether she welcomed sexual advances from him. By contrast, there was no evidence in this case that Ludlam knew of Swentek's past conduct or that he believed his conduct was welcomed by her. In fact, she says that she told him that his conduct was not welcome. Under these circumstances, it was improper for the trial judge to suggest that Swentek's past conduct meant that she welcomed Ludlam's behavior.[39]

4. Conduct Versus Invitation In order to be relevant, evidence must tend to show that a plaintiff actually invited the behavior, not simply that she, too, engaged in crude conduct. Compare the following cases:

Carr v. Allison Gas (1994)[40]

[Mary] Carr was a drill operator in GM's gas turbine division when, in August 1984, she entered the skilled trades in the division as a tinsmith apprentice. She was the first woman to work in the tinsmith shop, and her male coworkers were unhappy about working with a woman. They made derogatory comments of a sexual character to her on a daily basis (such as, "I won't work with any cunt"), continually referred to her in her presence by such terms as "whore," "cunt," and "split tail," painted "cunt" on her toolbox, and played various sex- or gender-related pranks on her, such as painting her toolbox pink and (without her knowledge) cutting out the seat of her overalls. They festooned her tool box and work area with signs, pictures, and graffiti of an offensive sexual character, hid and stole her tools, hid her toolbox, hung nude pin-ups around the shop, and would strip to their underwear in front of her when changing into and out of their work clothes. One of them placed an obscene Valentine Day's card, addressed to "Cunt," on her toolbox. The card shows a man carrying a naked woman upside down, and the text explains that the man has finally discovered why a woman has two holes — so that she can be carried like a six-pack. A worker named Beckham twice exhibited his penis. The first time, during an argument in which Carr told him the exit door "swings both ways," meaning that he could leave just as easily as she could, he replied that he had something that "swings," and he demonstrated. The second time, another male worker bet Beckham

---

39. 830 F.2d 552, 557 (4th Cir. 1987).
40. 32 F.3d 1007 (7th Cir. 1994).

$5 that he would not expose himself. He lost the bet, although it is unclear whether Carr was in front of Beckham or behind him. And it was Beckham who told Carr on another occasion that if he fell from a dangerous height in the shop she would have to give him "mouth to dick" resuscitation. Carr's male coworkers urinated from the roof of the shop in her presence, and, in her hearing, one of them accused a black employee who was only intermittently hostile to Carr of being "after that white pussy, that is why you want a woman here, you want some of that." A number of racist remarks and practical jokes of a racial nature were directed against this, the only black employee among the tinsmiths. A frequent remark heard around the shop was, "I'll never retire from this tinsmith position because it would make an opening for a nigger or a woman." Another of Carr's male coworkers threw a burning cigarette at her.

At first she disregarded the harassment but beginning in 1985 and continuing until 1989, when she quit—constructively discharged, she contends, the situation having become unbearable—she complained about the harassment repeatedly to her immediate supervisor, Jim Routh. To no avail. He testified that even though some of the offensive statements were made in his presence, not being a woman himself he was not sure that the statements would be considered offensive by a woman. His perplexity was such that when he heard the statements he would just chuckle and bite down harder on his pipe.

The district judge rejected the company's argument that the words and conduct that we have described were mere vulgar pleasantries, what is euphemistically known as "shop talk." . . .

So the behavior of Carr's coworkers was harassing, yet the district judge concluded that it was not actionable, because it had been "invited." "[S]he was not merely the recipient of crude behavior and crude language—she also dished it out." A female welder, who worked in proximity to the tinsmiths, considered Carr vulgar and unladylike, a "tramp," because she used the "F word" and told dirty jokes. This woman further testified that herself had no trouble with the men in the shop—though occasionally she did have to zap them with her welding arc to fend them off. Carr indeed used such terms as "fuck head" and "dick head," once placed her hand on the thigh of a young male worker, and, when shown a pornographic picture and asked to point out the clitoris, obliged. Once when her tool bench was moved (apparently not with hostile intent), she got into a shouting match with her coworkers. General Motors' brief describes her as "vulgar, confrontational, profane, lazy and vindictive." The district judge said that "she contributed just as much abusive language and crude behavior as did the male tinners, and therefore was just as responsible for any hostile sexual environment that consequently arose." "[T]he tinners' conduct, to the extent it may have constituted sexual harassment, was not unwelcome."

Of course it was unwelcome. A plaintiff's words, deeds, and deportment can cast light on whether her coworkers' treatment of her was unwelcome and should have been perceived as such by them and their supervisors, but we do not understand General Motors to be suggesting that Carr enjoyed or appeared to enjoy the campaign of harassment against her. . . . Carr's violent resentment of the conduct of her male coworkers toward her is plain. What the judge found, rather, was that Carr had *provoked* the misconduct of her coworkers. Had she been ladylike, he thought, like the welder, they would have left her alone—maybe; for remember that the welder had to use her welding arc to protect herself, and Carr was not so equipped.

Even if we ignore the question why "unladylike" behavior should provoke not a vulgar response but a hostile, harassing response, and even if Carr's testimony that she talked and acted as she did in an effort to be "one of the boys" is (despite its plausibility) discounted, her words and conduct cannot be compared to those of the men and used to justify their conduct and exonerate their employer. . . .[41]

Reed v. Shepard (1991)[42]

[JoAnn Reed worked as a civilian jailer for a county sheriff's department.] The trial was replete with grim stories concerning how the deputies and jailers liked to entertain themselves during slow periods at the jail. The district court's summary more than adequately sets the tone for the unprofessional atmosphere that prevailed during "slow time" at the jail.

> Plaintiff contends that she was handcuffed to the drunk tank and sally port doors, that she was subjected to suggestive remarks . . . , that conversations often centered around oral sex, that she was physically hit and punched in the kidneys, that her head was grabbed and forcefully placed in members laps, and that she was the subject of lewd jokes and remarks. She testified that she had chairs pulled out from under her, a cattle prod with an electrical shock was placed between her legs, and that they frequently tickled her. She was placed in a laundry basket, handcuffed inside an elevator, handcuffed to the toilet and her face pushed into the water, and maced. Perhaps others.

The record confirms these and a number of other bizarre activities in the jail office. By any objective standard, the behavior of the male deputies and jailers toward Reed revealed at trial was, to say the least, repulsive. But apparently not to Reed.

Reed not only experienced this depravity with amazing resilience, but she also relished reciprocating in kind. At one point during her job tenure Reed was actually put on probation for her use of offensive language

---

41. *Id.* at 1009–11.
42. 939 F.2d 484 (7th Cir. 1991).

at the jail. At the same time she was instructed to suspend the exhibition-istic habit she had of not wearing a bra on days she wore only a T-shirt to work. She also participated in suggestive giftgiving by presenting a softball warmer to a male co-worker designed to resemble a scrotum and by giv-ing another a G-string. Reed enjoyed exhibiting to the male officers the abdominal scars she received from her hysterectomy which necessarily involved showing her private area. Many witnesses testified that Reed rev-eled in the sexual horseplay, instigated a lot of it, and had "one of the foulest mouths" in the department. In other words, the trial revealed that there was plenty of degrading humor and behavior to go around.

The trial court further observed:

> ... several of the deputies and the Sheriff ... testified her propensity to use foul language is well known, and that she told many dirty jokes, often with sexual innuendos. No doubt some of the allegations on both sides are true, however the conclusion from the testimony must be that plaintiff participated freely in many of these antics and in fact instigated some of them.

. . . .

The district court in the present case found that "[Reed] ... admits that the [harassing] incidents charged by her did not affect her job per-formance." Additionally, the court found that "[Reed] was a willing and welcome participant until other incidences, not related at all to any harass-ment, cost her job."

Much of the evidence at trial emphasized Reed's enthusiastic recep-tiveness to sexually suggestive jokes and activities. The record of this case reveals numerous instances indicating that Reed's preferred method of dealing with co-workers was with sexually explicit jokes, suggestions and offers. As one witness put it, referring to the frequency of Reed's sex-related joking, "JoAnn—I mean, that was her way. There was not ever a time that I can recall of ever speaking to her that there wasn't some kind of sexual contact made with reference to rear-ends, ... or she would be the best or whatever." This sentiment was repeated often by other witnesses. From the foregoing, the district court is justified where it held: "The Court finds that language and sexually explicit jokes were used around plaintiff because of her personality rather than her sex."

Reed was quizzed on why she tolerated without complaint activity she now characterizes as harassing and abusive. At trial she claimed:

> Because it was real important to me to be accepted. It was important for me to be a police officer and if that was the only way that I could be accepted, I would just put up with it and kept [sic] my mouth shut. I had supervisors that would participate in this and you had a chain of

command to go through in order to file a complaint. One thing you don't do as a police officer, you don't snitch out [sic] another police officer. You could get hurt. [sic]

Although Reed suggests that tolerating and contributing to the crudeness of the jail was necessary for her career, other female employees testified that the male jail employees did not behave in this manner around women who asked them not to. The trial court's conclusion that Reed welcomed the sexual hijinx of her co-workers is strongly supported by the evidence presented at trial.[43]

Both Reed and Carr were women who worked in typically male-dominated workplaces, where crude language and sexualized behavior was the norm. Should the law penalize plaintiffs in such a situation for trying to blend in with the workplace culture even if it means not behaving like a "lady"? How relevant was the testimony of other female workers in each case that they did not participate in the workplace culture?

Consider, too, that even though the sexual conduct evidence in *Burns*, *Swentek*, and *Carr* was ultimately deemed irrelevant, it was still admitted into evidence by the lower courts (and presumably was a topic for discovery). Does this undermine the purpose of FRE 412, which is to encourage women to come forward with such complaints?

5. Subsequent History Note that the appellate court in *Burns* declined to issue a "*de facto* entry of judgment for Burns." The court explained that it "would not presume to substitute [its] view of the evidence for that of the experienced trial judge. . . ." Instead it remanded the case for further findings.

Upon remand, the lower court again found against Burns using the exact same reasoning. Burns appealed for a second time and the court again reversed, directing that judgment be entered for her. The second appellate court held:

On remand the trial court overlooked this court's earlier direction that "the threshold for determining that conduct is unwelcome" is whether it was uninvited and offensive.

. . . .

The plaintiff's choice to pose for a nude magazine outside work hours is not material to the issue of whether plaintiff found her employer's work-related conduct offensive. This is not a case where Burns posed in provocative and suggestive ways at work. Her private life, regardless how reprehensible the trier of fact might find it to be, did not provide lawful acquiescence to unwanted sexual advances at her work place by her employer. To hold otherwise would be contrary to Title VII's goal of ridding the work place of any kind of unwelcome sexual harassment. . . .

---

43. *Id.* at 486–92.

. . . .

The trial court made explicit findings that the conduct was not invited or solicited despite her posing naked for a magazine distributed nationally. The court believed, however, that because of her outside conduct, including her "interest in having her nude pictures appear in a magazine containing much lewd and crude sexually explicit material," the uninvited sexual advances of her employer were not "in and of itself offensive to her." The court explained that Burns "would not have been offended if someone she was attracted to did or said the same thing."

We hold that such a view is unsupported in law. If the court intended this as a standard or rationale for a standard, it is clearly in error. This rationale would allow a complete stranger to pursue sexual behavior at work that a female worker would accept from her husband or boyfriend. This standard would allow a male employee to kiss or fondle a female worker at the workplace. None of the plaintiff's conduct, which the court found relevant to bar her action, was work related. Burns did not tell sexual stories or engage in sexual gestures at work. She did not initiate sexual talk or solicit sexual encounters with co-employees. Under the trial court's rationale, if a woman taught part-time sexual education at a high school or college, a court would be compelled to find that sexual language, even though uninvited when directed at her in the work place, would not offend her as it might someone else who was not as accustomed to public usage of the terms.[44]

Consider the delay, trauma, and expense to the plaintiff of having to endure two trial determinations and two appeals. Could the first appellate court have crafted its opinion differently to avoid the outcome that resulted? Or did the first appellate court decide the case properly?

3. Element Four: Conduct That Affects the Terms, Conditions, or Privileges of Employment

In addition to raising questions about welcomeness, *Meritor* created confusion over other elements of the prima facie case for sexual harassment. For example, *Meritor* left unanswered what kind of "conduct has the purpose or effect of unreasonably interfering with an individual's work performance or creating an intimidating, hostile, or offensive working environment." What is unreasonable? By whose perspective does one evaluate reasonableness? Litigants struggled with how to measure and evaluate "severe or pervasive" behavior. Lower courts addressed the numerous ambiguities created in *Meritor* and arrived at differing conclusions.

---

44. 989 F.2d 959, 962–63 (8th Cir. 1993).

A. Defining a Hostile Work Environment

Rabidue v. Osceola Refining Company

805 F.2d 611 (6th Cir. 1986)

KRUPANSKY, Circuit Judge.

. . . .

. . . In 1973, the plaintiff [Vivienne Rabidue] was promoted to the position of administrative assistant and became a salaried rather than hourly employee. . . .

The plaintiff was a capable, independent, ambitious, aggressive, intractable, and opinionated individual. The plaintiff's supervisors and co-employees with whom plaintiff interacted almost uniformly found her to be an abrasive, rude, antagonistic, extremely willful, uncooperative, and irascible personality. . . .

The plaintiff's charged sexual harassment arose primarily as a result of her unfortunate acrimonious working relationship with Douglas Henry (Henry). . . . Henry was an extremely vulgar and crude individual who customarily made obscene comments about women generally, and, on occasion, directed such obscenities to the plaintiff. Management was aware of Henry's vulgarity, but had been unsuccessful in curbing his offensive personality traits during the time encompassed by this controversy. The plaintiff and Henry, on the occasions when their duties exposed them to each other, were constantly in a confrontation posture. The plaintiff, as well as other female employees, were annoyed by Henry's vulgarity. In addition to Henry's obscenities, other male employees from time to time displayed pictures of nude or scantily clad women in their offices and/or work areas, to which the plaintiff and other women employees were exposed.

The plaintiff was formally discharged from her employment at the company on January 14, 1977 as a result of her many job-related problems, including her irascible and opinionated personality and her inability to work harmoniously with co-workers and customers. . . .

. . . .

. . . A review of the record disclosed that the trial court's findings, namely that the company's predischarge actions toward the plaintiff did not evince an anti-female animus, were not clearly erroneous. Consequently, the trial court's conclusion that the plaintiff failed to establish violations of Title VII . . . is AFFIRMED.

. . . .

Unlike *quid pro quo* sexual harassment which may evolve from a single incident, sexually hostile or intimidating environments are characterized by multiple and varied combinations and frequencies of offensive exposures, which characteristics would dictate an order of proof that placed the burden upon the plaintiff to demonstrate that injury resulted not from a single or isolated offensive incident, comment, or conduct, but from incidents, comments, or conduct that occurred with some frequency. To accord appropriate protection to both plaintiffs and defendants in a hostile and/or abusive work environment sexual harassment case, the trier of fact, when judging the totality of the circumstances impacting upon the asserted abusive and hostile environment placed in issue by the plaintiff's charges, must adopt the perspective of a reasonable person's reaction to a similar environment under essentially like or similar circumstances. Thus, in the absence of conduct which would interfere with that hypothetical reasonable individual's work performance and affect seriously the psychological well-being of that reasonable person under like circumstances, a plaintiff may not prevail on asserted charges of sexual harassment anchored in an alleged hostile and/or abusive work environment regardless of whether the plaintiff was actually offended by the defendant's conduct. Assuming that the plaintiff has successfully satisfied the burden of proving that the defendant's conduct would have interfered with a reasonable individual's work performance and would have affected seriously the psychological well-being of a reasonable employee, the particular plaintiff would nevertheless also be required to demonstrate that she was actually offended by the defendant's conduct and that she suffered some degree of injury as a result of the abusive and hostile work environment.

Accordingly, a proper assessment or evaluation of an employment environment that gives rise to a sexual harassment claim would invite consideration of such objective and subjective factors as the nature of the alleged harassment, the background and experience of the plaintiff, her coworkers, and supervisors, the totality of the physical environment of the plaintiff's work area, the lexicon of obscenity that pervaded the environment of the workplace both before and after the plaintiff's introduction into its environs, coupled with the reasonable expectation of the plaintiff upon voluntarily entering that environment. Thus, the presence of actionable sexual harassment would be different depending upon the personality of the plaintiff and the prevailing work environment and must be considered and evaluated upon an ad hoc basis. As Judge Newblatt aptly stated in his opinion in the district court:

> Indeed, it cannot seriously be disputed that in some work environments, humor and language are rough hewn and vulgar. Sexual jokes, sexual conversations and girlie magazines may abound. Title VII was not meant to — or can — change this. It must never be forgotten that Title VII is the federal court mainstay in the struggle for equal employment opportunity for the female workers of America. But it is quite different to claim that Title VII was designed to bring about a magical transformation in the social mores of American workers. Clearly, the Court's qualification is necessary to enable 29 C.F.R. § 1604.11(a)(3) to function as a workable judicial standard.

> Rabidue [v. Osceola Ref. Co.], 584 F. Supp. [419,] . . . 430 [(E.D. Mich. 1984)].

To prevail in an action that asserts a charge of offensive work environment sexual harassment, the ultimate burden of proof is upon the plaintiff to additionally demonstrate respondeat superior liability by proving that the employer, through its agents or supervisory personnel, knew or should have known of the charged sexual harassment and failed to implement prompt and appropriate corrective action. [Ed.

note. This last element is no longer good law in the case of supervisor harassment.] The promptness and adequacy of the employer's response to correct instances of alleged sexual harassment is of significance in assessing a sexually hostile environment claim and the employer's reactions must be evaluated upon a case by case basis.

. . . It would appear that the most effective and efficient procedural format would implement the traditional practice of placing the ultimate burden of proof by a preponderance of the evidence upon the claimant followed by a proffer of defense and an opportunity for a plaintiff's rebuttal.

A review of the Title VII sexual harassment issue in the matter *sub judice* prompts this court to conclude that the plaintiff neither asserted nor proved a claim of "sexual advances," "sexual favors," or "physical conduct," or sexual harassment implicating subparts (a)(1) or (a)(2) of the EEOC definition, more specifically, those elements typically at issue in a case of *quid pro quo* sexual harassment. Thus, the plaintiff to have prevailed in her cause of action against the defendant on this record must have proved that she had been subjected to unwelcomed verbal conduct and poster displays of a sexual nature which had unreasonably interfered with her work performance and created an intimidating, hostile, or offensive working environment that affected seriously her psychological well-being.

In the case at bar, the record effectively disclosed that Henry's obscenities, although annoying, were not so startling as to have affected seriously the psyches of the plaintiff or other female employees. The evidence did not demonstrate that this single employee's vulgarity substantially affected the totality of the workplace. The sexually oriented poster displays had a de minimis effect on the plaintiff's work environment when considered in the context of a society that condones and publicly features and commercially exploits open displays of written and pictorial erotica at the newsstands, on prime-time television, at the cinema, and in other public places. In sum, Henry's vulgar language, coupled with the sexually oriented posters, did not result in a working environment that could be considered intimidating, hostile, or offensive under 29 C.F.R. § 1604.11(a)(3) as elaborated upon by this court. . . . Accordingly, the trial court's disposition of this issue is AFFIRMED.

. . . .

KEITH, Circuit Judge, concurring in part, dissenting in part.

. . . .

I dissent for several reasons. First, after review of the entire record I am firmly convinced, that although supporting evidence exists, the court is mistaken in affirming the findings that defendant's treatment of plaintiff evinced no anti-female animus and that gender-based discrimination played no role in her discharge. The overall circumstances of plaintiff's workplace evince an anti-female environment. For seven years plaintiff worked at Osceola as the sole woman in a salaried management position. In common work areas plaintiff and other female employees were exposed daily to displays of nude or partially clad women belonging to a number of male employees at Osceola. One poster, which remained on the wall for eight years, showed a prone woman who had a golf ball on her breasts with a man standing over her, golf club in hand, yelling "Fore." And one desk plaque declared "Even male chauvinist pigs need love." Plaintiff testified the posters offended her and her female co-workers.

In addition, Computer Division Supervisor Doug Henry regularly spewed anti-female obscenity. Henry routinely referred to women as "whores," "cunt," "pussy" and "tits." Of plaintiff, Henry specifically remarked "All that bitch needs is a good lay" and called her "fat ass." Plaintiff arranged at least one meeting of female employees to discuss Henry and repeatedly filed written complaints on behalf of herself and other female employees who feared losing their jobs if they complained directly. Osceola Vice President Charles Muetzel stated he knew that employees were "greatly disturbed" by Henry's language. However, because Osceola needed Henry's computer expertise, Muetzel did not reprimand or fire Henry. In response to subsequent complaints about Henry, a later supervisor, Charles Shoemaker, testified that he gave Henry "a little fatherly advice" about Henry's prospects if he learned to become "an executive type person."

In addition to tolerating this anti-female behavior, defendant excluded plaintiff, the sole female in management, from activities she needed to perform her duties and progress in her career. Plaintiff testified that unlike male salaried employees, she did not receive free lunches, free gasoline, a telephone credit card or entertainment privileges. Nor was she invited to the weekly golf matches. Without addressing defendant's disparate treatment of plaintiff, the district court dismissed these perks and business activities as fringe benefits. After plaintiff became credit manager defendant prevented plaintiff from visiting or taking customers to lunch as all previous male credit managers had done. Plaintiff testified that upon requesting such privileges, her supervisor, Mr. Muetzel, replied that it would be improper for a woman to take male customers to lunch and that she "might have car trouble on the road." Plaintiff reported that on another occasion, Muetzel asked her "how would it look for me, a married man, to take you, a divorced woman, to the West Branch Country Club in such a small town?" However, defendant apparently saw no problem in male managers entertaining female clients regardless of marital status. Plaintiff's subsequent supervisor, Charles Shoemaker, stated to another female worker, Joyce Solo, that "Vivienne (plaintiff) is doing a good job as credit manager, but we really need a man on that job," adding "She can't take customers out to lunch." Aside from this Catch-22, Mr. Shoemaker also remarked plaintiff was not forceful enough to collect slow-paying jobs. How plaintiff can be so abrasive and aggressive as to require firing but too timid to collect delinquent accounts is, in my view, an enigma.

. . . .

The record establishes plaintiff possessed negative personal traits. These traits did not, however, justify the sex-based disparate treatment recounted above. Whatever undesirable behavior plaintiff exhibited, it was clearly no worse than Henry's. I conclude the misogynous language and decorative displays tolerated at the refinery (which even the district court found constituted a "fairly significant" part of the job environment), the primitive views of working women expressed by Osceola super-visors and defendant's treatment of plaintiff as the only female salaried employee clearly evince anti-female animus.

Second, I dissent because I am unable to accept key elements of the standard for sexual harassment set forth in the majority opinion. Specifically, I would not impose on the plaintiff alleging hostile environment harassment an additional bur-den of proving respondeat superior liability where a supervisor is responsible for the harm. . . . Agency principles establish that an employer is normally liable for the acts of its supervisors and agents. . . . The creation of a discriminatory work environ-ment by a supervisor can only be achieved through the power accorded him by the employer. I see insufficient reason to add an element of proof not imposed on any other discrimination victim, particularly where agency principles and the "goals of Title VII law" preclude the imposition of automatic liability in all circumstances. . . .

. . . .

Nor do I agree with the majority holding that a court considering hostile envi-ronment claims should adopt the perspective of the reasonable person's reaction to a similar environment. In my view, the reasonable person perspective fails to account for the wide divergence between most women's views of appropriate sexual conduct and those of men. I would have courts adopt the perspective of the rea-sonable victim which simultaneously allows courts to consider salient sociological differences as well as shield employers from the neurotic complainant. Moreover, unless the outlook of the reasonable woman is adopted, the defendants as well as the courts are permitted to sustain ingrained notions of reasonable behavior fashioned by the offenders, in this case, men.

Which brings me to the majority's mandate to consider the "prevailing work envi-ronment," "the lexicon of obscenity that pervaded the environment both before and after plaintiff's introduction into its environs," and plaintiff's reasonable expectations upon "voluntarily" entering that environment. The majority suggests through these factors that a woman assumes the risk of working in an abusive, anti-female environ-ment. Moreover, the majority contends that such work environments somehow have an innate right to perpetuation and are not to be addressed under Title VII. . . .

In my view, Title VII's precise purpose is to prevent such behavior and attitudes from poisoning the work environment of classes protected under the Act. To con-done the majority's notion of the "prevailing workplace" I would also have to agree that if an employer maintains an anti-semitic workforce and tolerates a workplace in which "kike" jokes, displays of nazi literature and anti-Jewish conversation "may abound," a Jewish employee assumes the risk of working there, and a court must consider such a work environment as "prevailing." I cannot. As I see it, job related-ness is the only additional factor which legitimately bears on the inquiry of plain-tiff's reasonableness in finding her work environment offensive. In other words, the only additional question I would find relevant is whether the behavior com-plained of is required to perform the work. For example, depending on their job descriptions, employees of soft pornography publishers or other sex-related industries should reasonably expect exposure to nudity, sexually explicit language or even simulated sex as inherent aspects of working in that field. However, when that exposure goes beyond what is required professionally, even sex industry employees are protected under the Act from non-job related sexual demands, language or other offensive behavior by supervisors or co-workers. As I believe no woman should be subjected to an environment where her sexual dignity and reasonable sensibilities are visually, verbally or physically assaulted as a matter of prevailing male prerogative, I dissent.

The majority would also have courts consider the background of plaintiff's co-workers and supervisors in assessing the presence of actionable work environment sex harassment. The only reason to inquire into the backgrounds of the defendants or other co-workers is to determine if the behavior tolerated toward female employees is reasonable in light of those backgrounds. As I see it, these subjective factors create an unworkable standard by requiring the courts to balance a morass of perspectives. But more importantly, the background of the defendants or other workers is irrelevant. No court analyzes the background and experience of a supervisor who refuses to promote black employees before finding actionable race discrimination under Title VII. An equally disturbing implication of considering defendants' backgrounds is the notion that workplaces with the least sophisticated employees are the most prone to anti-female environments. Assuming *arguendo* this notion is true, by applying the prevailing workplace factor, this court locks the vast majority of working women into workplaces which tolerate anti-female behavior. I conclude that for actionable offensive environment claims, the relevant inquiry is whether the conduct complained of is offensive to the reasonable woman. Either the environment affects her ability to perform or it does not. The backgrounds and experience of the defendant's supervisors and employees is irrelevant.

Nor can I agree with the majority's notion that the effect of pin-up posters and misogynous language in the workplace can have only a minimal effect on female employees and should not be deemed hostile or offensive "when considered in the context of a society that condones and publicly features and commercially exploits open displays of written and pictorial erotica at newsstands, on prime-time television, at the cinema and in other public places." "Society" in this scenario must primarily refer to the unenlightened; I hardly believe reasonable women condone the pervasive degradation and exploitation of female sexuality perpetuated in American culture. In fact, pervasive societal approval thereof and of other stereotypes stifles female potential and instills the debased sense of self worth which accompanies stigmatization. The presence of pin-ups and misogynous language in the workplace can only evoke and confirm the debilitating norms by which women are primarily and contemptuously valued as objects of male sexual fantasy. That some men would condone and wish to perpetuate such behavior is not surprising. However, the relevant inquiry at hand is what the reasonable woman would find offensive, not society, which at one point also condoned slavery. I conclude that sexual posters and anti-female language can seriously affect the psychological well being of the reasonable woman and interfere with her ability to perform her job.

. . . .

In conclusion, I dissent because the record shows that defendant's treatment of plaintiff evinces anti-female animus and that plaintiff's gender played a role in her dismissal. I also believe the hostile environment standard set forth in the majority opinion shields and condones behavior Title VII would have the courts redress. Finally, in my view, the standard fails to encourage employers to set up internal complaint procedures or otherwise seriously address the problem of sexual harassment in the workplace.

Notes and Discussion

1. Factual Record Compare the majority's recitation of the facts with the dissent's. The majority described the language that plaintiff's supervisor used toward her and other women as "obscene" and "vulgar," but failed to set forth what language was actually used. The dissent, in contrast, listed the terms, including "whores," "cunt," "pussy," and "tits." Similarly, the majority described the material that was displayed in the workplace as "girlie magazines" and "sexually oriented poster displays." The dissent actually described the details of one such poster. Do these differences change your view of whether the facts constituted severe or pervasive behavior? Given the importance of the facts in reaching this threshold, consider how a plaintiff's lawyer can most effectively put forth the client's case: by including graphic detail, avoiding euphemisms, and pushing back against minimizing or dismissive language.

2. Severe *or* Pervasive Harassment The majority held that a plaintiff must "demonstrate that injury resulted not from a single or isolated offensive incident, comment, or conduct, but from incidents, comments, or conduct that occurred with some frequency." Is this an accurate reading of the standard set forth in *Meritor*? Could a hostile environment result from one particularly severe incident? The EEOC offers the following guidance:

> [A] single, unusually severe incident of harassment may be sufficient to constitute a Title VII violation; the more severe, the harassment, the less need to show a repetitive series of incidents. This is particularly true when the harassment is physical. . . .
>
> The Commission will presume that the unwelcome, intentional touching of a charging party's intimate body areas is sufficiently offensive to alter the conditions of her working environment and constitute a violation of Title VII.[45]

Is the EEOC Guidance persuasive? Why did the *Rabidue* majority depart from the Policy Guidance?

---

45. EEOC Policy Guidance on Current Issues of Sexual Harassment (March 19, 1990), https://www.eeoc.gov/policy/docs/currentissues.html.

3. Work Performance and Hostile Environment The EEOC's guidelines specify that actionable harassing conduct "has the purpose or effect of unreasonably interfering with an individual's work performance *or* creating an intimidating, hostile, or offensive working environment." Why is it important to include both of these options, in the disjunctive? Is it possible for harassment to lead to one outcome and not the other?

4. The Reasonable Person/Woman Standards The majority suggested that the trier of fact adopt a reasonable person's perspective in evaluating offensive behaviors. The dissent argued that the reasonable person standard "sustain[s] ingrained notions of reasonable behavior fashioned by the offenders, in this case, men[.]" Is that contention meritorious? Are men and women genuinely likely to perceive conduct differently, or does a "reasonable woman" standard only perpetuate sexist assumptions about the way men and women think? Is the opinion of other women at the workplace relevant in the evaluation of the objective reasonableness of the plaintiff's offense? Should it be determinative? Should courts permit expert testimony concerning the reasonableness of the plaintiff's response to and offense at certain behaviors? Note that this is an objective standard. The plaintiff must also demonstrate that she subjectively perceived the conduct to be offensive.

5. The Employment Environment The *Rabidue* majority held that courts should consider multiple factors when determining whether an environment is sexually harassing, including:

> the nature of the alleged harassment, the background and experience of the plaintiff, her coworkers, and supervisors, the totality of the physical environment of the plaintiff's work area, the lexicon of obscenity that pervaded the environment of the workplace both before and after the plaintiff's introduction into its environs, coupled with the reasonable expectation of the plaintiff upon voluntarily entering that environment. Thus, the presence of actionable sexual harassment would be different depending upon the personality of the plaintiff and the prevailing work environment and must be considered and evaluated on an ad hoc basis.[46]

Note at the same time the majority failed to discuss how the defendant excluded plaintiff from professional opportunities because she was a woman, a fact that is raised by the dissent. Why should a woman's "personality," "background and experience" be relevant to an evaluation of the objective hostility of the workplace?

The EEOC Guidelines, noted in footnote 5 by the majority, recommend that courts look to "the record as a whole and at the totality of the circumstances, such as the nature of the alleged sexual advances and the context in which the alleged incidents occurred." Was the majority correct that its approach "is not inconsistent with EEOC guidelines"? Is a case-by-case approach necessary even for conduct that clearly exceeds the bounds of acceptability?

---

46. *Rabidue*, 805 F.2d at 620.

Did the majority suggest, as the dissent claimed, that a plaintiff assumes the "risks" of working in an offensive workplace when he or she "voluntarily enter[s] the environment"? Professor Wendy Pollack concluded:

> Several themes run through many [sexual harassment] cases. . . . The first is the character assassination of the victim; second, misuse of the concept of assumption of risk to include voluntarily entering a hostile environment workplace; third, trivialization and isolation of the conduct so that it is not viewed as severe or pervasive.[47]

Are Pollack's conclusions fair? How much can any person know about a workplace environment prior to actually entering it? Why would any plaintiff "voluntarily" enter a hostile work environment? Consider *Meritor's* rejection of the involuntariness requirement, in favor of unwelcomeness. In light of this, is it appropriate for courts to make this inquiry? Should society permit such workers to assume the risk of their choices? By focusing on the plaintiff's expectations and his or her assumption of risk, does society somehow "blame" the target for a hostile workplace created by others? Does this approach vindicate the concerns raised by Susan Estrich?

Consider the quote from the district court, suggesting that Congress did not intend for Title VII to address workplaces replete with "sexual conversations and girlie magazines . . . [,] to bring about a magical transformation in the social mores of American workers. . . ." Would any court in the nation today make such an assertion? Consider Judge Edith Jones's dissent in *Waltman v. International Paper Co.*[48] in 1989 (finding sexual harassment, continuing violations and a prima facie showing of discriminatory failure to promote). She concluded, "We have so little social consensus in sexual mores nowadays that, short of incidents involving unwanted physical contact, it is impossible generally to categorize unacceptable sexual etiquette. It is likewise impossible to eradicate sexual conduct from the workplace—without unthinkable intrusiveness."[49] Is this still true today? Finally, consider Justice Scalia's more recent reference in *Oncale, infra,* to "ordinary socializing in the workplace—such as male on male horseplay or intersexual flirtation. . . ."

Do sexual displays and literature in the workplace have a "de minimis effect on the plaintiff's work environment when considered in the context of a society that condones and publicly features and commercially exploits open displays of written and pictorial erotica at the newsstands, on prime-time television, at the cinema, and in other public places"? Consider Susan Estrich's argument that "[i]t is precisely this attitude of easy acceptance, at least outside of work, which makes it so difficult to limit sexual harassment at work. The problem with the court decisions, and the attitudes they reflect, is that offensive sexuality is so routinely considered normal, abuse of power acceptable, and the dehumanizing of women in sexual relations

---

47. Pollack, *supra* note 38, at 70.
48. 875 F.2d 468 (5th Cir. 1989).
49. *Waltman*, 875 F.2d at 484 (Jones, J., dissenting).

unremarkable, that when we (or the courts, at least) see such things at work, it hardly seems a 'federal case.'"[50]

Finally, compare the majority's view of the "prevailing" American workplace with that of the dissent. The majority appears to treat the workplace as an extension of society, in which sexual images, jokes, and conversation are commonplace. Is this a correct way to determine workplace norms? As Professor Nancy Ehrenreich notes, the judge "essentially equated societal consensus with prevailing social practices. . . . [H]e seemed to conclude that the mere prevalence of pornography suggests general acceptance of the image of women contained within that pornography."[51] Is that true? In contrast, the dissent views the workplace as an environment that should be as free of such influences as possible, regardless of what might be more broadly accepted in society. Is the comparison with anti-Semitism in the workplace convincing?

Five years after the Sixth Circuit's *Rabidue* opinion, the Ninth Circuit explored many of the same issues in *Ellison v. Brady*. The *Ellison* majority discussed *Rabidue* and specifically disavowed its reasoning. Consider the differences in reasoning that underlie each decision.

Ellison v. Brady
924 F.2d 872 (9th Cir. 1991)

BEEZER, Circuit Judge:

Kerry Ellison appeals the district court's order granting summary judgment to the Secretary of the Treasury on her sexual harassment action brought under Title VII of the Civil Rights Act of 1964. 42 U.S.C. § 2000e (1982). This appeal presents two important issues: (1) what test should be applied to determine whether conduct is sufficiently severe or pervasive to alter the conditions of employment and create a hostile working environment, and (2) what remedial actions can shield employers from liability for sexual harassment by co-workers. The district court held that Ellison did not state a prima facie case of hostile environment sexual harassment. We reverse and remand.

. . . .

I.

Kerry Ellison worked as a revenue agent for the Internal Revenue Service in San Mateo, California. During her initial training in 1984 she met Sterling Gray, another trainee, who was also assigned to the San Mateo office. The two co-workers never became friends, and they did not work closely together.

---

50. Estrich, *supra* note 28, at 860.
51. Nancy Ehrenreich, *Pluralist Myth and Powerless Men: The Ideology of Reasonableness in Sexual Harassment Law*, 99 Yale L.J. 1177, 1206 (1990).

. . . Revenue agents in the San Mateo office often went to lunch in groups. In June of 1986 when no one else was in the office, Gray asked Ellison to lunch. She accepted. . . .

Ellison alleges that after the June lunch Gray started to pester her with unnecessary questions and hang around her desk. On October 9, 1986, Gray asked Ellison out for a drink after work. She declined, but she suggested that they have lunch the following week. She did not want to have lunch alone with him, and she tried to stay away from the office during lunch time. One day during the following week, Gray uncharacteristically dressed in a three-piece suit and asked Ellison out for lunch. Again, she did not accept.

On October 22, 1986 Gray handed Ellison a note he wrote on a telephone message slip which read:

> I cried over you last night and I'm totally drained today. I have never been in such constant term oil (sic). Thank you for talking with me. I could not stand to feel your hatred for another day.

When Ellison realized that Gray wrote the note, she became shocked and frightened and left the room. Gray followed her into the hallway and demanded that she talk to him, but she left the building.

Ellison later showed the note to Bonnie Miller, who supervised both Ellison and Gray. Miller said "this is sexual harassment." Ellison asked Miller not to do anything about it. She wanted to try to handle it herself. Ellison asked a male co-worker to talk to Gray, to tell him that she was not interested in him and to leave her alone. The next day, Thursday, Gray called in sick.

Ellison did not work on Friday, and on the following Monday, she started four weeks of training in St. Louis, Missouri. Gray mailed her a card and a typed, single-spaced, three-page letter. She describes this letter as "twenty times, a hundred times weirder" than the prior note. Gray wrote, in part:

> I know that you are worth knowing with or without sex. . . . Leaving aside the hassles and disasters of recent weeks. I have enjoyed you so much over these past few months. Watching you. Experiencing you from O so far away. Admiring your style and elan. . . . Don't you think it odd that two people who have never even talked together, alone, are striking off such intense sparks . . . I will [write] another letter in the near future.

Explaining her reaction, Ellison stated: "I just thought he was crazy. I thought he was nuts. I didn't know what he would do next. I was frightened."

She immediately telephoned Miller. Ellison told her supervisor that she was frightened and really upset. She requested that Miller transfer either her or Gray because she would not be comfortable working in the same office with him. . . .

. . . .

. . . Gray subsequently transferred to the San Francisco office on November 24, 1986. . . .

After three weeks in San Francisco, Gray filed union grievances requesting a return to the San Mateo office. The IRS and the union settled the grievances in Gray's favor, agreeing to allow him to transfer back to the San Mateo office provided that he spend four more months in San Francisco and promise not to bother Ellison. On January 28, 1987, Ellison first learned of Gray's request in a letter from Miller explaining that Gray would return to the San Mateo office. The letter indicated that management decided to resolve Ellison's problem with a six-month separation, and that it would take additional action if the problem recurred.

After receiving the letter, Ellison was "frantic." She filed a formal complaint alleging sexual harassment on January 30, 1987 with the IRS. She also obtained permission to transfer to San Francisco temporarily when Gray returned.

Gray sought joint counseling. He wrote Ellison another letter which still sought to maintain the idea that he and Ellison had some type of relationship.

The IRS employee investigating the allegation agreed with Ellison's supervisor that Gray's conduct constituted sexual harassment. In its final decision, however, the Treasury Department rejected Ellison's complaint because it believed that the complaint did not describe a pattern or practice of sexual harassment covered by the EEOC regulations. After an appeal, the EEOC affirmed the Treasury Department's decision on a different ground. It concluded that the agency took adequate action to prevent the repetition of Gray's conduct.

. . . .

II.

. . . .

Since *Meritor*, we have not often reached the merits of a hostile environment sexual harassment claim. In *Jordan v. Clark*, 847 F.2d 1368, 1373 (9th Cir. 1988) we explained that a hostile environment exists when an employee can show (1) that he or she was subjected to sexual advances, requests for sexual favors, or other verbal or physical conduct of a sexual nature, (2) that this conduct was unwelcome, and (3) that the conduct was sufficiently severe or pervasive to alter the conditions of the victim's employment and create an abusive working environment.

. . . .

III.

. . . .

We begin our analysis of the third part of the framework we set forth in *Jordan* with a closer look at *Meritor*. The Supreme Court in *Meritor* explained that courts may properly look to guidelines issued by the Equal Employment Opportunity Commission (EEOC) for guidance when examining hostile environment claims of sexual harassment. The EEOC guidelines describe hostile environment harassment as "conduct [which] has the purpose or effect of unreasonably interfering with an individual's work performance or creating an intimidating, hostile, or offensive working environment." . . .

The Supreme Court cautioned, however, that not all harassment affects a "term, condition, or privilege" of employment within the meaning of Title VII. For example, the "mere utterance of an ethnic or racial epithet which engenders offensive feelings in an employee" is not, by itself, actionable under Title VII. To state a claim under Title VII, sexual harassment "must be sufficiently severe or pervasive to alter the conditions of the victim's employment and create an abusive working environment."

. . . .

Although *Meritor* and our previous cases establish the framework for the resolution of hostile environment cases, they do not dictate the outcome of this case. Gray's conduct falls somewhere between forcible rape and the mere utterance of an epithet. . . .

The government asks us to apply the reasoning of other courts which have declined to find Title VII violations on more egregious facts. In *Scott v. Sears, Roebuck & Co.* (7th Cir. 1986), the Seventh Circuit analyzed a female employee's working conditions for sexual harassment. It noted that she was repeatedly propositioned and winked at by her supervisor. When she asked for assistance, he asked "what will I get for it?" Co-workers slapped her buttocks and commented that she must moan and groan during sex. The court examined the evidence to see if "the demeaning conduct and sexual stereotyping cause[d] such anxiety and debilitation to the plaintiff that working conditions were 'poisoned' within the meaning of Title VII." The court did not consider the environment sufficiently hostile.

Similarly, in *Rabidue v. Osceola Refining Co.* (6th Cir. 1986) the Sixth Circuit refused to find a hostile environment where the workplace contained posters of naked and partially dressed women, and where a male employee customarily called women "whores," "cunt," "pussy," and "tits," referred to plaintiff as "fat ass," and specifically stated, "All that bitch needs is a good lay." Over a strong dissent, the majority held that the sexist remarks and the pin-up posters had only a de minimis effect and did not seriously affect the plaintiff's psychological well-being.

We do not agree with the standards set forth in *Scott* and *Rabidue* and we choose not to follow those decisions. Neither *Scott*'s search for "anxiety and debilitation" sufficient to "poison" a working environment nor *Rabidue*'s requirement that a plaintiff's psychological well-being be "seriously affected" follows directly from language in *Meritor*. It is the harasser's conduct which must be pervasive or severe, not the alteration in the conditions of employment. Surely, employees need not endure sexual harassment until their psychological well-being is seriously affected to the extent that they suffer anxiety and debilitation. Although an isolated epithet by itself fails to support a cause of action for a hostile environment, Title VII's protection of employees from sex discrimination comes into play long before the point where victims of sexual harassment require psychiatric assistance.

We have closely examined *Meritor* and our previous cases, and we believe that Gray's conduct was sufficiently severe and pervasive to alter the conditions of Ellison's employment and create an abusive working environment. We first note that the required showing of severity or seriousness of the harassing conduct varies inversely with the pervasiveness or frequency of the conduct. . . .

Next, we believe that in evaluating the severity and pervasiveness of sexual harassment, we should focus on the perspective of the victim. If we only examined whether a reasonable person would engage in allegedly harassing conduct, we would run the risk of reinforcing the prevailing level of discrimination. Harassers could continue to harass merely because a particular discriminatory practice was common, and victims of harassment would have no remedy.

We therefore prefer to analyze harassment from the victim's perspective. A complete understanding of the victim's view requires, among other things, an analysis of the different perspectives of men and women. Conduct that many men consider unobjectionable may offend many women. *See, e.g.*, *Lipsett v. University of Puerto Rico* (1st Cir. 1988) ("A male supervisor might believe, for example, that it is legitimate for him to tell a female subordinate that she has a 'great figure' or 'nice legs.' The female subordinate, however, may find such comments offensive"). . . . *See also* Ehrenreich, *Pluralist Myths and Powerless Men: The Ideology of Reasonableness in Sexual Harassment Law*, 99 Yale L.J. 1177, 1207–1208 (1990) (men tend to view some forms of sexual harassment as "harmless social interactions to which only overly-sensitive women would object"); Abrams, *Gender Discrimination and the Transformation of Workplace Norms*, 42 Vand.L.Rev. 1183, 1203 (1989) (the characteristically male view depicts sexual harassment as comparatively harmless amusement).

We realize that there is a broad range of viewpoints among women as a group, but we believe that many women share common concerns which men do not necessarily share. For example, because women are disproportionately victims of rape and sexual assault, women have a stronger incentive to be concerned with sexual behavior.Women who are victims of mild forms of sexual harassment may understandably worry whether a harasser's conduct is merely a prelude to violent sexual assault. Men, who are rarely victims of sexual assault, may view sexual conduct in a vacuum without a full appreciation of the social setting or the underlying threat of violence that a woman may perceive.

In order to shield employers from having to accommodate the idiosyncratic concerns of the rare hyper-sensitive employee, we hold that a female plaintiff states a prima facie case of hostile environment sexual harassment when she alleges conduct which a reasonable woman would consider sufficiently severe or pervasive to alter the conditions of employment and create an abusive working environment.

We adopt the perspective of a reasonable woman primarily because we believe that a sex-blind reasonable person standard tends to be male-biased and tends to systematically ignore the experiences of women. The reasonable woman standard does not establish a higher level of protection for women than men. Instead, a gender-conscious examination of sexual harassment enables women to participate in the workplace on an equal footing with men. By acknowledging and not trivializing the effects of sexual harassment on reasonable women, courts can work towards ensuring that neither men nor women will have to "run a gauntlet of sexual abuse in return for the privilege of being allowed to work and make a living." *Henson v. Dundee*, 682 F.2d 897, 902 (11th Cir. 1982).

We note that the reasonable victim standard we adopt today classifies conduct as unlawful sexual harassment even when harassers do not realize that their conduct creates a hostile working environment. Well-intentioned compliments by co-workers or supervisors can form the basis of a sexual harassment cause of action if a reasonable victim of the same sex as the plaintiff would consider the comments sufficiently severe or pervasive to alter a condition of employment and create an abusive working environment. That is because Title VII is not a fault-based tort scheme. "Title VII is aimed at the consequences or effects of an employment practice and not at the . . . motivation" of co-workers or employers. *Rogers*, 454 F.2d at 239. To avoid liability under Title VII, employers may have to educate and sensitize their workforce to eliminate conduct which a reasonable victim would consider unlawful sexual harassment.

. . . .

. . . When Ellison learned that Gray arranged to return to San Mateo, she immediately asked to transfer, and she immediately filed an official complaint.

We cannot say as a matter of law that Ellison's reaction was idiosyncratic or hypersensitive. We believe that a reasonable woman could have had a similar reaction. After receiving the first bizarre note from Gray, a person she barely knew, Ellison asked a co-worker to tell Gray to leave her alone. Despite her request, Gray sent her a long, passionate, disturbing letter. He told her he had been "watching" and "experiencing" her; he made repeated references to sex; he said he would write again. Ellison had no way of knowing what Gray would do next. A reasonable woman could consider Gray's conduct, as alleged by Ellison, sufficiently severe and pervasive to alter a condition of employment and create an abusive working environment.

Sexual harassment is a major problem in the workplace. Adopting the victim's perspective ensures that courts will not "sustain ingrained notions of reasonable behavior fashioned by the offenders." *Lipsett*, 864 F.2d at 898, *quoting, Rabidue*, 805 F.2d at 626 (Keith, J., dissenting). Congress did not enact Title VII to codify prevailing sexist prejudices. . . . We hope that over time both men and women will learn what conduct offends reasonable members of the other sex. When employers and employees internalize the standard of workplace conduct we establish today, the current gap in perception between the sexes will be bridged.

. . . .

V.

We reverse the district court's decision that Ellison did not allege a prima facie case of sexual harassment due to a hostile working environment, and we remand for further proceedings consistent with this opinion. . . .

STEPHENS, District Judge, dissenting:

This case comes to us on appeal in the wake of the granting of a summary judgment motion. There was no trial, therefore no opportunities for cross examination of the witnesses. . . . Consequently, I believe that it is an inappropriate case with which to establish a new legal precedent which will be binding in all subsequent cases of like nature in the Ninth Circuit. I refer to the majority's use of the term "reasonable woman," a term I find ambiguous and therefore inadequate.

Nowhere in section 2000e of Title VII, the section under which the plaintiff in this case brought suit, is there any indication that Congress intended to provide for any other than equal treatment in the area of civil rights. . . . In fact, the Supreme Court has shown a preference against systems that are not gender or race neutral, such as hiring quotas. While women may be the most frequent targets of this type of conduct that is at issue in this case, they are not the only targets. I believe that it is incumbent upon the court in this case to use terminology that will meet the needs of all who seek recourse under this section of Title VII. Possible alternatives that are more in line with a gender neutral approach include "victim," "target," or "person."

. . . It is clear that the authors of the majority opinion intend a difference between the "reasonable woman" and the "reasonable man" in Title VII cases on the assumption that men do not have the same sensibilities as women. This is not necessarily true. A man's response to circumstances faced by women and their effect upon women can be and in given circumstances may be expected to be understood by men.

. . . .

The focus on the victim of the sexually discriminatory conduct has its parallel in rape trials in the focus put by the defense on the victim's conduct rather than on the unlawful conduct of the person accused. Modern feminists have pointed out that concentration by the defense upon evidence concerning the background, appearance and conduct of women claiming to have been raped must be carefully controlled by the court to avoid effectively shifting the burden of proof to the victim. It is the accused, not the victim who is on trial, and it is therefore the conduct of the accused, not that of the victim, that should be subjected to scrutiny. Many state legislatures have responded to this viewpoint, and rules governing the presentation of evidence in rape cases have evolved accordingly.

. . . .

The creation of the proposed "new standard" which applies only to women will not necessarily come to the aid of all potential victims of the type of misconduct that is at issue in this case. I believe that a gender neutral standard would greatly contribute to the clarity of this and future cases in the same area. Summary judgment is not appropriate in this case.

Notes and Discussion

1. Severe or Pervasive Conduct Did, as Ellison's supervisor suggested, the behavior on and before October 22, 1986, constitute severe or pervasive conduct amounting to "sexual harassment"? Why or why not? If not, when—if ever—did Gray's conduct constitute severe or pervasive harassment?

The majority held that there is an inverse relation between the severity and the pervasiveness of conduct in the sexual harassment calculus. Which factor—pervasiveness/frequency or severity—do you think is easier for a court to measure? How might this affect the analysis?

2. Psychological Impact The majority suggested, "Title VII's protection . . . comes into play long before the point where the victims of sexual harassment require psychiatric assistance." Should a survivor have to suffer any psychological impact before the offensive behavior becomes actionable? Why not leave all discussions of survivor harm to the damages phase of the trial? Some of these questions were answered definitively in *Harris*, discussed in the next section.

Proof of psychological harm, whether required or not, will strengthen both a plaintiff's prima facie case of hostile environment and her claim for emotional distress damages. What type of evidence could an advocate present to show psychological harm? Certainly, a report from a treating physician or psychologist would be useful, but what if the woman did not seek professional help? What other type of information would you use?

Even as they have an incentive to put forth a strong case, advocates will want to be careful about the amount and type of evidence they put forth to demonstrate emotional harm. Making such claims may place the plaintiff's medical and/or psychological condition at issue. Such claims open the door for discovery into other aspects of the plaintiff's medical and psychological history. In particular, the introduction of any treatment information into evidence may constitute a waiver of the psychotherapist-patient privilege that the Supreme Court articulated in *Jaffee v. Redmond*.[52] See, e.g., *Vann v. Lone Star Steakhouse & Saloon of Springfield, Inc.* (by endorsing her therapist as a witness, sexual harassment plaintiff waived her privilege).[53] Even if such information is to be kept confidential, plaintiffs may find such inquiries embarrassing and intrusive.

Whether or not a court will permit such discovery depends upon whether the court adopts a broad or narrow view of the waiver issue. Compare *Vanderbilt v. Town of Chilmark* (plaintiff waives the privilege only if she seeks to place her communications with her therapist at issue)[54] with *EEOC v. Danka Industries, Inc.* (simply requesting damage for emotional distress waives psychotherapist patient privilege and makes plaintiff's medical and psychological records discoverable).[55] Some courts have adopted a middle ground approach in which the plaintiff does not waive the privilege so long as she does not seek damages for more than "garden

---

52. 518 U.S. 1 (1996).
53. 967 F. Supp. 346 (C.D. Ill. 1997).
54. 174 F.R.D. 225 (D. Mass. 1997).
55. 990 F. Supp. 1138 (E.D. MO 1997).

variety emotional distress" and does not introduce expert testimony or a diagnosis in support of her claim.[56] In light of the fact that Title VII requires plaintiffs to demonstrate severity or pervasiveness as part of their prima facie case, how can courts balance plaintiffs' privacy interests against the rights of defendants to inquire into all potentially relevant subjects? Does this raise any ethical concerns for defense attorneys?

3. The Perpetrator's Perspective The *Ellison* majority suggested that "Title VII is not a fault-based tort scheme" and acknowledged that some "[w]ell-intentioned compliments by co-workers" might form the basis for a sexual harassment claim if the conduct was severe or pervasive. Should a trier of fact disregard the perpetrator's motivations?

Two years after *Ellison* marked a conflict with the Sixth Circuit's *Rabidue* opinion, the Supreme Court resolved the conflict and refined the definition of a hostile work environment. It also attempted to clarify the level of offense and trauma required before a target could sue. Consider whether the Court established a clear standard for evaluating severe or pervasive behavior.

Harris v. Forklift Systems, Inc.
510 U.S. 17 (1993)

O'CONNOR, J., delivered the opinion for a unanimous Court.

In this case we consider the definition of a discriminatorily "abusive work environment" (also known as a "hostile work environment"). . . .

I.

Teresa Harris worked as a manager at Forklift Systems, Inc., an equipment rental company, from April 1985 until October 1987. Charles Hardy was Forklift's president.

The Magistrate found that, throughout Harris' [sic] time at Forklift, Hardy often insulted her because of her gender and often made her the target of unwanted sexual innuendos. Hardy told Harris on several occasions, in the presence of other employees, "You're a woman, what do you know" and "We need a man as the rental manager"; at least once, he told her she was "a dumb ass woman." Again in front of others, he suggested that the two of them "go to the Holiday Inn to negotiate [Harris'] raise." Hardy occasionally asked Harris and other female employees to get coins from his front pants pocket. He threw objects on the ground in front of Harris and other women, and asked them to pick the objects up. He made sexual innuendos about Harris' and other women's clothing.

In mid-August 1987, Harris complained to Hardy about his conduct. Hardy said he was surprised that Harris was offended, claimed he was only joking, and apologized.

---

56. *See* Ruhlmann v. Ulster Country Dept. of Social Services, 194 F.R.D. 445 (N.D.N.Y. 2000).

He also promised he would stop, and based on this assurance Harris stayed on the job. But in early September, Hardy began anew: While Harris was arranging a deal with one of Forklift's customers, he asked her, again in front of other employees, "What did you do, promise the guy . . . some [sex] Saturday night?" On October 1, Harris collected her paycheck and quit.

Harris then sued Forklift, claiming that Hardy's conduct had created an abusive work environment for her because of her gender. The United States District Court for the Middle District of Tennessee, adopting the report and recommendation of the Magistrate, found this to be "a close case," but held that Hardy's conduct did not create an abusive environment. The court found that some of Hardy's comments "offended [Harris], and would offend the reasonable woman," but that they were not

> "so severe as to be expected to seriously affect [Harris'] psychological well-being. A reasonable woman manager under like circumstances would have been offended by Hardy, but his conduct would not have risen to the level of interfering with that person's work performance.

> "Neither do I believe that [Harris] was subjectively so offended that she suffered injury . . . . Although Hardy may at times have genuinely offended [Harris], I do not believe that he created a working environment so poisoned as to be intimidating or abusive to [Harris]."

In focusing on the employee's psychological well-being, the District Court was following Circuit precedent. *See* Rabidue v. Osceola Refining Co. The United States Court of Appeals for the Sixth Circuit affirmed in a brief unpublished decision.

We granted certiorari to resolve a conflict among the Circuits on whether conduct, to be actionable as "abusive work environment" harassment (no *quid pro quo* harassment issue is present here), must "seriously affect [an employee's] psychological well-being" or lead the plaintiff to "suffe[r] injury." *Compare* Rabidue (requiring serious effect on psychological well-being) . . . *with* Ellison v. Brady (9th Cir. 1991) (rejecting such a requirement).

II.

. . . When the workplace is permeated with "discriminatory intimidation, ridicule, and insult," [Meritor Savings Bank v. Vinson,] 477 U.S. at 65, that is "sufficiently severe or pervasive to alter the conditions of the victim's employment and create an abusive working environment," Title VII is violated.

This standard, which we reaffirm today, takes a middle path between making actionable any conduct that is merely offensive and requiring the conduct to cause a tangible psychological injury. As we pointed out in *Meritor*, "mere utterance of an . . . epithet which engenders offensive feelings in a employee," . . . does not sufficiently affect the conditions of employment to implicate Title VII. Conduct that is not severe or pervasive enough to create an objectively hostile or abusive work environment—an environment that a reasonable person would find hostile or abusive—is beyond Title VII's purview. Likewise, if the victim does not subjectively perceive the environment to be abusive, the conduct has not actually altered the conditions of the victim's employment, and there is no Title VII violation.

But Title VII comes into play before the harassing conduct leads to a nervous break-down. A discriminatorily abusive work environment, even one that does not seriously affect employees' psychological well-being, can and often will detract from employees' job performance, discourage employees from remaining on the job, or keep them from advancing in their careers. Moreover, even without regard to these tangible effects, the very fact that the discriminatory conduct was so severe or pervasive that it created a work environment abusive to employees because of their race, gender, religion, or national origin offends Title VII's broad rule of workplace equality. The appalling conduct alleged in *Meritor*, and the reference in that case to environments "so heavily polluted with discrimination as to destroy completely the emotional and psychological stability of minority group workers,'" merely present some especially egregious examples of harassment. They do not mark the boundary of what is actionable.

We therefore believe the District Court erred in relying on whether the conduct "seriously affected plaintiff's psychological well-being" or led her to "suffe[r] injury." Such an inquiry may needlessly focus the factfinder's attention on concrete psychological harm, an element Title VII does not require. Certainly Title VII bars conduct that would seriously affect a reasonable person's psychological well-being, but the statute is not limited to such conduct. So long as the environment would reasonably be perceived, and is perceived, as hostile or abusive, there is no need for it also to be psychologically injurious.

This is not, and by its nature cannot be, a mathematically precise test. We need not answer today all the potential questions it raises. . . . But we can say that whether an environment is "hostile" or "abusive" can be determined only by looking at all the circumstances. These may include the frequency of the discriminatory conduct; its severity; whether it is physically threatening or humiliating, or a mere offensive utterance; and whether it unreasonably interferes with an employee's work performance. The effect on the employee's psychological well-being is, of course, relevant to determining whether the plaintiff actually found the environment abusive. But while psychological harm, like any other relevant factor, may be taken into account, no single factor is required.

III.

Forklift, while conceding that a requirement that the conduct seriously affect psychological well-being is unfounded, argues that the District Court nonetheless correctly applied the *Meritor* standard. We disagree. Though the District Court did conclude that the work environment was not "intimidating or abusive to [Harris]," it did so only after finding that the conduct was not "so severe as to be expected to seriously affect plaintiff's psychological well-being," and that Harris was not "subjectively so offended that she suffered injury." The District Court's application of these incorrect standards may well have influenced its ultimate conclusion, especially given that the court found this to be a "close case."

We therefore reverse the judgment of the Court of Appeals, and remand the case for further proceedings consistent with this opinion.

Justice SCALIA, concurring.

. . . Today's opinion elaborates that the challenged conduct must be severe or pervasive enough "to create an objectively hostile or abusive work environment—an environment that a reasonable person would find hostile or abusive."

"Abusive" (or "hostile," which in this context I take to mean the same thing) does not seem to me a very clear standard—and I do not think clarity is at all increased by adding the adverb "objectively" or by appealing to a "reasonable person['s]" notion of what the vague word means. . . .

Be that as it may, I know of no alternative to the course the Court today has taken. One of the factors mentioned in the Court's nonexhaustive list—whether the conduct unreasonably interferes with an employee's work performance—would, if it were made an absolute test, provide greater guidance to juries and employers. But I see no basis for such a limitation in the language of the statute. Accepting *Meritor*'s interpretation of the term "conditions of employment" as the law, the test is not whether work has been impaired, but whether working conditions have been discriminatorily altered. I know of no test more faithful to the inherently vague statutory language than the one the Court today adopts. For these reasons, I join the opinion of the Court.

Notes and Discussion

1. Severe or Pervasive Clearly this Court rejected *Rabidue*, finding that the plaintiff need not prove a tangible psychological injury. The Court emphasized, however, that it was taking a "middle path" and that "merely offensive" behavior was not actionable under Title VII. Is it now clear where the Court would draw the line between merely offensive and severe or pervasive behavior? Is Justice Scalia's concurring opinion that the Court did not fashion a clear standard in defining what constitutes a "hostile" work environment persuasive?

Although *Harris* introduced some clarity into the analysis, the standard remains imprecise. Courts have struggled to articulate consistent principles, and cases vary widely with regard to the type and frequency of conduct required to constitute a hostile environment. The severe or pervasive test has been described as a "high bar" for plaintiffs to clear.[57]

As a general matter, courts most readily conclude that alleged conduct is sufficiently severe or pervasive when the behavior constitutes rape,[58] involves physical threats at work,[59] repeated solicitation for sex, repeated touching of intimate body parts, and/or daily or regular verbal harassment. The further the fact pattern strays

---

57. *See* EEOC v. Sunbelt Rentals, Inc., 521 F.3d 306 (4th Cir. 2008).

58. *See, e.g.*, Lapka v. Chertoff, 517 F.3d 974 (7th Cir. 2008).

59. *See, e.g.*, Kaytor v. Electric Boat Corp., 609 F.3d 537 (2d Cir. 2010).

from these obviously extreme situations, the more difficulty courts have. Read the following case summaries and try to identify consistent patterns or principles.

Cases finding the conduct to be insufficiently severe or pervasive to constitute actionable sexual harassment include:

- *Mendoza v. Borden*, 158 F.3d 1171 (11th Cir. 1999) (finding that over 11-month period, plaintiff's supervisor "constantly" followed her around, looked her up and down, twice stared at her groin while making a sniffing sound, and once rubbed his hip against hers while also touching her shoulder, and holding that such pattern of conduct falls "well short" of severe or pervasive harassment);

- *Shepherd v. Comptroller of Public Accounts of Texas*, 168 F.3d 871 (5th Cir. 1999) (holding that several incidents over a two-year period, including comment "your elbows are the same color as your nipples," another comment that plaintiff had big thighs, touching plaintiff's arm, and attempts to look down the plaintiff's dress, were insufficient to support hostile-environment claim);

- *Quinn v. Green Tree Credit Corp.*, 159 F.3d 759 (2d Cir. 1998) (holding that statement that plaintiff had the "sleekest ass" in office plus single incident of "deliberately" touching plaintiff's "breasts with some papers that he was holding in his hand" were insufficient to alter the terms or conditions of the plaintiff's employment);

- *Weiss v. Coca-Cola Bottling Co. of Chicago*, 990 F.2d 333 (7th Cir. 1993) (holding plaintiff's claims—supervisor repeatedly asked about her personal life, told her how beautiful she was, asked her on dates, called her a dumb blonde, put his hand on her shoulder at least six times, placed "I love you" signs in her work area, and tried to kiss her once at a bar and twice at work—were not sufficient for actionable sexual harassment);

- *Paul v. Northrop Grumman Ship Systems*, 309 Fed. Appx. 825 (5th Cir. 2009) (holding that conduct was not actionable where harasser came up to plaintiff and placed his chest against her breasts for 30 seconds, then followed her, forced his way through the door ahead of her and placed his hand on her stomach while he rubbed his pelvic region across her hips and buttocks, stating that "non-consensual physical touching" is only actionable where "chronic and frequent");

- *LeGrand v. Area Resources for Community and Human Services*, 394 F.3d 1098 (8th Cir. 2005) (evidence was insufficient to show actionable harassment, where the harasser forcibly kissed the plaintiff "in the mouth," grabbed the plaintiff's buttocks, reached for the plaintiff's genitals, gripped the plaintiff's thigh, and asked the plaintiff to watch pornographic movies with him);

- *Brooks v. City of San Mateo*, 214 F.3d 1082 (9th Cir. 2000) (harasser's conduct did not amount to severe or pervasive harassment, where the harasser touched the plaintiff's stomach while she was working and made a sexual comment, forced his hand underneath her sweater and bra to touch her bare breast, and then approached her as though he was going to "fondle her breasts again").

Cases finding the conduct to be sufficiently severe or pervasive to constitute actionable sexual harassment include:

- *Turner v. The Saloon, Ltd.*, 595 F.3d 679 (7th Cir. 2010) (evidence was sufficient to create a triable issue that the harassment was sufficiently severe or pervasive, where the harasser grabbed the plaintiff's genitals, asked the plaintiff to kiss her, pressed against the plaintiff asking if he missed her, grabbed his buttocks, and told him she missed seeing him naked when she saw plaintiff change into his work uniform);

- *Gerald v. University of Puerto Rico*, 707 F.3d 7 (1st Cir. 2013) (harasser's solicitation of sex on one occasion, touching the victim's breast on another occasion, and asking her in front of other co-workers why she would not have sex with him was sufficiently severe or pervasive to constitute actionable harassment);

- *Eich v. Bd. of Regents for Cent. Mo. State Univ.*, 350 F.3d 752 (8th Cir. 2003) (actionable harassment, where over a seven-year period, harasser brushed up against plaintiff's breasts, ran his fingers through her hair, and simulated sex acts with plaintiff while she was bent over during a handcuff training exercise, among other acts and behavior);

- *Redd v. New York State Div. of Parole*, 923 F. Supp. 2d 371 (2d Cir. 2012) (conduct was sufficiently severe or pervasive, where supervisor intentionally touched plaintiff's breasts on three occasions with hands);

- *Hawkins v. Anheuser-Busch, Inc.*, 517 F.3d 321 (6th Cir. 2008) (conduct sufficiently severe or pervasive, where harasser asked plaintiff to perform oral sex and have sex on multiple occasions, regularly tried to touch her, rubbed against her with his private parts, tried to grab her waist, made "lewd and sexual comments 'all the time,'" and made regular sexual references to her private body parts);

- *Hulsey v. Pride Rests., LLC*, 367 F.3d 1238 (11th Cir. 2004) (conduct sufficiently severe or pervasive, where harasser repeatedly propositioned plaintiff for sex, repeatedly attempted to touch her breasts, placed his hands down her pants, tried to pull off her pants, and enlisted others to hold her while he attempted to grope her).

What patterns, if any, do you see from these two sets? Does it appear that attitudes have changed over time?

2. Terms and Conditions of Employment The Court explained that "if the victim does not subjectively perceive the environment to be abusive, the conduct has not actually altered the conditions of the victim's employment, and there is no Title VII violation." Is this statement necessarily true? What if the target does not perceive a hostile environment because he or she has never known another kind of work environment? Consider the example of the African-American boy who boards a bus in the south in 1950. The driver orders him to the back of the bus and he complies, never considering that such a demand is insulting. Hasn't that little boy been discriminated against even though he did not subjectively "perceive" the insult? Should the law bar him from a discrimination suit if he does not perceive this insult (unwelcomeness) at the time?

3. The Totality of the Circumstances What factors should courts weigh when considering whether conduct amounts to severe or pervasive and, therefore, actionable behavior? Frequency—the number of times a particular action is taken—is an objective fact. Severity—how offensive a particular action is—is much more subjective. Does this subjectivity make it likely that courts will tend to emphasize the former, more easily discerned, factor over the latter?

4. Justice Ginsburg's Concurrence In her concurring opinion, Justice Ginsburg stated, "The critical issue, Title VII's text indicates, is whether members of one sex are exposed to disadvantageous terms or conditions of employment to which members of the other sex are not exposed." Is this what Title VII's text actually indicates? What happens if a supervisor discriminates against all women and one effeminate man? Does such a scenario preclude Title VII relief under Justice Ginsburg's rationale? Does this reasoning mean that Title VII provides no relief against the "equal opportunity" harasser? What if the environment contains workers of only one sex? Why did Justice Ginsburg author this concurrence?

B. The Reasonableness Standard

Note that the courts in both *Rabidue* and *Ellison* took different views on the proper standard for determining severity and pervasiveness of harassing conduct. *Rabidue* used a "reasonable person" standard. *Ellison* used that of a "reasonable woman." In presenting her case to the Court, Teresa Harris noted, "The parties agree that unwelcome workplace conduct should be considered from the viewpoint of a reasonable person in the position of the plaintiff."[60] Currently, the Ninth and Third Circuits employ a gender-specific standard,[61] while the Fifth, Sixth, Eighth, and Eleventh Circuits have clearly rejected a gender-specific standard.[62] The remaining circuits, the First, Second, Fourth, Seventh, and Tenth, apply the reasonable person standard in the great majority of cases, but have never actually rejected the use of the reasonable woman standard.[63]

---

60. Reply Brief for Petitioner at 9 n.4, *Harris*, 510 U.S. 17 (1993).

61. *Ellison*, 924 F.2d at 879; Andrews v. City of Philadelphia, 895 F.2d 1469, 1482 (3d Cir. 1990).

62. Watkins v. Bowden, 105 F.3d 1344, 1356 (11th Cir. 1997) (holding no reversible error in "reasonable person" standard after *Harris*); Gillming v. Simmons Indus., 91 F.3d 1168, 1172 (8th Cir. 1996) (finding the "reasonable person" standard appropriate after *Harris*); Hartleip v. McNeilab, Inc., 83 F.3d 767, 776 (6th Cir. 1996) (concluding "that a gender-conscious standard must be rejected"); DeAngelis v. El Paso Mun. Police Officers Ass'n, 51 F.3d 591, 594 (5th Cir. 1995) ("The test is an objective one, not a standard of offense to a 'reasonable woman.'"), *cert denied*, 516 U.S. 974 (1995).

63. *See, e.g.*, Valentin-Almeyda v. Municipality of Aguadilla, 447 F.3d 85, 94 (1st Cir. 2006) (applying the reasonable person standard); Jennings v. Univ. of N.C., 444 F.3d 255, 269 (4th Cir. 2006) (applying the reasonable person standard); Whittaker v. N. Ill. Univ., 424 F.3d 640, 645

Despite considerable controversy over the correct standard, the standard applied may have little relationship to whether the plaintiffs are able to meet the requirements for stating a prima facie case. An analysis of more than 200 hostile work environment cases from all federal districts indicates that a "reasonable woman" standard does not lead to a higher success rate for plaintiffs than a gender-neutral standard.[64]

Some scholars have critiqued the very concept of "reasonableness" as a factor that determines whether or not conduct constitutes a violation. Professor Nancy Ehrenreich asks:

> Why, for example, in the context of antidiscrimination statutes designed to reform society, is a standard that is explicitly tied to the status quo thought to be a proper vehicle for identifying discriminatory behavior? Why, despite recent scholarship revealing that judicial definitions of reasonableness often reflect the values and assumptions of a narrow elite, is the "objective test" seen as an accurate reflection of societal norms at all? In short, why is it that the test is still seen as the prototypical expression of the law's fairness and objectivity rather than, for example, as a mechanism for facilitating the coercive use of social power?[65]

Professor Ehrenreich points out that the very concept of reasonableness is indeterminate and predicated on the status quo. It encourages judges to use their own judgment of the "social consensus." Judicial opinions about what is acceptable workplace conduct lead to thorny questions. How is a judge supposed to reach this conclusion outside of his or her own judgment? How does such "consensus" reflect existing power structures that leave out vulnerable groups?

Moreover, Ehrenreich notes, when courts use "consensus" or prevailing norms to justify their views on reasonableness, this practice perpetuates two harms. First, it creates a false narrative of choice and marginalization, which leaves the complainant in a double-bind. Specifically, if she complains about prevailing workplace culture *she* is the aberrant one, and if she remains in the workplace she is acceding to this culture. Note also how this relates to Martha R. Mahoney's concept of the "ideology of exit," discussed in Chapter 2. Mahoney argues that staying and fighting for a job should be viewed less an act of acquiescence and more as an act of resistance. Second, Ehrenreich explains that the practice perpetuates an illusion of universality. More particularly, it equates the dominance of a viewpoint with its propriety and allows the judge to proceed under the guise of neutrality.

(7th Cir. 2005) (holding that hostile work environment requires both subjective and objective severity or pervasiveness); Petrosino v. Bell Atl., 385 F.3d 210, 221–22 (2d Cir. 2004) (considering reasonable woman, but applying the reasonable person standard); Stinnett v. Safeway, Inc., 337 F.3d 1213, 1219 (10th Cir. 2003) (applying the reasonable person standard).

64. *See* Nicole Newman, *The Reasonable Woman: Has She Made a Difference?*, 27 B.C. THIRD WORLD L.J. 529 (2007).

65. Ehrenreich, *supra* note 51, at 1178.

This debate regarding the proper standard has led some commentators to speculate that the shift from a "reasonable person" to a "reasonable woman" standard actually does more harm than good. In particular, it purports to make change without altering the underlying, male-dominated model.[66]

On the other hand, perhaps there is greater consensus in American society as to what constitutes a hostile environment. Professor Theresa Beiner reviewed progress in the courts, taking a sociological approach to sexual harassment law and the reasonableness standard. She found that, "there is, in actuality, considerable evidence that people do have a perception of what constitutes sexual harassment in the workplace and that, with respect to a wide range of behaviors, there is some agreement among workers about what they find harassing."[67] In fact, she concludes:

> My thesis is that judges often get assessments of harassment wrong. The average worker's beliefs encompass more behaviors than courts currently recognize. Instead, reasonable people believe that conduct is sexually harassing in situations that courts fail to acknowledge, but instead summarily dispose of by summary judgment or judgment as a matter of law. Thus, the perceptions of judges on what constitutes harassment to the reasonable person do not always square with what the reasonable person perceives as harassing.[68]

The reasonableness inquiry is inextricably bound up with racial, socioeconomic, and cultural perspectives. Differences in these characteristics may lead to differences in the type of conduct that is considered harassment, what an appropriate workplace culture consists of, and what the proper response of a harassment survivor should be.[69]

Notes and Discussion

1. Judicial Interpretation Do *Burns, Rabidue,* or *Ellison* support Professor Beiner's contention that "courts have not interpreted sexual harassment jurisprudence in a manner consistent with what many reasonable people believe is harassing"? If so, how?

2. The Reasonableness Standard Which view is preferable: a reasonable person standard, a reasonable woman standard, or a reasonable person in the position of the plaintiff standard? If the latter, how should people, who are *not* women or in the position of the plaintiff, make such determinations? In light of the concerns raised by Professor Ehrehreich, should the reasonableness standard be more sensitive to women's perspectives or would such a change simply mask the difficulty of implementing it without some form of bias?

---

66. *See* Leslie Bender, *A Lawyer's Primer on Feminist Theory and Tort*, 38 J. LEGAL EDUC. 3 (1988).
67. Theresa Beiner, *Let the Jury Decide: The Gap Between What Judges and Reasonable People Believe Is Sexually Harassing*, 75 S. CAL. L. REV. 791, 793–94 (2002).
68. *Id.* at 796.
69. Jennifer Zimbroff, *Cultural Differences in Perceptions of and Responses to Sexual Harassment*, 14 DUKE J. GENDER L. & POL'Y 1311 (2007).

3. Hostility to Employment Discrimination Cases Professor Beiner's research supports the conclusion that many advocates and scholars have reached: that sexual harassment plaintiffs fare better before juries than before judges. Given the significant number of harassment cases that judges resolve through summary judgment, should the "severe or pervasive" requirement be part of the plaintiff's prima facie case? Should judges simply allow juries to decide these issues on the merits? Or do judges serve an important screening role, preventing obviously deficient cases from going forward?

Of course, judges still can, and do, overturn jury verdicts on the question of hostile work environment. Megan E. Wooster notes how frequently courts grant judgment as a matter of law to defendants after jury verdicts for plaintiffs when those jurists determine that counsel actually failed to meet the hostile environment standard.[70]

4. Intersectionality Survivors of sexual harassment will also have group identities as members of racial, cultural, and socioeconomic groups. The intersection of these identities can contribute to a plaintiff's increased vulnerability to sexual harassment, as well as to difficulties for fact-finders. These issues are discussed thoroughly in Chapter 2. How might an intersectional approach reveal flaws with the reasonableness standard, judicial determinations, and jury verdicts?

5. Social Science Should courts use social science evidence in sexual harassment cases? Why or why not? Is more than 50% consensus enough to classify a specific behavior as sexual harassment? Would such evidence be admissible in guiding the judge's determination about whether conduct is actionable as a matter of law? Can Professor Beiner's suggested approach be reconciled with the concerns raised by Professor Ehrehreich? Explain.

6. Constructive Discharge The question of whether sexually harassing conduct is severe or pervasive, or unreasonably interferes with a plaintiff's work performance has obvious overlap with the issue of constructive discharge. The next chapter deals with this issue, along with questions of employer liability for harassment more generally.

4. Application of Law and Ethics
Hypothetical #3

Claudia Peters is a 28-year-old woman. She worked for 18 months as a research associate at Deletrex, a mid-sized technology firm. Her job required her to work on various projects as part of a Product Development team. There were multiple Product Development teams working at any given time at Deletrex. Each team was headed by a Vice President for Product Development. All five of these VPs were

---

70. Megan E. Wooster, *Sexual Harassment Law — The Jury Is Wrong as a Matter of Law*, 32 U. Ark. Little Rock L. Rev. 215 (2010).

male. Many of the senior engineers, software designers, and other technical positions were held by men. The research associates, who ranked the lowest in the firm's hierarchy, were evenly divided between men and women.

When she first started work, one of the other research associates took Claudia aside and told her that the work was intense and it was important for her to get along with the teams to which she was assigned. Positive feedback would lead to the best future assignments. If the word got out that she was difficult to work with, she would get sidelined.

The first team Claudia was assigned to work with was overall a good experience for her. The work was interesting and the team members all got along together. There was one thing that Claudia did not like: Some of the male team members would sit around in the open work space and discuss their sexual exploits and describe women in sexual terms. They never spoke this way about or to Claudia, and she never complained to them or anyone else.

Legal issue: Is this conduct sexual harassment?

After the project "wrapped," the team went out to a bar to celebrate. Many of the team members drank heavily, including Claudia, who was trying to fit in with the other team members. She ended up kissing and making out with a 32-year old team software designer named Louis. The next day she was mortified.

Claudia began work on another Product Development team, which thankfully did not include Louis. Still, Claudia knew that there was gossip about her at work. For a few months she would walk into a meeting and the other team members would snicker, or she would look up to see two team members chuckling and looking at her. A message was written on a white board: "Claudia gives great . . . research." She was too embarrassed to complain to anyone in management about this conduct and it finally stopped.

Legal issue: Is this conduct sexual harassment?

One evening the team leader, an older, married VP named Dennis Taylor summoned Claudia to his office to discuss the results of an issue that she had been researching. After she sat down in front of his desk, Dennis moved his chair around so that it was next to hers, saying that it was easier for people to communicate when they did not have a desk in between them. He leaned closer as she was talking, until he was only a few inches away from her. She became flustered and froze. At this point, Dennis said, "It's been really great having you on the team. I hope you feel the same way. I requested you specifically, you know. I heard about your performance on your last team and I knew you were special." Then he rubbed her thigh a few times. Claudia managed to say "thank you" and then quickly left.

Legal issue: Is this conduct sexual harassment?

After this episode, Claudia found it difficult to go back to the office. She used all of her personal days. Eventually she got a call from another researcher, telling her that people were not happy with her for taking so much unscheduled leave. Rather than go in and face anyone at Deletrex, she decided to quit.

1. Examine the different conduct that Claudia encountered at Deletrex and determine what her prima facie case for sexual harassment would be. Which conduct, if any, would be considered "severe or pervasive"? Can all of the conduct be described as both "unwelcome" and "based on sex"?

2. What defenses would Deletrex likely raise? Based on the cases in this chapter, how successful do you think these defenses would be?

3. Discuss any other issues that you believe merit further research or investigation by Deletrex.

5. Review

Professor Drobac's Severity Diagram

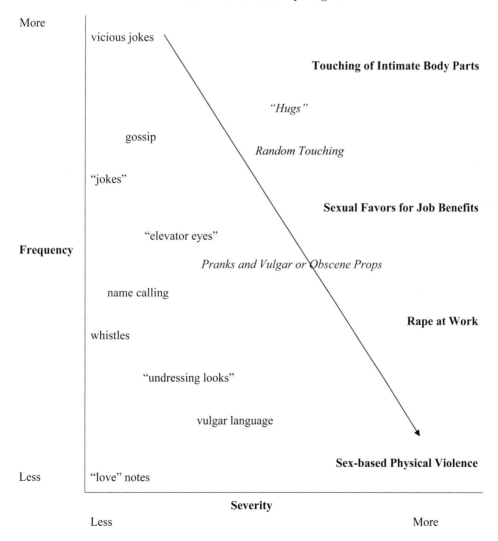

Chapter 4

Employer Liability for Workplace Sexual Harassment

1. Who Should Be Responsible?

The logical answer to the question of who is responsible for workplace harassment is the harassers. However, neither Title VII nor many state FEPS (fair employment practice statutes) hold individuals liable. Why not? With the passage of Title VII, Congress intended to protect small businesses from litigation costs for discrimination claims. Therefore, Title VII applies only to businesses with 15 or more employees.[1] Quoting a prior Ninth Circuit decision, the United States Court of Appeals for the First Circuit explained why courts have not found liability for employees as "agents" of employers. It noted Title VII's application limit and reasoned, "If Congress decided to protect small entities with limited resources from liability, it is inconceivable that Congress intended to allow civil liability to run against individual employees."[2]

A few states, including California, allow for such individual liability.[3] However, even if a plaintiff successfully proves a prima facie case and secures a jury or bench verdict, the individual harasser may suffer no meaningful consequence. Some harassers have no money to pay money damage awards. They are "judgment proof." Chapter 5 covers the types of remedies available under most antidiscrimination laws, but these remedies may not mandate that an employer fire or discipline an individual harasser. Without a mass movement and well-funded progressive support, those reformers, who would make individuals liable and force them to take responsibility for their conduct, face fierce resistance from some establishment interests. Finally, even when individual liability is available, some harassers do not change their behavior.

---

1. 42 U.S.C. § 2000e(b) (2012).

2. Fantini v. Salem State College, 557 F.3d 22, 28–31 (1st Cir. 2009) (quoting Miller v. Maxwell's Intern. Inc., 991 F.2d 583, 587 (9th Cir. 1993), *cert. denied*, 510 U.S. 1109 (1994)).

3. *See* CAL. GOV'T CODE § 12940 *et seq.* The National Women's Law Center (NWLC) tracks the statutes that provide for relief against individual harassers. In the District of Columbia, Massachusetts, Michigan, Montana, New Mexico, and Washington, law allows for actions against sexually harassing supervisors. In California, Iowa, and Vermont, state law provides for individual liability against any employee who harasses another employee. MAYA RAGHU & JOANNA SURIANI, NAT'L WOMEN'S LAW CTR. REPORT, #METOOWHATNEXT: STRENGTHENING WORKPLACE SEXUAL HARASSMENT PROTECTIONS AND ACCOUNTABILITY (Dec. 2017), https://nwlc.org/resources/metoowhatnext -strengthening-workplace-sexual-harassment-protections-and-accountability/.

Title VII holds employers liable for the conduct of individual harassers because employers have a duty to supervise workplace interactions to ensure equal opportunity and fair treatment. In their assessments under Title VII, courts consider factors such as the employer's knowledge, the offensive conduct itself, and the status of the harasser. Therefore, an understanding of the different types of harassers is useful. A well-informed human resources manager or employment lawyer can best advise organizations on strategies to neutralize those harassers, create a safe work environment, and enable the employer to avoid future problems.

A. Three Types of Harassers

Professor Drobac identifies at least three different kinds of harassers: the clueless, those who could not care less (the care-less), and the corrupt predators. She suggests that the clueless, once advised that their conduct is offensive, will feel remorse. They will try to make amends and change their behavior. Usually, the complainant need not sue these individuals for relief. A direct communication or complaint to a common supervisor or human resources professional, who can counsel the clueless party, cures the problem. These offenders take responsibility for their conduct and try to correct their behavior in the future. Drobac estimates that most mild workplace harassment comes from these types of harassers, male and female.[4]

More serious behavior more often occurs with the care-less. These people know that what they are doing is wrong *and they do not care*. They will not change their attitudes or behavior until threatened with unpleasant consequences, such as fines, unpaid leave, shift reductions, etc. The care-less feel empowered by their harassment and concomitant debasement of others. Individual liability can redirect their behavior, if not their attitudes. However, employer sanctions can also effectively combat abuse by the care-less. Meaningful employer control of the work environment, to create a safe and harmonious setting, protects vulnerable workers. Because the care-less will not spontaneously self-correct, only consistent and sustained employer/principal action ameliorates the situation for those complainants who live in the majority of states that still fail to provide for individual liability.

Drobac's third set of identified harassers, the corrupt predators, engage in the most serious types of workplace abuse and sex-based violence. These people have serious psychological problems or have become completely insensitive to their targets' trauma. Their sense of invincibility and power lead them to engage in the most depraved behavior. Think about Harvey Weinstein, Matt Lauer, Charlie Rose, Alex Kozinski, and Bill O'Reilly, to name just a few possible such predators. Most likely, these people will not reform. Even individual liability does not stop these predators because they are wealthy enough or powerful enough to pay the settlement fines and return to their degenerate, discriminatory tactics. Only employer/

---

4. For a good original source concerning differing behaviors, see Louise R. Fitzgerald et al., *The Incidence and Dimensions of Sexual Harassment in Academia and the Workplace*, 32 J. Voc. Behav. 152–75 (1988).

principal-directed employment termination and social disapprobation, in some circumstances, curb these iniquitous operators.

B. Targets Bear the Burden

This introduction makes clear that without strong, comprehensive employer-driven sanctions for sex-based harassment and assault, targets bear the physical, psychological, and financial burdens of their abuse by harassers. The targets become responsible for the costs and the cure. However, almost all targets fear that if they complain or try to resist, they will face retaliation. Such retaliation takes many forms, including social ostracism, reputational attacks, negative job consequences, and possibly even death threats.

Good reason exists for these fears. Retaliation is quite common—the most common issue alleged by federal workers and found in federal workplace complaints. On its website, the EEOC explains, "Nearly half of all complaints filed during fiscal year (FY) 2013 were retaliation complaints, with 42% of findings of discrimination based on retaliation."[5] In a special 2016 report, the EEOC found:

> The fears that stop most employees from reporting harassment are well-founded. One 2003 study found that 75% of employees who spoke out against workplace mistreatment faced some form of retaliation. Other studies have found that sexual harassment reporting is often followed by organizational indifference or trivialization of the harassment complaint as well as hostility and reprisals against the victim. Such responses understandably harm the victim in terms of adverse job repercussions and psychological distress. Indeed, as one researcher concluded, such results suggest that, in many work environments, the most "reasonable" course of action for the victim to take is to avoid reporting the harassment.[6]

These chilling statistics help explain why so many targets abandon their employment rather than report harassment. The final section of this chapter examines retaliation by employers in more detail.

Despite the shocking prevalence of retaliation by employers and co-workers, almost everyone agrees that targets should not bear the burden of sexual harassment or suffer retaliation for reporting it. However, they do, as documented in a December 2018 report. Researchers summarized their findings:

- About five million employees are sexually harassed at work every year
  - The overwhelming majority (99.8%) of people who experience sexual harassment at work never file formal charges.

5. U.S. Equal Emp. Opportunity Comm'n, *Retaliation—Making It Personal*, https://www.eeoc.gov/laws/types/retaliation_considerations.cfm.

6. Chai R. Feldblum & Victoria A. Lipnic, U.S. Equal Emp. Opportunity Comm'n, Select Task Force on the Study of Harassment in the Workplace: Report of Co-Chairs 16–17 (June 2016).

- Of those who file formal charges, very few—we estimate less than 1,500 per year—go to court.
- Most employers react punitively toward people who file formal sexual harassment charges.
  - 68% of sexual harassment charges include an allegation of employer retaliation; this rate is highest for black women.
  - 64% of sexual harassment charges are associated with job loss, and this rate is highest for white women and white men.
- Industries vary widely in their sexual harassment discrimination charge rates.
  - In all industries women are more likely than men to file charges, but this sex difference grows in male dominated industries.
- While the EEOC initially tends to judge sexual harassment charges as more likely than other discrimination complaints to sustain a finding of legal cause, most individuals benefit little from EEOC case processing.
  - 27% of employees who file a sexual harassment charge with the EEOC and continue to pursue redress receive any benefit
    - 23% receive some monetary compensation
    - the average award is $24,700, the median award is $10,000
    - less than 1% of awards are over $100,000
    - Only 12% of charges lead to a managerial agreement to change workplace practices
- Our conclusion from these results is that sexual harassment, and perhaps discrimination of all types, should be addressed proactively and affirmatively as managerial responsibilities, rather than leaving it to the targets of discrimination to pursue legal remedies as individuals.[7]

The law provides for employer liability to effectuate change, reduce the incidence of sex-based harassment and discrimination, and, in some small measure, compensate the targets of abuse. So why is the law not working? Why are studies like this calling for extralegal reforms? Consider the legal history, court enforcement (or lack thereof), and the law's evolution of employer liability.

2. Legal Background

Employer liability comprises the last element of the sexual harassment prima facie case. Whether or not a defendant is liable for an alleged wrong is always a part of any civil case, but in the employment discrimination context the inquiry becomes

---

7. Carly McCann, Donald Tomaskovic-Devey & M. V. Lee Badgett, Employer's Responses to Sexual Harassment 2 (Dec. 2018).

more complicated, particularly as it relates to sexual harassment claims. Almost all sexual harassment plaintiffs must impute liability for the individual harasser's acts of harassment to their employers as a matter of law.

Under the direction of Eleanor Holmes Norton, the EEOC promulgated its guidelines for employer liability in 1980. It recommended strict liability for harassment by a supervisor:

> Applying general Title VII principles, an employer is responsible for its acts and those of its agents and supervisory employees with respect to sexual harassment no matter whether the specific acts complained of were authorized or even forbidden by the employer and no matter whether the employer knew or should have known of their occurrence. The Commission will examine the circumstances of the particular employment relationship and the job functions performed by the individual in determining whether an individual acts in either a supervisory or agent capacity.[8]

In sum, if a supervisor acted in violation of Title VII, the EEOC advised that the employer-principal was "vicariously" liable, whether or not it knew about the harassment.

In contrast, the EEOC recommended a negligence standard for harassment by a co-worker or customer. The EEOC advised:

> With respect to conduct between fellow employees, an employer is responsible for acts of sexual harassment in the workplace where the employer (or its agents or supervisory employees) knows or should have known of the conduct, unless it can show that it took immediate and appropriate corrective action.

> An employer may also be responsible for the acts of non-employees, with respect to sexual harassment of employees in the workplace, where the employer (or its agents or supervisory employees) knows or should have known of the conduct and fails to take immediate and appropriate corrective action. In reviewing these cases the Commission will consider the extent of the employer's control and any other legal responsibility which the employer may have with respect to the conduct of such non-employees.[9]

So, if a worker harassed a peer or superior, the EEOC suggested that the employer-principal was liable for that conduct if it knew or should have known of the conduct and failed to take preventative and/or corrective action. The same standard applied if a customer or client harassed an employee.

This guidance was not congruent with the existing common law. The Second Restatement of Agency, as promulgated in 1958, stated that an employer is strictly liable for the harms committed by its employees who are acting within the scope

8. 29 C.F.R. § 1604.11(c) (no longer in force).
9. 29 C.F.R. § 1604.11(d), (e).

of their employment, a doctrine that is also referred to as respondeat superior or vicarious liability. The inverse is also true: an employer is not liable for the actions of its employees when they are acting outside of the scope of their employment. Sexual harassment is, almost by definition, considered to be conduct outside the scope of employment. (Although, ironically, the military treats sexual harassment as arising "out of or are in the course of activity incident to [military] service" and bars recovery under Title VII and the Federal Tort Claims Act.)

This classification is not fatal to employer liability, however, because there are four important exceptions to this exemption: (1) where the employer intended the conduct or the consequences, (2) where the employer was negligent or reckless, (3) where the conduct violated a non-delegable duty of the employer, or (4) where the employee purported to act or speak on behalf of the employer and there was reliance upon apparent authority, or he was aided in accomplishing the tort by the existence of the agency relation. Given the circumstances in which sexual harassment typically occurs, exceptions (2) and (4) are the ones most likely to come into play.

A. Early Case Law Regarding Employer Liability

As a result of the inconsistency between the EEOC guidance and traditional principles of tort and agency law, early courts struggled to determine the proper scope of employer liability for sexual harassment claims. The struggle grew more difficult as the doctrinal framework for sexual harassment cases grew more complex. While reading the following opinions (neither of which is an accurate statement of the law today), consider the courts' reasoning.

Barnes v. Costle
561 F.2d 983 (D.C. Cir. 1977)

MacKINNON, Circuit Judge, concurring:

. . . .

. . . The present case offers no suggestion that the sexual harassment was even arguably within the scope of employment and certainly it would not be so understood by any federal employee. The sexual harassment furthered no objective of the government agency, nor was it part of the supervisor's actual or ostensible authority, nor was it even within the outermost boundaries of what could be perceived to be his apparent authority.

To the general rule, however, the Second Restatement of Agency attaches four exceptions. The first three involve situations where culpability would naturally apply to the principal: "(a) the master intended the conduct or the consequences, or (b) the master was negligent or reckless, or (c) the conduct violated a non-delegable duty of the master. . . ." None of these are here relevant, though if the government had prior knowledge of the offending supervisor's propensity for sexual harassment of subordinate employees, liability might be based on negligence or reckless conduct. The fourth exception considers situations where "the servant purported to act or to speak on behalf of the principal and there was reliance upon apparent authority, or he was aided in accomplishing the tort by the existence of the agency relation."

The exception is stated in the disjunctive. The first part has no application here it could not be reasonably believed by an employee that the supervisor's demands derived from the employer or that in complying with such demands the employee actually relied upon the authority of the employer. Concerning the second part of the exception, at first reading it seems to argue too much. In every case where vicarious [strict] liability is at issue, the agent will have been aided in some way in committing the tort by the position that he holds. In this case, the male supervisor would not have been in a position to ask petitioner for an "after-hours affair" were it not for his position as her immediate "boss."

The examples provided in the Restatement commentary, however, indicate that a narrower concept is involved. The tort must be one accomplished by an instrumentality, or through conduct associated with the agency status.

. . . .

. . . Generally, liability has been premised on one of three (non-exhaustive) rationales: 1) if ambiguous conduct might be violative of the statute, the employer is in the best position to know the real cause, and to come forward with an explanation; 2) the employer, not the employee, can establish prophylactic rules which, without upsetting efficiency, could obviate the circumstances of potential discrimination; 3) the type of conduct at issue is questionable at best, and it is not undesirable to induce careful employers to err on the side of avoiding possibly violative conduct.

. . . .

1. The rationale of an employer's better position to know. Unlike the case of a standardized [and discriminatory] employment test, the employer or higher supervisor is not in the best position of anyone to know whether an employee has been unjustly damaged on her job. The sexual advance of a supervisor toward an employee is seldom a public matter; and the distinction between invited, uninvited-but-welcome, offensive-but-tolerated and flatly rejected advances ordinarily does not fall within the special ability of the employer or higher supervisor to discern.

However, once a complaint of offensive advances has been made, the employer's role becomes far more serious. One of the four district court opinions (besides the one currently before us) that have considered sexual advances, based employer liability precisely on this phase of the incident, "When a female employee registers a complaint of sexual abuse and the company chooses to fire her rather than investigate, the corporate response may constitute discrimination based on sex."

. . . .

From a more general perspective, respondeat superior should apply, and the common law rule should be ousted, whenever a plaintiff can show that, in addition to the particular sexual advance, and the retaliatory actions by the maker of that advance, other agents of the employer with knowledge of her charges assisted the retaliation or impeded the complaint. That type of showing suffices to shift to the defendant the burden of disproving that the agency had, at the least, a callous disregard of Title VII rights.

2. Employer's ability to take preventive steps in advance. An employer could promulgate a rule that no sexual advances were to be made by any supervisors to any employees. The unique problem with this kind of harassment, however, is that its potential is not confined to working hours. Even if a no-advances rule were adopted, it could only with great difficulty be made to apply to employees' "own time."

Hence, there is no basis under this rationale to oust the common law rule against respondeat superior for acts outside the scope of employment. Nor do the facts of this complaint demonstrate a narrowly definable opportunity for the employer to formulate a specific preventive rule short of prohibiting all off-hours social contacts between employees and supervisors which is of course out of the question.

As the analysis under this rationale unfolds, it is apparent that an employer could somewhat insulate itself from vicarious liability by taking certain preventive measures. At the least, an employer should be free from vicarious liability if it 1) posts the firm's (or government's) policy against sexual harassment by supervisors, and 2) provides a workable mechanism for the prompt reporting of sexual harassment, which mechanism 3) includes the rapid issuance of a warning to the supervisor complained of, or the mere notation of a rejected sexual advance for possible future reference in case an issue is made of voluntariness, and 4) affords the opportunity of the complainant remaining anonymous.

. . . [D]etailed [complaint] procedures along the lines suggested would demonstrate more sensitivity to the particular problem of sexual advances and subsequent discrimination, and, if conscientiously applied, would come close to assuring an employer of protection against vicarious liability in many cases.

3. Inducing extra caution. Sexual advances may not be intrinsically offensive, and no policy can be derived from the equal employment opportunity laws to discourage them. We are not here concerned with racial epithets or confusing union authorization cards, which serve no one's interest, but with social patterns that to some extent are normal and expectable. It is the abuse of the practice, rather than the practice itself, that arouses alarm.

Accordingly, there is no justification under this rationale to impose vicarious liability upon an employer.

. . . .

Henson v. Dundee

682 F.2d 897 (11th Cir. 1982)

VANCE, Circuit Judge:

. . . .

Respondeat superior. In a typical Title VII case, an employer is held liable for the discriminatory actions of its supervisors which affect the tangible job benefits of an employee on the basis of race, religion, or national origin. The reason for this stern rule is readily apparent:

> When (the employer gave) its (supervisory personnel) authority to fire employees, it also accepted responsibility to remedy any harm caused by (the supervisors') unlawful exercise of that authority. The modern corporate entity consists of the individuals who manage it, and little, if any, progress in eradicating discrimination in employment will be made if the corporate employer is able to hide behind the shield of individual employee action.

Tidwell v. American Oil Co., 332 F.Supp. at 436 (citation omitted).

It necessarily follows from this premise that an employer is strictly liable for sexual discrimination by supervisors that causes tangible job detriment. Sexual harassment resulting in tangible job detriment is a form of sex discrimination every bit as deleterious to the remedial purposes of Title VII as other unlawful employment practices. We hold that an employer is strictly liable for the actions of its supervisors that amount to sexual discrimination or sexual harassment resulting in tangible job detriment to the subordinate employee.

We recognize that this holding requires differing treatment of respondeat superior claims in the two types of sexual harassment cases. In the classic quid pro quo case an employer is strictly liable for the conduct of its supervisors, while in the work environment case the plaintiff must prove that higher management knew or should have known of the sexual harassment before the employer may be held liable. The rationale underlying this difference in the treatment of the two cases is easily stated. The environment in which an employee works can be rendered offensive in an equal degree by the acts of supervisors, coworkers, or even strangers to the workplace. The capacity of any person to create a hostile or offensive environment is not necessarily enhanced or diminished by any degree of authority which the employer confers upon that individual. When a supervisor gratuitously insults an employee, he generally does so for his reasons and by his own means. He thus acts outside the actual or apparent scope of the authority he possesses as a supervisor. His conduct cannot automatically be imputed to the employer any more so than can the conduct of an ordinary employee.

The typical case of quid pro quo sexual harassment is fundamentally different. In such a case, the supervisor relies upon his apparent or actual authority to extort sexual consideration from an employee. Therein lies the quid pro quo. In that case the supervisor uses the means furnished to him by the employer to accomplish the prohibited purpose. He acts within the scope of his actual or apparent authority to "hire, fire, discipline or promote." Because the supervisor is acting within at least the apparent scope of the authority entrusted to him by the employer when he makes employment decisions, his conduct can fairly be imputed to the source of his authority.

. . . .

Notes and Discussion

1. Scope of Employment and Authority Judge MacKinnon stated, "The present case offers no suggestion that the sexual harassment was even arguably within the scope of employment and certainly it would not be so understood by any federal employee." Is the Judge correct? Explain. He also declared, "The sexual harassment . . . was [not] even within the outermost boundaries of what could be perceived to be his apparent authority." Is this true? Explain.

2. Social Patterns Judge MacKinnon reasoned that sexual advances "may not be intrinsically offensive." He then found, "We are not here concerned with racial epithets or confusing union authorization cards, which serve no one's interest, but with social patterns that to some extent are normal and expectable." Does this comment remind you of the reasoning employed in the early district court sexual harassment cases? Recall that in *Corne v. Bausch & Lomb, Inc.*, Judge Frey referred to the respondent's conduct as "nothing more than a personal proclivity." Is sexual harassment normal, whether or not it's expectable? In other words, does Judge MacKinnon confuse sexual harassment with sexual advances that are "normal and expectable"? Does his attitude foreshadow a perspective found in the Supreme Court's *Oncale* opinion?

3. Complaint and Credibility Professor Nadine Taub ties the prevalence of stereotypes concerning women's credibility to standards for employer liability. She explains:

> There is, of course, good reason to believe . . . that many legitimate complaints go unmade. In addition to the reprisals risked by all discrimination complainants, a woman charging sexual harassment inevitably risks the counter charge that she invited this, and perhaps other, incidents. She may be greeted with condescension, ridicule and disbelief, compounding the humiliation and intimidation of the original incident. Since many women have internalized the view that they are to blame, shame and guilt, as well as concern for the aggressor's honor, further inhibit reporting. Underreporting in the analogous case of rape is well-known, no doubt for similar reasons. But whether underreporting is likely or not, what is really at issue is the complainant's credibility. There would seem to be no reason, other than a sexist stereotype of women, why the issue of credibility should not be dealt with in the same manner as other issues of credibility—by the trier of fact.

Here again, a new approach to discrimination may be helpful. To the extent that the court determines the conduct alleged amounts to discrimination, it uses a theory that sharpens its awareness of stereotypes, and it is less likely to impose unwarranted and sex-based obstacles to recovery.[10]

In this passage, Taub emphasizes that the view of women as fundamentally untrustworthy contributes to the failure to recognize sex discrimination and the reluctance to recompense survivors for their suffering.

Ultimately, Taub advocates for strict liability. Her arguments address why male employers and judges resist strict liability. She recommends:

Two facets of harassment are particularly relevant to making this possibility of strict liability a reality. One is understanding the important relation sexual harassment pairs to mental health, physical health, and worker productivity. The other is recognizing the way management can use harassment as a low-cost way of conveying status: the privilege to harass is a benefit management can confer in lieu of salary or other perquisites without obvious expenditure. Just as strict liability is now seen as an appropriate way of acknowledging and distributing the costs of industrial accidents, so too strict liability ultimately may be viewed as an appropriate way of acknowledging and distributing the costs of discrimination.[11]

Is Taub correct? Do employers fail to see that they permit compensatory oppression?

4. Employer Prevention Is it realistic that preventive measures, such as a policy, will end sexual harassment? Is the judges' focus on prevention and remediation a focus on liability limitation, abuse elimination, or both?

5. Authority The *Henson* majority found that "[t]he capacity of any person to create a hostile or offensive environment is not necessarily enhanced or diminished by the degree of authority which the employer confers upon that individual." Is this view reasonable?

B. Supreme Court Guidance?

Courts continued to debate the appropriate standard for employer liability for years following *Henson*. The Supreme Court's *Meritor* decision offered little clarity. Read *Meritor* and consider whether the concurrences highlight a flaw in the majority opinion. Or did the majority strike the right balance, given the underlying facts of the case?

---

10. Nadine Taub, *Keeping Women in Their Place: Stereotyping Per Se as a Form of Employment Discrimination*, 21 B.C. L. Rev. 345, 383–84 (1979–1980).

11. *Id.* at 386–87.

Meritor Savings Bank, FSB v. Vinson
477 U.S. 57 (1986)

Justice REHNQUIST delivered the opinion of the Court.

. . . .

Although the District Court concluded that respondent had not proved a violation of Title VII, it nevertheless went on to consider the question of the bank's liability. Finding that "the bank was without notice" of Taylor's alleged conduct, and that notice to Taylor was not the equivalent of notice to the bank, the court concluded that the bank, therefore, could not be held liable for Taylor's alleged actions. The Court of Appeals took the opposite view, holding that an employer is strictly liable for a hostile environment created by a supervisor's sexual advances, even though the employer neither knew nor reasonably could have known of the alleged misconduct. The court held that a supervisor, whether or not he possesses the authority to hire, fire, or promote, is necessarily an "agent" of his employer for all Title VII purposes, since "even the appearance" of such authority may enable him to impose himself on his subordinates.

The parties and *amici* suggest several different standards for employer liability. Respondent, not surprisingly, defends the position of the Court of Appeals. Noting that Title VII's definition of "employer" includes any "agent" of the employer, she also argues that "so long as the circumstance is work-related, the supervisor is the employer and the employer is the supervisor." Notice to Taylor that the advances were unwelcome, therefore, was notice to the bank.

Petitioner argues that respondent's failure to use its established grievance procedure, or to otherwise put it on notice of the alleged misconduct, insulates petitioner from liability for Taylor's wrongdoing. A contrary rule would be unfair, petitioner argues, since in a hostile environment harassment case the employer often will have no reason to know about, or opportunity to cure, the alleged wrongdoing.

The EEOC, in its brief as *amicus curiae*, contends that courts formulating employer liability rules should draw from traditional agency principles. Examination of those principles has led the EEOC to the view that where a supervisor exercises the authority actually delegated to him by his employer, by making or threatening to make decisions affecting the employment status of his subordinates, such actions are properly imputed to the employer whose delegation of authority empowered the supervisor to undertake them. Thus, the courts have consistently held employers liable for the discriminatory discharges of employees by supervisory personnel, whether or not the employer knew, should have known, or approved of the supervisor's actions.

The EEOC suggests that when a sexual harassment claim rests exclusively on a "hostile environment" theory, however, the usual basis for a finding of agency will often disappear. In that case, the EEOC believes, agency principles lead to "a rule that asks whether a victim of sexual harassment had reasonably available an avenue of complaint regarding such harassment, and, if available and utilized, whether that procedure was reasonably responsive to the employee's complaint. If the employer has an expressed policy against sexual harassment and has implemented a procedure specifically designed to resolve sexual harassment claims, and if the victim does not take advantage of that procedure, the employer should be shielded from liability absent actual knowledge of the sexually hostile environment (obtained, e.g., by the filing of a charge with the EEOC or a comparable state agency). In all other cases, the employer will be liable if it has actual knowledge of the harassment or if, considering all the facts of the case, the victim in question had no reasonably available avenue for making his or her complaint known to appropriate management officials."

Brief for United States and EEOC as *Amici Curiae* 26.

As respondent points out, this suggested rule is in some tension with the EEOC Guidelines, which hold an employer liable for the acts of its agents without regard to notice. The Guidelines do require, however, an "examin[ation of] the circumstances of the particular employment relationship and the job [f]unctions performed by the individual in determining whether an individual acts in either a supervisory or agency capacity."

This debate over the appropriate standard for employer liability has a rather abstract quality about it given the state of the record in this case. We do not know at this stage whether Taylor made any sexual advances toward respondent at all, let alone whether those advances were unwelcome, whether they were sufficiently pervasive to constitute a condition of employment, or whether they were "so pervasive and so long continuing . . . that the employer must have become conscious of [them]."

We therefore decline the parties' invitation to issue a definitive rule on employer liability, but we do agree with the EEOC that Congress wanted courts to look to agency principles for guidance in this area. While such common-law principles may not be transferable in all their particulars to Title VII, Congress' decision to define "employer" to include any "agent" of an employer, 42 U.S.C. §2000e(b), surely evinces an intent to place some limits on the acts of employees for which employers under Title VII are to be held responsible. For this reason, we hold that the Court of Appeals erred in concluding that employers are always automatically liable for sexual harassment by their supervisors. See generally Restatement (Second) of Agency §§219–237 (1958). For the same reason, absence of notice to an employer does not necessarily insulate that employer from liability.

Finally, we reject petitioner's view that the mere existence of a grievance procedure and a policy against discrimination, coupled with respondent's failure to invoke that procedure, must insulate petitioner from liability. While those facts are plainly relevant, the situation before us demonstrates why they are not necessarily dispositive. Petitioner's general nondiscrimination policy did not address sexual harassment in particular, and thus did not alert employees to their employer's interest in correcting that form of discrimination. Moreover, the banks grievance procedure apparently required an employee to complain first to her supervisor, in this case Taylor. Since Taylor was the alleged perpetrator, it is not altogether surprising that respondent failed to invoke the procedure and report her grievance to him. Petitioner's contention that respondent's failure should insulate it from liability might be substantially stronger if its procedures were better calculated to encourage victims of harassment to come forward.

. . . .

Justice MARSHALL, with whom Justice BRENNAN, Justice BLACKMUN, and Justice STEVENS join, concurring in the judgment.

I fully agree with the Court's conclusion that workplace sexual harassment is illegal, and violates Title VII. Part III of the Court's opinion, however, leaves open the circumstances in which an employer is responsible under Title VII for such conduct. Because I believe that question to be properly before us, I write separately.

The issue the Court declines to resolve is addressed in the EEOC Guidelines on Discrimination Because of Sex, which are entitled to great deference. The Guidelines explain:

"Applying general Title VII principles, an employer . . . is responsible for its acts and those of its agents and supervisory employees with respect to sexual harassment regardless of whether the specific acts complained of were authorized or even forbidden by the employer and regardless of whether the employer knew or should have known of their occurrence. The Commission will examine the circumstances of the particular employment relationship and the job [f]unctions performed by the individual in determining whether an individual acts in either a supervisory or agency capacity.

"With respect to conduct between fellow employees, an employer is responsible for acts of sexual harassment in the workplace where the employer (or its agents or supervisory employees) knows or should have known of the conduct, unless it can show that it took immediate and appropriate corrective action."

29 CFR §§ 1604.11(c), (d) (1985).

The Commission, in issuing the Guidelines, explained that its rule was "in keeping with the general standard of employer liability with respect to agents and supervisory employees. . . . [T]he Commission and the courts have held for years that an employer is liable if a supervisor or an agent violates the Title VII, regardless of knowledge or any other mitigating factor." 45 Fed. Reg. 74676 (1980). I would adopt the standard set out by the Commission.

An employer can act only through individual supervisors and employees; discrimination is rarely carried out pursuant to a formal vote of a corporation's board of directors. . . . Nonetheless, Title VII remedies, such as reinstatement and back-pay, generally run against the employer as an entity. The question thus arises as to the circumstances under which an employer will be held liable under Title VII for the acts of its employees.

The answer supplied by general Title VII law, like that supplied by federal labor law, is that the act of a supervisory employee or agent is imputed to the employer. . . . The courts do not stop to consider whether the employer otherwise had "notice" of the action, or even whether the supervisor had actual authority to act as he did. Following that approach, every Court of Appeals that has considered the issue has held that sexual harassment by supervisory personnel is automatically imputed to the employer when the harassment results in tangible job detriment to the subordinate employee.

The brief filed by the Solicitor General on behalf of the United States and the EEOC in this case suggests that a different rule should apply when a supervisor's harassment "merely" results in a discriminatory work environment. The Solicitor General concedes that sexual harassment that affects tangible job benefits is an exercise of authority delegated to the supervisor by the employer, and thus gives rise to employer liability. But, departing from the EEOC Guidelines, he argues that the case of a supervisor merely creating a discriminatory work environment is different because the supervisor "is not exercising, or threatening to exercise, actual or apparent authority to make personnel decisions affecting the victim." Brief for United States and EEOC as *Amici Curiae* 24. In the latter situation, he concludes, some further notice requirement should therefore be necessary.

The Solicitor General's position is untenable. A supervisor's responsibilities do not begin and end with the power to hire, fire, and discipline employees, or with the power to recommend such actions. Rather, a supervisor is charged with the day-to-day supervision of the work environment and with ensuring a safe, productive workplace. There is no reason why abuse of the latter authority should have different consequences than abuse of the former. In both cases it is the authority vested in the supervisor by the employer that enables him to commit the wrong: it is precisely because the supervisor is understood to be clothed with the employer's authority that he is able to impose unwelcome sexual conduct on subordinates. There is therefore no justification for a special rule, to be applied *only* in "hostile environment" cases, that sexual harassment does not create employer liability until the employee suffering the discrimination notifies other supervisors. No such requirement appears in the statute, and no such requirement can coherently be drawn from the law of agency.

Agency principles and the goals of Title VII law make appropriate some limitation on the liability of employers for the acts of supervisors. Where, for example, a supervisor has no authority over an employee, because the two work in wholly different parts of the employer's business, it may be improper to find strict employer liability. See 29 CFR § 1604.11(c) (1985). Those considerations, however, do not justify the creation of a special "notice" rule in hostile environment cases.

Further, nothing would be gained by crafting such a rule. In the "pure" hostile environment case, where an employee files an EEOC complaint alleging sexual harassment in the workplace, the employee seeks not money damages but injunctive relief. [Ed. note. Congress revised the panoply of damages available under Title VII in 1991. See *infra* Chapter 5.] Under Title VII, the EEOC must notify an employer of charges made against it within 10 days after receipt of the complaint. If the charges appear to be based on "reasonable cause," the EEOC must attempt to eliminate the offending practice through "informal methods of conference, conciliation, and persuasion." An employer whose internal procedures assertedly would have redressed the discrimination can avoid injunctive relief by employing these procedures after receiving notice of the complaint or during the conciliation period. Where a complainant, on the other hand, seeks backpay on the theory that a hostile work environment effected a constructive termination, the existence of an internal complaint procedure may be a factor in determining not the employer's liability but the remedies available against it. Where a complainant without good reason bypassed an internal complaint procedure she knew to be effective, a court may be reluctant to find constructive termination and thus to award reinstatement or backpay.

I therefore reject the Solicitor General's position. I would apply in this case the same rules we apply in all other Title VII cases, and hold that sexual harassment by a supervisor of an employee under his supervision, leading to a discriminatory work environment, should be imputed to the employer for Title VII purposes regardless of whether the employee gave "notice" of the offense.

Notes and Discussion

1. Framework Contradictions Professor David Oppenheimer addressed the apparent contradiction between the EEOC guidelines concerning employer liability and the *Meritor* opinion:

> When the Supreme Court agreed to hear *Vinson*, EEOC Chairman Thomas successfully lobbied Solicitor General Charles Fried to submit an *amicus curiae* brief. The Solicitor General's role in *Vinson* marked a major shift in the government's interpretation of Title VII cases. In all but six of those cases, the Solicitor General had sided with the employee. . . . In *Vinson*, however, the Solicitor General sided with the employer.

> Although the Solicitor General's *Vinson* brief purported to apply the EEOC Guidelines, its analysis disavowed them. The Solicitor General, on behalf of the EEOC, took the position that the district court correctly determined that Vinson had not been sexually harassed, and, further, that if the Court reached the issue of liability, it should hold that the court of appeals had erred in holding that employers were strictly liable for harassment by supervisors. To support its claim that there was insufficient evidence that Vinson had been harassed, the Solicitor General argued that Vinson had failed to complain until long after the alleged harassment occurred, had

declined opportunities to transfer to jobs away from the alleged harasser, and had not appeared to others to be frightened of or hostile toward her alleged harasser.

Turning to the question of employer liability, the Solicitor General urged that the court reject any application of vicarious liability for hostile work environment sexual harassment. The Solicitor General's brief argued that supervisors committing hostile work environment sexual harassment do not rely on their delegated authority; thus, unless an employer knows or should know of the harassment, it should not be subject to liability for its employees' wrongful acts. . . .

The Solicitor General supported this proposition by seriously misstating the law of agency. . . . [In addition,] the Solicitor General's brief was devoid of any discussion of the policies supporting the doctrine of *respondeat superior*. Most remarkably, nowhere did the brief admit that the Solicitor General's position represented a disavowal of the 1980 EEOC Guidelines.[12]

Why did EEOC Chairman Clarence Thomas lobby Solicitor General Charles Fried to take a position supporting the employer in this case? Why did the government disavow the EEOC Guidelines that call for vicarious liability? Is it true that because a supervisor is not exercising apparent authority to make a personnel decision in a hostile environment case, he is not "aided in accomplishing the tort by the existence of the agency relation"? Oppenheimer referred to the policies supporting the doctrine of *respondeat superior*. What are those policies?

2. Legal Theory Once the Supreme Court granted certiorari in *Meritor*, Catharine MacKinnon wrote the appellate brief.[13] Her participation highlights the value of legal academics' contributions in the practice arena. Law (both case law and legislation) evolves, in part, because of the contributions of legal theorists. What legal theory, if any, does *Meritor* use to find sexual harassment constitutes sex discrimination?

3. More Recent Developments Regarding Supervisor Harassment

In the years following the Supreme Court's *Meritor* decision, lower courts imposed vicarious (strict) liability when quid pro quo harassment had occurred, but not when supervisors had engaged in hostile work environment harassment unassociated with a tangible economic impact. For hostile work environment harassment by a supervisor, the courts ignored the EEOC guidelines and used a direct liability, negligence

---

12. David Benjamin Oppenheimer, *Exacerbating the Exasperating: Title VII Liability of Employers for Sexual Harassment Committed by Their Supervisors*, 81 CORNELL L. REV. 66, 124–28 (1995).

13. Anna-Maria Marshall, *Closing the Gaps: Plaintiffs in Pivotal Sexual Harassment Cases*, 23 LAW & SOC. INQUIRY 761, 787 (1998).

standard. Thus, lower courts found employer liability for hostile work environments only when the employer knew or should have known of the supervisor's harassing behavior and failed to take immediate and appropriate remedial action.

A. Supreme Court Cases That Changed the Title VII Standard for Employer Liability

Congress amended Title VII in 1991, but failed to design a protocol for employer liability.[14] Without clear guidance from Congress, the Court responded again to deal with circuit court variations. Twelve years after its *Meritor* decision, the Court provided a formula for employer liability in *Burlington Industries, Inc. v. Ellerth* and *Faragher v. City of Boca Raton*. In *Burlington Industries*, the Court applied its standard for a subordinate employee who refused a supervisor's unwelcome sexual advances and job-related threats but quit before she experienced any adverse tangible job consequences.

Burlington Industries, Inc. v. Ellerth

524 U.S. 742 (1998)

Justice KENNEDY delivered the opinion of the Court.

. . . .

I

From March 1993 until May 1994, [Kimberly] Ellerth worked as a salesperson in one of Burlington's divisions in Chicago, Illinois. During her employment, she alleges, she was subjected to constant sexual harassment by her supervisor, one Ted Slowik.

In the hierarchy of Burlington's management structure, Slowik was a midlevel manager. . . . Slowik was not Ellerth's immediate supervisor. Ellerth worked in a two-person office in Chicago, and she answered to her office colleague, who in turn answered to Slowik in New York.

Against a background of repeated boorish and offensive remarks and gestures which Slowik allegedly made, Ellerth places particular emphasis on three alleged incidents where Slowik's comments could be construed as threats to deny her tangible job benefits. In the summer of 1993, while on a business trip, Slowik invited Ellerth to the hotel lounge, an invitation Ellerth felt compelled to accept because Slowik was her boss. When Ellerth gave no encouragement to remarks Slowik made about her breasts, he told her to "loosen up" and warned, "you know, Kim, I could make your life very hard or very easy at Burlington."

---

14. *See* Civil Rights Act of 1991, Pub. L. No. 102-166, 105 Stat. 1072 (codified at 42 U.S.C. § 1981a (1994)).

In March 1994, when Ellerth was being considered for a promotion, Slowik expressed reservations during the promotion interview because she was not "loose enough." The comment was followed by his reaching over and rubbing her knee. Ellerth did receive the promotion; but when Slowik called to announce it, he told Ellerth, "you're gonna be out there with men who work in factories, and they certainly like women with pretty butts/legs."

In May 1994, Ellerth called Slowik, asking permission to insert a customer's logo into a fabric sample. Slowik responded, "I don't have time for you right now, Kim — unless you want to tell me what you're wearing." Ellerth told Slowik she had to go and ended the call. A day or two later, Ellerth called Slowik to ask permission again. This time he denied her request, but added something along the lines of, "are you wearing shorter skirts yet, Kim, because it would make your job a whole heck of a lot easier."

A short time later, Ellerth's immediate supervisor cautioned her about returning telephone calls to customers in a prompt fashion. In response, Ellerth quit. She faxed a letter giving reasons unrelated to the alleged sexual harassment we have described. About three weeks later, however, she sent a letter explaining she quit because of Slowik's behavior.

During her tenure at Burlington, Ellerth did not inform anyone in authority about Slowik's conduct, despite knowing Burlington had a policy against sexual harassment. In fact, she chose not to inform her immediate supervisor (not Slowik) because "'it would be his duty as my supervisor to report any incidents of sexual harassment.'" On one occasion, she told Slowik a comment he made was inappropriate.

. . . The District Court granted summary judgment to Burlington. The Court found Slowik's behavior, as described by Ellerth, severe and pervasive enough to create a hostile work environment, but found Burlington neither knew nor should have known about the conduct. There was no triable issue of fact on the latter point, and the Court noted Ellerth had not used Burlington's internal complaint procedures. Although Ellerth's claim was framed as a hostile work environment complaint, the District Court observed there was a *quid pro quo* "component" to the hostile environment. Proceeding from the premise that an employer faces vicarious liability for quid pro quo harassment, the District Court thought it necessary to apply a negligence standard because the quid pro quo merely contributed to the hostile work environment. The District Court also dismissed Ellerth's constructive discharge claim.

The Court of Appeals en banc reversed in a decision which produced eight separate opinions and no consensus for a controlling rationale. . . .

. . . .

The disagreement revealed in the careful opinions of the judges of the Court of Appeals reflects the fact that Congress has left it to the courts to determine controlling agency law principles in a new and difficult area of federal law. . . .

II

At the outset, we assume an important proposition yet to be established. . . . The premise is: A trier of fact could find in Slowik's remarks numerous threats to retaliate against Ellerth if she denied some sexual liberties. The threats, however, were not carried out or fulfilled. Cases based on threats which are carried out are referred to often as *quid pro quo* cases, as distinct from bothersome attentions or sexual remarks that are sufficiently severe or pervasive to create a hostile work environment. The terms *quid pro quo* and hostile work environment are helpful, perhaps, in making a rough demarcation between cases in which threats are carried out and those where they are not or are absent altogether, but beyond this are of limited utility.

. . . .

Nevertheless, as use of the terms grew in the wake of *Meritor*, they acquired their own significance. The standard of employer responsibility turned on which type of harassment occurred. If the plaintiff established a *quid pro quo* claim, the Courts of Appeals held, the employer was subject to vicarious liability. The rule encouraged Title VII plaintiffs to state their claims as *quid pro quo* claims, which in turn put expansive pressure on the definition. The equivalence of the *quid pro quo* label and vicarious liability is illustrated by this case. The question presented on certiorari is whether Ellerth can state a claim of *quid pro quo* harassment, but the issue of real concern to the parties is whether Burlington has vicarious liability for Slowik's alleged misconduct, rather than liability limited to its own negligence. The question presented for certiorari asks:

> "Whether a claim of *quid pro quo* sexual harassment may be stated under Title VII . . . where the plaintiff employee has neither submitted to the sexual advances of the alleged harasser nor suffered any tangible effects on the compensation, terms, conditions or privileges of employment as a consequence of a refusal to submit to those advances?"

. . . When a plaintiff proves that a tangible employment action resulted from a refusal to submit to a supervisor's sexual demands, he or she establishes that the employment decision itself constitutes a change in the terms and conditions of employment that is actionable under Title VII. For any sexual harassment preceding the employment decision to be actionable, however, the conduct must be severe or pervasive. Because Ellerth's claim involves only unfulfilled threats, it should be categorized as a hostile work environment claim which requires a showing of severe or pervasive conduct. For purposes of this case, we accept the District Court's finding that the alleged conduct was severe or pervasive. The case before us involves numerous alleged threats, and we express no opinion as to whether a single unfulfilled threat is sufficient to constitute discrimination in the terms or conditions of employment.

. . . .

III

We must decide, then, whether an employer has vicarious liability when a supervisor creates a hostile work environment by making explicit threats to alter a subordinate's terms or conditions of employment, based on sex, but does not fulfill the threat. We turn to principles of agency law, for the term "employer" is defined under Title VII to include "agents." In express terms, Congress has directed federal courts to interpret Title VII based on agency principles. Given such an explicit instruction, we conclude a uniform and predictable standard must be established as a matter of federal law. We rely "on the general common law of agency, rather than on the law of any particular State, to give meaning to these terms." The resulting federal rule, based on a body of case law developed over time, is statutory interpretation pursuant to congressional direction. This is not federal common law in "the strictest sense, *i.e.*, a rule of decision that amounts, not simply to an interpretation of a federal statute . . . , but, rather, to the judicial 'creation' of a special federal rule of decision." . . .

As *Meritor* acknowledged, the Restatement (Second) of Agency (1957) (hereinafter Restatement), is a useful beginning point for a discussion of general agency principles. Since our decision in *Meritor*, federal courts have explored agency principles, and we find useful instruction in their decisions, noting that "common-law principles may not be transferable in all their particulars to Title VII." The EEOC has issued Guidelines governing sexual harassment claims under Title VII, but they provide little guidance on the issue of employer liability for supervisor harassment.

A

. . . .

An employer may be liable for both negligent and intentional torts committed by an employee within the scope of his or her employment. Sexual harassment under Title VII presupposes intentional conduct. While early decisions absolved employers of liability for the intentional torts of their employees, the law now imposes liability where the employee's "purpose, however misguided, is wholly or in part to further the master's business."

As Courts of Appeals have recognized, a supervisor acting out of gender-based animus or a desire to fulfill sexual urges may not be actuated by a purpose to serve the employer. . . . The harassing supervisor often acts for personal motives, motives unrelated and even antithetical to the objectives of the employer. There are instances, of course, where a supervisor engages in unlawful discrimination with the purpose, mistaken or otherwise, to serve the employer. E.g., *Sims v. Montgomery County Comm'n*, 766 F. Supp. 1052, 1075 (MD Ala. 1990) (supervisor acting in scope of employment where employer has a policy of discouraging women from seeking advancement and "sexual harassment was simply a way of furthering that policy"). . . .

. . . .

The general rule is that sexual harassment by a supervisor is not conduct within the scope of employment.

B

Scope of employment does not define the only basis for employer liability under agency principles. In limited circumstances, agency principles impose liability on employers even where employees commit torts outside the scope of employment. The principles are set forth in the much-cited § 219(2) of the Restatement[.]

. . . .

Subsection 219(2)(d) concerns vicarious liability for intentional torts committed by an employee when the employee uses apparent authority (the apparent authority standard), or when the employee "was aided in accomplishing the tort by the existence of the agency relation" (the aided in the agency relation standard). As other federal decisions have done in discussing vicarious liability for supervisor harassment, e.g., *Henson v. Dundee*, 682 F.2d 897, 909 (11th Cir. 1982), we begin with § 219(2)(d).

C

As a general rule, apparent authority is relevant where the agent purports to exercise a power which he or she does not have, as distinct from where the agent threatens to misuse actual power. In the usual case, a supervisor's harassment involves misuse of actual power, not the false impression of its existence. Apparent authority analysis therefore is inappropriate in this context. If, in the unusual case, it is alleged there is a false impression that the actor was a supervisor, when he in fact was not, the victim's mistaken conclusion must be a reasonable one. Restatement § 8, Comment c ("Apparent authority exists only to the extent it is reasonable for the third person dealing with the agent to believe that the agent is authorized"). When a party seeks to impose vicarious liability based on an agent's misuse of delegated authority, the Restatement's aided in the agency relation rule, rather than the apparent authority rule, appears to be the appropriate form of analysis.

D

We turn to the aided in the agency relation standard. In a sense, most workplace tortfeasors are aided in accomplishing their tortious objective by the existence of the agency relation: Proximity and regular contact may afford a captive pool of potential victims. Were this to satisfy the aided in the agency relation standard, an employer would be subject to vicarious liability not only for all supervisor harassment, but also for all co-worker harassment, a result enforced by neither the EEOC nor any court of appeals to have considered the issue. The aided in the agency relation standard, therefore, requires the existence of something more than the employment relation itself.

At the outset, we can identify a class of cases where, beyond question, more than the mere existence of the employment relation aids in commission of the harassment: when a supervisor takes a tangible employment action against the subordinate. Every Federal Court of Appeals to have considered the question has found vicarious liability when a discriminatory act results in a tangible employment action. In *Meritor*, we acknowledged this consensus. Although few courts have elaborated how agency principles support this rule, we think it reflects a correct application of the aided in the agency relation standard.

In the context of this case, a tangible employment action would have taken the form of a denial of a raise or a promotion. The concept of a tangible employment action appears in numerous cases in the Courts of Appeals discussing claims involving race, age, and national origin discrimination, as well as sex discrimination. Without endorsing the specific results of those decisions, we think it prudent to import the concept of a tangible employment action for resolution of the vicarious liability issue we consider here. A tangible employment action constitutes a significant change in employment status, such as hiring, firing, failing to promote, reassignment with significantly different responsibilities, or a decision causing a significant change in benefits.

When a supervisor makes a tangible employment decision, there is assurance the injury could not have been inflicted absent the agency relation. A tangible employment action in most cases inflicts direct economic harm. As a general proposition, only a supervisor, or other person acting with the authority of the company, can cause this sort of injury. . . .

Tangible employment actions are the means by which the supervisor brings the official power of the enterprise to bear on subordinates. A tangible employment decision requires an official act of the enterprise, a company act. The decision in most cases is documented in official company records, and may be subject to review by higher level supervisors. The supervisor often must obtain the imprimatur of the enterprise and use its internal processes.

For these reasons, a tangible employment action taken by the supervisor becomes for Title VII purposes the act of the employer. Whatever the exact contours of the aided in the agency relation standard, its requirements will always be met when a supervisor takes a tangible employment action against a subordinate. In that instance, it would be implausible to interpret agency principles to allow an employer to escape liability, as *Meritor* itself appeared to acknowledge.

Whether the agency relation aids in commission of supervisor harassment which does not culminate in a tangible employment action is less obvious. Application of the standard is made difficult by its malleable terminology, which can be read to either expand or limit liability in the context of supervisor harassment. On the one hand, a supervisor's power and authority invests his or her harassing conduct with a particular threatening character, and in this sense, a supervisor always is aided by the agency relation. On the other hand, there are acts of harassment a supervisor might commit which might be the same acts a co-employee would commit, and there may be some circumstances where the supervisor's status makes little difference.

It is this tension which, we think, has caused so much confusion among the Courts of Appeals which have sought to apply the aided in the agency relation standard to Title VII cases. The aided in the agency relation standard, however, is a developing feature of agency law, and we hesitate to render a definitive explanation of our understanding of the standard in an area where other important considerations must affect our judgment. In particular, we are bound by our holding in *Meritor* that agency principles constrain the imposition of vicarious liability in cases of supervisory harassment. Congress has not altered *Meritor*'s rule even though it has made significant amendments to Title VII in the interim.

Although *Meritor* suggested the limitation on employer liability stemmed from agency principles, the Court acknowledged other considerations might be relevant as well. For example, Title VII is designed to encourage the creation of antiharassment policies and effective grievance mechanisms. Were employer liability to depend in part on an employer's effort to create such procedures, it would effect Congress' intention to promote conciliation rather than litigation in the Title VII context and the EEOC's policy of encouraging the development of grievance procedures. To the extent limiting employer liability could encourage employees to report harassing conduct before it becomes severe or pervasive, it would also serve Title VII's deterrent purpose. As we have observed, Title VII borrows from tort law the avoidable consequences doctrine and the considerations which animate that doctrine would also support the limitation of employer liability in certain circumstances.

In order to accommodate the agency principles of vicarious liability for harm caused by misuse of supervisory authority, as well as Title VII's equally basic policies of encouraging forethought by employers and saving action by objecting employees, we adopt the following holding in this case and in *Faragher v. Boca Raton, post*, also decided today. An employer is subject to vicarious liability to a victimized employee for an actionable hostile environment created by a supervisor with immediate (or successively higher) authority over the employee. When no tangible employment action is taken, a defending employer may raise an affirmative defense to liability or damages, subject to proof by a preponderance of the evidence. The defense comprises two necessary elements: (a) that the employer exercised reasonable care to prevent and correct promptly any sexually harassing behavior, and (b) that the plaintiff employee unreasonably failed to take advantage of any preventive or corrective opportunities provided by the employer or to avoid harm otherwise. While proof that an employer had promulgated an anti-harassment policy with complaint procedure is not necessary in every instance as a matter of law, the need for a stated policy suitable to the employment circumstances may appropriately be addressed in any case when litigating the first element of the defense. And while proof that an employee failed to fulfill the corresponding obligation of reasonable care to avoid harm is not limited to showing any unreasonable failure to use any complaint procedure provided by the employer, a demonstration of such failure will normally suffice to satisfy the employer's burden under the second element of the defense. No affirmative defense is available, however, when the supervisor's harassment culminates in a tangible employment action, such as discharge, demotion, or undesirable reassignment.

. . . .

Justice THOMAS, with whom Justice SCALIA joins, dissenting.

The Court today manufactures a rule that employers are vicariously liable if supervisors create a sexually hostile work environment, subject to an affirmative defense that the Court barely attempts to define. This rule applies even if the employer has a policy against sexual harassment, the employee knows about that policy, and the employee never informs anyone in a position of authority about the supervisor's conduct. As a result, employer liability under Title VII is judged by different standards depending upon whether a sexually or racially hostile work environment is alleged. The standard of employer liability should be the same in both instances: An employer should be liable if, and only if, the plaintiff proves that the employer was negligent in permitting the supervisor's conduct to occur.

I

Years before sexual harassment was recognized as "discriminat[ion] . . . because of . . . sex," 42 U.S.C. § 2000e-2(a)(1), the Courts of Appeals considered whether, and when, a racially hostile work environment could violate Title VII.[1] In the landmark case *Rogers v. EEOC*, 454 F.2d 234 (1971), *cert. denied*, 406 U.S. 957 (1972), the Court of Appeals for the Fifth Circuit held that the practice of racially segregating patients in a doctor's office could amount to discrimination in "'the terms, conditions, or privileges'" of employment, thereby violating Title VII. . . .

. . . .

In race discrimination cases, employer liability has turned on whether the plaintiff has alleged an adverse employment consequence, such as firing or demotion, or a hostile work environment. If a supervisor takes an adverse employment action because of race, causing the employee a tangible job detriment, the employer is vicariously liable for resulting damages. This is because such actions are company acts that can be performed only by the exercise of specific authority granted by the employer, and thus the supervisor acts as the employer. If, on the other hand, the employee alleges a racially hostile work environment, the employer is liable only for negligence: that is, only if the employer knew, or in the exercise of reasonable

---

1. This sequence of events is not surprising, given that the primary goal of the Civil Rights Act of 1964 was to eradicate race discrimination and that the statute's ban on sex discrimination was added as an eleventh-hour amendment in an effort to kill the bill. *See* Barnes v. Costle, 561 F.2d 983, 987 (C.A.D.C. 1997).

care should have known, about the harassment and failed to take remedial action. Liability has thus been imposed only if the employer is blameworthy in some way.

This distinction applies with equal force in cases of sexual harassment. When a supervisor inflicts an adverse employment consequence upon an employee who has rebuffed his advances, the supervisor exercises the specific authority granted to him by his company. His acts, therefore, are the company's acts and are properly chargeable to it.

If a supervisor creates a hostile work environment, however, he does not act for the employer. As the Court concedes, a supervisor's creation of a hostile work environment is neither within the scope of his employment, nor part of his apparent authority. Indeed, a hostile work environment is antithetical to the interest of the employer. In such circumstances, an employer should be liable only if it has been negligent. That is, liability should attach only if the employer either knew, or in the exercise of reasonable care should have known, about the hostile work environment and failed to take remedial action.

Sexual harassment is simply not something that employers can wholly prevent without taking extraordinary measures—constant video and audio surveillance, for example—that would revolutionize the workplace in a manner incompatible with a free society. Indeed, such measures could not even detect incidents of harassment such as the comments Slowick allegedly made to respondent in a hotel bar. The most that employers can be charged with, therefore, is a duty to act reasonably under the circumstances. . . .

Under a negligence standard, Burlington cannot be held liable for Slowick's conduct. Although respondent alleged a hostile work environment, she never contended that Burlington had been negligent in permitting the harassment to occur, and there is no question that Burlington acted reasonably under the circumstances. The company had a policy against sexual harassment, and respondent admitted that she was aware of the policy but nonetheless failed to tell anyone with authority over Slowick about his behavior. Burlington therefore cannot be charged with knowledge of Slowick's alleged harassment or with a failure to exercise reasonable care in not knowing about it.

II

Rejecting a negligence standard, the Court instead imposes a rule of vicarious employer liability, subject to a vague affirmative defense, for the acts of supervisors who wield no delegated authority in creating a hostile work environment. This rule is a whole-cloth creation that draws no support from the legal principles on which the Court claims it is based. Compounding its error, the Court fails to explain how employers can rely upon the affirmative defense, thus ensuring a continuing reign of confusion in this important area of the law.

. . . .

Section 219(2)(d) of the Restatement provides no basis whatsoever for imposing vicarious liability for a supervisor's creation of a hostile work environment. Contrary to the Court's suggestions, the principle embodied in §219(2)(d) has nothing to do with a servant's "power and authority," nor with whether his actions appear "threatening." Rather, as demonstrated by the Restatement's illustrations, liability under §219(2)(d) depends upon the plaintiff's belief that the agent acted in the ordinary course of business or within the scope of his apparent authority. In this day and age, no sexually harassed employee can reasonably believe that a harassing supervisor is conducting the official business of the company or acting on its behalf. Indeed, the Court admits as much in demonstrating why sexual harassment is not committed within the scope of a supervisor's employment and is not part of his apparent authority.

Thus although the Court implies that it has found guidance in both precedent and statute — ("The resulting federal rule, based on a body of case law developed over time, is statutory interpretation pursuant to congressional direction") — its holding is a product of willful policymaking, pure and simple. The only agency principle that justifies imposing employer liability in this context is the principle that a master will be liable for a servant's torts if the master was negligent or reckless in permitting them to occur; and as noted, under a negligence standard, Burlington cannot be held liable.

The Court's decision is also in considerable tension with our holding in *Meritor* that employers are not strictly liable for a supervisor's sexual harassment. Although the Court recognizes an affirmative defense — based solely on its divination of Title VII's gestalt — it provides shockingly little guidance about how employers can actually avoid vicarious liability. Instead, it issues only Delphic pronouncements and leaves the dirty work to the lower courts. . . .

What these statements mean for district courts ruling on motions for summary judgment — the critical question for employers now subject to the vicarious liability rule — remains a mystery. Moreover, employers will be liable notwithstanding the affirmative defense, *even though they acted reasonably*, so long as the plaintiff in question fulfilled *her* duty of reasonable care to avoid harm. In practice, therefore, employer liability very well may be the rule. But as the Court acknowledges, this is the one result that it is clear Congress did *not* intend.

The Court's holding does guarantee one result: There will be more and more litigation to clarify applicable legal rules in an area in which both practitioners and the courts have long been begging for guidance. It thus truly boggles the mind that the Court can claim that its holding will effect "Congress' intention to promote conciliation rather than litigation in the Title VII context."

. . . .

Notes and Discussion

1. Statutory Interpretation The Court asserted that it employed the common law of agency in determining employer liability. Federal courts are typically not supposed to create federal common law. The *Ellerth* Court specifically denied making "federal common law in 'the strictest sense, i.e., a rule of decision that amounts, not simply to an interpretation of a federal statute . . . , but, rather, to the judicial "creation" of a special federal rule of decision.'"[15] Did the Court simply interpret statutory law in accordance with the common law of agency? Is the EEOC interpreting statutory law when it issues guidelines concerning Title VII? Does it matter to the consideration of whether the Court engaged in statutory interpretation or the creation of federal common law that the Court announced an affirmative defense that was not contemplated in the common law of agency? Are Justices Scalia and Thomas correct when they allege that "the Court recognizes an affirmative defense—based solely on its divination of Title VII's gestalt"?[16]

2. EEOC Guidelines The Court declared that the EEOC guidelines "provide little guidance on the issue of employer liability for supervisor harassment."[17] Is that true? Do the EEOC guidelines influence the evaluation about whether the Court engaged in statutory interpretation or created federal common law?

3. Scope of Employment The Court concluded that sexual harassment did not fall within the scope of employment. Professor David Oppenheimer suggested, however, that it did:

b. *The Requirement that the Servant Be Acting Within the Scope of Employment*

> The law of agency determines whether a servant is acting within the master's delegated authority by determining whether his act falls within the "scope of employment." Generally, an employee's wrongful conduct is within the scope of employment if it is the kind of conduct he is employed to perform and if the conduct substantially adheres to the authorized time and space limits of the work assignment. Some courts further require that the conduct be motivated, at least in part, by a business purpose, although the growing trend is to substitute a requirement that the misconduct be foreseeable. Conduct may be within the scope of employment even when it is an intentionally wrongful act.

> i. *The requirement that the wrongful conduct be the kind of conduct the employee is employed to perform, occurring substantially within the time and space limits of the employment*

> This Article assumes that employers typically do not employ supervisors to sexually harass employees, or to commit other wrongful acts. Thus, one

---

15. Burlington Indust., Inc. v. Ellerth, 524 U.S. 742, 755 (1998).

16. *Id.* at 773 (Thomas, J., dissenting).

17. *Id.* at 755 (majority opinion).

might assume that sexual harassment falls outside the scope of a supervisor's employment, rendering the theory of vicarious liability inapplicable. However, the doctrine of respondeat superior focuses on the relationship between the supervisor's job responsibilities and the wrong he committed; it mandates that the "kind of conduct" inquiry consider not the authority to harass, but the authority to supervise. This element of respondeat superior has generated a great deal of confusion. Many courts and commentators have fundamentally erred by assuming that the relevant authority is the authority to harass. As numerous cases and the Restatement illustrate, this view is simply wrong.

. . . In the context of sexual harassment, where a supervisor's harassment of an employee occurs on the work-site, during working hours, and within the supervisor-subordinate relationship, it meets the scope of authority standards for respondeat superior imposed by the Restatement. The fact that the employer has not authorized the supervisor to harass the employee is irrelevant.

ii. *The requirement that the employee be motivated, at least in part, by a purpose to serve the master*

The Restatement takes the position that in order to apply respondeat superior, the employee must be motivated, at least in part, by an intent to serve the employer. Where this rule is retained, the courts accept any connection between the motivation for the wrongful act and the employee's work as sufficient to bring the conduct within the scope of employment. . . .

In all but the most remarkable circumstances, a supervisor engaging in sexual harassment will have some personal purpose other than serving the interests of the employer. But even when the business-purpose test is applied, the existence of a personal motive does not alone relieve the employer of liability. The Restatement finds that conduct may be within the scope of employment, even when the motivation is largely to serve the employee's private interests. The Comment to §236 explains:

> The fact that the predominant motive of the servant is to benefit himself or a third person does not prevent the act from being within the scope of employment. If the purpose of serving the master's business actuates the servant to any appreciable extent, the master is subject to liability if the act otherwise is within the service. . . .

The Restatement illustrates the purpose-to-serve-the-master principle by using the example of a speeding delivery person. The purpose of employment is to deliver goods, not to speed. In fact, the employer may specifically direct the driver not to speed. However, the driver may speed in order to finish early, or to win a race—reasons independent from serving the employer. Nonetheless, the speeding is within the scope of the delivery person's employment. Thus, if the driver's speeding causes an accident, the employer is vicariously liable.

. . . .

The comparison of a hypothetical harassing supervisor to the speeding delivery person is helpful in determining whether the supervisor's harassment falls within the scope of his employment. The driver's business purpose is to deliver goods, and the supervisor's business purpose is to oversee the work of subordinate employees. As long as the supervisor's conduct mixes work-related and non-work-related functions, his sexual harassment is incidental to the performance of the job. Just as the delivery driver's speeding is within the scope of his employment, the supervisor's interactions with subordinate employees, including his harassment, are incidental to, and thus within the scope of, his employment. Therefore, unless the non-work-related interactions can be surgically separated so as to have no relation to the supervisor-subordinate relationship, all of the supervisor's harassment of subordinates falls within the scope of his employment. . . .

iii. *The inclusion of intentional wrongful acts*

The fact that harassment may be intentional and consciously wrongful will not prevent the application of respondeat superior. [T]he employer's liability under respondeat superior extends to willful and malicious torts, as well as negligence. For example, in *Agarwal v. Johnson*, the California Supreme Court upheld a verdict against an employer whose supervisor fired an employee shortly after calling him a "black nigger, member of an inferior race." The court explained that "the rule in this state is that the employer is liable for the willful misconduct of his employees acting in a managerial capacity. The reason for the imposition of liability is to encourage careful selection and control of persons placed in important management positions."

Recognition of the supervisor's harassment as within the scope of employment depends to some extent on the point of view of the observer. From the point of view of the employer, the supervisor's harassment may bear no relation to the job the supervisor was hired to perform. The employer may thus view the harassment as not simply outside the scope of employment, but as a completely private matter between the supervisor and employee, in which the existence of an employee-supervisor relationship is irrelevant. From the viewpoint of the supervisor himself, he may or may not consciously regard his ability to subject the employee to his unwanted conduct as a privilege of his employment position. But from the employee's point of view, the supervisor's ability to harass her is created precisely by the agency relationship, which affords the supervisor the authority to call her into his presence, to retain her in his presence over her objections, to use his responsibility to act as the voice of the employer to place her in a compromising position, and to take liberties with her personal privacy beyond the reach of a co-equal acquaintance, or a stranger. The authority that the employer has given him to supervise leaves her vulnerable to his wrongful acts.[18]

Is the Court or Oppenheimer more persuasive on sexual harassment and the scope of employment?

4. Aided in the Agency Relation Does this provision of the Restatement ever apply to co-workers? If not, why did the Court decide not to use it, in conjunction with supervisor harassment, without "something more"? If a supervisor harasses a worker—as a co-worker could—is it possible that the supervisor is aided in the agency relation? Is it true that "there may be some circumstances where the supervisor's status makes little difference"?[19]

5. The Affirmative Defense What were the policy considerations the Court discussed in its decision to limit vicarious liability for employers? Are these considerations consistent with the limitations of the affirmative defense? Does the affirmative defense convert what would otherwise be a strict liability scheme into a negligence system? Why or why not?

The Court announced that an employer will avoid liability when "the employer exercised reasonable care to prevent and correct promptly any sexually harassing behavior, and . . . the plaintiff employee unreasonably failed to take advantage of any preventive or corrective opportunities provided by the employer or to avoid harm otherwise."[20] Did the Court define what constituted "reasonable care" in the prevention and correction of sexual harassment? What steps would insulate an employer from liability? What factors might result in a conclusion that the employer failed to act reasonably? Might the prevalence of expert testimony with respect to the employer's duty of care increase? Will industry standards develop to use as benchmarks? Why or why not?

Did the Court clarify what constitutes an unreasonable failure on the part of the employee? Might an employee act reasonably in failing to avail himself or herself of procedures designed by the employer to prevent or correct sexual harassment?

6. From *Meritor* to *Burlington* The similarity between the affirmative defense adopted in *Burlington* and the government's proposal, filed in the EEOC's amicus brief in the *Meritor* case, is striking. The two are almost identical. About the *Meritor* brief, Martha Chamallas commented:

> [T]he Solicitor General's brief urged the Court to impose liability only in cases where employers failed to provide victims with an avenue of complaint or were unresponsive to an employee's complaint. Particularly given the notorious reluctance of sexual harassment victims to report incidents of

---

18. Oppenheimer, *supra* note 12, at 81–88.
19. *Burlington Indust., Inc.*, 524 U.S. at 763.
20. *Id.* at 765.

harassment to company officials, the proposed limit would likely have had the effect of insulating the large majority of employers that adopt internal anti-harassment policies and grievance procedures.

. . . In this respect, the Solicitor General's brief represented an early backlash attempt to curtail Title VII coverage even before the Supreme Court formally endorsed sexual harassment claims.[21]

Is *Burlington*'s affirmative defense a more successful curtailment of Title VII coverage? Do the statistics showing a dearth of formal complaints noted at the beginning of this chapter reinforce Chamallas's point?

7. **The Dissent** Given the similarities between the Solicitor General's *Meritor* brief and *Burlington*'s affirmative defense, why did Justice Thomas (the Chairman of the EEOC when *Meritor* was argued) dissent in *Burlington*?

Were Justices Scalia and Thomas correct that the majority "manufactures a rule that employers are vicariously liable if supervisors create a sexually hostile work environment . . . [and that this] is a whole-cloth creation that draws no support from the legal principles"?[22] Why or why not? Does Justice Thomas's participation in the government's *Meritor* amicus brief influence your analysis?

Referring to the Restatement's illustrations, Justice Thomas asserted that the plaintiff must have the belief that the agent acted within his apparent authority. The comment states more:

Clause (d) includes primarily situations in which the principal's liability is based upon conduct which is within the apparent authority of a servant, as where one purports to speak for his employer in defaming another or interfering with another's business. See § 247–249. Apparent authority may also be the basis of an action of deceit (§ 257–264), and even physical harm. See § 265–267. *In other situations, the servant may be able to cause harm because of his position as agent*, as where a telegraph operator sends false messages purporting to come from third persons. See § 261. Again, the manager of a store operated by him for an undisclosed principal is enabled to cheat the customers because of his position. See § 222. *The enumeration of such situations is not exhaustive, and is intended only to indicate the area within which a master may be subjected to liability for acts of his servants not in scope of employment.*[23]

Did the Justices give short shrift to the "aided in the agency relation" provision of § 219(2)(d)?

---

21. Martha Chamallas, *Two Very Different Stories: Vicarious Liability Under Tort and Title VII Law*, 75 Ohio St. L.J. 1315, 1322 (2014).

22. *Burlington Indust., Inc.*, 524 U.S. at 766 (Thomas, J., dissenting).

23. Restatement (Second) of Agency § 219(2)(d) cmt. e (Am. Law. Inst. 1958) (emphasis added).

Is the Court's *Burlington* decision in tension with *Meritor* as the dissenters alleged? Should courts limit employer liability for supervisor harassment to only those situations in which the employer was negligent, as advocated by Justices Thomas and Scalia? Were Justices Thomas and Scalia correct that the Court has created different standards for sexual and racial harassment? Is it true that "[t]here will be more and more litigation to clarify applicable legal rules" of Title VII?[24]

On the same day that the Justices decided *Burlington*, the Court also dealt with the circumstances under which the Court would find an employer liable for supervisor hostile environment harassment in *Faragher v. City of Boca Raton*. In this case, neither the supervisors nor the City took formal action to undermine Ms. Faragher's employment status. The Court again endorsed the concept of vicarious liability with an affirmative defense.

Faragher v. City of Boca Raton
524 U.S. 775 (1998)

Justice SOUTER delivered the opinion of the Court.

. . . .

I

Between 1985 and 1990, while attending college, petitioner Beth Ann Faragher worked part time and during the summers as an ocean lifeguard for the Marine Safety Section of the Parks and Recreation Department of respondent, the City of Boca Raton, Florida (City). During this period, Faragher's immediate supervisors were Bill Terry, David Silverman, and Robert Gordon. In June 1990, Faragher resigned.

In 1992, Faragher brought an action against Terry, Silverman, and the City. . . . [T]he complaint alleged that Terry and Silverman created a "sexually hostile atmosphere" at the beach by repeatedly subjecting Faragher and other female lifeguards to "uninvited and offensive touching," by making lewd remarks, and by speaking of women in offensive terms. The complaint contained specific allegations that Terry once said that he would never promote a woman to the rank of lieutenant, and that Silverman had said to Faragher, "Date me or clean the toilets for a year." Asserting that Terry and Silverman were agents of the City, and that their conduct amounted to discrimination in the "terms, conditions, and privileges" of her employment, 42 U.S.C. § 2000e-2(a)(1), Faragher sought a judgment against the City for nominal damages, costs, and attorney's fees.

---

24. *Burlington Indust., Inc.*, 524 U.S. at 774 (Thomas, J., dissenting).

... Silverman and Gordon were responsible for making the lifeguards' daily assignments, and for supervising their work and fitness training.

. . . .

In February 1986, the City adopted a sexual harassment policy, which it stated in a memorandum from the City Manager addressed to all employees. In May 1990, the City revised the policy and reissued a statement of it. Although the City may actually have circulated the memos and statements to some employees, it completely failed to disseminate its policy among employees of the Marine Safety Section, with the result that Terry, Silverman, Gordon, and many lifeguards were unaware of it.

. . . .

II

A

. . . .

While indicating the substantive contours of the hostile environments forbidden by Title VII, our cases have established few definite rules for determining when an employer will be liable for a discriminatory environment that is otherwise actionably abusive. Given the circumstances of many of the litigated cases, including some that have come to us, it is not surprising that in many of them, the issue has been joined over the sufficiency of the abusive conditions, not the standards for determining an employer's liability for them. In such instances, the combined knowledge and inaction may be seen as demonstrable negligence, or as the employer's adoption of the offending conduct and its results, quite as if they had been authorized affirmatively as the employer's policy.

Nor was it exceptional that standards for binding the employer were not in issue in *Harris, supra*. In that case of discrimination by hostile environment, the individual charged with creating the abusive atmosphere was the president of the corporate employer, who was indisputably within that class of an employer organization's officials who may be treated as the organization's proxy. *Burns v. McGregor Electronic Industries, Inc.*, (employer-company liable where harassment was perpetrated by its owner). . . .

Finally, there is nothing remarkable in the fact that claims against employers for discriminatory employment actions with tangible results, like hiring, firing, promotion, compensation, and work assignment, have resulted in employer liability once the discrimination was shown.

. . . .

Meritor's statement of the law is the foundation on which we build today. Neither party before us has urged us to depart from our customary adherence to stare decisis in statutory interpretation. And the force of precedent here is enhanced by Congress's amendment to the liability provisions of Title VII since the Meritor decision, without providing any modification of our holding.

B

The Court of Appeals identified, and rejected, three possible grounds drawn from agency law for holding the City vicariously liable for the hostile environment created by the supervisors. It considered whether the two supervisors were acting within the scope of their employment when they engaged in the harassing conduct. The court then enquired whether they were significantly aided by the agency relationship in committing the harassment, and also considered the possibility of imputing Gordon's knowledge of the harassment to the City. Finally, the Court of Appeals ruled out liability for negligence in failing to prevent the harassment. Faragher relies principally on the latter three theories of liability.

. . . [The Court rejected the scope of employment grounds.]

2

The Court of Appeals also rejected vicarious liability on the part of the City insofar as it might rest on the concluding principle set forth in § 219(2)(d) of the Restatement, that an employer "is not subject to liability for the torts of his servants acting outside the scope of their employment unless . . . the servant purported to act or speak on behalf of the principal and there was reliance on apparent authority, or he was aided in accomplishing the tort by the existence of the agency relation." Faragher points to several ways in which the agency relationship aided Terry and Silverman in carrying out their harassment. She argues that in general offending supervisors can abuse their authority to keep subordinates in their presence while they make offensive statements, and that they implicitly threaten to misuse their supervisory powers to deter any resistance or complaint. Thus, she maintains that power conferred on Terry and Silverman by the City enabled them to act for so long without provoking defiance or complaint.

. . . .

We therefore agree with Faragher that in implementing Title VII it makes sense to hold an employer vicariously liable for some tortious conduct of a supervisor made possible by abuse of his supervisory authority, and that the aided-by-agency-relation principle embodied in § 219(2)(d) of the Restatement provides an appropriate starting point for determining liability for the kind of harassment presented here. . . . The agency relationship affords contact with an employee subjected to a supervisor's sexual harassment, and the victim may well be reluctant to accept the risks of blowing the whistle on a superior. When a person with supervisory authority discriminates in the terms and conditions of subordinates' employment, his actions necessarily draw upon his superior position over the people who report to him, or those under them, whereas an employee generally cannot check a supervisor's abusive conduct the same way that she might deal with abuse from a co-worker. When a fellow employee harasses, the victim can walk away or tell the offender where to go, but it may be difficult to offer such responses to a supervisor, whose "power to supervise—[which may be] to hire and fire, and to set work schedules and pay rates—does not disappear . . . when he chooses to harass through insults and offensive gestures rather than directly with threats of firing or promises of promotion." Estrich, *Sex at Work*, 43 Stan. L. Rev. 813, 854 (1991). Recognition of employer liability when discriminatory misuse of supervisory authority alters the terms and conditions of a victim's employment is underscored by the fact that the employer has a greater opportunity to guard against misconduct by supervisors than by common workers; employers have greater opportunity and incentive to screen them, train them, and monitor their performance.

In sum, there are good reasons for vicarious liability for misuse of supervisory authority. That rationale must, however, satisfy one more condition. We are not entitled to recognize this theory under Title VII unless we can square it with *Meritor*'s holding that an employer is not "automatically" liable for harassment by a supervisor who creates the requisite degree of discrimination and there is obviously some tension between that holding and the position that a supervisor's misconduct aided by supervisory authority subjects the employer to liability vicariously; if the "aid" may be the unspoken suggestion of retaliation by misuse of supervisory authority, the risk of automatic liability is high. To counter it, we think there are two basic alternatives, one being to require proof of some affirmative invocation of that authority by the harassing supervisor, the other to recognize an affirmative defense to liability in some circumstances, even when a supervisor has created the actionable environment.

. . . [The Court rejected the first alternative as difficult to implement.]

The other basic alternative to automatic liability would avoid this particular temptation to litigate, but allow an employer to show as an affirmative defense to liability that the employer had exercised reasonable care to avoid harassment and to eliminate it when it might occur, and that the complaining employee had failed to act with like reasonable care to take advantage of the employer's safeguards and otherwise to prevent harm that could have been avoided. This composite defense would, we think, implement the statute sensibly, for reasons that are not hard to fathom.

Although Title VII seeks "to make persons whole for injuries suffered on account of unlawful employment discrimination," its "primary objective," like that of any statute meant to influence primary conduct, is not to provide redress but to avoid harm. As long ago as 1980, the Equal Employment Opportunity Commission (EEOC), charged with the enforcement of Title VII, 42 U.S.C. § 2000e-4, adopted regulations advising employers to "take all steps necessary to prevent sexual harassment from occurring, such as . . . informing employees of their right to raise and how to raise the issue of harassment," and in 1990 the Commission issued a policy statement enjoining employers to establish a complaint procedure "designed to encourage victims of harassment to come forward [without requiring] a victim to complain first to the offending supervisor." It would therefore implement clear statutory policy and complement the Government's Title VII enforcement efforts to recognize the employer's affirmative obligation to prevent violations and give credit here to employers who make reasonable efforts to discharge their duty. Indeed, a theory of vicarious liability for misuse of supervisory power would be at odds with the statutory policy if it failed to provide employers with some such incentive.

. . . .

In order to accommodate the principle of vicarious liability for harm caused by misuse of supervisory authority, as well as Title VII's equally basic policies of encouraging forethought by employers and saving action by objecting employees, we adopt the following holding in this case and in *Burlington Industries, Inc. v. Ellerth*, 524 U.S. 742 (1998) also decided today. An employer is subject to vicarious liability to a victimized employee for an actionable hostile environment created by a supervisor with immediate (or successively higher) authority over the employee. When no tangible employment action is taken, a defending employer may raise an affirmative defense to liability or damages, subject to proof by a preponderance of the evidence, see Fed. Rule. Civ. Proc. 8(c). The defense comprises two necessary elements: (a) that the employer exercised reasonable care to prevent and correct promptly any sexually harassing behavior, and (b) that the plaintiff employee unreasonably failed to take advantage of any preventive or corrective opportunities provided by the employer or to avoid harm otherwise. While proof that an employer had promulgated an antiharassment policy with complaint procedure is not necessary in every instance as a matter of law, the need for a stated policy suitable to the employment circumstances may appropriately be addressed in any case when litigating the first element of the defense. And while proof that an employee failed to fulfill the corresponding obligation of reasonable care to avoid harm is not limited to showing an unreasonable failure to use any complaint procedure provided by the employer, a demonstration of such failure will normally suffice to satisfy the employer's burden under the second element of the defense. No affirmative defense is available, however, when the supervisor's harassment culminates in a tangible employment action, such as discharge, demotion, or undesirable reassignment. See *Burlington*, 534 U.S., at 762–763.

Applying these rules here, we believe that the judgment of the Court of Appeals must be reversed. The District Court found that the degree of hostility in the work environment rose to the actionable level and was attributable to Silverman and Terry. It is undisputed that these supervisors "were granted virtually unchecked authority" over their subordinates, "directly controlling and supervis[ing] all aspects of [Faragher's] day-to-day activities." It is also clear that Faragher and her colleagues were "completely isolated from the City's higher management." The City did not seek review of these findings.

While the City would have an opportunity to raise an affirmative defense if there were any serious prospect of its presenting one, it appears from the record that any such avenue is closed. The District Court found that the City had entirely failed to disseminate its policy against sexual harassment among the beach employees and that its officials made no attempt to keep track of the conduct of supervisors like Terry and Silverman. The record also makes clear that the City's policy did not include any assurance that the harassing supervisors could be bypassed in register- ing complaints. Under such circumstances, we hold as a matter of law that the City could not be found to have exercised reasonable care to prevent the supervisors' harassing conduct. Unlike the employer of a small workforce, who might expect that sufficient care to prevent tortious behavior could be exercised informally, those responsible for city operations could not reasonably have thought that precautions against hostile environments in any one of many departments in far-flung locations could be effective without communicating some formal policy against harassment, with a sensible complaint procedure.

. . . .

Justice THOMAS, with whom Justice SCALIA joins, dissenting.

For the reasons given in my dissenting opinion in *Burlington Industries v. Ellerth*, 524 U.S. 742 (1998), absent an adverse employment consequence, an employer cannot be held vicariously liable if a supervisor creates a hostile work environ- ment. Petitioner suffered no adverse employment consequence; thus the Court of Appeals was correct to hold that the City is not vicariously liable for the conduct of Chief Terry and Lieutenant Silverman. Because the Court reverses this judgment, I dissent.

. . . .

Notes and Discussion

1. Direct Liability: Proxy Versus Agent Before launching into its discussion of vicarious liability, the Court distinguished among an employer's agent, a supervi- sor, and an employer's proxy. The Court confirmed that Title VII fixes liability on an employer when a proxy for the organization, such as an owner or President— someone who clearly speaks for the company—engages in abusive conduct. Profes- sors Daniel Hemel and Dorothy Lund explain:

> Lower courts have applied this last rule—known as the alter ego doctrine— in cases involving high-ranking corporate officials below the officer level. Beyond evidence of high rank, the key to proving that strict liability is appropriate is to show that the employee exercised "exceptional authority and control" within the organization.
>
> In sum, companies can expect to be held strictly liable for harassment by high-ranking corporate officials with substantial control over corporate affairs.[25]

---

25. Daniel Hemel & Dorothy S. Lund, *Sexual Harassment and Corporate Law*, 118 COLUM. L. REV. 1583, 1603 (2018). Hemel and Lund cite several cases to support their point, including: Townsend v. Benjamin Enters., 679 F.3d 41, 53–55 (2d Cir. 2012) (leaving for the jury the question of whether alter ego liability applies in the case of a vice president who "exercised a significant

2. A Tripartite Scheme for Vicarious Liability In his law review note, Justin Smith succinctly summarized the *Faragher* and *Ellerth* holdings:

> Thus, *Faragher* and *Burlington Industries* introduced a tripartite regime in which liability varies depending both on the type of harassment and on the status of the harasser. The three resulting liability standards currently in place are: (1) for harassment by a supervisor that results in a tangible employment action, the employer is subject to strict vicarious liability; (2) for harassment by a supervisor that does not result in a tangible employment action, the employer is subject to strict vicarious liability, but it can offer an affirmative defense that it was non-negligent and the harassment victim was negligent; and (3) for harassment by nonsupervisory coworkers, the employer is subject to vicarious liability based on negligence (dicta).
>
> In practice, this regime requires a court to make a series of inquiries. First, it has to determine the status of the harasser. If the harasser is a supervisor, employer liability is strict; if the harasser is a nonsupervisory coworker, employer liability is based on negligence. If the court initially determines that the harasser was a supervisor, it then proceeds to determine the type of harassment. If the harassment results in a tangible employment action, the employer is automatically liable; if the harassment does not result in a tangible employment action, the employer can attempt to establish the affirmative defense.[26]

Does this scheme further congressional intent to end workplace discrimination and harassment? Why or why not? Justin Smith suggested that "varying liability standards by the status of the harasser [as the EEOC did in 1980] was in many ways more straightforward than the regime the majority of circuits chose to follow after *Meritor*—dividing the liability regime by the type of harassment."[27] Did the Court simplify matters in *Faragher* and *Ellerth*?

3. Scope of Employment The *Faragher* Court reasoned that "courts have emphasized that harassment consisting of unwelcome remarks and touching is motivated solely by individual desires and serves no purpose of the employer. For this reason, courts have likened hostile environment sexual harassment to the classic 'frolic and detour' for which an employer has no vicarious liability."[28] Does this language sound

---

degree of control over corporate affairs" and whose family held all corporate shares); Mallinson-Montague v. Pocrnick, 224 F.3d 1224, 1232–33 (10th Cir. 2000) (holding an alter ego liability jury instruction appropriate in the case of a senior vice president of consumer lending who had hiring, firing, and supervisory authority over employees in one department, retained ultimate authority to disapprove all consumer loans, and reported directly to the president) and Helm v. Kansas, 656 F.3d 1277, 1286 (10th Cir. 2011). *Id.* at 1603, nn.115–116.

26. Justin P. Smith, *Note, Letting the Master Answer: Employer Liability for Sexual Harassment in the Workplace After* Faragher *and* Burlington Industries, 74 N.Y.U. L. Rev. 1786, 1795 (1999).

27. *Id.* at 1804–05.

28. Faragher v. City of Boca Raton, 524 U.S. 775, 794 (1998).

reminiscent of other court decisions? Compare this reasoning with that in *Corne*, in which the court found for the defense:

> In the present case, Mr. Price's conduct appears to be nothing more than a personal proclivity, peculiarity or mannerism. By his alleged sexual advances, Mr. Price was satisfying a personal urge. Certainly no employer policy is here involved; rather than the company being benefited in any way by the conduct of Price, it is obvious it can only be damaged by the very nature of the acts complained of.[29]

Does this passage employ the same reasoning as that in *Faragher*? If so, did American sexual harassment jurisprudence regress by 20 years with the *Faragher* and *Ellerth* decisions? Explain.

Is it true, as the Court suggested, that "there is no reason to suppose that Congress wished courts to ignore the traditional distinction between acts falling within the scope and acts amounting to what the older law called frolics or detours from the course of employment. . . ."[30] What was Congress's purpose? Might all discrimination be considered a "frolic and detour"—not just sexual harassment but also race discrimination, sex discrimination, etc.? If so, why treat sexual harassment differently? The behavior is defined as unwelcome, so why should it be treated differently from racial harassment or race discrimination?

4. Aided by the Agency Relation Is it true that supervisors are aided in the agency relationship with the employer in a way that co-workers are not? In *Dillon v. Frank*, the court noted, "Management allegedly did nothing more than admonish the harassers, and hold meetings detailing the policy against sexual harassment in place at the center. Dillon alleged that management finally threw up their hands in despair, telling Dillon not to waste their time with his complaints. . . ."[31] Does it appear that the postal service had "a greater opportunity to guard against misconduct by supervisors than by common workers"?[32]

Is it true that *Meritor* does not allow for strict liability in the case of a supervisor aided by the agency relation? Explain.

5. The Avoidance of Harm If the Court is correct that Title VII's primary purpose is the avoidance of harm, would imposition of strict liability for supervisorial conduct defeat that purpose? Might such a liability standard encourage employer monitoring of supervisorial behavior and result in the avoidance of harm? Would employers have less incentive to effectuate protective policies if they were held strictly liable for supervisorial malfeasance? If the target unreasonably fails to avoid the harm, might

---

29. Corne v. Bausch & Lomb, Inc., 390 F. Supp. 161, 163 (D. Ariz. 1975), *rev'd*, 562 F.2d 55 (9th Cir. 1977).
30. *Faragher*, 524 U.S. at 776.
31. Dillon v. Frank, 952 F.2d 403, No. 90-2290, 1992 WL 5436, at *1 (6th Cir. Jan. 15, 1992).
32. *Faragher*, 524 U.S. at 803.

it make sense to lessen her damages rather than restrict employer liability generally? If not, why not?

6. The Rationale for Employer Liability Is the rationale for holding employers liable for supervisorial offenses — foreseeable social behavior — the same as that for holding employers liable for co-worker harassment?

7. The Dissent Is it true, as the dissent contended, that "[p]etitioner suffered no adverse employment consequence"?[33] Is the suffering of humiliation, fear, and abuse not an adverse employment consequence? If not, why not?

B. Post *Faragher* and *Burlington* Interpretations

While the decisions in *Faragher* and *Burlington* answered some questions, their creation of an affirmative defense raised new ones. For example, imagine that an employer implements an effective sexual harassment policy and an employee reasonably avails herself of it. Is the employer still liable for the harassing conduct? Is it liable for only the conduct that occurred up to the point of a reasonably prompt complaint? What if the harassment consists of one severe incident — an attempted rape? Consider how the Eighth Circuit handled a Supreme Court reversal of one of its decisions following the Court's holdings in *Faragher* and *Burlington*.

Todd v. Ortho Biotech, Inc.
175 F.3d 595 (8th Cir. 1999)

LOKEN, Circuit Judge.

Lori Todd, a former sales representative for Ortho Biotech, Inc. ("Ortho"), was sexually assaulted by James Moreland, Ortho's Director of Trade Relations, while attending Ortho's 1992 national sales meeting in Boston. Todd sued Ortho, claiming Moreland's assault constituted a hostile work environment violation of Title VII of the Civil Rights Act of 1964, and actionable sexual harassment under the Minnesota Human Rights Act. [Review of this Minnesota claim is omitted.] A jury found Ortho liable under Title VII, and the court imposed additional damages under the state law claim. Ortho appealed. Based upon the jury's finding that Ortho took prompt and effective remedial action after learning of the assault, we reversed. Todd petitioned the Supreme Court for a writ of certiorari, and that Court vacated our judgment and remanded for further consideration in light of newly decided *Burlington Industries, Inc. v. Ellerth* and *Faragher v. City of Boca Raton*. For the following reasons, we remand Todd's Title VII hostile work environment claim to the district court for further proceedings.

---

33. *Id.* at 810 (Thomas, J., dissenting).

I. The Title VII Claim.

In *Ellerth* and *Faragher*, the Supreme Court articulated a new standard for determining when a supervisor's sexual harassment subjects the employer to hostile work environment liability under Title VII. . . . This holding overrules the Eighth Circuit standard we applied in *Todd*, 138 F.3d at 736, at least in some situations.

A. To determine the impact of *Ellerth* and *Faragher* on our initial decision, we must first consider whether the new *Ellerth/Faragher* standard applies to the facts of this case. That question is problematic for at least two reasons.

1. In deciding *Todd*, 138 F.3d at 736, this court assumed, as did Ortho, that a single severe act of sexual harassment can, without more, constitute a hostile work environment that is actionable under Title VII. Neither the Supreme Court nor this court has squarely addressed this issue, and portions of the opinions in *Ellerth* and *Faragher* cast doubt on its resolution. The Supreme Court's new affirmative defense was adopted to avoid "automatic" employer liability and to give credit to employers who make reasonable efforts to prevent and remedy sexual harassment. But that defense, adopted in cases that involved ongoing sexual harassment in a workplace, may not protect an employer from automatic liability in cases of single, severe, unanticipatable sexual harassment unless, for example, the harassment does not ripen into an actionable hostile work environment claim until the employer learns that the harassment has occurred and fails to take proper remedial action. Though this is an issue of law, it is the kind of issue that is more properly addressed by the district court in the first instance.

2. The new *Ellerth/Faragher* vicarious liability standard is limited to cases of harassment by a "supervisor with immediate (or successively higher) authority over the employee." The Court did not further explain what it meant by "supervisor." Ortho argues that Moreland was not a supervisor under *Ellerth* and *Faragher* because he was not in Todd's "chain of command" at the time of the assault. Todd responds that Moreland had retained supervisory authority over Todd and, at any rate, appeared to Todd to possess such authority. The contours of the term "supervisor" as used in the new *Ellerth/Faragher* standard is another question more appropriately addressed by the district court in the first instance.

B. Assuming the new *Ellerth/Faragher* standard applies to this case, there are fact questions that we cannot answer on the present record and that prevent us from deciding, as a matter of law, which side should prevail.

1. The district court's vicarious liability instruction did not accurately forecast the new *Ellerth/Faragher* standard. The court instructed:

> An employer is liable for the sexual harassment committed by its supervisor if the supervisor used his actual or apparent authority to further the harassment, or if he was otherwise aided in accomplishing the harassment by the existence of his supervisory powers. . . . Apparent authority means such authority as an employer knowingly permits a manager to assume, or

which it holds the manager out as possessing; such authority as the manager appears to have by reason of his or her actual authority; or such authority as a reasonably prudent person, using diligence and discretion, would naturally suppose the manager to possess.

In *Ellerth* and *Faragher*, the Supreme Court stated that "[a]pparent authority analysis therefore is inappropriate in this context." Because the jury may have found Ortho liable for Moreland's harassment solely by reason of his apparent authority, we cannot conclude that the jury's verdict was tantamount to a finding of liability under *Ellerth* and *Faragher*. On the other hand, had the jury been properly instructed in accordance with the new standard, the evidence appears sufficient to support a verdict in Todd's favor. Thus, Ortho is entitled to a new trial, but not judgment as a matter of law, on this issue.

2. The district court's instructions did not ask the jury whether Ortho proved the *Ellerth/Faragher* affirmative defense, an essential component of the new standard. The jury found that Ortho took timely and effective action in response to Moreland's assault, the affirmative defense under prior Eighth Circuit law. Because the law has changed dramatically on this key issue, our review of the present record does not reveal whether a reasonable jury could have found for Ortho on the new affirmative defense. In these circumstances, the appropriate disposition is to remand for a new trial.

This survey of certain issues is intended only to illustrate why Todd's Title VII hostile work environment claim must be remanded. Our discussion should not be read as dictating a particular resolution of these issues, nor does it foreclose the parties from raising on remand additional issues concerning the proper application of *Ellerth* and *Faragher* to this case.

. . . .

RICHARD S. ARNOLD, Circuit Judge, concurring in the judgment.

I agree that a remand is appropriate in this case, at least to allow the employer to try to prove the new affirmative defense established by the recent Supreme Court opinions in *Ellerth* and *Faragher*. There are a few other aspects of today's opinion, however, with which I am not in entire agreement, and I desire to add a few words of explanation.

First, I have no doubt that a single severe act of sexual harassment can amount to a hostile work environment actionable under Title VII. I see nothing in *Ellerth* or *Faragher* to negative this proposition. The Court expresses the fear that employer liability might be automatic if a single severe act is allowed to create liability. This result, the Court says, would be inconsistent with the Supreme Court's reasons for creating the new affirmative defense. The affirmative defense set out in the two recent Supreme Court opinions, however, is not always a complete defense to liability. It can also be a defense to damages only. If a supervisor abuses his authority to commit a sufficiently severe act of harassment, the employer's affirmative defense, if established, should serve to reduce the damages, but I don't understand why it should always erase the tort completely.

Second, I cannot agree that apparent-authority analysis would be inappropriate in the present case. Maybe it's just a question of words, but if the plaintiff reasonably believed that the supervisor in this case, despite not being any longer in the direct chain of command, still possessed a substantially equivalent power to affect her career, that would be enough, in my view, for Mr. Moreland to be treated as a "supervisor" within the meaning of the new rule. The Court quotes a passage from *Ellerth* as holding that "[a]pparent authority analysis . . . is inappropriate in this context." When the entire paragraph in which this sentence appears is read, however, it seems that the Supreme Court was not laying down a flat rule of law. A fuller quotation from the *Ellerth* opinion should make this clear:

> In the usual case, a supervisor's harassment involves misuse of actual power, not the false impression of its existence. Apparent authority analysis therefore is inappropriate in this context.

The present case may be an "unusual" one in the terms of this analytical approach. Here, Mr. Moreland was not in the direct chain of command, but he was still a high ranking official in the area of sales, and, as I have said, the plaintiff may reasonably have believed that he had not lost much of his power, if any. It seems to me not inappropriate to characterize this approach as involving the concept of apparent authority. I believe the Court unduly restricts the analysis when it rules apparent authority out as a matter of law.

Notes and Discussion

1. A Single Incident The court labeled Moreland's behavior a sexual assault and remanded this case, in part, for a determination concerning whether a severe incident of harassment is actionable as a hostile environment. The first appellate court's recitation of the facts provided more details and, therefore, guidance on this remand question:

> After a full day of conferences, Todd stopped at the hospitality suite, where she agreed to go to a jazz club with two other product specialists and James Moreland, Ortho's Director of Trade Relations. The group later went to a local bar, where Moreland drank shots of vodka and exchanged sexually oriented jokes with Todd. Back at the hotel, their companions returned to the hospitality suite, leaving Todd and Moreland alone in an empty elevator. Moreland grabbed Todd and attempted to kiss her but she pushed him away, asking "What are you doing?" Moreland apologized and suggested Todd accompany him to his room for a complete apology. Todd said that was unnecessary, but complied when Moreland persisted, fearful of upsetting a high-ranking Ortho official. Once inside the room, Moreland overpowered Todd, pinned her to the bed, and attempted to rape her. When

Todd began hyperventilating, Moreland allowed her to escape from the room.

The next evening, Todd reported the attack to another product specialist, who urged her to report the incident to Charles Ball, Ortho's Director of Management Development. Todd approached Ball the next morning and asked for a private meeting, without telling him she had been attacked. Ball agreed to meet at the end of that day's conferences. Todd attended the scheduled meetings that day, including a skit she found sexually offensive. She met Ball in her hotel room that evening, told him about the attack and, at his urging, also told Craig Mangean, Director of Employee Relations. Ball was shocked and sympathetic. Mangean told Todd that she had a right to inform the police, but she declined to do so. She said that Mangean could tell the company attorney of the incident but asked that Moreland's superiors not be informed. At Todd's request, Ball and Mangean accompanied her to dinner. After dinner, Todd reported the incident to her immediate supervisor, Division Manager John Hess. She returned to her room, where she received a brief phone call from Moreland. Todd reported the call to Ball, who offered to move her to another room. She declined, saying she felt safe in her own room. Todd returned to Minnesota the next day, where she later obtained medical attention, including treatment for depression and anxiety.[34]

Might the full recitation of the facts have influenced someone's interpretation of the severity of this case? On remand, was it likely that the district court would reject an attempted rape as creating a hostile work environment? The first appellate court noted, "In this case, Ortho quite properly concedes that an attempted rape at a national sales meeting is sufficiently severe misconduct to be actionable sexual harassment. The issue, then, is whether Ortho is liable for Moreland's misconduct."[35] If a defendant admits that behavior constitutes actionable sexual harassment, can he later deny actionable harassment?

The majority asserted that *Faragher* and *Burlington* cast doubt on the viability of single incident hostile work environment claims. Is the majority or concurring judge correct about the proper reading of *Faragher* and *Burlington*? Do *Meritor* or *Harris* offer guidance on the viability of one severe incident? What about the EEOC?

2. Prompt Remedial Action The court failed to elaborate on how Ortho Biotech responded to Todd's complaint but the first appellate decision gave more detail:

Officials at Ortho's headquarters in New Jersey contacted Moreland promptly after receiving Todd's complaint and confronted him early the following week with Todd's accusations. Moreland denied assaulting Todd and claimed he was being targeted because he is an African-American.

34. Todd v. Ortho Biotech, Inc., 138 F.3d 733, 735–36 (8th Cir. 1998), *vacated*, 525 U.S. 802 (1998).
35. *Id.* at 736.

After a three-week investigation, Ortho discharged Moreland but gave him a severance package worth over $100,000 in exchange for his release of all claims against Ortho, including Title VII claims.

. . . .

In this case, Ortho had a published policy against sexual harassment. After hearing Todd's complaint, Ball and Mangean expressed shock and sympathy, asked Todd what she would like them to do, offered to move her to another hotel room, and helped her return home. In Minnesota, Ortho offered to pay Todd's uninsured therapy costs (which she declined); urged her to move her therapy day to a work day, with full pay; and granted her substantial paid leave. Ortho's senior management confronted Moreland when he returned from the sales conference, investigated Todd's complaint thoroughly, and fired Moreland when Todd's complaint was found to be credible. These actions are similar to employer responses the Minnesota courts have found to be timely and appropriate remedial action.

The district court concluded that Ortho did not take timely and appropriate remedial action primarily for three reasons: its investigation of Todd's complaint took thirty days, Moreland was given a valuable severance package when terminated, and Todd's subsequent requests for transfer and additional leave were not accommodated. In our view, these facts do not justify rejecting the jury's finding of timely and appropriate remedial action. When confronted, Moreland vigorously denied Todd's allegations. He accused Ortho of race discrimination when it credited Todd's version of the events in question and threatened litigation if he was terminated. Ortho cannot be faulted for carefully investigating two conflicting versions of a serious incident that could not be independently corroborated. . . .

Likewise, we do not fault Ortho for its decision to buy peace with Moreland with a severance package. By terminating this high-ranking minority employee with two decades of experience and no complaints on his record on the ground that he sexually harassed a relatively new employee, Ortho showed its commitment to preventing sexual harassment in its workplace, not timidity in the face of controversy. Finally, Ortho's failure to accommodate Todd's later requests for a transfer from Minnesota to Houston and for a lengthy personal leave, and her complaint that some at Ortho treated her as a "non-person," cannot nullify Ortho's timely and appropriate remedial action in response to her complaint of sexual harassment. These subsequent events occurred months after the Moreland assault and were the basis for Todd's separate Title VII claim of unlawful retaliation. The jury found that Ortho did not retaliate.[36]

---

36. *Id.* at 736, 739.

Does it appear that Ortho took prompt remedial action in response to Todd's complaints? If it did, should it be held liable for Moreland's alleged attempted rape?

3. Defining "Supervisor" The court questioned whether it could label Moreland a supervisor under *Faragher* and *Burlington*. Is the dissent correct that an apparent authority analysis might be appropriate in this case, or is the majority correct that *Burlington* discredited such an analysis?

4. The Affirmative Defense How should a new jury decide the issue of whether Ortho can qualify for the affirmative defense?

5. Inconclusive Results The first appellate court noted that Moreland denied assaulting Todd. What should an employer do in the case of conflicting testimony or in a "he said/she said" case? Cautious employers inform the parties that their findings were inconclusive and take nondisciplinary, remedial actions such as minimizing contact between the parties, recirculating the sexual harassment policy, and providing sensitivity training.

6. The Future Impact of Evolving Standards *Todd* highlights the interpretation challenges that the liability standard created. Four years before the Supreme Court crafted the affirmative defense, the Ninth Circuit forecast, "As time goes by and harassers learn that they can no longer victimize their prey at will, their actions become less overt."[37] Is it likely that employment discrimination has become more subtle than "tangible"? How might harassers camouflage their behavior? What might employers do to respond to and combat such subterfuge?

C. Theoretical Responses to *Burlington* and *Faragher*

As additional lower courts interpreted *Ellerth* and *Faragher* precedent, legal scholars analyzed the courts' responses. Some academic theorists, including Professor Joanna Grossman, called for revisions to the standard for employer liability. Others, such as Professor John H. Marks, advocated for the proper implementation of the affirmative defense.

In her article *The First Bite Is Free: Employer Liability for Sexual Harassment*, Professor Grossman compares the *Ellerth/Faragher* liability formula to common law that insulates dog owners from liability for the first injury caused by their biting dog.[38] She disputes that the formula creates liability for employers who might be blameless. She suggests that the *Faragher* and *Ellerth* "decisions, far from imposing additional liability on innocent employers, had instead created a virtual safe harbor that protects employers from liability unless their own conduct is found wanting."[39]

---

37. Nichols v. Frank, 42 F.3d 503, 512 (9th Cir. 1994), *abrogated in part by* Burrell v. Star Nursery, Inc., 170 F.3d 951 (9th Cir. 1999).

38. Joanna L. Grossman, *The First Bite Is Free: Employer Liability for Sexual Harassment*, 61 U. PITT. L. REV. 671 (2000).

39. *Id*. at 675.

She maintains that the Court expected that the affirmative defense might limit damages or liability, but that lower courts used it to limit liability. She argues that courts should never permit respondents to avoid liability in this way.

Grossman summarizes the potential consequences of an application of the affirmative defense. She suggests that the defense "undermines Title VII's goal of compensating victims . . . while not serving its deterrence rationale." She argues that the use of this defense "to bar liability in some or all cases is inconsistent with the agency principles that underlie the rule, as well as the doctrine of avoidable consequences that the Court tried to implement."[40] Grossman also explains that the defense "unfairly penalizes women who do not file formal complaints, despite the well-documented reality that most sexual harassment victims do not report such conduct through internal grievance mechanisms."[41] She concludes that the affirmative defense dramatically circumscribes compensation for women injured by sexual harassment. It also fails to promote workplace equality.

As part of her analysis, Grossman reviews the *Todd* case. She asserts that "[t] he majority correctly recognized that the employer [Ortho] would be subject to automatic liability for the assault because the plaintiff's prompt complaint would deprive it of the affirmative defense."[42] However, Grossman points out that *Todd* quotes the portion of the *Ellerth* and *Faragher* opinions that confirm the affirmative defense "was adopted to *avoid* 'automatic' employer liability and to give credit to employers who make reasonable efforts to prevent and remedy sexual harassment."[43] Ultimately, she discredits the *Todd* appellate court:

> To protect the employer from liability for harassment that matured before the employer had the opportunity to respond, the *Todd* majority suggested that a single, severe act of harassment could never constitute an actionable hostile environment. Such an approach prevents a plaintiff from recovering for any initial act of harassment as long as the employer subsequently responds. Thus, . . . *Todd* interprets *Faragher* and *Ellerth* to hold employers liable only based on their own misconduct or inaction, absolving them of liability for the first bite.[44]

In this passage, Grossman interprets the *Todd* decision as a definitive rejection of absolute liability for severe single-action supervisor conduct. Scholars may debate whether the *Todd* decision, and by implication *Ellerth* and *Faragher*, close the door to automatic liability or merely cast doubt on such automatic determinations. However, Grossman makes clear that the *Ellerth/Faragher* affirmative defense and its interpretation by lower courts undermine Title VII's protections for targets.

---

40. *Id.* at 677.
41. *Id.*
42. *Id.* at 713.
43. *Id.* at 714 (emphasis added).
44. *Id.*

A second result of the *Ellerth* and *Faragher* decisions, contends Grossman, was a shift in goals. She reminds us that the Supreme Court had recognized a dual purpose for Title VII: compensation and deterrence. She argues that "in *Faragher* and *Ellerth*, the Supreme Court elevated deterrence to the 'primary' goal and left compensation by the wayside. The Court's reconstructionist history paved the way for a framework designed primarily to prevent harassment from occurring, at the cost of undercompensating victims when prevention fails."[45]

In response to the *Ellerth* and *Faragher* decisions, Professor Grossman urges Congress to amend Title VII again. She suggests that "employers who respond diligently upon learning of hostile environment harassment should be rewarded, if at all, in terms of remedy."[46] She recommends that automatic liability should apply for supervisor misconduct, no matter the employer response "and that the affirmative defense operate only to reduce or eliminate damages rather than avoid liability. . . ."[47] Congress has not responded to Grossman's call.

Having read Joanna Grossman's critique of the affirmative defense, Professor John H. Marks offers a different perspective in his article, *Smoke, Mirrors, and the Disappearance of "Vicarious" Liability: The Emergence of a Dubious Summary-Judgment Safe Harbor for Employers Whose Supervisory Personnel Commit Hostile Environment Workplace Harassment*.[48] He argues that the affirmative defense consists of not just two prongs, but contains three elements. He suggests that courts must first consider: "Did the employer act reasonably to prevent and correct workplace harassment?" The second question is whether the plaintiff unreasonably failed "to use the employer's preventive and corrective measures or otherwise avoid harm." Finally, if the plaintiff did unreasonably fail to avoid harm, Marks says that courts should ask if "the employer [is] entitled to complete liability avoidance, or just reduced damages." In other words, would "the reasonable person have avoided all harm, or just some harm?"[49] Marks reasons that an employer should avoid liability only if it prevails on all three questions, not just on the first or the first two.

Based on his interpretation, Marks expected that fewer employer summary judgment motions would succeed. He admits that he was wrong in that expectation and argues that lower courts have in fact greatly weakened the standard for liability: "Approving summary dismissal at a rate of more than 50%, post-*Ellerth* lower courts are essentially adjudicating the 'vicarious' right out of 'vicarious liability' and are resurrecting outdated barriers to the civil rights of harassment victims."[50]

---

45. *Id.* at 721.

46. *Id.* at 735.

47. *Id.* at 736.

48. John H. Marks, *Smoke, Mirrors, and the Disappearance of "Vicarious" Liability: The Emergence of a Dubious Summary-Judgment Safe Harbor for Employers Whose Supervisory Personnel Commit Hostile Environment Workplace Harassment*, 38 Hous. L. Rev. 1401 (2002).

49. *Id.* at 1421–22.

50. *Id.* at 1404.

Marks contends that the remedy for the problem is not a new liability standard or a congressional amendment of Title VII. He asserts that "Professor Grossman's solution, however, would guarantee victory for all plaintiffs and thus would, in some cases, replace one windfall with another."[51] Marks explains that because many of these cases were dismissed via summary judgment, juries did not have the opportunity to consider the facts. Therefore, reviewing scholars and courts cannot know whether compensation was unjustly denied. He suggests that the inappropriate award of summary judgment, which has benefited employers, does not justify a new windfall for complainants.

Marks examines the *Ellerth* defense and concludes that the Supreme Court "comprehensively resolved the employer liability question, leaving no independent immunity for purportedly innocent employers in cases of rapid-onset harassment— not when at least equally innocent employees have suffered unavoidable supervisory abuse."[52] He stresses, "There is simply no independent immunity for an innocent employer when an at least equally innocent employee could not have avoided harm. Sleight-of-hand attempts to distinguish *Ellerth* and *Faragher* . . . resurrect an independent reasonable-employer immunity that the Supreme Court, in fact, plainly overturned in those cases."[53]

In addition, Marks rejects the notion that the defense simulates a contributory negligence scheme (in which the employer can avoid or limit liability by proving the plaintiff's unreasonable failure to complain). Instead, he claims that the Court created a system of "causal apportionment." He explains:

> Under the Court's rule, full dismissal on summary judgment is not proper in cases of even presumably dilatory plaintiffs unless the reasonable person in the plaintiff's position would have complained in advance of the work environment becoming hostile—indeed, far enough in advance to allow completely preemptive employer intervention. Accordingly, an employer seeking full dismissal on summary judgment against a presumably dilatory plaintiff still must negate any factual issues as to: (1) the point when the work environment became hostile, and (2) some time frame, beforehand, during which the reasonable person necessarily would have complained and the presumably responsive employer would have successfully intervened.[54]

Based on this reasoning, Marks concludes that triable issues of fact will remain as to whether a plaintiff failed to mitigate or avoid harm. Therefore, any court award of summary judgment without the proofs noted above, "results in an unjustified invasion on the province of the jury, and denies vindication for at least some

---

51. *Id.* at 1459.
52. *Id.* at 1405.
53. *Id.* at 1405–06.
54. *Id.* at 1406.

undoubtedly victimized persons who may be entitled to at least nominal damages for an initially unavoidable civil rights violation."[55]

Marks submits that, if properly applied, the affirmative defense "should accomplish at least some of the results Professor Grossman seeks with a rule of automatic liability. Her rule, after all, allows for mitigation, as does the second prong of the *Ellerth* defense."[56] He proposes that the difference between Grossman's rule and the *Ellerth* defense "is that the Court's rule can result in complete liability avoidance if the plaintiff should have avoided all harm."[57] He doubts, however, that juries would often select complete liability avoidance.

Three years after she first analyzed the *Faragher* affirmative defense, Professor Grossman evaluated the then-current state of sexual harassment law and found it inadequate.

The Culture of Compliance:
The Final Triumph of Form Over Substance
in Sexual Harassment Law

Joanna L. Grossman[58]

. . . .

The rules of liability for sexual and other forms of harassment have created an elaborate scheme of incentives. Employers must attempt to prevent harassment by enacting anti-harassment policies and communicating them to their work force. They must also attempt to remedy harassment with prompt and effective internal investigations. Victims must file prompt, internal complaints when harassment occurs. In litigation, response to these incentives is cause for reward, while failure to respond is cause for penalty. Thus, rule compliance has become the benchmark by which employers and victims are measured.

However, social science literature suggests that a near-perfect state of rule compliance can peaceably co-exist with an uncomfortably high level of harassment. The problem is that the rules of liability were developed in a vacuum, without consideration of the real-world problem of harassment and its causes. While some of the preventative efforts encouraged by the law may have the incidental effect of reducing harassment, the same is not true of all of them. In fact, the only measure with any proven ability to affect the level of harassment—anti-harassment training—is encouraged, but not required by the law. Even there, the type of training that satisfies any legal duty may not be the same type that works. Those measures that are considered legally sufficient have little evidence to support their effectiveness.

---

55. *Id.*
56. *Id.* at 1460.
57. *Id.* at 1461.
58. 26 HARV. WOMEN'S L.J. 3, 70–75 (2003).

The same criticism holds for legally required corrective measures. The requirement that victims complain immediately upon experiencing unwelcome sexual conduct does not account for the reality that very few report, nor is it accompanied by any measures to improve the level of reporting. Moreover, the emphasis on internal investigations is made without consideration of the problems endemic to them. The responses of the typical employer (who will likely respond to the incentives given) and the typical victim (who will not) create no assurance that harassment will be addressed, either in terms of prevention or correction. Both sets of rules overlook the significant control employers exercise over the workplace and their ability to establish norms of respect and equality, to respond to problems in a manner that both resolves them and encourages future victims to come forward, and to discipline offenders.

The reevaluation of the current legal regime dictates both doctrinal reform and extralegal efforts. Three doctrinal changes can take the focus away from rule compliance and toward effective prevention and adequate compensation: elimination of the affirmative defense, greater availability of punitive damages, and the recognition of individual liability. The affirmative defense is doctrinally unjustifiable for a variety of reasons. It thwarts Title VII's stated purposes, misallocates risk to victims rather than employers, deprives victims of attorneys' fees that make civil rights enforcement possible, and is inconsistent with the treatment of other victims of discrimination. The lessons learned from social science about employer, harasser, and victim behavior countenance its elimination as well.

Research suggests that the affirmative defense rewards compliance without ensuring success. A rule of automatic liability, without such a defense, will produce the same set of incentives for employers to combat harassment, but will reward them only if their actions work. Such an approach will induce employers not only to take their preventative and corrective efforts seriously, but also to adapt standard measures to idiosyncratic problems they may face and to take additional measures to establish workplace norms that are inhospitable to harassment. They may also be spurred to evaluate the efficacy of the measures they do adopt—something rarely done—and to continue to experiment with potentially more effective strategies.

This approach will not garner support from most commentators, many of whom have either praised the affirmative defense as a fair and appropriate interpretation of Title VII or have criticized it for imposing too much liability on employers. The bulk of this commentary has been critical of the second prong of the affirmative defense, which makes the employer's liability turn on the independent actions of the victim. The possibility exists that even if the employer has acted reasonably in its preventive and corrective measures, it may nonetheless be held liable for harassment if the victim files a prompt complaint. That strikes many as unfair, including several courts that have simply refused to apply the second prong of the affirmative defense for fear of "punishing" an employer who has, in their view, done nothing wrong.

This concern, however, is overstated and, in any event, both descriptively and normatively unjustified. It is unlikely that an employer who has done "nothing wrong" will be sanctioned, because employer liability accrues only when actionable harassment occurs. An employer who responds quickly and adequately to a victim's complaint of harassment is likely to prevent the harassment from rising to that level and thus avoid liability for the initial harassment. Only when an initial act of harassment is so severe as to independently create a hostile environment prior to a victim's prompt complaint will an employer be held liable despite its "reasonable" conduct.

Moreover, an empirical study of federal court decisions in the first eighteen months following *Faragher* and *Ellerth* revealed that employer behavior heavily influenced not only the first prong of the affirmative defense, but the second prong as well. In cases where the employer behaved responsibly, courts were more likely to find that the victim behaved unreasonably. Based on a content analysis of these opinions, the authors of this study concluded that "[s]uch factors as whether an employer has a good sexual harassment policy and responds well to an allegation may prove sufficient to satisfy prongs one and two, independent of what an employee may or may not do." Thus, plaintiffs in those cases were found to have acted unreasonably when they delayed even a short time before reporting the harassment or complained to the wrong party.

Even if courts were not influenced by employer conduct, liability on the employer is appropriate for harassment that becomes actionable before the victim can complain. Because the employer is in a better position to prevent such acts by screening and monitoring supervisors, it should bear the risk of loss when those measures fail.

Others have praised the affirmative defense for preventing victims from remaining silent in the face of harassment and then later complaining when nothing was done to help them. This criticism would be more convincing if the legal regime were calculated to increase victim reporting. Instead, as discussed above, the regime punishes victims for failing to report harassment without building in any incentives to increase the likelihood that they will.

. . . .

. . . [E]xtralegal changes may help . . . with the problem of victims underreporting harassment. Because the existing framework does not contain any incentives to increase victim reporting, other approaches that target victim behavior may be necessary. As long as the affirmative defense survives, it is incumbent upon women's and employees' advocates to disseminate greater information about the responsibilities the affirmative defense imposes on victims to file prompt complaints about sexual harassment. Potential victims need to be educated about what constitutes sexual harassment, why it is wrong and should not happen, and how to respond when it does occur. Greater education could, at a minimum, improve levels of compensation for victims to the extent they fulfill their obligations imposed by this new regime.

While the changes proposed in this Article may help reduce workplace harassment, they will not eliminate it. Perhaps one of the most important lessons from social science is that law cannot, by itself, change culture or behavior. While legal incentives have some capacity to produce a response, they work less effectively on disaggregated groups like victims than they do on mobilized, well-advised employers. And they only work in a meaningful way on employers if the incentives induce effective responses to combating harassment. It may thus be that advocating for doctrinal change may reveal the same myopia that effected the creation of the legal regime in the first instance.

That the law has limited power to change the workplace culture in which harassment thrives is evidenced by many things, including survey data that show no decrease in the prevalence of unwanted sexual attention despite more than twenty years of litigation and the development of stronger and stronger rules of liability. In the context of discrimination law, courts seem confident in their ability to change workplace culture through the development of liability rules. Yet, experience with anti-discrimination laws shows that they sometimes have the effect of simply replacing overt acts of discrimination with covert ones. And, while those who point out that the under-enforcement of legal rights creates a background that allows discrimination to occur are surely right, the converse is not necessarily true. The faithful, even strong enforcement of anti-discrimination laws may be insufficient to change a culture in which sexual harassment thrives.

Notes and Discussion

1. "**The First Bite Is Free**" Did the *Ellerth* affirmative defense, as applied, establish a "one bite" rule as Professor Grossman argues? If so, is that a problem that the law should attempt to address? In other words, is this rule not an improvement over the employer negligence (knew or should have known) standard formerly applied to supervisor hostile work environment harassment?

2. **The Solution** What solution does Professor Grossman propose to deal with the "first bite" problem? Are her arguments convincing? Or is Marks correct? Are juries as reasonable as Marks predicts? If courts have already misapplied the affirmative defense, is it prudent to count on them to apply it correctly going forward?

In response to this question, one might examine the First Circuit's use of the affirmative defense in *Chaloult v. Interstate Brands Corp.*[59] The court reviewed whether an employer was vicariously liable based upon a lateral supervisor's knowledge of sexual harassment, given that the employer's sexual harassment policy required all supervisors to report any known misconduct. The court found, despite a resignation letter in which Chaloult stated that she felt uncomfortable working for her

---

59. Chaloult v. Interstate Brands Corp., 540 F.3d 64 (1st Cir. 2008).

immediate supervisor, Chaloult had not complained. Therefore, interpreting the affirmative defense, it declined to extend liability.

In a *Chaloult* case comment, Lauren P. Gearty explains how the First Circuit applied the affirmative defense:

> Chaloult asserted that Interstate could not establish the *Faragher-Ellerth* affirmative defense because Anderson, who acted as Interstate's agent [and knew about much of the harassment], failed to take proper corrective measures to eliminate the harassment. Interstate moved for summary judgment on grounds that it established the *Faragher-Ellerth* affirmative defense to vicarious liability. The district court agreed and granted summary judgment in favor of Interstate, finding that Anderson's failure to report the harassment did not create any issue of material fact as to whether Interstate acted reasonably to prevent and correct the sexual harassment. On appeal, the First Circuit affirmed, holding that Interstate's sexual-harassment policy, requiring that all supervisors report any harassment, would not increase its liability under Title VII.[60]

Was the *Chaloult* outcome reasonable?

3. Reconstructionist History Did the Court engage in reconstructionist history, as Grossman alleged, by leaving Title VII's "compensation goal by the wayside"? If so, where is the harm?

4. Failure to Complain In her *First Bite* article, Professor Grossman cites a number of cases that criticized the complainant's failure to notify the employer or use its procedures. These cases detail what will *not* support a failure to complain. Those factors include: "generalized fears [of retaliation,]" "embarrassment and fear of reprisal[,]" "concern about the reaction of co-workers[,]" "plaintiff's fear of retaliation," "a threat of termination, without more. . . .").[61]

Not all courts consider a failure to complain fatal to a Title VII sexual harassment claim. For example, in *Minarsky v. Susquehanna Cty.*, the plaintiff sued the county's Department of Veterans Affairs (VA) for years of sexual harassment by her

---

60. Lauren P. Gearty, Comment, *Labor and Employment Law—Vicarious Liability Not Defined By Employer's Own Sexual-Harassment Policy*—Chaloult v. Interstate Brands Corp., *540 F.3d 64 (1st Cir. 2008)*, 42 Suffolk U. L. Rev. 399, 401 (2009).

61. Grossman, *supra* note 39, at 700 n.142. For examples of courts finding plaintiffs unreasonable, see *Macias v. Southwest Cheese Co.*, LLC, 181 F. Supp. 3d 883 (D.N.M. 2016) (ruling that the plaintiff was unreasonable for waiting to complain until "roughly five months after the commencement of the alleged harassment and roughly four months after Plaintiff's termination."), *Helm v. Kansas*, 656 F.3d 1277 (10th Cir. 2011) (holding that the plaintiff who professed ignorance of the sexual harassment policy was unreasonable because she signed an acknowledgement that she had read and understood the policies), and *Anderson v. Deluxe Homes of PA, Inc.*, 131 F. Supp. 2d 637 (M.D. Pa. 2001) ("While courts in this circuit have given little guidance on the second prong of the affirmative defense, we note that courts in other circuits have held that failing to complain due solely to a subjective fear of termination is unreasonable as a matter of law.").

supervisor Yadlosky.[62] During her deposition, Minarsky explained that she had never reported the behavior because she feared retaliation. She recounted that the VA had twice warned Yadlosky about his conduct with other women but that his inappropriate behavior continued. The district court had dismissed Minarsky's Title VII claim, holding that the VA had satisfied both prongs of the affirmative defense. The district court explained, "no reasonable jury could find that Plaintiff acted reasonably in failing to avail herself of the protections of the sexual harassment policy."[63]

The Third Circuit reversed. Exploring Minarsky's failure to report Yadlosky's offensive kissing and touching, the appellate court wrote, "She claims that Yadlosky knew that her young daughter was ill and thus knew Minarsky depended on her employment to pay medical bills. She states that she feared speaking up to him in any context, let alone to protest his harassment, because he would react and sometimes become "nasty."[64] The court then concluded:

> Although we have often found that a plaintiff's outright failure to report persistent sexual harassment is unreasonable as a matter of law, particularly when the opportunity to make such complaints exists, we write to clarify that a mere failure to report one's harassment is not per se unreasonable. Moreover, the passage of time is just one factor in the analysis. Workplace sexual harassment is highly circumstance-specific, and thus the reasonableness of a plaintiff's actions is a paradigmatic question for the jury, in certain cases. If a plaintiff's genuinely held, subjective belief of potential retaliation from reporting her harassment appears to be well-founded, and a jury could find that this belief is objectively reasonable, the trial court should not find that the defendant has proven the second *Faragher-Ellerth* element as a matter of law. Instead, the court should leave the issue for the jury to determine at trial.

> Here, Minarsky asserts several countervailing forces that prevented her from reporting Yadlosky's conduct to Beamer or a County Commissioner: her fear of Yadlosky's hostility on a day-to-day basis and retaliation by having her fired; her worry of being terminated by the Chief Clerk; and the futility of reporting, since others knew of his conduct, yet it continued. All of these factors were aggravated by the pressing financial situation she faced with her daughter's cancer treatment.[65]

---

62. Minarsky v. Susquehanna Cty., 895 F.3d 303 (3d Cir. 2018).

63. *Id.* at 312 (quoting Minarsky v. Susquehanna Cty., 2017 WL 4475981, at *1 (M.D. Pa. June 28, 2017)).

64. *Id.* at 307.

65. *Id.* at 314. *See also* Sotoj v. Nashville Aquarium, Inc., No. 3:14-CV-00754, 2016 WL 3568591, at *10 (M.D. Tenn. July 1, 2016) (finding that "[r]easonableness is a question of fact, and a delay in reporting harassment does not always constitute an unreasonable failure to take advantage of corrective opportunities to avoid harm").

Whether other courts will follow this approach remains to be seen. How should courts deal with a complainant's failure to report? Is a complaint requirement likely to produce cultural change and result in the empowerment of women?

5. Compliance but No Success Is Professor Grossman correct that the affirmative defense promotes compliance but not success? What could employers do to encourage targets to report? Have the #MeToo and #TimesUp campaigns changed culture and behavior? In a review of the *Minarsky* case, one law firm suggested, "Against the backdrop of #MeToo, employers should understand that employees are often afraid to report harassing conduct. After the Third Circuit's ruling in *Minarsky,* an employee's failure to report misconduct may not necessarily result in the automatic dismissal of a subsequent harassment lawsuit."[66] What suggestions might a member of this law firm or a VA employee make to change workplace culture, address discriminatory behavior, and eradicate the toleration of sexual harassment?

4. Constructive Discharge

Another issue that arises in liability assessment centers on constructive discharge. Can an employer be held liable for the "virtual" (but not actual) termination of an employee who abandons her employment because she believes that the environment is hostile or untenable? Employees quit to avoid harassing or abusive behavior. They also leave because, after complaining, they think that the employer has not adequately remedied the situation. Or the situation has gotten worse.

In the following sex-based harassment case, the Supreme Court evaluated the circumstances under which an employee might bring a successful constructive discharge case against an employer.

Pennsylvania State Police v. Suders
542 U.S. 129 (2004)

Justice GINSBURG delivered the opinion of the Court.

Plaintiff-respondent Nancy Drew Suders alleged sexually harassing conduct by her supervisors, officers of the Pennsylvania State Police (PSP), of such severity she was forced to resign. The question presented concerns the proof burdens parties bear when a sexual harassment/constructive discharge claim of that character is asserted under Title VII of the Civil Rights Act of 1964.

To establish hostile work environment, plaintiffs like Suders must show harassing behavior "sufficiently severe or pervasive to alter the conditions of [their]

---

66. Young Conaway Stargatt & Taylor, LLP, *Ellerth/Faragher In #Metoo Era: What if Harassment Isn't Reported?*, 23 No. 10 DEL. EMP. L. LETTER 7, Oct. 2018.

employment." *Meritor Savings Bank, FSB v. Vinson*, 477 U.S. 57, 67 (1986). . . . [W]e hold, to establish "constructive discharge," the plaintiff must make a further showing: She must show that the abusive working environment became so intolerable that her resignation qualified as a fitting response. An employer may defend against such a claim by showing both (1) that it had installed a readily accessible and effective policy for reporting and resolving complaints of sexual harassment, and (2) that the plaintiff unreasonably failed to avail herself of that employer-provided preventive or remedial apparatus. This affirmative defense will not be available to the employer, however, if the plaintiff quits in reasonable response to an employer-sanctioned adverse action officially changing her employment status or situation, for example, a humiliating demotion, extreme cut in pay, or transfer to a position in which she would face unbearable working conditions. In so ruling today, we follow the path marked by our 1998 decisions in *Burlington Industries, Inc. v. Ellerth*, 524 U.S. 742, and *Faragher v. Boca Raton*, 524 U.S. 775.

I

Because this case was decided against Suders in the District Court on the PSP's motion for summary judgment, we recite the facts, as summarized by the Court of Appeals, in the light most favorable to Suders. In March 1998, the PSP hired Suders as a police communications operator for the McConnellsburg barracks. Suders' supervisors were Sergeant Eric D. Easton, Station Commander at the McConnellsburg barracks, Patrol Corporal William D. Baker, and Corporal Eric B. Prendergast. Those three supervisors subjected Suders to a continuous barrage of sexual harassment that ceased only when she resigned from the force.

Easton "would bring up [the subject of] people having sex with animals" each time Suders entered his office. He told Prendergast, in front of Suders, that young girls should be given instruction in how to gratify men with oral sex. Easton also would sit down near Suders, wearing spandex shorts, and spread his legs apart. Apparently imitating a move popularized by television wrestling, Baker repeatedly made an obscene gesture in Suders' presence by grabbing his genitals and shouting out a vulgar comment inviting oral sex. Baker made this gesture as many as five-to-ten times per night throughout Suders' employment at the barracks. Suders once told Baker she "'d[id]n't think [he] should be doing this'"; Baker responded by jumping on a chair and again performing the gesture, with the accompanying vulgarity. Further, Baker would "rub his rear end in front of her and remark 'I have a nice ass, don't I?'" Prendergast told Suders "'the village idiot could do her job'"; wearing black gloves, he would pound on furniture to intimidate her.

In June 1998, Prendergast accused Suders of taking a missing accident file home with her. After that incident, Suders approached the PSP's Equal Employment Opportunity Officer, Virginia Smith-Elliott, and told her she "might need some help." Smith-Elliott gave Suders her telephone number, but neither woman followed up on the conversation. On August 18, 1998, Suders contacted Smith-Elliott again, this time stating that she was being harassed and was afraid. Smith-Elliott told Suders to file a complaint, but did not tell her how to obtain the necessary form. Smith-Elliott's response and the manner in which it was conveyed appeared to Suders insensitive and unhelpful.

Two days later, Suders' supervisors arrested her for theft, and Suders resigned from the force. The theft arrest occurred in the following circumstances. Suders had several times taken a computer-skills exam to satisfy a PSP job requirement. Each time, Suders' supervisors told her that she had failed. Suders one day came upon her exams in a set of drawers in the women's locker room. She concluded that her supervisors had never forwarded the tests for grading and that their reports of her failures were false. Regarding the tests as her property, Suders removed them from the locker room. Upon finding that the exams had been removed, Suders' supervisors devised a plan to arrest her for theft. The officers dusted the drawer in which the exams had been stored with a theft-detection powder that turns hands blue when touched. As anticipated by Easton, Baker, and Prendergast, Suders attempted to return the tests to the drawer, whereupon her hands turned telltale blue. The supervisors then apprehended and handcuffed her, photographed her blue hands, and commenced to question her. Suders had previously prepared a written resignation, which she tendered soon after the supervisors detained her. Nevertheless, the supervisors initially refused to release her. Instead, they brought her to an interrogation room, gave her warnings under *Miranda v. Arizona*, 384 U.S. 436 (1966), and continued to question her. Suders reiterated that she wanted to resign, and Easton then let her leave. The PSP never brought theft charges against her.

In September 2000, Suders sued the PSP in Federal District Court, alleging, *inter alia*, that she had been subjected to sexual harassment and constructively discharged, in violation of Title VII of the Civil Rights Act of 1964. At the close of discovery, the District Court granted the PSP's motion for summary judgment. Suders' testimony, the District Court recognized, sufficed to permit a trier of fact to conclude that the supervisors had created a hostile work environment. The court nevertheless held that the PSP was not vicariously liable for the supervisors' conduct.

In so concluding, the District Court referred to our 1998 decision in *Faragher*. . . .

Suders' hostile work environment claim was untenable as a matter of law, the District Court stated, because she "unreasonably failed to avail herself of the PSP's internal procedures for reporting any harassment." Resigning just two days after she first mentioned anything about harassment to Equal Employment Opportunity Officer Smith-Elliott, the court noted, Suders had "never given [the PSP] the opportunity to respond to [her] complaints." The District Court did not address Suders' constructive discharge claim.

The Court of Appeals for the Third Circuit reversed and remanded the case for disposition on the merits. The Third Circuit agreed with the District Court that Suders had presented evidence sufficient for a trier of fact to conclude that the supervisors had engaged in a "pattern of sexual harassment that was pervasive and

regular." But the appeals court disagreed with the District Court in two fundamental respects. First, the Court of Appeals held that, even assuming the PSP could
assert the affirmative defense described in *Ellerth* and *Faragher*, genuine issues
of material fact existed concerning the effectiveness of the PSP's "program ... to
address sexual harassment claims." Second, the appeals court held that the District
Court erred in failing to recognize that Suders had stated a claim of constructive
discharge due to the hostile work environment.

A plaintiff alleging constructive discharge in violation of Title VII, the Court of
Appeals stated, must establish:

> "(1) he or she suffered harassment or discrimination so intolerable that
> a reasonable person in the same position would have felt compelled to
> resign ... ; and (2) the employee's reaction to the workplace situation—
> that is, his or her decision to resign—was reasonable given the totality of
> circumstances ...."

. . . .

This Court granted certiorari to resolve the disagreement among the Circuits on
the question whether a constructive discharge brought about by supervisor harassment ranks as a tangible employment action and therefore precludes assertion of
the affirmative defense articulated in *Ellerth* and *Faragher*. We conclude that an
employer does not have recourse to the *Ellerth/Faragher* affirmative defense when a
supervisor's official act precipitates the constructive discharge; absent such a "tangible employment action," however, the defense is available to the employer whose
supervisors are charged with harassment. We therefore vacate the Third Circuit's
judgment and remand the case for further proceedings.

II

A

Under the constructive discharge doctrine, an employee's reasonable decision to
resign because of unendurable working conditions is assimilated to a formal discharge for remedial purposes. The inquiry is objective: Did working conditions
become so intolerable that a reasonable person in the employee's position would
have felt compelled to resign?

. . . .

B

. . . .

1

The constructive discharge here at issue stems from, and can be regarded as
an aggravated case of, sexual harassment or hostile work environment. For an
atmosphere of sexual harassment or hostility to be actionable, we reiterate, the
offending behavior "must be sufficiently severe or pervasive to alter the conditions of the victim's employment and create an abusive working environment." A

hostile-environment constructive discharge claim entails something more: A plaintiff who advances such a compound claim must show working conditions so intolerable that a reasonable person would have felt compelled to resign.

Suders' claim is of the same genre as the hostile work environment claims the Court analyzed in *Ellerth* and *Faragher*. Essentially, Suders presents a "worse case" harassment scenario, harassment ratcheted up to the breaking point. Like the harassment considered in our pathmarking decisions, harassment so intolerable as to cause a resignation may be effected through co-worker conduct, unofficial supervisory conduct, or official company acts. Unlike an actual termination, which is *always* effected through an official act of the company, a constructive discharge need not be. A constructive discharge involves both an employee's decision to leave and precipitating conduct: The former involves no official action; the latter, like a harassment claim without any constructive discharge assertion, may or may not involve official action.

To be sure, a constructive discharge is functionally the same as an actual termination in damages-enhancing respects. As the Third Circuit observed, both "en[d] the employer-employee relationship," and both "inflic[t] . . . direct economic harm." But when an official act does not underlie the constructive discharge, the *Ellerth* and *Faragher* analysis, we here hold, calls for extension of the affirmative defense to the employer. As those leading decisions indicate, official directions and declarations are the acts most likely to be brought home to the employer, the measures over which the employer can exercise greatest control. Absent "an official act of the enterprise," as the last straw, the employer ordinarily would have no particular reason to suspect that a resignation is not the typical kind daily occurring in the work force. And as *Ellerth* and *Faragher* further point out, an official act reflected in company records — a demotion or a reduction in compensation, for example — shows "beyond question" that the supervisor has used his managerial or controlling position to the employee's disadvantage. Absent such an official act, the extent to which the supervisor's misconduct has been aided by the agency relation, as we earlier recounted is less certain. That uncertainty, our precedent establishes justifies affording the employer the chance to establish, through the *Ellerth/Faragher* affirmative defense, that it should not be held vicariously liable.

. . . .

We note, finally, two recent Court of Appeals decisions that indicate how the "official act" (or "tangible employment action") criterion should play out when constructive discharge is alleged. Both decisions advance the untangled approach we approve in this opinion. In *Reed v. MBNA Marketing Systems, Inc.*, 333 F.3d 27 (C.A.1 2003), the plaintiff claimed a constructive discharge based on her supervisor's repeated sexual comments and an incident in which he sexually assaulted her. The First Circuit held that the alleged wrongdoing did not preclude the employer from asserting the *Ellerth/Faragher* affirmative defense. As the court explained in *Reed*, the supervisor's behavior involved no official actions. Unlike, "*e.g.,* an extremely dangerous job assignment to retaliate for spurned advances," the supervisor's conduct in *Reed* "was exceedingly unofficial and involved no direct exercise of company authority"; indeed, it was "exactly the kind of wholly unauthorized conduct for which the affirmative defense was designed." In contrast, in *Robinson v. Sappington*, 351 F.3d 317 (C.A.7 2003), after the plaintiff complained that she was sexually harassed by the judge for whom she worked, the presiding judge decided to transfer her to another judge, but told her that "her first six months [in the new post] probably would be 'hell,'" and that it was in her "'best interest to resign.'" The Seventh Circuit held that the employer was precluded from asserting the affirmative defense to the plaintiff's constructive discharge claim. The *Robinson* plaintiff's decision to resign, the court explained, "resulted, at least in part, from [the presiding judge's] official actio[n] in transferring" her to a judge who resisted placing her on his staff. The courts in *Reed* and *Robinson* properly recognized that *Ellerth* and *Faragher*, which divided the universe of supervisor-harassment claims according to the presence or absence of an official act, mark the path constructive discharge claims based on harassing conduct must follow.

2

. . . Following *Ellerth* and *Faragher*, the plaintiff who alleges no tangible employment action has the duty to mitigate harm, but the defendant bears the burden to allege and prove that the plaintiff failed in that regard. The plaintiff might elect to allege facts relevant to mitigation in her pleading or to present those facts in her case in chief, but she would do so in anticipation of the employer's affirmative defense, not as a legal requirement.

* * *

We agree with the Third Circuit that the case, in its current posture, presents genuine issues of material fact concerning Suders' hostile work environment and constructive discharge claims.[11] We hold, however, that the Court of Appeals erred in declaring the affirmative defense described in *Ellerth* and *Faragher* never available in constructive discharge cases. Accordingly, we vacate the Third Circuit's judgment and remand the case for further proceedings consistent with this opinion.

. . . .

Justice THOMAS, dissenting.

. . . .

. . . If a supervisor takes an adverse employment action because of sex that directly results in the constructive discharge, the employer is vicariously liable. But, where the alleged constructive discharge results only from a hostile work environment, an employer is liable if negligent. Because respondent has not adduced sufficient

---

11. Although most of the discriminatory behavior Suders alleged involved unofficial conduct, the events surrounding her computer-skills exams were less obviously unofficial.

evidence of an adverse employment action taken because of her sex, nor has she proffered any evidence that petitioner knew or should have known of the alleged harassment, I would reverse the judgment of the Court of Appeals.

Notes and Discussion

1. Summary Judgment Did the *Suders* district court grant summary judgment for reasons that mirrored Professors Grossman and Marks's concerns? If so, how? Did the Third Circuit respond appropriately to the appeal? Why did the Supreme Court take this case? Why is reliance on the appellate process to correct improper summary judgment problematic? Does the appellate process disfavor particular classes of aggrieved litigants?

2. The Affirmative Defense According to *Suders*, when is the affirmative defense unavailable in a constructive discharge case? What might constitute an "official action"? What was the official action in *Suders*?

3. Thomas's Dissent Is it true that Suders did not present sufficient evidence of an adverse employment action? Where should courts draw the line on what constitutes such an action?

4. The Future of Constructive Discharge Will employees continue to bring constructive discharge cases based on tangible employment actions or will employers and their supervisors become increasingly more "subtle" with fewer tangible consequences? Does the outcome of *Suders* make sense? Explain.

5. Retaliation as Title VII Harassment and Discrimination

In addition to substantive prohibitions on discrimination and harassment, Title VII also prohibits retaliation against employees who engage in specific protected activities:

Title VII Retaliation Provisions
42 U.S.C. § 2000e-3 (2012)

§ 2000e-3. Other unlawful employment practices

(a) **Discrimination for making charges, testifying, assisting, or participating in enforcement proceedings**

It shall be an unlawful employment practice for an employer to discriminate against any of his employees or applicants for employment, for an employment agency, or joint labor-management committee controlling apprenticeship or other training or retraining, including on—the-job training programs, to discriminate against any individual, or for a labor organization to discriminate against any member thereof or applicant for membership, because he has opposed any practice made an unlawful employment practice by this subchapter, or because he has made a charge, testified, assisted, or participated in any manner in an investigation, proceeding, or hearing under this subchapter.

According to the EEOC, "retaliation is the most common issue alleged by federal employees and the most common discrimination finding in federal sector cases. Nearly half of all complaints filed during fiscal year (FY) 2013 were retaliation complaints, with 42% of findings of discrimination based on retaliation."[67] The EEOC also confirms that "retaliation has been the most frequently alleged basis of discrimination in the federal sector since fiscal year 2008. In addition, the number of discrimination findings based on a retaliation claim has outpaced other bases of discrimination."[68]

The EEOC defines retaliation as "a materially adverse action [taken by an employer] because an individual has engaged, or may engage, in activity in furtherance of the EEO laws the Commission enforces."[69] It defines "protected activity" as either participation in an EEO process or the opposition to conduct made unlawful by an EEO law.[70] The EEOC explains:

> [T]he "participation clause," provides protection from retaliation for many actions, including filing or serving as a witness for any side in an administrative proceeding or lawsuit alleging discrimination in violation of an EEO law. The participation clause applies even if the underlying allegation is not meritorious or was not timely filed. . . . The opposition clause of Title VII has an "expansive definition," and "great deference" is given to the EEOC's interpretation of opposing conduct."[71]

This EEOC guidance indicates that controversies arise over what constitutes opposition to discrimination. Courts have offered further guidance on what qualifies as protected activity and retaliation.

Crawford v. Metro. Gov't. of Nashville and Davidson Cnty. Tenn.

555 U.S. 271 (2009)

Justice SOUTER delivered the opinion of the Court.

Title VII . . . forbids retaliation by employers against employees who report workplace race or gender discrimination. The question here is whether this protection

---

67. U.S. Equal Emp. Opportunity Comm'n, *supra* note 5.

68. *Id.*

69. Equal Emp. Opportunity Comm'n, EEOC Enforcement Guidance on Retaliation and Related Issues, No. 915.004, 2 (Aug. 25, 2016), https://www.eeoc.gov/laws/guidance/retaliation -guidance.cfm.

70. *Id.* at 4.

71. *Id.* at 6, 10.

extends to an employee who speaks out about discrimination not on her own initiative, but in answering questions during an employer's internal investigation. We
hold that it does.

I

In 2002, respondent Metropolitan Government of Nashville and Davidson
County, Tennessee (Metro), began looking into rumors of sexual harassment by the
Metro School District's employee relations director, Gene Hughes. When Veronica
Frazier, a Metro human resources officer, asked petitioner Vicky Crawford, a 30-year
Metro employee, whether she had witnessed "inappropriate behavior" on the part of
Hughes, Crawford described several instances of sexually harassing behavior: once,
Hughes had answered her greeting, "Hey Dr. Hughes, [w]hat's up?,'" by grabbing his
crotch and saying "'[Y]ou know what's up'"; he had repeatedly "'put his crotch up
to [her] window'"; and on one occasion he had entered her office and "'grabbed her
head and pulled it to his crotch,'" . . . Two other employees also reported being sexually harassed by Hughes. Although Metro took no action against Hughes, it did fire
Crawford and the two other accusers soon after finishing the investigation, saying in
Crawford's case that it was for embezzlement. Crawford claimed Metro was retaliating for her report of Hughes's behavior and filed a charge of a Title VII violation with
the Equal Employment Opportunity Commission (EEOC), followed by this suit in
the United States District Court for the Middle District of Tennessee.

The Title VII antiretaliation provision has two clauses, making it "an unlawful
employment practice for an employer to discriminate against any of his employees . . .
[1] because he has opposed any practice made an unlawful employment practice by
this subchapter, or [2] because he has made a charge, testified, assisted, or participated in any manner in an investigation, proceeding, or hearing under this subchapter." The one is known as the "opposition clause," the other as the "participation
clause," and Crawford accused Metro of violating both.

The District Court granted summary judgment for Metro. It held that Crawford could not satisfy the opposition clause because she had not "instigated or initiated any complaint," but had "merely answered questions by investigators in an
already-pending internal investigation, initiated by someone else." It concluded
that her claim also failed under the participation clause, which Sixth Circuit precedent confined to protecting "'an employee's participation in an employer's internal investigation . . . where that investigation occurs pursuant to a pending EEOC
charge'" (not the case here).

The Court of Appeals affirmed on the same grounds. . . . [The Court briefly
reviews the Sixth's Circuit's decision and notes a split amongst the Circuits, justify-
ing the grant of certiorari.]

. . . .

II

The opposition clause makes it "unlawful . . . for an employer to discriminate against any . . . employe[e] . . . because he has opposed any practice made . . . unlawful . . . by this subchapter." The term "oppose," being left undefined by the statute, carries its ordinary meaning: "[t]o resist or antagonize . . . ; to contend against; to confront; resist; withstand,". . . . Although these actions entail varying expenditures of energy, "RESIST frequently implies more active striving than OPPOSE."

The statement Crawford says she gave to Frazier is thus covered by the opposition clause, as an ostensibly disapproving account of sexually obnoxious behavior toward her by a fellow employee, an answer she says antagonized her employer to the point of sacking her on a false pretense. Crawford's description of the louche goings-on would certainly qualify in the minds of reasonable jurors as "resist[ant]" or "antagoni[stic]" to Hughes's treatment, if for no other reason than the point argued by the Government and explained by an EEOC guideline: "When an employee communicates to her employer a belief that the employer has engaged in . . . a form of employment discrimination, that communication" virtually always "constitutes the employee's *opposition* to the activity." It is true that one can imagine exceptions, like an employee's description of a supervisor's racist joke as hilarious, but these will be eccentric cases, and this is not one of them.[2]

. . . .

"Oppose" goes beyond "active, consistent" behavior in ordinary discourse, where we would naturally use the word to speak of someone who has taken no action at all to advance a position beyond disclosing it. Countless people were known to "oppose" slavery before Emancipation, or are said to "oppose" capital punishment today, without writing public letters, taking to the streets, or resisting the government. And we would call it "opposition" if an employee took a stand against an employer's discriminatory practices not by "instigating" action, but by standing pat, say, by refusing to follow a supervisor's order to fire a junior worker for discriminatory reasons. There is, then, no reason to doubt that a person can "oppose" by responding to someone else's question just as surely as by provoking the discussion, and nothing in the statute requires a freakish rule protecting an employee who reports discrimination on her own initiative but not one who reports the same discrimination in the same words when her boss asks a question.

Metro and its *amici* support the Circuit panel's insistence on "active" and "consistent" opposition by arguing that the lower the bar for retaliation claims, the less likely it is that employers will look into what may be happening outside the executive suite. As they see it, if retaliation is an easy charge when things go bad for an

---

2. Metro suggests in passing that it was unclear whether Crawford actually opposed Hughes's behavior because some of her defensive responses were "inappropriate," such as telling Hughes to "bite me" and "flip[ping] him a bird." This argument fails not only because at the summary judgment stage we must "view all facts and draw all reasonable inferences in [Crawford's] favor," but also because Crawford gave no indication that Hughes's gross clowning was anything but offensive to her.

employee who responded to enquiries, employers will avoid the headache by refusing to raise questions about possible discrimination.

The argument is unconvincing, for we think it underestimates the incentive to enquire that follows from our decisions in *Burlington Industries, Inc. v. Ellerth* and *Faragher v. Boca Raton,. Ellerth* and *Faragher* hold "[a]n employer . . . subject to vicarious liability to a victimized employee for an actionable hostile environment created by a supervisor with . . . authority over the employee." Although there is no affirmative defense if the hostile environment "culminates in a tangible employment action" against the employee, an employer does have a defense "[w]hen no tangible employment action is taken" if it "exercised reasonable care to prevent and correct promptly any" discriminatory conduct and "the plaintiff employee unreasonably failed to take advantage of any preventive or corrective opportunities provided by the employer or to avoid harm otherwise,". . . Employers are thus subject to a strong inducement to ferret out and put a stop to any discriminatory activity in their operations as a way to break the circuit of imputed liability. The possibility that an employer might someday want to fire someone who might charge discrimination traceable to an internal investigation does not strike us as likely to diminish the attraction of an *Ellerth-Faragher* affirmative defense.

That aside, we find it hard to see why the Sixth Circuit's rule would not itself largely undermine the *Ellerth-Faragher* scheme, along with the statute's "'primary objective'" of "avoid[ing] harm" to employees. If it were clear law that an employee who reported discrimination in answering an employer's questions could be penalized with no remedy, prudent employees would have a good reason to keep quiet about Title VII offenses against themselves or against others. This is no imaginary horrible given the documented indications that "[f]ear of retaliation is the leading reason why people stay silent instead of voicing their concerns about bias and discrimination." The appeals court's rule would thus create a real dilemma for any knowledgeable employee in a hostile work environment if the boss took steps to assure a defense under our cases. If the employee reported discrimination in response to the enquiries, the employer might well be free to penalize her for speaking up. But if she kept quiet about the discrimination and later filed a Title VII claim, the employer might well escape liability, arguing that it "exercised reasonable care to prevent and correct [any discrimination] promptly" but "the plaintiff employee unreasonably failed to take advantage of . . . preventive or corrective opportunities provided by the employer." Nothing in the statute's text or our precedent supports this catch-22.[3]

---

3. Metro also argues that "[r]equiring the employee to actually initiate a complaint . . . conforms with the employee's 'obligation of reasonable care to avoid harm' articulated in *Faragher* and *Ellerth*." But that mitigation requirement only applies to employees who are suffering discrimination and have the opportunity to fix it by "tak[ing] advantage of any preventive or corrective opportunities provided by the employer," . . . ; it is based on the general principle "that a victim has a duty 'to use such means as are reasonable under the circumstances to avoid or minimize . . . damages,'" . . . We have never suggested that employees have a legal obligation to report discrimination against others to their employer on their own initiative, let alone lose statutory protection by failing to speak.

. . . .

Notes and Discussion

1. Opposition to Harassment Metro claimed that it fired Crawford for embezzlement. Crawford contended that the true reason for her firing was retaliation for her participation in the investigation into Gene Hughes's conduct. The dispute essentially boils down to Metro's motives: were they permissive (it believed Crawford was embezzling), unlawful (retaliation), or a mixture of both? Recall the prima facie case requirements for substantive claims that are discussed in Chapter 3. A plaintiff who alleges harassment typically does not need to delve into arguments about the employer's, or the harasser's, motivations. Other than the fact that it must be "because of sex," the motivation behind a harasser's behavior is, for the most part, irrelevant. What matters is what he did and how his actions affected the plaintiff.

For other substantive discrimination claims in which more than one motivation may exist for the employer's conduct, the court, per Title VII, must use a "mixed motives" standard (or instruct the jury on this standard).[72] This proof requires a finding for the plaintiff as long as there is evidence that an unlawful discriminatory motive played any part in the defendant's decision-making. But it also permits a limited affirmative defense, if the defendant can prove it would have taken the negative action absent the discriminatory motive.

Retaliation claims are brought under a different part of the statute, one that is not subject to the "mixed motives" analysis that applies to substantive claims.[73] Thus, in order to prevail, the plaintiff must prove that retaliation was the primary or controlling factor that led to the defendant's action. The "mixed motives" analysis was developed by Congress and the courts because of the difficulty that a plaintiff might have in proving which of two motives caused an employer to act. Does that concern exist for retaliation plaintiffs, too? Other than the fact that the statute treats the different forms of unlawful treatment differently, why treat retaliation claims any differently from "regular" discrimination claims?

2. Opposition, #MeToo, and #TimesUp Recent publicity regarding sexual harassment has focused on bystander intervention. The idea is that bystanders can help to disable harassers and support targets. Are bystanders protected under *Crawford* reasoning? Explain.

Extending the mitigation requirement so far would make no sense; employees will often face retaliation not for opposing discrimination they themselves face, but for reporting discrimination suffered by others. Thus, they are not "victims" of anything until they are retaliated against, and it would be absurd to require them to "mitigate" damages they may be unaware they will suffer.

72. 42 U.S.C. § 2000e-2(m) (2012) ("Except as otherwise provided in this subchapter, an unlawful employment practice is established when the complaining party demonstrates that race, color, religion, sex, or national origin was a motivating factor for any employment practice, even though other factors also motivated the practice.").

73. *See* Univ. of Texas S.W. Medical Center v. Nassar, 570 U.S. 338 (2013).

The conservative composition of the Supreme Court after two appointments by President Trump suggests that Court modification of the current Title VII employer liability standards for complainants is unlikely. The House of Representatives, controlled by Democrats since the 2018 election, may introduce Title VII legislative revisions to enhance employer liability and reform standards. However, without the support of the current Republican-controlled Senate, any reform measures are likely to fail there. That said, in December 2018, Congress passed legislation (later signed by President Trump) that reforms the way Congress deals with sexual misconduct within its ranks. In part, the new law "mandates an annual report of all settlements and awards and eliminates the confidentiality agreements required for accusers at the beginning of the existing process."[74] In sum, much depends on future elections for the determination of legislative reforms.

Social media and a free press remain outstanding beacons of hope for oppressed and abused workers. Public pressure on employers and a robust competitive market for talented workers may do more than traditional legal strategies to hold employers accountable for the sexual harassment that occurs at work.

6. Application of Law and Ethics

Hypothetical #4
(based on several actual cases)

Part I.

Aimee retains Patty to pursue a sexual harassment and wrongful termination case against Philter Engineering and her supervisor Greg. Aimee tells Patty that on her first day of work, Greg said when he met her, "It will be a pleasure working with such an attractive assistant." At lunch, Aimee found a banana at her desk with a yellow post-it attached that said, "Eat me!" Shocked, Aimee saved the note but did nothing further. An African American, Aimee had been called "a stupid monkey" at another job and was concerned that the banana might involve a reference to her race.

Legal issue: Is this sexual harassment? Is it race harassment? Should Aimee complain now?

Over the months, Greg continued to make sexual overtures toward Aimee who began to find the attention flattering as she came to "know" Greg and that he meant no harm. They began a consensual sexual relationship despite the fact that inter-office affairs were strictly forbidden at Philter. *See supra* Chapter XII. Aimee began seeing a psychotherapist to deal with the stress and the concern that she might get fired for this "affair."

---

74. Elise Viebeck, *Congress Sends Trump Bill to Make Lawmakers Liable for Harassment Settlements*, WASH. POST (Dec. 13, 2018).

Legal issue: Can Philter legally forbid such office romances?

Aimee broke off the relationship when she discovered through office gossip that Greg was sexually involved with other women. Aimee relays to Patty that despite her rejections, Greg continued to pursue her (Aimee) daily. Aimee recalls, "He must have sensed that I still loved him." When Aimee continued to rebuff him, Greg became angry and threatened to pull her off an important research project, among other retaliatory acts.

Legal issue: Is this sexual harassment? Should Aimee have complained?

Several months after her break-up with her boss Greg, Aimee discovered she had contracted a sexually transmitted disease (STD). She confronted Greg. When Greg admitted that he had given two other women in the office the same STD, Aimee became hysterical. She screamed at him to leave her alone. Aimee described that Greg then tried to embrace her in an effort to seduce her and quiet her anger. Just as Aimee pushed Greg away from her with such force that he fell to the ground, Aimee's co-worker, Whitney Ness, entered the lab. The next day, Philter (Greg and his boss) fired Aimee for insubordination and violent behavior against Greg.

Legal Issue: If Aimee files a Title VII claim against Philter, will the company be able to use the Burlington/Faragher *affirmative defense?*

Aimee's attorney Patty wrote Philter a letter, requesting an investigation of these events and the immediate rehire of Aimee. Philter's counsel, Barbara, responded that Philter would rehire Aimee while it investigated the incident but that both Aimee and Greg had to remain at home on paid administrative leave until the matter was resolved. Barbara also counseled Greg not to speak with Aimee or Patty.

Legal Issue: Has Philter "exercised reasonable care to prevent and correct promptly any sexually harassing behavior"? Has Aimee (through Patty) acted "to take advantage of any preventive or corrective opportunities provided by the employer or to avoid harm otherwise"?

Part II.

Philter and Barbara investigate Aimee's discrimination, harassment, and wrongful termination claims. Four months later, Barbara informs Patty that Philter has been unable to confirm the discrimination and sexual harassment charges.

Legal Issues: Has Philter responded promptly to Patty's request for an investigation? Why would this matter?

Philter has determined that both Aimee and Greg violated company policies, however, including the anti-fraternization rule. Both Aimee and Greg must voluntarily leave their employment or face immediate termination.

Legal Issue: Is Philter's proposed choice retaliatory?

Philter offers Aimee an unusual severance package should she decide to leave her employment. In exchange for $90,000.00 (a year's salary) and an agreement not to contest unemployment benefits, Aimee must tender her immediate resignation, promise not to seek rehire at Philter, and release any and all claims she may have against Philter and Greg.

Practice Issue: Do you think this offer is a fair resolution of the matter?

In addition, Barbara wants assurances from Patty that she does not represent any other Philter employees and that Patty will agree to act as a "consulting" attorney for Philter for the next year. Patty's "consulting" fee will be the contingency fee she earns in Aimee's case. Barbara sends Patty a proposed "consulting" contract that explains the details.

Ethics Issue: Why is Philter's requirement of Patty problematic? What ethics issues might it raise? Should Patty sign the "consulting" contract?

7. Review

Definitions

1. Respondeat Superior "Let the master answer"—A legal doctrine that holds the employer liable for the employee-agent's unlawful acts committed within the scope of employment.

2. Constructive Discharge Occurs when an employee reasonably abandons her employment to escape the hostile work environment and other illegal conduct created or tolerated by the employer. Note that an *Ellerth/Faragher* affirmative defense is available to employers unless the plaintiff has suffered a tangible economic detriment associated with her employment (apart from her departure).

3. Retaliation The EEOC declares, "A manager may not fire, demote, harass or otherwise 'retaliate' against an individual for filing a complaint of discrimination, participating in a discrimination proceeding, or otherwise opposing discrimination." It emphasizes that the laws (including Title VII) that prohibit discrimination also protect persons who oppose discrimination.[75]

Liability Review

The Liability Table below gives a compact way of identifying whom courts will find liable under different statutory schemes. Examine Title VII's liability provisions, as interpreted in the Ninth Circuit, and compare them with those under California's state fair employment practice statute, FEHA (the Fair Employment and Housing Act). Note the differences in how the two systems treat supervisor and co-worker harassment in both hostile work environment and quid pro quo cases in which a tangible employment action (TEA) results.

---

75. EQUAL EMP. OPPORTUNITY COMM'N, *supra* note 5.

California Liability Table

SYSTEM/TYPE	EMPLOYER	SUPERVISOR	WORKER
FED 9th—TEA (tangible employment action)	Vicarious or direct liability	No individual liability[T]	N/A
State [CA]—TEA	Vicarious* or direct liability	Yes, but not for sex "discrimination"[✓]	N/A
FED 9th—no TEA—SUPERVISOR	Vicarious or direct liability with affirmative defense	No individual liability[T]	N/A
CA—no TEA—SUPERVISOR	Vicarious* or direct liability	Direct liability for harasser) / knew or should have known (if not accused harasser)	N/A
FED 9th—no TEA—CO-WORKER	Direct liability—if knew or should have known	No individual liability[T]	No individual liability[T]
CA—no TEA—CO-WORKER	Direct liability—if knew or should have known	Direct liability—if knew or should have known	Direct liability

Notes: For punitive damages, the plaintiff must show ratification, malice, or reckless disregard. For vicarious liability for supervisor harassment, the supervisor must be a managing agent.

*An officer, director, or managing agent must know of the harassment or be involved.

[✓]Under California employment law, sex discrimination involves an employer policy for which individuals are not usually liable.

[T]Certain districts in some circuits provide for agent liability.

Chapter 5

Title VII Remedies, Attorneys' Fees, and Costs

Unlike a settlement in which only the creativity of the parties constrains the outcome, a verdict results in a limited array of remedies. Consider the relief originally provided for under Title VII and the expanded remedies allowed under the Civil Rights Act of 1991. Evaluate whether, collectively, these provisions can restore plaintiffs to the position they would have occupied but for the offenses.

1. Equitable Remedies

Under the original Title VII, a prevailing party was entitled to recover only equitable remedies such as back pay, front pay, injunctive relief, and reinstatement, as well as reasonable attorneys' fees. The operative provisions of the statute follow.

Title VII Enforcement Provisions
42 U.S.C. § 2000e-5 (2012)

§ 2000e-5. Enforcement provisions

. . . .

(g) **Injunctions; appropriate affirmative action; equitable relief; accrual of back pay; reduction of back pay; limitations on judicial orders**

(1) If the court finds that the respondent has intentionally engaged in or is intentionally engaging in an unlawful employment practice charged in the complaint, the court may enjoin the respondent from engaging in such unlawful employment practice, and order such affirmative action as may be appropriate, which may include, but is not limited to, reinstatement or hiring of employees, with or without back pay (payable by the employer, employment agency, or labor organization, as the case may be, responsible for the unlawful employment practice), or any other equitable relief as the court deems appropriate. Back pay liability shall not accrue from a date more than two years prior to the filing of a charge with the Commission. Interim earnings or amounts earnable with reasonable diligence by the person or

persons discriminated against shall operate to reduce the back pay otherwise allowable.

. . . .

(k) **Attorney's fee; liability of Commission and United States for costs**

In any action or proceeding under this subchapter the court, in its discretion, may allow the prevailing party, other than the Commission or the United States, a reasonable attorney's fee (including expert fees) as part of the costs, and the Commission and the United States shall be liable for costs the same as a private person.

Many courts awarded injunctive relief—particularly in hostile work environment cases where the plaintiff had not lost her job and could not support a claim for back pay. The cessation of offending behaviors does not automatically render the plaintiff's request for injunctive relief moot. The *Bundy* appellate court reasoned:

Common sense tells us that the men who harassed Bundy may well have ceased their actions solely because of the pendency of her complaint and lawsuit. Moreover, the law tells us that a suit for injunctive relief does not become moot simply because the offending party has ceased the offending conduct, since the offending party might be free otherwise to renew that conduct once the court denied the relief.[1]

Courts also consider the class of people they protect, as well as the individual plaintiffs, when fashioning injunctive relief. The *Robinson* court noted:

The history of management's condonation and approval of sexually harassing conditions, together with the past failures to redress effectively those instances of sexual harassment of which management disapproved, argues forcefully for affirmative relief that provides guidance for all employees regarding acceptable and offensive conduct, provides confidence to female employees that their valid complaints of sexual harassment will be remedied, and provides male employees who transgress the boundaries of sexual harassment with notice that their conduct will be penalized commensurate with the seriousness of the offense.[2]

Two factors can weigh against the award of injunctive relief. When a plaintiff no longer works for the accused employer, courts typically find the plaintiff lacks standing to request such relief. Second, when an employer takes prompt remedial action beyond merely ceasing the harassment, injunctive relief may become unnecessary.

In addition to notification, training, and other affirmative relief orders, courts can order the plaintiff's reinstatement. However, courts cannot order the plaintiff's reinstatement if nondiscriminatory grounds also justify a termination.[3]

---

1. Bundy v. Jackson, 641 F.2d 934, 946 n.13 (D.D.C. 1981).
2. Robinson v. Jacksonville Shipyards, Inc., 760 F. Supp. 1486, 1534 (M.D. Fla. 1991).
3. 42 U.S.C. § 2000e-5(g)(2)(B) (2012).

Reinstatement may also be inappropriate if irreparable hostility exists or if the court could not adequately monitor employee interactions in a small, closely held organization. Finally, the plaintiff's emotional health or other factors may counsel against reinstatement. In such cases, the court may order back pay, calculated from the time the employee left the job to the time of the judgment, and front pay, calculated from the time of the judgment to a reasonable period in the future. Consider how these issues arise in the following case.

Hansel v. Public Service Co. of Colorado

778 F. Supp. 1126 (D. Colo. 1991)

BABCOCK, District Judge.

. . . .

I.

Findings of Fact

Plaintiff Victoria Lynn Hansel (Hansel) . . . brought this action in June 1988 against Public Service Company of Colorado (PSC) alleging that defendant maintained and failed to correct a sexually hostile work environment in violation of Title VII of the Civil Rights Act of 1964. . . . Hansel had previously filed a similar complaint with the EEOC in December, 1987.

Hansel was hired in March, 1980 as an auxiliary tender in the operations department of the Comanche Power Plant in Pueblo, Colorado. The job of auxiliary tender is the entry level position in plant operations and requires employees to operate and maintain various machinery. . . .

When Hansel was hired, there was only one other woman employed as an auxiliary tender and there were no women in higher job categories within the operations department. Because all the operations employees are required to work rotating shifts, Hansel was often the only woman working in the plant during her shift.

. . . .

. . . As with all new hires, Hansel was placed on a 120 day training and probation period. She satisfactorily completed her training, and on her 121st day, she was given her "white helmet." On that day, one of her male co-workers hit her over the head with a crescent wrench with such force that Hansel's helmet was dented. He told her that this was her "initiation." New employees were often subjected to this initiation. However, their helmets were not on their heads when the helmet was struck.

After Hansel's probation, her co-workers began a continuous and concerted campaign of sexual harassment and discrimination intended to force her out of plant operations, previously an all-male environment. . . .

When Hansel asked a co-worker a job-related question, he replied to her "I have something you want, you have something I want."

When Hansel was working by herself, a co-worker had hidden himself in the shadows above and behind her. He dropped a large bolt that nearly hit her head.

Hansel was slapped on her buttocks on more than 10 occasions by more than five different co-workers. This conduct often occurred in front of other workers, who laughed at Hansel's attempts to stop this conduct.

On at least three occasions, different co-workers grabbed and fondled Hansel's breasts. On one of these occasions, Hansel's arms were held while another co-worker assaulted her.

When Hansel came into work one day with an Ace bandage on her wrist, she was greeted with the comment "Out fucking dogs all night and one bit you." This comment was made in the break room, in front of several co-workers.

After accepting a ride from two co-workers, Hansel was held down by one in the front seat of the car while the other sexually assaulted her by fondling her genitals.

While her car was parked in the employee parking lot, Hansel's windshield was broken twice and a side window broken once. She often found "spit" on her windshield.

Hansel's work gloves were a focus of this harassment. Once, they were filled with bathroom cleaner. Another time, they were filled with sunflower seed shells. At yet another time, her gloves were filled with lime powder. The employee who filled her gloves with bathroom cleaner later apologized and bought Hansel a new pair of gloves.

Hansel came out of a stall in the ladies room one day to find a male co-worker in the bathroom holding a hangman's noose. He told her it would be better if she just killed herself.

At another time, two male co-workers came into the ladies room and asked Hansel if she needed any help.

One day, Hansel came back to the desk used by auxiliary tenders to find one of her used tampax placed over the nozzle of a spray bottle.

There was sexually explicit graffiti throughout the plant, some of which was explicitly directed at Hansel.

Generally, Hansel was continually insulted and made to feel "stupid" by her co-workers.

Hansel did not report the majority of these incidents to her supervisors. However, she reported the broken windshields and one incident concerning her gloves. Hansel felt that if she reported the harassment it would only get worse. She thought that if she kept quiet her co-workers would eventually accept her and the harassment would stop.

The harassment severely affected Hansel's work and personal life. She was afraid to ask job-related questions. She found it hard to concentrate on her tasks. She felt continually fearful and threatened at work. She never knew when the next incident would occur. She even considered suicide during this period.

During her annual performance review in 1982, Hansel told her supervisor, Mr. North, that she was having problems with sexual harassment. However, she refused to provide him with names and specific details, fearing retaliation. North told her that nothing could be done unless she came forward with that information. He also told her to "work on your peer relations" and to try to "fit in better."

Again at her performance review in January, 1983 with her supervisor, Walt O'Hara, she complained of sexual harassment, but refused to provide him with names and specific details. Hansel felt that she would lose her job if she provided this information. At this meeting, Hansel became hysterical and was hospitalized later that day for a nervous breakdown. She returned to work a month later, where she was then ridiculed as a "mental case", despite management's promise to keep the nature of her hospitalization confidential.

After talking with her union representative, Hansel requested a meeting with plant management to file charges of sexual harassment. At that meeting on May 10, 1983, Hansel identified six co-workers and set out the specifics of many of the incidents detailed above.

In response to Hansel's charges, Roitsch and other management at the plant discussed the allegations with four of the six workers identified by Hansel. These men denied her charges and were never formally disciplined. In notes dated May 12, 1983, Roitsch indicated that he would discuss sexual harassment generally with his supervisors, although it is unclear whether this discussion ever took place. In those notes, Roitsch listed four ways for Hansel to respond to the sexual harassment:

1. Get help from Supv. Supt. or Manager immediately
2. Thin skinned about words
3. Tries too hard to be liked
4. Develop coping techniques
   a. replies
   b. belt knife or 10″ crescent
   c. Other gals discuss — support group

PSC took no other remedial action in 1983.

The sexual harassment did not end after Hansel filed these charges. The overt, physical harassment declined, but the hostile and abusive work environment continued, manifesting itself in different ways.

After the May 10 meeting, Hansel was told by one co-worker that she had "really screwed up" and that from then on it would be "total isolation." During the next year, Hansel was shunned and ostracized by her co-workers.

After 1983, the sexually explicit graffiti at the plant intensified. Much of this graffiti was directed at Hansel by name. For example, one graffiti read "V.H. sucks all cocks." Another said "Dog Face Hansel." Yet another depicted the lower half of a female body with the words "Shot cunt V.H." written over it and "Sweet Lips" written underneath. Plant management knew of the graffiti, and, although some of it was removed by management, much of it remained on the walls at the plant for months and even years. The sexually explicit graffiti was prevalent throughout the period of Hansel's active employment at the plant.

There were also pornographic and sexually explicit magazines, pinups, and calendars at the plant. On at least two occasions, this material was left where Hansel would find it. This kind of material was prevalent throughout the plant from 1980 until 1988–89.

After 1983, cartoons began appearing on the bulletin boards disparaging Hansel. For example, a sign posted in the control room in the summer of 1987 read: "SEXUAL HARASSMENT IN THIS AREA WILL NOT BE REPORTED HOWEVER, IT WILL BE GRADED." One of PSC's own policy statements dated October 2, 1987 on equal employment opportunity was altered to read that sexual advances were "welcome."

During her performance reviews in 1985, 1986 and 1987, Hansel was told by her supervisor that women should not be in power plants and that women are not mechanically inclined.

PSC had a company policy forbidding sexual harassment from at least 1985. . . . However, PSC had no effective means to monitor whether there was a sexually hostile work environment at any of its plants. . . .

. . . .

PSC never effectively disciplined or terminated any of the male co-workers who were subjecting Hansel to the sexual harassment.

Hansel suffered a job related injury at the plant on July 13, 1990. She returned to light duty for a few weeks in August, but since then she has not been released by her physician to return to work. She did not establish when she stopped receiving her salary. However, to the date of trial, Hansel continues to receive her employee benefits and she is carried on the personnel roster as an employee on "no time" status.

. . . .

Hansel's treating psychologist, Dr. Aldrich, and expert witness, Dr. Ricci, agree that Hansel is suffering from post traumatic stress disorder. Both psychologists believe that it would be detrimental to plaintiff's mental health to return to work at Comanche, because many of the men who harassed plaintiff are still employed at the plant and some of them would now supervise her.

Evidence was admitted that Hansel was paid approximately $29,000 a year and received benefits worth $12,412 a year. PSC introduced no evidence on whether plaintiff fulfilled her duty to mitigate her damages with respect to either back pay or front pay.

. . . .

II.

Conclusions of Law

. . . .

D. Damages

Under Title VII, I may award back pay, reinstatement, or "any other equitable relief as the court deems appropriate." In determining what relief is appropriate, I look to the purposes of Title VII. "It is . . . the purpose of Title VII to make persons whole for injuries suffered on account of unlawful employment discrimination."

> [W]here a legal injury is of an economic character "the general rule is, that when a wrong has been done, and the law gives a remedy, the compensation shall be equal to the injury. The latter is the standard by which the former is measured. The injured party is to be placed, as near as may be, in the situation he would have occupied if the wrong had not been committed."

I cannot award back pay here because Hansel's counsel introduced no evidence as to when she stopped receiving her salary. However, based upon the testimony of Drs. Ricci and Aldrich, I conclude that reinstatement is an impossible option for Hansel. Not only would returning to Comanche jeopardize her mental health, but many of the men who were her worst harassers are now in supervisory positions. The usual remedy in Title VII cases where reinstatement is not possible is "front pay."

Here, I am faced with a unique situation because Hansel is still technically an employee of PSC. She does not receive a salary, but she does receive benefits and she is carried on the personnel roster. Therefore, this case is not one of typical constructive discharge.

However, merely because this action does not fit the usual constructive discharge mold does not mean that an award of front pay is inappropriate under my charge, in equity, to make Title VII claimants "whole." Under Title VII, I have broad discretion to fashion appropriate equitable relief. This discretionary power should be exercised to allow the most complete achievement of the objectives of Title VII attainable under the facts and circumstances of the specific case.

I conclude that Hansel is entitled to an award of front pay to compensate her for the continuing future effects of defendant's hostile work environment. Plaintiff is not receiving a salary now and she cannot return to her employment with PSC at Comanche. Therefore, front pay will make her whole.

However, quantification of front pay cannot be speculative. There must be some basis in the record upon which to base an award of future earnings. An award of front pay must specify an ending date and must take into account any amount that the plaintiff could earn using reasonable efforts. Here, to alleviate the speculative nature of a future damage award, I must take evidence concerning Hansel's salary and benefits at the time she stopped receiving them, any potential increase in her salary through regular promotions and cost of living adjustments, her work and life expectancy, the reasonable availability of other work opportunities for her, the period within which she may become reemployed with reasonable efforts, and methods to discount any award to net present value.

Because evidence was not proffered on these factors, I must set the question of the amount of front pay for a full hearing. Hansel bears the initial burden of proof concerning the amount of front pay and PSC bears the burden of proof on any issue in the nature of mitigation.

. . . .

Accordingly, IT IS ORDERED THAT:

(1) Partial judgment shall enter in favor of plaintiff on her sexual harassment claim and against defendant determining that defendant has violated Title VII;

(2) A hearing on the amount of front pay to be awarded plaintiff shall be set;

(3) Partial judgment shall enter in favor of defendant and against plaintiff on her disparate treatment claim determining that defendant has not violated Title VII; and,

(4) Costs are awarded to plaintiff.

Notes and Discussion

1. Back Pay If the court had found a constructive discharge, it could have ordered back pay from the date of the constructive termination. Judge Babcock determined that he could not order back pay because Hansel's counsel had not introduced evidence of when Hansel stopped receiving her salary. Could the court have allowed this evidence at the hearing about front pay? Why or why not? Did counsel commit malpractice by failing to introduce that evidence? Explain.

Assume PSC stopped paying Hansel on August 31, 1990. For what period could the court award back pay? If PSC had stopped paying her August 31, 1989, for what period could the court award back pay? Would the court deduct anything from that back pay award? If so, what?

2. Mitigation Plaintiffs have a duty to mitigate their harm, which means obtaining substitute employment when possible.[4] The plaintiff's new earnings will offset her recovery of backpay. However, a plaintiff need not accept a demotion or change career paths. See, e.g., *Wheeler v. Snyder Buick, Inc.*, 794 F.2d 1128 (7th Cir. 1986) (holding that Title VII did not require plaintiff to accept less pay in another line of work). Moreover, she need not take a job offered on the condition that she settle all

---

4. 42 U.S.C. § 2000e-5(g)(1) (2012).

discrimination claims with her employer. See *Odima v. Westin Tucson Hotel*, 53 F.3d 1484 (9th Cir. 1995). If a plaintiff does successfully mitigate her harm, what happens to the defendant's duty to make her whole? In the absence of damages, does the mitigation requirement allow defendants to get off the hook?

Occasionally, special circumstances prompt a court to be more lenient with the mitigation requirement. For example, in *E.E.O.C. v. Gurnee Inn Corp.*, the court held that the failure of a 15-year-old high school student and 20-year-old college student to look for employment following a constructive discharge due to sexual harassment did not bar an award of back pay. The court stated, "[t]he district court acted within its discretion in concluding that 'it would not be unreasonable for a young woman having gone through the experience of these women to feel "gun shy" about looking for a similar position.'"[5]

As with front pay, back pay includes all forms of compensation, such as medical and dental coverage, annuity or pension payments, sales commissions, overtime, cost-of-living increases, bonuses, raises, tips, vacation, and sick pay. It is the plaintiff's responsibility to provide this evidence so that the court can make a proper determination.

3. Reinstatement Did the court properly exclude reinstatement as a relief option? Suppose an employer offers reinstatement into a "cured" environment to avoid an award of front pay. Suppose further that the plaintiff's primary argument against reinstatement is that she feels "uncomfortable and embarrassed" about returning to work in the environment. Should the judge still order reinstatement? If not, should she order the remittitur of any front pay damages awarded by a jury? Explain.

4. Front Pay Did the court properly award front pay? Review the factors that influence the calculation of front pay. Are there other factors that a court might consider? If a plaintiff mitigates her damages but still suffers an economic loss in the form of a lesser hourly rate, can a court award front pay amounting to the difference?

While some plaintiffs may have received adequate remedies under Title VII, the lack of damages prevented many sexual harassment plaintiffs from being fully compensated for their injuries. Consider a woman who, like Victoria Hansel, is harassed for years by her co-workers. Despite her complaints, nothing is done. The harassment is severe enough to cause the woman emotional trauma, but (unlike Hansel) she does not stop working. Under a purely equitable framework, what could a court do for her? She would not be entitled to front or back pay because she has not missed time from work. It is likely the only available remedy would be an injunction requiring the employer to put a stop to the harassment. While the plaintiff would undoubtedly appreciate this, it does not come close to making her whole. Or consider the real-life example of Beth Ann Faragher, the plaintiff in *Faragher v.*

---

5. U.S. E.E.O.C. v. Gurnee Inn Corp., 914 F.2d 815, 818 n.4 (7th Cir. 1990).

City of Boca Raton.[6] She was sexually harassed for five years while working as a lifeguard when she was in college. She left her employment when she graduated, moved to another state, and then filed her lawsuit. Although the harassment was severe and caused her significant emotional distress, because it occurred prior to the 1991 Amendments, the court could only award her nominal damages of $1.00.[7]

Similarly, equitable remedies have a limited deterrent effect on employers. An employer may have to pay attorney's fees (for both itself and for the plaintiff) but have little other tangible costs as the result of losing a lawsuit involving serious misconduct.

It was these concerns that led Congress to amend the statute.

2. Compensatory and Punitive Damages

In 1991, Congress significantly amended Title VII to include compensatory and punitive damages for targets of intentional discrimination (i.e., not claims brought under the disparate impact theory).

Title VII Damages Provisions

42 U.S.C. § 1981a (2012)

§ 1981a. Damages in cases of intentional discrimination in employment

(a) **Right of recovery**

(1) **Civil Rights**

In an action brought by a complaining party under section 706 or 717 of the Civil Rights Act of 1964 . . . against a respondent who engaged in unlawful intentional discrimination . . . the complaining party may recover compensatory and punitive damages as allowed in subsection (b) of this section, in addition to any relief authorized by section 706(g) of the Civil Rights Act of 1964 [42 U.S.C.A. § 2000e-5(g)], from the respondent.

. . . .

(b) **Compensatory and punitive damages**

(1) Determination of punitive damages

A complaining party may recover punitive damages under this section against a respondent (other than a government, government agency or political subdivision) if the complaining party demonstrates that the

---

6. Faragher v. City of Boca Raton, 524 U.S. 775 (1998); *see supra* Chapter 4 for an in-depth discussion.

7. For an interesting first-person account of this case, see Beth Ann Faragher, Faragher v. City of Boca Raton: *A Personal Account of a Sexual Harassment Plaintiff*, 22 Hofstra Lab. & Emp. L.J. 417 (2005).

285

respondent engaged in a discriminatory practice or discriminatory practices with malice or with reckless indifference to the federally protected rights of an aggrieved individual.

(2) Exclusions from compensatory damages

Compensatory damages awarded under this section shall not include backpay, interest on backpay, or any other type of relief authorized under section 706(g) of the Civil Rights Act of 1964 [42 U.S.C.A. § 2000e-5(g)].

(3) Limitations

The sum of the amount of compensatory damages awarded under this section for future pecuniary losses, emotional pain, suffering, inconvenience, mental anguish, loss of enjoyment of life, and other nonpecuniary losses, and the amount of punitive damages awarded under this section, shall not exceed, for each complaining party—

(A) in the case of a respondent who has more than 14 and fewer than 101 employees in each of 20 or more calendar weeks in the current or preceding calendar year, $50,000;

(B) in the case of a respondent who has more than 100 and fewer than 201 employees in each of 20 or more calendar weeks in the current or preceding calendar year, $100,000; and

(C) in the case of a respondent who has more than 200 and fewer than 501 employees in each of 20 or more calendar weeks in the current or preceding calendar year, $200,000; and

(D) in the case of a respondent who has more than 500 employees in each of 20 or more calendar weeks in the current or preceding calendar year, $300,000.

. . . .

(c) Jury trial

If a complaining party seeks compensatory or punitive damages under this section—

(1) any party may demand a trial by jury; and

(2) the court shall not inform the jury of the limitations described in subsection (b)(3) of this section.

Notes and Discussion

1. How Caps Apply Awards for front pay and back pay closely resemble compensatory damages, but they are technically considered equitable relief. Thus, they are not subject to the statutory caps.[8]

---

8. *See* Pollard v. E.I. DuPont de Nemours & Co., 532 U.S. 843 (2001).

The statute makes clear that the caps apply to "each complaining party" rather than to each claim. Thus, a plaintiff with multiple claims under Title VII is still limited to the single, capped amount. Both punitive and compensatory damages are combined under the single cap. Additional claims under other federal statutes or state law are not subject to the caps.

2. The Effect of Caps After concluding that damages were necessary to deter bad behavior, Congress nevertheless capped the damages a plaintiff can receive. The legislative history makes clear that this was done as a compromise measure necessary to ensure the law's passage. The cap amounts have not been raised since they were set in 1991.

Consider the basis upon which the damages are capped: according to the number of employees that the employer has. Why do you think Congress used this as the benchmark? Commentators have argued that setting caps in this manner fails to meet the dual purposes of any damages regime, which are to make the plaintiff whole and to deter misconduct. As Professor Lynn Ridgeway Zehrt observes:

> These caps are not based on the extent of a victim's injuries. Nor are the caps variable based on the egregiousness of the employer's conduct. They also are not designed to deter and punish, given that the only loose connection to an employer's net worth is an assessment of the number of employees it retained during the relevant calendar year.[9]

Is Zehrt correct? Is there a fairer and more effective benchmark?

In addition, commentators point out the specific disadvantage that damage caps create for plaintiffs claiming sex discrimination. A plaintiff who alleges discrimination based on race or national origin may also state a claim under 42 U.S.C. § 1981, which mandates racial and ethnic equality in contracts (including employment relationships). Claims under § 1981 have no damage caps. Thus, a victim of racial harassment could get full compensation and punitive damages for her claim, but a victim of sexual harassment with no attendant racial component is limited by the caps.

Professor Zehrt argues that this disparity was, in fact, intentional, as demonstrated by the legislative history surrounding the Amendment:

> [N]umerous days of testimony before congressional committees and subcommittees were devoted to the problem of sexual harassment and the inadequacies of remedies available to women under Title VII. Yet despite this convincing testimony, congressional leaders in both houses of Congress exchanged sharp words of disagreement over the scope of damages that should be afforded to victims of sex discrimination. This included the testimony of several witnesses who offered discriminatory justifications for

---

9. Lynn Ridgeway Zehrt, *Twenty Years of Compromise: How the Caps on Damages in the Civil Rights Act of 1991 Codified Sex Discrimination*, 25 YALE J.L. & FEMINISM 249, 252 (2014).

the availability of only limited damages to victims of sex discrimination, including the view that sex discrimination was an unavoidable "social problem." Given the inevitability of flirtations between men and women in the workplace, some Republican congressional leaders expressed the concern that providing women with unlimited tort damages would "open the floodgates" and overburden the federal courts with sexual harassment claims.[10]

These concerns were similar to reasons given by courts in the early 1970s to dismiss sexual harassment cases under Title VII. Are these concerns legitimate?

3. Taxes Historically, the United States tax code excluded personal injury damage awards from income taxation. In 1996, however, Congress added a provision to the Small Business Job Protection Act making all punitive and compensatory damages awarded for "non-physical" injuries taxable income.[11]

The amended statute also explicitly states that emotional distress is not within the definition of physical injuries or sickness, unless the plaintiff incurred medical expenses as a result. On the other hand, if a claim for emotional distress is attached to a physical personal injury, compensatory damages received for emotional distress can be excluded from the individual's gross income. Put another way, if an individual receives a compensatory damage award or settlement stemming from a physical personal injury and related emotional distress, the entire award would be excludable from taxation. In contrast, if an individual were to recover compensatory damages stemming solely from non-physical emotional distress, the entire award would be taxable. This is particularly relevant for sexual harassment cases, in which emotional distress and punitive damages are likely to make up a significant portion of the plaintiff's total recovery. Why do you think Congress created this dichotomy in the tax treatment of damages awards? Does it imply that harms from sexual harassment are less real or less important than harms from other injurious conduct? For an extension of this argument, see Marisa J. Mead, *Taxing the Victims: Compensatory Damage Awards and Attorney's Fees in Sexual Harassment Lawsuits*, 11 J.L. & Pol'y 801 (2003).

Until recently, businesses were allowed to deduct the costs of settlement payments or court-ordered payments for compensatory damages. Congress limited this ability somewhat in 2017 when it inserted a provision in the Tax Cuts and Jobs Act to deny a business deduction for "any settlement or payment related to sexual harassment or sexual abuse if such settlement or payment is subject to a nondisclosure agreement."[12]

4. Juries By authorizing money damages under Title VII, Congress also granted plaintiffs who seek such damages the right to a jury trial. Previously, Title VII cases that did not include any other causes of action could only be tried to judges. Do you

---

10. *Id.* at 262.
11. 26 U.S.C. § 104(a) (2003).
12. 26 U.S.C. § 162(q) (2017).

believe outcomes are likely to be different for plaintiffs who choose a jury trial over a bench trial? Why?

Why does the 1991 Act forbid the revelation of damage caps to the jury? Research into jury behavior has found that when jurors are provided with damage cap information, a number of decision-making paradigms and heuristics are likely to influence the ultimate awards. As Professors Rebecca Hollander-Blumoff and Matthew T. Bodie note:

> Psychological research has marshaled strong evidence for the phenomena of anchoring and adjustment, in which the first number with which a decision-maker is presented has a demonstrable effect on that person's ultimate choice. In essence, the first number heard becomes the place away from which any adjustment is made. Anchoring effects are powerful, widespread, and have been found in a variety of contexts. The source of the anchoring first number need not even be tied to any rational source; indeed, the groundbreaking initial research on anchoring demonstrated that anchoring effects were robust even when subjects believed the first number to be randomly generated.[13]

Professors Hollander-Blumoff and Bodie also note other psychological phenomena that can distort decision-making when jurors are presented with concrete numbers, including scaling (where the presentation of a number creates a mental scale that individuals use to calculate choices), and prospect theory/loss aversion (where, in the absence of a cap any award is viewed as a gain to the plaintiff, while the presence of a cap makes any award lower than the cap seem like a loss to the plaintiff). Interestingly, the research does not clearly point to directionality of these effects on verdicts. Put another way, it is not obvious whether revelation of the damage caps leads to higher or lower jury verdicts.

Does it create a fairness problem, or even a Seventh Amendment (which guarantees the right to a civil jury trial) problem, when a jury awards a sexual harassment plaintiff a multimillion dollar judgment, only to have the award cut back to a fraction of that by the judge? Hollander-Blumoff and Bodie argue that jurors' perception of the justice system may be harmed by such a phenomenon, and that "[i]t seems not only inefficient but also irrational to endorse or even require knowledge of the law in most situations but ignorance of the law in some small subset."[14]

Moreover, with knowledge of the caps, a jury might strategically allocate damage awards in cases that contain multiple claims under other federal statutes, state laws, or local ordinances. Courts disagree on the question of whether such "cap evasion" is acceptable. In *Martini v. Federal National Mortgage Association*,[15] the plaintiff had

---

13. Rebecca Hollander Blumoff & Matthew T. Bodie, *The Effects of Jury Ignorance About Damage Caps: The Case of the 1991 Civil Rights Act*, 90 Iowa L. Rev. 1361, 1378 (2005).

14. *Id.* at 1397.

15. Martini v. Federal Nat'l Mortg. Ass'n, 178 F.3d 1336 (D.C. Cir. 1999).

filed a complaint alleging sexual harassment and retaliation under Title VII and the D.C. Human Rights Act (HRA). The jury was given a single set of instructions for both sets of claims. It returned a verdict for the plaintiff, with millions of dollars of compensatory and punitive damages under Title VII, and lesser (but still significant) awards under the D.C. HRA. The judge remitted the Title VII damages to fit the caps. On appeal, the court overturned the remittitur:

> Because the jury used exactly the same instructions in evaluating Martini's Title VII and D.C. law claims, and because the jury had no knowledge of Title VII's damages cap, it had no legal basis for distinguishing between the two statutes. Thus, for any one claim against any one defendant, distinguishing between damages that the jury awarded under Title VII and damages that it awarded under the D.C. Human Rights Act makes no sense. For example, although the jury awarded punitive damages of $2 million under Title VII and $1 million under D.C. law against Fannie Mae on Martini's retaliation claim, there is no basis for saying that the jury intended to impose a $2 million award specifically under Title VII, plus a $1 million award specifically under D.C. law. Instead, the most sensible inference is that the jury sought to impose a total of $3 million in punitive damages against Fannie Mae for retaliation. To be sure, only $300,000 of that amount may be awarded under Title VII. But we see no reason why Martini should not be entitled to the balance under the D.C. Human Rights Act, since the local law contains the same standards of liability as Title VII but imposes no cap on damages.
>
> Were we not to treat damages under federal and local law as fungible where the standards of liability are the same, we would effectively limit the local jurisdiction's prerogative to provide greater remedies for employment discrimination than those Congress has afforded under Title VII.[16]

Compare this with the approach of the United States Court of Appeals for the Fourth Circuit in *Sasaki v. Class*.[17] There, the plaintiff's counsel encouraged the jury to adjust its damages allocation between her state and federal claims, apparently to evade the caps:

> The jury therefore appears to have faithfully followed Sasaki's counsel's directions with regard to the award. In awarding a significantly larger amount of damages for the "lesser included" state conduct and injury, the jury almost undoubtedly adjusted its award to account for the federal cap. Although the basis for the jury's decision can, of course, never be known to a certainty, when a jury's damages award itself indicates so strongly that the error substantially influenced the jury's verdict, the error cannot be dismissed as harmless. . . .

---

16. *Id.* at 1349–50.
17. Sasaki v. Class, 92 F.3d 232 (4th Cir. 1996).

The district court's admonition to the jury that statements and arguments "of counsel are not evidence," did not "cure" the error resulting from counsel's improper mention of the cap. Even if the jurors properly obeyed this instruction, as we assume they did, this would not have prevented them from following the improper legal suggestion of Sasaki's counsel—to award limited damages on the federal claim and "more generous" damages on the state claims to avoid the federal cap. The jury here likely reacted in precisely the manner that Congress specifically feared, and which it attempted to preclude through the enactment of 42 U.S.C. § 1981a....

. . . .

The jury in this case was given a special verdict form. The form required the jury to set forth separately its findings as to whether Class sexually harassed, assaulted, or battered Sasaki. The form also required the jury to determine whether Class's conduct was egregious enough to warrant punitive damages. Finally, the form required the jury to assess damages. The jury specifically found that Class did sexually harass, did assault and batter Sasaki, and that his conduct did warrant punitive damages. The jury then made its damages assessment. [W]e must reverse the damages assessment due to the error in Sasaki's counsel's reference to the cap on damages.[18]

Should courts try to effectuate the intent of the jury in such circumstances, or should they adhere to the intent of Congress in imposing the caps?

5. Common Law and Other Claims As discussed above, some lawyers add other claims to avoid the damage caps and to protect against dismissal if the Title VII claim fails for any reason (such as its short statute of limitations). Three general categories of claims serve these purposes: common law claims, claims brought under other federal statutes, and claims brought under state fair employment practice statutes (FEPS). Plaintiffs can bring many of these claims in conjunction with a Title VII claim. Some of the alternative claims, however, do not provide for punitive damages and some do not allow for recovery of attorneys' fees.

Typical common law claims used in sexual harassment cases include breach of public policy, breach of an implied contract and covenant of good faith and fair dealing, tortious interference with contractual relations, loss of consortium, negligent hiring and retention, intentional and negligent infliction of emotional distress, assault and battery, false imprisonment, invasion of privacy, defamation, and misrepresentation. Common law tort remedies allow for the recovery of punitive damages, but common law breach of contract claims do not. Typically, common law claims do not allow for the prevailing party to collect attorneys' fees.[19]

---

18. *Id.* at 238.

19. *See* Kevin Gomez, Melissa McClure & Destine McCulley, *State Regulation of Harassment*, 18 GEO. J. GENDER & L. 815 (2017); Krista J. Schoenheider, *A Theory of Tort Liability for Sexual Harassment in the Workplace*, 134 U. PA. L. REV. 1461 (1986); Sarah E. Wald, *Alternatives to Title VII: State*

3. Punitive Damages

Sometimes a plaintiff will collect more in punitive damages than in compensatory damages. Faced with large punitive damages awards, some defendants in other types of non-Title VII cases argued that allowing a jury to impose unlimited punitive damages violated their due process rights. In response, the Supreme Court provided some guidance. In *BMW v. Gore* (a fraud case),[20] the Court set forth three guideposts: (1) the degree of reprehensibility of the defendant's conduct, (2) the ratio between the compensatory damages and the damages (a reasonable relationship), and (3) the sanctions for comparable conduct. In *State Farm v. Campbell* (an insurance case),[21] the Court suggested that a ratio of more than 9 to 1 (punitive to compensatory damages) is presumptively unconstitutional. Although this issue is less likely to arise in Title VII cases because of the damage caps, it may still present itself if the jury awards very low compensatory damages and the highest allowable punitive damages. It may also arise when the Title VII claim is combined with other claims that are not subject to the caps.

A plaintiff can overcome the *State Farm* presumption, however, with a showing that a greater award is fair under the circumstances, and courts have shown themselves willing to permit deviations from the suggested ratio. For example, in *Seitzinger v. Trans-Lux Corp.*, the New Mexico Supreme Court upheld a $400,000 punitive damages award (26 to 1 ratio) in a sexual harassment case brought under the state's human rights law.[22] In *Wilson v. Brinker Int'l*, the trial court upheld a $163,400 punitive damages award despite the fact that the jury had only awarded the plaintiff nominal compensatory damages of $1.00.[23]

Under what circumstances a jury can award punitive damages against an employer for the misconduct of its employee, however, has engendered much debate. The discussion is similar to imputing liability to the employer for the harassing behavior of an employee, and the courts look to the common law of agency. A 1999 Supreme Court decision concerning punitive damages in Title VII cases clarifies this important issue.

Kolstad v. American Dental Association
527 U.S. 526 (1999)

Justice O'CONNOR delivered the opinion of the Court.

Under the terms of the Civil Rights Act of 1991 (1991 Act), punitive damages are available in claims under Title VII of the Civil Rights Act of 1964 (Title VII).

Statutory and Common-Law Remedies for Employment Discrimination, 5 Harv. WOMEN'S L.J. 35 (1982).

20. 517 U.S. 559 (1996).
21. 538 U.S. 408 (2003).
22. 40 P.3d 1008 (N.M. 2002).
23. 248 F. Supp. 2d 856 (D. Minn. 2003).

Punitive damages are limited, however, to cases in which the employer has engaged in intentional discrimination and has done so "with malice or with reckless indifference to the federally protected rights of an aggrieved individual." We here consider the circumstances under which punitive damages may be awarded in an action under Title VII.

I

A

[Carole Kolstad, was employed by the American Dental Association. She applied for a promotion, but ultimately a man, Spangler, was chosen for the position. Kolstad sued for discrimination under Title VII.]

B

. . . .

The District Court denied petitioner's request for a jury instruction on punitive damages. The jury concluded that respondent had discriminated against petitioner on the basis of sex and awarded her backpay totaling $52,718. Although the District Court subsequently denied respondent's motion for judgment as a matter of law on the issue of liability, the court made clear that it had not been persuaded that respondent had selected Spangler over petitioner on the basis of sex, and the court denied petitioner's requests for reinstatement and for attorney's fees.

Petitioner appealed from the District Court's decisions denying her requested jury instruction on punitive damages and her request for reinstatement and attorney's fees. . . . In a split decision, a panel of the Court of Appeals for the District of Columbia Circuit reversed the District Court's decision denying petitioner's request for an instruction on punitive damages. In so doing, the court rejected respondent's claim that punitive damages are available under Title VII only in "'extraordinarily egregious cases.'" The panel reasoned that, "because 'the state of mind necessary to trigger liability for the wrong is at least as culpable as that required to make punitive damages applicable,'" the fact that the jury could reasonably have found intentional discrimination meant that the jury should have been permitted to consider punitive damages. The court noted, however, that not all cases involving intentional discrimination would support a punitive damages award. Such an award might be improper, the panel reasoned, in instances where the employer justifiably believes that intentional discrimination is permitted or where an employee engages in discrimination outside the scope of that employee's authority. Here, the court concluded, respondent "neither attempted to justify the use of sex in its promotion decision nor disavowed the actions of its agents."

The Court of Appeals subsequently agreed to rehear the case en banc[.] The en banc majority concluded that, "before the question of punitive damages can go to the jury, the evidence of the defendant's culpability must exceed what is needed to show intentional discrimination." Based on the 1991 Act's structure and legislative history, the court determined, specifically, that a defendant must be shown to have engaged in some "egregious" misconduct before the jury is permitted to consider a request for punitive damages. Although the court declined to set out the "egregiousness" requirement in any detail, it concluded that petitioner failed to make the requisite showing in the instant case. . . .

We granted certiorari to resolve a conflict among the Federal Courts of Appeals concerning the circumstances under which a jury may consider a request for punitive damages under § 1981a(b)(1).

II

A

. . . .

The 1991 Act limits compensatory and punitive damages awards, however, to cases of "intentional discrimination—that is, cases that do not rely on the "disparate impact" theory of discrimination. 42 U.S.C. § 1981a(a)(1). Section 1981a(b)(1) further qualifies the availability of punitive awards:

> "A complaining party may recover punitive damages under this section against a respondent (other than a government, government agency or political subdivision) if the complaining party demonstrates that the respondent engaged in a discriminatory practice or discriminatory practices with malice or *with reckless indifference to the federally protected rights of an aggrieved individual*." (Emphasis added.)

The very structure of § 1981a suggests a congressional intent to authorize punitive awards in only a subset of cases involving intentional discrimination. Section 1981a(a)(1) limits compensatory and punitive awards to instances of intentional discrimination, while § 1981a(b)(1) requires plaintiffs to make an additional "demonstrat[ion]" of their eligibility for punitive damages. Congress plainly sought to impose two standards of liability—one for establishing a right to compensatory damages and another, higher standard that a plaintiff must satisfy to qualify for a punitive award.

The Court of Appeals sought to give life to this two-tiered structure by limiting punitive awards to cases involving intentional discrimination of an "egregious" nature. We credit the en banc majority's effort to effectuate congressional intent, but, in the end, we reject its conclusion that eligibility for punitive damages can only be described in terms of an employer's "egregious" misconduct. The terms "malice" and "reckless" ultimately focus on the actor's state of mind. While egregious misconduct is evidence of the requisite mental state, § 1981a does not limit plaintiffs to this form of evidence, and the section does not require a showing of egregious or outrageous discrimination independent of the employer's state of mind. Nor does the statute's structure imply an independent role for "egregiousness" in the face of congressional silence. On the contrary, the view that § 1981a provides for punitive awards based solely on an employer's state of mind is consistent with the 1991 Act's distinction between equitable and compensatory relief. Intent determines which remedies are open to a plaintiff here as well; compensatory awards are available only where the employer has engaged in "intentional discrimination."

Moreover, § 1981a's focus on the employer's state of mind gives some effect to Congress' apparent intent to narrow the class of cases for which punitive awards are available to a subset of those involving intentional discrimination. The employer must act with "malice or with reckless indifference *to [the plaintiff's] federally protected rights.*" § 1981a(b)(1) (emphasis added). The terms "malice" or "reckless indifference" pertain to the employer's knowledge that it may be acting in violation of federal law, not its awareness that it is engaging in discrimination.

We gain an understanding of the meaning of the terms "malice" and "reckless indifference," as used in § 1981a, from this Court's decision in *Smith v. Wade*, 461 U.S. 30 (1983). . . . Employing language similar to what later appeared in § 1981a, the Court concluded in *Smith* that "a jury may be permitted to assess punitive damages in an action under § 1983 when the defendant's conduct is shown to be motivated by evil motive or intent, or when it involves reckless or callous indifference to the federally protected rights of others." While the *Smith* Court determined that it was unnecessary to show actual malice to qualify for a punitive award, its intent standard, at a minimum, required recklessness in its subjective form. The Court referred to a "subjective consciousness" of a risk of injury or illegality and a "'criminal indifference to civil obligations.'" The Court thus compared the recklessness standard to the requirement that defendants act with "'knowledge of falsity or reckless disregard for the truth'" before punitive awards are available in defamation actions, a subjective standard. Applying this standard in the context of § 1981a, an employer must at least discriminate in the face of a perceived risk that its actions will violate federal law to be liable in punitive damages.

There will be circumstances where intentional discrimination does not give rise to punitive damages liability under this standard. In some instances, the employer may simply be unaware of the relevant federal prohibition. There will be cases, moreover, in which the employer discriminates with the distinct belief that its discrimination is lawful. The underlying theory of discrimination may be novel or otherwise poorly recognized, or an employer may reasonably believe that its discrimination satisfies a bona fide occupational qualification defense or other statutory exception to liability. . . .

At oral argument, respondent urged that the common law tradition surrounding punitive awards includes an "egregious misconduct" requirement. We assume that Congress, in legislating on punitive awards, imported common law principles governing this form of relief. Moreover, some courts and commentators have described punitive awards as requiring both a specified state of mind and egregious or aggravated misconduct.

Most often, however, eligibility for punitive awards is characterized in terms of a defendant's motive or intent. Indeed, "[t]he justification of exemplary damages lies in the evil intent of the defendant." Accordingly, "a positive element of conscious wrongdoing is always required."

Egregious misconduct is often associated with the award of punitive damages, but the reprehensible character of the conduct is not generally considered apart from the requisite state of mind. Conduct warranting punitive awards has been characterized as "egregious," for example, *because* of the defendant's mental state. *See* Restatement (Second) of Torts § 908(2) (1979) ("Punitive damages may be awarded for conduct that is outrageous, because of the defendant's evil motive or his reckless indifference to the rights of others"). Respondent, in fact, appears to endorse this characterization. That conduct committed with the specified mental state may be characterized as egregious, however, is not to say that employers must engage in conduct with some independent, "egregious" quality before being subject to a punitive award.

To be sure, egregious or outrageous acts may serve as evidence supporting an inference of the requisite "evil motive." "The allowance of exemplary damages depends upon the bad motive of the wrong-doer *as exhibited by his acts.*" Likewise, under § 1981a(b)(1), pointing to evidence of an employer's egregious behavior would provide one means of satisfying the plaintiff's burden to "demonstrat[e]" that the employer acted with the requisite "malice or . . . reckless indifference." Again, however, respondent has not shown that the terms "reckless indifference" and "malice," in the punitive damages context, have taken on a consistent definition including an independent, "egregiousness" requirement.

B

The inquiry does not end with a showing of the requisite "malice or . . . reckless indifference" on the part of certain individuals, however. 42 U.S.C. § 1981a(b)(1). The plaintiff must impute liability for punitive damages to respondent. The en banc dissent recognized that agency principles place limits on vicarious liability for punitive damages. Likewise, the Solicitor General as *amicus* acknowledged during argument that common law limitations on a principal's liability in punitive awards for the acts of its agents apply in the Title VII context.

. . . While we decline to engage in any definitive application of the agency standards to the facts of this case, it is important that we address the proper legal standards for imputing liability to an employer in the punitive damages context. This issue is intimately bound up with the preceding discussion on the evidentiary showing necessary to qualify for a punitive award, and it is easily subsumed within the question on which we granted certiorari. . . . "On a number of occasions, this Court has considered issues waived by the parties below and in the petition for certiorari because the issues were so integral to decision of the case that they could be considered 'fairly subsumed' by the actual questions presented." . . . Accordingly, we conclude that these potential limitations on the extent of respondent's liability are properly considered in the instant case.

The common law has long recognized that agency principles limit vicarious liability for punitive awards. This is a principle, moreover, that this Court historically has endorsed. Courts of Appeals, too, have relied on these liability limits in interpreting 42 U.S.C. § 1981a.

We have observed that, "[i]n express terms, Congress has directed federal courts to interpret Title VII based on agency principles." Observing the limits on liability that these principles impose is especially important when interpreting the 1991 Act. In promulgating the Act, Congress conspicuously left intact the "limits of employer liability" established in *Meritor*.

Although jurisdictions disagree over whether and how to limit vicarious liability for punitive damages, our interpretation of Title VII is informed by "the general common law of agency, rather than ... the law of any particular State." The common law as codified in the Restatement (Second) of Agency (1957), provides a useful starting point for defining this general common law. The Restatement of Agency places strict limits on the extent to which an agent's misconduct may be imputed to the principal for purposes of awarding punitive damages:

> "Punitive damages can properly be awarded against a master or other principal because of an act by an agent if, but only if:
>
> (a) the principal authorized the doing and the manner of the act, or
>
> (b) the agent was unfit and the principal was reckless in employing him, or
>
> (c) the agent was employed in a managerial capacity and was acting in the scope of employment, or
>
> (d) the principal or a managerial agent of the principal ratified or approved the act." Restatement (Second) of Agency, *supra*, § 217 C.

The Restatement, for example, provides that the principal may be liable for punitive damages if it authorizes or ratifies the agent's tortious act, or if it acts recklessly in employing the malfeasing agent. The Restatement also contemplates liability for punitive awards where an employee serving in a "managerial capacity" committed the wrong while "acting in the scope of employment." "Unfortunately, no good definition of what constitutes a 'managerial capacity' has been found," and determining whether an employee meets this description requires a fact-intensive inquiry. "In making this determination, the court should review the type of authority that the employer has given to the employee, the amount of discretion that the employee has in what is done and how it is accomplished." Suffice it to say here that the examples provided in the Restatement of Torts suggest that an employee must be "important," but perhaps need not be the employer's "top management, officers, or directors," to be acting "in a managerial capacity."

Additional questions arise from the meaning of the "scope of employment" requirement. The Restatement of Agency provides that even intentional torts are within the scope of an agent's employment if the conduct is "the kind [the employee] is employed to perform," "occurs substantially within the authorized time and space limits," and "is actuated, at least in part, by a purpose to serve the" employer. According to the Restatement, so long as these rules are satisfied, an employee may be said to act within the scope of employment even if the employee engages in acts "specifically forbidden" by the employer and uses "forbidden means of accomplishing results." On this view, even an employer who makes every effort to comply with Title VII would be held liable for the discriminatory acts of agents acting in a "managerial capacity."

Holding employers liable for punitive damages when they engage in good faith efforts to comply with Title VII, however, is in some tension with the very principles underlying common law limitations on vicarious liability for punitive damages—that it is "improper ordinarily to award punitive damages against one who himself is personally innocent and therefore liable only vicariously." Where an employer has undertaken such good faith efforts at Title VII compliance, it "demonstrat[es] that it never acted in reckless disregard of federally protected rights."

Applying the Restatement of Agency's "scope of employment" rule in the Title VII punitive damages context, moreover, would reduce the incentive for employers to implement antidiscrimination programs. In fact, such a rule would likely exacerbate concerns among employers that § 1981a's "malice" and "reckless indifference" standard penalizes those employers who educate themselves and their employees on Title VII's prohibitions. Dissuading employers from implementing programs or policies to prevent discrimination in the workplace is directly contrary to the purposes underlying Title VII. The statute's "primary objective" is "a prophylactic one"; it aims, chiefly, "not to provide redress but to avoid harm[.]" With regard to sexual harassment, "[f]or example, Title VII is designed to encourage the creation of anti-harassment policies and effective grievance mechanisms." The purposes underlying Title VII are similarly advanced where employers are encouraged to adopt antidiscrimination policies and to educate their personnel on Title VII's prohibitions.

In light of the perverse incentives that the Restatement's "scope of employment" rules create, we are compelled to modify these principles to avoid undermining the objectives underlying Title VII. Recognizing Title VII as an effort to promote prevention as well as remediation, and observing the very principles underlying the Restatements' strict limits on vicarious liability for punitive damages, we agree that, in the punitive damages context, an employer may not be vicariously liable for the discriminatory employment decisions of managerial agents where these decisions are contrary to the employer's "good-faith efforts to comply with Title VII." As the dissent recognized, "[g]iving punitive damages protection to employers who make good-faith efforts to prevent discrimination in the workplace accomplishes" Title VII's objective of "motivat[ing] employers to detect and deter Title VII violations."

. . . .

For the foregoing reasons, the decision of the Court of Appeals is vacated, and the case is remanded for proceedings consistent with this opinion.

Notes and Discussion

1. Egregious Conduct Did the Court properly interpret Title VII as not requiring egregious conduct for the award of punitive damages? How would a plaintiff go about demonstrating that her employer's conduct (as opposed to her harasser's conduct) recklessly disregarded her federally protected rights?

2. Good Faith What constitutes a "good faith effort to comply with Title VII" such that an employer can insulate itself from punitive damages liability? Is the adoption of a sexual harassment policy sufficient? What if the employer does not consistently enforce that policy? Courts usually find that the mere existence of a written sexual harassment policy does not provide a per se good-faith defense if, for example, the policy is not disseminated to employees (*Faragher*), if the employer minimizes or fails to investigate complaints (*Ogden v. Wax Works*, 214 F.3d 999 (8th Cir. 2000)), or where managers observe sexual harassment and fail to take any action to stop it (*Wilson v. Brinker Int'l*, 248 F. Supp. 2d 856 (D. Minn. 2003)). See also *Lopez v. Aramark Uniform & Career Apparel, Inc.*, 426 F. Supp. 2d 914 (2006) (finding that an employer could not escape liability for punitive damages, when the sexual harassment training it provided for its staff consisted of a video available only in English despite the employer's high number of Spanish-speaking employees).

The result is that if employers have, disseminate, and follow a minimally adequate sexual harassment policy, they are likely to be relieved of punitive damages liability. Professor Joanna Grossman argues that *Kolstad*'s emphasis on the good-faith efforts of employers has created a system in which employers can insulate themselves from punitive damages by instituting pro forma measures that do little to actually address the problem of sexual harassment:

> The Supreme Court, in *Kolstad*, adopted a good-faith standard, holding that employers should not face punitive damages if they had made a good-faith effort to comply with Title VII. Enacting anti-discrimination policies and procedures were precisely the measures the Court mentioned as constituting "good-faith." This standard reinforces the problem with the underlying liability standard: an employer can be relieved of liability because it made some effort to prevent or remedy harassment, even if its efforts were so ineffective that a serious incident of harassment nonetheless occurred. Punitive damages, instead, should be evaluated on a case-by-case basis, leaving juries free to punish employers who have perhaps paid mere lip service to prevention while permitting a culture of harassment to proliferate.[24]

Is Professor Grossman's proposal reasonable? By now, many employers have sexual harassment policies in place, but the number of reported sexual harassment claims has only increased in recent years. Does this suggest that the policies are not

---

24. Joanna L. Grossman, *The Culture of Compliance: The Final Triumph of Form Over Substance in Sexual Harassment Law*, 26 HARV. WOMEN'S L.J. 3, 73–74 (2003).

effective in actually reducing harassment in the workplace? Should the good-faith defense be revisited in light of this?

3. Vicarious Liability Does the Court convincingly justify its decision to modify agency principles (once again)? If so, how? Do you agree that the application of agency principles would work as a disincentive for employers to implement anti-discrimination programs? Is shielding employers from punitive damages liability necessary to effectuate the purposes of Title VII? Consider how the *Harvard Law Review* answered some of these questions:

> In 1991, Congress believed that punitive damages would serve as a more effective deterrent for unlawful discrimination than the existing equitable remedies.
>
> . . . .
>
> In deciding the vicarious liability question, the *Kolstad* Court examined the effect of such liability on employers' adoption of antidiscrimination policies. The Court thus focused its inquiry too narrowly; it should have examined the effect of vicarious liability on the broader deterrent purpose of Title VII and the 1991 Act. The deterrent purpose of these laws extends beyond encouraging employers to adopt antidiscrimination policies to preventing employers from engaging in unlawful discrimination. Had the Court examined the effect of vicarious liability on the prevention of unlawful discrimination — the broader purpose of Title VII — it would have seen that holding employers vicariously liable for punitive damages would not have undermined, but instead would have furthered, the deterrent purposes of Title VII and the 1991 Act. Potential liability for punitive damages would encourage employers to take the steps necessary to adhere to Title VII. Limiting the potential for punitive liability leaves employers with the pre-1991 incentives to adhere to Title VII — the incentives that Congress deemed inadequate.
>
> . . . .
>
> The Court based its decision on the idea that the best way to induce compliance with Title VII is to provide employers with positive incentives. This opinion conflicts with Congress's decision that the best way to induce Title VII compliance is by providing a negative incentive — punishment — to those who engage in intentional discrimination. The difference in the two liability regimes is the amount of effort that employers will make to comply with Title VII by preventing unlawful discrimination. Under the regime the Court established in *Kolstad*, employers will be interested in establishing antidiscrimination policies with two components: a component indicating that it is not company policy to discriminate against individuals on the basis of race, color, religion, sex, or national origin; and a component detailing a procedure for addressing claims of discrimination. Alternatively, if the Court had allowed employers to be vicariously

liable for punitive damages, then employers would institute antidiscrimination policies that actively ensure compliance with Title VII and ensure that employers seriously address potential violations. By making punitive damages available to victims of intentional employment discrimination, Congress intended to do more than to ask employers to try to comply with Title VII—it intended to punish them if they failed to comply.[25]

Was the *Law Review* accurate that limiting vicarious punitive liability undermines the deterrent effect that Congress intended with the 1991 Act? Is discrimination generally covert and will this covert nature make it more difficult to punish reckless employers? Which approach to discrimination eradication works better: the carrot or stick method? Or did Congress allow for both and did *Kolstad* take away the stick?

4. Trial Courts as Barriers Despite the availability of punitive damages for Title VII plaintiffs in theory, in practice courts often create barriers to recovery. For example, Professor Joseph Steiner conducted an empirical analysis of employment discrimination cases in the federal courts after *Kolstad*. He found that very few resulted in meaningful punitive damages—just 24 reported cases in the two-year time frame of his analysis. In part, he attributes this to trial courts taking the issue away from the jury, either by refusing to give an instruction on punitive damages or by vacating or reducing awards that a jury has given. This leads him to conclude that "punitive damages are simply not achieving their intended [deterrent] purpose."[26]

Professor Sandra Sperino points out that courts may also make errors when conducting the excessiveness review suggested by the Supreme Court in *Gore* and *State Farm*. In particular, because back pay and front pay are not technically compensatory damages (recall that they are considered equitable relief), courts sometimes ignore them when calculating the ratio of compensatory to punitive damages. Back and front pay are in the nature of compensatory relief, Professor Sperino argues, because they help to make the plaintiff whole, and so they should be included on the compensatory side of the ratio. She notes a number of Title VII cases in which courts failed to consider high-value back pay awards and then reduced punitive damages awards to correspond to the artificially low compensatory damages.

Professor Sperino also addresses the interplay between the excessiveness review for punitive damages and the statutory caps. She argues that when a jury returns both compensatory and punitive damages awards that exceed the cap, courts should allocate the total amount of the cap to compensatory damages:

> This approach is preferable to splitting the capped amount between compensatory and punitive damages for several reasons related to judicial

25. *Civil Rights Act of 1991—Employer Liability for Punitive Damages in Title VII Claims*, 113 HARV. L. REV. 359, 364–68 (1999).
26. Joseph A. Seiner, *The Failure of Punitive Damages in Employment Discrimination Cases: A Call for Change*, 50 WM & MARY L. REV. 735, 775 (2008).

efficiency. Courts that split the amount must be careful that such a split does not introduce an error into the *Gore* calculation — making a comparison between the reduced compensatory damages and the reduced punitive damages. Such a comparison is inappropriate, because the Title VII damages caps, as applied to compensatory damages, do not represent the amount of harm suffered by the plaintiff, but rather the maximum amount of harm for which the defendant may be held liable.

. . . .

When a court reduces compensatory damages to comport with the statutory cap, it should not use the reduced amount in conducting the *Gore* analysis. The second *Gore* guidepost calls for a comparison of the actual or potential harm incurred by the plaintiff and the punitive damages award. The harm suffered by the plaintiff is represented by the compensatory damages award before imposition of the statutory cap. In a stand-alone Title VII case, awarding compensatory damages first alleviates the conceptual error that occurs when a court compares the reduced amount of compensatory damages to the punitive damages.

Additionally, splitting the capped damages between compensatory and punitive damages is likely to draw three different requests for review: a request for remittitur of compensatory damages, a request for remittitur of punitive damages, and a request for excessiveness review of punitive damages. Allocating all of the capped damages to compensatory damages limits the types of review the court may be asked to undertake, thereby promoting judicial efficiency and reducing the possibilities of analytical missteps.[27]

Is Professor Seiner's conclusion, that punitive damages are not a meaningful deterrent in Title VII cases, correct? Might the threat of punitive damages and the incentives that *Kolstad* creates operate as a significant deterrent?

4. Attorneys' Fees and Costs

Title VII provides for attorneys' fees and costs to the prevailing party. Without such a provision, many plaintiffs would otherwise find it difficult to hire competent counsel to prosecute a sexual harassment case. Most sexual harassment targets cannot afford high hourly legal fees, especially since many targets face unemployment and financial worries as a result of the harassment they suffered. The contingency model might not work well, either. Other factors (such as damage caps, low pay rates resulting in fewer compensatory damages, etc.) might result in lower damages, such that a reasonable percentage of the jury award fails to equal the market value of the

---

27. Sandra Sperino, *The New Calculus of Punitive Damages for Employment Discrimination Cases*, 62 Okla. L. Rev. 701, 725–26 (2010).

time that it takes competent lawyers to prosecute a case. The attorneys' fees provision gives plaintiff's counsel the assurance that, if successful, she will probably be paid for her time. This encourages the prosecution of civil rights claims that might not otherwise be prosecuted.

In *Farrar v. Hobby*,[28] the Supreme Court resolved a conflict among the circuits as to whether an award of nominal damages confirms the plaintiff as a prevailing party. The Court reasoned:

> [A] plaintiff "prevails" when actual relief on the merits of his claim materially alters the legal relationship between the parties by modifying the defendant's behavior in a way that directly benefits the plaintiff.
>
> . . . .
>
> . . . A judgment for damages in any amount, whether compensatory or nominal, modifies the defendant's behavior for the plaintiff's benefit by forcing the defendant to pay an amount of money he otherwise would not pay. . . .[29]

Thus, an award of either injunctive relief or nominal damages supports a claim for attorneys' fees and costs.

Courts have been reluctant, however, to award attorneys' fees to prevailing defendants. In *Christiansburg Garment Co. v. EEOC*, the Supreme Court required that defendants, seeking a fee shift, must show that a discrimination suit was "frivolous, unreasonable, or without foundation."[30]

The calculation of attorneys' fees and costs entails an evaluation of what constituted reasonable time to prosecute a case multiplied by the reasonable market rate per hour for professional services. This is commonly referred to as the "lodestar." While federal courts rarely award fee enhancements in the form of multipliers, many state courts do. Consider the award of attorneys' fees and costs in the following cases and whether these decisions seem reasonable from a public policy perspective.

Weeks v. Baker & McKenzie
74 Cal. Rptr. 2d 510 (Cal. Ct. App. 1998)

STEIN, Associate Justice.

A jury found that Martin R. Greenstein, a partner in the law firm of Baker & McKenzie, sexually harassed his secretary, plaintiff Rena Weeks and awarded her $50,000 in compensatory damages from both Greenstein and Baker & McKenzie. The jury further awarded Weeks $225,000 in punitive damages from Greenstein and $6.9 million in punitive damages from Baker & McKenzie. The latter award was

---

28. Farrar v. Hobby, 506 U.S. 103 (1992).
29. *Id.* at 111, 113.
30. Christiansburg Garment Co. v. Equal Emp. Opportunity Comm'n, 434 U.S. 412, 421 (1978).

reduced to $3.5 million by the trial court. The court awarded Weeks $1,847,437.86 in attorney fees and expenses. This figure was calculated, in part, by fixing reasonable hourly fees for each legal professional representing Weeks, multiplying those figures by the number of hours reasonably devoted by the respective professional to the case, and multiplying that amount by a factor of 1.7.

. . . .

Fee enhancements by means of multipliers or otherwise are well recognized in California. Under California law, the trial court begins by fixing a "lodestar" or "touchstone" reflecting a compilation of the time spent and reasonable hourly compensation of each attorney or legal professional involved in the presentation of the case. The court then adjusts this figure in light of a number of factors that militate in favor of augmentation or diminution. The purpose of a fee enhancement is not to reward attorneys for litigating certain kinds of cases, but to fix a reasonable fee in a particular action. In *Press v. Lucky Stores, Inc.* (1983), California's Supreme Court implicitly found that it would be appropriate to enhance an award by means of a multiplier "'to reflect the broad public impact of the results obtained and to compensate for the high quality of work performed and the contingencies involved in undertaking this litigation.'" This does not mean, however, that the trial courts should enhance the lodestar figure in every case of uncertain outcome or where the work performed was of high quality. The challenge to the trial courts is to make an award that provides fair compensation to the attorneys involved in the litigation at hand and encourages litigation of claims that in the public interest merit litigation, without encouraging the unnecessary litigation of claims of little public value.

. . . .

[The federal approach] is to enhance the lodestar figure only in exceptional cases. The United States Supreme Court thus has identified a strong presumption that the product of reasonable hours times a reasonable rate represents a reasonable fee, and has held that in most cases this rate should not be enhanced. . . .

. . . California does not follow the approach to fee awards adopted by the federal courts. Therefore, although there is appeal in the high court's finding that many of the factors commonly used to enhance a lodestar figure more properly are considered in determining the lodestar figure at the outset, under present California law the relevant factors are considered only after the lodestar figure has been determined, and are used to augment or diminish it. As a result, an upward or downward adjustment from the lodestar figure will be far more common under California law than under federal law. Nonetheless, the ultimate goal in California, as under federal law, still is to determine a "reasonable" attorney fee, and not to encourage unnecessary litigation of claims that serve no public purpose either because they have no broad public impact or because they are factually or legally weak.

. . . .

In enhancing the lodestar figure the trial court applied a number of [factors.] The trial court thus found an upward adjustment to be warranted by the contingent nature of the award, the difficulty of the litigation, the skill displayed in conducting it, the amounts involved and the results obtained, the fact that Weeks's attorneys had turned down other cases in order to represent Weeks and the delay in receiving payment. The application of these factors must be analyzed in light of the underlying purpose of fee awards—to encourage litigation of certain kinds of claims— but also in light of the danger of encouraging litigation of claims of dubious merit from either an individual or a public policy point of view.

Looking first to the contingent nature of the award, [there was no question that the attorneys would be entitled to an award of fees if they prevailed]. The contingent nature of the litigation, therefore, was the risk that Weeks would not prevail. Such a risk is inherent in any contingency fee case and is managed by the decision of the attorney to take the case and the steps taken in pursuing it. When the public value of the case is great and the risk of loss results from the complexity of the litigation or the uncertainty of the state of the law, fee enhancement may be proper. Fee enhancement, however, should not be a tool that encourages litigation of claims where the actual injury to the plaintiff was slight. It should not compel a defendant to settle frivolous claims under threat that the weaker the claim the more likely it is that any fees awarded will be enhanced should the plaintiff manage to prevail. We do not intend to imply that Weeks's claim lacked factual or legal merit, although we do note that the jury concluded that her damages were not overwhelming. We do, however, mean to urge caution in awarding enhanced fees, particularly in private actions, that will then encourage future litigation of questionable claims.

As to the factor of novelty or difficulty of litigation, the trial court found that litigation was difficult not because of the novelty or complexity of the issues, but because of the inherent difficulty of proving sexual harassment. "Witnesses to harassing conduct are rare, issues of credibility abound, victims are often reluctant to testify, damages are difficult to quantify, and settlements frequently are difficult to obtain." This statement is, of course, correct. As the court also noted, however, the same will be true for many sexual harassment actions. Indeed, it often will be true for other claims of harassment or discrimination in the workplace. Other factors cited by the court, such as delay in payment or turning down other cases in order to litigate this action, also are factors common to many cases. There is at least partial compensation for these problems, however, in the availability of statutory attorney fees. In addition, because Government Code section 12965 permits the court to award reasonable fees, and does not limit fees to a percentage of the plaintiff's recovery, the attorney who takes such a case can anticipate receiving full compensation for every hour spent litigating a claim against even the most polemical opponent.

As to the skill of the attorneys in litigating the case, that factor necessarily is reflected in the lodestar figure. The more skillful and experienced the attorney the higher his or her hourly charges will be. It follows that the skill of an attorney will justify enhancing the lodestar figure only if the skills exhibited are beyond those that might be expected of attorneys of comparable expertise or experience. This case, as litigated in the trial court, did not involve novel or complex legal issues. The attorneys were not required to demonstrate skills above and beyond those that would be expected of persons of their stature and experience.

As the trial court found, the factor of amounts involved and results obtained militate against enhancing the fee award. The amount of compensatory damages actually awarded was relatively modest. The amount obtained was extraordinary because of the substantial award of punitive damages. Such damages have been characterized as a "windfall" and do not justify enhancement of attorney fees. The purpose of a fee award is not to punish the defendant, but to ensure that the plaintiff will be fully compensated and will not have to bear the expense of litigation. When the plaintiff receives a substantial punitive damages award, that purpose is fulfilled. Enhancement may be appropriate when an attorney who obtained a significant result otherwise would receive but meager compensation. Where the attorney will be fully compensated for his or her efforts, however, the fact that the client receives a windfall in the form of punitive damages neither justifies paying the attorney an increased amount nor exacting an increased amount from the defendant. The fact that Weeks obtained a substantial award of punitive damages, therefore, does not support enhancement of the fee award.

Although we find that the award of fees in the first instance was proper, we cannot find sufficient public or private reason in the factors cited by the trial court for the use of a multiplier of 1.7 in this case. . . .

Forshee v. Waterloo Industries, Inc.

178 F.3d 527 (8th Cir. 1999)

LOKEN, Circuit J.

[Melissa Forshee filed suit against Waterloo Industries, alleging that she was discharged from her employment after she refused her supervisor's demand for sexual favors.] A jury returned a verdict in her favor, awarding $10,369 in back pay damages, $9,631 in compensatory emotional distress damages, and $14,733 in attorneys' fees. . . .

. . . .

III. The Award of Attorneys' Fees

Conceding that Forshee as prevailing party is entitled to an attorneys' fee award, *see* 42 U.S.C. § 2000e5(k), Waterloo argues the district court abused its discretion by awarding Forshee's lead attorney an enhanced fee based upon an hourly rate above his normal hourly rate. We agree. Forshee's motion for an attorneys' fees award represented that attorney Murrey Grider's normal hourly rate was $100 per hour and requested that this rate be enhanced to $150 per hour because Grider represented Forshee "on a contingency basis." Without explanation, the district court based its award on an hourly rate of $125 for attorney Grider.

. . . In *City of Burlington v. Dague* (1992), the Supreme Court held that "enhancement for contingency is not permitted under [federal] feeshifting statutes." Thus, Forshee's motion to the district court requested a fee enhancement for an impermissible reason.

An upward adjustment to an attorney's lodestar hourly rate is permissible "in certain 'rare' and 'exceptional' cases, supported by both 'specific evidence' on the record and detailed findings by the lower courts." "Because the lodestar amount may already compensate the applicant for exceptionally good service and results, however, the fee applicant must do more than establish outstanding service and results. The applicant also must establish that the quality of service rendered and the results obtained were superior to what one reasonably should expect in light of the hourly rates charged and the number of hours expended." Here, the case was not unusually difficult or complex to prepare and try, the result while favorable to Forshee was not exceptional, Forshee gave only an impermissible reason for enhancement, and the district court made no "detailed findings" that would justify an enhanced fee award. In these circumstances, we conclude that an award to attorney Grider based upon an hourly rate above his normal hourly rate of $100 per hour was an abuse of discretion. Finally, we reject Waterloo's contention that the district court abused its discretion in awarding a fee based upon the hours attorney M. Joseph Grider spent in assisting attorney Murrey Grider prepare for and attend the trial. The court reasonably reduced the hours claimed by Joseph Grider to eliminate any duplicative effort.

. . . .

Shea v. Galaxie Lumber & Construction Co., Ltd.

6 Wage & Hour Cas. 2d (BNA) 1435 (N.D. Ill. 1999)

LEINENWEBER, J.

. . . .

. . . Shea sued Galaxie Lumber & Construction Company, Ltd. in this court, raising unpaid overtime and retaliation claims under the Fair Labor Standards Act, and a sexual harassment claim under Title VII of the Civil Rights Act of 1964. [Before trial, Galaxie made a Rule 68 offer to settle Shea's overtime claim for $3,000, which Shea's attorneys failed to respond to.] Upon conclusion of a jury trial, the jury returned a verdict in Shea's favor on both her FLSA claims and sexual harassment claim. [The award for her overtime claim, however, was only $1,207.50. The court then granted a defense motion to set aside the punitive damages award on Shea's FLSA claim.]

[Shea moved for attorneys fees and] this court adjusted the lodestar to account for the market rate and redundant entries and determined the potential fee award to be $104,207.50. Nevertheless, based on Shea's limited success at trial, this court found that granting the full potential fee award was unreasonable, and reduced the award to 20% of that amount, to $20,841.50. This court also awarded Shea $2,642.97 in costs, after adjusting the requested amount of $5,694.15 to exclude excessive photocopying expenses, the expert accountant witness fees and all costs incurred after March 1, 1996, as Galaxie's offer of judgment regarding the FLSA overtime claim was rejected and a lower award ultimately received. The court ultimately awarded Shea a total of $23,484.47.

[Shea appealed the attorneys fee decision, as well as the court's refusal to grant liquidated damages on her FLSA claim. The court of appeals ruled that liquidated damages should have been granted, vacated the court's decision on attorneys fees and costs, and remanded the case.]

Lodestar Fee

Shea asserts that based on the Seventh Circuit's decision her results can no longer be characterized as a "limited success," and should receive the entire lodestar fee. Galaxie responds that the court of appeals did not specifically order that this court enter an award equal to the previously determined lodestar fee. Galaxie contends that the reduced award should not be altered because Shea, despite the appellate court ruling, still has only achieved limited success. Galaxie asserts that the factors which this court considered post-trial in reducing the fee remain unchanged. Galaxie points out that Shea rejected an offer of judgment which was more than what she received at trial, and is still more than what she received on appeal. Before trial, Galaxie made a Rule 68 offer to settle Shea's overtime claim for $3,000. At trial Shea was awarded $1,207.50 in back overtime wages. On appeal, the Seventh Circuit vacated this award and granted liquidated damages by doubling the amount to $2,415. Galaxie asserts that because the resulting judgment, $2,415, is still less than the original offer of $3,000, the court should consider this factor as an indicator that Shea has still only achieved limited success. Shea responds that this argument should be rejected, asserting that a Rule 68 offer does not affect the district court's award of attorneys fees.

In addition, Galaxie argues that the outcome of Shea's sexual harassment claim remains unchanged and that the reinstatement of the award of punitive damages on Shea's constructive discharge claim only indicates a marginal increase on Shea's level of success. Further, Galaxie argues that Shea spent most of the time on the sexual harassment claim at trial, and therefore, the reduction in the lodestar fee should not be changed. Shea counters generally that she has now achieved "excellent results," by obtaining a favorable verdict on each of her claims under the FLSA. In addition, Shea posits that this court's determination that the lodestar fee was $104,207.50 is a finding of fact that should not be disturbed on remand.

Although this court is revisiting the issue of attorneys fees on remand, it remains a fact-based issue, and thus, this court retains considerable discretion in again deciding the reasonableness of attorneys fees. This court has already calculated the unreduced lodestar fee, $104,207.50, which will not be disturbed for purposes of the proper starting point. Now the court turns to Shea's level of success on appeal. The court agrees with Shea that she has achieved greater overall success after appeal, in that Shea received liquidated damages in an amount double the overtime wage claim she received at trial, and had her punitive damages reinstated on her overtime wage claim. In short, Shea has achieved greater overall financial success.

This result, however, does not change the other factors which the court found important in previously calculating the attorneys fees. These factors generally remain unchanged, even after appeal. Specifically, it remains true that the amount Shea received on her overtime wage claim, albeit in liquidated damages ($2,415), is less than the amount of the Rule 68 offer ($3,000) Shea and her counsel refused to consider. The court continues to be skeptical of the motives behind Shea's counsel actions in allowing a settlement offer to lapse without response, not discussing a second offer with his client, refusing to consider any settlement at several pretrial conferences before the court and instead demanding the right to go to trial. In giving weight to these particular facts, the court sees eye to eye with the Ninth Circuit in *Haworth v. State of Nevada*, 56 F.3d 1048, 1052 (9th Cir. 1995). In *Haworth*, the court noted that, due to the attorneys fees provisions in the statute, it is often the plaintiff's attorney, rather than the client, who benefits most from pursuing litigation after a Rule 68 offer is made, stating, "clients, and not the attorney, are the ones to decide whether to accept a settlement offer . . . [j]ust because a plaintiff has an FLSA violation in her pocket does not give [the attorney] a license to go to trial, run up the attorney fees and then recover them from the defendant." *Id.* Furthermore, this court is acutely aware that this case is not the first time a federal district court has suspected a possible manipulation or abuse of billing practices with regard to Shea's counsel in a FLSA case. *See Uphoff v. Elegant Bath, Ltd.,* No. 96 C 4645, 1998 WL 42312, at *3 (N.D.Ill. 1998) ("[t]his court having read many of Rossiello's fee motions is all too familiar with their format and content"). Although Shea has achieved an increased level of financial success, Shea has still received, even after appeal, only a fraction of the amounts she sought at trial on her overtime wage claim, $125,000 in punitive damages and $5,000 in compensatory damages plus her overtime wages. With regard to Shea's sexual harassment claim, the court of appeals left the verdict undisturbed, reflecting no increased success with regard to that claim. Therefore, having carefully considered all the foregoing factors, the court will grant attorneys fees in the amount of 60% of the lodestar amount, $62,524.50.

. . . .

Prejudgment Interest

Shea requests that the court award prejudgment interest on attorneys fees and costs. The court agrees that enhancement for delay in payment is appropriate, by either awarding the fees and costs using current attorney rates or past rates with interest. Because this court calculated the lodestar fee and costs using past rates, it will award prejudgment interest on the awards. . . .

. . . .

Notes and Discussion

1. Multipliers Are multipliers necessary or advisable in sexual harassment cases? Explain. Was the *Weeks* court correct that 1.7 was too high?

2. State Laws Note the multimillion dollar verdict awarded in *Weeks v. Baker & McKenzie*. Clearly Rena Weeks did not sue under Title VII, which would have capped her compensatory and punitive damages at $300,000. Rather, she sued under California's FEHA. Often plaintiffs with strong cases who use state law and common law claims can recover awards in the hundreds of thousands, if not millions, of dollars. See, e.g., *Dial Settles U.S. Suit Over Sexual Harassment*, N.Y. TIMES, April 30, 2003, at C7 (describing a $10 million settlement in the *Dial* case and a $34 million settlement in the larger 1998 *Mitsubishi* sexual harassment settlement).

3. Fee and Hour Adjustments *Shea* makes clear that when a plaintiff fails to prevail on all of her claims, the court can award a reduced fee amount. Is this fair? Why or why not? Did the *Shea* court's original reduction to just 20% seem unusually harsh? Why did the court ultimately award only 60% of the requested lodestar amount?

4. Rule 68 Offer of Judgment Federal Rule of Civil Procedure 68 states: "At least 14 days before the date set for trial, a party defending against a claim may serve on an opposing party an offer to allow judgment on specified terms, with the costs then accrued. . . . If the judgment that the offeree finally obtains is not more favorable than the unaccepted offer, the offeree must pay the costs incurred after the offer was made." Thus, when the plaintiff fails to recover at trial an amount that exceeds a Rule 68 offer, she cannot recover her post-offer costs (and included attorneys' fees). Why did Shea's counsel argue that Rule 68 did not affect the court's award of attorneys' fees?

5. Interest Why do courts often award pre-judgment and post-judgment interest in discrimination cases?

5. Application of Law and Ethics
Hypothetical #5

Alice has worked for two years on an assembly line in a small manufacturing plant with roughly 75 employees. She makes $11 an hour. She is one of the few women in her work area and her immediate supervisors are all men. Since her first days on the job, Alice has been the subject of sexual jokes and language. Her co-workers make comments about her body, talk about sex acts, and leave offensive notes and graffiti in the break room about her. Sometimes her work station is sabotaged so that she has to clean it up before the line starts, which puts her behind. She complains to management. The whole line is ordered to watch a 30-minute sexual harassment prevention video. Nothing changes except now Alice's co-workers joke about the video.

One day, two co-workers grab her in the parking lot and force her head down to a third co-worker's crotch so that it looks like she is performing oral sex. One of them yells, "This would make a much better video!" Alice quits that day. She is emotionally exhausted, fearful, and angry. She finds a lawyer who is willing to take her case for a contingency fee, with the expectation of a reasonable fee award as well. After a few weeks, Alice also finds a new job at a grocery store, where she makes $9 an hour.

The lawyer files suit against the company claiming violations of Title VII, state law, and common law torts.

Legal Issues:

1. Under a pre-1991 regime, to what relief would Alice be entitled? Has she sufficiently mitigated her damages?

2. What compensatory damages might Alice receive? How should they be computed?

3. Are punitive damages appropriate in this case? Why?

4. Suppose a jury awards Alice $200,000 in punitive damages and $200,000 in compensatory damages, without specifying to which cause of action each corresponds. How should the judge respond? How could the judge allocate the award to ensure a maximum recovery for Alice?

Ethics Issue:

1. Are there any problems with the attorney taking a contingency fee, as well as receiving compensation for her hours through fee shifting? What if the jury awards only a few thousand dollars, only fraction of what Alice was seeking?

6. Review

Damages and Costs (including Attorneys' Fees) available in Sexual Harassment Cases

Remedy→ / Source of Law↓	Declaratory Relief	Injunctive Relief	Back Pay (certain)	Front Pay	Equitable Relief	Attorneys' Fees*	Costs	Interest (Pre- and post-judgment)	Nominal Damages	Compensatory Damages	Punitive Damages	Expert Witness Fees
'64 Title VII	√	√	√	√	√	√	√					
'91 Amendment	'64	'64	'64	'64	'64	'64	'64			√©	√© (Kolstad Standard)	√
'99 After Acquired Evidence	√	√ No reinstatement	√ Cuts off at discovery			√	√	√		√©	√©	√
'99 Mixed Motive Defense	√	√ No reinstatement				√	√	√				√
'99 Defense Verdict						√ Rarely						
CA FEP (FEHA)	√	√	√	√	√	√	√	√	√	√	√	√
Other Misc. Law			≠	≠	≠	£®	®	√		≠	♣ (Not available w/Gov't.Δ)	

Symbols:

*   Available to prevailing party (via verdict, Rule 68, nominal damages, settlement, or voluntary relief).
©   Capped!
≠   Duty to mitigate damages.
£   Calculate lodestar (hours x rate) and add enhancement if available.
®   Rule 11 also available.
♣   Malice, etc. required . . . influenced by the defendant's wealth.

Chapter 6

Sexual Harassment at School

Courts first elucidated sexual harassment law when interpreting Title VII in employment discrimination cases; however, sexual harassment clearly occurs outside of the workplace. Anywhere that one encounters an imbalance of power between people, one might find abuse and sexual exploitation. Depending upon the context, unique factors may accompany the abuse of power through "sex" and produce distinct harms. For example, in the employment context, sexual harassment threatens a target's physical and emotional well-being, as well as income and financial security. In schools, sexual harassment distinctly imperils a student's education and, potentially, future job prospects.

This chapter explores the development of sexual harassment law for schools and students of all ages. It considers legal questions unique to the academic setting where legal concepts and requirements, applied to the sexual abuse of adults in the workplace, may not translate well. For example, should courts require that schoolchildren indicate that the sexual attention of their teachers is unwelcome (the unwelcomeness element, covered in Chapter 3)? Consider that adult-juvenile sexual conduct is often already illegal. Under state statutory rape and other criminal laws, the age of the child and the nature of the behavior determine the level of the sex crime offense. Arguably, therefore, criminal law should influence the interpretation and application of civil sexual harassment law for youth, who do not have the legal capacity to consent to sex with an adult. Another question that arises is whether courts should hold schools and universities legally responsible for peer sexual harassment on their campuses. If so, should there be limits on legal liability? Should the standards be the same as those under Title VII?

An exhaustive survey of sexual harassment in all contexts is beyond the scope of this textbook. However, an examination of several different forms of sexual harassment and the associated laws in this and the next several chapters reveals important differences in the nature of and response to sexual harassment. As noted, this chapter addresses sexual harassment at schools for all ages. Chapter 7 covers sexual harassment in housing. Chapter 8 deals with sexual harassment in the heavily regulated prison and military environments. Finally, Chapter 9 briefly examines sexual harassment in relatively unregulated public places and between adults in cyberspace. In these chapters, analyze how courts have adapted Title VII law, within alternate statutory schemes, to these other contexts. In particular, examine how a target's prima facie case differs in contexts other than the workplace. Additionally, consider the unique factors pertinent to the different contexts, starting with schools.

Before launching into a review of the statutes applicable to schools, however, Section 1 of this chapter reviews the prevalence of sexual harassment at schools. Section 2 introduces Title IX, the federal statute that prohibits sex-based discrimination at schools. Sections 3 and 4 explore case law interpretation of Title IX. Section 5 examines the prohibition of sexual harassment off campus and Section 6 discusses recent Title IX developments, as well as the GenZ student movement. Sexual harassment at school is a complex topic involving a variety of issues that depend on the ages and maturity of the parties, as well as the diverse educational environments. Hopefully, these sections convey the complexity of the problem and its remediation.

1. The Prevalence of Sexual Harassment

Sexual harassment encompasses a wide variety of behaviors. Working beyond legal definitions, Psychology Professor Louise Fitzgerald offered an excellent classification system that allows investigators to identify sexually harassing behavior. She first highlighted the exploitation of power: "Sexual harassment consists of the sexualization of an instrumental relationship through the introduction or imposition of sexist or sexual remarks, requests or requirements, in the context of a formal power differential."[1] She acknowledged, however, "Harassment can also occur where no such formal differential exists, if the behavior is unwanted by or offensive to the woman. Instances of harassment can be classified into the following general categories: gender harassment, seductive behavior, solicitation of sexual activity by promise of reward or threat of punishment, and sexual imposition or assault."[2]

Sexual harassment occurs in grade schools and in university graduate programs. It happens between young peers, between adults, and between adults and their juvenile students. This chapter first focuses on sexual harassment in high schools by peers and then by adult teachers. Next, it discusses the problem on college campuses. By examining these two limited contexts, one can begin to understand the array of factors that complicate this problem.

A. In High Schools by Peers[3]

In a 2001 study, the American Association of University Women (AAUW) found that 83% of girls and 79% of boys reported experiencing sexually harassing behavior at some point during their school career.[4] These are staggering numbers. Ten years

---

1. Louise F. Fitzgerald, *Sexual Harassment: The Definition and Measurement of a Construct, in* Sexual Harassment on College Campuses: Abusing the Ivory Power 25, 41 (Michele A. Paludi ed., 1996).

2. *Id.* at 41.

3. Adapted from Jennifer Ann Drobac, Sexual Exploitation of Teenagers: Adolescent Development, Discrimination & Consent Law (Univ. of Chicago Press, 2016).

4. AAUW, Hostile Hallways: Bullying, Teasing, and Sexual Harassment in School 4, 32 (2001).

later the AAUW published results from another survey but limited the time frame to one academic year, 2010–11. It still found that almost half of the students (48%) in grades 7–12 reported being sexually harassed during that year and noted that, "nearly all the behavior documented in the survey was peer-to-peer sexual harassment."[5] Educating a projected 16 million students in U.S. high schools alone,[6] schools are dealing with a huge problem—almost 7 million sexually harassed teenagers.

The AAUW survey covered a range of behavior:

In Person

- Having someone make unwelcome sexual comments, jokes, or gestures to or about you
- Being called gay or lesbian in a negative way
- Being touched in an unwelcome sexual way
- Having someone flash or expose themself to you
- Being shown sexy or sexual pictures that you didn't want to see
- Being physically intimidated in a sexual way
- Being forced to do something sexual

Through Text, E-Mail, Facebook, or Other Electronic Means

- Being sent unwelcome sexual comments, jokes, or pictures or having someone post them about or of you
- Having someone spread unwelcome sexual rumors about you
- Being called gay or lesbian in a negative way[7]

Note that most of this behavior, in isolation, would not constitute legally actionable sexual harassment under Title VII's severe or pervasive standard. It probably would also not merit legal action under Title IX's severe and pervasive standard, discussed below. However, offensive behaviors may still constitute sex-based harassment and discrimination, even if they do not meet the thresholds set by courts for legal action.

Studies of offensive sex-based conduct, other than those by the AAUW, found similar rates of sexual harassment in schools.[8] "Some researchers claim that sexual harassment is so common for girls that many fail to recognize it as sexual harassment

---

5. CATHERINE HILL & HOLLY KEARL, AAUW, CROSSING THE LINE: SEXUAL HARASSMENT AT SCHOOL 3, 11 (2011).

6. Nat'l Ctr. for Educ. Statistics [hereinafter NCES], U.S. Dep't of Educ. [hereinafter ED], *Digest of Education Statistics: 2011* tbl. A (2012), http://nces.ed.gov/programs/digest/d11/ch_1.asp.

7. HILL & KEARL, *supra* note 5, at 10.

8. *See, e.g.*, Amy M. Young et al., *Adolescents' Experiences of Sexual Assault by Peers: Prevalence and Victimization Occurring Within and Outside of School*, 38 J. YOUTH ADOLESCENCE 1072 (2008) (finding about 50% of high school girls reported being sexually assaulted).

when it happens."[9] For example, many girls might not consider a smack on the butt by a coach to be harassment. However, this conduct is almost never acceptable at the workplace and is not appropriate at school.[10] Certainly, one smack on the butt is neither severe nor indicative of pervasive harassment. However, such behavior multiplied could add to the creation of a hostile educational environment. Just as juveniles may not recognize discrimination and gender-based slurs, they may not immediately identify sexual harassment. Thus, the prevalence of sexual harassment in schools may be even higher than that reported by the AAUW researchers or other scholars.

The high incidence of reported harassing behaviors suggests that schools, parents, and other adults could do more to educate and protect all students and appropriately discipline transgressing students. Professor Nan Stein argues that sexual harassment is a form of gendered violence that students learn is acceptable when adults fail to intervene. She suggests the need for greater intervention.[11]

A 2018 AAUW report cautioned that schools are either not seeking or not recording the information they need to deal with this problem:

> AAUW also analyzed 2015–16 data from the Civil Rights Data Collection (CRDC) from 96,000 public and public charter P-12 educational institutions—including magnet schools, special education schools, alternative schools, and juvenile justice facilities. More than three-fourths (79 percent) of the 48,000 public schools with students in grades 7 through 12 disclosed zero reported allegations of harassment or bullying on the basis of sex. These numbers do not square with what research shows students experience. Far more students experience sexual harassment than schools report in the CRDC. This is a cause for concern.[12]

If schools are not adequately tracking this problem or think that they do not have a problem, those factors are both problematic. Until adults realize the scope and nature of the sexual harassment on school grounds, they are unlikely to eradicate such misconduct. Thus, peer sexual harassment remains a significant ongoing problem in U.S. schools.

---

9. Campbell Leaper & Christia Spears Brown, *Perceived Experiences with Sexism Among Adolescent Girls*, 79 Child Dev. 685 (2008).

10. *See* Jennifer Ann Drobac, *The* Oncale *Opinion: A Pansexual Response*, 30 McGeorge L. Rev. 1269, 1287–88 (1999) (reviewing Oncale v. Sundowner Offshore Serv. Inc., 523 U.S. 75, 81–82 (1998) and discussing the stereotypical assumptions in Justice Scalia's classification of butt smacking on a playing field as not sexual harassment).

11. Bruce G. Taylor, Elizabeth A. Mumford & Nan D. Stein, *Effectiveness of "Shifting Boundaries" Teen Dating Violence: Prevention Program for Subgroups of Middle School Students*, 56 J. Adolescent Health S20–S26 (2015); Nan Stein, *Sexual Harassment in School: The Public Performance of Gendered Violence*, 65 Harv. Edu. Rev. 145–63 (1995).

12. Kevin Miller, *Schools Are Still Underreporting Sexual Harassment and Assault*, AAUW Education & Training (Nov. 2, 2018).

B. In High Schools by Adults

In contrast to peer sexual harassment, there is even less information about educator sexual misconduct. A 2004 study prepared for the Department of Education (ED) by Professor Charol Shakeshaft found "few empirical studies of educator sexual misconduct. . . . The report recommends a series of studies to deepen the understanding of educator sexual misconduct and strategies to prevent the abuse of students."[13]

While the AAUW surveys focused on peer sexual harassment, Professor Shakeshaft analyzed the data from AAUW reports predating the 2011 study that also contained information on educator sexual misconduct. In her 2003 article, she determined that almost *10%* (9.6%) of students in the eighth through twelfth grades had experienced *unwanted* educator sexual misconduct.[14] The 2004 Shakeshaft ED report explained, "Teachers whose job description includes time with individual students, such as music teachers or coaches, are more likely to sexually abuse than other teachers. . . . The majority of allegations of educator sexual misconduct are not reported to the police by the school districts."[15] It also found, "There are no systematic studies of false accusations of educators, but studies of child sexual abuse in general indicate that false allegations are not common."[16] Shakeshaft concluded, "Based on the assumption that the AAUW surveys accurately represent the experiences of all K-12 students, more than 4.5 *million* students are subject to sexual misconduct by an employee of a school sometime between kindergarten and 12th grade."[17]

Compulsory education laws in every U.S. state mandate that parents send their children to school (or homeschool them under guidelines).[18] Sexual harassment at school has been a focus of attention for more than 20 years, since the two Supreme Court Title IX cases from 1998 (reviewed later in this chapter). The question arises why the ED Office of Civil Rights (OCR) and schools, to which parents must send their children, do not track and publish this information. More rigorous scientific analysis and legal reform is arguably late in coming to protect high school students from their peers and teachers.

---

13. Charol Shakeshaft, ED, Office of The Under Secretary, Educator Sexual Misconduct: A Synthesis of Existing Literature 3, 51 (2004) [hereinafter Shakeshaft, Educator Sexual Misconduct].

14. *Id.* at 17–18 (citing Charol Shakeshaft, *Educator Sexual Abuse*, Hofstra Horizons, Spring 2003, at 10–13).

15. *Id.* at 22, 48.

16. *Id.* at 36.

17. *Id.* at 18 (emphasis added). We conducted an intensive literature search to find more recent statistics concerning educator sexual misconduct. Citations continue to point to Shakeshaft's 2003 and 2004 works.

18. *See, e.g.,* Ind. Code § 20-33-2-6 (West 2019); *see generally* Michael Katz, The History of Compulsory Education Laws (1975), https://files.eric.ed.gov/fulltext/ED119389.pdf.

C. At Colleges and Universities

In 2015, several studies found that large numbers of college and university students, mostly female, had experienced sexual assault by their peers. A *Washington Post*/Kaiser Family Foundation poll reported that 20% of women in college said that they had been violated.[19] The AAUW surveyed 150,000 students at 27 colleges and universities across the country and published that 27.2% of female college seniors recounted that they had experienced an unwanted sexual contact since entering college.[20]

A 2015 documentary film titled *The Hunting Ground* also explored this topic. The film retells the stories of university assault survivors, including the 2011 case of third-year Harvard Law student, Kamilah Willingham.[21] This film elevated the profile of sexual assault on college campuses. Critics challenged the film's claims but the filmmakers provided citations to the studies noted above in the film and on its website.[22]

A page from The Department of Justice (DOJ) archives, dated September 22, 2016, estimates an even higher percentage of assaults:

> A recent survey conducted by OVW [Office on Violence Against Women] and the Bureau of Justice Statistics found that an average of *one in four* undergraduate females experience sexual assault by the time they finish college. Younger students as well as lesbian, gay, bisexual, and transgender (LGBT) students experience the highest rates of sexual violence on campuses nationwide. It's clear that, as far as we've come in recognizing these problems, much still needs to be done to make campuses safe for all students.[23]

Sadly, most of the links at this site no longer work. Like a ghost town, this site is abandoned. This archived and abandoned material demonstrates that, even in the aftermath of #MeToo, campus sexual violence against women and some male students is not a priority for many people in power, including the Trump administration DOJ.

Fortunately, the U.S. Department of Health & Human Services Office on Women's Health (OWH) has an active website. According to OWH, one in five women experience sexual assault at college. Colleges are required to report sexual assault but many

19. Bianca DiJulio et al., *Survey of Current and Recent College Students on Sexual Assault*, KFF POLLING (Jun. 12, 2015), https://www.kff.org/other/poll-finding/survey-of-current-and-recent-college-students-on-sexual-assault/; Nick Anderson & Scott Clement, *1 in 5 College Women Say They Were Violated*, WASH. POST (June 12, 2015).

20. DAVID CANTOR ET AL., AAUW/WESTAT, REPORT ON THE AAU CAMPUS CLIMATE SURVEY ON SEXUAL ASSAULT AND SEXUAL MISCONDUCT xiv, 23, 65, 81 tbl.3-20 (Oct. 20, 2017).

21. THE HUNTING GROUND (CNNFilms 2015) (a documentary about sexual assault on college campuses, produced by Amy Zierling and, ironically, distributed by The Weinstein Company).

22. *The Facts of The Hunting Ground*, http://thehuntinggroundfilm.com/the-facts/.

23. *National Campus Safety Awareness Month: Changing The Institutional Response to Change the Statistics*, DEP'T OF JUSTICE, OFFICE OF VIOLENCE AGAINST WOMEN (Sept. 22, 2016), https://www.justice.gov/archives/ovw/blog/national-campus-safety-awareness-month-changing-institutional-response-change-statistics.

assault survivors do not report the attack to police.[24] Therefore, experts predict that sexual harassment (the more inclusive umbrella term for sex-based misconduct) on college campuses is vastly underreported. Later in this chapter, Section 6 reviews other issues regarding university and college campus sexual assault and harassment.

2. Title IX's Debut and Application

In 1964, Title VII did not cover discrimination against people employed at educational institutions.[25] Title VI, also enacted in 1964, banned race discrimination in federally funded private and public entities; however, it did not prohibit sex discrimination. Working with NOW and the Women's Equity Action League (WEAL) in 1971, Bernice R. Sandler began to lobby for legislation to fill the gap. Backed by Representatives Edith Green and Patsy Mink, and Senator Birch Bayh, Title IX became law in 1972 when President Richard Nixon signed the legislation.[26]

Title IX specifies, "No person in the United States shall, on the basis of sex, be excluded from participation in, be denied the benefits of, or be subjected to discrimination under any education program or activity receiving Federal financial assistance. . . ."[27] This language is simple and clear. It indicates that Title IX protects employees, students, and third parties since "no person" shall "be subjected to discrimination." However, the statute did not provide much more guidance regarding Title IX's scope and application.

During the late 1970s, several important court cases and events resolved key Title IX questions. In 1977, the NCAA (National Collegiate Athletic Association) unsuccessfully challenged the legality of Title IX.[28] Later, in *Cannon v. Univ. of Chicago* (1979), the Supreme Court ruled that a private right of action was available

---

24. *Sexual Assault on College Campuses*, U.S. Dep't of Health & Human Services Office on Women's Health (Sept. 2016), https://www.womenshealth.gov/relationships-and-safety/sexual-assault-and-rape/college-sexual-assault#8 (citing Krebs, C., Lindquist, C., et al., Bureau of Justice Statistics, U.S. Dep't of Justice, Campus Climate Survey Validation Study Final Technical Report (Jan. 2016), https://www.bjs.gov/content/pub/pdf/ccsvsftr.pdf)).

25. "This Title shall not apply to . . . an educational institution with respect to the employment of individuals to perform work connected with the educational activities of such institution." Civil Rights Act of 1964, Pub. L. No. 88-352, 78 Stat. 241; Kim Turner, *The Rights of School Employee Coaches Under Title VII and Title IX in Educational Athletic Programs*, 32 ABA J. Labor & Empl. L. 229, 231 (2017) (noting that Title VII was amended to include educational institutions several months before the passage of Title IX).

26. *See generally* Welch Suggs, A Place on the Team: The Triumph and Tragedy of Title IX (2005); Iram Valentin, *Title IX: A Brief History*, WEEA Equity Res. Ctr., Aug. 1997, http://www2.edc.org/WomensEquity/pdffiles/t9digest.pdf; *Overview of Title IX of The Education Amendments of 1972, 20 U.S.C.A. § 1681 et. seq.*, U.S. Dept. of Justice (Aug. 7, 2015), https://www.justice.gov/crt/overview-title-ix-education-amendments-1972-20-usc-1681-et-seq.

27. 20 U.S.C. § 1681 *et seq.* (2013).

28. *Title IX Legislative Chronology*, Women's Sports Foundation (Sept. 13, 2011), https://www.womenssportsfoundation.org/advocate/title-ix-issues/history-title-ix/history-title-ix/.

under Title IX.[29] The following year, in *Alexander v. Yale* (1980), the Second Circuit held that sexual harassment of a female student constituted actionable sex discrimination under Title IX.[30] Additionally, the ED was created and given oversight of Title IX.[31] Not until more than a decade later (and 20 years after Title IX's passage) did the Supreme Court recognize the availability of monetary damages in *Franklin v. Gwinnett Co. Pub. Sch.* (1992), a Title IX sexual harassment case.[32] Court action and ED guidance now confirm that Title IX applies to all federally funded educational institutions and all age groups. It covers peer-student conduct and conduct involving adults.

A. Defining Sexual Harassment under Title IX

Before 2017, the Equal Employment Opportunity Commission (EEOC) and the ED's OCR definitions of sexual harassment were quite similar. The Trump administration, however, narrowed the Title IX definition to create a new one by using 1999 phrasing from the Supreme Court Title IX decisions featured in this chapter. The OCR website now states, "Sexual harassment is unwelcome conduct of a sexual nature[,] . . . unwelcome sexual advances, requests for sexual favors, and other verbal, nonverbal, or physical conduct. . . ."[33] This first part tracks the Title VII definition and the former Title IX definition. Relatively recent adaptations of the definition clarify that sex-based harassment includes sexual violence and gender-based harassment.[34] However, the new definition continues, "Sex-based harassment creates a hostile environment if the conduct is sufficiently serious that it denies or limits a student's ability to participate in or benefit from the school's program."[35] This second aspect narrows the scope of what ED recognizes as sexual harassment. If the ED fails to label misconduct as sexual harassment until it actually limits or denies a student access to education, then interim remediation before the problem escalates is practically impossible.

The new OCR definition retains the requirement that the conduct be unwelcome. However, the unwelcomeness requirement is problematic when applied to children who, under state criminal law, do not have the legal capacity to consent to sex. States have passed strict liability statutory rape laws because adults believe that it is harmful for minors below a certain age (and that age varies by state) to engage in sex, particularly with adults.

---

29. 441 U.S. 677, 717 (1979); *see also* Turner, *supra* note 25, at 242.

30. Alexander v. Yale, 631 F.2d 178 (2d Cir. 1980).

31. *Overview and Mission Statement*, ED, https://www2.ed.gov/about/landing.jhtml.

32. 503 U.S. 60 (1992).

33. *Sex Discrimination: Frequently Asked Questions, What Is Sexual Harassment?*, OCR (last modified Sept. 25, 2018) [hereinafter *FAQ*], https://www2.ed.gov/about/offices/list/ocr/frontpage /faq/sex.html.

34. *Sex-Based Harassment, Issues* [hereinafter *Issues*], OCR (last modified Sept. 25, 2018), https://www2.ed.gov/about/offices/list/ocr/frontpage/pro-students/issues/sex-issue01.html.

35. *Id.*

The notion is that a more mature, powerful adult will take advantage of and manipulate a minor into a sexual encounter. Because of children's relative biological and psychological immaturity and their lack of wisdom and experience, adults have concluded that most children do not have the capacity to give informed, legally significant consent. Given this conclusion, can children "welcome" sexual conduct under civil law when they do not have legal capacity to consent to sex? For example, suppose that a physics teacher, Mr. Smith, flatters a teenage student with sexual attention? Is it still harassment, even though she "welcomed" the kisses and caresses?[36] Should it depend on her age? What if she is 12? What if she is 17? The answer is not simple or clear under Title IX or Title VII (if this student also works for Mr. Smith, say as a lab assistant).

In contrast, some clubs and youth-oriented associations use a broader definition than the one first developed by the EEOC for sexual harassment by adults at work.[37] For example, Rotarians do not require that conduct be "unwelcome." They also acknowledge sexual harassment as grooming behavior, behavior engaged in by a sexual predator intent on serious sexual exploitation.[38] Adult seduction and molestation of adolescents at work, school, or play are fundamentally different from adult abuse of other adults. These minor targets are not adults and, because of their developmental immaturity, do not function like adults.[39]

Professor Drobac has written extensively on the sexual harassment of teens, their developmental maturation, and criminal statutory rape laws. She explores how neuro-psychology, limited legal rights, economic dependence, political disenfranchisement, and other factors further contribute to thwart children and their parents who wish to address sexual harassment at school. She contends that even the definition of sexual harassment can limit statutory efforts to curb sex-based abuse

---

36. *See, e.g.,* Doe v. Willits Unified Sch. Dist., No. C-09-03655-JSW (DMR), 2010 WL 2524587 (N.D. Cal. Jun. 23, 2010) (involving a 38-year-old physics and math teacher who was charged with lewd acts, oral copulation, and sexual penetration of his 15-year-old student); *see also* Glenda Anderson, *Jail Term for Former Willits Teacher Who Had Sex with Student,* Press Democrat (Aug. 4, 2009) (Santa Rosa, Cal.).

37. *See, e.g.,* U.S. Figure Skating Board of Directors, *U.S. Figure Skating Harassment and Abuse Policy—Revised* 1 (Nov. 2013); *see also* Shakeshaft, Educator Sexual Misconduct, *supra* note 13, at 2 (referring to Canada's Ontario College of Teachers definition). The Ontario College of Teachers refers to child sexual abuse by teachers as "educator sexual misconduct" because that phrase emphasizes the conduct of the responsible adult. Its list of abusive conduct is not limited to unwelcome behaviors but includes, for example, "[a]ny activity directed toward establishing a sexual relationship such as sending intimate letters; engaging in sexualized dialogue in person, via the Internet, in writing or by phone; making suggestive comments; dating a student." *Id.* (paraphrasing Ontario College of Teachers, *Professional Advisory on Professional Misconduct Related to Sexual Abuse and Sexual Misconduct* 2–3 (2002)).

38. Rotary International, *Abuse and Harassment Prevention Training Manual and Leader's Guide* 2 (2002). The Rotarians define sexual harassment as "[s]exual advances, requests for sexual favors, or verbal or physical conduct of a sexual nature. In some cases, sexual harassment precedes sexual abuse and is a technique used by sexual predators to desensitize or groom their victims." *Id.* at 2.

39. *See, e.g.,* Surviving R. Kelly (Lifetime 2019).

and discrimination. She proposes another, more comprehensive definition of sexual harassment. She suggests: "*To sexually harass is to dominate another person physically or psychologically by annoying, frightening, demeaning, or taking unfair advantage of that person through the exploitation of human sexuality or gender stereotypes.*"[40] This definition condemns the conduct of Mr. Smith, noted above, and other savvy predators who would exploit minors, as well as adults.

B. State Statutory Rape Laws, Title IX, and the Unwelcomeness Requirement[41]

Professor Drobac proffers her revised definition of sexual harassment, in part to break with a tradition of criminal prosecution and definition of illicit sexual behavior. She explains that statutory rape laws historically defined "the age of consent" as a girl's age when her consent to sexual intercourse earned legal significance and insulated the male participant from criminal prosecution. During the nineteenth century, states raised the age of consent from 10 to as high as 21. As late as 1994, only 35 states had gender-neutral laws protecting both male and female minors. Now all states protect both sexes but they do not set the age of consent consistently. Additionally, many have different ages at which minors may consent to particular types of behavior with partners of varying ages and personal characteristics. In 2015, when Drobac last surveyed state laws, 38% of the states set the age of consent below the age of majority (typically 18) when minors become adults for most legal purposes. The lay term for underage sex with a minor is statutory rape. However, states use a variety of titles for sex crimes, including: debauching a minor, statutory sexual seduction, child molestation, corruption of a minor, minor sexual abuse, and others.[42] Thus, under state criminal law, Mr. Smith's student might legally consent to and welcome her teacher's attention, depending upon her age and the state in which they live.

Drobac also explains that not all state civil laws congruently track their respective criminal laws. In about a dozen states, including New York, state criminal laws give no legal effect to juvenile consent but state civil laws credit that same consent.[43] In other words, a minor's consent to sex is no defense for a criminal law defendant, but it may provide a complete defense for a civil suit respondent. In these states, it is not clear whether Mr. Smith would face civil liability under state law for the seduction of an "underage" student. California used to fall into this collection of states, where criminal and civil law approaches to juvenile consent yield polar opposite

---

40. Drobac, *supra* note 3, at 18.
41. *See generally* Drobac, *supra* note 3.
42. *Id.* at 80, 82. Drobac's Appendix Two contains a complete table of state ages of consent and related state sex crime laws. *Id.* at 243–62.
43. *Id.* at 111–12, 183–84.

outcomes. But in 2016, prompted in part by Drobac's research, California changed its civil law to remedy this conflict of laws.[44]

The treatment of a minor's consent and legal capacity to consent relates to the law's requirement that sexual harassment be unwelcome. If a minor cannot consent to sex, can that same minor welcome sex such that the initiator could avoid civil liability? Explanatory OCR literature once discussed the unwelcomeness requirement under Title IX. This guidance has been archived, presumably in anticipation of Trump administration revision of the OCR's implementation of Title IX. Whether this archived material is still applicable is not clear, but it may still be important given the Trump administration's retention of the unwelcomeness requirement. For example, in its own, now-archived, educational pamphlet, the OCR posed the question, "Must the sexual conduct be unwelcome?"[45] The answer reads, "Yes. Conduct is considered unwelcome if the student did not request or invite it and considered the conduct to be undesirable or offensive."[46] The OCR added, "The age of the student, the nature of the conduct and other relevant factors affect whether a student *was capable* of welcoming the sexual conduct. A student's submission to the conduct or failure to complain does not *always* mean that the conduct was welcome."[47] This answer suggests that some students may, under federal law, welcome the sexual advances of their teachers.

The current OCR guidance is no more helpful. It fails to explain the unwelcomeness requirement and also conflates the definition of sexual violence and sexual harassment. It declares, "Sexual violence, as OCR uses the term, refers to physical sexual acts perpetrated against a person's will or where a person is *incapable of giving consent*. A number of different acts fall into the category of sexual violence, including rape, sexual assault, sexual battery, sexual abuse, and sexual coercion."[48]

Does this mean that all sexual harassment against underage children is sexual violence? No, not necessarily. In the OCR's current answers to frequently asked questions, the OCR clarifies:

> Sexual violence is a form of sexual harassment. Sexual violence, as OCR uses the term, refers to physical sexual acts perpetrated against a person's will or where a person is incapable of giving consent (*e.g.*, due to the student's age or use of drugs or alcohol, or because an intellectual or other disability prevents the student from having the capacity to give consent).[49]

---

44. *Id.* at 238. California Civil Code Section 1708.5.5 specifies that "consent shall not be a defense in any civil action under Section 1708.5 [sexual battery] if the person who commits the sexual battery is an adult who is in a position of authority over the minor."

45. *Sexual Harassment: It's Not Academic* 5, OCR, U.S. Dep't of Educ. (Sept. 2008) [hereinafter *Not Academic*].

46. *Id.*

47. *Id.* (emphasis added).

48. *Issues, supra* note 34 (emphasis added).

49. *FAQ, supra* note 33 (emphasis added).

This passage suggests that a child's age matters but it does not clarify how it matters. Inconsistent state "age of consent" laws may direct whether a minor is capable of welcoming sexual advances by Mr. Smith or any other adult but the OCR does not specifically say so. The OCR has left the welcomeness question for courts to resolve. The next section provides some examples of how courts have approached this question.

C. Borrowing from Title VII and the Unwelcomeness Requirement Pertaining to Youth

In *Doe v. Oberweis Dairy* (2006), the U.S. Court of Appeals for the Seventh Circuit attempted to deal with the "welcomeness" issue in a Title VII employment case involving a teenager.[50] Doe was a 16-year-old ice cream scooper who, through her parents (because she did not have the legal capacity to sue on her own behalf), alleged sexual harassment by her 20-something supervisor. Despite the fact that the age of consent in Illinois is 17 and Doe was underage at the time, the *Oberweis* federal district court dismissed the case. It reasoned that Doe had not complained of the unwelcome conduct.[51] Additionally, it had found that the conduct was not severe or pervasive. The district court judge found that the alleged facts had not reached the threshold level for a federal case. The court declared, "Here, it is undisputed that through Plaintiff's approximately eight-month employment with Defendant, Nayman [the supervisor] only touched Plaintiff on 15 occasions."[52]

The Seventh Circuit court reversed this district court decision, emphasizing the age disparity between Nayman and Doe. The court found that, although Nayman had not committed forcible rape, he had committed statutory rape.[53] The court reasoned that statutory rape is a crime because minors may be unable to make responsible decisions about whether to engage in sex.

Acknowledging the unwelcomeness requirement under Title VII, the *Oberweis* appellate court devised a plan for dealing with adolescent consent to sex. Writing for the court, Judge Posner explained that the court wanted to avoid reclassifying sex that a state deems to be nonconsensual, as consensual. Posner avoided "intractable inquiries into maturity that legislatures invariably pretermit by basing entitlements to public benefits (right to vote, right to drive, right to drink, right to own a gun, etc.) on specified ages rather than on a standard of maturity."[54] He suggested that, in reference to Title VII, courts should defer to the state's age of consent,

---

50. 456 F.3d 704 (7th Cir. 2006).

51. Doe v. Oberweis Dairy, No. 03 C 4774, 2005 WL 782709, *6–7 (N.D. Ill. Apr. 6, 2005), *rev'd*, 456 F.3d 704 (7th Cir. 2006).

52. *Id*. at *7.

53. *Oberweis Dairy*, 456 F.3d at 713. The court cited to the Illinois statutory rape law. *Id.*; *see* 720 Ill. Comp. Stat Ann. 5/12–15(c), 16(d) (West 2011).

54. *Oberweis Dairy*, 456 F.3d at 713 (internal quotations omitted).

which reflects the judgment of average maturity for sexual matters. Judge Posner cautioned against an effort to determine whether a minor was able to welcome the sexual overtures of an adult. Thus, the court concluded that, for Title VII cases, the age of consent should determine whether a minor has to show unwelcomeness to prove sexual harassment.[55]

Judge Posner's plan, however, contains a serious flaw. Judge Posner acknowledged that the protection afforded to teenage employees by Title VII varies by state age-of-consent laws, but he mistakenly calculated that the variance would be limited to a "fairly narrow band."[56] In fact, those ages range for various conduct from 14 in states such as Texas to 18 in New York. Businesses such as Burger King and Starbucks, which operate nationally, must conform within a complex network of various ages of consent which, according to Judge Posner, should apply in civil sexual harassment cases. In states such as New York, where state criminal and civil law conflict, Posner's formula provides minimal guidance on how to treat adolescent nonresistance or consent for the purposes of civil liability in a Title VII sexual harassment case.

Notes and Discussion

1. **Definitions of Sexual Harassment under Title IX** Is the ED's definition of sexual harassment helpful or problematic? What about Professor Drobac's definition? How should schools or the ED define sexual harassment with respect to minors?

2. **The Unwelcomeness Requirement** With respect to the unwelcomeness requirement, is it appropriately applied in a Title IX case? Explain. Should it be applied to teenagers in Title VII cases? Why or why not? How will the OCR, or even an expert psychologist or psychiatrist, know whether the minor was "capable of welcoming the conduct" when it happened? Adults will be evaluating the teen's capacity months or years after-the-fact when the issue lands in the superintendent's office or in court. How will judges and jurors, who conceivably have no training in adolescent development, know if the teen or youth was mature and capable when the alleged incidents occurred? And, does this question not miss the point? Arguably, society outlaws sex with minors because they *do not* have the *legal capacity* to consent. Why would OCR presume juvenile legal capacity to welcome sex with an adult when many criminal laws deny that very same capacity?

3. Court Treatment of the Unwelcomeness Requirement Under Title IX

Courts that have addressed the unwelcomeness standard under Title IX have had difficulty transferring precedent from Title VII to sexual harassment of children at

---

55. *Id.*
56. *Id.* at 714.

school. The Title IX school environment is very different from a Title VII work environment. Moreover, as noted, the severity standard for Title IX liability is even more onerous than that for Title VII. Courts have taken differing approaches, depending in part on their own state laws. Consider a few of those approaches and determine if courts are implementing Title IX properly.

A. *Mary M. v. North Lawrence Community School Corp.* (1997)

In *Mary M. v. North Lawrence Community School Corp.*, the Seventh Circuit reviewed a Title IX claim by a 13-year-old eighth-grader, Diane M., against a 21-year-old cafeteria worker, Andrew Fields. The trial court had allowed evidence at trial concerning Diane's responses to Fields's sexual advances and whether Diane welcomed his attention. It had also permitted a jury instruction regarding whether Diane found the conduct unwelcome.[57] The instruction read:

> In order to find in favor of the Plaintiff, you must find first that the alleged sexual advances and/or abuses occurred, and if it did, that the advances and/or abuses were unwelcome by her. Conduct is unwelcome if Diane M. did not solicit or incite it, and if she regarded the conduct as undesirable or offensive. In determining whether the conduct was unwelcome, you should consider such things as Diane M.'s receptiveness to the alleged sexual advances and/or abuse in light of her words, acts and demeanor; her emotional predisposition, if any; the age disparity between her and Andrew Fields; any power disparity between them due to Diane M.'s status as a student and Andrew Field's status as a school employee.[58]

Despite the fact that this girl was 13, this instruction tracks the unwelcomeness requirement established for Title VII cases. However, consistent with the ED/OCR guidance, this instruction also acknowledges the potential power disparity between an adult school worker and a minor. Recall that the OCR directs administrators to consider "[t]he age of the student, the nature of the conduct and other relevant factors affect whether a student *was capable* of welcoming the sexual conduct."[59]

The *Mary M.* appellate court reversed the district court, ruling that a 13-year-old student, who was an "elementary school student" under state law, could not welcome the advances of an adult school employee. The *Mary M.* appellate court listed six reasons why sexual harassment at school deserves a special analysis. First, the court noted the greater ability of teachers and school officials to control behavior in the classroom, suggesting that "students look to their teachers for guidance as well as for protection." Second, the court explained that school harassment leaves

---

57. 131 F.3d 1220, 1220–23 (7th Cir. 1997).
58. *Id.* at 1224.
59. *Not Academic, supra* note 45, at 5 (emphasis added).

a "longer lasting impact on its younger victims and institutionalizes sexual harassment as accepted behavior." Third, the court reasoned that while adults can leave a hostile work environment, children can rarely leave school without legal penalty. Fourth, the court emphasized that children need a nondiscriminatory environment in which to maximize their intellectual growth. The court stated: "A sexually abusive environment inhibits, if not prevents, the harassed student from developing her full intellectual potential and receiving the most from the academic program." Fifth, the court admonished that schools act *in loco parentis* while employers do not. Finally, the court concluded that "employees are older and (presumably) know how to say no to unwelcome advances, while children may not even understand that they are being harassed."[60]

The third and sixth reasons reveal that the *Mary M.* appellate court assumed a workplace populated by adult workers. If one reviews the court's reasoning and substitutes adolescent workers for the adults, the court's analysis weakens, and the two environments (school and work) appear less distinct. For example, one might argue that sexual harassment at work leaves a lasting impact on young workers, just as it does on young students. Additionally, as noted previously, many youth may not understand they are experiencing sexual harassment. Arguably, the court should have distinguished two different targets of sexual harassment—children and adults—in addition to two different environments. In other words, the unwelcomeness requirement may be appropriate as applied to adults (although many other feminists would dispute this assertion) but not as applied to minors, whether they are at school or at work.

Like many similar tort cases, the *Mary M.* case also raised the relevance of the criminal law's definition of the age of consent. Rejecting the idea of setting criminal and civil law at odds, the *Mary M.* court concluded:

> An opposite holding would defeat the purposes of Title IX and make children claiming sexual discrimination under Title IX subject to intense scrutiny. . . . If welcomeness were properly an issue for the jury in cases involving elementary students, the very children bringing the suits would be subject to intense scrutiny regarding their responses to their alleged abusers. Trial transcripts would be replete with insinuations that a child dressed or acted in such a manner as to ask for the very conduct she or he is seeking to redress. . . . We decline to allow the inference that an elementary school student is presumed to have not consented to molestation by a twenty-one year old in a criminal case, but welcomed the same conduct in a civil case.[61]

In this passage, the court acknowledged the inconsistency of a failure to apply a criminal law presumption in a civil case. More importantly, the *Mary M.* court

---

60. *Id.* at 1226–27 (citing Davis v. Monroe County Bd. of Educ., 74 F.3d 1186, 1193 (11th Cir. 1996)).

61. *Id.* at 1227.

understood that once a child's consent comes into evidence, the child goes on trial. The *Mary M.* court eschewed the notion of putting a child on trial.[62] The *Mary M.* court "refused to transfer the onus on the child to prove that in fact she or he did not welcome the complained-of advances."[63]

B. *Chancellor v. Pottsgrove School District* (2007)

In *Chancellor v. Pottsgrove School District*, the court emphasized several themes noted in *Mary M.*, including the unique power dynamic between teachers and students and legal capacity. However, it emphasized the custodial role of school teachers and staff. It also explicitly disavowed the OCR guidance in resolving a case for a high school student.

Chancellor was a Title IX and § 1983 case involving a 17-year-old student, Jeanette Chancellor, and her 29-year-old band teacher, Christian Oakes.[64] In addition to noting her age, the Chancellor court added, "From an early age, Plaintiff [Jeanette] struggled with depression, anorexia, and bulimia."[65] Presumably, the court added this information to indicate Jeanette's fragile condition and to alert the reader that Jeanette may not have had the fortitude to resist an adult seducer. Jeanette and Oakes engaged in sex on more than 45 occasions during band camp, in the band room closet at school, in Oakes's car, and at a hotel during a band school trip. Allegedly, Oakes had sex with a second female student, A.P., in 2004. A.P.'s mother reported her suspicions to police officers who investigated and interviewed Jeanette. Police later arrested Oakes, who pled guilty to two counts of corruption of a minor. "Following Oakes's arrest, Plaintiff attempted suicide and was repeatedly hospitalized for psychiatric reasons, including major depressive disorder."[66] The *Chancellor* court ultimately ruled for the plaintiff, finding that Jeanette did not have the capacity to consent and that the principal's alleged conduct had been outrageous.[67]

The *Chancellor* court focused on "two helpful analogs in determining whether Plaintiff had the capacity to consent to sex with Oakes." First, the court identified the custodial nature of the adult-teen relationship. The court suggested that the adult "by virtue of his position of custody or authority over" the minor renders her "incapable of offering her effective consent." To support this argument, the court offered an analogy to "a prisoner [who] lacks the capacity to consent to sex with her prison guard."[68]

---

62. *Compare id., with* Doe by Roe v. Orangeburg County Sch., 518 S.E.2d 259, 261 (S.C. 1999). Ironically, the *Orangeburg* court took its guidance from *Barnes v. Barnes*, 603 N.E.2d 1337 (Ind. 1992), an Indiana case. The *Mary M.* case also originated in Indiana.
63. *Mary M.*, 131 F.3d at 1227.
64. 501 F. Supp. 2d 695 (E.D. Pa. 2007).
65. *Id.* at 699.
66. *Id.*
67. *Id.* at 695.
68. *Id.* at 705 (footnote omitted).

"The second helpful analog is the premise of statutory rape (or statutory sexual assault) and ages of consent. A minor under a certain age is legally unable to offer her consent . . . even if the sexual conduct was free of coercion or duress."[69] The *Chancellor* court announced:

> Pottsgrove [the school], however, conflates the question of whether Plaintiff "consented" to Oakes's sexual advances with the question of whether Plaintiff (a high school student in Oakes's class) had the legal capacity to consent to the sex. If Plaintiff lacked the capacity to consent, of course, she did not have the capacity to "welcome" Oakes's sexual advances.[70]

The *Chancellor* court continued:

> [M]any states have "corruption of minors" laws, [prohibiting] sexual conduct with sixteen- and seventeen-year-olds — minors who are above the age of consent for statutory rape purposes. . . . In other words, at least in the corruption of minors context, a minor lacks the capacity to consent to sex with an adult.[71]

However, in finding for Jeanette, the *Chancellor* court rejected guidance from the ED's OCR. The *Chancellor* court acknowledged that it took a stance different from the one endorsed by the OCR. *Chancellor* criticized the OCR's guidance for three reasons. First, *Chancellor* accused ED of "conflat[ing] consent with the capacity to consent," the same error committed by the Pottsgrove School District. The *Chancellor* court emphasized that *actual* consent is not the same as *legal* consent and may not signal legal capacity to consent. Second, the *Chancellor* court stressed that OCR imported the "totality of the circumstances" test from Title VII jurisprudence. The *Chancellor* court reasoned that *capacity* to welcome a supervisor's conduct or advance are not part of the Title VII inquiry. Rather the question under Title VII centers on whether the target actually welcomed the conduct. Therefore, Title VII does not work for an evaluation focused on juveniles.

Finally, the *Chancellor* court rejected the OCR guidance as unworkable, practically speaking. The court explained that, under the OCR's guidance, a high school teacher might violate Title IX with one student but not with another in the same class because "they [the students] are of a different age or mental capacity or the sex occurs under slightly different circumstances. . . . In this situation, a murky line is worse than a bright one."[72] Additional interpretive legal exchanges between a court and the ED/OCR are discussed in Section 6 of this chapter.

---

69. *Id.* at 706.
70. *Id.* at 705 (footnote omitted).
71. *Id.* at 706 (citations omitted).
72. *Id.* at 708.

C. *Benefield v. Board of Trustees of the University of Alabama* (2002)

Another complicating aspect of the unwelcomeness requirement under Title IX is that it applies to college undergraduates and university graduate students, as well as to grammar and high school students. These are dramatically different populations. The application of the same standards and guidelines for young children and maturing college students challenges courts. For example, in *Benefield* the Alabama federal trial court considered whether a 15-year-old college student could sue her university under Title IX for sexual harassment by classmates. While this was not a case of adult-student harassment, it serves to highlight problems regarding the effect of the unwelcomeness requirement.

The *Benefield* court ultimately ruled that "[t]o constitute sexual harassment, the behavior in question must be unwelcome."[73] Because the court conflated acquiescence and consent, and did not consider capacity at all, it ruled that Benefield's consent constituted a complete defense. The *Benefield* court distinguished college students from elementary and secondary school students and rejected Benefield's claim, holding that the university did not stand *in loco parentis*.[74]

Black's Law Dictionary defines *in loco parentis* to mean "[a]cting as a temporary guardian or caretaker of a child, taking on all or some of the responsibilities of a parent."[75] When an adult acts *in loco parentis*, typically the law will impose upon that person a higher duty of care for the child supervised. Ironically, when defining the phrase, Black's Dictionary refers to "[s]upervision of a young adult by an administrative body such as a university."[76] Possibly, *because* Benefield sued as a college student, the court interpreted Title IX more strictly.

Notes and Discussion

1. Comparing Approaches Which court took the best approach — *Mary M.*, *Chancellor*, or *Benefield*? Explain. According to these cases, why does school sexual harassment merit specialized consideration?

2. Variations on *Benefield* Did the court correctly decide *Benefield*? If Benefield had been an older student, an adult, her legal capacity would not have been an issue. In that case, and if still dealing with a peer, she might have had the power and ability to establish that the behavior was unwelcome. However, what if Benefield's harasser had been a professor or someone on her Ph.D. dissertation defense panel? Would it have been reasonable to assume that she possessed the capacity to consent? Would the law deny the autonomy of an adult student if it rejected her consent in this context? Or should society feel comfortable in prohibiting teacher-student liaisons

---

73. 214 F. Supp. 2d 1212, 1215, 1220 (N.D. Ala. 2002).
74. *Id.* at 1218, 1220.
75. *In loco parentis*, BLACK'S LAW DICTIONARY (10th ed. 2014).
76. *Id.*

between "consenting adults." These are tough questions that courts deal with in the context of Title IX.

4. Supreme Court Analysis of Sexual Harassment Under Title IX

Title IX's statutory language, the unique circumstances of an academic environment, the particular dynamics of the adult-student and peer relationships, and other complicating factors led to Supreme Court review of Title IX's application. While the Supreme Court has not opined on the unwelcomeness requirement in the context of Title IX, it has established the proper standard for review of misconduct. To the question of whether a school administrator must treat each allegation of inappropriate behavior as a legal matter, the answer is probably "no." The Court also declined to adopt Title VII's severe or pervasive standard. Instead, Supreme Court cases in the late 1990s confirmed a severe *and* pervasive standard under Title IX. Consider whether the Supreme Court's treatment of school sexual harassment is consistent with Title IX's prohibitions and whether it will lead to equal access to educational benefits.

A. Supreme Court Analysis of Teacher-Student Harassment under Title IX

Gebser v. Lago Vista Independent School District

524 U.S. 274 (1998)

Justice O'CONNER, delivered the opinion of the Court.

The question in this case is when a school district may be held liable in damages in an implied right of action under Title IX of the Education Amendments of 1972, . . . 20 U.S.C. § 1681 *et seq.* (Title IX), for the sexual harassment of a student by one of the district's teachers. We conclude that damages may not be recovered in those circumstances unless an official of the school district, who at a minimum has authority to institute corrective measures on the district's behalf, has actual notice of, and is deliberately indifferent to, the teacher's misconduct.

I

In the spring of 1991, when petitioner Alida Star Gebser was an eighth-grade student at a middle school in respondent Lago Vista Independent School District (Lago Vista), she joined a high school book discussion group led by Frank Waldrop, a teacher at Lago Vista's high school. Lago Vista received federal funds at all pertinent times. During the book discussion sessions, Waldrop often made sexually suggestive comments to the students. Gebser entered high school in the fall and was assigned to classes taught by Waldrop in both semesters. Waldrop continued to make inappropriate remarks to the students, and he began to direct more of his suggestive comments toward Gebser, including during the substantial amount of time that the two were alone in his classroom. He initiated sexual contact with Gebser in the spring, when, while visiting her home ostensibly to give her a book, he kissed and fondled her. The two had sexual intercourse on a number of occasions during the remainder of the school year. Their relationship continued through the summer and into the following school year, and they often had intercourse during class time, although never on school property.

Gebser did not report the relationship to school officials, testifying that while she realized Waldrop's conduct was improper, she was uncertain how to react and she wanted to continue having him as a teacher. In October 1992, the parents of two other students complained to the high school principal about Waldrop's comments in class. The principal arranged a meeting, at which, according to the principal, Waldrop indicated that he did not believe he had made offensive remarks but apologized to the parents and said it would not happen again. The principal also advised Waldrop to be careful about his classroom comments and told the school guidance counselor about the meeting, but he did not report the parents' complaint to Lago Vista's superintendent, who was the district's Title IX coordinator. A couple of months later, in January 1993, a police officer discovered Waldrop and Gebser engaging in sexual intercourse and arrested Waldrop. Lago Vista terminated his employment, and subsequently, the Texas Education Agency revoked his teaching license. During this time, the district had not promulgated or distributed an official grievance procedure for lodging sexual harassment complaints; nor had it issued a formal anti-harassment policy.

... [The Court reviewed how the district court denied liability, finding no discriminatory school policy. Additionally, the district court held that the school had only one complaint concerning Waldrop, not enough to establish actual or constructive notice that Waldrop was sexually involved with a student. The Fifth Circuit declined to impose strict liability for a teacher's sexual harassment of a student. It agreed that there was insufficient evidence to find that the school should have known about Waldrof's liaison with Gebser. Finally, it rejected common law vicarious liability, to avoid the creation of liability in every case of teacher-student harassment.] The Fifth Circuit's analysis represents one of the varying approaches adopted by the Courts of Appeals in assessing a school district's liability under Title IX for a teacher's sexual harassment of a student. ...

II

Title IX provides in pertinent part: "No person ... shall, on the basis of sex, be excluded from participation in, be denied the benefits of, or be subjected to discrimination under any education program or activity receiving Federal financial assistance." 20 U.S.C. § 1681(a). The express statutory means of enforcement is administrative: The statute directs federal agencies that distribute education funding to establish requirements to effectuate the nondiscrimination mandate, and permits the agencies to enforce those requirements through "any ... means authorized by law," including ultimately the termination of federal funding. [The Court reaffirmed that Title IX is enforceable through an implied private right of action for monetary and other damages.]

. . . .

Whether educational institutions can be said to violate Title IX based solely on principles of *respondeat superior* or constructive notice was not resolved by [*Franklin v. Gwinnett County Public Schools*, 503 U.S. 60 (1992)]'s citation of *Meritor*. . . . *Meritor*'s rationale for concluding that agency principles guide the liability inquiry under Title VII rests on an aspect of that statute not found in Title IX: Title VII, in which the prohibition against employment discrimination runs against "an employer," 42 U.S.C. § 2000e-2(a), explicitly defines "employer" to include "any agent," § 2000e(b). Title IX contains no comparable reference to an educational institution's "agents," and so does not expressly call for application of agency principles.

In this case, moreover, petitioners seek not just to establish a Title IX violation but to recover *damages* based on theories of *respondeat superior* and constructive notice. It is that aspect of their action, in our view, that is most critical to resolving the case. Unlike Title IX, Title VII contains an express cause of action, § 2000e-5(f), and specifically provides for relief in the form of monetary damages, § 1981a. Congress therefore has directly addressed the subject of damages relief under Title VII and has set out the particular situations in which damages are available as well as the maximum amounts recoverable. § 1981a(b). With respect to Title IX, however, the private right of action is judicially implied, see [*Cannon v. University of Chicago*, 441 U.S. 677 , 717 (1979)], and there is thus no legislative expression of the scope of available remedies, including when it is appropriate to award monetary damages. . . .

III

Because the private right of action under Title IX is judicially implied, we have a measure of latitude to shape a sensible remedial scheme that best comports with the statute. . . . To guide the analysis, we generally examine the relevant statute to ensure that we do not fashion the scope of an implied right in a manner at odds with the statutory structure and purpose.

Those considerations, we think, are pertinent not only to the scope of the implied right, but also to the scope of the available remedies. We suggested as much in *Franklin*, where we recognized "the general rule that all appropriate relief is available in an action brought to vindicate a federal right," but indicated that the rule must be reconciled with congressional purpose. . . .

Applying those principles here, we conclude that it would "frustrate the purposes" of Title IX to permit a damages recovery against a school district for a teacher's sexual harassment of a student based on principles of *respondeat superior* or constructive notice, *i.e.*, without actual notice to a school district official. Because Congress did not expressly create a private right of action under Title IX, the statutory text does not shed light on Congress' intent with respect to the scope of available remedies.

Instead, "we attempt to infer how the [1972] Congress would have addressed the issue had the . . . action been included as an express provision in the" statute.

As a general matter, it does not appear that Congress contemplated unlimited recovery in damages against a funding recipient where the recipient is unaware of discrimination in its programs. When Title IX was enacted in 1972, the principal civil rights statutes containing an express right of action did not provide for recovery of monetary damages at all, instead allowing only injunctive and equitable relief. It was not until 1991 that Congress made damages available under Title VII, and even then, Congress carefully limited the amount recoverable in any individual case, calibrating the maximum recovery to the size of the employer. Adopting petitioners' position would amount, then, to allowing unlimited recovery of damages under Title IX where Congress has not spoken on the subject of either the right or the remedy, and in the face of evidence that when Congress expressly considered both in Title VII it restricted the amount of damages available.

Congress enacted Title IX in 1972 with two principal objectives in mind: "[T]o avoid the use of federal resources to support discriminatory practices" and "to provide individual citizens effective protection against those practices." The statute was modeled after Title VI of the Civil Rights Act of 1964, which is parallel to Title IX except that it prohibits race discrimination, not sex discrimination, and applies in all programs receiving federal funds, not only in education programs. See 42 U.S.C. § 2000d *et seq.* The two statutes operate in the same manner, conditioning an offer of federal funding on a promise by the recipient not to discriminate, in what amounts essentially to a contract between the Government and the recipient of funds.

That contractual framework distinguishes Title IX from Title VII, which is framed in terms not of a condition but of an outright prohibition. Title VII applies to all employers without regard to federal funding and aims broadly to "eradicat[e] discrimination throughout the economy." Title VII, moreover, seeks to "make persons whole for injuries suffered through past discrimination." Thus, whereas Title VII aims centrally to compensate victims of discrimination, Title IX focuses more on "protecting" individuals from discriminatory practices carried out by recipients of federal funds. That might explain why, when the Court first recognized the implied right under Title IX in *Cannon*, the opinion referred to injunctive or equitable relief in a private action, but not to a damages remedy.

Title IX's contractual nature has implications for our construction of the scope of available remedies. When Congress attaches conditions to the award of federal funds under its spending power, U.S. Const., Art. I, § 8, cl. 1, as it has in Title IX and Title VI, we examine closely the propriety of private actions holding the recipient liable in monetary damages for noncompliance with the condition. Our central concern in that regard is with ensuring that "the receiving entity of federal funds [has] notice that it will be liable for a monetary award." . . . If a school district's liability for a teacher's sexual harassment rests on principles of constructive notice or *respondeat superior,* it will likewise be the case that the recipient of funds was unaware of the discrimination. It is sensible to assume that Congress did not envision a recipient's liability in damages in that situation.

Most significantly, Title IX contains important clues that Congress did not intend to allow recovery in damages where liability rests solely on principles of vicarious liability or constructive notice. Title IX's express means of enforcement — by administrative agencies — operates on an assumption of actual notice to officials of the funding recipient. The statute entitles agencies who disburse education funding to enforce their rules implementing the nondiscrimination mandate through proceedings to suspend or terminate funding or through "other means authorized by law." Significantly, however, an agency may not initiate enforcement proceedings until it "has advised the appropriate person or persons of the failure to comply with the requirement and has determined that compliance cannot be secured by voluntary means." The administrative regulations implement that obligation, requiring resolution of compliance issues "by informal means whenever possible," 34 CFR § 100.7(d) (1997), and prohibiting commencement of enforcement proceedings until the agency has determined that voluntary compliance is unobtainable and "the recipient . . . has been notified of its failure to comply and of the action to be taken to effect compliance," § 100.8(d); see § 100.8(c).

. . . .

Presumably, a central purpose of requiring notice of the violation "to the appropriate person" and an opportunity for voluntary compliance before administrative enforcement proceedings can commence is to avoid diverting education funding from beneficial uses where a recipient was unaware of discrimination in its programs and is willing to institute prompt corrective measures. The scope of private damages relief proposed by petitioners is at odds with that basic objective. When a teacher's sexual harassment is imputed to a school district or when a school district is deemed to have "constructively" known of the teacher's harassment, by assumption the district had no actual knowledge of the teacher's conduct. Nor, of course, did the district have an opportunity to take action to end the harassment or to limit further harassment.

It would be unsound, we think, for a statute's *express* system of enforcement to require notice to the recipient and an opportunity to come into voluntary compliance while a judicially *implied* system of enforcement permits substantial liability without regard to the recipient's knowledge or its corrective actions upon receiving notice. Moreover, an award of damages in a particular case might well exceed a recipient's level of federal funding. See Tr. of Oral Arg. 35 (Lago Vista's federal funding for 1992–1993 was roughly $120,000). Where a statute's express enforcement scheme hinges its most severe sanction on notice and unsuccessful efforts to obtain compliance, we cannot attribute to Congress the intention to have implied an enforcement scheme that allows imposition of greater liability without comparable conditions.

IV

Because the express remedial scheme under Title IX is predicated upon notice to an "appropriate person" and an opportunity to rectify any violation, 20 U.S.C. § 1682, we conclude, in the absence of further direction from Congress, that the implied damages remedy should be fashioned along the same lines. An "appropriate person" under § 1682 is, at a minimum, an official of the recipient entity with authority to take corrective action to end the discrimination. Consequently, in cases like this one that do not involve official policy of the recipient entity, we hold that a damages remedy will not lie under Title IX unless an official who at a minimum has authority to address the alleged discrimination and to institute corrective measures on the recipient's behalf has actual knowledge of discrimination in the recipient's programs and fails adequately to respond.

We think, moreover, that the response must amount to deliberate indifference to discrimination. The administrative enforcement scheme presupposes that an official who is advised of a Title IX violation refuses to take action to bring the recipient into compliance. The premise, in other words, is an official decision by the recipient not to remedy the violation. That framework finds a rough parallel in the standard of deliberate indifference. Under a lower standard, there would be a risk that the recipient would be liable in damages not for its own official decision but instead for its employees' independent actions. Comparable considerations led to our adoption of a deliberate indifference standard for claims under § 1983 alleging that a municipality's actions in failing to prevent a deprivation of federal rights was the cause of the violation.

Applying the framework to this case is fairly straightforward, as petitioners do not contend they can prevail under an actual notice standard. The only official alleged to have had information about Waldrop's misconduct is the high school principal. That information, however, consisted of a complaint from parents of other students charging only that Waldrop had made inappropriate comments during class, which was plainly insufficient to alert the principal to the possibility that Waldrop was involved in a sexual relationship with a student. Lago Vista, moreover, terminated Waldrop's employment upon learning of his relationship with Gebser. Justice STE-VENS points out in his dissenting opinion that Waldrop of course had knowledge of his own actions. Where a school district's liability rests on actual notice principles, however, the knowledge of the wrongdoer himself is not pertinent to the analysis.

Petitioners focus primarily on Lago Vista's asserted failure to promulgate and publicize an effective policy and grievance procedure for sexual harassment claims. They point to Department of Education regulations requiring each funding recipient to "adopt and publish grievance procedures providing for prompt and equitable resolution" of discrimination complaints and to notify students and others that "it does not discriminate on the basis of sex in the educational programs or activities which it operates." Lago Vista's alleged failure to comply with the regulations, however, does not establish the requisite actual notice and deliberate indifference. And in any event, the failure to promulgate a grievance procedure does not itself constitute "discrimination" under Title IX. Of course, the Department of Education could enforce the requirement administratively: Agencies generally have authority to promulgate and enforce requirements that effectuate the statute's non-discrimination mandate even if those requirements do not purport to represent a definition of discrimination under the statute. We have never held, however, that the implied private right of action under Title IX allows recovery in damages for violation of those sorts of administrative requirements.

V

The number of reported cases involving sexual harassment of students in schools confirms that harassment unfortunately is an all too common aspect of the educational experience. No one questions that a student suffers extraordinary harm when subjected to sexual harassment and abuse by a teacher, and that the teacher's conduct is reprehensible and undermines the basic purposes of the educational system. The issue in this case, however, is whether the independent misconduct of a teacher is attributable to the school district that employs him under a specific federal statute designed primarily to prevent recipients of federal financial assistance from using the funds in a discriminatory manner. Our decision does not affect any right of recovery that an individual may have against a school district as a matter of state law or against the teacher in his individual capacity under state law or under 42 U.S.C. § 1983. Until Congress speaks directly on the subject, however, we will not hold a school district liable in damages under Title IX for a teacher's sexual harassment of a student absent actual notice and deliberate indifference. We therefore affirm the judgment of the Court of Appeals.

It is so ordered.

Justice STEVENS, with whom Justice SOUTER, Justice GINSBURG, and Justice BREYER join, dissenting.

...As a basis for its decision, the majority relies heavily on the notion that because the private cause of action under Title IX is "judicially implied," the Court has "a measure of latitude" to use its own judgment in shaping a remedial scheme. This assertion of lawmaking authority is not faithful either to our precedents or to our duty to interpret, rather than to revise, congressional commands. Moreover, the majority's policy judgment about the appropriate remedy in this case thwarts the purposes of Title IX.

. . . .

II

We have already noted that the text of Title IX should be accorded "'a sweep as broad as its language.'" That sweep is broad indeed. "No person . . . shall, on the basis of sex, . . . be subjected to discrimination under any education program or activity receiving Federal financial assistance. . . ." As Judge Rovner has correctly observed, the use of passive verbs in Title IX, focusing on the victim of the discrimination rather than the particular wrongdoer, gives this statute broader coverage than Title VII.

. . . .

The Court nevertheless holds that the law does not provide a damages remedy for the Title IX violation alleged in this case because no official of the school district with "authority to institute corrective measures on the district's behalf" had actual notice of Waldrop's misconduct. That holding is at odds with settled principles of agency law, under which the district is responsible for Waldrop's misconduct because "he was aided in accomplishing the tort by the existence of the agency relation." This case presents a paradigmatic example of a tort that was made possible, that was effected, and that was repeated over a prolonged period because of the powerful influence that Waldrop had over Gebser by reason of the authority that his employer, the school district, had delegated to him. As a secondary school teacher, Waldrop exercised even greater authority and control over his students than employers and supervisors exercise over their employees. His gross misuse of that authority allowed him to abuse his young student's trust.

Reliance on the principle set out in §219(2)(b) of the Restatement comports with the relevant agency's interpretation of Title IX. The United States Department of Education, through its Office for Civil Rights, recently issued a policy "Guidance" stating that a school district is liable under Title IX if one of its teachers "was aided in carrying out the sexual harassment of students by his or her position of authority with the institution." As the agency charged with administering and enforcing Title IX, the Department of Education has a special interest in ensuring that federal funds are not used in contravention of Title IX's mandate. It is therefore significant that the Department's interpretation of the statute wholly supports the conclusion that respondent is liable in damages for Waldrop's sexual abuse of his student, which was made possible only by Waldrop's affirmative misuse of his authority as her teacher.

The reason why the common law imposes liability on the principal in such circumstances is the same as the reason why Congress included the prohibition against discrimination on the basis of sex in Title IX: to induce school boards to adopt and enforce practices that will minimize the danger that vulnerable students will be exposed to such odious behavior. The rule that the Court has crafted creates the opposite incentive. As long as school boards can insulate themselves from knowledge about this sort of conduct, they can claim immunity from damages liability. Indeed, the rule that the Court adopts would preclude a damages remedy even if every teacher at the school knew about the harassment but did not have "authority to institute corrective measures on the district's behalf." . . .

III

The Court advances several reasons why it would "frustrate the purposes" of Title IX to allow recovery against a school district that does not have actual notice of a teacher's sexual harassment of a student. . . .

. . . .

The majority's inappropriate reliance on Title IX's administrative enforcement scheme to limit the availability of a damages remedy leads the Court to require not only actual knowledge on the part of "an official who at a minimum has authority to address the alleged discrimination and to institute corrective measures on the recipient's behalf," but also that official's "refus[al] to take action," or "deliberate indifference" toward the harassment. Presumably, few Title IX plaintiffs who have been victims of intentional discrimination will be able to recover damages under this exceedingly high standard. The Court fails to recognize that its holding will virtually "render inutile causes of action authorized by Congress through a decision that *no* remedy is available."

IV

We are not presented with any question concerning the affirmative defenses that might eliminate or mitigate the recovery of damages for a Title IX violation. . . . A rule providing an affirmative defense for districts that adopt and publish such policies pursuant to the regulations would not likely be helpful to respondent, however, because it is not at all clear whether respondent adopted any such policy, and there is no evidence that such a policy was made available to students, as required by regulation.

A theme that seems to underlie the Court's opinion is a concern that holding a school district liable in damages might deprive it of the benefit of the federal subsidy—that the damages remedy is somehow more onerous than a possible termination of the federal grant. It is possible, of course, that in some cases the recoverable damages, in either a Title IX action or a state-law tort action, would exceed the amount of a federal grant. That is surely not relevant to the question whether the school district or the injured student should bear the risk of harm—a risk against which the district, but not the student, can insure. It is not clear to me why the well-settled rules of law that impose responsibility on the principal for the misconduct of its agents should not apply in this case. As a matter of policy, the Court ranks protection of the school district's purse above the protection of immature high school students that those rules would provide. Because those students are members of the class for whose special benefit Congress enacted Title IX, that policy choice is not faithful to the intent of the policymaking branch of our Government.

I respectfully dissent.

Justice GINSBURG, with whom Justice SOUTER and Justice BREYER join, dissenting.

Justice STEVENS' [dissenting] opinion focuses on the standard of school district liability for teacher-on-student harassment in secondary schools. I join that opinion, which reserves the question whether a district should be relieved from damages liability if it has in place, and effectively publicizes and enforces, a policy to curtail and redress injuries caused by sexual harassment. I think it appropriate to answer that question for these reasons: (1) the dimensions of a claim are determined not only by the plaintiff's allegations, but by the allowable defenses; (2) this Court's pathmarkers are needed to afford guidance to lower courts and school officials responsible for the implementation of Title IX.

In line with the tort law doctrine of avoidable consequences, I would recognize as an affirmative defense to a Title IX charge of sexual harassment, an effective policy for reporting and redressing such misconduct. School districts subject to Title IX's governance have been instructed by the Secretary of Education to install procedures for "prompt and equitable resolution" of complaints, 34 CFR § 106.8(b) (1997), and the Department of Education's Office for Civil Rights has detailed elements of an effective grievance process, with specific reference to sexual harassment, 62 Fed. Reg. 12034, 12044–12045 (1997).

The burden would be the school district's to show that its internal remedies were adequately publicized and likely would have provided redress without exposing the complainant to undue risk, effort, or expense. Under such a regime, to the extent that a plaintiff unreasonably failed to avail herself of the school district's preventive and remedial measures, and consequently suffered avoidable harm, she would not qualify for Title IX relief.

Notes and Discussion

1. Facts Did the principal act correctly in response to the parents' complaints? Would the principal's reporting the incidents to the Title IX coordinator have made a difference? Explain. In footnote 17, Justice Stevens noted, "The district's superintendent stated that she did not remember if any handbook alerting students to grievance procedures was disseminated to students." He added, "Gebser herself stated: 'If I had known at the beginning what I was supposed to do when a teacher starts making sexual advances towards me, I probably would have reported it. I was bewildered and terrified and I had no idea where to go from where I was.'" How likely is it that Gebser would have reported Waldrop?

Neither the Supreme Court nor the Fifth Circuit court opinions mention Waldrop's age. However, a journalist reported that Waldrop was a 50-year-old teacher at Lago Vista's high school.[77] (To put Waldrop's age in context, note that he was six years younger than Justices Scalia and Kennedy, who dissented, and six years older than Justice Thomas, who joined Justices O'Connor and Rehnquist in the majority opinion.)[78] The Fifth Circuit opinion relates that Waldrop's wife was Gebser's eighth grade honors class teacher and referred Gebser, then 13, to her husband's book group. They believed Gebser needed more academic challenge.[79]

The Supreme Court's failure to mention Waldrop's age in their opinion as they recounted Gebser's age is surprising. Why might it have avoided this fact? The Fifth Circuit court conveys the facts this way:

---

77. Mary Deibel, *Court Sides with Schools on Abuse Harassment Victims Can't Sue Institution Unless Incident Report Ignored*, Denver Rocky Mountain News, June 23, 1998, at 2A.

78. Richard E. Berg-Andersson, *United States Supreme Court Justices*, TheGreenPapers.com (updated Oct. 6, 2018) (listing birth dates of the justices).

79. Doe v. Lago Vista Indep. Sch. Dist., 106 F.3d 1223 1224 (5th Cir. 1997).

Waldrop initiated sexual contact with her at her home in the spring of 1992. Knowing she would be alone, he visited under the pretext of returning a book and proceeded to fondle her breasts and unzip her pants. During the summer, Waldrop had sex on a regular basis with Doe [Gebser], who was by then fifteen years old. None of the encounters took place on school property. The relationship ended in January of 1993, when a Lago Vista police officer happened to discover Waldrop and Doe having sex.[80]

Neither the Supreme Court nor the Fifth Circuit court opinion details that "Waldrop was given a ten-year suspended jail sentence after pleading no-contest to attempted sexual assault."[81] Is a suspended sentence for *attempted* sexual assault surprising? Or was it an appropriate outcome for this case? Note that the age of consent in Texas is 17. A criminal court handed down this sentence after police found Waldrop naked in the woods with Gebser.[82] Concerning civil liability, Texas abandoned its promiscuity defense (suggesting the complainant's promiscuity should absolve the accused of any liability) to statutory rape only in 1993.[83] The year 1993 was the same year that police found Waldrop naked with Gebser in the woods. While these details may not be critical to an analysis of Title IX, they explain sociocultural conditions at the time and add to a complete understanding of the case brought before the federal civil courts.

2. Agency Liability Would the application of agency liability "result in school district liability in essentially every case of teacher-student harassment"? Does the lack of a reference to an agent in Title IX necessarily preclude the imposition of agency liability? In his dissent, Justice Stevens explained, "The United States Department of Education, through its Office for Civil Rights, recently issued a policy 'Guidance' stating that a school district is liable under Title IX if one of its teachers 'was aided in carrying out the sexual harassment of students by his or her position of authority with the institution.'" Was the majority justified in rejecting that contemporary OCR Guidance? Did the Court engage in a "rather dramatic departure from settled law" on agency liability, as Justice Stevens contended? What were the majority's reasons for rejecting agency liability? Was the majority correct?

3. Damages The Court concluded that Congress intended limited damages under Title IX. How did the Court reach that conclusion? In contrast, isn't it possible that Congress intended any reasonable measure of damages that would end discrimination in education? Did the Court usurp Congress's authority by legislating a damages provision where there was none? Was the concern over excessive damage awards a significant, if not the primary, motivation in this case? Did the Court rank "protection of the school district's purse above the protection of immature high school students. . . ." as Justice Stevens suggested in his dissent?

---

80. *Id.* at 1224–25.
81. Deibel, *supra* note 77.
82. *Id.*
83. Hernandez v. State, 861 S.W.2d 908 (Tex. 1993).

4. Legislative Intent The Court suggested in *Gebser* that "Title VII aims centrally to compensate victims of discrimination, [whereas] Title IX focuses more on 'protecting' individuals from discriminatory practices carried out by recipients of federal funds." Is this statement consistent with other assertions by the Court regarding Title VII's purpose?

Recall that in *Faragher*, decided just days after *Gebser*, the Court found that Title VII's "'primary objective,' like that of any statute meant to influence primary conduct, is not to provide redress but to avoid harm." Is the Court confused or confusing (or neither)? Does the threat of damages liability provide an incentive for actors to avoid harm? Is there a public policy argument for providing more protection for young students under Title IX than for adult employees under Title VII rather than less protection as the court did in *Gebser*? Professor Drobac argues that the unique effects of sexual abuse on minors justifies stricter legislative sanctions.[84]

5. Deliberate Indifference Does the express language of the Title IX remedial scheme mandate a deliberate indifference standard? What, if anything, justifies the imposition of this standard? Professor William Kaplin concluded:

> In effect, the Court has insisted on a standard of actual notice, while at the same time tacitly admitting that the school district had not provided students directions or channels for giving that notice, and has insisted on a standard of deliberate indifference, while at the same time declining to consider lack of a harassment policy and grievance procedure as evidence of that indifference.[85]

Is Kaplin's summation accurate or not?

6. Actual Notice The *Gebser* Court emphasized the need for actual notice before Title IX liability might attach. Professors Sandra J. Perry and Tanya M. Marcum explored how courts have dealt with this requirement in the succeeding years. They determined that a minority interpret the requirement quite strictly.[86]

For example, in *Baynard v. Malone*, the Fourth Circuit found that a principal, who learned of allegations of a teacher's past sexual abuse of a student, did not satisfy the *Gebser* standard regarding new allegations. The court explained, "Although [Principal] Malone certainly should have been aware of the potential for such abuse, and for this reason was properly held liable under § 1983, there is no evidence in the record to support a conclusion that Malone was in fact aware that a student was being abused." The court also held "that Malone was [not] invested with the power to take corrective action on behalf of the ACSB [school district]." It

---

84. Drobac, *supra* note 3, at 68–75.

85. William A. Kaplin, *A Typology and Critique of Title IX Sexual Harassment Law After* Gebser *and* Davis, 26 J.C. & U.L. 615, 621–22 (2000).

86. Sandra J. Perry & Tanya M. Marcum, *Liability for School Sexual Harassment Under Title IX: How the Courts Are Failing Our Children*, 30 U. La Verne L. Rev. 3, 18–29 (2008).

concluded that the district had not invested Malone with "the authority to hire and terminate employees."[87]

In contrast, Perry and Marcum found that a majority require only "actual notice of a substantial risk of abuse." They explained, "Under this standard, there is generally a jury question presented to determine whether the evidence shows that the school was on notice."[88]

7. Authority Did Waldrop wield the "authority to institute corrective measures on the district's behalf"? Was Justice Stevens correct that Waldrop exhibited a lack of will, not authority? Did Waldrop's delegated authority as a teacher enable him to harass Gebser?

8. An Affirmative Defense Justice Stevens noted that the parties did not raise the issue of affirmative defenses. Would an affirmative defense, similar to the one crafted in *Burlington* and *Faragher*, be appropriate for middle and high school students? Should children be responsible for avoiding the consequences of teacher sexual harassment? Why or why not? Justice Ginsburg recommended placing the burden on school districts to show that their sexual harassment procedures caused no "undue risk, effort or expense" for the complaining students. Is this recommendation realistic? Why or why not? How would the Court have applied such a defense in this case and to what result? Should the same considerations, or other factors, apply to different types of educational institutions (i.e., ones that are not public secondary schools)? How about to private schools (where conserving public resources is not at issue) or to colleges and universities?

9. Respondeat Superior Is a teacher's sexual harassment of a student "so unusual or startling that it would seem unfair to include the loss resulting from it among other costs of the employer's business"?[89] Does it make a difference that a school is not (usually) a for-profit business? Does society grant teachers "extraordinary power and authority over" children? Should the community bear the costs resulting from

---

87. 268 F.3d 228, 238–239 (4th Cir. 2001); *see also* Delgado v. Stegall, 367 F.3d 668, 672 (7th Cir. 2004) (finding that the plaintiff "must prove actual knowledge of misconduct, not just actual knowledge of the risk of misconduct, and must also prove that the officials having that knowledge decided not to act on it."); Bostic v. Smyrna Sch. Dist., No. 01-0261 KAJ, 2003 U.S. Dist. LEXIS 3458 (D. Del. 2003), *aff'd* 418 F.3d 355 (3d Cir. 2005).

88. Perry & Marcum, *supra* note 86, at 25, 24–30. *See* Tesoriero v. Syosset Cent. Sch. Dist., 382 F. Supp. 2d 387, 397 (E.D.N.Y. 2005) (stating, "Most federal courts appear to agree that the "actual knowledge" need only be of facts indicating that the teacher has the potential to abuse a student."); Doe v. Green, 298 F. Supp. 2d 1025 (D. Nev. 2004) (quoting *Johnson v. Galen Health Institutes, Inc.*, 267 F. Supp. 2d 679, 688 (W.D. Ky. 2003), "[c]onsistent with the majority of other courts, the Court thus finds that the actual notice standard is met when an appropriate official has actual knowledge of a substantial risk of abuse to students based on prior complaints by other students.").

89. The California Supreme Court explored this reasoning for respondeat superior liability in *Farmers Ins. Grp. v. Co. Santa Clara*, 47 Cal. Rptr. 2d 478, 486 (1995).

the misuse of power "because of the substantial benefits that the community derives from the lawful exercise of" a teacher's power?[90] Discuss.

10. A "Special Relationship" Do schools have a custodial relationship with students? Should they? Professors Catherine Fisk and Erwin Chemerinsky concluded:

> If ever there were a "special relationship" deserving of legal recognition, it must be the relationship between a school and the children entrusted to its care. School children are at the mercy of the schools in a way that employees and most other victims of discrimination are not. A student who is victimized by discrimination by school employees does not have the option employees do, as Justice Souter said in *Faragher*, of "walking away or telling the offender where to go." Students cannot quit school, they cannot refuse to attend class, and they cannot tell their teachers "where to go." Although they can tell harassing classmates "where to go," if words alone are ineffective to stop the harassment, or if the students are too intimidated, they cannot distance themselves from harassing classmates by switching classes or transferring themselves to another school. . . . The Court's holding in *Gebser v. Lago Vista Independent School District* essentially says that schools usually are not responsible for the harms students suffer at school. This holding is astounding given that the victims of the harm are children and that the law requires them to spend most of their waking hours in the school's care.[91]

Are Fisk and Chemerinsky persuasive? Do children's "developing capacities" mandate a higher level of protection than that afforded adults?[92]

Gebser remains the only guidance from the Supreme Court concerning adult-teen sexual relations under Title IX. Because Gebser's "consent" to Waldrop's sexual solicitations was not at issue in *Gebser*, lower courts continue to struggle with not only "deliberate indifference" and the nature of notice appropriate for a federally funded recipient, but also with the legal meaning of "consent" following the *Gebser* decision. The only other Supreme Court guidance regarding Title IX and sexual harassment focuses on peer harassment, the most prevalent kind.

B. Supreme Court Analysis of Peer-Student Sexual Harassment under Title IX

The year after the Supreme Court decided *Gebser* and the issue of teacher-student harassment, the Court resolved a split in the circuit courts regarding peer student

---

90. *Id.* at 495.

91. Catherine Fisk & Erwin Chemerinsky, *Civil Rights Without Remedies: Vicarious Liability Under Title VII, Section 1983 and Title IX*, 7 Wm. & Mary Bill Rts. J. 755, 793 (1999).

92. *See* Jennifer Ann Drobac, *Sex and the Workplace: "Consenting" Adolescents and a Conflict of Laws*, 79 Wash. L. Rev. 471 (2004) (introducing the notion of adolescent "developing capacity" with regard to the legal treatment of adolescent consent).

harassment. Does peer harassment create unequal educational opportunities? Should courts impose liability on school districts for harassing behavior by students? Consider under what standard courts should evaluate peer harassment. Should courts apply a reasonable student standard? Should students be required to endure more from their peers than adult workers do from theirs? Evaluate the Court's response on the liability issue and think about what issues remain unaddressed.

Davis v. Monroe County Board of Education
526 U.S. 629 (1999)

Justice O'CONNOR delivered the opinion of the Court.

Petitioner brought suit against the Monroe County Board of Education and other defendants, alleging that her fifth-grade daughter had been the victim of sexual harassment by another student in her class. Among petitioner's claims was a claim for monetary and injunctive relief under Title IX of the Education Amendments of 1972 (Title IX), 20 U.S.C. § 1681 *et seq.* The District Court dismissed petitioner's Title IX claim on the ground that "student-on-student," or peer, harassment provides no ground for a private cause of action under the statute. The Court of Appeals for the Eleventh Circuit, sitting en banc, affirmed. We consider here whether a private damages action may lie against the school board in cases of student-on-student harassment. We conclude that it may, but only where the funding recipient acts with deliberate indifference to known acts of harassment in its programs or activities. Moreover, we conclude that such an action will lie only for harassment that is so severe, pervasive, and objectively offensive that it effectively bars the victim's access to an educational opportunity or benefit.

I

. . . .

A

Petitioner's minor daughter, LaShonda, was allegedly the victim of a prolonged pattern of sexual harassment by one of her fifth-grade classmates at Hubbard Elementary School, a public school in Monroe County, Georgia. According to petitioner's complaint, the harassment began in December 1992, when the classmate, G.F., attempted to touch LaShonda's breasts and genital area and made vulgar statements such as "'I want to get in bed with you'" and "'I want to feel your boobs.'" Similar conduct allegedly occurred on or about January 4 and January 20, 1993. LaShonda reported each of these incidents to her mother and to her classroom teacher, Diane Fort. Petitioner, in turn, also contacted Fort, who allegedly assured petitioner that the school principal, Bill Querry, had been informed of the incidents. Petitioner contends that, notwithstanding these reports, no disciplinary action was taken against G.F.

G.F.'s conduct allegedly continued for many months. In early February, G.F. purportedly placed a door stop in his pants and proceeded to act in a sexually suggestive manner toward LaShonda during physical education class. LaShonda reported G.F.'s behavior to her physical education teacher, Whit Maples. Approximately one week later, G.F. again allegedly engaged in harassing behavior, this time while under the supervision of another classroom teacher, Joyce Pippin. Again, LaShonda allegedly reported the incident to the teacher, and again petitioner contacted the teacher to follow up.

Petitioner alleges that G.F. once more directed sexually harassing conduct toward LaShonda in physical education class in early March, and that LaShonda reported the incident to both Maples and Pippen. In mid-April 1993, G.F. allegedly rubbed his body against LaShonda in the school hallway in what LaShonda considered a sexually suggestive manner, and LaShonda again reported the matter to Fort.

The string of incidents finally ended in mid-May, when G.F. was charged with, and pleaded guilty to, sexual battery for his misconduct. The complaint alleges that LaShonda had suffered during the months of harassment, however; specifically, her previously high grades allegedly dropped as she became unable to concentrate on her studies, and, in April 1993, her father discovered that she had written a suicide note. The complaint further alleges that, at one point, LaShonda told petitioner that she "'didn't know how much longer she could keep [G.F.] off her.'"

Nor was LaShonda G.F.'s only victim; it is alleged that other girls in the class fell prey to G.F.'s conduct. At one point, in fact, a group composed of LaShonda and other female students tried to speak with Principal Querry about G.F.'s behavior. According to the complaint, however, a teacher denied the students' request with the statement, "'If [Querry] wants you, he'll call you.'"

Petitioner alleges that no disciplinary action was taken in response to G.F.'s behavior toward LaShonda. In addition to her conversations with Fort and Pippen, petitioner alleges that she spoke with Principal Querry in mid-May 1993. When petitioner inquired as to what action the school intended to take against G.F., Querry simply stated, "'I guess I'll have to threaten him a little bit harder.'" Yet, petitioner alleges, at no point during the many months of his reported misconduct was G.F. disciplined for harassment. Indeed, Querry allegedly asked petitioner why LaShonda "'was the only one complaining.'"

Nor, according to the complaint, was any effort made to separate G.F. and LaShonda. On the contrary, notwithstanding LaShonda's frequent complaints, only after more than three months of reported harassment was she even permitted to change her classroom seat so that she was no longer seated next to G.F. Moreover, petitioner alleges that, at the time of the events in question, the Monroe County Board of Education (Board) had not instructed its personnel on how to respond to peer sexual harassment and had not established a policy on the issue.

B

. . . [The Court discussed the procedural history of this case and the dismissals at the district and appellate court levels.]

We granted certiorari in order to resolve a conflict in the Circuits over whether, and under what circumstances, a recipient of federal educational funds can be liable in a private damages action arising from student-on-student sexual harassment. We now reverse.

II

. . . .

A

. . . It is Title IX's "unmistakable focus on the benefited class," rather than the perpetrator, that, in petitioner's view, compels the conclusion that the statute works to protect students from the discriminatory misconduct of their peers.

Here, however, we are asked to do more than define the scope of the behavior that Title IX proscribes. We must determine whether a district's failure to respond to student-on-student harassment in its schools can support a private suit for money damages. . . . Because we have repeatedly treated Title IX as legislation enacted pursuant to Congress' authority under the Spending Clause, however, private damages actions are available only where recipients of federal funding had adequate notice that they could be liable for the conduct at issue. . . .

. . . .

We agree with respondents that a recipient of federal funds may be liable in damages under Title IX only for its own misconduct. The recipient itself must "exclud[e] [persons] from participation in, . . . den[y] [persons] the benefits of, or . . . subjec[t] [persons] to discrimination under" its "program[s] or activit[ies]" in order to be liable under Title IX. The Government's enforcement power may only be exercised against the funding recipient, see § 1682, and we have not extended damages liability under Title IX to parties outside the scope of this power.

We disagree with respondents' assertion, however, that petitioner seeks to hold the Board liable for G. F.'s actions instead of its own. Here, petitioner attempts to hold the Board liable for its *own* decision to remain idle in the face of known student-on-student harassment in its schools. . . . .

[In *Gebser*,] . . . we rejected the use of agency principles to impute liability to the district for the misconduct of its teachers. Likewise, we declined the invitation to impose liability under what amounted to a negligence standard—holding the district liable for its failure to react to teacher-student harassment of which it knew or *should have* known. Rather, we concluded that the district could be liable for damages only where the district itself intentionally acted in clear violation of Title IX by remaining deliberately indifferent to acts of teacher-student harassment of which it had actual knowledge. . . .

. . . .

We consider here whether the misconduct identified in *Gebser*—deliberate indifference to known acts of harassment—amounts to an intentional violation of

Title IX, capable of supporting a private damages action, when the harasser is a student rather than a teacher. We conclude that, in certain limited circumstances, it does. As an initial matter, in *Gebser* we expressly rejected the use of agency principles in the Title IX context, noting the textual differences between Title IX and Title VII. Additionally, the regulatory scheme surrounding Title IX has long provided funding recipients with notice that they may be liable for their failure to respond to the discriminatory acts of certain nonagents. The Department of Education requires recipients to monitor third parties for discrimination in specified circumstances and to refrain from particular forms of interaction with outside entities that are known to discriminate.

The common law, too, has put schools on notice that they may be held responsible under state law for their failure to protect students from the tortious acts of third parties. In fact, state courts routinely uphold claims alleging that schools have been negligent in failing to protect their students from the torts of their peers.

This is not to say that the identity of the harasser is irrelevant. On the contrary, both the "deliberate indifference" standard and the language of Title IX narrowly circumscribe the set of parties whose known acts of sexual harassment can trigger some duty to respond on the part of funding recipients. Deliberate indifference makes sense as a theory of direct liability under Title IX only where the funding recipient has some control over the alleged harassment. A recipient cannot be directly liable for its indifference where it lacks the authority to take remedial action.

. . . .

Where, as here, the misconduct occurs during school hours and on school grounds—the bulk of G.F.'s misconduct, in fact, took place in the classroom—the misconduct is taking place "under" an "operation" of the funding recipient. In these circumstances, the recipient retains substantial control over the context in which the harassment occurs. More importantly, however, in this setting the Board exercises significant control over the harasser. We have observed, for example, "that the nature of [the State's] power [over public schoolchildren] is custodial and tutelary, permitting a degree of supervision and control that could not be exercised over free adults." *Vernonia School Dist. 47J v. Acton*, 515 U.S. 646, 655 (1995). On more than one occasion, this Court has recognized the importance of school officials' "comprehensive authority . . . consistent with fundamental constitutional safeguards, to prescribe and control conduct in the schools." *Tinker v. Des Moines Independent Community School Dist.*, 393 U.S. 503, 507 (1969); see also *New Jersey v. T.L.O.*, 469 U.S. 325, 342, n. 9 (1985) ("The maintenance of discipline in the schools requires not only that students be restrained from assaulting one another, abusing drugs and alcohol, and committing other crimes, but also that students conform themselves to the standards of conduct prescribed by school authorities"); 74 F.3d, at 1193 ("The ability to control and influence behavior exists to an even greater extent in the classroom than in the workplace . . ."). The common law, too, recognizes the school's disciplinary authority. We thus conclude that recipients of federal funding may be liable for "subject[ing]" their students to discrimination where the recipient is deliberately indifferent to known acts of student-on-student sexual harassment and the harasser is under the school's disciplinary authority.

. . . .

We stress that our conclusion here—that recipients may be liable for their deliberate indifference to known acts of peer sexual harassment—does not mean that recipients can avoid liability only by purging their schools of actionable peer harassment or that administrators must engage in particular disciplinary action. We thus disagree with respondents' contention that, if Title IX provides a cause of action for student-on-student harassment, "nothing short of expulsion of every student accused of misconduct involving sexual overtones would protect school systems from liability or damages." Likewise, the dissent erroneously imagines that victims of peer harassment now have a Title IX right to make particular remedial demands. In fact, as we have previously noted, courts should refrain from second-guessing the disciplinary decisions made by school administrators.

School administrators will continue to enjoy the flexibility they require so long as funding recipients are deemed "deliberately indifferent" to acts of student-on-student harassment only where the recipient's response to the harassment or lack thereof is clearly unreasonable in light of the known circumstances. The dissent consistently mischaracterizes this standard to require funding recipients to "remedy" peer harassment and to "ensur[e] that . . . students conform their conduct to" certain rules. Title IX imposes no such requirements. On the contrary, the recipient must merely respond to known peer harassment in a manner that is not clearly unreasonable. This is not a mere "reasonableness" standard, as the dissent assumes. In an appropriate case, there is no reason why courts, on a motion to dismiss, for summary judgment, or for a directed verdict, could not identify a response as not "clearly unreasonable" as a matter of law.

. . . We believe . . . that the standard set out here is sufficiently flexible to account both for the level of disciplinary authority available to the school and for the potential liability arising from certain forms of disciplinary action. A university might not, for example, be expected to exercise the same degree of control over its students that a grade school would enjoy and it would be entirely reasonable for a school to refrain from a form of disciplinary action that would expose it to constitutional or statutory claims.

While it remains to be seen whether petitioner can show that the Board's response to reports of G.F.'s misconduct was clearly unreasonable in light of the known circumstances, petitioner may be able to show that the Board "subject [ed]" LaShonda to discrimination by failing to respond in any way over a period of five months to complaints of G.F.'s in-school misconduct from LaShonda and other female students.

B

. . . Students are not only protected from discrimination, but also specifically shielded from being "excluded from participation in" or "denied the benefits of" any "education program or activity receiving Federal financial assistance." § 1681(a).

The statute makes clear that, whatever else it prohibits, students must not be denied access to educational benefits and opportunities on the basis of gender. We thus conclude that funding recipients are properly held liable in damages only where they are deliberately indifferent to sexual harassment, of which they have actual knowledge, that is so severe, pervasive, and objectively offensive that it can be said to deprive the victims of access to the educational opportunities or benefits provided by the school.

The most obvious example of student-on-student sexual harassment capable of triggering a damages claim would thus involve the overt, physical deprivation of access to school resources. Consider, for example, a case in which male students physically threaten their female peers every day, successfully preventing the female students from using a particular school resource—an athletic field or a computer lab, for instance. District administrators are well aware of the daily ritual, yet they deliberately ignore requests for aid from the female students wishing to use the resource. The district's knowing refusal to take any action in response to such behavior would fly in the face of Title IX's core principles, and such deliberate indifference may appropriately be subject to claims for monetary damages. It is not necessary, however, to show physical exclusion to demonstrate that students have been deprived by the actions of another student or students of an educational opportunity on the basis of sex. Rather, a plaintiff must establish sexual harassment of students that is so severe, pervasive, and objectively offensive, and that so undermines and detracts from the victims' educational experience, that the victim-students are effectively denied equal access to an institution's resources and opportunities. *Cf. Meritor Savings Bank, FSB v. Vinson*, 477 U.S., at 67.

Whether gender-oriented conduct rises to the level of actionable "harassment" thus "depends on a constellation of surrounding circumstances, expectations, and relationships," *Oncale v. Sundowner Offshore Services, Inc.*, 523 U.S. 75, 82 (1998), including, but not limited to, the ages of the harasser and the victim and the number of individuals involved, see OCR Title IX Guidelines 12041–12042. Courts, moreover, must bear in mind that schools are unlike the adult workplace and that children may regularly interact in a manner that would be unacceptable among adults. See, e.g., Brief for National School Boards Association et al. as *Amici Curiae* 11 (describing "dizzying array of immature . . . behaviors by students"). Indeed, at least early on, students are still learning how to interact appropriately with their peers. It is thus understandable that, in the school setting, students often engage in insults, banter, teasing, shoving, pushing, and gender-specific conduct that is upsetting to the students subjected to it. Damages are not available for simple acts of teasing and name-calling among school children, however, even where these comments target differences in gender. Rather, in the context of student-on-student harassment, damages are available only where the behavior is so severe, pervasive, and objectively offensive that it denies its victims the equal access to education that Title IX is designed to protect.

. . . .

Moreover, the provision that the discrimination occur "under any education program or activity" suggests that the behavior be serious enough to have the systemic effect of denying the victim equal access to an educational program or activity. Although, in theory, a single instance of sufficiently severe one-on-one peer harassment could be said to have such an effect, we think it unlikely that Congress would have thought such behavior sufficient to rise to this level in light of the inevitability of student misconduct and the amount of litigation that would be invited by entertaining claims of official indifference to a single instance of one-on-one peer harassment. By limiting private damages actions to cases having a systemic effect on educational programs or activities, we reconcile the general principle that Title IX prohibits official indifference to known peer sexual harassment with the practical realities of responding to student behavior, realities that Congress could not have meant to be ignored. Even the dissent suggests that Title IX liability may arise when a funding recipient remains indifferent to severe, gender-based mistreatment played out on a "widespread level" among students.

. . . .

C

Applying this standard to the facts at issue here, we conclude that the Eleventh Circuit erred in dismissing petitioner's complaint. Petitioner alleges that her daughter was the victim of repeated acts of sexual harassment by G.F. over a 5-month period, and there are allegations in support of the conclusion that G.F.'s misconduct was severe, pervasive, and objectively offensive. The harassment was not only verbal; it included numerous acts of objectively offensive touching, and, indeed, G.F. ultimately pleaded guilty to criminal sexual misconduct. Moreover, the complaint alleges that there were multiple victims who were sufficiently disturbed by G.F.'s misconduct to seek an audience with the school principal. Further, petitioner contends that the harassment had a concrete, negative effect on her daughter's ability to receive an education. The complaint also suggests that petitioner may be able to show both actual knowledge and deliberate indifference on the part of the Board, which made no effort whatsoever either to investigate or to put an end to the harassment.

. . . Accordingly, the judgment of the United States Court of Appeals for the Eleventh Circuit is reversed, and the case is remanded for further proceedings consistent with this opinion.

Justice KENNEDY, with whom THE CHIEF JUSTICE, Justice SCALIA, and Justice THOMAS join, dissenting.

. . . .

. . . In order to make its case for school liability for peer sexual harassment, the majority must establish that Congress gave grant recipients clear and unambiguous notice that they would be liable in money damages for failure to remedy discriminatory acts of their students. The majority must also demonstrate that the statute gives schools clear notice that one child's harassment of another constitutes "discrimination" on the basis of sex within the meaning of Title IX, and that—as applied to individual cases—the standard for liability will enable the grant recipient to distinguish inappropriate childish behavior from actionable gender discrimination. The majority does not carry these burdens.

. . . .

The only certainty flowing from the majority's decision is that scarce resources will be diverted from educating our children and that many school districts, desperate to avoid Title IX peer harassment suits, will adopt whatever federal code of student conduct and discipline the Department of Education sees fit to impose upon them. The Nation's schoolchildren will learn their first lessons about federalism in classrooms where the Federal Government is the ever-present regulator. The Federal Government will have insinuated itself not only into one of the most traditional areas of state concern but also into one of the most sensitive areas of human affairs. This federal control of the discipline of our Nation's schoolchildren is contrary to our traditions and inconsistent with the sensible administration of our schools. Because Title IX did not give States unambiguous notice that accepting federal funds meant ceding to the Federal Government power over the day-to-day disciplinary decisions of schools, I dissent.

I

. . . .

Given the state of gender discrimination law at the time Title IX was passed . . . there is no basis to think that Congress contemplated liability for a school's failure to remedy discriminatory acts by students or that the States would believe the statute imposed on them a clear obligation to do so. When Title IX was enacted in 1972, the concept of "sexual harassment" as gender discrimination had not been recognized or considered by the courts. See generally C. MacKinnon, Sexual Harassment of Working Women: A Case of Sex Discrimination 59–72 (1979). The types of discrimination that were recognized—discriminatory admissions standards, denial of access to programs or resources, hiring, etc.—could not be engaged in by students.

2

The majority nonetheless appears to see no need to justify drawing the "enough control" line to encompass students. In truth, however, a school's control over its students is much more complicated and limited than the majority acknowledges. A public school does not control its students in the way it controls its teachers or those with whom it contracts. Most public schools do not screen or select students, and their power to discipline students is far from unfettered.

Public schools are generally obligated by law to educate all students who live within defined geographic boundaries. Indeed, the Constitution of almost every State in the country guarantees the State's students a free primary and secondary public education. In at least some States, moreover, there is a continuing duty on schools to educate even students who are suspended or expelled. Schools that remove a harasser from the classroom and then attempt to fulfill their continuing-education obligation by placing the harasser in any kind of group setting, rather than by hiring expensive tutors for each student, will find themselves at continuing risk of Title IX suits brought by the other students in the alternative education program.

In addition, federal law imposes constraints on school disciplinary actions. This Court has held, for example, that due process requires, "[a]t the very minimum," that a student facing suspension "be given some kind of notice and afforded some kind of hearing." *Goss v. Lopez*, 419 U.S. 565, 579 (1975).

The Individuals with Disabilities Education Act (IDEA), 20 U.S.C. § 1400 *et seq.* (1994 ed., Supp. III), moreover, places strict limits on the ability of schools to take disciplinary actions against students with behavior disorder disabilities, even if the disability was not diagnosed prior to the incident triggering discipline. "Disability," as defined in the IDEA, includes "serious emotional disturbance," § 1401(3)(A)(i), which the DOE, in turn, has defined as a "condition exhibiting . . . over a long period of time and to a marked degree that adversely affects a child's educational performance," an "inability to build or maintain satisfactory interpersonal relationships with peers and teachers," or "[i]nappropriate types of behavior or feelings under normal circumstances." 34 CFR § 300.7(b)(9) (1998). If, as the majority would have us believe, the behavior that constitutes actionable peer sexual harassment so deviates from the normal teasing and jostling of adolescence that it puts schools on clear notice of potential liability, then a student who engages in such harassment may have at least a colorable claim of severe emotional disturbance within the meaning of the IDEA. When imposing disciplinary sanction on a student harasser who might assert a colorable IDEA claim, the school must navigate a complex web of statutory provisions and DOE regulations that significantly limit its discretion.

The practical obstacles schools encounter in ensuring that thousands of immature students conform their conduct to acceptable norms may be even more significant than the legal obstacles. School districts cannot exercise the same measure of control over thousands of students that they do over a few hundred adult employees. The limited resources of our schools must be conserved for basic educational services. Some schools lack the resources even to deal with serious problems of violence and are already overwhelmed with disciplinary problems of all kinds.

Perhaps even more startling than its broad assumptions about school control over primary and secondary school students is the majority's failure to grapple in any meaningful way with the distinction between elementary and secondary schools, on the one hand, and universities on the other. The majority bolsters its argument that schools can control their students' actions by quoting our decision in *Vernonia School Dist. 47J v. Acton*, 515 U.S. 646, 655 (1995), for the proposition that "'the nature of [the State's] power [over public school children] is custodial and tutelary, permitting a degree of supervision and control that could not be exercised over free adults.'" Yet the majority's holding would appear to apply with equal force to universities, which do not exercise custodial and tutelary power over their adult students.

A university's power to discipline its students for speech that may constitute sexual harassment is also circumscribed by the First Amendment. A number of federal courts have already confronted difficult problems raised by university speech codes designed to deal with peer sexual and racial harassment.

The difficulties associated with speech codes simply underscore the limited nature of a university's control over student behavior that may be viewed as sexual harassment. Despite the fact that the majority relies on the assumption that schools exercise a great deal of control over their students to justify creating the private cause of action in the first instance, it does not recognize the obvious limits on a university's ability to control its students as a reason to doubt the propriety of a private cause of action for peer harassment. It simply uses them as a factor in determining whether the university's response was reasonable.

. . . .

II

. . . .

The law recognizes that children—particularly young children—are not fully accountable for their actions because they lack the capacity to exercise mature judgment. See, e.g., 1 E. Farnsworth, Contracts §4.4 (2d ed. 1998) (discussing minor's ability to disaffirm a contract into which he has entered). It should surprise no one, then, that the schools that are the primary locus of most children's social development are rife with inappropriate behavior by children who are just learning to interact with their peers. The *amici* on the front lines of our schools describe the situation best:

> "Unlike adults in the workplace, juveniles have limited life experiences or familial influences upon which to establish an understanding of appropriate behavior. The real world of school discipline is a rough-and-tumble place where students practice newly learned vulgarities, erupt with anger, tease and embarrass each other, share offensive notes, flirt, push and shove in the halls, grab and offend." Brief for National School Boards Association et al. as *Amici Curiae* 10–11 (hereinafter Brief for School *Amici*).

No one contests that much of this "dizzying array of immature or uncontrollable behaviors by students," is inappropriate, even "objectively offensive" at times, and that parents and schools have a moral and ethical responsibility to help students learn to interact with their peers in an appropriate manner. It is doubtless the case, moreover, that much of this inappropriate behavior is directed toward members of the opposite sex, as children in the throes of adolescence struggle to express their emerging sexual identities.

It is a far different question, however, whether it is either proper or useful to label this immature, childish behavior gender discrimination. Nothing in Title IX suggests that Congress even contemplated this question, much less answered it in the affirmative in unambiguous terms.

. . . .

Contrary to the majority's assertion, however, respondents have made a cogent and persuasive argument that the type of student conduct alleged by petitioner should not be considered "sexual harassment," much less gender discrimination actionable under Title IX:

> "[A]t the time Petitioner filed her complaint, no court, including this Court had recognized the concept of sexual harassment in any context other than the employment context. Nor had any Court extended the concept of sexual harassment to the misconduct of emotionally and socially immature children. The type of conduct alleged by Petitioner in her complaint is not new. However, in past years it was properly identified as misconduct which was addressed within the context of student discipline. The Petitioner now asks this Court to create out of whole cloth a cause of action by labeling childish misconduct as 'sexual harassment,' to stigmatize children as sexual harassers, and have the federal court system take on the additional burden of second guessing the disciplinary actions taken by school administrators in addressing misconduct, something this Court has consistently refused to do."

Likewise, the majority's assertion that *Gebser* and *Franklin* settled the question is little more than *ipse dixit*.[93] *Gebser* and *Franklin* themselves did nothing more than cite *Meritor Savings Bank, FSB v. Vinson,* 477 U.S. 57, 64 (1986), a Title VII case, for the proposition that "when a supervisor sexually harasses a subordinate because of the subordinate's sex, that supervisor 'discriminate[s]' on the basis of sex." To treat that proposition as establishing that the student conduct at issue here is gender discrimination is to erase, in one stroke, all differences between children and adults, peers and teachers, schools and workplaces.

In reality, there is no established body of federal or state law on which courts may draw in defining the student conduct that qualifies as Title IX gender discrimination. Analogies to Title VII hostile environment harassment are inapposite, because schools are not workplaces and children are not adults. The norms of the adult workplace that have defined hostile environment sexual harassment are not easily translated to peer relationships in schools, where teenage romantic relationships and dating are a part of everyday life. Analogies to Title IX teacher sexual harassment of students are similarly flawed. A teacher's sexual overtures toward a student are always inappropriate; a teenager's romantic overtures to a classmate (even when persistent and unwelcome) are an inescapable part of adolescence.

The majority admits that, under its approach, "[w]hether gender-oriented conduct rises to the level of actionable 'harassment' . . . 'depends on a constellation of

---

93. *Ipse dixit*, BLACK'S LAW DICTIONARY (10th ed. 2014) ("Something asserted but not proved").

surrounding circumstances, expectations, and relationships,' including, but not limited to, the ages of the harasser and the victim and the number of individuals involved." The majority does not explain how a school is supposed to discern from this mishmash of factors what is actionable discrimination. Its multifactored balancing test is a far cry from the clarity we demand of Spending Clause legislation.

The difficulties schools will encounter in identifying peer sexual harassment are already evident in teachers' manuals designed to give guidance on the subject. For example, one teachers' manual on peer sexual harassment suggests that sexual harassment in kindergarten through third grade includes a boy being "put down" on the playground "because he wants to play house with the girls" or a girl being "put down because she shoots baskets better than the boys." Minnesota Dept. of Education, Girls and Boys Getting Along: Teaching Sexual Harassment Prevention in the Elementary Classroom 65 (1993). Yet another manual suggests that one student saying to another, "You look nice," could be sexual harassment, depending on the "tone of voice," how the student looks at the other, and "who else is around." N. Stein & L. Sjostrom, Flirting or Hurting? A Teacher's Guide on Student-to-Student Sexual Harassment in Schools (Grades 6 through 12), p. 14 (1994). Blowing a kiss is also suspect. This confusion will likely be compounded once the sexual harassment label is invested with the force of federal law, backed up by private damages suits.

The only guidance the majority gives schools in distinguishing between the "simple acts of teasing and name-calling among school children," said not to be a basis for suit even when they "target differences in gender," and actionable peer sexual harassment is, in reality, no guidance at all. The majority proclaims that "in the context of student-on-student harassment, damages are available only where the behavior is so severe, pervasive, and objectively offensive that it denies its victims the equal access to education that Title IX is designed to protect." The majority does not even purport to explain, however, what constitutes an actionable denial of "equal access to education." Is equal access denied when a girl who tires of being chased by the boys at recess refuses to go outside? When she cannot concentrate during class because she is worried about the recess activities? When she pretends to be sick one day so she can stay home from school? It appears the majority is content to let juries decide.

The majority's reference to a "systemic effect" does nothing to clarify the content of its standard. The majority appears to intend that requirement to do no more than exclude the possibility that a single act of harassment perpetrated by one student on one other student can form the basis for an actionable claim. That is a small concession indeed.

The only real clue the majority gives schools about the dividing line between actionable harassment that denies a victim equal access to education and mere inappropriate teasing is a profoundly unsettling one: On the facts of this case, petitioner has stated a claim because she alleged, in the majority's words, "that the harassment had a concrete, negative effect on her daughter's ability to receive an education." In petitioner's words, the effects that might have been visible to the school were that her daughter's grades "dropped" and her "ability to concentrate on her school work [was] affected." Almost all adolescents experience these problems at one time or another as they mature.

III

The majority's inability to provide any workable definition of actionable peer harassment simply underscores the myriad ways in which an opinion that purports to be narrow is, in fact, so broad that it will support untold numbers of lawyers who will prove adept at presenting cases that will withstand the defendant school districts' pretrial motions. Each of the barriers to runaway litigation the majority offers us crumbles under the weight of even casual scrutiny.

For example, the majority establishes what sounds like a relatively high threshold for liability — "denial of equal access" to education — and, almost in the same breath, makes clear that alleging a decline in grades is enough to survive Federal Rule of Civil Procedure 12(b)(6) and, it follows, to state a winning claim. The majority seems oblivious to the fact that almost every child, at some point, has trouble in school because he or she is being teased by his or her peers. The girl who wants to skip recess because she is teased by the boys is no different from the overweight child who skips gym class because the other children tease her about her size in the locker room; or the child who risks flunking out because he refuses to wear glasses to avoid the taunts of "four-eyes"; or the child who refuses to go to school because the school bully calls him a "scaredy-cat" at recess. Most children respond to teasing in ways that detract from their ability to learn. The majority's test for actionable harassment will, as a result, sweep in almost all of the more innocuous conduct it acknowledges as a ubiquitous part of school life.

The string of adjectives the majority attaches to the word "harassment" — "severe, pervasive, and objectively offensive" — likewise fails to narrow the class of conduct that can trigger liability, since the touchstone for determining whether there is Title IX liability is the effect on the child's ability to get an education. Indeed, the Court's reliance on the impact on the child's educational experience suggests that the "objective offensiveness" of a comment is to be judged by reference to a reasonable child at whom the comments were aimed. Not only is that standard likely to be quite expansive, it also gives schools — and juries — little guidance, requiring them to attempt to gauge the sensitivities of, for instance, the average seven-year-old.

The majority assures us that its decision will not interfere with school discipline and instructs that, "as we have previously noted, courts should refrain from second-guessing the disciplinary decisions made by school administrators." The obvious reason for the majority's expressed reluctance to allow courts and litigants to second-guess school disciplinary decisions is that school officials are usually in the best position to judge the seriousness of alleged harassment and to devise an appropriate response. The problem is that the majority's test, in fact, invites courts and juries to second-guess school administrators in every case, to judge in each instance whether the school's response was "clearly unreasonable." A reasonableness standard, regardless of the modifier, transforms every disciplinary decision into a jury question.

Another professed limitation the majority relies upon is that the recipient will be liable only where the acts of student harassment are "known." The majority's enunciation of the standard begs the obvious question: known to whom? Yet the majority says not one word about the type of school employee who must know about the harassment before it is actionable.

The majority's silence is telling. The deliberate indifference liability we recognized in *Gebser* was predicated on notice to "an official of the recipient entity with authority to take corrective action to end the discrimination." The majority gives no indication that it believes the standard to be any different in this context and—given its extensive reliance on the *Gebser* standard throughout the opinion—appears to adopt the *Gebser* notice standard by implication. At least the courts adjudicating Title IX peer harassment claims are likely to so conclude.

By choosing not to adopt the standard in explicit terms, the majority avoids having to confront the bizarre implications of its decision. In the context of teacher harassment, the *Gebser* notice standard imposes some limit on school liability. Where peer harassment is the discrimination, however, it imposes no limitation at all. In most cases of student misbehavior, it is the teacher who has authority, at least in the first instance, to punish the student and take other measures to remedy the harassment. The anomalous result will be that, while a school district cannot be held liable for a teacher's sexual harassment of a student without notice to the school board (or at least to the principal), the district can be held liable for a teacher's failure to remedy peer harassment. The threshold for school liability, then, appears to be lower when the harasser is a student than when the harasser is a teacher who is an agent of the school. The absurdity of this result confirms that it was neither contemplated by Congress nor anticipated by the States.

The majority's limitations on peer sexual harassment suits cannot hope to contain the flood of liability the Court today begins. The elements of the Title IX claim created by the majority will be easy not only to allege but also to prove. A female plaintiff who pleads only that a boy called her offensive names, that she told a teacher, that the teacher's response was unreasonable, and that her school performance suffered as a result, appears to state a successful claim.

There will be no shortage of plaintiffs to bring such complaints. Our schools are charged each day with educating millions of children. Of those millions of students, a large percentage will, at some point during their school careers, experience something they consider sexual harassment. A 1993 study by the American Association of University Women Educational Foundation, for instance, found that "fully 4 out of 5 students (81%) report that they have been the target of some form of sexual harassment during their school lives." Hostile Hallways: The AAUW Survey on Sexual Harassment in America's Schools 7 (1993). The number of potential lawsuits against our schools is staggering.

The cost of defending against peer sexual harassment suits alone could overwhelm many school districts, particularly since the majority's liability standards will allow almost any plaintiff to get to summary judgment, if not to a jury. In addition, there are no damages caps on the judicially implied private cause of action under Title IX. As a result, school liability in one peer sexual harassment suit could approach, or even exceed, the total federal funding of many school districts. Petitioner, for example, seeks damages of $500,000 in this case. Respondent school district received approximately $679,000 in federal aid in 1992–1993. The school district sued in *Gebser* received only $120,000 in federal funds a year. Indeed, the entire 1992–1993 budget of that district was only $1.6 million.

The limitless liability confronting our schools under the implied Title IX cause of action puts schools in a far worse position than businesses; when Congress established the express cause of action for money damages under Title VII, it prescribed damages caps. Adopting petitioner's position would amount, then, to allowing unlimited recovery of damages under Title IX where Congress has not spoken on the subject of either the right or the remedy, and in the face of evidence that when Congress expressly considered both in Title VII it restricted the amount of damages available"). In addition, in contrast to Title VII, Title IX makes no provision for agency investigation and conciliation of complaints (prior to the filing of a case in federal court) that could weed out frivolous suits or settle meritorious ones at minimal cost.

The prospect of unlimited Title IX liability will, in all likelihood, breed a climate of fear that encourages school administrators to label even the most innocuous of childish conduct sexual harassment. It would appear to be no coincidence that, not long after the DOE issued its proposed policy guidance warning that schools could be liable for peer sexual harassment in the fall of 1996, a North Carolina school suspended a 6-year-old boy who kissed a female classmate on the cheek for sexual harassment, on the theory that "[u]nwelcome is unwelcome at any age." Los Angeles Times, Sept. 25, 1996, p. A11. A week later, a New York school suspended a second grader who kissed a classmate and ripped a button off her skirt. Buffalo News, Oct. 2, 1996, p. A16. The second grader said that he got the idea from his favorite book "Corduroy," about a bear with a missing button. School administrators said only, "We were given guidelines as to why we suspend children. We follow the guidelines."

At the college level, the majority's holding is sure to add fuel to the debate over campus speech codes that, in the name of preventing a hostile educational environment, may infringe students' First Amendment rights. Indeed, under the majority's control principle, schools presumably will be responsible for remedying conduct that occurs even in student dormitory rooms. As a result, schools may well be forced to apply workplace norms in the most private of domains.

Even schools that resist overzealous enforcement may find that the most careful and reasoned response to a sexual harassment complaint nonetheless provokes litigation. Speaking with the voice of experience, the school *amici* remind us, "[h]istory shows that, no matter what a school official chooses to do, someone will be unhappy. Student offenders almost always view their punishment as too strict, and student complainants almost always view an offender's punishment as too lax."

A school faced with a peer sexual harassment complaint in the wake of the majority's decision may well be beset with litigation from every side. One student's demand for a quick response to her harassment complaint will conflict with the alleged harasser's demand for due process. Another student's demand for a harassment-free classroom will conflict with the alleged harasser's claim to a mainstream placement under the IDEA [Individuals with Disabilities Education Act] or with his state constitutional right to a continuing, free public education. On college campuses, and even in secondary schools, a student's claim that the school should remedy a sexually hostile environment will conflict with the alleged harasser's claim that his speech, even if offensive, is protected by the First Amendment. In each of these situations, the school faces the risk of suit, and maybe even multiple suits, regardless of its response.

. . . .

. . . Federalism and our struggling school systems deserve better from this Court. I dissent.

Notes and Discussion

1. The Facts or Hidden Sexism Is this a case about "childish misconduct"? A case involving a "dizzying array of immature or uncontrollable behaviors" by G.F.? Does the criminal battery charge make a difference in the analysis of this case? Justice Kennedy said, "[M]uch of this inappropriate behavior is directed toward members of the opposite sex, as children in the throes of adolescence struggle to express their emerging sexual identities." In essence, is Kennedy saying, "Boys will be boys"? If not, is this statement still a minimization of the *Monroe* facts? Might "much of this inappropriate behavior" be considered predatory and deliberately mean? Explain.

Are teenage and adult dating habits so very different, as Justice Kennedy suggested? Explain. If "a teenager's romantic overtures to a classmate (even when persistent and unwelcome) are an inescapable part of adolescence[,]" does that mean they should be? What about at school?

What is the significance, if any, of the principal's conduct?

In October 2018, the U.S. Senate confirmed Brett Kavanaugh to the Supreme Court,[94] following allegations by Dr. Christine Blasey-Ford that he sexually assaulted her when they were in high school.[95] Assuming the truth of the allegation, was Kavanaugh's behavior "childish misconduct" or just another example of a "dizzying array of immature or uncontrollable behaviors"? Does this allegation change the way people might perceive school harassment or is it incomparable because the

---

94. *Everything on Brett Kavanaugh, the Senate Vote and the Fallout*, N.Y. Times (Oct. 2, 2018, updated Oct. 6, 2018).

95. Elizabeth Williamson et al., *For Christine Blasey Ford, a Drastic Turn From a Quiet Life in Academia*, N.Y. Times (Sept. 19, 2018).

alleged assault by Kavanaugh occurred at a high school party and not on school grounds?

2. Off Campus Harassment The *Monroe* Court emphasized for liability purposes that the harassment occurred at school. The Court stressed, "Where, as here, the misconduct occurs during school hours and on school grounds . . . the misconduct is taking place 'under' an 'operation' of the funding recipient. In these circumstances, the recipient retains substantial control over the context in which the harassment occurs." What if G.F. had harassed or "bullied" Davis via email or Facebook or Instagram? How should schools (and courts) handle e-harassment? For one answer, see *Feminist Majority Foundation v. Hurley* (2018), featured below.

3. Sexual Harassment Standards The Court specified that "an action will lie only for harassment that is so severe, pervasive, and objectively offensive that it effectively bars the victim's access to an educational opportunity or benefit." How is this standard different from that for teacher-student harassment or for harassment under Title VII? Who needs to know about peer harassment in order for liability to attach?

Should the same Title IX standards apply to universities as apply to grammar and secondary schools? Does *Monroe* provide any incentive for schools to develop innovative policies and procedures to address and prevent sexual harassment?

4. Deliberate Indifference Was this standard consistent in the *Gebser* and *Monroe* decisions? Professor Julie Davies thought not and explained:

> Not surprisingly, courts are confused about the meaning of the deliberate indifference standard. In *Gebser*, the Court indicated that deliberate indifference must amount to an official decision by the recipient (school district) not to remedy the violation. In *Davis* the Court reaffirmed the deliberate indifference requirement, but defined it as an institutional response that is "clearly unreasonable." Some lower courts believe that the only instance when the requirement could be met is where a decision has been made not to remedy the complaint. Under this interpretation, virtually any response, or even negligent failure to process a complaint, seemingly would insulate the institution from liability. Several decisions interpret the deliberate indifference standard to be the same as the standard for punitive damages, thus requiring proof of subjective consciousness of a risk of injury or illegality. A different interpretation would view an institution's decision not to remedy a situation as but one example of deliberate indifference. Courts with this view believe they are permitted to assess the reasonableness of the decision maker's actions, albeit with a strong preference for protecting institutional discretion in crafting resolutions.

> It is a serious mistake to view deliberate indifference as requiring an explicit decision to ignore reported harassment. While clearly such a refusal would suffice, many other scenarios also warrant such a finding. As the cases reveal, deliberate indifference to reported sexual harassment may arise in a wide variety of circumstances; it is an issue with a much greater

factual nuance than either the *Gebser* or *Davis* decisions convey. . . . Deliberate indifference may exist even if a school district did not make a decision to ignore the harassment.[96]

Did Davies raise a valid point?

5. Sex Discrimination Did the school discriminate against LaShonda? If so, how?[97] Justice Kennedy, who joined in the *Gebser* majority opinion, authored the *Monroe* dissent. In *Monroe*, he suggested that to violate Title IX, "discrimination must actually be 'controlled by'—that is, be authorized by, pursuant to, or in accordance with, school policy or actions." Is there any inconsistency between this statement and a vote with the majority in *Gebser*? Explain. Is severe and pervasive student harassment that administrators ignore also "'under' the operations of the school"? Why or why not? Is a "decline in grades" a "'denial of equal access' to education," as the dissent claimed?

Might *Monroe* be viewed not as a sexual harassment case but as a disparate protection case? In other words, would administrators have responded the same way if LaShonda had been Lamar, a boy? What if school administrators had worn equal opportunity blinders and ignored harassment against both males and females? Would that failure to act have still been actionable under Title IX?[98]

6. Other Types of Discrimination or Simple Misconduct What if sexually harassing conduct is typically the result of a protected disability (under the IDEA) to which administrators cannot respond with discipline? Is G.F. a bully and, therefore, discrimination law does not apply? Nan Stein cautions against the conflation of bullying and sex-based harassment. She makes three important points regarding the label "bullying" in schools. First, she contends that the term "bullying" is "imprecise and vague, and used as a default, a crutch, and a place holder." Second, she maintains that "there is no agreement on the definition of 'bullying,' and neither state laws nor researchers can agree on a common definition." Third, she says that "claims of effectiveness of classroom interventions/curriculum on bullying reduction are often inflated, exaggerated, and self-serving, and should be met with skepticism."[99] Is she correct? Why or why not?

---

96. Julie Davies, *Assessing Institutional Responsibility for Sexual Harassment in Education*, 77 Tul. L. Rev. 387, 427–28 (2002). For a thorough discussion of the deliberate indifference standard, see Deborah L. Brake, *School Liability for Peer Harassment After Davis: Shifting from Intent to Causation in Discrimination Law*, 12 Hastings Women's L.J. 5, 14–29 (2001).

97. *See* Joan E. Schaffner, *Dispelling the Misconceptions Raised by the* Davis *Dissent*, 12 Hastings Women's L.J. 141, 156–62 (2001) (demonstrating that sexual harassment at school is sex discrimination).

98. *See* Brake, *supra* note 96, at 8–10 (explaining that the Court rejected a comparative approach and equal opportunity harassment at school is actionable under Title IX).

99. Nan Stein, *Sexual Harassment Left Behind: What the Bullying Framework Is Doing to Civil Rights Laws and Framework*, Audiocast, Wellesley Centers for Women Lunchtime Seminar Series, Nov. 4, 2010.

7. Defendants and Defenses Does it seem a bit far removed to allow a suit against the County Board of Education for harassment between peers? Should administrators face personal liability? Does the Court's holding encourage a see-no-evil blindness and a head-in-the-sand defense? Does curbing verbal sexual harassment constitute a violation by the school of the free speech clause of the First Amendment? See *infra* Chapter 9.

8. Notice and the Spending Clause Was it really unclear to the Board, or to the school, that school administrators violate the law when they fail to maintain an educational environment free of sexual harassment and sex discrimination? If so, what did they think Title IX meant? Or is this case about knowledge regarding financial liability, not discrimination? Will "scarce resources be diverted from educating our children" because of *Monroe*, as the dissent asserted?

9. Identifying Peer Harassment Will schools have trouble identifying severe, pervasive, and objectively offensive sexual harassment as the dissent suggested? Was the dissent correct that the majority offered no guidance? Will schools suspend six-year-olds regularly or were the dissent's examples isolated cases of poor judgment? Has the majority created a "Federal Student Civility Code," as the dissent claimed?

10. Uniform Standards The dissent took issue with the majority's adoption of a liability standard based on whether "the harassment had a concrete, negative effect on her daughter's [Davis's] ability to receive an education." It suggested that many students suffer negative effects for a variety of reasons, which could be difficult to ascertain. Additionally, the dissent argued that this standard might subject schools to liability for trivial misconduct. It discussed a variety of state responses by different school systems. The majority conceded, "A university might not, for example, be expected to exercise the same degree of control over its students that a grade school would enjoy and it would be entirely reasonable for a school to refrain from a form of disciplinary action that would expose it to constitutional or statutory claims." Should the majority have created different standards for grammar schools, high schools, and colleges? Or is a uniform standard helpful? Explain.

Aspects of *Monroe* present interesting questions for colleges and universities. As the Court noted, a university does not have the same control that a secondary school has. What are other significant differences between a high school campus and a university environment that might contribute to implementation issues under Title IX?

11. Floodgates *Monroe* did not open the litigation floodgates as the dissent predicted. However, the dissent's prophecy should sound familiar. Early employment sexual harassment decisions made similar predictions (see Chapter 1). Are there other parallels between *Monroe* and the early employment cases?

12. Federalism Did this case concern federalism as the dissent asserted? Professor Joan Schaffner agreed:

> I believe it is a matter of federalism, properly understood, and that the decision was in fact consistent with federalism principles. Title IX was enacted pursuant to Congress' spending power but reflects and enforces Fourteenth

Amendment principles of equal protection. By labeling the conduct as mere "discipline," and comparing it to teasing based on weight or wearing glasses, the dissent failed to recognize the important federal interest at stake. If one accepts that actionable student-on-student sexual harassment constitutes sex discrimination, then one must recognize that it is a matter of national concern and requires a uniform, national approach to address the concern. This is not a case in need of state experimentation or a diverse approach to satisfy local interests. Rather, we as a society have established a principle of equal protection under the laws and equal treatment of the sexes as a fundamental right guaranteed to all citizens. Thus, it is consistent with the underlying tenets of federalism to create a federal case out of student-on-student sexual harassment that rises to the level of sex discrimination.[100]

13. **Alliances** Notice that Justice O'Connor authored both *Gebser* and *Monroe*; however, the majority and dissent alliances flip-flopped completely. Why? Is it significant that neither of the female justices joined in the *Monroe* dissent?

5. Off-Campus Harassment

The *Gebser* and *Monroe* decisions addressed both adult and peer sex-based harassment but did so within a traditional, on-campus frame. However, much educational advancement happens off-campus or outside of brick and mortar buildings. Consider that college residences may be off-campus. Online classrooms and discussion groups may be located in cyberspace—not technically on-campus. Students meet each other and their teachers or coaches on Facebook and Instagram. Students obtain learning and work experience in private labs, on the job with employers running businesses, and in governmental agencies. How should schools deal with sexual harassment in these contexts. How should courts?

Some administrators refer to online harassment as cyberbullying. Cyberbullying is often a misnomer. When offensive conduct is sex-based, arguably it should be called out as sex discrimination. A bullying label minimizes the sometimes subtle oppression and reflects society's denial of the discriminatory nature of the behavior. However, a sexual harassment label carries such political implications (i.e., that the accusers are "femi-nazis" or radicals, etc.) that some school administrators do not want to use it. They would rather address bullying successfully than fail to get permission or public buy-in to curb discriminatory (and perhaps already illegal) harassment.

This section examines two different types of off-campus harassment under Title IX; online sex-based harassment and the harassment of student interns. Consider whether these problems should be handled differently or whether the courts took the proper approach.

---

100. Schaffner, *supra* note 97, at 144.

A. Online Harassment

A recent Pew study shows that two-thirds of young adults ages 18–29 have been subject to some type of online sexual harassment, and this behavior disproportionately targets women, people of color, LGBTQ individuals, and those with disabilities.[101] In a groundbreaking decision in December 2018, *Feminist Majority Foundation v. University of Mary Washington*, the Fourth Circuit Court of Appeals ruled that universities cannot ignore student complaints about anonymous, online sexual harassment. The Court ruled that Title IX and the Equal Protection Clause require schools to address cyberharassment, and that threats to kill or injure others are not protected by the First Amendment.

Feminist Majority Foundation v. Hurley
911 F.3d 674 (4th Cir. 2018)

KING, Circuit Judge:

Plaintiffs Feminist Majority Foundation [FMF], Feminists United on Campus, and several Feminists United members appeal from the district court's dismissal of their civil action, filed pursuant to Title IX of the Education Amendments of 1972, as well as 42 U.S.C. § 1983 ["a § 1983 claim against UMW's [University of Mary Washington's] former president, Dr. Richard Hurley, for violating the Equal Protection Clause of the Fourteenth Amendment"]. . . . As explained below, we affirm the dismissal of the § 1983 claim and part of the Title IX retaliation claim. We vacate, however, the dismissal of the Title IX sex discrimination claim and the balance of the retaliation claim. We therefore remand for further proceedings.

I.

A.

. . . Plaintiff Feminists United is a student organization at UMW and a local affiliate of plaintiff Feminist Majority Foundation, a national organization. During the 2014–2015 academic year, plaintiffs Paige McKinsey, Julia Michels, Kelli Musick, Jordan Williams, and Alexis Lehman were UMW students who served on Feminists United's executive board.

1.

In November 2014, UMW's student senate voted to authorize male-only fraternities at the University. During a campus town hall meeting following the senate's authorization, Feminists United members questioned the wisdom of having such fraternities at UMW, in light of "research that showed that Greek life on campus increased the number of [on-campus] sexual assaults." Plaintiff McKinsey was particularly troubled by the vote of approval, and she believed that UMW had failed

---

101. Maeve Duggan, Pew Research Center, Online Harassment 2017 (July 11, 2017), http://www.pewinternet.org/2017/07/11/online-harassment-2017/.

to support victims of sexual assault in the past. Soon after the town hall meeting, UMW students debated the Greek life vote on Yik Yak, a now-defunct social media application. Yik Yak allowed its users within a limited geographic range to create and view anonymous messages known as "Yaks." Within the Yik Yak conversational thread available at UMW, several students expressed—in offensive terms—strong criticism of Feminists United and its members for their opposition to on-campus fraternities.

On November 21, 2014, several Feminists United members met with UMW's Title IX coordinator, Dr. Leah Cox, to explain their concerns about the University's past failures in responding to student sexual assault complaints. As the Feminists United members walked home from the meeting, other UMW students drove by and screamed, "Fuck the feminists!"

Two days later, on November 23, a UMW student videotaped members of the UMW men's rugby team performing a chant that glorified violence against women, including rape and necrophilia. Later that month, the student who recorded the rugby team video provided it to the UMW administration and informed plaintiff McKinsey about the video. Members of Feminists United subsequently met with then-President Hurley to discuss the rugby team's offensive chant. They were assured by Hurley that some unspecified "action" was being taken in response thereto.

. . . .

On February 20, 2015, members of the UMW men's rugby team approached plaintiff McKinsey in the University's dining hall and confronted her about the newspaper article ["explaining '[w]hy UMW is not a feminist friendly campus."]. That same day, McKinsey informed Dr. Cox—UMW's Title IX coordinator—that McKinsey felt unsafe on the UMW campus after her encounter with the rugby team members, particularly in light of the threats lodged against her and other Feminists United members on Yik Yak and the school newspaper's website. McKinsey requested that the UMW administration take "some sort of action."

. . . .

On March 11, 2015, UMW held an open forum about sexual assault on campus, at which President Hurley downplayed the seriousness of the rugby team's chant. . . .

. . . .

On March 19, 2015, after several UMW students expressed outrage on Facebook over the rugby team's chant, President Hurley announced that all rugby activities had been suspended indefinitely and that the rugby players would be required to participate in anti-sexual assault and violence training. Immediately after Hurley's announcement, a flurry of harassing and threatening Yaks were directed at members of Feminists United, blaming them for the rugby team's suspension. The Yaks named plaintiffs McKinsey and Musick, along with Feminists United member Grace Mann, and contained threats of physical and sexual violence. By way of example, the Yaks threatened:

- "Gonna tie these feminists to the radiator and [g]rape them in the mouth";

- "Dandy's about to kill a bitch . . . or two"; and

- "Can we euthanize whoever caused this bullshit?"

Several of the offending Yaks, as alleged in the Complaint, also referred to Feminists United members by such terms as "femicunts, feminazis, cunts, bitches, hoes, and dikes."

. . . .

On March 25, plaintiff Michels sent an email to President Hurley, Dr. Cox, and UMW's vice president, Douglas Searcy. The email explained that Feminists United members had documented "nearly 200 examples of students using Yik Yak to post either violent, vitriolic hate or threats against [them]," and that they feared for their safety on the UMW campus. Michels therein requested a meeting between Feminists United and the UMW administration to address the Feminists United members' safety concerns. As a result, Cox, Searcy, and other UMW employees met with Feminists United members the next day. The members then requested that the UMW administration take a number of steps. Those requests included: (1) contacting Yik Yak to have the Yik Yak application disabled on UMW's campus; (2) barring access to Yik Yak on UMW's wireless network; (3) communicating "more transparent[ly]" with students; (4) announcing to UMW's student body that Feminists United "had no role in . . . [UMW's] decision [to suspend rugby activities];" and (5) hosting an "assembly to explain rape culture and discuss harassment, cyber bullying[,] and social media issues."

Rather than grant the requests of Feminists United, Dr. Cox sent a schoolwide email on March 27, 2015, addressing the University's recent cyberbullying issues. Cox asserted that nothing could be done, that is, the University had "no recourse for such cyber bullying." Instead, she encouraged UMW students to report any threatening online comments to Yik Yak or other platforms where such comments were made. Disappointed with Cox's approach to the ongoing threats, plaintiff Michels responded and urged Cox and UMW administrators to "take the lead against this problem."

On March 30, 2015, following plaintiff Michels's response to Dr. Cox, another member of Feminists United emailed President Hurley and suggested that UMW's hands-off response to the offending Yaks had contravened the statutory mandate of Title IX. By that time, more than 700 harassing and threatening Yaks had been directed at Feminists United and its members.

. . . .

On April 17, 2015—in an event later determined to be unrelated to the offending Yaks—UMW student and Feminists United member Grace Mann was killed by another student who was her roommate. During the immediate aftermath of that terrible event, Feminists United members were unaware that it had no apparent connection to the harassing and threatening Yaks. Mann's demise prompted one Feminists United member to send an email to UMW administrators chastising the University for its failure to respond to the Yik Yak bullying and threats. UMW administrators did not respond to that email.

2.

On May 7, 2015, the plaintiffs filed a complaint with the Department of Education's Office of Civil Rights (the "OCR complaint"), alleging that UMW had contravened Title IX by failing to address the hostile environment at the University resulting from the sexually harassing and threatening online posts. The plaintiffs also held a press conference on UMW's campus to announce the OCR complaint. That same day, UMW issued a statement denying the allegations in the OCR complaint. After the University's denials, several messages were posted on Yik Yak that again harassed Feminists United members, and also criticized the filing of the OCR complaint.

. . . .

B.

In May 2017, the plaintiffs withdrew the OCR complaint and initiated this lawsuit in the Eastern District of Virginia, alleging, inter alia, the three claims now on appeal. First, the Complaint alleges that UMW contravened Title IX by being deliberately indifferent to student-on-student sex discrimination (the "sex discrimination claim"). In support of the sex discrimination claim, the Complaint specifies that UMW's deliberate indifference served to create and foster a campus atmosphere so hostile that Feminists United members refrained from leaving their homes, attending classes, and participating in campus events. Second, the Complaint alleges that UMW retaliated against the plaintiffs for advocating against sexual assault and reporting sexual harassment, also in violation of Title IX (the "retaliation claim"). According to the Complaint, UMW retaliated against the plaintiffs in two ways: (1) the University was deliberately indifferent to UMW students harassing and threatening members of Feminists United for engaging in protected conduct; and (2) President Hurley prepared and released his June 2015 letter, which made false accusations against—and was intended to disparage—members of Feminists United. Third, under § 1983 of Title 42, the Complaint alleges that Hurley infringed on the plaintiffs' equal protection rights under the Fourteenth Amendment (the "equal protection claim"). The Complaint alleges that Hurley contravened the plaintiffs' equal protection rights by, inter alia, failing to act against those UMW students who had sexually harassed members of Feminists United.

. . . .

III.

. . . .

2.

. . . .

The district court explained that the sexual harassment endured by members of Feminists United "took place in a context over which UMW had limited, if any, control." Furthermore, the court concluded that UMW was not deliberately indifferent to such harassment because it "t[ook] some action," including coordinating listening circles and sending a campus police officer to attend two student events. To the extent the plaintiffs faulted UMW for failing to respond to the harassment in their preferred manner, the court observed that "Title IX does not require [a university] to meet the particular remedial demands of its students." The court also emphasized that one of those demands — "banning Yik Yak from the campus wireless network" — might expose the University to First Amendment liability.

3.

. . . .

a.

The district court determined that UMW had little — if any — control over the context in which the Feminists United members were harassed, because nearly all of that harassment occurred through Yik Yak. We are satisfied, however, that the court's decision in that regard is undermined by the Complaint's factual allegations. In so ruling, we remain mindful that the Supreme Court's decision limits an educational institution's Title IX liability for student-on-student sexual harassment to those situations where the defendant institution "exercises substantial control over both the harasser and the context in which the known harassment occurs."

We begin the substantial control analysis by identifying the context in which the sexual harassment occurred and UMW's control over that context. The Complaint alleges that much of the harassment occurred through Yik Yak. Although that harassment was communicated through cyberspace, the Complaint shows that UMW had substantial control over the context of the harassment because it actually transpired on campus. Specifically, due to Yik Yak's location-based feature, the harassing and threatening messages originated on or within the immediate vicinity of the UMW campus. In addition, some of the offending Yaks were posted using the University's wireless network, and the harassers necessarily created those Yaks on campus. Moreover, the harassment concerned events occurring on campus and specifically targeted UMW students.

Furthermore, to the extent the sexual harassment was communicated through UMW's wireless network, the Complaint alleges that the University could have disabled access to Yik Yak campuswide. The Complaint also alleges that the University could have sought to identify those students using UMW's network to harass and threaten Feminists United members. If the University had pinpointed the harassers, it could then have circumscribed their use of UMW's network. Indeed, it is widely known that a university can control activities that occur on its own network. A university may, for example, bar a student caught downloading music or movies in violation of copyright laws from accessing its network.

Beyond the University's technical capacity to control the means by which the harassing and threatening messages were transmitted, the Complaint demonstrates that UMW could have exercised control in other ways that might have corrected the hostile environment. For instance, UMW administrators could have more clearly communicated to the student body that the University would not tolerate sexually harassing behavior either in person or online. The University also could have conducted mandatory assemblies to explain and discourage cyberbullying and sex discrimination, and it could have provided anti-sexual harassment training to the entire student body and faculty. In these circumstances, we are satisfied that the Complaint sufficiently alleges UMW's substantial control over the context in which the alleged harassment occurred.

The substantial control analysis also requires us to consider the educational institution's control over the harasser, especially its "disciplinary authority." Under the Complaint, UMW had the ability to punish those students who posted sexually harassing and threatening messages online. Indeed, the Complaint recounts that UMW had previously disciplined students—members of the men's rugby team—for derogatory off-campus speech. If UMW could punish students for offensive off-campus speech that was not aimed at any particular students, the University also could have disciplined students for harassing and threatening on-campus speech targeted at Feminists United members. In fact, according to the Complaint, Dr. Cox actually advised Feminists United members to contact her if they felt threatened by an "identified member[ ] of [the] community." Viewed in the proper light, Cox's statement demonstrates UMW's capacity to exercise control over students engaging in threatening online behavior.

To the extent the University contends it was unable to control the harassers because the offending Yaks were anonymous, we readily reject that proposition. The Complaint alleges that the University never sought to identify the students who posted the offending messages on Yik Yak, even though some of those messages were facilitated by (i.e., posted through the use of) UMW's network. Nor did the University ever ask Yik Yak to identify those users who had harassed and threatened UMW students. The University cannot escape liability based on facially anonymous posts when, according to the Complaint, UMW never sought to discern whether it could identify the harassers.

At bottom, in assessing whether UMW—under the Complaint—had sufficient control over the harassers and the context of the harassment, we cannot conclude that UMW could turn a blind eye to the sexual harassment that pervaded and disrupted its campus solely because the offending conduct took place through cyberspace. Rather, we are satisfied that the Complaint sufficiently alleges that UMW could exert substantial control over the context in which the harassment occurred and could exercise disciplinary authority over those UMW students who sexually harassed and threatened the Feminists United members.

b.

The district court also ruled that the sex discrimination claim fails because the Complaint does not sufficiently allege UMW's deliberate indifference to sexual harassment. We again disagree. Simply put, the Complaint demonstrates that—although

UMW was not entirely unresponsive to allegations of harassment—the University did not engage in efforts that were "reasonably calculated to end [the] harassment." Indeed, the Complaint portrays repeated instances of UMW students targeting and harassing Feminists United members with threats and other sex-based hostility. Those harassing activities were reported to the University on multiple occasions over many months. UMW's administrators, however, merely responded with two listening circles, a generic email, and by sending a campus police officer with a threatened student on one evening after particularly aggressive and targeted Yaks.

The University faces serious difficulties in its effort to convince us that the Complaint does not sufficiently allege deliberate indifference. . . . The University, however, never investigated the harassment and threats, and never asked any law enforcement agencies to investigate them.

On the allegations of the Complaint, we are satisfied that the plaintiffs sufficiently allege that UMW exhibited deliberate indifference to known instances of sexual harassment. Although the Complaint acknowledges that UMW took limited steps in response to the harassing and threatening Yaks, those actions do not preclude Title IX liability at this stage. UMW's decision to have a campus police officer at two student meetings was a short-term countermeasure—a one-off—that failed to address the more than six-month harassment campaign directed at Feminists United and its members. Moreover, viewed in the proper light, UMW's position is undermined by the fact that its campus environment was such that a police officer's presence was necessary at two student meetings.

As for the listening circles, we agree that university administrators listening to students' reports of harassment and threats is an important step in seeking to rectify a sexually hostile environment. But the mere act of listening to students is not a remedy in and of itself. Significantly, after the Feminists United members placed the UMW administration on notice of the hostile environment permeating the campus, the University made no real effort to investigate or end the harassment and threats contained in the Yaks.

Rather than seeking to end the online harassment and threats, Dr. Cox—as UMW's Title IX coordinator—simply advised the Feminists United members that the University was powerless to address the offending conduct. President Hurley likewise declined to take any meaningful action to curtail the online harassment and publicly downplayed the seriousness of the threats aimed at the Feminists United members. Under the Complaint, we are therefore unable to conclude at the pleading stage that UMW's response to the sexual harassment of Feminists United members was not "clearly unreasonable."

c.

In its deliberate indifference analysis, the district court also agreed with the University that the First Amendment circumscribed UMW's ability to respond to the online harassment and threats suffered by the plaintiffs. On appeal, the University maintains that two actions requested by the plaintiffs implicate the First

Amendment, namely that students be punished for their speech, and that students be barred from accessing Yik Yak on UMW's wireless network. As explained below, First Amendment concerns do not render the University's response to the sexual harassment and threats legally sufficient for two sound reasons: (1) true threats are not protected speech, and (2) the University had several responsive options that did not present First Amendment concerns.

(1)

We first address the University's expressed apprehension about punishing students for their speech. Put simply, we are satisfied that its First Amendment concerns about penalizing speech lack a proper basis. The University could have vigorously responded to the threatening Yaks without implicating the First Amendment because "true threats" are not protected speech. See *Virginia v. Black*, 538 U.S. 343, 359 (2003) (recognizing that "true threats" are not constitutionally protected and describing them as "statements where the speaker means to communicate a serious expression of an intent to commit an act of unlawful violence to a particular individual or group of individuals").

The Supreme Court and our Court have consistently recognized the principle that threatening speech is not protected by the Constitution. See, e.g., *Watts v. United States*, 394 U.S. 705, 707 (1969) (upholding constitutionality of statute making it illegal to threaten president with physical violence); *United States v. Maxton*, 940 F.2d 103, 105–06 (4th Cir. 1991) ("Threats to kidnap or injure persons are legislatively proscribable, falling within that group of expressions, such as fighting words, which are not constitutionally protected pure speech." Moreover, both federal law and Virginia law criminalize the communication of threats to kill or injure others.

. . . .

(2)

Furthermore, the Complaint alleges that UMW could have taken other steps in response to the harassment that would not have implicated any First Amendment concerns. For example, the University could have more vigorously denounced the harassing and threatening conduct, clarified that Feminists United members were not responsible for the rugby team's suspension, conducted a mandatory assembly of the student body to discuss and discourage such harassment through social media, or hired an outside expert to assist in developing policies for addressing and preventing harassment. Additionally, UMW could have offered counseling services for those impacted by the targeted harassment. To be sure, Title IX required none of those specific actions. Consideration of an educational institution's remedial options, however, inheres in the deliberate indifference analysis. In other words, when an educational institution claims that it has done all it can to address instances of sexual harassment and threats, a reviewing court should consider whether the institution failed to take other obvious and reasonable steps. The Complaint thus adequately alleges that UMW could have addressed the harassing and threatening Yaks without exposing itself to First Amendment liability.

d.

At bottom, we are satisfied that the plaintiffs have sufficiently alleged a sex discrimination claim under Title IX, predicated on UMW's deliberate indifference to the specified student-on-student harassment. We will therefore vacate the dismissal of that claim.

. . . [A thorough and lengthy discussion of remaining claims is omitted.]

AGEE, Circuit Judge, dissenting in part and concurring in part:

. . . .

B.

. . . .

I. Title IX: Deliberate Indifference to Peer Discrimination

The majority opinion contorts the cause of action recognized in *Davis*, beyond recognition. In *Davis*, the Supreme Court held that a recipient of federal education funds may be liable under Title IX for peer harassment that occurs in a context controlled by the funding recipient only when its response to actual notice of that harassment is clearly unreasonable. But the majority's unprecedented view of a Title IX *Davis* claim exposes a funding recipient to liability even when the allegations show that neither the student victims nor their school knows who the harassers are, much less has control over them, and the school has no control over the environment in which the harassment occurred. Because a faithful application of *Davis* requires affirming the district court's dismissal of the Complaint's Title IX sex discrimination claim, I respectfully dissent.

. . . .

In sum, FMF fails to adequately allege the threshold requirement of control over the harasser. Because the Yaks were anonymous, they could have been posted by anyone within a geographic area that extended well beyond the University's campus. The Complaint contains only the "naked assertion," that students posted them and that allegation is insufficient as a matter of law to plead a cognizable Title IX claim. Consequently, the district court's dismissal of the deliberate indifference to discrimination claim should be affirmed on this basis alone.

2.

Even if FMF's Complaint had adequately alleged substantial control over the harassers, that would not end the threshold control inquiry necessary to hold a funding recipient liable. *Davis* separately requires that the funding recipient also exercise substantial control over the context of the harassment. FMF's allegations do not plausibly claim that the University exercised such control over Yik Yak or the offensive Yaks. This deficiency independently supports the district court's dismissal of FMF's deliberate indifference claim.

Davis' context requirement is most readily satisfied when the harassment occurs on a school's campus. That was the case in *Davis*: a student harassed another student "during school hours and on school grounds," and principally "in the classroom." . . .

This is not to say that a school never has substantial control over the context of harassment when the underlying events occur off campus. But there must be some additional proof that the school exercised dominion over the environment in which the alleged harassment occurred. For example, relying on *Davis*, a funding recipient may be found to have exercised substantial control when the underlying harassment occurred on other property controlled by the defendant, such as a school bus, or during a school-supervised activity off campus. In all events, the essential hook under *Davis* is that the school has "substantial control" over where the harassment occurred such that it has authority to take remedial action in that place.

. . . .

[B]ecause FMF's claim arises from alleged harassment that occurred in the ether, on a social media app, the location of the harassment is several degrees removed from the traditional geographic consideration: the funding recipient's real property. Thus, at a basic level, the context of the harassment in this case is markedly different from prior *Davis* claims. Online harassment will never, by its nature, occur on a school's grounds or other physical location controlled by a funding recipient in the same way that in-person harassment will. In short, the manner in which in-person harassment can be found to satisfy the context inquiry will necessarily differ from the way in which online harassment could be found to satisfy that inquiry. Even so, *Davis*' context inquiry must be satisfied before a funding recipient can be said to incur any liability.

. . . .

That the alleged harassment occurred online is not necessarily dispositive, however, because *Davis*' physical location requirements may have virtual counterparts. For example, a funding recipient may own or otherwise have a property interest in the online forum where the harassment occurred or the means the harasser used to access that forum. But neither circumstance has been alleged here. Specifically, the Complaint does not allege that the University owned Yik Yak or otherwise exercised any control over its content or operation. From all that can be reasonably inferred from the Complaint, Yik Yak was a third-party social media app that was unrelated to the University and open to students and non-students alike. Hence, nothing in the Complaint allows the conclusion that the University had any authority to control what happened on Yik Yak.

. . . .

The absence of allegations concerning the wireless network merits a brief additional discussion because the majority opinion asserts otherwise, claiming that "some of the offending Yaks were posted using the University's wireless network, and the harassers necessarily created those Yaks on campus." This is baseless speculation without support in the Complaint. At no point does the Complaint allege any facts that connect any of the Yaks to the University's wireless network.

. . . .

The Complaint simply fails to plead a fundamental part of a *Davis* claim: that the University substantially controlled the context where the harassment occurred. When comparing the hallmarks of the context inquiry under *Davis* against the Complaint's allegations, the Complaint fails to plausibly allege facts sufficient to satisfy this threshold requirement. As such, the University cannot be held liable under Title IX.

. . . .

Because the Complaint failed to plausibly allege facts that the University exercised control over Yik Yak or the means the harassers were using to access Yik Yak, the Complaint fails to meet the minimal pleading requirement that the University controlled the context of the harassment at issue in this case. And because a litigant must satisfy *Davis'* context inquiry in order to bring suit, the district court appropriately granted the University's motion to dismiss for failure to state a deliberate indifference claim.

. . . .

Only by distorting and ignoring the original principles set out in *Davis* can the majority reach its preferred result, holding that the Complaint states a plausible claim of deliberate indifference against the University. The majority has repositioned the once high bar for a *Davis* claim to a new low. As demonstrated, the Complaint does not contain factual allegations that satisfy *Davis'* harasser or context inquiries. And because the Complaint does not survive 12(b)(6) review concerning these threshold requirements for a deliberate indifference claim, there's no need to proceed further and consider whether the University's response was clearly unreasonable. The district court's decision to dismiss this claim should be affirmed.

. . . .

Notes and Discussion

1. Technical Control Does it matter whether the harassers were students? Was it sufficient that, per the majority, the University controlled the "context"? Or is the dissent correct that the plaintiffs needed to demonstrate that the University controlled Yik Yak? Does it matter for liability under Title IX whether harassers posted Yaks on campus, using campus equipment if they were known students? Would off-campus posts from private devices of known students have triggered Title IX? Is the dissent's concern valid? Or would an outcome dictated by the dissent merely encourage schools to remain ignorant and avoid investigation of similar problems? Can anyone control cyberspace? Should they?

2. Deliberate Indifference Did the University demonstrate deliberate indifference to sex-based harassment, threats, and hostility? Explain. Does the court make clear how it determined the threshold for deliberate indifference? Should *any* responsive action insulate a school from Title IX liability?

376 SEXUAL HARASSMENT AT SCHOOL

3. First Amendment Chapter 9 addresses the First Amendment defense in more detail. Consider returning to these questions about *Hurley* after review of that section. Were the Yaks "free speech"? Were they merely speech or were they oppressive actions or cyber abuse? How about the rugby team chant? Explain. What is the difference between "pure" speech protected by the Constitution's First Amendment and "hate" speech, "fighting words," or "pornography"? Is the First Amendment a valid defense to censorship in this context? If the Yaks had threatened to set off a bomb on campus, would that speech have been protected by the First Amendment?

4. Cheap Speech Whether or not the Yaks were threats or hate speech, one could argue that they were "cheap speech." Cheap speach is a phrase coined by Professor Eugene Volokh in his 1995 article, *Cheap Speech and What It Will Do*,[102] to describe inexpensive communications and publications. Volokh suggests that the regulation of electronic speech should track the treatment of more traditional messages. However, he acknowledges that the electronic format creates new issues that did not exist with older communication methods. Volokh cautions:

> The proto-infobahn of today — the Internet, bulletin boards, and various commercial services — has already generated quite a few First Amendment controversies. . . .

> . . . For instance, there's already a lively debate about the propriety of regulating sexually harassing speech; harassing speech on electronic bulletin boards should just be a special case of this. . . .

> . . . The law of speech is premised on certain (often unspoken) assumptions about the way the speech market operates. If these assumptions aren't valid for new technologies, the law may have to evolve to reflect the changes.[103]

His point is that the unique nature of electronic speech may require adaptation of legal regulations. Should the law should regulate sexually harassing cheap speech under Title IX? Explain.

5. Reliance on *Davis* versus Enforcement of Title IX In its discussion of law, the majority reiterated Title IX's prohibition. It held, "Beginning with the plaintiffs' sex discrimination claim against UMW, we recognize that Title IX provides . . ." that "[n]o person . . . shall, on the basis of sex, be excluded from participation in, be denied the benefits of, or be subjected to discrimination under any education program or activity receiving Federal financial assistance." The dissent suggested, "That the alleged harassment occurred online is not necessarily dispositive, however, because *Davis*'s physical location requirements may have virtual counterparts." Did the dissent rely too heavily on *Davis*'s physical location requirements? Is *Davis* even relevant to this cyber context? That is, does reliance on *Davis* too narrowly circumscribe the reach of Title IX? Or is the dissent correct that *Hurley* lacks the virtual counterparts for Title IX application? Explain.

---

102. 104 YALE L.J. 1805 (1995).
103. *Id.* at 1843–44.

B. Harassment of Student Interns

Title IX protects against discrimination at school and, at least currently in the Fourth Circuit, in school-affiliated cyberspace. However, many students receive some educational instruction and practice training at worksites or other occupational centers as student interns or externs. While some states have laws that protect student interns, Title VII typically applies only if the student receives payment for work. The question arises whether Title IX applies in the case of a student intern sexually harassed on the job.[104] Who is liable? The school? The employer? Anyone?

In their article, *Legal Limbo of The Student Intern: The Responsibility of Colleges and Universities to Protect Student Interns Against Sexual Harassment*,[105] Professors Cynthia Grant Bowman and MaryBeth Lipp explore how some student interns may fall through the gaps between Title VII and Title IX. They demonstrate that, under current law, no one may be held liable for the sexual harassment of unpaid student interns. They emphasize, however, that Title IX should address this problem. They argue, "While students have many classes with different professors, an intern remains in the same environment each day, all day long, and may even work exclusively for one person. Harassment in this environment hinders a student intern's ability to complete an internship effectively."[106] Therefore, Bowman and Lipp contend that "a bright-line rule immunizing universities from liability for harassment of interns at off-campus sites is inconsistent with Title IX's purpose of ensuring a genuinely equal education to male and female students." They recommend that courts examine the university's involvement in the internship by considering a number of factors. "Such factors would include, for example, the proximity of the setting to the university, the amount of experience the university has had with placing interns at that site, and the existence and terms of any contract between the school and the employment setting."[107]

Two cases showcase the issues presented for student interns. Consider the differences between them.

O'Connor v. Davis
126 F.3d 112 (2d Cir. 1997)

Walker, Circuit Judge:

. . . .

While enrolled as a student at Marymount College ("Marymount"), a private Catholic college located in Tarrytown, New York, Bridget O'Connor majored in

---

104. *See, e.g.*, Blair Hickman and Christie Thompson, *How Unpaid Interns Aren't Protected Against Sexual Harassment*, ProPublica (Aug. 9, 2013).

105. 23 Harv. Women's L.J. 95 (2000).

106. *Id.* at 100.

107. *Id.* at 120.

social work. As a component of her major, O'Connor was required during her senior year to perform 200 hours of field work at one of several Marymount-approved organizations. . . . Marymount arranged for O'Connor to be placed for her senior-year internship [in September 1994] with Rockland, a hospital for the mentally disabled operated by New York State. Because this internship was considered to be "work study" for financial aid purposes, O'Connor received, through Marymount, federal work study funds for the time she spent performing her volunteer work with Rockland.

. . . .

Dr. James Davis ("Davis") worked as a licensed psychiatrist at Rockland. Approximately two days after O'Connor began her internship, Davis referred to O'Connor, in her presence, as "Miss Sexual Harassment"—a term Davis later explained was intended, as a compliment, to convey the idea that O'Connor was physically attractive and, as such, was likely to be the object of sexual harassment. O'Connor promptly complained about Davis's comment to [her Rockland supervisor Lisa] Punzone, who explained that Davis made similar comments to her, and that O'Connor should try her best to ignore him.

Not only did Davis continue to address O'Connor as "Miss Sexual Harassment," he added to his repertoire of inappropriate sexual remarks. For instance, on one Monday morning, Davis told O'Connor that she looked tired, and that she and her boyfriend must have had "a good time" the night before. On another occasion, Davis pointed to a picture in a newspaper of a woman dressed only in underwear and announced that O'Connor was the woman photographed. He also suggested to O'Connor (and other women present) that they should participate in an "orgy." Finally, on yet another occasion, Davis told O'Connor to remove her clothing in preparation for a meeting with him; he explained, "Don't you always take your clothes off before you go in the doctor's office?"

O'Connor was apparently not Davis's only target; he also commented regularly on the physical appearance of a number of women employed at Rockland, and directed sexual jokes and sexually suggestive noises at them—particularly, as Davis put it, on occasions when he thought the women "looked very well that day." Davis also made "jokes" about female patients—suggesting in one instance that a women patient would benefit from sterilization and, on another occasion, when considering a woman patient who was an incest victim, stating: "the family that plays together stays together."

Although O'Connor reported a good deal of this conduct to Punzone, Punzone did not report any of O'Connor's complaints to James Wagner, her own supervisor, until January of 1995. And when Wagner learned of O'Connor's encounters with Davis, he, like Punzone, did nothing to remedy the situation.

Also in January of 1995, O'Connor complained to Virginia Kaiser, Marymount's social work field instructor, who in turn brought Davis's conduct to the attention of Madeline Connolly, Rockland's director of social work. Connolly then notified

Wilbur T. Aldridge, Rockland's affirmative action administrator, who thereafter investigated O'Connor's complaint.

Finally, at some point in January of 1995, O'Connor left Rockland; however, Marymount arranged for her to complete her internship at another facility.

In March of 1995, O'Connor filed the instant action against Marymount, Rockland, the State of New York, and various Marymount and Rockland employees, alleging, inter alia, sexual harassment in violation of Title VII, and Title IX. The action was eventually discontinued against Marymount, Punzone, Wagner, Connolly, and Davis himself. The remaining defendants (Rockland and New York State) moved for summary judgment on several grounds. First, they argued that the plaintiff's Title VII claim should be dismissed because O'Connor was not an "employee" of Rockland within the meaning of Title VII. Second, the defendants argued that the Title IX claim should be dismissed because Rockland was not an "educational institution" as set forth in Title IX. Finally, the defendants argued that O'Connor failed to establish a prima facie case of sexual harassment.

In an opinion and order dated May 20, 1996, the district court granted the defendants' summary judgment motion, agreeing that O'Connor was not an "employee" under Title VII and that Rockland was not an "educational institution" under **Title IX.1** Because of this disposition, the district court did not reach the defendants' assertion that O'Connor failed to establish a prima facie case of sexual harassment.

I. Title VII

. . . [The court gave a detailed review of the application of Title VII.]

Because the absence of either direct or indirect economic remuneration or the promise thereof is undisputed in this case, we agree with the district court that O'Connor was not a Rockland employee within the meaning of Title VII and thus that her discrimination claim under that statute must fail.

II. Title IX

O'Connor's second argument is that the district court erred in dismissing her Title IX claim in the belief that Title IX did not apply to Rockland because Rockland is not an "education program or activity." O'Connor urges that because Rockland both receives federal financial assistance either through the state, its patients, or its employees, and also operates "vocational training through an organized educational program," it is subject to Title IX's prohibition against sex discrimination — proscribed conduct that includes sexual harassment.

. . . .

Although the term "education" is not defined by the regulations governing Title IX and has not been construed by this court, O'Connor argues that because Rockland provides its volunteers with some modicum of on-the-job training, Rockland therefore provides vocational training, and, on that basis, may be considered to operate an organized educational program. We decline, however, to convert

Rockland's willingness to accept volunteers into conduct analogous to administering an "education program" as contemplated by Title IX.

Preliminarily, in light of O'Connor's contention that Rockland's internship program is analogous to vocational training, it is instructive to look to 34 C.F.R. § 106.2, which defines for Title IX purposes the term "institution of vocational education" as:

> a school or institution (except an institution of professional or undergraduate higher education) which has as its primary purpose preparation of students to pursue a technical, skilled, or semiskilled occupation or trade . . . , whether or not the school or institution offers certificates, diplomas, or degrees and whether or not it offers fulltime study.

24 C.F.R. § 106.2(n) (emphasis supplied). Rockland plainly does not satisfy this definition, as its "primary purpose" is in no sense to educate: it accepts no tuition, has no teachers, has no evaluation process, and requires no regular hours or course of study for its volunteer workers.

Not only is Rockland's internship program not classifiable as a vocational program, Rockland also cannot be said more generally to operate an "education program" because the institution maintains none of the characteristics associated with being an educator. The environment at Rockland is not, for example, analogous to a teaching hospital's "mixed employment-training context," . . . Nor is Rockland's acceptance of volunteers comparable to running an educational or vocational program at a state correctional facility, as such programs typically provide instructors, evaluations, and offer a particular course of training.

Finally, the fact that Marymount operates an "education program" may not be imputed to Rockland simply because O'Connor was a student at the former while she performed volunteer work with the latter. Factors that could lead to a different conclusion simply are not present here: the two entities have no institutional affiliation; there is no written agreement binding the two entities in any way; no staff are shared; no funds are circulated between them; and, indeed, Marymount students had previously volunteered at Rockland on only a few occasions. The only hint of a connection between Marymount and Rockland lies in the fact that (1) Marymount contacted Rockland for the purpose of placing O'Connor in an internship, and (2) Marymount appears to base its evaluation of its students' performance during their internships in part on an evaluation prepared by the person who supervised the student on-site—which, in O'Connor's case, would have been Lisa Punzone of Rockland. Such connections are insufficient to establish Rockland as an agent or arm of Marymount for Title IX purposes. Rather, we think it clear that Rockland is a state-funded psychiatric hospital, with no affiliation to any educational institution whatsoever, that allows volunteers from a nearby college to perform (with minimal supervision) volunteer work at its facility. Rockland thus does not conduct an "education program or activity," and O'Connor's Title IX claim was properly dismissed.

Doe v. Mercy Catholic Medical Center

850 F.3d 545 (3d Cir. 2017)

Fisher, Circuit Judge.

I

Medical residencies are a vital component of American medical education. They provide new doctors a supervised transition between the pure academics of medical school and the realities of practice. Generally they do so successfully: Our nation's residency programs reliably produce some of the "finest physicians and medical researchers in the world." But as this case shows, these programs aren't exempt from charges of sex discrimination. Here we must decide whether an ex-resident, proceeding anonymously as Jane Doe, can bring private causes of action for sex discrimination under Title IX against Mercy Catholic Medical Center, a private teaching hospital operating a residency program. The District Court held she cannot and dismissed her complaint in its entirety. We will affirm in part and reverse in part that order. Doe's Title IX retaliation and quid pro quo claims endure. Her Title IX hostile environment claim is, however, time-barred.

. . . .

Under a residency agreement, Doe joined Mercy's diagnostic radiology residency program in 2011 as a second-year, or R2. The program [affiliated with Drexel University's College of Medicine] offered training in all radiology subspecialties in a community-hospital setting combining hands-on experience with didactic teaching. As required, Doe attended daily morning lectures presented by faculty and afternoon case presentations given by residents under faculty or attending physicians' supervision. She took a mandatory physics class taught on Drexel's campus, attended monthly radiology lectures and society meetings, joined in interdepartmental conferences, and sat for annual examinations to assess her progress and competence.

Doe says the director of Mercy's residency program, whom she calls Dr. James Roe, sexually harassed her and retaliated against her for complaining about his behavior, resulting in her eventual dismissal. Early on, Dr. Roe inquired about her personal life and learned she was living apart from her husband. He found opportunities to see and speak with her more than would otherwise be expected, often looking at her suggestively. This made Doe uncomfortable, especially when the two were alone. From these interactions she surmised Dr. Roe was sexually attracted to her and wished to pursue a relationship, though they both were married.

Three months into her residency Doe sent Dr. Roe an email voicing concern that others knew about his interest in her. She wanted their relationship to remain professional, she said, but Dr. Roe persisted, stating he wanted to meet with her while they attended a conference in Chicago. She replied with text messages to clear the air that she didn't want to pursue a relationship with him. Apparently displeased, Dr. Roe reported these messages to Mercy's human resources department, or HR.

In response, HR called Doe to a meeting where she described Dr. Roe's conduct, like how he'd touched her hand at work, and said his unwelcome sexual attention was negatively affecting her training. The next day HR referred Doe to a psychiatrist, noting that her attendance was optional. Doe, however, believed Mercy would use it against her if she didn't go, given her complaints against Dr. Roe. She thus attended three sessions and complained there about Dr. Roe's conduct, but she heard nothing more from HR. Later Dr. Roe apologized to Doe for reporting her. He did it, he said, for fear he'd be reprimanded for having an inappropriate relationship with her. Thereafter two male faculty members, both close with Dr. Roe, trained her significantly less than they had before.

In Fall 2012 Dr. Roe learned Doe was getting divorced. His overtures intensified. He too was getting divorced, he told her, and he wanted a relationship with her. He suggested they go shooting and travel together. He said he was uncomfortable with her going to dinner for fellowship interviews and unhappy about her leaving Philadelphia post-residency. During this time Doe asked Dr. Roe and another faculty member for fellowship recommendation letters. They agreed but wrote short, cursory, and perfunctory ones. Dr. Roe even told the fellowship's director that Doe was a poor candidate. When Doe called Dr. Roe to ask why, he said it was to teach her a lesson before hanging up on her.

In response to Doe's complaints about Dr. Roe, Mercy's vice president, Dr. Arnold Eiser, called Doe to a meeting with Dr. Roe and others. There Doe complained about Dr. Roe's conduct again but was told to wait outside. A short time later Dr. Eiser escorted her to Mercy's psychiatrist. As they walked Dr. Eiser told Doe her second in-service examination score was poor, an issue she needed to address. Later, however, Doe learned this wasn't true: Her score was in the 70th percentile, and Dr. Eiser had received misinformation. She asked Dr. Roe to report her improvement to the fellowship she'd applied to, but he refused. Mercy later told Doe that to remain in the program, she'd have to agree to a corrective plan. Reluctantly, she signed on.

Dr. Roe's conduct continued into Spring 2013. Once while Doe was sitting alone with Dr. Roe at a computer reviewing radiology reports, he reached across her body and placed his hand on hers to control the mouse, pressing his arm against her breasts in the process. She pushed herself back in her chair, stood up, and protested. Another time, when a physician expressed interest in Doe, Dr. Roe became jealous and told Doe she shouldn't date him. Later, in April 2013 Dr. Roe told another resident to remove Doe's name as coauthor from a research paper she'd contributed to. Doe complained, but Dr. Roe said she was acting unprofessionally and ordered her to another meeting with Dr. Eiser. At that meeting Doe again told Dr. Eiser about Dr. Roe's conduct over the past year. Dr. Eiser, however, said the other residents loved Dr. Roe and told her to apologize to him. She did, but Dr. Roe wouldn't accept it, calling it insincere. Dr. Eiser suspended Doe, recommending another visit to the psychiatrist.

Thereafter on April 20, 2013 Doe received a letter from Mercy stating she'd been terminated but could appeal. She appeared before an appeals committee four days later where she described Dr. Roe's behavior. Dr. Roe appeared there too advocating for her dismissal. He did so, she says, because she'd rejected his advances. The committee upheld Doe's dismissal, giving her five days to bring another appeal. She declined and quit the program, with Mercy accepting her resignation. Since then, no other residency program has accepted her, blocking her from full licensure.

. . . .

III

. . . .

A

. . . Title IX's language says, "No person in the United States shall, on the basis of sex, be excluded from participation in, be denied the benefits of, or be subjected to discrimination under *any education program or activity* receiving Federal financial assistance," 20 U.S.C. § 1681(a) (emphasis added). We must decide, then, if Mercy's operation of a residency program makes it an "education program or activity" under Title IX.

. . . .

The Supreme Court has twice instructed us that, to give Title IX the scope its origins dictate, we're to accord it a sweep as broad as its language. . . .

Like the Second Circuit we hold that a "program or activity" under § 1687 is an "education program or activity" under § 1681(a) if it has "features such that one could reasonably consider its mission to be, at least in part, educational." *O'Connor v. Davis*, 126 F.3d 112, 117 (2d Cir. 1997). This accords with Title IX's text and structure. It lines up with the Eighth and Ninth Circuits' applications of Title IX beyond educational institutions "in the sense of schooling" to entire state-prison systems offering inmates educational programs. It's consistent with the First Circuit's application of Title IX to a university's medical residency program. And it's in step with how twenty-one federal agencies, including the Departments of Education and Health and Human Services, have interpreted the statute.

. . . .

We note first that Title IX's application turns primarily on whether the defendant-entity's questioned program or activity has educational characteristics. The plaintiff's characteristics—for example, whether she's a student, employee, or something else—may be relevant in some cases, but they aren't necessarily dispositive. That caveat aside, we highlight here several features that support deeming a "program or activity" an "education program or activity" under Title IX, emphasizing that particular features (or other features not here listed) may be more or less relevant depending on the unique circumstances of each case. In no particular order, these features are that (A) a program is incrementally structured through a particular course of study or training, whether full- or part-time; (B) a program allows participants to earn a degree or diploma, qualify for a certification or certification examination, or pursue a specific occupation or trade beyond mere on-the-job training;

(C) a program provides instructors, examinations, an evaluation process or grades, or accepts tuition; or (D) the entities offering, accrediting, or otherwise regulating a program hold it out as educational in nature. These guidelines are, we think, in keeping with the common understanding of the word "education" prevalent when Title IX was enacted.

. . . .

Applying this reading, we identify two plausible ways Mercy's residency program makes it an "education program or activity" under Title IX.

First Doe's allegations raise the plausible inference that Mercy is a private organization principally engaged in the business of providing healthcare, whose operation of an ACGME [Accreditation Council for Graduate Medical Education]-accredited residency program makes its mission, at least in part, educational. Doe says, and we accept as true, that she was enrolled in a multiyear regulated program of study and training in diagnostic radiology at Mercy. That program required her to learn and train under faculty members and physicians, attend lectures and help present case presentations under supervision, participate in a physics class on a university campus, and sit for annual examinations. Had Doe completed Mercy's program, she would have been eligible to take the American Board of Radiology's certification examinations, and passing scores there would have certified her to practice for six years. Doe also says Mercy held out its residency programs as educational in nature and that the ACGME calls residency programs "structured educational experience[s]." . . .

. . . .

Second we find it plausible Mercy's operation of a residency program makes its mission, at least in part, educational under Title IX because of Mercy's "affiliat[ion]" with Drexel Medicine, a university program plausibly covered by Title IX. Two decisions guide us—*Lam v. Curators of UMKC Dental School*, 122 F.3d 654 (8th Cir. 1997), and *O'Connor* from the Second Circuit.

In *Lam* a clinician hired a university dental student to work at his private office "[un]affiliated" with the university. Alleging the clinician sexually assaulted her there, the student sued the university under Title IX. The university argued that she failed to show a "nexus" between the private office and the university and the Eighth Circuit agreed, holding that the "independent, private dental practice" wasn't a "program or activity of the University" under Title IX. An education program, the court explained, is one "controlled by" and that inures "some benefit" to the covered institution. In the student's case, it found, the clinician conferred "no benefit" to the university by operating a "separate, competing" clinic, as the university exercised "no control" over it and didn't provide it "staff, funding," or "any other support."

. . . [The court next discussed the *O'Connor* facts and holding.]

Our case is different. Unlike *Lam* where the private dental office was "[un]affiliated" with the university, here we accept as true that Mercy's residency program is "affiliated" with Drexel Medicine. Doe supports that contention with allegations that she took a physics class "taught on Drexel's campus" and that Mercy provided the "clinical bases" for Drexel Medicine's emergency medicine residency. It's thus plausible, we think, that Mercy's residency program inured "some benefit" to Drexel Medicine (and vice versa) and that these entities shared "staff, funding," and "other support."

O'Connor is distinguishable too. There the hospital accepted student-interns from a college with which it had "no institutional affiliation." Here, in contrast, Doe expressly alleges such an affiliation between Mercy and Drexel Medicine. And given her supporting allegations, we find it plausible to infer an "agreement binding" them and the sharing of "staff" and "funds." Given these alleged connections, it's plausible Mercy's operation of a residency program affiliated with Drexel Medicine makes its mission, at least in part, educational under Title IX, satisfying § 1681(a). We will therefore vacate the District Court's order so far as it concludes otherwise.

. . . [The court also analyzed whether *Cannon v. University of Chicago*, 441 U.S. 677 (1979) extends a Title IX cause of action by a student intern to retaliation, quid pro quo, and hostile environment claims. It found that Title IX provides relief for all three.] *First* private-sector employees aren't "limited to Title VII" in their search for relief from workplace discrimination. The Supreme Court has so held despite Title VII's "range" and "design as a comprehensive solution" for "invidious discrimination in employment."

Second it is a matter of "policy" left for Congress's constitutional purview whether an alternative avenue of relief from employment discrimination might undesirably allow circumvention of Title VII's administrative requirements. *North Haven* [*Board of Education v. Bell*, 456 U.S. 512 (1982)] is particularly illuminating. Dissenting there, Justice Powell described vividly the putative inefficiencies, redundancies, and contradictions of parallel enforcement in private-sector employment under Titles VII and IX. But given Congress's use of the expansive term "person" in § 1681(a), six Justices rejected those views, signifying they carry little, if indeed any, weight in our analysis.

Third the provision implying Title IX's private cause of action encompasses employees, not just students. Because § 1681(a) "neither expressly nor impliedly excludes employees from its reach," we're to interpret it as "covering and protecting these 'persons,'" for Congress easily could have substituted "'student' or 'beneficiary' for the word 'person' if it had wished to restrict" § 1681(a)'s scope.

Fourth Title IX's implied private cause of action extends explicitly to employees of federally-funded education programs who allege sex-based retaliation claims under Title IX. Retaliation against a "person," including an employee, because she "complained of sex discrimination" is another form of "intentional sex discrimination" actionable under Title IX. . . .

We note the Fifth and Seventh Circuits have held categorically that Title VII provides the "exclusive remedy for individuals alleging employment discrimination on the basis of sex in federally funded educational institutions." Allowing any private Title IX claim to proceed there, these courts held, would "disrupt" Title VII's "carefully balanced remedial scheme for redressing employment discrimination." Given the four principles described above, we decline to follow *Lakoski* [*v. James*, 66 F.3d 751 (5th Cir. 1995)] and *Waid* [*v. Merrill Area Pub. Schs.*, 91 F.3d 857 (7th Cir. 1996), *abrogated in part on other grounds by* Fitzgerald [*v. Barnstable Sch. Comm.*, 555 U.S. 246, 255 (2009)], both of which went against the First and Fourth Circuits' decisions recognizing employees' private Title IX claims. [The court further discredits these two circuit court cases.] We thus question the continued viability of *Lakoski* and *Waid* and see fit here to deviate from them.

. . . .

Notes and Discussion

1. The Facts Do the facts regarding O'Connor's internship and Mercy Doe's residency sound unusual? Why would an intern or medical resident decide not to report sexual harassment to management, especially if she has written and documented proof?

2. Power Is the power imbalance between a worker and a student intern different from that between a worker and any other new entry-level employee? If so, how?

3. *O'Connor, Lam,* and *Mercy* Did the Second Circuit court decide *O'Connor* correctly? If so, should O'Connor have recovered for any lost employment opportunities, disrupted academic progress, emotional distress, etc. in some other way? How? What are the differences between *O'Connor, Lam*, and *Mercy*? How might a school ensure that its students will be protected in an internship off campus? Or at an institution in a foreign country, organized as a "study abroad" program?

4. Title IX and the Department of Education Office for Civil Rights Does Title IX apply to off-campus internships even if a business controls the internship site? Are courts likely to impose liability under Title IX when a school has no control over an alleged harasser? Do student interns have any incentive to complain under Title IX?

In his article on student interns, Professor David Yamada addressed some of these issues:

> Bowman and Lipp provide insightful commentary on the legal and practical issues concerning school liability in internship settings. From the standpoint of public policy, however, in many instances Title IX should not be the primary source of legal relief for sexual discrimination in an internship setting. First, although Bowman and Lipps [sic] aptly note that many internship programs are affiliated with post-secondary institutions, a significant portion of internship programs are not so affiliated. Focusing excessive attention on school liability thus risks overlooking the countless internship programs that are independently run and maintained [by employers]. Second, even in situations where off-site internships are formally affiliated with schools, practically and legally speaking, the schools

are not ideally suited to prevent or respond to sexual discrimination in those outside placements. On a practical level, the schools are not in the best position to police the conduct of employers and employees in an off-site internship placement. Furthermore, the holdings in neither *Gebser* nor *Davis* give schools the legal authority to insist that an internship provider implement preventive measures to reduce the likelihood of sexual discrimination or harassment.

. . . .

Compensation for one's labor and freedom from discrimination and sexual harassment are chief among the legal issues implicated by the Intern Economy. As noted above, roughly half of all student internships are unpaid. Stronger enforcement of the minimum wage provisions of the federal Fair Labor Standards Act and adoption of more appropriate standards for determining employee status under the FLSA would help to remedy this situation. Furthermore, many interns and internship applicants are not protected by laws prohibiting discrimination and sexual harassment. A legislative amendment that explicitly covers bona fide interns would be the best response to this problem.

It is not clear whether the political impetus for these legal and legislative changes currently exists. As noted above, student interns have little incentive to blow the whistle on employers that do not pay them. Furthermore, an intern or applicant for an internship is taking a significant risk by raising a harassment or discrimination complaint. Legal actions by a few bold individuals could trigger a more widespread awareness of the legal plight of student interns. In addition, advocacy groups that deal with higher education could raise these issues and press for change via legislative and administrative means.

In all likelihood, internships will remain a key point of entry into the job market. Against this backdrop, there is no principled reason to deny student interns the basic legal protections that are afforded to traditional employees.[108]

Is Yamada correct that Title IX should not be the primary source of relief for interns? Why or why not? Yamada suggested that the political impetus might not exist for legislative changes to protect interns. Why not?

5. Contractual Obligations Might explicit contractual obligations, including the incorporation of a university's sexual harassment policy, affect whether Title IX applies to a particular internship? If so, give an example of such a provision. Might schools rewrite those contractual agreements to avoid liability? Can students insist

---

108. David C. Yamada, *The Employment Law Rights of Student Interns*, 35 Conn. L. Rev. 215, 249–50, 256–57 (2002).

on contractual protection by their home academic institutions? If so, how? How likely is it that students will insist on such protection? Explain.

6. Recent Title IX Developments and The GenZ Student Movement

Students have shown a willingness to insist on protection—when they learn that Title IX exists and prohibits more than discrimination on the athletic field. Many of them are not aware, however.[109] Years before #MeToo or #TimesUp campaigns, newly informed student sexual assault survivors began lobbying for better enforcement of Title IX, more remedial action from universities and government agencies, and greater consciousness everywhere. Professor Drobac calls this cause-driven effort a GenZ (Generation Z) movement, a new student movement.[110] Similar to the champions of the 1960s and 1970s women's and civil rights movements, these youth are politically active and are coordinating efforts. They are speaking out and with each other.

Reminiscent of the college student protest movement of the 1960s during the Vietnam War, leaders of this GenZ movement use the media and performance to raise awareness. For example, Emma Sulkowicz wore a 50-pound mattress on their (Sulkowicz identifies as non-binary) back in a performance-art protest, *Mattress Performance (Carry that Weight)* (2014–2015). They were protesting their alleged 2012 rape by fellow Columbia University student Paul Nungesser. Following an investigation, Columbia determined that it would not hold Nungesser responsible.[111] Nungesser later filed a Title IX claim against Columbia that the University settled in 2017.[112] This particular controversy reveals the difficulties that schools can encounter in balancing one student's rights against another's.

---

109. *See, e.g.*, Mahroh Jahangiri, *Betsy DeVos Met with Men's Rights Groups About Campus Rape. As A Survivor, I'm Terrified.*, Vox, (July 19, 2017). Ms. Jahangiri writes, "At the time, I did not know that outside of a racist criminal system, Title IX provides survivors with the civil right to access the resources they need—free counseling services, extensions on papers, or getting moved out of a class shared with a rapist—to stay in school after an assault." *Id.*

110. One popular culture source, Wikipedia, defines Generation Z as "the demographic cohort after the Millennials. Demographers and researchers typically use the early-1990s to mid-2000s as starting birth years. There is little consensus regarding ending birth years. Most of Generation Z have used the Internet since a young age and are comfortable with technology and social media." *Generation Z*, WIKIPEDIA (last visited May 22, 2019).

111. Soraya Nadia McDonald, *It's Hard to Ignore a Woman Toting a Mattress Everywhere She Goes, Which Is Why Emma Sulkowicz Is Still Doing It*, WASH. POST (Oct. 29, 2014),.; Max Kutner, *The Anti-Mattress Protest: Paul Nungesser's Lawsuit Against Columbia University*, NEWSWEEK, Apr. 28, 2015.

112. T. Rees Shapiro, *Columbia University Settles Title IX Lawsuit with Former Student Involving 'Mattress Girl' Case*, WASH. POST (July 13, 2017).

The GenZ movement also understands the root problems, including gendered violence. GenZ advocates often pursue their goals by using multiple forms of legal and extralegal action. They have learned from historical movements that political and social activism are sometimes more effective than legal action alone in addressing civil rights violations. In 2013, Dana Bolger and Alexandra Brodsky created Know Your IX, "a survivor- and youth-led project of Advocates for Youth that aims to empower students to end sexual and dating violence in their schools." These youth leaders "envision a world in which all students can pursue their civil right to educations free from violence and harassment." They explain on their website:

> We recognize that gender violence is both a cause of inequity and a consequence of it, and we believe that women, transgender, and gender nonconforming students will not have equality in education or opportunity until the violence ends. We draw upon the civil rights law Title IX as an alternative to the criminal legal system — one that is more just and responsive to the educational, emotional, financial, and stigmatic harms of violence.[113]

Know Your IX is just one of many student-led or inspired initiatives regarding the epidemic of sexual exploitation, assault, and harassment. Know Your IX's co-founders Bolger and Brodsky continue in their efforts to end campus sexual violence.[114]

Another group that finds much of its power in youth activism is It's On Us. A 2014 White House task force, formed by Barack Obama to address sexual assault on campus, conceived of It's On Us. According to the It's On Us website,

> It's On Us is a national movement to end sexual assault. The campaign was launched following recommendations from the White House Task Force to Prevent Sexual Assault that noted the importance of engaging everyone in the conversation to end sexual violence. It's On Us asks everyone — students, community leaders, parents, organizations, and companies — to step up and realize that the conversation changes with us. It's a rallying cry to be a part of the solution. The campaign combines innovative creative content and grassroots organizing techniques to spark conversation on a national and local level.[115]

As this passage makes clear, It's On Us stresses the need for everyone to engage in the effort to eradicate sexual assault. The website discusses bystander intervention and other tools that work to spread awareness and call out behavior or "language that perpetuates rape culture."[116] These extralegal approaches enhance more traditional legal ones first taken by President Obama and his administration.

---

113. *Learn About Know Your IX*, KNOW YOUR IX, https://www.knowyourix.org/about/.

114. *See, e.g.*, Dana Bolger & Alexandra Brodsky, *Sexual Assault Survivor Activists Launch 'Know Your IX' Campaign*, HUFFINGTON POST (Jan. 23, 2014); Dana Bolger & Alexandra Brodsky, *How Two Girls Are Teaching Students Their Rights to Fight Campus Sexual Assault*, TEEN VOGUE (Jan. 14, 2016).

115. *Our Story*, IT'S ON US, https://www.itsonus.org/our-story/.

116. *Tools*, IT'S ON US, https://www.itsonus.org/tools/.

Even before the creation of the 2014 Task Force, Obama's Department of Education confirmed the administration's focus on Title IX enforcement. Among other initiatives, the 2011 "Dear Colleague Letter" ("DCL") approved many reforms of Title IX implementation. In part, the DCL advanced the preponderance of the evidence standard, already used by a majority of educational institutions for sexual misconduct cases. This standard, less onerous than the "clear and convincing evidence" or criminal law's "beyond a reasonable doubt" standard, requires that schools hold the accused responsible if the evidence shows, more likely than not, that a violation occurred.

President Obama's administration was dedicated to the enforcement of Title IX and the eradication of campus sexual violence. Vice President Joe Biden, who had 26 years earlier chaired the Senate Judiciary Committee for the confirmation of Clarence Thomas to the Supreme Court, actively served at the forefront of this issue. In January 2017, Biden published a letter to college leaders regarding campus sexual assaults.[117] With it, Biden issued a guide for the prevention and remediation of campus sexual misconduct.[118] The guide notes the Obama administration's strong commitment to Title IX enforcement:

> The White House Task Force to Protect Students from Sexual Assault ("Task Force") was established in 2014 to focus on the seriousness and urgency of addressing sexual misconduct at colleges and universities. The Task Force has developed resources, reports, and a website that offer action steps and recommendations for conducting campus climate surveys, engaging men and women to assist in developing solutions, effectively responding to reports of sexual misconduct, and increasing transparency and enforcement of campus policies and procedures established to address sexual misconduct. Since then, efforts have been concentrated on identifying promising practices used by schools around the country.[119]

These enforcement efforts to eradicate sex-based discrimination and abuse at schools arguably came to a halt following the 2016 election of President Donald Trump. In July 2017, President Trump's Department of Education (ED) Secretary Betsy DeVos met with men's rights groups to discuss concerns about the Obama administration's Title IX policies.[120] Those groups included several that advocate for men accused of sexual assault, including the National Coalition for Men (NCFM). According to *Vox* reporter, Anna North, "The president of NCFM once defended

---

117. Andy Thomason, *In Letter to College Presidents, Biden Urges Continued Fight Against Sexual Assault*, CHRONICLE OF HIGHER ED. (Jan. 5, 2017).

118. WHITE HOUSE TASK FORCE TO PROTECT STUDENTS FROM SEXUAL ASSAULT, PREVENTING AND ADDRESSING CAMPUS SEXUAL MISCONDUCT: A GUIDE FOR UNIVERSITY AND COLLEGE PRESIDENTS, CHANCELLORS, AND SENIOR ADMINISTRATORS (Jan. 2017).

119. *Id.* at 2.

120. Erin Dooley, Janet Weinstein & Meridith McGraw, *Betsy DeVos' Meetings with 'Men's Rights' Groups over Campus Sex Assault Policies Spark Controversy*, ABC NEWS (Jul .14, 2017); Jahangiri, *supra* note 109.

football player Ray Rice after he was caught on camera assaulting his then-girlfriend, saying, 'If she hadn't aggravated him, she wouldn't have been hit.' The group has also posted photographs and names online of women who have accused men of rape."[121]

North further reported that "the fact that she [DeVos] was willing to give a group like NCFM equal time stoked fears that she did not have survivors' concerns at heart."[122] It's not clear, however, that the ED actually gave equal time to or even seriously considered survivors and their advocates. DeVos is known for her support of those accused of sexual misconduct. *The Washington Post* explains, "DeVos's family foundation has previously donated $25,000 to FIRE (Foundation for Individual Rights in Education), a civil liberties group that often represents students accused of sexual assault and has argued that the 2011 guidelines jeopardize due process."[123]

The woman who organized the ED listening sessions was Candice Jackson, DeVos's Acting Assistant Secretary for Civil Rights. From her 2005 book, *Their Lives: The Women Targeted by the Clinton Machine*,[124] one might assume that she is an advocate for sexual assault survivors. However, Jackson has also spoken out against feminism and called the women who accused Trump of sexual violence "fake victims" who lied "for political gain."[125] In the same month that Jackson organized the listening sessions for DeVos, Jackson commented on Title IX guidance. *The New York Times* quoted Jackson:

> Investigative processes have not been "fairly balanced between the accusing victim and the accused student," Ms. Jackson argued, and students have been branded rapists "when the facts just don't back that up." In most investigations, she said, there's "not even an accusation that these accused students overrode the will of a young woman."
>
> "Rather, the accusations—90 percent of them—fall into the category of 'we were both drunk,' 'we broke up, and six months later I found myself under a Title IX investigation because she just decided that our last sleeping together was not quite right,'" Ms. Jackson said.[126]

Jackson later apologized for the last remark.[127] Two months later, DeVos announced that she would roll back the 2011 guidelines, which she claimed were denying accused students "due process."[128]

---

121. Anna North, *"This Will Make Schools Less Safe": Why Betsy DeVos's Sexual Assault Rules Have Advocates Worried*, Vox (Nov. 16, 2018).

122. *Id.*

123. Katie Mettler, *Trump Official Apologizes for Saying Most Campus Sexual Assault Accusations Come After Drunken Sex, Breakups*, Wash. Post (July 13, 2017).

124. Candice E. Jackson, Their Lives: The Women Targeted by the Clinton Machine (2005).

125. Mettler, *supra* note 123.

126. Erica L. Green and Sheryl Gay Stolberg, *Campus Rape Policies Get a New Look as the Accused Get DeVos's Ear*, N.Y. Times (July 12, 2017).

127. Mettler, *supra* note 123.

128. North, *supra* note 121.

Later, in November 2018, DeVos issued new proposed rules (subject to a comment period) that could ultimately govern Title IX investigations.[129] These new rules would implement several important changes. Professor Jeannie Suk Gersen commented, "The truth is that there is much to criticize in DeVos's proposal but also much that would help to make schools' processes for handling sexual misconduct fairer to all parties."[130] Review of all the potential changes to Title IX implementation is beyond the scope of this chapter. However, several deserve specific mention.

First, the Trump rules allow schools to use either the "preponderance of the evidence" standard or the higher "clear and convincing evidence" standard. Arguably, this change could make it more difficult for complainants to prove a sexual harassment case in schools that abandon the civil law standard for the stricter one.[131] Professor Gersen also notes, "Disturbingly, DeVos would give schools discretion to use the higher standard for sexual cases while using the lower one for nonsexual ones. That seems discriminatory." Gersen suggests, "It would be fairest simply to require symmetry and equalization of the standards."[132]

Second, the Obama guidelines defined sexual harassment as "unwelcome conduct of a sexual nature." The Trump rules define it as "unwelcome conduct on the basis of sex that is so severe, pervasive and objectively offensive that it denies a person access to the school's education program or activity."[133] This new definition initially expands the range of what Title IX prohibits by explicitly including nonsexual, but sex-based conduct. However, the definition then grossly constricts what is covered by requiring a high threshold of egregious behavior and impact. Professor Gersen explains, "But a rape could be severe but not pervasive. And a compliment of one's appearance isn't necessarily severe or objectively offensive but may be pervasive, if repeated enough times, and certainly could create a hostile environment."[134]

One could argue that the definition merely incorporates the *Gebser* and *Monroe* threshold requirements for a Title IX case. However, a viable legal case is quite different from a baseline definition of sexual harassment and misconduct. By incorporating the mandate that the conduct be so "severe, pervasive and objectively offensive that it denies a person access to the school's education program or activity," the Trump administration reframes what constitutes sexual harassment. This

---

129. *Title IX of the Education Amendments of 1972: Notice of Proposed Rulemaking*, OCR (Nov. 16, 2018) [hereinafter *Notice*].

130. Jeannie Suk Gersen, *Assessing Betsy DeVos's Proposed Rules on Title IX and Sexual Assault*, NEW YORKER (Feb. 1, 2019).

131. OCR, *Notice, supra* note 129, at 60; *see also* North, *supra* note 121; Sarah Brown & Katherine Mangan, *What You Need to Know About the Proposed Title IX Regulations*, THE CHRONICLE OF HIGHER EDUC. (Nov. 16, 2018).

132. Gersen, *supra* note 130.

133. *Notice, supra* note 129, at 18, 23, 133; *see also* North, *supra* note 121; Brown & Mangan, *supra* note 131.

134. Gersen, *supra* note 130.

re-conception may cause schools to be reluctant to respond to conduct until it effectively denies access to education—a point too late to prevent damage.

Third, the Trump rules specify that "due process" for the accused requires that the accused or his representative be allowed to cross-examine the complainant. The rules provide in part:

> Cross examination is the "greatest legal engine ever invented for the discovery of truth." *California v. Green*, 399 U.S. 149, 158 (1970) (quoting John H. Wigmore, 5 Evidence § 1367, at 29 (3d ed., Little, Brown & Co. 1940)). The Department [of Education] recognizes the high stakes for all parties involved in a sexual harassment investigation, and recognizes that the need for recipients to reach reliable determinations lies at the heart of Title IX's guarantees for all parties. Indeed, at least one federal circuit court has held that in the Title IX context cross-examination is not just a wise policy, but is a Constitutional requirement of Due Process. *Doe v. Baum*, 903 F.3d 575, 581 (6th Cir. 2018) ("Not only does cross-examination allow the accused to identify inconsistencies in the other side's story, but it also gives the fact-finder an opportunity to assess a witness's demeanor and determine who can be trusted").
>
> The Department has carefully considered how best to incorporate the value of cross-examination for proceedings at both the postsecondary level and the elementary and secondary level. Because most parties and many witnesses are minors in the elementary and secondary school context, sensitivities associated with age and developmental ability may outweigh the benefits of cross-examination at a live hearing. Proposed section 106.45(b)(3)(vi) allows—but does not require—elementary and secondary schools to hold a live hearing as part of their grievance procedures. With or without a hearing, *the complainant and the respondent must have an equal opportunity to pose questions to the other party* [italics added] and to witnesses prior to a determination of responsibility, with each party being permitted the opportunity to ask all relevant questions and follow-up questions, including those challenging credibility, and a requirement that the recipient explain any decision to exclude questions on the basis of relevance. If no hearing is held, each party must have the opportunity to conduct its questioning of other parties and witnesses by submitting written questions to the decision-maker, who must provide the answers to the asking party and allow for additional, limited follow-up questions from each party.
>
> In contrast, the Department has determined that at institutions of higher education, where most parties and witnesses are adults, grievance procedures must include live cross examination at a hearing. Proposed section 106.45(b)(3)(vii) requires institutions to provide a live hearing, *and to allow the parties' advisors to cross-examine the other party and witnesses.* [Italics added.] If a party does not have an advisor at the hearing, the recipient must provide that party an advisor aligned with that party to conduct

cross-examination. Cross-examination conducted by the parties' advisors (who may be attorneys) must be permitted notwithstanding the discretion of the recipient under subsection 106.45(b)(3)(iv) to otherwise restrict the extent to which advisors may participate in the proceedings. In the context of institutions of higher education, the proposed regulation balances the importance of cross-examination with any potential harm from personal confrontation between the complainant and the respondent by requiring questions to be asked by an advisor aligned with the party. Further, the proposed regulation allows either party to request that the recipient facilitate the parties being located in separate rooms during cross-examination while observing the questioning live via technological means. The proposed regulations thereby provide the benefits of cross-examination while avoiding any unnecessary trauma that could arise from personal confrontation between the complainant and the respondent. *Cf. Baum*, 903 F.3d at 583 ("Universities have a legitimate interest in avoiding procedures that may subject an alleged victim to further harm or harassment. And in sexual misconduct cases, allowing the accused to cross-examine the accuser may do just that. But in circumstances like these, the answer is not to deny cross-examination altogether. Instead, the university could allow the accused student's agent to conduct cross-examination on his behalf. After all, an individual aligned with the accused student can accomplish the benefits of cross-examination—its adversarial nature and the opportunity for follow-up—without subjecting the accuser to the emotional trauma of directly confronting her alleged attacker.").[135]

This guidance is somewhat vague regarding what is required or permitted regarding cross-examination. For example, in grammar and high schools, "the complainant and the respondent must have an equal opportunity to pose questions to the other party to directly cross-examine their accusers." Does this mean that a high school senior who allegedly sexually assaults a freshman can cross-examine this accuser about the alleged event and any alleged consent? It appears so.

At the college and university level, the rules require a live hearing. They allow the parties to have representatives (provided by the school, and presumably at school expense, if a party does not have a lawyer or other advisor) to cross-examine the opposing party.

The cross-examination rules also cite twice to *Doe v. Baum*.[136] In that Sixth Circuit case, the court reviewed an alleged sexual assault by a University of Michigan junior ("Doe") of a freshman ("Roe") at a fraternity party. Doe and his witnesses claim that Roe consented to intercourse and that she was not obviously intoxicated. Roe and her witnesses called the conduct rape because she was much too intoxicated

---

135. *Notice, supra* note 129, at 56–58; *see also* North, *supra* note 121; Brown & Mangan, *supra* note 131.

136. Doe v. Baum, 903 F.3d 575 (6th Cir. 2018).

to consent. The court held that Michigan's failure to permit Doe or his advisor to cross-examine Roe in a live hearing deprived him of his procedural due process.

When exploring the need for cross-examination in Title IX cases, the *Baum* court explained:

> Instead, the university must allow for some form of *live* questioning *in front of* the fact-finder. See *Univ. of Cincinnati*, 872 F.3d at 402–03, 406 (noting that this requirement can be facilitated through modern technology, including, for example, by allowing a witness to be questioned via Skype "without physical presence").
>
> That is not to say, however, that the accused student always has a right to *personally* confront his accuser and other witnesses. Universities have a legitimate interest in avoiding procedures that may subject an alleged victim to further harm or harassment. And in sexual misconduct cases, allowing the accused to cross-examine the accuser may do just that. See *Univ. of Cincinnati*, 872 F.3d at 403. But in circumstances like these, the answer is not to deny cross-examination altogether. Instead, the university could allow the accused student's agent to conduct cross-examination on his behalf. After all, an individual aligned with the accused student can accomplish the benefits of cross-examination—its adversarial nature and the opportunity for follow-up—without subjecting the accuser to the emotional trauma of directly confronting her alleged attacker.[137]

The court acknowledged the trauma that a complainant might feel in a direct confrontation with the accused.

By leaving vague how schools might implement *Baum* and the new Title IX ED guidance, ED set up the response that University of Michigan implemented at the end of 2018.[138] Following the *Baum* appellate decision, Michigan announced that it would revise its misconduct policy. "Under the [new] investigative resolution process, students can ask questions of each other and witnesses at an in-person hearing conducted by a trained hearing officer."[139] The Michigan policy allows for advisors but cautions, "The adviser may not present evidence on a party's behalf, present argument, examine witnesses, testify, disrupt, or otherwise obstruct the meeting or proceedings."[140] Arguably, this process allows even an alleged rapist to cross-examine the accuser about the events and her alleged consent.

Critics of the Michigan resolution process and the ED Title IX proposals, as well as other survivor advocates, have mobilized. "The University of California—among

---

137. *Id.* at 583.

138. *See* University of Michigan, *The University of Michigan Interim Policy and Procedures on Student Sexual and Gender-Based Misconduct and Other Forms of Interpersonal Violence* ("*The Michigan Policy*") (effective January 9, 2019).

139. Martin Slagter, *Revised University of Michigan Student Sexual Misconduct Policy Includes In-Person Hearing*, MLIVE.COM (Dec. 10, 2018).

140. *The Michigan Policy, supra* note 138, at 26.

the largest university systems in the nation—blasted the proposal, in large part because of the new live hearing requirement. 'It's inherently intimidating,' Suzanne Taylor, the UC system's Title IX coordinator . . . 'This change more than almost any other will discourage complainants from coming forward.'"[141] In October 2018, SurvJustice, Equal Rights Advocates, and Victim Rights Law Center amended their lawsuit, which alleges that the Trump Administration's Title IX policy "is unlawfully based on government officials' discriminatory stereotypes about the credibility of women and girls who report sexual violence."[142] Clearly, these issues will not be resolved any time soon.

Notes and Discussion

1. The GenZ Student Movement Are there additional examples of GenZ activism? Has the GenZ movement had a unique impact on social problems and politics? Explain.

2. Politics, Title IX, and Due Process What are the differences between the Obama administration's interpretation and enforcement of Title IX and that of the Trump administration? Is the "preponderance of the evidence standard" or the "clear and convincing evidence standard" better suited to a Title IX investigation? Why? Has Title IX implementation afforded accused students too little due process? Explain.

3. Cross-Examination and the New Title IX ED Guidance What did the Trump administration mandate regarding Title IX investigations and cross-examination? What did *Baum* require? Do you think that the Michigan policy correctly interpreted *Baum*? Should other schools or courts endorse this Michigan policy (i.e., will it discourage possible complainants?)? What other alternatives might work at a school like Michigan?

7. Application of Law and Ethics
Ethics Hypothetical #6
(based on a true story)

Kurt and Janice teach at New Columbia Law School. At a social gathering away from the law school, Kurt, a tenured professor, requests sexual favors from Janice, an untenured professor who teaches sexual harassment law, among other courses. Janice refuses his advances and attributes his offensive behavior to excessive alcohol

141. Benjamin Wermund, *The Biggest Sticking Point in DeVos' Title IX Rules*, Politico (Nov. 19, 2018).

142. Press Release, Equal Rights Advocates, BREAKING: New Evidence Strengthens Claim that Trump's Title IX Policy Was Based on Sexist Stereotypes, Rendering It Unconstitutional (Oct. 31, 2018), https://www.equalrights.org/breaking-amended-federal-lawsuit-against-devos-shows-title-ix-policy-was-based-on-sexist-stereotypes-is-unconstitutional/; Juana Summers, *Civil Rights Groups Sue Betsy DeVos over Sexual Assault Policy*, CNN (Jan. 25, 2018).

consumption. Over the next several weeks, Kurt makes inappropriate comments to Janice when he is clearly sober. One day at the office, Kurt again tries to kiss Janice. Furious with Kurt and with herself for failing to recognize common predatory behavior, Janice tells two tenured New Columbia friends about Kurt's conduct but specifically directs both not to take action for her unless they hear of other inappropriate conduct by Kurt. They take no action.

Legal Issues: Does Kurt's conduct constitute sexual harassment? Did the two faculty friends act appropriately?

Believing that hers is a "he said; she said" case, Janice documents the problem but keeps the memorandum in a drawer. Janice makes no formal complaint until she discovers several days later that Kurt has hugged and kissed students who found the behavior offensive. One student, Lena, also works part-time as Kurt's administrative assistant in exchange for a tuition reduction. Janice and Lena lodge a formal, written complaint of harassment against Kurt. The Dean promises to take immediate action, including consulting with university counsel. The Dean also asks Janice to act as an intermediary with Lena and the other student targets, and to propose a resolution of the matter based upon her expertise in this area of the law. The University of New Columbia ultimately determines that sexual harassment occurred and puts a formal letter of reprimand into Kurt's personnel file.

Legal Issue: Assume that New Columbia refused to take action because of the accused's tenured status, so that Lena and other complaining students opted to sue. Should Lena bring a Title IX or Title VII claim?

Additional Questions:[143]

1. Did Kurt violate any legal or ethical rules by sexually harassing the targets he chose?

2. Did Janice violate any legal or ethical rules by failing to report Kurt's behavior after the first episode? After the subsequent comments? After the final episode?

3. Did Janice's two tenured friends violate any legal or ethical rules by failing to report Kurt's alleged conduct?

4. Can Janice ethically act as a liaison for the targets and university administration?

5. Can Janice ethically advise the Dean regarding a resolution to the matter?

6. Did the Dean violate any ethical rules by his conduct?

---

143. In addition to the American Bar Association *Model Rules of Professional Conduct,* consider the American Association of University Professors (AAUP) *Statement on Professional Ethics* to assist in exploring these ethics questions.

Chapter 7

Title VIII — Sexual Harassment in Housing

1. Introduction to Sexual Harassment in Housing

Sexual harassment in housing occurs when a housing provider — typically a landlord, property manager, or maintenance worker — subjects tenants to sexually harassing behavior. There is a dearth of research about this phenomenon, although there is no shortage of reported cases and administrative complaints. Most of what is known comes from a few studies and a review of existing cases and complaints. These sources overwhelmingly indicate that low-income women, for whom access to decent, affordable housing is a significant challenge, are likely to experience sexual harassment in housing. There is a power imbalance when low-income women, who are likely to have multiple, intersectional vulnerabilities, seek housing, a basic human need, because housing is largely controlled by male landlords. Other women who are less socioeconomically marginalized may also be harassed by their landlords, but little evidence currently supports this notion.

In 2008, Dr. Griff Tester analyzed 137 sexual harassment in housing complaints made to the Ohio Civil Rights Commission (OCRC) between 1990 and 2003.[1] He was the first to obtain data on the race of the targets and perpetrators and he found that 68% of the reported targets were African American or "other women of color" while virtually all of the perpetrators were white men. Most of the harassment occurred in private rentals as opposed to public housing, although OCRC files were not clear whether the targets were receiving housing subsidies at the time.[2] The landlords tended to represent small, privately owned housing rather than large rental companies with structured management and procedures. OCRC did not collect specific data about the complainants' socioeconomic status, although information in the files indicated that many women were poor and in need of housing assistance.

---

1. Griff Tester, *An Intersectional Analysis of Sexual Harassment in Housing*, 22 GENDER & SOC'Y 349 (2008).

2. Housing subsidies are typically administered in the form of a Housing Choice Voucher (commonly known as "Section 8") by the Office of Housing and Urban Development (HUD). The voucher is used to help defray the costs of housing in the private market.

Professor Rigel Oliveri conducted a more recent pilot study of sexual harassment in housing, which sought information about the targets, perpetrators, and the type of housing.[3] She conducted detailed interviews with 100 randomly selected low-income women. Of those, 10% had experienced actionable sexual harassment by their landlords. The women were very young at the time they were harassed — all but one was under 25 and several were 20 or younger. All but one of the women were black. All were living in private rental housing at the time they were harassed; none lived in public housing, shelters, or other institutional facilities. Three of the 10 women were receiving housing subsidies in the form of Housing Choice Vouchers (often referred to as "Section 8") at the time they were harassed. Whether or not a woman had a subsidy did not appear to increase the likelihood of harassment, although it did positively correlate to whether she was able to remain in the housing after experiencing the harassment.

The landlords who perpetrated the harassment were all owner-operators of their rental properties. They did not work for or employ a rental management company. They were significantly older than the tenants they harassed — with an estimated average age difference of 20 years. They were usually white. The harassment itself took two forms: (1) almost all of the women described being explicitly asked to provide sex in lieu of rent and; (2) half of the women also reported experiencing serious, likely criminal conduct such as home invasion, indecent exposure, and unwanted touching. These behaviors are consistent with findings of a team of researchers who analyzed landlord conduct in several dozen depositions and published opinions from sexual harassment in housing cases. The team noted:

> Despite overall similarities to its workplace counterpart, a number of distinctive characteristics of residential harassment were evident; in particular, the phenomena of home invasion and masculine possessiveness have no apparent workplace parallels. Housing sexual harassment often takes place in the victim's home, creating an intensely threatening atmosphere.[4]

Only one of the women in Professor Oliveri's pilot study reported the harassment. She contacted the police, who apparently took no action. The remaining women did not complain because they did not know to whom to direct a complaint and because they did not want to risk jeopardizing their housing situations.

Even though Professor Oliveri's pilot study found harassment in only private housing, it is clear that sexual harassment occurs in other housing settings, such as homeless shelters and public housing.[5]

---

3. Rigel C. Oliveri, *Sexual Harassment of Low-Income Women in Housing: Pilot Study Results*, 83 Mo. L. Rev. 597 (2018).

4. Maggie E. Reed et al., *There's No Place Like Home*, 11 Psychol. Pub. Pol'y & L. 439 (2005).

5. *See, e.g.*, Banks v. Housing Authority of Bossier City, No. 11-0551, 2011 WL 4591899, at *1 (W.D. La. Sept. 30, 2011) (female public housing tenant alleged sexual harassment by maintenance technician); Woods v. Foster, 884 F. Supp. 1169, 1171 (N.D. Ill. 1995) (female residents of homeless shelter sexually harassed by shelter directors).

Professor Oliveri identifies the root cause of housing harassment as "the fact that so many poor women are left to their own devices to find housing in a private rental market that is spectacularly ill-suited for meeting the existing need."[6] She notes:

> We live in a nation where an individual earning minimum wage cannot afford a two-bedroom apartment and where 75% of people who qualify for housing assistance do not receive it because of resource constraints. Waiting lists for public housing and Section 8 Vouchers are years long in many places and are frequently closed to new applicants, so new families cannot even sign up.[7]

. . . .

No one who is unemployed, on disability, or working in a low-wage and/ or part-time job can consistently afford to pay market rate rent without a housing subsidy or some other form of assistance. This group will never be "qualified" in the manner contemplated by the employment cases, and without access to affordable housing, they will always be in need of a break. Too often, this "break" comes in the form of an exploitative offer from the landlord to trade sex for rent. Unfortunately, this may be viewed by a court — or a jury — less as a hostile gesture by the landlord and more akin to a business proposal in which the woman is complicit in keeping open the possibility of gaining something of value that she could otherwise not afford. Another way to describe such a situation is that it amounts to solicitation of prostitution. This is not to say that the victims are prostitutes but rather that the landlords clearly view them as needy enough to consider using sex as currency.

. . . .

The women in the Pilot Study have much in common with the subjects featured in Matthew Desmond's powerful ethnography, *Evicted: Poverty and Profit in the American City*, which chronicles the inability of poor families to maintain stable housing and the terrible toll that the cycle of eviction and forced moves takes on their relationships, children, employment prospects, and mental health. [As with the Pilot Study, the landlords that Desmond observed] rent to low-income populations knowing fullwell that their tenants will never be able to stay current on rent. While the landlords may view themselves as providing a necessary service (or even being charitable), in reality, some of these landlords have devised ways to profit from the situation — for example, by charging the tenants high rent, keeping their security deposits, making no improvements or repairs to the properties, and flipping the properties frequently as poor families cycle in and out. "Exploitation," Desmond observes, "thrives when it comes to the

---

6. Oliveri, *supra* note 3, at 637.
7. *Id.*

essentials, like housing[.]" While the exploitation that Desmond chronicles is economic, the Pilot Study makes clear that there is a subset of landlords who seek to exploit this population of renters sexually as well.[8]

Notes and Discussion

1. Lack of Attention Few academic studies of sexual harassment in housing document the scope of the problem. News media and public discourse focus on employment harassment. It is clear, however, that a significant problem exists. Why have housing cases received so little attention? What are the consequences of a lack of awareness about the problem by courts, legislators, and the public? Activists have worked to raise awareness about sexual harassment in housing for decades.[9] In April 2018, the Department of Justice announced a nationwide initiative to combat sexual harassment in housing.[10] The initiative contains three components: (1) a joint task force, involving the DOJ and the HUD, to coordinate and improve training, data sharing, and outreach, (2) a toolkit for U.S. attorneys' offices to use for enforcement, and (3) a public awareness campaign.

2. Exclusion Versus Exploitation Some legal theorists have framed the problem of workplace harassment as one in which men use harassment to deny women access to the benefits of a male-dominated workplace or to punish them for encroaching on it. For example, in her influential article, Professor Vicki Schultz argues:

> [M]en's desire to exploit or dominate women sexually may not be the exclusive, or even the primary, motivation for harassing women at work. Instead, a drive to maintain the most highly rewarded forms of work as domains of masculine competence underlies many, if not most, forms of sex-based harassment on the job. Harassment has the form and function of denigrating women's competence for the purpose of keeping them away from male-dominated jobs or incorporating them as inferior, less capable workers.[11]

In the housing setting, there is no male-dominated realm from which the women are being excluded. There is no comparable group of low-income male renters gaining access to housing on more favorable terms. Rather, the sex-for-rent proposition is a landlord's way of taking advantage of the low-income woman's structurally vulnerable position to extort sex. In this way, sexual harassment in housing is also different from other forms of housing discrimination. As one commentator points out:

> A neighbor who burns a cross in the lone African-American family's yard is presumably intending to force that family out of its home. The same result

8. *Id.* at 626–628.

9. For example, in 1996 an attorney with the NOW Legal Defense published a primer for lawyers to use in such cases. *See* Sherry Leiwant, *Sexual Harassment in Housing: A Primer* (1996), https://www.povertylaw.org/files/docs/article/chr_1996_december_leiwant.pdf.

10. Press Release, Dep't of Justice, Justice Department Announces Nationwide Initiative to Combat Sexual Harassment in Housing (Apr. 12, 2018), https://www.justice.gov/opa/pr/justice-department-announces-nationwide-initiative-combat-sexual-harassment-housing.

11. Vicki Schultz, *Reconceptualizing Sexual Harassment*, 107 YALE L.J. 1683, 1755 (1998).

is likely intended when insults and religious epithets are scrawled outside a Jewish family's house. But the landlord who sexually harasses his tenant is not intending to drive her out; instead, he is attempting to draw her in . . . to satisfy his own desire to control and exploit.[12]

How important is this distinction? Will it matter in determining how a plaintiff should frame her prima facie case? What sorts of evidence and arguments do you think advocates might have to put forward in order to support cases like this? What evidence and arguments might a defense lawyer raise?

3. Home as a Haven A number of commentators have argued that the social, psychological, and legal significance of the home should prompt courts to apply a more nuanced and particularized analysis to sexual harassment in housing than they do currently. Their arguments often emphasize the importance of privacy rights within the home.

In 1987, Professor Regina Cahan wrote the first major law review article on housing harassment. She drew on the concept of the home as a place of refuge from the world, noting:

> When sexual harassment occurs at work, at that moment or at the end of the workday, the woman may remove herself from the offensive environment. She will choose whether to resign from her position based on economic and personal considerations. In contrast, when the harassment occurs in a woman's home, it is a complete invasion in her life. Ideally, home is the haven from the troubles of the day. When home is not a safe place, a woman may feel distressed and, often, immobile.[13]

2. Introduction to the Law

The primary federal statute for addressing sexual harassment in housing is the Fair Housing Act (FHA), which is Title VIII of the Civil Rights Act of 1968.[14] In 1974, Congress passed an amendment adding "sex" to the FHA's list of prohibited bases of discrimination. The statute's language mirrors Title VII in many respects, although there are some significant differences. The most commonly used provisions for sexual harassment cases follow.

A. Denials of Housing: Section 3604(a)

This section makes it unlawful to refuse to rent or "otherwise make unavailable or deny" housing to a person because of sex. This provision resembles the language

---

12. Aric K. Short, *Slaves for Rent: Sexual Harassment in Housing as Involuntary Servitude*, 86 Neb. L. Rev. 838, 841–42 (2008).

13. Regina Cahan, *Home Is No Haven: An Analysis of Sexual Harassment in Housing*, 1987 Wis. L. Rev. 1061, 1073 (1987).

14. 42 U.S.C. § 3601 (2012).

in Title VII, which makes it unlawful "to fail or refuse to hire or to discharge any individual" based on protected characteristics. It would apply in the sexual harassment context if a landlord evicted or failed to rent to a tenant because of her refusals to engage in sexual activity. It might also apply in situations where the harassment is so severe that it causes the tenant to move out, thus constituting a constructive eviction.

B. Discriminatory Terms and Conditions: Section 3604(b)

Section 3604(b) prohibits discrimination "against any person in the terms, conditions, or privileges of sale or rental of a dwelling, or in the provision of services or facilities in connection therewith" because of sex. This language closely mirrors Title VII's language making it unlawful "to discriminate against any individual with respect to his compensation, terms, conditions, or privileges of employment" because of sex. As such, counsel commonly use it to bring hostile environment sexual harassment claims under the FHA, particularly when the landlord has not evicted the woman or forced her to move.

C. Discriminatory Statements: Section 3604(c)

This section makes it unlawful "[t]o make, print, or publish, . . . any notice, statement, or advertisement, with respect to the sale or rental of a dwelling that indicates any preference, limitation, or discrimination based on . . . [sex]." The language of this provision is similar to a provision in Title VII that makes it unlawful for an employer "to print or publish . . . any notice or advertisement relating to employment . . . indicating any preference, limitation, specification, or discrimination, based on [sex]." Section 3604(c) goes beyond its Title VII counterpart, however, by banning discriminatory "statements" as well as discriminatory "notices" and "advertisements." By extending its prohibitions to discriminatory statements, § 3604(c) provides a source of law that would seem to cover some types of verbal harassment that are not explicitly addressed by Title VII. For example, an employer's single utterance of a phrase disparaging women might not be considered severe or pervasive enough to violate Title VII. The same statement by a landlord to a female apartment-seeker, however, could violate this portion of the FHA.

D. Intimidation and Interference: Section 3617

Section 3617 declares it illegal to "coerce, intimidate, threaten, or interfere with any person in the exercise or enjoyment of . . . any right" granted or protected by the Fair Housing Act. This provision also has a counterpart in Title VII, which makes it unlawful for an employer to discriminate against any individual employee "because he has opposed any practice made an unlawful employment practice by this title, or because he has made a charge, testified, assisted or participated in any manner in an investigation, proceeding or hearing under this title." The language of the FHA's provision is clearly broader than Title VII's, which is likely due to the congressional purpose behind this section. When Congress first passed the FHA, one of its goals was to address the practice of whites using violence and threats to prevent blacks from moving into segregated neighborhoods. Title VII's prohibition is limited to retaliation against an individual for her opposition to practices condemned by the statute. Section 3617 covers not only retaliation but other types of discriminatory behavior as well. By its terms, § 3617 specifically prohibits a wide variety of practices, including coercion, intimidation, threats, and — most importantly for present purposes — "interfere[nce] with any person in the exercise or enjoyment of . . . any right granted or protected by" the FHA. Certainly, sexual harassment could be characterized as a form of "interference" with a female tenant's right to enjoy her housing on a nondiscriminatory basis.

The FHA also contains a criminal provision, which makes it a crime to willfully injure, intimidate, or interfere with a person for selling, purchasing, renting, financing, or occupying a dwelling based on protected characteristics.[15] Legislators intended this provision to reach violent and threatening behavior such as fire-bombing or cross-burning. It has never been used to prosecute a defendant for sexual harassment.

3. Title VIII Cases and Title VII Precedent

The law of sexual harassment in housing developed well after and in virtual lockstep with the law of sexual harassment in employment, which is unsurprising given the textual similarity between the FHA and Title VII. Thus, the same prima facie case concept applies, with similar requirements for unwelcomeness, behavior "based on sex," and the severe or pervasive standard. Application of this latter standard has been a particular point of contention. In the early years, many courts simply interpreted the FHA to prohibit sexual harassment to the same degree as Title VII prohibits it in the employment setting. The first court to consider a sexual harassment in housing case did so in 1983, after the United States Court of Appeals for the Eleventh Circuit's decision in *Henson v. Dundee* but before the United States Supreme Court's decision in *Meritor v. Vinson*. Note how closely this opinion adopts *Henson's* Title VII analysis, including the definition of the prima facie case and the characterization of cases as quid pro quo and/or hostile environment.

Shellhammer v. Lewallen

No. C 82-689 (W.D. Ohio, Nov. 22, 1983)

. . . .

This is a civil rights case in which the parties have consented to the entry of final judgment by the undersigned. In their complaint the plaintiffs allege that the

---

15. 42 U.S.C. § 3631 (2012).

defendants have violated the Fair Housing Act by discriminating on the basis of sex. The gravaman of the complaint is that the defendant Norman Lewallen, with the acquiescence of his wife, the defendant Jacqueline Lewallen, conditioned the rental of premises owned by them upon the performance by female tenants of sexual acts with Mr. Lewallen. If the tenants refused, then, according to the allegations of the complaint, the tenants were evicted.

. . . .

The named plaintiffs are Tammy and Thomas Shellhammer. In essence. They claim that the defendant Norman Lewallen solicited Mrs. Shellhammer to pose for nude photographs and, later, to have sexual intercourse with him. Upon her refusal to accede to either of these requests, plaintiffs allege, eviction proceedings were brought against them on the pretextual basis that they had not paid their rent.

The named plaintiffs also allege that the conduct of the defendant Lewallen against Mrs. Shellhammer and the later eviction proceedings are representative of a pattern and practice of similar conduct on Mr. Lewallen's part towards several of his female tenants. On their own behalf and on behalf of the class which they purport to represent, the named plaintiffs seek equitable and legal relief.

At the trial of the named plaintiffs' complaint against the defendants, several former tenants, in addition to the named plaintiffs, were called to testify. These witnesses testified about Mr. Lewallen's activities and actions towards them while they were tenants in property owned by him and his wife. This testimony described requests to pose for nude photographs, acceptance of sexual favors in lieu of payment of security deposits, unconsented entry into apartments and solicitation of other sexual favors. Some of the witnesses testified that they had acquiesced in some of these requests. While others rebuffed them. Following such rejection, eviction proceedings were brought; often, however, the stated basis for such action was nonpayment of rent.

The plaintiffs base their complaint upon cases developed under the equal employment opportunity statute. During the past ten years courts have accepted the contention that sexual harassment at the workplace constitutes employment discrimination on the basis of sex. Though this concept appears to be generally accepted under Title VII, the equal employment statute, it has yet to be applied under Title VIII, the Fair Housing Act.

Plaintiffs encounter, therefore, an initial question about the applicability of the sexual harassment doctrine, as established under Title VII, to cases brought under Title VIII. In opposition to adopting this doctrine in the context of a fair housing case, the defendants make two general arguments: first, that no other court has taken such step, and second, that the focus of the fair housing statute differs from the purpose of the equal employment act.

For several reasons, these are not very persuasive arguments. Sexual harassment is not specifically addressed in either Title VII or its legislative history. Nonetheless, courts have had little difficulty in interpreting and applying Title VII to claims of such harassment, and concluding that such activity falls within the broad reach of that statute. At one time, there were no decisions to that effect; that has not, however, inhibited judicial development of the doctrine.

Defendants' second argument focuses on the fact that Title VII prohibits discrimination in employment, whereas Title VIII prohibits discrimination in housing. This argument cannot avoid the fact that both statutes are designed to eradicate the effects of bias and prejudice. Their purposes are, clearly, the same; only their field of operation differs. . . .

. . . .

In view of the policy of broad interpretation of the Fair Housing Act, the statute's remedial purposes, and the absence of any persuasive reason in support of the defendants' contentions that sexual harassment is not actionable under the Act, I conclude that it is entirely appropriate to incorporate this doctrine into the fair housing area. Defendants' motion to dismiss on the basis that no cause of action has been stated, made at the close of the plaintiffs' case, and renewed at the conclusion of the trial, should, therefore, be overruled.

Guidance for defining the elements of sexual harassment in the context of this case can be found in the Eleventh Circuit's recent and exhaustive opinion in Henson [v. City of Dundee (11th Cir. 1982)]. In that case the court described two basic varieties of actionable consequences from conduct generally referred to as sexual harassment: a) creation of an "offensive environment," and b) extracting or seeking to extract "sexual consideration in exchange for job benefits. In the context of housing. sexual harassment would consist of either creating an "offensive environment," or conditioning tenancy, or continued tenancy, upon sexual consideration.

Plaintiff Tammy Shellhammer asserts that she was subjected to both forms of sexual harassment during her tenancy in the defendants' building. First, she contends that the request to pose nude and the later solicitation of sexual intercourse created an offensive environment. Second, she asserts that the defendants' actions in seeking to evict her and her husband were motivated by her refusal to grant sexual favors in response to her landlord's requests.

In Henson the court defined the elements of each claim. These are readily adaptable to claims of sexual harassment in housing, and I conclude that the elements of each of plaintiff's claims may be expressed as follows.

First, the hostile environment claim consists of five elements:

1. Membership in the protected group.

2. Being subjected to unwelcome and extensive sexual harassment, in the form of sexual advances, requests for sexual favors, and other verbal or physical conduct of a sexual nature, which has not been solicited or desired by the plaintiff, and which is viewed as undesirable or offensive.

3. The harassment was based upon sex; i.e., but for the plaintiff's gender, the harassment would not have occurred.

4. The harassment makes continued tenancy burdensome and significantly less desirable than if the harassment were not occurring, and

5. If vicarious liability is asserted, the plaintiff must show that the owner knew or should have known about the particular harassment and failed to remediate the situation promptly.

Like the court in Henson, I am persuaded that plaintiff must show, in order to establish her claim that the defendant's conduct created an offensive environment, that the landlord's actions were pervasive and persistent. An occasional statement or request would not suffice. However, once the requisite frequency and pervasiveness have been established, then, in my opinion, the effect of that conduct should be ascertained on a subjective, rather than an objective standard. Conduct or statements which one person finds intolerable might be viewed as simply annoying or even amusing by another person. In view of the personal and subjective nature of the tenant's response, she should be able to prevail upon a showing that her tenancy was made burdensome for her, and significantly less desirable than if the harassment had not occurred. Liability should not be defeated, however, on the basis that someone else felt, or a reasonable person might have felt a different reaction to the landlord's conduct.

With reference to the second type of sexual harassment claim (namely, that the landlord conditioned tenancy or continued tenancy upon the extension of sexual consideration), the following elements must be established by the plaintiff in order to prevail:

1. Membership in the protected group;

2. A demand for sexual favors, which has not been solicited or desired by the tenant (or prospective tenant);

3. The request was based upon the plaintiff's sex (i.e., but for the plaintiff's gender, the request would not have been made);

4. The plaintiff's reaction to the request affected one or more tangible terms, conditions, or privileges of tenancy, in that she was denied or deprived or tenancy or a substantial benefit thereof as a result of her response to the landlord's demand for sexual favors; and

5. If vicarious liability is asserted. The plaintiff must show that the owner knew or should have known about the particular harassment and failed to remediate the situation promptly.

Where the plaintiff's claim is that her reaction to sexual harassment had an adverse effect upon her tenancy, then, in my opinion, she need not show that the landlord's demands were frequent. If she establishes that her rejection of a single request for a sexual favor led to a reaction by the landlord which adversely affected a tangible component of her tenancy, then she should prevail.

With reference to plaintiffs first claim—that the landlord's conduct subjected her to a hostile environment as a result of her sex, it is clear that she has failed to satisfy the elements of this claim as defined above. She points to two requests during the three or four months of her tenancy. This does not amount to the pervasive and persistent conduct which is a predicate to finding that the sexual harassment created a burdensome situation which caused the tenancy to be significantly less desirable than it would have been had the harassment not occurred. The plaintiffs, therefore, are not entitled to relief on the first aspect of her claim.

I find, however, that the plaintiffs have established the second aspect of their claim — namely, that as a consequence of Mrs. Shellhammer's rejection of Mr. Lewallan's sexual advances, eviction proceedings were instituted against the plaintiffs.

In reaching this conclusion, I have adapted the [prima facie case from Title VII] to the order and burden of proof in this case. First, the plaintiffs had the burden of establishing a prima facie case. Then the burden was upon the defendants to articulate a legitimate, non-discriminatory reason for their actions. Finally, the burden remained on the plaintiffs to prove that the articulated reason was not, in fact, the reason which motivated the defendants.

There can be no question, in my opinion, that the plaintiffs met their initial burden of establishing a prima facie case that their eviction had been motivated by Mrs. Shellhammer's response to the defendant's sexual advances. In addition to the plaintiff's testimony in support of this contention, there was the testimony of several other former tenants which suggested a pattern or practice of conduct.

At this point, the defendants had the burden of articulating a legitimate, non-discriminatory reason. They met this burden by coming forward with evidence, which, if believed, would establish that the plaintiffs willfully defaulted on the July, 1981, rent obligation. Unless plaintiffs failed to meet the burden of proving that this was not, in fact, the motivating factor, then the defendants would be entitled to judgment.

I am persuaded, however, that the plaintiffs met their ultimate burden of proving that the articulated reason was not the exclusive factor, and that the eviction proceedings were, to a significant extent, brought in response to Mrs. Shellhammer's rejection of Mr. Lewallen's request that she pose in the nude, and his later response that she have sex with him.

. . . .

This finding is based upon the evidence of record which shows that Mr. Lewallen's conduct in this instance is representative, and follows a pattern of action of his part in similar situations. The testimony of the plaintiffs' witnesses showed that requests for sexual favors were a recurrent element of Mr. Lewallen's landlordship. That testimony also shows that, when such requests were rejected, eviction proceedings or other retaliatory actions ensued.

Several witnesses testified that Mr. Lewallen offered to make "arrangements" in lieu of a security deposit. At least two of the witnesses — Michael and Reasoner — acquiesced. Ms. Michael testified, however, that Mr. Lewallen reniged [sic] on his initial agreement, which had caused her to refuse to pay rent. This, in turn, led to her eviction. Similarly, Ms. Reasoner testified that after she had initially acquiesced in Mr. Lewallen's "arrangements" for the security deposit, he changed the arrangements by offering to pay her five or ten dollars, rather than giving her a further rebate on the security deposit. She, likewise, was evicted for nonpayment of rent, which she acknowledged but attributed to "getting tired" of Mr. Lewallen.

Another witness, Ms. Upchurch, testified that she too had gone to bed with the defendant rather than paying the security deposit. It does not appear, however, that further requests were either made or rejected. Though Ms. Upchurch declined later requests by Mrs. Lewallen for the security deposit, there is no indication that eviction proceedings were brought against her. Instead, according to her testimony, she moved voluntarily.

A comparison of the sequence of events relating to Ms. Michael and Ms. Reasoner with the testimony of Ms. Upchurch provides support for the plaintiffs' claims that the eviction proceedings against them were motivated by Mrs. Shellhammer's refusal to accede to the defendant's request for sexual favors. Ms. Michael and Ms. Reasoner, in time, rebuffed similar requests: thereafter eviction proceedings were instituted. Ms. Upchurch, like Ms. Michael and Ms. Reasoner, initially acceded as well. Because no further requests, apparently, were made, none were refused. And her tenancy continued undisturbed until she voluntarily vacated her apartment.

The testimony of other witnesses produced by the plaintiffs also supported their contentions. Ms. Jackson testified that two weeks after she had moved in, she was propositioned. and refused the defendant's request. Thereafter, though she offered to pay her rent following receipt of her [Aid to Families with Dependent Children (ADC)] check, her offer was refused by the defendant, who had told her previously that he did not want her on his premises. Eviction proceedings were commenced, as were self-help repossession techniques.

A similar sequence was described by Ms. Miles, who was asked to pose for pictures, which were to be taken after she had "satisfied" the defendant. She refused both requests, which had been made shortly after she had become a tenant. Thereafter. She was told to move by the defendant: she refused to pay rent and following filing of an eviction suit, she left.

Another tenant, Ms. Miles, who had declined a request to "fool around" with the defendant, was thereafter notified to quit when she failed to pay the following month's rent on its due date. She testified that her ADC check was late that month, which accounted for her failure to pay her rent when due. Though her check later came, proceedings were instituted against her, and she moved out without paying rent for that month.

Delay in receiving her ADC check also caused Ms. Kennedy to fail to pay her rent on the first of the month. Three weeks earlier she had hit the defendant after he had fondled her. Her proffer of the following month's rent, made by her after her check had come, was refused, and she was forced to vacate her apartment. Similarly, Ms.

Kincaid testified that after she had rebuffed the defendant's sexual passes her things had been moved out of her apartment on the first of the following month, though she was willing to pay her rent for that month.

In my opinion, the testimony of these witnesses establishes a pattern of conduct on the part of Mr. Lewallen whereby he would solicit sexual favors of various kinds from tenants. In time, those who refused would be subjected to eviction proceedings. In many instances, though they would be in technical default, they were willing and able to become current on their rent obligations. In some of those instances the failure to pay rent when due was caused by no fault on their part—ADC checks arrived late.

In light of this evidence, it is apparent that the eviction proceedings brought against the plaintiffs were motivated in part by Mrs. Shellhammer's refusal to accede to the defendant's requests that she pose in the nude and have sex with him. Though these requests were made several weeks apart, and the later request also predated the eviction proceedings by more than a month, nonetheless, in light of the other evidence of record, I find that the eviction was motivated in part by Mrs. Shellhammer's response to the defendant's sexual advances.

I also find that Mrs. Lewallen, as a coowner of the properties, and as an active participant in the collection of rents and institution of eviction proceedings, is, in light of her knowledge of her husband's conduct, vicariously liable. Several witnesses told her about her husband's actions, but she declined to take any remedial steps, though in a position to do so as general manager of the properties. Consequently, she is jointly liable as a result of her acquiescence in her husband's discriminatory conduct.

In light of the foregoing, I make the following factual findings:

1. The plaintiff, Mrs. Shellhammer, is a member of the protected group.

2. The defendant, Mr. Lewallen, sought unsolicited sexual favors from Mrs. Shellhammer, she, in turn, rejected these requests;

3. Those requests were motivated by Mrs. Shellhammer's sex, female.

4. Following such rejection, Mr. Lewallen caused eviction proceedings to be instituted against the plaintiffs;

5. Mr. Lewallen's motivation in bringing such proceedings was in part based upon Mrs. Shellhammer's refusal to acquiesce in his requests for sexual favors;

6. The defendant Mrs. Lewallen was aware of Mr. Lewallen's practices with reference to his female tenants; she was in a position, but failed to take steps to remedy such conduct and its effects.

In light of the foregoing, I conclude, as a matter of law, that the defendants have discriminated against the plaintiff, Mrs. Shellhammer, on the basis of her sex in violation of 42 U.S.C. § 3604(b). They are, consequently, liable to her for damages under the statute.

I conclude further that both Mrs. Shellhammer and her husband, Mr. Shellhammer, have standing to maintain this action. He has established that, as a result of the actions taken by Mr. Lewallen against his wife, he, likewise, "has suffered a 'distinct and palatable injury.'"

. . . .

Notes and Discussion

1. Proper Defendants Note that Mr. Lewallen faced individual liability under the FHA, which would not have occurred if the case had proceeded under Title VII. Individual liability is another characteristic that distinguishes Title VIII from Title VII.[16] This difference is significant because many properties are owned and managed by a single person. Professor Oliveri's study revealed that individual owner-operators are the most likely perpetrators of sexual harassment in housing. Without individual liability, those solo owner-operators would not face consequences under Title VIII.

Additionally, the FHA has no limitation on the size of a defendant corporation, whereas Title VII applies only to employers with 15 or more employees. The FHA does, however, contain an exception to § 3604 for landlords who own four or fewer units and reside in one of the units. This provision, § 3603(b)(2), exempts "rooms or units in dwellings containing living quarters occupied or intended to be occupied by no more than four families living independently of each other, if the owner actually maintains and occupies one of such living quarters as his residence."

The language makes clear that the exemption (sometimes referred to as the "Mrs. Murphy exemption") applies to people who rent out rooms in their homes and also those who own and live in small apartment buildings. Why did Congress include this exemption? The Mrs. Murphy exemption does *not* apply to § 3617. Thus, a plaintiff may still be able to state a claim for harassment even if the property is otherwise exempt from the statute.

Note, as well, that Mr. Lewallen's wife was also a proper defendant because she co-owned and managed the properties with her husband, was aware of the complaints against him, and took no action. Therefore, under the FHA, it appears that simple negligence is the standard of liability for those who are in a position to address harassment but take no action. Moreover, Department of Housing and Urban Development (HUD) regulations (discussed *infra*) make clear that the Title VII affirmative defense to an employer's vicarious liability for a supervisor's hostile environment harassment does *not* apply to cases brought pursuant to the FHA.

2. Proper Plaintiffs Note that Mr. Shellhammer also had standing to maintain a claim against Mr. Lewallen based upon his own injury—being evicted—that resulted from his wife's refusal to accede to Mr. Lewallen's sexual demands. Sexual harassment in housing can affect every person who lives in a unit—including partners,

---

16. *See* 42 U.S.C. § 3602(d) (2012) (defining persons covered by the statute to include individuals as well as corporations).

children, and roommates—even though they are not the direct targets. Any of these individuals can be considered "aggrieved individuals" under the statute and can be parties to the suit.

3. Additional Targets The court heard testimony from several women who were propositioned by Mr. Lewallen. They had hoped to proceed as a class, represented by the Lewallens, but the court denied their request. While their testimony clearly bolstered that of the Shellhammers, they did not recover any damages because they were not permitted to proceed as plaintiffs. There is no record of any of these women filing their own lawsuits against Mr. Lewallen. Why do you think this was the case?

It is not uncommon for the same landlord to sexually harass multiple tenants. Indeed, for some like Mr. Lewallen, attempts to extract sex from low-income women appears to be part of their business model. Many reported complaints and cases involve multiple aggrieved parties. These cases, however, tend to be brought by the Department of Justice (DOJ) under its "pattern or practice" authority to enforce the FHA, or by fair housing organizations who operate using state and federal grants. Why is it common for plaintiffs to be represented by organizations or the government rather than by private attorneys?

Is there any danger in a court relying on Title VII precedents for sexual harassment that occurs in the housing context? Courts that heard early housing cases and imported the Title VII harassment analysis wholesale often reached conclusions that observers found to be troubling and not grounded in reality. For example, the *Shellhammer* court held that the landlord's behavior did *not* create a hostile environment. Recall that Mr. Lewallen's conduct toward Mrs. Shellhammer included his asking her to pose for nude photographs and later asking her to have sex with him over a three- to four-month period. Is this determination defensible? Would the same behavior in the workplace amount to "severe or pervasive" conduct under Title VII?

The *Shellhammer* decision could be explained by the fact that it was decided when sexual harassment law was still developing and housing harassment was virtually unheard of. But judicial reliance on employment precedents to resolve harassment in housing continued for decades and resulted in a number of cases that have provoked intense criticism. Consider the following case.

Dicenso v. Cisneros
96 F.3d 1004 (7th Cir. 1996)

BAUER, Circuit Judge.

This case raises the question of whether one incident of harassment was sufficiently egregious to create a hostile environment sex discrimination cause of action under the Fair Housing Act. An Administrative Law Judge ("ALJ") thought it was not, but the Housing and Urban Development ("HUD" or "the Department") Secretary's Designee disagreed, and remanded the case to the ALJ for a determination of damages. On remand, the ALJ awarded Christina Brown $5,000 in compensatory damages, assessed a $5,000 civil penalty, and entered injunctive relief. The landlord who committed the harassment now seeks relief from the Secretary's Order. We reverse.

Background

The events of this lawsuit arose in the context of Christina Brown's tenancy at 522½ West Allen Street in Springfield, Illinois. Brown, who at the time was 18 years old, lived in one of the four apartment units with Thomas Andrews and their infant daughter Sara. Beginning in June 1990, they leased the apartment from Albert DiCenso, who owned and managed the building, did most of the cleaning and maintenance, and collected the rents.

. . . .

Sometime in mid-October or early November, DiCenso came to Brown's apartment to collect the rent. According to the ALJ's findings, the following exchange took place:

> While [Brown] stood at the door, [DiCenso] asked about the rent and simultaneously began caressing her arm and back. He said to her words to the effect that if she could not pay the rent, she could take care of it in other ways. [Brown] slammed the door in his face. [DiCenso] stood outside calling her names — a "bitch" and "whore," and then left.

On January 15, 1991, DiCenso again went to the apartment to collect the monthly rent. While there, he became involved in a confrontation with Andrews and the police were called. DiCenso informed the police that the disagreement was over Andrews' refusal to pay the rent. Brown and Andrews told DiCenso that they would be leaving the apartment within the next ten days. According to the police report, the two parties "both came to the decision of settling the matter in court."

Brown and Andrews did not move out, however, and in late January, DiCenso served them with a five-day notice to quit the premises. On January 31, Brown filed a housing discrimination complaint alleging that DiCenso had harassed her and her boyfriend, and had made sexual advances toward her. DiCenso denied the allegations, and asserted that he had had problems collecting the December 1990 and January 1991 rent, and that Andrews not only refused to pay the rent, but had threatened to hurt him. DiCenso felt that the discrimination complaint was a "plot" by Brown and Andrews to avoid paying the rent that was due.

The Department investigated Brown's complaint and determined that reasonable cause existed to believe that discrimination had occurred. On June 22, 1994 the Department issued a charge against DiCenso for violations of sections 804(b) and 818 of the Fair Housing Act. A HUD ALJ conducted a hearing on October 25, 1994.

On March 20, 1995, the ALJ issued a thorough decision, in which she . . . found Brown more credible than DiCenso. However, the ALJ also found that Brown's testimony established only one act of sexual harassment by DiCenso — the mid-October incident. On this set of facts, the ALJ concluded that DiCenso's conduct did not rise to the level of severity required to create a hostile housing environment.

Consequently, the ALJ found that Brown had failed to establish a claim of sex discrimination and dismissed the complaint.

The Department, acting on Brown's behalf, sought review of the ALJ's order pursuant to 42 U.S.C. § 3612(h). The HUD Secretary's Designee affirmed the ALJ's findings of fact, but reached a different conclusion on the issue of whether the single incident amounted to a hostile housing environment for purposes of the Fair Housing Act. Finding for Brown on the issue of liability, the Secretary's Designee vacated the ALJ's decision and remanded the case for a determination of damages. The ALJ awarded Brown $5,000 in compensatory damages, assessed a $5,000 civil penalty against DiCenso and entered injunctive relief. DiCenso filed a petition for review in this court.

Analysis

A. Standard of Review

Before addressing whether DiCenso's conduct constitutes unlawful discrimination, we first must address the applicable standard of review. . . .

. . . In *Meritor Savings Bank, FSB v. Vinson*, the Supreme Court commented on the deference given to EEOC guidelines defining sexual harassment as a form of sex discrimination. Although those guidelines "constitute a body of experience and informed judgment to which courts and litigants may properly resort for guidance," they are not "controlling upon the courts by reason of their authority." In this case, by contrast, HUD has not even enacted guidelines regarding hostile housing environment sex discrimination. [Ed. note: this is no longer the case.] Rather, as the HUD Secretary's Designee acknowledged, a determination of what constitutes a hostile environment in the housing context requires the same analysis courts have undertaken in the Title VII context. Such a determination does not require deference to an administrative agency.

Despite the concession in its initial brief, the Department now argues that we should subject determinations of whether an incident of harassment is sufficiently egregious to constitute sex discrimination to a clearly erroneous standard. . . . In this case, the existence of harassment is not at issue. The sole question is whether the incident of harassment that occurred is sufficient to state a cause of action under the Fair Housing Act. This is purely a question of law which we review *de novo*.

B. Hostile Environment Sex Discrimination

Title VII of the Civil Rights Act of 1964 allows a cause of action for harassment that creates a hostile or offensive working environment. Claims of hostile environment sex discrimination in the housing context have been far less frequent. . . . [C]ourts that have found harassment to create an actionable form of housing discrimination also have incorporated Title VII doctrines into their analyses.

Like the Tenth Circuit, we recognize a hostile housing environment cause of action, and begin our analysis with the more familiar Title VII standard. For sexual harassment to be actionable in the Title VII context, it must be sufficiently severe or pervasive to alter the conditions of the victim's employment and create an abusive working environment. . . . Applied to the housing context, a claim is actionable "when the offensive behavior unreasonably interferes with use and enjoyment of the premises." Whether an environment is "hostile" or "abusive" can be determined only by looking at all the circumstances. . . .

We repeatedly have held that isolated and innocuous incidents do not support a finding of sexual harassment [in the workplace]. For example, in *Saxton v. American Tel. & Tel. Co.,* 10 F.3d 526 (7th Cir. 1993), the defendant on one occasion put his hand on the plaintiff's leg and kissed her until she pushed him away. Three weeks later, the defendant lurched at the plaintiff from behind some bushes and unsuccessfully tried to grab her. While these incidents were subjectively unpleasant, the defendant's conduct was not frequent or severe enough to create a hostile environment. Similarly, in *Weiss v. Coca-Cola Bottling Co. of Chicago,* 990 F.2d 333 (7th Cir. 1993), the defendant asked the plaintiff for dates on repeated occasions, placed signs which read "I love you" in her work area, and twice attempted to kiss her. These incidents also were too isolated and insufficiently severe to create a hostile work environment. Common to all of these examples is an emphasis on the frequency of the offensive behavior. "Though sporadic behavior, if sufficiently abusive, may support a [discrimination] claim, success often requires repetitive misconduct."

In this context, the problem with Brown's complaint is that although DiCenso may have harassed her, he did so only once. Moreover, DiCenso's conduct, while clearly unwelcome, was much less offensive than other incidents which have not violated Title VII. DiCenso's comment vaguely invited Brown to exchange sex for rent, and while DiCenso caressed Brown's arm and back, he did not touch an intimate body part, and did not threaten Brown with any physical harm. There is no question that Brown found DiCenso's remarks to be subjectively unpleasant, but this alone did not create an objectively hostile environment.

We stress in closing that our decision today should not be read as giving landlords one free chance to harass their tenants. We do not condone DiCenso's conduct, nor do we hold that a single incident of harassment never will support an actionable claim. Considering the totality of the circumstances in this case, we agree with the ALJ that DiCenso's conduct was not sufficiently egregious to create an objectively hostile housing environment.

Conclusion

For the foregoing reasons, we grant DiCenso's petition and reverse the decision of the HUD Secretary Designee.

Notes and Discussion

1. The Housing Context Does conduct that might be viewed one way in the workplace take on a more threatening tone when it is undertaken inside a person's home? Consider the workplace examples that the *DiCenso* court cites. In *Saxton,* the defendant put his hand on the plaintiff's leg and kissed her until she pushed him away, and a few weeks later "lurched at" her from behind some bushes and unsuccessfully tried to grab her. Would it be more disturbing if the defendant were a property manager trying to kiss his tenant in her living room, and lurching at her from behind the bushes next to her front door? Similarly, in *Weiss*, the defendant asked the plaintiff for dates, placed signs which read "I love you" in her work area, and twice attempted to kiss her. What if he were her landlord, and instead used his keys to enter her house and leave "love notes" on her nightstand?

For a more recent example, consider *Tagliaferri v. Winter Park Housing Authority* (2012), in which the plaintiffs alleged that the maintenance man at their apartment complex set up a video camera at their bedroom window.[17] A three-judge panel of the Eleventh Circuit was asked to review the district court's dismissal of the case for failure to state a claim under FHA. The panel relied heavily on a Title VII sexual harassment case, *Mendoza v. Borden, Inc.* (1999), in which the plaintiff alleged a hostile work environment based, in part, on the allegation that her supervisor was constantly watching, following, and staring at her.[18] The *Mendoza* court had found that this behavior did not constitute severe or pervasive conduct because "the everyday observation of fellow employees in the workplace is also a natural and unavoidable occurrence when people work together in close quarters or when a supervisor keeps an eye on employees." The *Tagliaferri* court, relying on this precedent, upheld the lower court's dismissal of the case. Should the court have noted the difference between a woman being watched by her supervisor at work and having the maintenance man of her apartment building set up a video camera facing her bedroom window?

Understanding the home as a uniquely protected place has led commentators to conclude that harassing conduct should be held to violate the FHA even if it would not be egregious enough to be actionable under Title VII. Thus, for example, Professor Deborah Zalesne has argued that landlords should be held "to a heightened standard where they have significant power over their tenants."[19] Similarly, Professor Michelle Adams has advocated that, because "[s]exual harassment at home must be recognized and understood as a distinct and significant civil rights issue," a housing provider's harassing activities should be evaluated based on "the nature and importance of home in the American cultural imagination," which would likely change the result in favor of liability in many FHA cases.[20] Professor Adams goes on to argue:

> While the application of employment law principles to sexual harassment at home is somewhat useful, it fails to address central issues raised

---

17. 486 Fed. App'x 771, 774 (11th Cir. 2012).

18. 195 F.3d 1238 (11th Cir. 1999).

19. Deborah Zalesne, *The Intersection of Socioeconomic Class and Gender in Hostile Housing Environment Claims Under Title VIII: Who Is the Reasonable Person?*, 38 B.C. L. Rev. 861 (1997).

20. Michelle Adams, *Knowing Your Place: Theorizing Sexual Harassment at Home*, 40 Ariz. L. Rev. 44 (1998).

in the sexual-harassment-at-home cases. The intimacy of the relationship between landlord and tenant make sexual harassment at home different from sexual harassment at work. Sexual harassment at home can, I believe, be understood as a form of "intimate violence," particularly given the economic and cultural backdrop [in which housing harassment occurs].[21]

The view that harassment in housing must be evaluated within the unique context of the home finds some support in other cases. For example, in *Beliveau v. Caras*, a district court quoted Professor Cahan's statement set forth at the beginning of the chapter, and then concluded that the defendant's alleged conduct constituted sexual harassment because it "was committed (1) in plaintiff's own home, where she should feel (and be) less vulnerable, and (2) by one whose very role was to provide that safe environment."[22]

2. "One Free Chance?" Did the *DiCenso* court authorize "one free chance" for landlords to harass their tenants? How much more severe would a single instance of bad conduct need to be to rise to the level of actionable harassment?

Note that the Seventh Circuit focused exclusively on the fact that DiCenso touched the plaintiff's back while insinuating that she could pay her rent through sexual activity. It appears to have ignored the additional ALJ finding that after she rejected him, he stood outside of her door screaming clearly gendered epithets that she was a "bitch" and a "whore." Could this have pushed DiCenso's conduct across the "severe or pervasive" threshold? Why did the Seventh Circuit fail to consider it?

3. The Administrative Law Judge Under the FHA, plaintiffs can bring claims to HUD, which handles them according to its administrative process. This process, which is quasi-judicial, can culminate in a hearing before an Administrative Law Judge (ALJ). The decisions of the ALJ can be reviewed by a federal court of appeals. Such was the case in *DiCenso*. The benefit of this process is that it is free for the complainant, who is represented by a HUD attorney. One potential drawback, however, is that there is no jury. Would the outcome have been different if the case had been tried to a jury?

4. Fact or Law? The Seventh Circuit appeared to treat the question of whether a single instance of harassing behavior could constitute a violation of the FHA as a question of law that was settled by prior Title VII precedent. Should such a question, which contains an evaluation of the underlying facts of the harassing behavior, actually be one of fact for a jury? This distinction matters less in the *DiCenso* case because that case was first tried in an administrative hearing, for which a jury is unavailable. However, even in regular court proceedings, judges can take issues

---

21. *Id.* at 44.
22. 873 F. Supp. 1393, 1397–98 (C.D. Cal. 1995). Subsequently, two other trial court decisions — *Williams v. Poretsky Management, Inc.*, 955 F. Supp. 490 (D. Md. 1996) and *Reeves v. Carrollsburg Condominium Unit Owners Ass'n*, No. CIV.A. 96-2496RMU, 1997 WL 1877201 (D.D.C. Dec. 18, 1997) — cited this part of the *Beliveau* opinion with approval.

away from juries by granting summary judgment or ordering judgment as a matter of law.

Consider another important early case, in which the Tenth Circuit upheld such a move by the trial court. Pay particular attention to the dissenting judge's argument as to why this was improper.

Honce v. Vigil
1 F.3d 1085 (10th Cir. 1993)

PAUL KELLY, Jr., Circuit Judge.

. . . .

In August 1990, Ms. Honce arranged to rent a lot in Mr. Vigil's mobile home park. Ms. Honce placed a mobile home on the property in mid-September and moved in at the beginning of October. Mr. Vigil invited Ms. Honce to accompany him socially on three occasions in September, prior to her moving in. Finally, two days before moving in, Mr. Vigil asked, "When can we go out?" She responded that she did not wish to go out with him at any time. He told her that he had only wanted to be friends and did not ask her out again. . . .

After Ms. Honce moved in, she and Mr. Vigil had a series of disputes over the property . . . [which culminated in] a shouting match, during which he threatened to evict her. As Mr. Vigil entered his truck to leave, Ms. Honce's dog ran in front of the vehicle. Mr. Vigil "revved" the engine and Ms. Honce retrieved her dog, fearing that the dog would be hit. That night, Ms. Honce went to the sheriff's department for advice and was told that she should be concerned for her safety. She left the next day and moved the trailer out on November 11.

. . . .

Mr. Vigil testified that he believes there is a "conspiracy" against him, led by his former girlfriend and the sheriff's department. Relationships with most of his tenants quickly break down because of this conspiracy, and the problems are often with women. He has evicted between ten and twenty-five tenants in the past, both male and female, including his own nephew.

. . . .

Ms. Honce alleges that Mr. Vigil's actions amount to sexual discrimination and harassment, which forced her to leave the trailer park. The district court granted judgment as a matter of law for Mr. Vigil, following the conclusion of Plaintiff's evidence. The court found no disparate treatment in Mr. Vigil's equally poor treatment of all his tenants, and no evidence of sexual harassment. As for constructive eviction, the court found that the sheriff's advice, not her landlord's actions, caused her to vacate.

Discussion

. . . .

B. Sexual Harassment

. . . .

. . . Mr. Vigil made no quid pro quo threat based on sexual favors. Ms. Honce contends, though, that the threat was implicit, and that the landlord's subsequent actions were in direct response to her rejection. She failed to provide any evidence of a connection, however. She rejected her landlord's advances prior to moving in to the park. Mr. Vigil did not "retaliate" for the rejection by attempting to stop her from moving in. The disputes which occurred after she moved in involved . . . [aspects of the property].

Although Defendant may not be the most rational actor, Title VIII does not make irrational rental policies illegal. Ms. Honce failed to present evidence of a causal connection, and a conclusional allegation is insufficient to create a question of fact. We agree that no reasonable jury could find quid pro quo harassment here.

C. Hostile Housing Environment

Ms. Honce raises the related claim that Mr. Vigil's harassment created a hostile housing environment. In the employment context an employer violates Title VII by creating a discriminatory work environment, even if the employee loses no tangible job benefits, because the harassment is a barrier to equality in the workplace. Applied to housing, a claim is actionable when the offensive behavior unreasonably interferes with use and enjoyment of the premises. The harassment must be "sufficiently severe or pervasive" to alter the conditions of the housing arrangement. The offensive acts need not be purely sexual; it is sufficient that they would not have happened but for claimant's gender. Evidence of harassment of other female tenants is relevant to plaintiff's claim.

In *Hicks*, we remanded for a determination of whether sexual touching, sexual remarks and threats of violence in the workplace constituted a hostile environment. Hostile environment claims usually involve a long-lasting pattern of highly offensive behavior. In *Shellhammer*, the Sixth Circuit affirmed a district court finding that two explicit sexual propositions from a landlord during four months of tenancy did not prove a hostile housing environment because it did not create a "burdensome situation" that would make the tenancy undesirable.

The offensive behavior here did not include sexual remarks or requests, physical touching, or threats of violence. Mr. Vigil asked Ms. Honce to accompany him socially on three occasions, all prior to her occupying the premises. The contact between them after that involved arguments over plumbing, stepping stones and a fence. The landlord's behavior here was eccentric, and probably unwarranted, but was not directed solely at Ms. Honce. Other tenants of both sexes endured similar treatment. Because the conduct was neither sexual nor directed solely at women, it is not actionable under the hostile housing environment theory.

. . . .

SEYMOUR, Circuit Judge, dissenting.

. . . .

The majority also concludes that a directed verdict was proper on Ms. Honce's claim of quid pro quo sexual harassment. . . . I must disagree. The majority improperly bases its conclusion on a view of the record that favors Mr. Vigil. Ms. Honce's quid pro quo claim required her to present evidence that Mr. Vigil conditioned the quality of her home environment upon her positive response to his personal overtures. The majority concludes that Ms. Honce failed to establish any connection between her refusals to go out with Mr. Vigil and his commencement of abusive behavior toward her. In support of this conclusion, the majority states that Ms. Honce rejected Mr. Vigil's advances before she moved in and that Mr. Vigil did not attempt to stop her from moving in. However, Mr. Vigil's own testimony undercuts the majority's characterization of the situation. Ms. Honce moved the trailer into the park in mid-September and then began moving her belongings in piecemeal after that. Although she did not physically move into the trailer herself until October 1, she had signed a rental agreement in August. Mr. Vigil testified that in his view Ms. Honce had possession upon signing the rental agreement on August 25. He stated that after she signed the agreement, "[N]obody else could have lived there. The minute I sign, no one can live—I had given her possession. It's immaterial when she decides to move in. And it's immaterial when the mobile home moves in." Moreover, Mr. Vigil testified that he and Ms. Honce "had a very, very good relationship up until about a week *after* she moved in." The majority seemingly believes that a single mother of a young child who has just borrowed money to buy a mobile home and has signed a rental agreement for the lot onto which she has moved it somehow is completely free to abandon the lease and leave the premises upon finding the conduct of her new landlord offensive. This inference, adversely drawn by the majority against Ms. Honce, is belied by Mr. Vigil's insistent testimony that Ms. Honce was in severe financial straits, and by the fact that she ultimately was required to borrow $1,000 from her parents to pay the cost of moving the mobile home. It also defies common sense regarding the economic realities of single working mothers such as Ms. Honce.

In view of our obligation to view the record most favorably to the nonmoving party and to give her the benefit of all reasonable inferences to be drawn from the evidence, in my judgment the record raises a jury issue on whether Mr. Vigil retaliated against Ms. Honce because she refused to go out with him. Ms. Honce testified that Mr. Vigil's attitude toward her changed abruptly after she made it clear to him at the very end of September that she did not wish to see him socially. She testified that when she next spoke to Mr. Vigil to discuss a plumbing problem and her dog run, he became very upset and hung up the phone. Their relationship continued to deteriorate until the October 24 encounter witnessed by the fence installers at which Mr. Vigil threatened to evict her. In the context of retaliation under Title VII, we have held that "[t]he causal connection may be demonstrated by evidence of circumstances that justify an inference of retaliatory motive, such as protected conduct closely followed by adverse action." I believe the jury could reasonably infer from the circumstances here that Mr. Vigil's conduct, culminating in his eviction threat, was in retaliation for her refusal of his invitations.

Finally, I am particularly troubled by the majority's treatment of Ms. Honce's claim that she was the victim of a discriminatory hostile housing environment. This circuit's law with respect to hostile environment claims is set out in *Hicks v. Gates Rubber Co.*, [an employment case] in which we adopted the District of Columbia Court of Appeals' definition of sexual harassment.

> "We have never held that sexual harassment or other unequal treatment of an employee or group of employees that occurs because of the sex of an employee must, to be illegal under Title VII, take the form of sexual advances or of other instances with clearly sexual overtones. And we decline to do so now. Rather, we hold that any harassment or other unequal treatment of an employee or group of employees that would not occur but for the sex of the employee or employees may, if sufficiently patterned or pervasive, comprises an illegal condition of employment under Title VII."

The majority's review of the evidence supports my conclusion that it has again viewed the evidence most favorably to Mr. Vigil. The majority states that "[t]he offensive behavior here did not include sexual remarks or requests, physical touching, or threats of violence." It then concludes there is no evidence of disparate treatment because Mr. Vigil treated women the same as men. Id. Finally, it states that "[b]ecause the conduct was neither sexual nor directed solely at women, it is not actionable under the hostile housing environment theory."

The fact that Mr. Vigil's conduct was not sexual in nature is irrelevant under *Hicks* so long as that conduct would not have occurred but for Ms. Honce's gender. Moreover, when the record is evaluated under a standard that gives effect to our holding in *Hicks*, the evidence I have set out in discussing the disparate treatment claim indisputably supports the inference that Mr. Vigil's conduct created a hostile environment for women. This evidence indicates that numerous women, including Ms. Honce, Mrs. Haenner, and others to whom Mr. Vigil himself referred, had felt compelled to move out as a result of Mr. Vigil's behavior or had been evicted by him. The majority's statement that "tenants of both sexes endured similar treatment" from Mr. Vigil, is simply without evidentiary support. The record contains specific references to only two male tenants, Mr. Haenner and Mr. Vigil's nephew. As set out above, Mr. Vigil did not direct any hostile behavior to Mr. Haenner. Although Mr. Vigil was attempting to evict his nephew, the record does not reveal the details of Mr. Vigil's conduct toward the nephew during this proceeding. In sum, the majority simply fails to recognize that a landlord may violate the Fair Housing Act even when he does provide equal rental services if, in so doing, he creates a hostile environment for women. Because I believe Ms. Honce has raised a jury question with respect to her Fair Housing Act claims, I would reverse the grant of a directed verdict.

. . . .

Notes and Discussion

1. Factual Interpretations Does the dissenting opinion offer a convincing interpretation of the facts in *Honce*? Could a reasonable jury have found in favor of the plaintiff?

2. HUD Guidelines The Supreme Court has recognized that HUD's views about the meaning of the FHA are entitled to great weight. The *DiCenso* court noted that, at the time, HUD had not passed any guidance, in the form of administrative regulations, for sexual harassment cases. Such guidance did not issue until 2013, when HUD formally passed a regulation about sexual harassment in housing:

Title VIII Harassment in Housing Regulation
24 C.F.R. § 100.600 (2013)

§ 100.600 Quid pro quo and hostile environment harassment.

(a) General. Quid pro quo and hostile environment harassment because of . . . sex . . . may violate sections [3604 and 3617] of the Act, depending on the conduct. The same conduct may violate one or more of these provisions.

(1) Quid pro quo harassment. Quid pro quo harassment refers to an unwelcome request or demand to engage in conduct where submission to the request or demand, either explicitly or implicitly, is made a condition related to: The sale, rental or availability of a dwelling; the terms, conditions, or privileges of the sale or rental, or the provision of services or facilities in connection therewith; or the availability, terms, or conditions of a residential real estate-related transaction. An unwelcome request or demand may constitute quid pro quo harassment even if a person acquiesces in the unwelcome request or demand.

(2) Hostile environment harassment. Hostile environment harassment refers to unwelcome conduct that is sufficiently severe or pervasive as to interfere with: The availability, sale, rental, or use or enjoyment of a dwelling; the terms, conditions, or privileges of the sale or rental, or the provision or enjoyment of services or facilities in connection therewith; or the availability, terms, or conditions of a residential real estate-related transaction. Hostile environment harassment does not require a change in the economic benefits, terms, or conditions of the dwelling or housing-related services or facilities, or of the residential real-estate transaction.

(i) Totality of the circumstances. Whether hostile environment harassment exists depends upon the totality of the circumstances.

(A) Factors to be considered to determine whether hostile environment harassment exists include, but are not limited to, the nature of the conduct, the context in which the incident(s) occurred, the severity, scope, frequency, duration, and location of the conduct, and the relationships of the persons involved.

(B) Neither psychological nor physical harm must be demonstrated to prove that a hostile environment exists. Evidence of psychological or physical harm may, however, be relevant in determining whether a hostile environment existed and, if so, the amount of damages to which an aggrieved person may be entitled.

(C) Whether unwelcome conduct is sufficiently severe or pervasive as to create a hostile environment is evaluated from the perspective of a reasonable person in the aggrieved person's position.

(ii) Title VII affirmative defense. The affirmative defense to an employer's vicarious liability for hostile environment harassment by a supervisor under Title VII of the Civil Rights Act of 1964 does not apply to cases brought pursuant to the Fair Housing Act.

(b) Type of conduct. Harassment can be written, verbal, or other conduct, and does not require physical contact.

(c) Number of incidents. A single incident of harassment because of race, color, religion, sex, familial status, national origin, or handicap may constitute a discriminatory housing practice, where the incident is sufficiently severe to create a hostile environment, or evidences a quid pro quo.

Does this regulation add anything new to the current understanding of the law? Do you think it will result in more consistent outcomes from courts in sexual harassment cases? Would these regulations have changed the outcome in early decisions like *Shellhammer* and *DiCenso*?

4. Additional Issues

A number of additional issues can arise in harassment in housing cases that are unique to the housing context because of specific language in the FHA. The Supreme Court has never heard a sexual harassment in housing case, so many of the issues remain unresolved, with courts divided. Guidance from HUD provides some clarity. The nature of the underlying right — housing — also gives rise to some additional considerations with respect to damages and other causes of action.

A. "In connection with the sale or rental of a dwelling" Post-Acquisition Claims

Recall that § 3604(b) and (c) of the FHA prohibit sexually harassing behavior or comments that are made "in connection with the sale or rental of a dwelling." Some courts, most notably the Seventh Circuit in the case of *Halprin v. Prairie Single Family Homes Ass'n.*,[23] have interpreted this language to mean that only discrimination or

---

23. 388 F.3d 327 (7th Cir. 2004).

harassment that occurs at the point of sale or rental will be actionable. Put another way, these courts held that sexual harassment that occurred *after* a woman had taken occupancy of her apartment could not be reached by the FHA. This approach has come under considerable academic criticism. Professor Rigel Oliveri argues:

> A detailed analysis of the flaws in the reasoning behind *Halprin* should not obscure one of the most problematic aspects of the opinion: It leads to extremely anomalous results. According to *Halprin* it would not violate § 3604(b) for a Condo Association to prevent a disabled person from using the laundry facilities, or for a landlord to refuse to provide maintenance to his Hispanic tenants. Similarly, it would not violate § 3604(b) for a landlord to sexually harass a tenant or to raise the rent only of Jewish tenants. It would not violate § 3604(c) for a landlord to use racial slurs to or about existing tenants — or even to spray-paint such a slur on someone's door. Nor would it violate § 3604(c) for a Homeowner's Association to print up flyers denigrating a particular resident due to her religious faith and post them throughout the neighborhood. Despite the FHA's prohibitions of such conduct, all of these behaviors would be beyond the law's purview solely because of when they occurred.
>
> Most practitioners and scholars (indeed, most laypeople), would likely be alarmed to discover that the nation's remedial and comprehensive fair housing legislation — whose stated purpose is to provide "for fair housing . . . throughout the United States" — had such a limited reach. And with good reason: Such a regime would eviscerate nearly 40 years of fair housing jurisprudence, particularly in the landlord-tenant context, and would invalidate the results of hundreds of cases.[24]

Not all courts agreed with *Halprin*. Many adopted the approach set out in the following case. Consider the differences and whether the *Koch* precedent improves the law.

United States v. Koch
352 F. Supp. 2d 970 (2004)

URBOM, District Judge.

[The defendant landlord was accused of sexually harassing a number of his low-income, female tenants. The harassment took the form of requests for sex and strip-tease dances in lieu of rent, home invasions, unwanted groping, and indecent exposure. At least three women engaged in sexual activity because they were afraid of being evicted by the defendant. Most of the harassment took place after the women had become tenants, but some of the harassment occurred while the women were at the lease-signing stage. For example, the defendant asked one woman to

---

24. Rigel C. Oliveri, *Is Acquisition Everything? Protecting the Rights of Occupants Under the Fair Housing Act*, 43 Harv. C.R.-C.L. L. Rev. 1, 32–33 (2008).

write her measurements on her lease application and then sit on his lap. He told another that he would rent to her only if she "flashed" him. This matter proceeded to trial, and at the conclusion of the plaintiff's case in chief, the defendant moved for judgment as a matter of law on the post-acquisition claims.]

. . . .

The defendant first "seeks judgment as a matter of law on all post-residence acquisition Fair Housing Act [c]laims asserted pursuant to 42 U.S.C. § 3604(a–c) as they cannot be maintained under the plain language of the statute." In addition, the defendant claims that these "post-residence acquisition" claims cannot proceed under 42 U.S.C. § 3617. In other words, the defendant argues that to the extent the aggrieved persons claim that they suffered discriminatory treatment after they moved into the defendant's properties, their claims cannot be maintained under sections 3604 or 3617 of the Fair Housing Act.

. . . .

In support of his position, the defendant relies chiefly upon the district court's and Seventh Circuit's opinions in *Halprin v. Prairie Single Family Homes of Dearborn Park Ass'n*. In *Halprin*, the co-owners of a home located in the Prairie Single Family Homes subdivision filed a complaint against several defendants, including the subdivision's homeowners' association and a Mr. Ormond, who was a resident of the subdivision and a member and officer of the homeowners' association. The complaint was based upon a number of incidents, including Mr. Ormond's alleged vandalism of the plaintiffs' home; the defendants' alteration and destruction of records in an attempt to conceal Ormond's threats against the plaintiffs; the defendants' threats to force the plaintiffs to sell their home due to an alleged violation of the association's covenants; the defendants' application of unwanted chemicals to the plaintiffs' lawn; and the defendants' enactment of "several new rules targeted solely at restricting the freedom of plaintiffs to enjoy the use of their home." "[T]he entire campaign of harassment was caused or at least influenced by the religion of the Jewish plaintiff."

The plaintiffs alleged that the defendants' actions amounted to violations of 42 U.S.C. §§ 3604(b)–(c) and 3617. The district court disagreed and dismissed each of these claims. According to the court, the plaintiffs' complaint failed to state a claim under section 3604(b) because "Plaintiffs already owned their home and none of plaintiffs' allegations involve the sale or rental of housing." For the same reason, the court concluded that the complaint failed to state a claim under section 3604(c). Finally, the court determined that the section 3617 claim ought to be dismissed for two reasons. First, the court noted that "the Seventh Circuit has instructed that when the alleged violation of § 3617 involves the same conduct and the same party responsible for a violation of § 3604, and the court finds the underlying § 3604 claim meritless, the court should also find the § 3617 claim meritless." Since the plaintiffs failed to state a claim under section 3604, the court held that the section 3617 claim must also fail. Secondly, the court concluded that the plaintiff's allegations were not severe enough to support a claim under section 3617, because that section only applies to "threatening, intimidating, or extremely violent discriminatory conduct designed to drive an individual out of his home," such as "cross-burning, fire-bombing homes or cars, shooting shotguns, physical assaults, or throwing Molotov cocktails."

On appeal, the Seventh Circuit affirmed the district court's conclusion that the plaintiffs failed to state a claim under section 3604, stating, "Our plaintiffs . . . are complaining not about being prevented from acquiring property but about being harassed by other property owners." . . . The court [reasoned that:]

> Title VII protects the job holder as well as the job applicant, so an employer who resorts to harassment to force an employee to quit is engaged in job discrimination within the meaning of the Act. The Fair Housing Act contains no hint either in its language or its legislative history of a concern with anything but access to housing. Behind the Act lay the widespread practice of refusing to sell or rent homes in desirable residential areas to members of minority groups. Since the focus was on their exclusion, the problem of how they were treated when they were included, that is, when they were allowed to own or rent homes in such areas, was not at the forefront of congressional thinking. That problem — the problem not of exclusion but of expulsion — would become acute only when the law forced unwanted associations that might provoke efforts at harassment, and so it would tend not to arise until the Act was enacted and enforced. There is nothing to suggest that Congress was trying to solve that future problem, an endeavor that would have required careful drafting in order to make sure that quarrels between neighbors did not become a routine basis for federal litigation.

Thus, the Seventh Circuit concluded that the "plaintiffs have no claim under section 3604."

. . . .

The defendant asks that I apply in this case the rules derived in *Halprin*. More specifically, the defendant argues that to the extent the aggrieved persons' claims are based upon incidents that occurred after they took possession of the rental properties, their claims cannot proceed under 42 U.S.C. § 3604. For the following reasons, I reject the defendant's arguments.

. . . .

[A]fter studying the *Halprin* opinions, I find that I am not persuaded by their analyses of the intended scope of Title VIII. Specifically, it seems to me that the courts' analyses are questionable in two key respects: they counsel that a narrow interpretation ought to be given to the language of section 3604, and they depend greatly upon a narrow view of the FHA's legislative history. I shall elaborate upon each of these criticisms in turn.

In *Halprin*, the district court interpreted the terms of section 3604(b) narrowly, holding that the prohibition of discrimination "against any person in the terms, conditions, or privileges of sale or rental of a dwelling, or in the provision of services or facilities in connection therewith," cannot be read to apply to acts of discrimination that occur after a home is sold. However, there is authority that the terms of the Fair Housing Act are to be construed generously in order to promote the replacement of segregated ghettos with "truly integrated and balanced living patterns." In any event, the Seventh Circuit acknowledged in *Halprin* that post-sale discrimination might be encompassed within the statutory language of section 3604 "as a purely semantic matter," because the "'privileges of sale or rental' might conceivably be thought to include the privilege of inhabiting the premises." In my view, it is difficult to imagine a privilege that flows more naturally from the purchase or rental of a dwelling than the privilege of residing therein; therefore the Fair Housing Act should be (and has been) read to permit the enjoyment of this privilege without discriminatory harassment. Thus, and in view of the authorities counseling a broad interpretation of the language of the FHA, I cannot share the *Halprin* courts' cramped interpretation of the scope of section 3604(b).

I also disagree with the Seventh Circuit's analysis of the legislative history of the FHA. As I noted above, the court granted — albeit somewhat grudgingly — that section 3604(b) might be read to prohibit unlawful discrimination against the privilege of inhabiting the premises that one has purchased or rented. However, the court relied upon the legislative history of the FHA to rule out this interpretation, stating, "The Fair Housing Act contains no hint either in its language or its legislative history of a concern with anything but access to housing," and arguing that there is no reason to conclude that Congress gave any thought to problems that might arise when "[minorities] were allowed to own or rent homes" in "desirable residential areas." I cannot agree with this assessment. . . .

As for the legislative history of the FHA, it is true that the congressional records reflect a deep concern about exclusionary housing practices; in particular, it is clear that the legislation was motivated by a desire to eliminate discriminatory business practices that confined African-Americans to harsh inner-city living conditions. However, it does not necessarily follow that Congress did not intend for the FHA to reach discrimination that occurs after housing has been acquired. On the contrary, Congress was "committed to the principle of living together," and sought to promote integrated neighborhoods where residents of different races would live together in "harmony." Congress hoped that its promotion of these principles would lead to the reduction of the deleterious effects of ghettos on the employment and education of the Americans trapped therein. To achieve these goals, Congress sought to pass "measures that have teeth and meaning, in the eyes of every American, black or white." It seems to me that little progress could have been made toward Congress's goals — and its measures would appear to have few teeth — if the basic privilege of residing within one's home were not protected from the evils of discriminatory harassment.

In sum, it is the Seventh Circuit's view that Congress sought to allow members of minority groups to acquire housing without facing discrimination but was not concerned with allowing such people to live in that housing without facing discrimination. I do not believe that this interpretation of the scope of the FHA is mandated by the Act's language or its legislative history. . . .

. . . .

Notes and Discussion

1. Right of Access Versus Right of Occupancy Which court has the better argument? Is it possible to protect access to housing without also protecting the rights of occupancy? Note that the Seventh Circuit significantly retreated from its decision in *Halprin* in a later case, *Bloch v. Frischholz*, 587 F.3d 771 (7th Cir. 2009) ("Upon careful review of the FHA and our prior opinion in *Halprin*, we conclude that in some circumstances homeowners have an FHA cause of action for discrimination that occurred after they moved in.").

2. Congressional Intent Consider the differing views of congressional intent that the cases present. It is true that Congress passed the FHA in large part to open access to housing for African Americans and to break up segregated living patterns. Does a focus on access and integration make sense when it comes to sexual harassment by landlords?

B. The Independent Utility of § 3617

Recall that § 3617, the FHA provision that prohibits interference and coercion, is in a different section of the statute than the other substantive prohibitions, which are contained in § 3604. As a result, courts and scholars have debated its utility as an independent source of law to challenge harassment in housing. Put another way, can a plaintiff assert a § 3617 claim without also asserting (or prevailing on) a § 3604 claim?

This question is important because there are certain circumstances under which § 3604 does not apply. For example, § 3617 is not subject to the Mrs. Murphy exemption, which exempts certain landlords from § 3604. In addition, a plaintiff may not succeed in stating a claim under any of the subsections of § 3604 but may still wish to argue that she has experienced interference or coercion in violation of § 3617. Finally, § 3604 has long been interpreted to apply only to housing professionals or providers, such as landlords, property managers, or others who are acting (in the statute's words) "in connection with the sale or rental of housing."

Section 3617 contains no language requiring a connection to housing sale or rental, and thus might be applied to other people, including neighbors, who commit acts of harassment. Indeed, this appears to have been part of Congress's reason for including § 3617.

A number of potential issues arise with the independent application of § 3617. First, some courts have held that the term "interfere" in § 3617 — coming as it does after the words "coerce, intimidate, [and] threaten" — should be interpreted to require a certain level of force. Such a requirement might mean that the type of offensive and unwelcome, albeit non-threatening, behavior that often forms the basis for hostile environment claims would not be actionable under § 3617. Other courts, however, have given a more generous interpretation of this term. These courts hold that non-physical acts of sexual harassment may sufficiently "interfere" with a female tenant's enjoyment of her apartment to establish a § 3617 violation.[25] In these cases, however, the defendant's harassment was also severe enough to constitute quid pro quo harassment in violation of the complainant's rights under § 3604.

The concluding language of § 3617 creates another potential stumbling block. The last part requires that the interference be with a person's exercise or enjoyment of a right "granted or protected by" §§ 3603–3606. To assert a § 3617 claim, therefore, a harassment target apparently must assert a right covered by these other substantive provisions. While this part does not mean that a § 3617 claim always requires an outright violation of §§ 3603–3606, at least some sort of connection to a right covered by these other substantive provisions must exist.

The problem is that if the "predicate" right in a § 3617 harassment case is based on the substantive provision of the statute, then the fact that these provisions are subject to the restrictive Title VII standards in sexual harassment cases may mean that § 3617 cannot be used without reference to these standards. For example, if a plaintiff's claim of hostile environment harassment fails because the conduct does not meet the "severe or pervasive" standard, some courts might determine that a claim under § 3617 necessarily fails too. The *Halprin* court suggested this. The *Koch* court disagreed:

> To the extent that the *Halprin* courts hold that a violation of section 3617 cannot lie absent a violation of section [3604], I respectfully disagree. As another district judge in this circuit has aptly noted, "such a construction renders § 3617 a redundant section." Similarly, other circuit courts have concluded that section 3617 may be violated when "no discriminatory housing practice may have occurred at all." I agree with these decisions, and I find that even if section 3604 were given a narrow interpretation, such that it does not prohibit post-possession discrimination, it does not necessarily follow that no violation of section 3617 can lie.[26]

Some of the confusion on this point has been cleared up by a HUD regulation interpreting § 3617 in a manner that suggests it does not need to be tied to another asserted statutory violation.

---

25. Quigley v. Winter, 598 F.3d 938 (8th Cir. 2010) (landlord's sexual harassment of tenant, which consisted of entering her home uninvited and making sexual comments, was coercive and intimidating in violation of § 3617); HUD v. Krueger, 2A Fair Hous.-Fair Lending (Aspen L. & Bus.) at 26,026 (holding that landlord's sexual harassment of female tenant interfered with the "quiet enjoyment of her apartment" in violation of § 3617).

26. 352 F. Supp. 2d at 978.

Title VIII Prohibitions Regulation

24 C.F.R. § 100.400 (2013)

§ 100.400 Prohibited interference, coercion or intimidation.

(a) This subpart provides the Department's interpretation of the conduct that is unlawful under section [3617] of the Fair Housing Act.

(b) It shall be unlawful to coerce, intimidate, threaten, or interfere with any person in the exercise or enjoyment of, or on account of that person having exercised or enjoyed, or on account of that person having aided or encouraged any other person in the exercise or enjoyment of, any right granted or protected by this part.

(c) Conduct made unlawful under this section includes, but is not limited to, the following:

(1) Coercing a person, either orally, in writing, or by other means, to deny or limit the benefits provided that person in connection with the sale or rental of a dwelling or in connection with a residential real estate-related transaction because of . . . sex. . . .

(2) Threatening, intimidating or interfering with persons in their enjoyment of a dwelling because of the . . . sex . . . of such persons, or of visitors or associates of such persons.

. . . .

Notes and Discussion

1. Section 3617 and "Serious" Harassment Harassment plaintiffs usually prevail on § 3617 claims when the harassment is also serious enough to violate other portions of the statute. In these cases, does § 3617 add anything to the plaintiff's claim? Does the language of § 3617 seem to limit it to these situations? Is there a harassment scenario where the defendant's conduct violates § 3617 but is not found to be severe or pervasive enough to violate § 3604(b)?

2. Neighbor Harassment As discussed previously, Congress included § 3617 in the statute in order to address the then-widespread problem of whites using threats and intimidation to keep blacks from integrating neighborhoods. As such, it makes sense that § 3617 should apply to harassment by neighbors, even though neighbors would not be covered by the substantive provisions of the statute. Several early courts applied § 3617 to racial harassment by neighbors absent a claim under § 3604.[27]

---

27. *See, e.g.*, Stirgus v. Benoit, 720 F. Supp. 119, 121, 123 (N.D. Ill. 1989) (holding that the plaintiff's allegation that firebombing of her home was sufficient to support a § 3617 claim); Seaphus v. Lilly, 691 F. Supp. 127, 138–39 (N.D. Ill. 1988) (holding that the plaintiffs allegation that the defendants attempted to force the plaintiff from his home might support a claim under § 3617); Waheed v. Kalafut, No. 86 C 6674, 1988 WL 9092, at *4 (N.D. Ill. Feb. 2, 1988) (holding that the allegation that the defendant attempted to oust an African-American family from their home was sufficient

Commentary to HUD Regulation 100.400 also makes clear that that "persons who are not involved in any aspect of the sale or rental of a dwelling are nonetheless prohibited from engaging in conduct to coerce, intimidate, threaten or interfere with persons in connection with protected activities."[28] There are no reported cases of plaintiffs successfully suing their neighbors for sexual harassment under the FHA.

Plaintiffs who have been harassed by their neighbors have successfully brought claims under §3617 against their landlords for failure to respond to the harassment.[29] In these cases, the courts apply a negligence standard to the landlords: that they knew or should have known about the harassment and failed to take proper action.

C. Damages

The FHA allows courts to award a successful complainant actual and punitive damages, injunctive relief, and attorneys' fees and costs.[30] Unlike Title VII, there are no caps or limitations on the amounts that a court can award. The FHA originally had a $1,000 cap on punitive damages but Congress repealed this in 1988 with the express purpose of encouraging private litigants to bring cases. Cases that proceed through HUD's administrative process and go to trial do so before an ALJ. The ALJ has the authority to award the complainant compensatory damages, injunctive relief, and attorneys' fees but not punitive damages.[31]

In many sexual harassment cases involving low-income women, courts may not find significant "actual damages," because even if a woman is actually or constructively evicted due to the harassment, the value of the housing at issue may be low. A few months' rent is not likely to amount to much. Thus, most of the damages for a sexual harassment in housing plaintiff take the form of emotional distress and punitive damages. Even without a statutory cap, Supreme Court precedent may

---

to support a §3617 claim); Stackhouse v. DeSitter, 566 F. Supp. 856 (N.D. Ill. 1983) (defendant's firebombing of plaintiff's car, which was intended to intimidate the plaintiff and drive him out of the neighborhood, was prohibited by §3617).

28. Implementation of Fair Housing Amendments Act of 1988, 54 Fed. Reg. 3257 (Jan. 23, 1989) (codified at 24 C.F.R. pt. 100).

29. *See, e.g.,* Neudecker v. Bosclair Corp., 351 F.3d 361, 365 (8th Cir. 2003) ("While Neudecker does not allege that Boisclair's agents themselves harassed him, he does allege that tenants . . . constantly harassed and threatened him based on his disability; that he repeatedly complained to Bosclair management about the harassment to no avail; and that he ultimately moved from his apartment out of concerns for his health stemming from the harassment."); Fahnbulleh v. GFZ Realty, LLC, 795 F. Supp. 2d 360, 364 (D. Md. 2011) ("[C]onduct is imputable to a landlord, if the landlord knew or should have known of the harassment, and took no effectual action to correct the situation."); Reeves v. Carrollsburg Condo. Unit Owners Ass'n, No. CIV. A. 96-2495RMU, 1997 WL 1877201, at *7 (D.D.C. Dec. 18, 1997) (finding that a defendant condominium association could be held liable for creation of a hostile housing environment by fellow condo owner where the defendant "knew or should have known of the [racial and sexual] harassment, and took no effectual action to correct the situation").

30. 42 U.S.C. §3613(c) (2012).

31. 42 U.S.C. §3612 (2012).

limit the amount of punitive damages.[32] The FHA also provides for attorneys' fees. This provision is particularly important for low-income plaintiffs who otherwise could not afford counsel. Courts calculate the amount of these fees according to the lodestar method.[33]

Consider how the following case handles a cross-appeal on the issue of whether a plaintiff who claimed sexual harassment in housing was entitled to a jury instruction concerning punitive damages and attorneys' fees. Did the court err in reducing the amount of both?

Quigley v. Winter
598 F.3d 938 (8th Cir. 2010)

RILEY, Circuit Judge.

. . . .

Having found no reversible trial error, we turn to [plaintiff] Quigley's claims on appeal. Quigley claims the district court (1) improperly reduced the jury's punitive damage award from $250,000.00 to $20,527.50, and (2) failed to conduct a proper analysis of Quigley's entitlement to attorney fees and awarded an insufficient amount of attorney fees to Quigley. Conversely, Winter claims the district court erred in submitting punitive damages to the jury and in awarding any amount of punitive damages or attorney fees to Quigley.

1. Punitive Damages

a. Punitive Damages Jury Instruction

We first address [defendant] Winter's contention that the district court erred in allowing the jury to consider punitive damages. "The [FHA] provides for the recovery of punitive damages by victims of discriminatory housing practices." We apply the same standard for punitive damages in [FHA] cases as we do in employment discrimination and 42 U.S.C. § 1983 civil rights cases. "Punitive damages are appropriate in a federal civil rights action when the defendant's conduct is shown to be motivated by evil motive or intent, or when it involves reckless or callous indifference to the federally protected rights of others." In *Kolstad*, a gender discrimination case, the Supreme Court held "[t]he terms 'malice' and 'reckless [indifference]' ultimately focus on the actor's state of mind." They "pertain to the [defendant's] knowledge that [he] may be acting in violation of federal law, not [his] awareness that [he] is engaging in discrimination." Thus, "it is sufficient that a defendant 'discriminate in the face of a perceived risk that [his] actions will violate federal law to be liable in punitive damages.'"

---

32. *See* BMW of North America, Inc. v. Gore, 517 U.S. 559 (1996); State Farm Mut. Auto. Ins. Co. v. Campbell, 538 U.S. 408 (2003). Chapter 5, *supra*, reviews these cases.

33. *See supra* Chapter 5.

The district court determined Quigley had presented sufficient evidence to justify instructing the jury on punitive damages, because Winter admitted at trial he knew sexual harassment was unlawful, he had been a landlord for many years and managed many properties, he had worked with various governmental agencies to provide subsidized housing, and his lease agreement with Quigley stated he, as the landlord, was not to discriminate on the basis of sex. We agree with the district court. The district court did not err in submitting punitive damages for the jury's consideration.

b. Reasonableness of the Punitive Damages Award

The jury found Quigley was entitled to punitive damages in the amount of $250,000.00, and the district court entered judgment. Winter then filed a motion to amend the judgment to reduce the punitive damages award. The district court noted the punitive damages award was more than eighteen times the compensatory damages award ($13,685.00) and found the award was excessive and did not comport with due process. The district court reduced the award to $20,527.50, which amounted to one and a half times the compensatory damages award, "for the simple reason that [Winter's] conduct . . . can be considered only as to what he said and did directly to [Quigley]."

Quigley challenges the district court's analysis, arguing the jury's punitive damages award complied with due process and the original award should be reinstated. "We review a district court's legal conclusions regarding punitive damages de novo." We also review the proportionality determination de novo.

> The factual findings made by the district courts in conducting the excessiveness inquiry, of course, must be accepted unless clearly erroneous. . . .
> But the question whether a [punitive damages award] is constitutionally excessive calls for the application of a constitutional standard to the facts of a particular case, and in this context de novo review of that question is appropriate.

To assess the reasonableness or excessiveness of a punitive damages award, we consider: (1) "the degree of reprehensibility of the defendant's conduct," (2) the ratio between punitive damages and actual harm (compensatory damages), and (3) "the civil or criminal penalties that could be imposed for comparable misconduct."

i. Reprehensibility

In *Gore*, the Supreme Court declared the degree of reprehensibility was "[p]erhaps the most important indicium of the reasonableness of a punitive damages award." In assessing the degree of reprehensibility, we must consider whether

> "the harm caused was physical as opposed to economic; the tortious conduct evinced an indifference to or a reckless disregard of the health or safety of others; the target of the conduct had financial vulnerability; the conduct involved repeated actions or was an isolated incident; and the harm was the result of intentional malice, trickery, or deceit, or mere accident."

The district court determined Winter's conduct was not sufficiently reprehensible to justify the jury's punitive damages award. The district court may have based this finding on an assumption the jury considered Winter's conduct toward other tenants, and not just the conduct directed toward Quigley, in arriving at the punitive damages amount. However, as Quigley notes, the jury instruction on punitive damages clearly stated the jury was to consider "[Winter]'s conduct only as against [Quigley]" in assessing punitive damages. We have no reason to believe the jury disregarded the district court's instructions.

Winter's conduct was reprehensible. Quigley lived alone with small children at the time of Winter's harassment, and she had few, if any, alternative housing options. Quigley's financial vulnerability was evidenced by her need for Section 8 housing vouchers. Winter held a certain level of power over Quigley and her family. Winter repeatedly subjected Quigley to inappropriate conduct during Quigley's tenancy, and Winter's conduct was unquestionably intentional and more than churlish. Most significant, Winter's conduct intruded upon Quigley's sense of security in her own home. However, as we explain below, we do not believe the degree of reprehensibility of Winter's conduct justifies the jury's large punitive damages award.

ii. Ratio Between Punitive Damages and Actual Harm

The second *Gore* factor, the ratio between punitive and compensatory damages, is the "most commonly cited indicium of an unreasonable or excessive punitive damages award." Punitive "damages must bear a 'reasonable relationship' to compensatory damages." What constitutes a "reasonable relationship" varies from case to case. The Supreme Court "ha[s] consistently rejected the notion that the constitutional line is marked by a simple mathematical formula, even one that compares actual and potential damages to the punitive award." The Court explained,

> low awards of compensatory damages may properly support a higher ratio than high compensatory awards, if, for example, a particularly egregious act has resulted in only a small amount of economic damages. A higher ratio may also be justified in cases in which the injury is hard to detect or the monetary value of noneconomic harm might have been difficult to determine.

Yet, later, in *Campbell*, the Court declared, "Our jurisprudence and the principles it has now established demonstrate ... few awards exceeding a single-digit ratio between punitive and compensatory damages, to a significant degree, will satisfy due process." The Court continued, "Single-digit multipliers are more likely to comport with due process, while still achieving the State's goals of deterrence and retribution." The Court reiterated there was "a long legislative history, dating back over 700 years and going forward to today, providing for sanctions of double, treble, or quadruple damages to deter and punish." The district court then declared, "While these ratios are not binding, they are instructive."

. . . .

Recognizing we are not bound by a rigid mathematical formula, we nevertheless, are persuaded a single digit multiplier is appropriate in the present case. We take our guidance from the Supreme Court's assessment of single-digit multipliers. Quigley was awarded $13,685.00 in compensatory damages, which is not a nominal amount. We find the circumstances of this case and due process do not justify a punitive damages award eighteen times greater than the compensatory damages and, agreeing with the district court, conclude the jury's punitive damage award was excessive.

iii. Sanctions for Comparable Misconduct

We turn then to the final *Gore* factor, a comparison between the punitive damages award and the civil and criminal penalties available for comparable misconduct. "[A] reviewing court engaged in determining whether an award of punitive damages is excessive should 'accord "substantial deference" to legislative judgments concerning appropriate sanctions for the conduct at issue.'"

Quigley points out 42 U.S.C. § 3614 permits the Attorney General to commence a civil action against "any person . . . engaged in a pattern or practice of resistance to the full enjoyment of any of the rights granted by the [FHA]." Section 3614(d)(1) (C) . . . states a court may grant [a civil penalty] for a first violation in an amount not exceeding $55,000.

While we agree with the district court that the jury's punitive damage award was excessive, we disagree with the district court's assessment that $20,527.50, which is one and a half times the compensatory award, sufficiently reflects the reprehensibility of Winter's conduct. We conclude an appropriate punitive damages award in this case is $54,750. This amount is four times greater than Quigley's compensatory damages ($13,685.00), which we find is an appropriate ratio under the circumstances of this case. This amount comports with due process, while achieving the statutory and regulatory goals of retribution and deterrence.

2. Attorney Fees

Finally, Quigley contests the district court's judgment with respect to the attorney fee award. The district court granted Quigley's motion for attorney fees, but only awarded her $20,000.00 of the $117,066.50 Quigley requested. "'We review the district court's award of attorney fees for abuse of discretion'."

a. Entitlement to Attorney Fees

"The prevailing party in FHA litigation may be awarded costs and a reasonable attorney's fee." Winter does not contest Quigley was a prevailing party; however, Winter suggests Quigley may not be entitled to attorney fees because she had a contingency fee agreement with her attorneys. Quigley's attorney stated, "[W]e have agreed with [Quigley] . . . that we would take a contingency fee amount, which is 33 1/3 [%], or what the court would grant us in statutorily granted attorney fees. That's an either/or. We don't get both."

Winter cites two 1986 cases from outside our circuit in support of his proposition that the existence of a contingency agreement bars an award of attorney fees. We consider [these cases] inapplicable and not contrary to our decision. As Quigley notes, these two cases were decided before the 1988 amendments to the FHA. Before the amendments, an award of attorney fees under the FHA was only available to "a prevailing plaintiff [who was] not financially able to assume said attorney fees." The current version of the FHA does not limit attorney fees to plaintiffs or to those who are not financially able to assume the fees; rather, "the prevailing party, other than the United States, [may recover] a reasonable attorney's fee." 42 U.S.C. § 3613(c)(2) (emphasis added). "The attorney's fees provided for in a contingent-fee agreement is not a ceiling upon the fees recoverable." The district court did not err in finding Quigley was entitled to attorney fees.

b. Amount of Attorney Fees

We now consider whether the district court erred in its manner of calculation or in the amount of attorney fees awarded to Quigley. The Supreme Court has stated,

> The most useful starting point for determining the amount of a reasonable fee is the number of hours reasonably expended on the litigation multiplied by a reasonable hourly rate. This calculation provides an objective basis on which to make an initial estimate of the value of a lawyer's services. The party seeking an award of fees should submit evidence supporting the hours worked and rates claimed. Where the documentation of hours is inadequate, the district court may reduce the award accordingly.
>
> The district court also should exclude from this initial fee calculation hours that were not "reasonably expended." Cases may be overstaffed, and the skill and experience of lawyers vary widely. Counsel for the prevailing party should make a good-faith effort to exclude from a fee request hours that are excessive, redundant, or otherwise unnecessary, just as a lawyer in private practice ethically is obligated to exclude such hours from his fee submission.

The district court's explanation for its award of attorney fees is puzzling. The court stated, "There is no need to discuss the lodestar calculations or the skill and experience of the plaintiff's lawyers." Instead, the district court relied upon the "*Kloberdanz* theory." This *Kloberdanz* theory apparently came from an unpublished district court case, *United States v. Kloberdanz*, No. CR 76-2013 (N.D. Iowa Nov. 30, 1976) (McManus, J.), which did not address the issue of attorney fees. According to the district court, *Kloberdanz* involved the criminal prosecution of a postal employee for theft, and the *Kloberdanz* court found there was no need for an excessive fine because, in the district court's words, "it was a two bit case and he was going to receive a two bit fine." The district court then noted Quigley's case "is not a two bit case . . . [but] there is still a matter of justice, there is still a matter of basic fairness, there is still a matter of equity." The district court declared its belief that it was "appropriate to determine or consider the effect on [Winter], whether he can pay [the attorney fees] or not." The district court concluded, "[W]hile they certainly are good lawyers and they certainly did a good job, . . . attorney fees in the sum of $20,000.00 are appropriate."

The district court's failure, under the circumstances here, to analyze Quigley's entitlement to attorney fees under the lodestar approach was an abuse of discretion.

Furthermore, we find the district court erred in its consideration of Winter's ability to pay. Even if a defendant's ability to pay could be an appropriate consideration in awarding attorney fees, the record in this case adequately supports Winter is a substantial owner of real estate, and Winter did not submit any evidence of his financial situation or his net worth to address any issue of his inability to pay a substantial fee award.

In lieu of remanding the case to the district court, Quigley requests us to conduct a lodestar calculation and award the appropriate amount of attorney fees. Quigley insists a remand to the district court would create a "serious risk of substantial continued litigation," because, based on the district court's previous decision, Quigley believes "another appeal to [our court] may be necessary if the issue is remanded."

"A request for attorney's fees should not result in a second major litigation." The Eleventh Circuit has interpreted this command to authorize circuit courts to "determine for ourselves, once we conclude that the district court has abused its discretion, how many hours were reasonably spent in litigation." We have not located any cases from our circuit where we have foregone a remand under these circumstances. However, like the First and Eleventh Circuits, we believe the record before us is clear, remand would be inefficient, and it is necessary for us to determine an appropriate attorney fees award in this case in order to comply with the Supreme Court's command that "[a] request for attorney's fees should not result in a second major litigation."

While we agree with Quigley that the district court abused its discretion in significantly reducing Quigley's requested attorney fees without conducting the proper analysis and in basing its decision on unsupported considerations, we do agree with the district court's determination that Quigley's attorney fees request was excessive. We have reviewed in depth Quigley's supporting documentation. According to one of Quigley's attorneys, Scott Moore, the preparation of Quigley's case involved 437.7 hours of work performed by six attorneys and two paralegals from Baird Holm, LLP, an Omaha, Nebraska, law firm. These lawyers and their firm are deservedly highly respected, and their success in this case is commendable. Although we do not question the ethics or abilities of these attorneys, in our view, the complexity of the issues in this case simply did not warrant the requested amount of "lawyering." We also conclude there was a significant amount of duplicative work, in part caused by transitions in the attorneys of record. For those reasons, we determine it is reasonable and appropriate to reduce the hours expended by each of the attorneys and paralegals by one-third, while leaving their hourly rates undisturbed.

Using the adjusted number of hours, and multiplying by the respective hourly rates, we arrive at the following lodestar calculation . . . [for a total of $78,044.33]. "The product of reasonable hours times a reasonable rate does not end the inquiry." There remain other considerations that may lead the district court to adjust the fee upward or downward, including the important factor of the results obtained. Quigley obtained excellent results, as the jury found in her favor on all claims. We conclude no other upward or downward adjustments are mandated in this case. We thus conclude a reasonable attorney fee award in this case is $78,044.33. . . .

Notes and Discussion

1. Punitive Damages Do the factors from *Gore* and *Campbell* provide appropriate guidance for courts in reviewing punitive damage awards? How did the district court come to its conclusion in *Quigley*? How did the Eighth Circuit's analysis differ? Does tying the punitive damages, at least somewhat, to the amount of compensatory damages create a more systematic method of analysis?

2. Attorneys' Fees Why did the district court in *Quigley* award so little in attorneys' fees? By all accounts, the plaintiff's attorneys did an excellent job. Why did the Eighth Circuit award less than the plaintiff was requesting? Recall that harassment in housing complainants have the option of proceeding through the HUD administrative process. For complaints that go to hearing, HUD provides an attorney. Similarly, aggrieved persons may have their interests represented by the DOJ if they elect to proceed in federal court or if the DOJ files suit under its pattern and practice authority. Government lawyers do not charge or receive attorneys' fees.

D. Other Legal Provisions

Virtually every state has a state fair housing statute that provides at least as much protection as the federal law, although many states have passed additional protections.[34] Similar to other types of sexual harassment, sexual harassment in housing can also give rise to a number of tort claims. Depending on the facts of the case, the plaintiff may claim assault, battery, intentional infliction of emotional distress, or other torts. The housing context provides for additional state common law and statutory remedies based on property, contract, and landlord-tenant law.

For example, plaintiffs might pursue an action for breach of the covenant of quiet enjoyment. In every lease, the landlord impliedly covenants that the tenant shall have quiet enjoyment and possession of the premises. Many states' laws explicitly prohibit a landlord from engaging in any action that would interrupt a tenant's beneficial use and enjoyment of the leased premises. The covenant protects the tenant from any act by the landlord that interferes with the tenant's right to use and enjoy the premises for the purposes contemplated by the tenancy. Thus, a landlord who sexually harasses his tenant has arguably breached the covenant of quiet enjoyment. However, this argument is limited because courts typically require an eviction, either actual or constructive, before finding a breach of the covenant of quiet enjoyment.

---

34. *See, e.g.,* CAL. GOV'T CODE § 12940 *et seq.* (West 2019).

Only two fair housing cases have addressed the issue of quiet enjoyment, *Beliveau v. Caras*[35] and *Honce v. Vigil*.[36] In *Beliveau*, the plaintiff claimed that her landlord's manager sexually assaulted her in her apartment when he was there to repair her bathroom. This assault, the plaintiff argued, breached the covenant of quiet enjoyment. The court, interpreting California law, held that only an actual or constructive eviction could breach the covenant. Because the plaintiff alleged in her complaint that she was still residing at her apartment, the court summarily found there was no actual or constructive eviction. Therefore, it found no breach of the covenant of quiet enjoyment.

The *Honce* majority also required an actual or constructive eviction to maintain a breach of the covenant of quiet enjoyment claim. The court defined constructive eviction as when a landlord substantially deprives a tenant of the beneficial uses of the premises and the tenant vacates. Alternately, constructive eviction results when the landlord's actions are extremely meritless, done in malice or bad faith, and so severe it interferes with the tenant's peaceful enjoyment of the premises. The *Honce* majority, which earlier held that the plaintiff failed to prove either quid pro quo or hostile environment harassment, applied this standard and held there was no constructive eviction, even though the plaintiff had moved out. Therefore, the court found no breach of the covenant of quiet enjoyment.

Another potential claim is for the breach of the implied warranty of habitability. Every residential lease carries with it an implied promise that the premises are fit for occupancy. Some scholars have argued that this includes an implied warranty of freedom from sexual harassment.[37] This cause of action is limited, however, because the warranty will be breached only if the conduct renders the dwelling unfit for occupancy.

In addition, the remedies under both of these approaches are lacking. Both likely require the landlord to compensate the target only for any rent she paid during the time that the implied warranty or covenant was breached. And, if the woman remained in the housing for any length of time, this fact would undercut her argument that the landlord's conduct effectively made the dwelling uninhabitable or constituted a constructive eviction. If the woman is already in arrears with the rent, she may have little to recover as damages.

Finally, every contract imposes on all parties the duty of good faith and fair dealing in the contract's performance and enforcement. Leases are contracts. Arguably every lease carries an implied good faith promise that neither party will act illegally in regard to the lease. A landlord who sexually harasses a tenant is not performing his obligations under the lease in good faith. The benefit of pleading a breach of the

---

35. 873 F. Supp. 1393 (C.D. Cal. 1995).

36. 1 F.3d 1085 (10th Cir. 1993).

37. Theresa Keeley, *An Implied Warranty of Freedom from Sexual Harassment: The Solution for Harassed Tenants Where the Fair Housing Act Has Failed*, 38 Univ. Mich. J.L. Reform 397 (2005).

covenant of good faith and fair dealing, instead of or in addition to a breach of the covenant of quiet enjoyment, is that the plaintiff need not establish a constructive or actual eviction. For a court to find a violation of the covenant of good faith and fair dealing, however, the lease must be in a jurisdiction that applies the covenant to residential leases. Many jurisdictions do not. Moreover, a court would likely limit the remedy to the amount of rent paid during the time of breach.

In light of these drawbacks, it usually makes the most sense for plaintiffs to proceed under federal and state fair housing statutes.

5. Application of Law and Ethics
Hypothetical #7

Tasha is a 26-year-old, African-American, single mother of two young children. She works part-time for a housecleaning service, a job that pays minimum wage and does not have regular hours. Her income is low enough that she qualifies for a housing subsidy but the waiting list is closed. She has rented many apartments in the past few years. Typically, she is able to pay the rent for the first few months but then her hours get cut or she misses work because she cannot find child care. When this happens, she falls behind on rent and gets evicted. She then stays with relatives or in shelters until she is able to save up enough money for another down payment and rent a new apartment.

Tasha and her children have been staying at her aunt's apartment for the last few months but the place is very crowded and the aunt has made clear that Tasha's family needs to go. Tasha has saved her money and, after much looking, she finds a listing for a two-bedroom house that is in her price range ($600 a month).

When she goes to see the house, the landlord—who looks to be in his mid-fifties and is white—asks her if she has any evictions on her record. She admits that she has a few but she tells him that she is working and can pay the down payment and first month's rent in cash. "I normally don't like tenants with eviction records," he says, "but you seem very sweet and nice. Maybe we can have an agreement that as long as you stay nice and sweet you can live here, and if you have any problems with the rent, we can just work out an arrangement."

Tasha agrees because she really wants the house. As they sign the lease papers the landlord mentions to her, "Also, I don't want to see any boyfriends coming over here. I know a sexy girl like you could have different guys staying over all the time. And I will be watching to make sure that doesn't happen." Before she leaves, he asks Tasha for a hug "to seal the deal," which she reluctantly gives him. Tasha and her children move in to the house.

Early on, she notices the landlord in the front yard looking in the windows. She also sees him parked in his car across the street. His behavior makes her uneasy but she figures he is just trying to make sure she isn't having men over.

One evening he knocks on the door, saying "I was just in the neighborhood and I thought I'd come see how things are." She lets him in. He looks around, then sits down on the couch and lights up a cigarette. Tasha feels intensely uncomfortable and is not sure if she is allowed to ask him to leave. Instead she tells him she has to go put her children to bed. She stays in their bedroom until she hears the landlord exit.

A few weeks later a pipe starts leaking in the kitchen. Tasha calls the landlord to report the problem. The next day she wakes up and walks to the kitchen in her nightshirt. She is surprised to find him in her house. He says he is just there to check the pipe and did not want to disturb her by knocking. When she asks if he can call and make an appointment next time, he looks her up and down and says, "only if you promise to wear that." Tasha laughs in embarrassment and says "OK, sure, whatever." A month goes by. The landlord does not fix the pipe, so Tasha constantly stuffs towels under the sink.

The landlord continues to loiter around and sometimes drops by unannounced. Tasha is increasingly alarmed. She keeps the curtains pulled and asks friends to come over in the evenings in case he comes by. One day, the landlord approaches her in the driveway. "I saw you partying here last night. I said no boyfriends." Tasha tells him it was just friends, and then asks if he is ever going to fix the pipe. "Why should I fix anything, if you are just using this as a whore house?" he demands.

The next month, Tasha's hours get cut at work. When the landlord stops by to collect the rent, she is $80 short. "No problem," he says, "just let me see you in that night shirt again." Tasha does not want to, but she is afraid of being evicted again. She tells him it will have to be sometime when her kids are not at home. She is able to put him off for another month, mostly by staying away from her house during the day when her children are at school. Eventually, he catches her at home and asks for his "show." She puts on the nightshirt and comes back into the living room. "Nice," he says, "now take it off." Tasha cannot do it and starts to cry. The landlord mutters, "This is bullshit. You're just a tease." and stomps out, slamming the door behind him.

Tasha knows that she cannot make up the $80, much less the next month's rent, which will be due soon. Afraid of what the landlord will do, Tasha moves her family out without giving notice. They stay in a homeless shelter.

Legal Issues:

1. What is Tasha's prima facie case for sexual harassment under the Fair Housing Act?

2. Would the conduct she has experienced constitute a violation of Title VII if she had experienced it in the workplace? Can the conduct she has experienced be translated into a workplace context?

3. Does Tasha have a claim under any common law torts? Has she been constructively evicted? Why or why not?

4. What defenses might the landlord bring? Can he argue that he actually treated her more favorably, by renting to her in the first place despite her eviction record? Does it matter that she initially acquiesced to some of his requests? That she was able to stay in the house for almost a month without paying rent?

5. What will Tasha's damages likely consist of? What kind of compensatory damages does she have, tangible and intangible? Does she have a case for punitive damages?

Chapter 8

Sexual Harassment in Prisons and the Military

In preceding chapters, you learned about sex-based harassment and assault at work, school, and home. Different laws serve in each of those contexts to prevent and remedy sex-based discrimination: Title VII, Title IX, and Title VIII, respectively. However, sex-based misconduct occurs beyond those borders. While an exhaustive discussion of every environment is beyond the scope of this textbook, this chapter surveys two of those other contexts: prisons and the military.

In prisons and in the military, power hierarchies differ completely from those in civilian environments. In both locations, power serves a valuable purpose. In prisons, correctional officers use power to subdue and control inmates, who are physically segregated from the rest of the world during the terms of their imprisonment. In the military, officers use power to train, organize, and deploy military personnel to protect our nation. However, as in the civilian context, some persons in prisons and in the military manipulate and abuse power by sexually harassing those people with less power. The law operates differently to combat sexual harassment in these highly regulated settings. Of course, standard antidiscrimination laws do not apply to prisoners or military personnel.

1. Sexual Harassment in Prison — Harassment by Inmates

Sexual harassment in prisons occurs primarily between and within two groups of people: the correctional officers and the inmates. Some courts have held that prison service providers, such as supervisors in prison work programs, also violate the Constitution if they assault prisoners.[1] Harassed employees of most prison systems can sue under Title VII or other antidiscrimination laws. Inmates enjoy much less protection from correctional officers, third parties, and each other under the law. Usually, the Eighth Amendment to the U.S. Constitution, which guards against the infliction of "cruel and unusual punishments," serves as the only serious federal legal protection for inmates. Most state legislatures have now passed laws that criminalize rape or

---

1. *See, e.g.*, Smith v. Cochran, 339 F.3d 1205 (10th Cir. 2003).

sexual assault of an inmate by a correctional officer.[2] Since rape and sexual assault are already state crimes, it is not clear how much these measures add.

In 2003, Congress passed the Prison Rape Elimination Act (PREA), but it authorizes little more than the collection of data.[3] Mike Farrell commented, "Now, the National Prison Rape Elimination Commission meets periodically to 'study the impact of prisoner rape.' While they study, rape continues."[4] In 2012, the Department of Justice "issued its first set of national standards requiring that detention facilities not only give inmates multiple ways to report sexual abuse but also investigate every allegation."[5]

The Bureau of Justice Statistics (BJS) now compiles information annually, as mandated by the PREA. In June 2018, the BJS reported its highlights:

- Correctional administrators reported 24,661 allegations of sexual victimization in 2015, nearly triple the number recorded in 2011 (8,768 allegations).

- Substantiated allegations rose from 902 in 2011 to 1,473 in 2015 (up 63%). (Substantiated allegations are those in which an investigation determined that an event occurred, based on a preponderance of the evidence.)

- In 2014, unfounded allegations (8,372) exceeded unsubstantiated allegations (7,783) for the first time in [Survey of Sexual Victimization] data collection. Prior to 2014, more allegations were unsubstantiated than were unfounded. (Unfounded allegations are those in which an investigation determined that an event did not occur. Unsubstantiated allegations are those in which an investigation concluded that evidence was insufficient to determine whether an event occurred.)

- Among the 24,661 allegations of sexual victimization in 2015, a total of 1,473 were substantiated, 10,142 were unfounded, 10,313 were unsubstantiated, and 2,733 were still under investigation.

- The sharp rise in unfounded or unsubstantiated allegations of sexual victimization coincided with the release of the National Standards to Prevent, Detect, and Respond to Prison Rape in 2012. It reflects improvements in data collection and reporting by correctional authorities, and increased reporting of allegations by inmates.[6]

---

2. For a 2001 overview of these laws, state-by-state, see AMNESTY INTERNATIONAL, ABUSE OF WOMEN IN CUSTODY: SEXUAL MISCONDUCT AND SHACKLING OF PREGNANT WOMEN (2001). The Washington College of Law's Project on Addressing Prison Rape also has a website that contains more current information on this topic. *Project on Addressing Prison Rape*, AM. UNIV., https://www.wcl.american.edu/impact/initiatives-programs/endsilence/legislative/.

3. Robert Weisberg & David Mills, *Violence Silence: Why No One Really Cares About Prison Rape*, SLATE (Oct. 1, 2003).

4. Mike Farrell, *Ending the Hidden, Savage Routine of Prison Rape*, HUFFINGTON POST (Mar. 17, 2008, updated May 25, 2011).

5. Alysia Santo, *Prison Rape Allegations Are on the Rise*, MARSHALL PROJECT (July 25 2018).

6. Jessica Stroop, *PREA Data Collection Activities, 2018*, BJS, June 29, 2018.

Civil rights advocates challenge the numbers of unfounded reports. Additionally, Allen Beck, BJS senior statistical advisor, acknowledged, "We know there are many victims who don't feel comfortable coming forward, and correction administrators only know what comes to their attention."[7] Given the statistics, likely biases, and known failures to report, one can predict that sexual harassment and violent sexual assault remain serious problems for prison inmates.

Consider what makes sexual harassment in prisons different from that in the workplace and evaluate whether the Eighth Amendment adequately protects the more than two million inmates in prisons and jails across the United States.[8]

Cruel and Unusual Punishment in United States Prisons: Sexual Harassment Among Male Inmates

James E. Robertson[9]

. . . .

I. Introduction

Sexual harassment is not locked out of prison. Among male inmates it is commonplace and often involves the doing of other inmates. Like the sexual harassment of women, sexual harassment among male inmates is unwanted, offensive, and frequently results in acute fear of sexual assault. Consequently, one penal expert states that sexual harassment of inmates "constitutes one of the most crippling aspects of the prison climate." Nonetheless, many prison officials are incapable or unwilling to reasonably safeguard targeted inmates.

. . . .

This Article advances the following theses: the Eighth Amendment imposes upon prison staff a constitutional duty not to be deliberately indifferent to sexual harassment among male inmates; and conditions within many prisons suggest that this duty is frequently ignored. . . .

II. A Portrait of Inmate Sexual Harassment

A. Defining Sexual Harassment in the Prison Setting

1. Title VII and Inmate Sexual Harassment

. . . [Title VII discussed.]

Title VII solely addresses workplace harassment and thus does not provide a remedy for inmates sexually harassed by other inmates. Nonetheless, prisons and

---

7. Santo, *supra* note 5.

8. The Sentencing Project, *Fact Sheet: Trends in U.S. Corrections*, https://www.cfgnh.org/Portals/0/Uploads/Documents/Articles/nh%20healthystart/inc_Trends_in_Corrections_Fact_sheet.pdf (citing the Bureau of Justice Statistics Prisoners Series).

9. 36 Am. Crim. L. Rev. 1 (1999) (some footnotes omitted). Because many of Professor Robertson's footnotes are quite useful, we provide some of them here, along with the original footnote number.

the workplace bear certain similarities that invite comparable definitions of sexual harassment.

Like many corporate workplaces, prisons are highly stratified given the immutable distinction between the correctional staff ("the keepers") and the inmate population ("the kept").[16] Thus, prisons readily breed conduct resembling Title VII quid pro quo harassment, in which a superior pressures a subordinate to concede to his or her sexual demands. The facts of *Thomas v. District of Columbia*[18] illustrate quid pro quo harassment in prison: a correctional officer allegedly sought to coerce the plaintiff-inmate into sexual relations by threatening to label him a "snitch."[19]

Prisons, like the workplace, also create environments conducive to same-sex harassment. Indeed, the inmate subculture includes sex roles grounded in aggression . . . and submission. . . . For inmates assigned to the latter roles, prison life resembles the Supreme Court's description of hostile environment harassment—an environment "permeated with discriminatory intimidation, ridicule, and insult." . . .

. . . .

2. The Constituent Elements of Inmate Sexual Harassment

Sexual harassment among male inmates consists of uninvited sexual comments or conduct made by and directed at male inmates that would be perceived by reasonable male inmates as offensive and/or coercive. Four key elements constitute the above definition. First, target selection is sexual in nature but not necessarily sex-based: while the subject matter is sexual—such as the overt or implicit references to fellatio and/or anal sex—the victim is usually not selected because of his sex. Most sexual aggressors in prison are neither homosexual nor bisexual; they are heterosexuals who define sexual aggression as affirmation of heterosexuality even though their victims are of the same sex. It is this component that fundamentally distinguishes sexual harassment among male inmates from opposite-sex harassment.

Second, sexual harassment in prison almost invariably arises from a premeditated desire to humiliate, intimidate, and/or coerce inmates. Unlike opposite-sex harassment, it cannot be attributed to miscommunication born from gender socialization.

The third distinguishing feature is its non-consensual nature; the victim neither requests nor invites this conduct. As unwelcome conduct, sexual harassment among male inmates parallels Title VII sexual harassment.

---

16. *See* GRESHAM M. SYKES, THE SOCIETY OF CAPTIVES 41 (1958). . . .

18. 887 F. Supp. 1 (D.D.C. 1995).

19. *See id.* at 6. Sykes defined a "rat," i.e., a "snitch," as follows:
   [I]n the prison the word rat or squealer carries an emotional significance far greater than that usually encountered in the free community. The name is never applied lightly as a joking insult. . . . Instead, it represents the most serious accusation that one inmate can level at another for it implies a betrayal that transcends the specific act of disclosure. The rat is a man who has betrayed not just one inmate or several; he has betrayed inmates in general.

Sykes, *supra* note 16 at 87.

The final element posits that a reasonable male inmate would consider the words or conduct offensive and/or coercive. Because incarceration heightens a man's sensitivity to words and conduct that impugn his masculinity, sexual harassment in prison should not be gauged by a gender-neutral, reasonable person standard. Correspondingly, the Ninth Circuit Court of Appeals employed a reasonable woman standard in a Title VII opposite-sex harassment suit because men and women can disagree as to what is offensive.

B. Types of Inmate Sexual Harassment

1. Verbal Harassment

a. Statements Which Feminize the Inmate

The first type of sexual harassment consists of comments intended to feminize the target and are thus offensive to most inmates. Such comments include: "Guys would whistle at me or say I got a nice ass . . ." and "You are cute." Feminization of inmates allows predatory heterosexual inmates to rationalize the sexual victimization of other men.

b. Sexual Propositions

Most inmates define themselves as heterosexual. Consequently, propositions for sex, even if they are politely presented, are likely to be offensive to a reasonable inmate. Unless they are forcefully rebutted, propositions can mark the targeted inmate as a homosexual.

c. Sexual Extortion

One variation of sexual extortion occurs when an inmate pressures another inmate to pay a debt via a sexual act. As one inmate confided: "I owed this guy gambling losses and he has supplied me with some pot, cigarettes, and other things—now he told me I could settle the account by giving him some head." First-time inmates are particularly susceptible to this type of sexual extortion; predatory inmates offer them "loans" upon their arrival and they soon find themselves unable to honor their debts. Another variation of sexual extortion involves pressuring an inmate to submit to sexual acts in exchange for protection from other victimizers. . . .

2. Physical Harassment, i.e., Kissing, Touching, or Fondling Intimate Body Areas

In an atmosphere charged with suspicion and fear of aggression, inmates often perceive touching and grabbing as sexual. As one inmate recounted, "He kept putting his hands on me and he was touching my shoulder and arm, patting my hand and constantly around, ridiculous crap. But enough so it would be aggravating." Acts such as these are rarely mistaken for expressions of genuine caring or concern: "You can't be sensitive in here. That or being kind is a sign of weakness. When you see someone who is emotional or kind, he is a mark. . . . You gotta be hard." Furthermore, sexual aggressors sometimes communicate by bodily contact because of limited verbal skills and/or a reluctance to overtly display force.

C. Explaining Inmate Sexual Harassment

Sexual harassment among male inmates, like other inmate behavior, can be attributed to the conditions of confinement as well as the cultural and subcultural values that inmates bring with them to prison. These two causal factors share a common theme: that sexual harassment among male inmates is an act of sexual aggression born from a need to dominate others.

. . . .

In his classic study of a maximum security prison, [Gresham] Sykes observed that three "pains of imprisonment" are especially injurious to an inmate's masculine self-image. First, imprisonment deprives the great majority of inmates heterosexual relationships, a hardship that imposes symbolic "castration."[54] Second, the many prison regulations governing an inmate's life "involve a profound threat to the prisoner's self image because they reduce the prisoner to the weak, helpless, dependent status of childhood. . . ." Finally, inmates reside in a subculture without women. . . .

In need of affirming their masculinity, some inmates turn to a strategy not denied them by imprisonment — victimizing their fellow inmates.[58] They do so as a result of the pre-prison cultural and subcultural values they hold [which equate aggression and dominance with masculinity]. . . . As the premier act of domination, prison rape is thus transformed into a statement of one's masculinity and strength[.]

. . . .

Within this context, sexual harassment among male inmates performs three functions. First, predatory heterosexual inmates employ sexual harassment as a means of feminizing inmates targeted for sexual exploitation. . . .

Sexual harassment of another inmate also communicates aggressive intentions. . . .

Finally, sexual harassment among male inmates promotes involuntary identity transformation and role assignment within the inmate social world. . . .

. . . .

E. Victims and Victimizers

In the unisex prison, attributes that mark inmates as effeminate or weak make them likely targets of sexual harassment. . . .

Being of slight stature or being a young, non-Hispanic white male also stigmatizes one as both effeminate and weak and thus prime sexual fodder. . . .

---

54. [Sykes, *supra* note 16 at 70. *See generally* Bonnie E. Carlson, *Conjugal Visits, in* ENCYCLO-PEDIA OF AMERICAN PRISONS 105, 105–106 (Marilyn D. McShane & Frank P. Williams III eds., 1996) (stating that only nine states allow conjugal visits and most states restrict the privilege to low security risk inmates).

58. *See, e.g.,* ANTHONY M. SCACCO, JR., RAPE IN PRISON 3 (1975) (defining sexual victimization as "an act whereby one male (or group of males) seeks testimony to what he considers is an outward validation of his masculinity"). . . .

. . . .

Lastly, imprisonment renders homosexuals likely victims of harassment. Their sexual orientation per se signifies femininity and weakness in the inmate subculture. Racial characteristics may also be significant given that non-Hispanic white homosexuals reported a greater frequency of sexual harassment than African-Americans and Hispanics in the Wooden and Parker study.

African-American inmates disproportionately comprise the population of sexual harassers. Lockwood found that they constituted seventy-eight percent of the prison's sexually aggressive inmates. Davis noted that fifty-six percent of the sexual incidents he studied involved black aggressors and white victims. Other researchers similarly found that most victims of prison rape were white and most assailants were black.

The causal relationship between race, sexual harassment, and/or prison rape is complex, if not unclear. Lockwood asserted that young, non-Hispanic whites were inviting targets because of their presumed naiveté, perceived femininity, and reluctance to retaliate if one of their own were attacked. Similarly, Chonco concluded that sexual assault of white inmates is related to their perceived weakness rather than their race per se.

III. The Case Law on Sexual Harassment of Male Inmates

A. Sexual Harassment Absent Significant Physical Contact

Case law has long posited that words alone—be they harassing, abusive, vulgar, racially charged, or threatening—do not violate the Eighth Amendment. As one court observed, "Not every unpleasant experience a prisoner might endure while incarcerated constitutes cruel and unusual punishment. . . ." Allegations of sexual harassment are not exempted from this rule: "The fact that verbal harassment is gender-specific gives it no greater claim as a constitutional violation than verbal harassment generally," asserted the Tenth Circuit Court of Appeals in a recent decision.

Three cases are instructive. In *Ellis v. Meade*,[123] a correctional officer allegedly tapped or spanked the plaintiff's buttocks between two and ten times and commented, "How's the little guy doing?" The court held that this remark did not violate the inmate's constitutional rights because it was isolated, carried no threat of violence, and may not have been sexual in nature.[125]

In *Adkins v. Rodriquez*,[126] a jail deputy made comments to a female inmate about "her body, his own sexual prowess, and his sexual conquests" on one occasion and later entered her cell, stood over her bed, and remarked as he exited, "By the way,

---

123. 887 F. Supp. 324 (D. Me. 1995).

125. *See id.* at 329. The court treated the spanking incident as a distinct basis for relief, ruling that spanking an inmate could be a rational means of promoting a penal objective and noting that the spanking was isolated and not painful. *See id.* at 300.

126. 59 F.3d 1034 (10th Cir. 1995).

you have nice breasts." The court characterized the deputy's conduct as "outrageous and unacceptable" but not tantamount to the "physical intimidation" required by the Eighth Amendment.

Lastly, in *McClean v. Seco*,[130] the plaintiff alleged that correctional officers "verbally threatened and abused" him by declaring that he should fear for his safety because of his notoriety as a sex offender. In granting a summary judgment for the defendants, the trial court found no reason to depart from the "well established" rule that threats alone do not state a constitutional claim even if the threatened inmate has a particular vulnerability to assault.

Meanwhile, a few courts have broken with precedent to hold that some forms of verbal harassment can inflict cruel and unusual punishment. Three decisions involved the threatened use of lethal weapons. For instance, in *Burton v. Livingstone*,[134] the petitioner alleged that a correctional officer pointed a cocked pistol at him and exclaimed, "[N]igger run so I can blow your Goddamn brains out;" "I want you to run so I'll be justified [sic]. . . ." In reinstating his cause of action, the court explained that "the day has passed when an inmate must show a court the scars of torture in order to make out a . . . [constitutional] complaint."

A fourth case, *Parrish v. Johnson*,[137] addressed a guard's mistreatment of paraplegic inmates, including his "paraplegic slurs" directed at one of the plaintiffs. In finding an Eighth Amendment violation in the totality of prison conditions, the court characterized the verbal abuse as "strip[ping] . . . the inmate of his dignity. . . ."

Finally, *Thomas v. District of Columbia*[140] concerned allegations that a correctional officer "forcibly touched or attempted to touch plaintiff's penis on at least two occasions, sexually harassed and intimidated plaintiff, and threatened to, and then did, spread rumors that . . . the plaintiff is a homosexual and a 'snitch.'" The court deemed conduct of this sort "simply not part of the penalty that criminal offenders pay for their offenses against society" and, thus, cruel and unusual punishment.

B. Sexual Harassment With Significant Physical Contact

Case law, both old and new, posits that *de minimis* touching does not violate the Eighth Amendment. . . .

Three decisions speak to the frequency and degree of bodily contact needed to elevate officer-inmate sexual harassment into an Eighth Amendment claim. In *Gilson v. Cox*,[146] the plaintiff alleged that a female correctional officer "made various sexual advances toward him and physically abused him by grabbing his genitals and buttocks." The court held that these allegations failed to state an Eighth Amendment claim because, if true, they were not "literally shocking to the conscience."

---

130. 876 F. Supp. 695 (E.D. Pa. 1995).
134. 791 F.2d 97 (8th Cir. 1986).
137. 800 F.2d 600 (6th Cir. 1986).
140. 887 F. Supp. 1 (D.D.C. 1995).
146. 711 F. Supp. 354 (E.D. Mich. 1989).

Nonetheless, the court did find a "right to be free of sexual abuse" and allowed the suit to proceed under a substantive due process claim.

In *Boddie v. Schnieder*,[150] the Second Circuit Court of Appeals addressed an inmate's allegations that a female correctional officer made "'a pass' at him;" and later "squeezed his hand, touched his penis and said, '[Y]ou know your [sic] sexy black devil, I like you' and on another occasion bumped into him . . . 'with her whole body vagina against penis [sic]. . . .'" Nonetheless, the court ruled that he failed to state an Eighth Amendment claim because the incidents were few in number and no single incident was "sufficiently serious." The court did indicate that "severe or repetitive sexual abuse of an inmate" can impose a punishment "objectively, sufficiently serious enough" to breach the Eighth Amendment.

Finally, in *Watson v. Jones*,[154] the Eighth Circuit Court of Appeals reversed the trial court's summary judgment for a female prison officer accused of engaging in sexually harassing pat-down searches of two male inmates. These searches allegedly occurred on a daily basis for two months and represented "ongoing sexual advances. . . ." The plaintiffs claimed that the searches included "prolonged rubbing and fondling of the genitals and anus areas."

IV. Sexual Harassment as Cruel and Unusual Punishment

A. The Deliberate Indifference Test

. . . .

In the current decade, the Court has decided two cases, *Wilson v. Seiter*[179] and *Farmer v. Brennan*,[180] that speak to the duty of prison staff to safeguard inmates from one another. In *Wilson*, the Court posited that all challenges to conditions-of-confinement, including "the protection . . . to be afforded against other inmates," are to be decided by the following two-part test. The first component, which the Court characterized as "objective" in nature, requires that the deprivation be "sufficiently serious." Speaking for the Court, Justice Scalia observed that a deprivation of this magnitude "den[ies] 'the minimal civilized measure of life's necessities.'" Justice Scalia also articulated a "subjective component" in conditions-of-confinement claims, namely, whether the defendant prison officials were "deliberate[ly] indifferen[t]" to this deprivation.

In *Farmer v. Brennan*, the Court elaborated upon the deliberate indifference standard advanced in *Wilson*. The petitioner, Dee Farmer, a preoperative transsexual with a feminine appearance, had been transferred to the general population of a high-security federal prison. Inmates at this prison beat and raped him, and while the Court made no mention of sexual harassment, incarcerated transsexuals are likely targets. Because inmate Farmer did not inform prison staff that he feared for

---

150. 105 F.3d 857 (2d Cir. 1997).
154. 980 F.2d 1165 (8th Cir. 1992).
179. 501 U.S. 294 (1991).
180. 511 U.S. 825 (1994).

his safety, the trial court granted summary judgment for the defendants. The Seventh Circuit Court of Appeals affirmed.

The Supreme Court in *Farmer* rejected the petitioner's call for an objective ("ought to have known") standard of deliberate indifference. Like the trial court, the *Farmer* Court held that deliberate indifference arises when the prison staff fails to take reasonable safeguards despite their "actual knowledge" of an "excessive" or "substantial" risk to the inmate's safety. Unlike the trial court, Justice Souter's majority opinion expressly warned prison staff that they would not be permitted to ignore obvious risks to inmates:

> Whether a prison official had the requisite knowledge of a substantial risk is . . . subject to [proof] in the usual ways, including inference from circumstantial evidence. . . . For example, if [a] . . . plaintiff presents evidence showing that a substantial risk of inmate attacks was "long-standing, pervasive, well documented, or expressly noticed by prison officials in the past, and the circumstances suggest that the defendant-official being sued had been exposed to information concerning the risk and thus 'must have known' about it, then such evidence could be sufficient to permit a trier of fact to find the defendant-official had actual knowledge of the risk."

The *Farmer* Court also indicated that the requisite "substantial" risk of harm can arise from threats specifically addressed to the petitioner as well as from his possessing characteristics common to vulnerable inmates. As Justice Souter explained:

> The question under the Eighth Amendment is whether prison officials, acting with deliberate indifference, exposed a prisoner to substantial "risk of serious damage to his future health," . . . and it does not matter whether the risk comes from a single source or multiple sources, any more than it matters whether the prisoner faces an excessive risk of attack for reasons personal to him or because all prisoners in his situation face such a risk.

Lastly, Justice Souter stressed that to be of constitutional dimension "the deprivation [inflicted upon inmate Farmer] must be, objectively, 'sufficiently serious'. . . ." He did not elaborate on the identifying qualities of such a risk perhaps because the Court had previously spoken to this issue. In *Estelle v. Gamble*,[196] the Court had ruled that an Eighth Amendment violation occurs when staff are deliberately indifferent to "serious medical needs." More recently, in *Wilson v. Seiter*, the Court spoke of a sufficiently severe injury as depriving "a single, identifiable human need such as food, warmth, or exercise. . . ." Later, in *Hudson v. McMillian*,[200] the Court stated that "extreme deprivations are required to make out a conditions-of-confinement claim." Finally, in *Helling v. McKinney*,[202] the Court held that an injury need not have

---

196. 429 U.S. 97 (1976).
200. 503 U.S. 1 (1992).
202. 509 U.S. 25 (1993).

occurred to state an Eighth Amendment claim as long as the inmate was exposed to "an unreasonable risk of serious damage to his future health."

Whether the requisite "serious" harm can be of a mental or psychological nature awaits a definitive answer by the Court. Nothing in the Court's modern pronouncements indicates that such harm falls outside the ban on cruel and unusual punishment. Indeed, the Court in *Rhodes v. Chapman*[204] stated that "the Eighth Amendment prohibits punishments which, although not physically barbarous, 'involved the unnecessary and wanton infliction of pain,' or are grossly disproportionate to the severity of the crime." As Justice Blackmun observed in his concurring opinion in *Hudson v. McMillian*, "The Eighth Amendment prohibits the unnecessary and wanton infliction of 'pain,' rather than 'injury'. . . . 'Pain' in its ordinary meaning surely includes a notion of psychological harm." Furthermore, psychological harm must have been contemplated by the Court when it stated in *Hudson v. Palmer*[208] that "calculated harassment of inmates by prison staff unrelated to prison needs" can violate the Eighth Amendment.

The circuit courts of appeal are generally in accord that Eighth Amendment pain includes emotional as well as physical injury if the former is "serious" or "significant." For instance, in *Scher v. Engelke*,[211] the Eighth Circuit addressed whether Eighth Amendment pain can arise from cell searches undertaken to harass an inmate. The defendant correctional officer had searched the plaintiff inmate's cell ten times in nineteen days. He did so in retaliation of plaintiff's earlier report of misconduct by another staff member. The trial court awarded plaintiff nominal and punitive damages. In affirming the trial court's denial of defendant's motion for judgment notwithstanding the verdict, the court of appeals ruled that "the scope of Eighth Amendment protection is broader than the mere infliction of physical pain . . . and evidence of fear, mental anguish, and misery inflicted through frequent retaliatory cell searches . . . could suffice as the requisite injury for an Eighth Amendment claim."

B. Applying the "Deliberate Indifference" Test

1. The Objective Prong: Does Sexual Harassment Among Male Inmates Result in Eighth Amendment Pain?

a. The Intersection Between Sexual Harassment and Fear

Fear of sexual victimization is the "the dominant metaphor in terms of which almost every other aspect of 'prison reality' is interpreted." A new, first-time inmate's foremost fear is rape. The rate of prison rapes is unknown. Estimates range from as low as one percent of the prison population to as high as twenty-eight percent. Inmates perceive rape to be widespread. There is judicial support for this perception:

---

204. 452 U.S. 337 (1981).
208. 468 U.S. 517 (1984).
211. 943 F.2d 921 (8th Cir. 1991).

"A youthful inmate," wrote Justice Blackmun, "can expect to be subjected to homosexual gang rape his first night in jail. . . ."

. . . .

Sexual harassment greatly contributes to the fear of rape. "[I]t is the frequency of sexual harassment (insults and offensive propositions) that may lead some observers to believe that rape is rampant in prisons, a belief that is largely attributable to the level of fear generated." Fifty-five percent of the targeted inmates studied by Lockwood reported that they consequently feared for their safety. They had good reason to fear for their safety given that harassment invariably precedes sexual assault.

. . . .

b. Psychological and Physical Injuries Arising from Sexual Harassment

Fear born from sexual harassment results in both psychological and physical injuries. Lockwood described the psychological consequences as "devastating and debilitating," causing anxiety and crises in some instances. Nearly one-fourth of the targeted inmates experienced anxiety. Lockwood's inmates told of "shaking, crying, stuttering, weakness, and inability to sleep or concentrate." . . .

Lockwood also found that inmates in crises sometimes injure themselves or commit suicide. He attributed this self-destructive behavior to a situation "where one becomes suicidal to avoid victimization which he convinces himself is certain."

The more common physical injuries, however, arise from combat between harasser and target. In a sample of 114 violent transactions, Lockwood determined that forty-two began with offensive sexual overtures, while another thirty-six were started by polite propositions. Sylvester's study of murder in prison found that sexual approaches constituted the motive in thirty percent of single-assailant killings. . . .

A harassed inmate's willingness to risk the injuries of combat is often a prerequisite for achieving "real man" status. As Robertson wrote, "In addition to fending off predators, it [target violence] can transform the vulnerable inmate's prison identity—from being "unmanly," and thus an appropriate target, to someone "sport[ing] the stigmata of manliness." The following incident is illustrative:

> One of the larger inmates stood in front of him and stated his simple proposition: "fuck or fight." The proper response for the untested inmate was to immediately strike the propositioning con, thereby starting a fight. This spontaneous response assured him that he would not be considered to be a sexual fodder for all the wolves.

Inmates reluctant to risk combat harassment only enhance their vulnerability to sexual exploitation. They are "fair game" for further harassment as well as rape unless they become "kids," who trade sexual services in exchange for protection.

c. The Constitutional Threshold

Several federal courts have held that substantial fear of assault, sexual or otherwise, when coupled with the staff's deliberate indifference, imposes cruel and unusual punishment. As one court explained: "Subjecting prisoners to violent attacks or sexual assaults, or constant fear of such violence, shocks modern sensibilities and serves no legitimate penological purpose. We reject as below any level of decency the theory that sexual or other assaults are a legitimate part of a prisoner's punishment."

Fear of prison rape reaches the constitutional threshold when sexual assaults are commonplace either within the general prison population or an identifiable subgroup of offenders, such as inmates of slight stature. For instance, in *Martin v. White*,[247] inmate Martin brought suit after his fellow inmates "sexually threatened" him on three or more occasions. The court concluded that prison officials had been appraised of a pervasive risk of harm to inmate White by virtue of the prison's fifty-nine reported assaults as well as some 300 "claimed assaults" during a four-year period.

Measuring fear through reported rapes, however, is seriously flawed. First, many assaults go unreported. Second, some harassed inmates give in to threats of assault by becoming "punks" or "kids," who engage in apparently consensual sexual relations. Finally, many harassed inmates fight off would-be rapists. . . .

. . . .

Perhaps the best measure of fear is the frequency of violent encounters between the targeted inmate and his harasser. Lockwood found that fifty-seven percent of the sexual overtures that included offensive remarks and gestures led to violence, and one-third of polite sexual propositions erupted into physical confrontations initiated by either the target or the harasser. Case law holds that assault rates of this magnitude evidence a pervasive and thus constitutionally unacceptable degree of fear of assault.

2. The Subjective Prong: Are Prison Staff Deliberately Indifferent to Sexual Harassment Among Male Inmates?

a. Do Prison Staff Possess Actual Knowledge of Sexual Harassment?

1) First Indicium: Direct Evidence of a Specific Threat

"A prisoner normally proves actual knowledge of impending harm," observed the Seventh Circuit Court of Appeals, "by showing that he complained to prison officials about a specific threat to his safety." For example, in *Porm v. White*,[261] inmate Porm allegedly informed Officer Tindle but not Officer White that he had been threatened by a group of inmates harassing "young pretty white guys." Tindle failed to take protective measures, and one of the harassers subsequently stabbed Porm. On appeal, the court ruled that a reasonable jury could find deliberate indifference only on Tindle's part.

---

247. 742 F.2d 469 (8th Cir. 1984).
261. 762 F.2d 635 (8th Cir. 1985).

Most inmates, however, will not report sexual harassment out of fear of being labeled a "snitch." The facts of *McGill v. Duckworth*[266] are instructive. McGill, an Indiana inmate of slight physical stature, received "suggestive notes and comments" from his fellow prisoners when he entered an Indiana prison for a murder that, according to a prison rumor, had "homosexual overtones." Later he was verbally harassed by two inmates, who subsequently made sexually suggestive comments and threats as they followed him to the shower room. On the way, McGill spoke with two correctional officers about an unrelated matter but did not inform them of the harassment. In the shower room one of his harassers raped him.

In the resulting failure-to-protect suit, the court in McGill observed that "[o]ther circuits have held that failure to tell prison officials about threats is fatal and have dismissed such claims at the pleading stage." Characterizing this case law as "sound," the court held for the defendants.

2) Second Indicium: Inferential Evidence of a Non-Specific Threat

The subsequent Supreme Court ruling in *Farmer v. Brennan* spares many sexually harassed inmates the Hobson's choice of "ratting" on their tormentors or forgoing the staff's intervention. While *Farmer* required a showing of prison officials' actual knowledge of a serious risk of harm, the Court permitted the fact-finder to infer such knowledge when (1) "all prisoners . . . [or those inmates similarly situated] face such a risk" and (2) the risk is "long-standing, pervasive, well-documented, or expressly noted by prison officials in the past. . . ." As documented below, prison officials' actual knowledge of sexual harassment can be readily inferred via the *Farmer* standards.

First, inmates who are fodder to sexual harassers possess shared attributes: victims tend to be non-Hispanic whites, slightly built, and/or homosexual. Knowledge of these risk factors dates back at least to Davis's widely publicized 1968 study of sexual victimization in Philadelphia's jails.

Furthermore, the frequency of sexual harassment and the consequent fear of violence are pervasive and adequately documented. Twenty-eight percent of the inmates in the Lockwood study and twenty-nine percent of the inmates in the Nacci and Kane study experienced some form of sexual victimization. In addition, seventy-one percent of non-Hispanic white inmates and fifty-three percent of homosexuals were sexually targeted. Also recall that over half the targeted inmates interviewed by Lockwood feared for their safety (and wisely so, given the frequency of violence arising from sexual overtures).

Lastly, interviews with prison staff suggest their familiarity with sexual harassment of inmates and the resulting dangers. Wooden and Parker found that correctional officers agreed with the following: (1) "forced or pressured sexual encounters are very common;" (2) "homosexual inmates have a more difficult time than

---

266. 944 F.2d 344 (7th Cir. 1991).

heterosexual inmates, due to [sexual] pressure . . . ;" and (3) "it is a very common occurrence for young, straight boys to be turned out, or forced into being punks."

In turn, Eigenberg's survey of 166 Texas correctional officers revealed that eighty-six percent of them "disagreed" or "strongly disagreed" that prison rape is rare.[285] Because sexual harassment "invariably" precedes sexual assault, one could extrapolate that an equally high percentage of the officers would disagree that sexual harassment is rare. The officers were most likely to believe young inmates and inmates owing debts who reported being raped. Eigenberg found that a smaller majority of officers were willing to believe homosexuals.

Finally, Lockwood provided the most conclusive proof of staff's familiarity with sexual harassment. He determined that they knew of two-thirds of the sexual incidents experienced by targeted inmates. Most incidents came to their attention through reports filed by the victims, personal observation, or informal channels of information.

b. How Do Prison Staff Respond to Sexual Harassment?

1) First Indicium: Staff Attitudes Toward Sexual Harassment

A new correctional officer confronts sexual harassment amid an organizational environment that tolerates, if not legitimates, this behavior. He or she quickly learns that many co-workers do little to safeguard inmates from sexual aggression.

Greatly outnumbered, policing less than "defensible space," plagued by structural limitations on their power, confronting strong prison gangs, yet provided with inadequate resources, correctional officers often struggle to maintain simply the semblance of order. "In some contemporary institutions they have withdrawn to the walls, leaving inmates to intimidate, rape, maim, and kill each other with alarming frequency."

Indeed, it appears that many prison workers believe that targeted inmates, not the staff, are primarily responsible for warding off sexual aggressors via combat. As one inmate recounted:

> I went [to the company officer] and said, "Look, this guy is bothering me, man. He keeps coming out with these sexual remarks and I want somebody to do something about this guy—tell him something." He said, "Well, there is nothing that we can do about it, and there is nothing that the brass can do about it, so hit him." He came right out and told me just like that.

In some instances, staff will overlook target violence rather than discipline an inmate fighting for his dignity, if not his survival. In turn, inmates who do not fight are seen by some prison workers as unworthy of protection. Lockwood attributed

---

285. [Helen Eigenberg, *Male Rape: An Empirical Examination of Correctional Officers' Attitudes Toward Rape in Prison*, 69 PRISON J. 39, 47 tbl.3 (1989)] (stating that 50% "disagreed that rape is rare and another 35.5% of officers "strongly disagreed").

these attitudes to the staff's embrace of lower-class norms equating masculinity with dominance.

One empirical study addresses this issue. Nacci and Kane surveyed 500 correctional officers employed by the Federal Bureau of Prisons. When queried about their motivation to protect inmates from sexual assaults, the officers averaged just 5.5 on a 7-point scale, with 4.0 being a neutral response. Their willingness to deter so-called "consensual" homosexual acts fell to a 5.0 average. Furthermore, the officers were inclined to assume consensuality in sex acts involving homosexual or bisexual inmates (the very individuals likely to be harassed or otherwise sexually exploited). Nacci and Kane also found that "something 'switches off'" many officers as their careers progress, leading to their diminished motivation to prevent sexual exploitation.

2) Second Indicium: Prison Rules Addressing Sexual Harassment

Three of every four companies possess sexual harassment policies. While the presence of a sexual harassment policy does not ensure its enforcement, its absence signifies institutional indifference to sexual exploitation. A similar conclusion can be drawn when the prison's code of inmate discipline lacks explicit prohibitions of sexual harassment among male inmates.

The disciplinary codes of a mere six departments of corrections—Idaho, Michigan, New Mexico, North Dakota, Oregon, and Tennessee—specifically proscribe sexual harassment among male inmates. Oregon officials drafted the most comprehensive ban:

> An inmate commits . . . sexual harassment if he/she directs offensive language or gestures towards another person or group, or about another person or group, or subjects another to physical contact, because of the other person's . . . sex. . . .

A. Essential elements

1. Offensive language or gestures; and 2. Directed toward another person or group or about another person or group; or 3. Physical contact motivated because of the other person or groups [sic] . . . sex[.]

The remaining five states provide staff and inmates comparatively brief prohibitions. Michigan bars "words or actions of a sexual nature directed at another person in order to harass or degrade that person." Similarly, New Mexico punishes "abusive words or gestures to any person that . . . constitute . . . sexual harassment. . . ." North Dakota bans "unwelcome sexual advances, requests for sexual favors, sexually motivated physical conduct or other verbal or physical conduct or communication of a sexual nature." Idaho, without elaboration, prohibits "sexually harassing another person." Lastly, Tennessee forbids "making sexually related comments, gestures or written communication to another person."

Four additional states sanction harassing behavior per se. California bars "[h]arassment of another person, group, or entity. . . ." Minnesota prohibits "harass[ment] . . .

with gestures, acts, or remarks." Illinois' ban on harassment is subsumed under the offense of insolence, which is defined as "talking, touching, gesturing, or other behavior which harasses, annoys, or shows disrespect." Connecticut addresses harassment under the offense of "[c]ausing a [di]sruption."

Several of the remaining forty state departments of corrections prohibit acts that constructively constitute one or more of the four forms of sexual harassment. Sixteen states employ an open-ended ban on abusive, degrading, or insulting language. Eighteen prison systems sanction sexual propositions. The departments of corrections in Arizona and Nebraska stand alone in punishing inmates for "pressuring" for sex. Finally, twelve states expressly bar kissing, fondling, or other contact of a sexual nature.

. . . .

V. Conclusion

A. Recommendations

Presently, sexually harassed inmates are fortunate if they can successfully cope with their perilous situation. Besides resorting to violence, they may join with fellow inmates in a protective clique. Others simply stay in their cells. Some secure a transfer to another institution. Lastly, inmates enter protective custody, where they are segregated from the general prison population.

Many inmates do not successfully cope. They experience continuing sexual harassment, fall victim to sexual assault, and/or become "kids" or "punks." While staff can aid inmates in developing effective coping strategies, such assistance ought not to satisfy constitutional minima. Coping strategies ultimately accommodate sexual harassment. As a wholly gratuitous punishment, offensive and/or coercive sexual conduct must be banished rather than accommodated.

. . . .

Accordingly, inmate disciplinary codes should directly proscribe the various forms of sexual harassment and staff should fairly and consistently enforce these prohibitions. Furthermore, inmates known or predicted to be sexually aggressive should be appropriately classified, housed, counseled, and in some instances removed from the general prison population. Conversely, inmates at risk should be confined in protective custody only as a last resort; to do otherwise would revictimize them through the stigma and isolation entailed by this form of segregation.

To further counter sexual harassment, prison staff should undertake direct and continuous supervision of inmates. Historically, inmate control has been based on the intermittent surveillance of inmates, an approach that falsely assumes that prison architecture and visual surveillance can control inmates with limited direct supervision by correctional staff. The direct supervision model, on the other hand, divides inmates into small, manageable groups and houses them in podular living units where staff work among rather than apart from the residents. As one commentator wrote, this approach to inmate management "is predicated on the belief that inmates must be continuously and directly supervised by custodial staff to prevent opportunities for illicit inmate behavior and activities, and to reinforce *institutional* as opposed to *inmate* control." The direct supervision approach is credited with reducing violence in several penal facilities.

While the causes of sexual harassment among male inmates are partly rooted in pre-prison experiences, they are exacerbated by the deprivations of prison life. Besides enhanced security, a prison regime committed to deterring sexual harassment must provide for the legitimate needs and aspirations of inmates. Indeed, responding to sexual harassment simply through tighter control of inmates may be counterproductive because such measures further challenge an inmate's masculinity, making him more likely to engage in sexual harassment as well as other forms of prison violence.

. . . .

B. Summary

Sexual harassment among male inmates plagues American prisons and constitutes "a major punishment for some prisoners." It takes several forms: (1) statements that feminize the targeted inmate; (2) sexual propositions; (3) sexual extortion; (4) and unwanted kissing, touching, or fondling intimate body areas. These behaviors arise from the deprivations imposed by incarceration as well as subcultural values that inmates bring with them to prison. The impact of sexual harassment on targeted inmates is often profound, with fear being the most common injury. The fear experienced by targeted inmates brings sexual harassment into the ambit of the Eighth Amendment: several courts have held that reasonable fear of sexual assault can inflict a constitutional violation. Nonetheless, prison staff do little to stop sexual harassment despite their long-standing knowledge of this form of victimization. To counter sexual harassment among male inmates, this Article advocates the following: (1) prison rules that explicitly bar the four forms of sexual harassment; (2) consistent enforcement of these rules; (3) segregation of inmates known or predicted to be sexually assaultive; (4) a prison regime that engages in the direct and continuous supervision of inmates under conditions that promote their legitimate needs and aspirations.

Notes and Discussion

1. Sex Discrimination Is prison sexual harassment discrimination "because of . . . sex"? Professor Robertson argued that "target selection is sexual in nature but not necessarily sex-based. . . ." Is that statement completely true, given his description of the environment? Why or why not? Professor Robertson's account of prison sexual harassment arguably reveals a hole in Justice Ginsburg's explanation of conduct based on sex in her *Harris* concurrence. Justice Scalia later quoted that explanation in *Oncale*. How does Ginsburg's explanation of conduct based on sex fail to explain prison harassment? Is this failure a problem in sexual harassment jurisprudence?

2. Sex, Sexuality, and Aggression Does Robertson's description of same-sex sexual aggression, as a means of establishing heterosexuality, demonstrate the stereotyped interconnection of sexuality and gender? Is the nature of sex-based aggression in prison different from that in civilian life? More particularly, does the fact of confinement make a difference for inmates? Masculine aggression exists outside of prison in the form of rampant domestic abuse. What is the difference between domestic violence and prison sexual violence? Is it only that someone else is watching in the prisons?

According to Gresham Sykes, prisoners equate the denial of heterosexual relationships with symbolic castration. Is it really the denial of the relationship or the authoritarian control of prisoners, manifested in a variety of ways, that conflicts with stereotypical notions of masculinity? For example, do military men feel "castrated" when denied heterosexual relationships because of war or training? Isn't any kind of authoritarian control a form of masculine castration for those who perceive masculinity in a stereotyped fashion? Might a strict hierarchical workplace lead to similar feelings, although less pronounced, for those men at the bottom of "the pecking order"? Why or why not? Do prisoners resent the "status of childhood," as Sykes contended, or do they resent their feminization?

3. **Power** Does the power element associated with prison harassment highlight or minimize the power abuse associated with workplace harassment? What about with housing harassment or school harassment? Explain. Is prison harassment that is designed to "humiliate, intimidate, and/or coerce" as different from opposite-sex harassment as Robertson suggests?

4. **Reasonableness** Is the reasonableness standard described by Robertson consistent with the one mentioned in *Oncale*? Explain.

5. **Intersectionality** Race seemed to influence the dynamics of prison sexual harassment. How? What conclusions can be drawn, if any, about race, class, and sexual orientation as they pertain to sexual harassment in prison? Might class-based and homophobic attitudes held by prison guards exacerbate the sexually exploitative environment? Explain.

6. **The Eighth Amendment** If the less egregious forms of sexual harassment often lead to sexual assault, where should courts draw the line to define a "sufficiently serious" deprivation? The deliberate indifference standard requires actual knowledge of a "substantial" risk to an inmate's safety. How likely are inmates to prevail given this standard? What are some of the predictable challenges that prisoners will face?

2. Sexual Harassment in Prison — Harassment by Prison Guards

While male inmates commit most of the abuses suffered by their peers, prison guards more often sexually abuse female inmates.[10] Moreover, the form of the

---

10. *See* Cheryl Bell et al., *Rape and Sexual Misconduct in the Prison System: Analyzing America's Most "Open" Secret*, 18 YALE L. & POL'Y REV. 195, 202 (1999).

victimization sometimes differs from that perpetrated against men. Cheryl Bell and her colleagues explain:

> Sexual abuse takes various forms in American prisons. Allegations by female inmates of sexual abuse include reports of guards forcing sex on female inmates, and of prison staff demanding sex in exchange for drugs, favors and promises of more lenient treatment. Prison officials have also been accused of leering at female inmates while the inmates undress, take showers, and use the toilet. Female inmates have also reported that guards improperly touch them while performing body searches. Further allegations of abuse extend beyond prison walls. At the Women's Community Correctional Center in Oahu, Hawaii, for example, inmates charged that guards ran a prostitution ring at a nearby hotel and used female inmates as call girls.

> . . . .

> Retaliation against prisoners who report sexual abuse is all too common and can sometimes result in prisoners having to serve longer terms. In Michigan, for example, researchers found that corrections officials retaliate against women prisoners who complain about sexual harassment or abuse by writing up disciplinary "tickets" for specious violations of prison rules or regulations. A guard will sometimes force a confrontation to occur in order to create a minor violation for which he can write a ticket. For example, a guard could refuse to give a female inmate permission to go to the bathroom, so that he can write her up for insubordination when she insists that she needs to go. Another tactic is for a guard to ask a colleague to write up a ticket, whether for a false violation or for a minor one, so that the retaliation cannot be traced back to him. A prisoner with several tickets may be punished in a number of ways, including a loss of "good time" accrued toward early release.

> Guards also threaten to retaliate against women prisoners who dare to report sexual abuse by denying them visitation rights with their children. This can be devastating, not only for the women prisoners, but also for their children. More than two-thirds of all incarcerated women have at least one child under eighteen, and the majority of those women are single mothers.[11]

Consider the following cases and whether they highlight the problems noted by the legal scholars. Evaluate whether these cases are different from those involving a hostile work environment.

Barney v. Pulsipher
143 F.3d 1299 (10th Cir. 1998)

SEYMOUR, Chief Judge.

. . . .

---

11. *Id.* at 203, 210–11.

In accordance with state law requiring "the separation of prisoners by sex," women inmates at Box Elder County Jail are placed in solitary confinement in a cell specifically designated for females. . . .

Several closed circuit television cameras are in the jail and linked to monitors in the dispatch area to aid jail officials in maintaining the security of the facility. No cameras monitor the outside exercise area commonly known as the "bullpen." Although dispatchers generally watch the monitors in concert with their dispatch duties, they are under no obligation to view them continuously.

The Jail Policies and Procedures Manual specifically instructs jailers to "give notification prior to entering the cell blocks of the opposite sex" to the dispatcher who "will monitor the cell block." Moreover, male jailers are prohibited from "remov[ing] female inmates from their cells without another officer being physically present." Ordinarily two jailers are required to be on duty per shift, but when one jailer is sick or on vacation a second jailer is usually not called in due to understaffing and budgetary constraints. The manual further prohibits jailers from accepting sex or other favors from prisoners, forbids staff members from taking any prisoners out of the jail for any reason except to perform authorized jail work assignments, and prohibits discrimination against any prisoner on the basis of sex.

As a result of overcrowding in the jail, the indoor exercise area and library are used to house overflow male prisoners, and women are therefore excluded from using these spaces. Because of the lack of monitoring and services available to women inmates, a report evaluating the jail concluded "[t]he present configuration of space dictates that the facility not house women inmates for periods of time longer than several hours." . . .

Early in the morning of May 15, 1993, Kathy Christensen arrived at Box Elder County Jail to serve a 48-hour sentence for a DUI conviction and was placed in the female cell. Later that day, Gerald Pulsipher, the only jailer on duty at the time, removed Ms. Christensen from her cell without informing the dispatcher as required by jail policy and led her outside to the unmonitored "bullpen" area where he sexually assaulted her. Mr. Pulsipher threatened to keep Ms. Christensen in jail longer than 48 hours if she did not perform oral sex as he demanded. After completing her sentence, Ms. Christensen did not report the incident of assault to the County.

On July 10, 1993, Susan Barney was placed in the female cell at Box Elder County Jail to serve a 48-hour sentence for shoplifting. Mr. Pulsipher, who once again was the only jailer on duty, took Ms. Barney to the same unmonitored area without informing the dispatcher and sexually assaulted her. Ms. Barney also did not report the incident to the County upon her release. However, Ms. Barney showed her drug counselor a sexually explicit note Mr. Pulsipher had written her while in jail and told her counselor about the assault. The counselor reported Mr. Pulsipher's conduct to Ms. Barney's probation officer, who in turn reported the incident to Sheriff Limb. The County subsequently learned that Ms. Christensen had also been previously assaulted by Mr. Pulsipher.

On August 24, 1993, Sheriff Limb terminated Mr. Pulsipher's employment. Criminal charges were filed against Mr. Pulsipher, who pled guilty to forcible sexual abuse of Ms. Christensen. As part of the plea agreement, the criminal charges relating to the sexual assault of Ms. Barney were dismissed.

. . . [The court discussed details of Mr. Pulsipher's hire and training. It also reviewed the role, or lack thereof, of senior administrators and commissioners in the functioning of the jail.]

The sexual assaults on Ms. Christensen and Ms. Barney were the only incidents of sexual misconduct by Box Elder County jailers of which Sheriff Limb was aware during his more than thirty-year tenure as the County's sheriff. The Commissioners likewise lacked knowledge of any alleged sexual misconduct by jailers or any complaints about inadequate conditions at the jail for female inmates prior to the Christensen and Barney incidents. The record reveals the only problem Sheriff Limb mentioned to one of the Commissioners was that of overcrowding, which resulted in his having to send prisoners elsewhere due to lack of space in the jail.

Susan Barney brought this action against Gerald Pulsipher, Box Elder County, Sheriff Limb and Commissioners Allen, White, and Jensen in their official and individual capacities under 42 U.S.C. § 1983 for the sexual assault by Mr. Pulsipher and other conditions of confinement arising out of her two-day incarceration at Box Elder County Jail. Ms. Barney alleges that defendants' inadequate policies and facilities for women inmates, their failure to adequately staff, train, and supervise jailers, and their failure to take reasonable measures to protect her well-being and bodily integrity violated her rights under the First, Eighth, Ninth, and Fourteenth Amendments of the United States Constitution. She seeks monetary damages, declaratory and injunctive relief, and attorneys' fees and costs.

Ms. Christensen also brought a section 1983 action against the same defendants, alleging similar constitutional violations and seeking similar relief for her two-day incarceration at the jail. These actions were subsequently consolidated by the district court.

The district court granted the motions of the County, Sheriff Limb, and Commissioners Allen, White, and Jensen for summary judgment. The court was persuaded that defendants had not acted with the required "deliberate indifference" to violate the Eighth Amendment, noting the absence of any previously reported incidents of sexual misconduct by Mr. Pulsipher or any jailers, and holding that the conditions of plaintiffs' confinement did not rise to the level of cruel and unusual punishment in light of the brevity of their stay. The court further found no evidence in the record demonstrating that jail conditions for female prisoners violated clearly established equal protection rights, and concluded that defendants' policy of holding women inmates in solitary confinement when arrangements could not be made to transport them to other jails was reasonably related to the legitimate penal interest of providing separate housing for men and women prisoners. The court thus granted the individual defendants qualified immunity on all damage claims and granted judgment in favor of defendants on all claims in the complaint.

II

. . . [The court reviewed how the county had no discriminatory policies or procedures and could not be found liable.]

III

Ms. Barney and Ms. Christensen also sued the Sheriff and the Commissioners in their individual capacities. Qualified immunity is an affirmative defense against section 1983 damage claims available to public officials sued in their individual capacities. Government officials are shielded from liability if "their conduct does not violate clearly established statutory or constitutional rights of which a reasonable person would have known." Plaintiffs maintain the district court erred in granting qualified immunity to the individual defendants, contending defendants violated their clearly established rights under the Eighth Amendment and Equal Protection Clause.

"In analyzing qualified immunity claims, we first ask if a plaintiff has asserted the violation of a constitutional right at all, and then assess whether the right was clearly established at the time of a defendant's actions." . . .

A. Eighth Amendment

Prison officials are required to provide humane conditions of confinement by ensuring inmates receive the basic necessities of adequate food, clothing, shelter, and medical care and by taking reasonable measures to guarantee the inmates' safety. Plaintiffs contend Sheriff Limb and the Commissioners violated their Eighth Amendment rights by failing to protect them from Mr. Pulsipher's sexual harassment and assaults and by the inhumane conditions they allegedly suffered during their two-day incarcerations.[10]

In order to hold prison officials liable for violating an inmate's right to humane conditions of confinement, two requirements must be met. First, the deprivation alleged must be objectively "sufficiently serious," depriving the inmate of "'the minimal civilized measure of life's necessities.'" Second, the official must have a "sufficiently culpable state of mind," which in this context means the official must exhibit "deliberate indifference" to a substantial risk of serious harm to an inmate. Thus, the deliberate indifference standard in a prison-conditions case is a "subjective" and not an "objective" requirement. That is, a prison official is liable only if the "official knows of and disregards an excessive risk to inmate health and safety." It is not enough to establish that the official should have known of the risk of harm.

---

10. Although plaintiffs generally invoke other constitutional amendments in their complaints, their claims concerning conditions of confinement "remain[ ] bounded by the Eighth Amendment, the explicit textual source of constitutional protection in the prison context."

With regard to plaintiffs' sexual assault claims,[11] we have expressly acknowledged that an "inmate has a constitutional right to be secure in her bodily integrity and free from attack by prison guards." *Hovater v. Robinson*, 1 F.3d 1063, 1068 (10th Cir. 1993). Clearly plaintiffs' deprivations resulting from the sexual assaults are sufficiently serious to constitute a violation under the Eighth Amendment. Nevertheless, Ms. Barney and Ms. Christensen have not shown that Sheriff Limb and the Commissioners were deliberately indifferent in failing to protect them from Mr. Pulsipher's assaults. Plaintiffs maintain defendants knew of the substantial risk posed by permitting Mr. Pulsipher to be the sole guard on duty and consciously disregarded that risk. To support their claims of defendants' knowledge, plaintiffs rely primarily on defendants' official policy requiring two jailers to be present when female prisoners were removed from their cell. This policy, in plaintiffs' view, clearly reflects defendants' understanding that a substantial risk of sexual misconduct to female inmates existed when only one male jailer was present.

We explicitly rejected this argument in *Hovater*, which involved very similar facts and controls here. There, Mr. Robinson, a detention officer, called Ms. Hovater, a female inmate, from her cell to the library. In violation of jail policy which required that female inmates be accompanied by either a female officer or at least two male officers, Ms. Hovater was left alone with Mr. Robinson, who then sexually assaulted her. Prior to this incident, neither the sheriff nor the county commissioners knew of any complaints from female inmates about sexual misconduct by Mr. Robinson or any other jail officer. We held Ms. Hovater failed to establish that the sheriff and the county commissioners acted with deliberate indifference—i.e., that the defendants "disregarded an obvious risk to the safety of female inmates by allowing a single male guard to have custody of a female inmate absent any indication that the guard would assault her." We further stated:

> [T]he mere existence of the policy at issue does not establish an obvious risk that females left alone with male guards are likely to be assaulted.

> Sheriff Hill had no knowledge that Mr. Robinson was a threat to the female inmates. Any known harm could stem only from the mere fact of Mr. Robinson's gender. To find harm present in these circumstances would, in effect, require the conclusion that every male guard is a risk to the bodily integrity of a female inmate whenever the two are left alone. There is absolutely no evidence in this record to support that conclusion.

---

11. Although plaintiffs allege Mr. Pulsipher subjected them to severe verbal sexual harassment and intimidation, these acts of verbal harassment alone are not sufficient to state a claim under the Eighth Amendment. Plaintiffs' claims of verbal harassment are only actionable "[i]n combination" with the assaults. *See, e.g.,* Women Prisoners v. District of Columbia, 877 F. Supp. 634, 665 (D.D.C. 1994) (observing that "when officers make sexual remarks in an environment where sexual assaults of women prisoners by officers are well known and inadequately addressed" such conduct "mutually heighten[s]" the injury to women prisoners). . . . We therefore focus on plaintiffs' sexual assault claims.

Nor does the record here contain any evidence to indicate that male guards at Box Elder County Jail, if left alone with female inmates, posed a risk to their health and safety. As in *Hovater,* we decline to find knowledge by Sheriff Limb and the Commissioners of a substantial risk of harm from the mere fact of Mr. Pulsipher's gender. Without any evidence of sexual misconduct in Mr. Pulsipher's background or any evidence of previous incidents of sexual misconduct by Box Elder County jailers, plaintiffs have failed to raise a fact question on whether the Sheriff and the Commissioners acted with deliberate indifference under either an objective or subjective standard.

. . . .

B. Equal Protection

Ms. Barney and Ms. Christensen contend defendants discriminated against them on the basis of their sex in violation of the Equal Protection Clause by subjecting them to sexual harassment and assault,[15] placing them in solitary confinement when male inmates are not ordinarily placed in solitary confinement, and denying them access to educational and recreational facilities and programs offered to male inmates. The Equal Protection Clause requires the government to treat similarly situated people alike. In order to assert a viable equal protection claim, plaintiffs must first make a threshold showing that they were treated differently from others who were similarly situated to them.

Plaintiffs have not come forward with any evidence indicating that women serving two-day sentences at Box Elder County Jail received treatment different from men serving similar lengths of time. Nor have they presented evidence of the relative number of men and women prisoners, the average length of stays of men and women prisoners, and what programs are offered to male prisoners. Absent any relevant information about male prisoners at Box Elder County Jail, plaintiffs cannot make the required threshold showing that they were treated differently from male inmates who were similarly situated to them. Plaintiffs' equal protection claims therefore fail. *See Women Prisoners v. District of Columbia*, 93 F.3d 910, 925–26 (D.C. Cir. 1996) (female inmates at co-correctional facility foreclosed from making equal protection claim because no evidence regarding programs available to male inmates at same facility).[17]

---

15. Plaintiffs assert that sexual harassment and sexual assault are actionable as an equal protection violation under 42 U.S.C. § 1983 without a showing that a comparable group of males are likewise being harassed, citing *Starrett v. Wadley*, 876 F.2d 808, 814 (10th Cir. 1989). Starrett involved a suit brought by a female county employee against the county and her male supervisor for sexual harassment and retaliatory discharge. We are not confronted here with a charge of sexual harassment in the employment context. Claims of sexual harassment and assault of inmates by prison guards are more properly analyzed under the Eighth Amendment. The Equal Protection Clause in the prison-conditions context is usually invoked to remedy disparities in educational, vocational, and recreational programs offered to male and female inmates.

17. Moreover, considering that state law requires the separation of men and women inmates and that the jail houses primarily male prisoners while female inmates are ordinarily detained for

In sum, plaintiffs failed to meet their burden of presenting sufficient facts to show that Sheriff Limb and the Commissioners violated either the Eighth Amendment or the Equal Protection Clause. Consequently, the district court properly granted summary judgment for these defendants.

IV

As the County defendants readily concede, Mr. Pulsipher's conduct towards Ms. Barney and Ms. Christensen was inexcusable and "outrageous." Such outrageous conduct by Mr. Pulsipher, without more, is not enough to impose liability on the County, or the Sheriff and the Commissioners in their individual capacities. Mr. Pulsipher has been criminally convicted for his behavior and the section 1983 suit against him is pending below. Ms. Barney and Ms. Christensen are therefore not left entirely without relief.

. . . .

Newby v. The District of Columbia

59 F. Supp. 2d 35 (D. D.C. 1999)

SPORKIN, District Judge.

. . . In instances where a "party has been fully heard on an issue and there is no legally sufficient evidentiary basis for a reasonable jury to find for that party", the Court may direct a verdict against that party. Such is the case here.

The undisputed facts adduced before this Court during the trial are as follows:

Plaintiff, Jacquelyn Newby, was incarcerated in Southeast I at the D.C. Jail in July, 1995. Over the course of the month, prison guards forced Ms. Newby, along with other female inmates, to participate in strip-shows and exotic dancing on three occasions. The female prisoners, including Ms. Newby, wore only g-strings during the dancing and at least on one occasion danced in the nude. On each of the three dancing occasions the three prison guards on duty directed that the dancing take place. On one occasion, male prison guards were allowed in to observe. On no occasion were supervisory prison officials present, or on duty in the area of the jail where the dancing took place. The number of inmates housed in this section of the jail at the time numbered between eighty and one-hundred.

Bonita Pryor, a former inmate in the D.C. Jail in July 1995 testified that she refused to participate in the strip-shows. On either July 26th or July 27th of 1999, Ms. Pryor was beaten by a prison guard. Even though the reason for the beating is in dispute, (Ms. Pryor says it was because she refused to dance, the defendants say

---

only brief periods of time and contracted out to neighboring jails, the County defendants' policy of keeping women in solitary confinement reflects a legitimate and rational decision to provide for the safety of inmates and the efficient running of the jail. We hesitate to interfere with prison officials' decisions concerning the day-to-day administration of prisons, to which we must accord deference.

it was for other reasons) the City government concedes it was improper for such a beating to have taken place. Another female inmate, Ms. Shawnez Williams, testified without contradiction that she participated in the dancing against her will out of fear of physical retaliation from prison guards if she refused.

During the month of July, 1995, Ms. Newby also engaged in a sexual relationship with a prison guard, Quida Graham. The nature of this relationship included private meetings in an empty cell where the two would fondle and kiss one another. Such meetings which occurred on more than one occasion are concededly against the law.[1]

On December 13, 1994 United States District Judge June L. Green, issued an Opinion in Lockwood, 877 F. Supp. 634 (D.D.C. 1994). In her opinion, Judge Green made the following findings of fact, among others: (1) that there were incidents of sexual misconduct between prison employees and female prisoners in the D.C. Jail, the Lorton Minimum Security Annex, and the Correctional Treatment Facility; (2) that a general acceptance of sexual relationships between prison staff and inmates existed in the D.C. Department of Corrections that created a "sexualized environment"; (3) that the District of Columbia's responses to the complaints of female inmates about the sexualized environment was inadequate; (3) that the District of Columbia did not adequately investigate complaints of sexual misconduct brought to their attention by female inmates. Based on these findings Judge Green found the District of Columbia violated the Eighth Amendment of the U.S. Constitution by subjecting the women prisoners in their custody to cruel and unusual punishment as well as 42 U.S.C. § 1983 by maintaining a governmental custom of sexual harassment in the three D.C. Correctional facilities (including the City jail which is the facility at issue in this case), notwithstanding the existence of official policies prohibiting such behavior.

The District of Columbia has a duty to provide those under its custody a safe place of incarceration. *See* D.C. Code § 24-442 (The Department of Corrections shall be responsible for the safekeeping, care, protection, instruction, and discipline of all persons committed to such institutions). In her Opinion, Judge Green explicitly directed the city to take remedial steps to put an end to, and to prevent in the future, the gross abuses of the rights of female prisoners she found existed throughout the city's correctional system. Judge Green's opinion dated December 13, 1994 was issued just seven months before the concededly unlawful activities that occurred in this case took place. Other than putting out a policy statement regarding sexual conduct between prison guards and female inmates, and implementing certain training procedure concerning sexual harassment, the District did little else to ensure the cessation of guards engaging in proscribed activities with inmates. Most significantly, the District failed to institute a meaningful system of

---

1. The District of Columbia's "Anti-Sexual Abuse Act of 1994" prohibits prison officials from engaging in "a sexual act" with any person under their custody. *See* D.C. Law 10–257 (1995).

supervision that would provide some reasonable assurance that D.C. Code § 24-442 and the city's concomitant other legal responsibilities would be properly discharged.

In this case the facts are not in dispute that on the three occasions in July 1995 where female inmates participated in sex shows[2] including nude and semi-nude dancing, and whose sexual encounters between correctional officer Quida Graham and Ms. Newby occurred, there were no supervisory persons present at Southeast I. Even to this date the District of Columbia has taken no steps to monitor what occurs in the jail, either by the placement of surveillance cameras or directing supervisory officials to be present with prison guards during their daily prison rounds. The District of Columbia has stated that the structure and age of the D.C. Jail prevent the installation of monitoring equipment. With the City's past history of sexual misconduct at the jail, it is incumbent upon the city to find some way to monitor the common areas at the jail.

With or without the use of monitoring equipment, the City clearly had the duty to assure supervisory personnel on July 1995 were present in the common areas of Southeast I, in order to safeguard the rights of the prisoners. At a minimum, the city should have made sure supervisory officials on duty took the necessary steps to have prevented the sexual dancing that occurred. The District of Columbia has the duty, not only to train its officers in matters relating to sexual contact between prison guards and inmates, but also has the responsibility to actively devise and implement a system of supervision of its first level corrections officers in accordance with the law.

The City has failed to explain where were its supervisory personnel at the time the "sexual dancing" was taking place. What is particularly troubling is that these horrendous activities that took place at the City jail only surfaced when Plaintiff Newby and inmate Pryor complained about them. It is inconceivable how improper sexual activities involving the entire prison population of Southeast I, with inmates numbering between eighty and one-hundred and three prison guards on duty as well as the presence of other prison guards from other parts of the prison could have occurred with no one in a supervisory role putting an immediate stop to them. Where such conditions obtain, the City itself has clearly violated Plaintiff's constitutional and section 1983 rights. This is so whether the City can be deemed to have endorsed such violative activities or actually participated in them by failing to actively supervise its prison facilities. The District has woefully failed to carry out its responsibilities under both Federal law and the laws of the District of Columbia. Accordingly, it is liable to plaintiff Newby, for whom this Court is directing a verdict under Fed. R. Civ. P. 50. The only issue remaining for the jury to decide, and which will be submitted to them, is the amount of damages to which the plaintiff is entitled.

---

2. On one occasion during the dancing the prison guards on duty ordered one of the "dancing" inmates to place a cigarette in her vagina.

Howard v. Everett

208 F.3d 218 (8th Cir. 2000)

Before RICHARD S. ARNOLD, BOWMAN, and BEAM, Circuit Judges.

PER CURIAM.

Steven Howard, an inmate at the North Central Unit (NCU) in Arkansas, submitted a 42 U.S.C. § 1983 complaint against NCU employees Robert Henderson and Dustin Foret, among others, alleging that they verbally sexually harassed him in violation of the Eighth Amendment. The District Court denied Henderson's and Foret's motion for summary judgment based on qualified immunity, and Henderson and Foret appeal. We reverse.

. . . Qualified immunity shields government officials from suit unless their conduct violated "clearly established statutory or constitutional rights of which a reasonable person would have known."

In determining defendants' entitlement to immunity, we determine whether the plaintiff has alleged a deprivation of constitutional magnitude, and, if so, whether that right was so clearly established that defendants would have known their conduct violated the Constitution at the time of their acts. "[B]ecause the sexual harassment or abuse of an inmate by a corrections officer can never serve a legitimate penological purpose and may well result in severe physical and psychological harm, such abuse can, in certain circumstances, constitute the 'unnecessary and wanton infliction of pain' forbidden by the Eighth Amendment."

We disagree with the District Court that Howard alleged a deprivation of constitutional magnitude. Although defendants' sexual comments and gestures were reprehensible, Howard specifically alleged that Henderson and Foret never touched him. We believe this sexual harassment, absent contact or touching, does not constitute unnecessary and wanton infliction of pain. *Cf. Seltzer-Bey v. Delo*, 66 F.3d 961, 962–63 (8th Cir. 1995) (allegations that prison guard conducted daily strip searches, made sexual comments about prisoner's penis and buttocks, and rubbed prisoner's buttocks with nightstick were sufficient to withstand motion for summary judgment); *Watson v. Jones*, 980 F.2d 1165, 1165–66 (8th Cir. 1992) (allegations in verified complaint that prison guard performed almost daily pat-down searches, tickled inmates, and deliberately examined genital, anus, lower stomach and thigh areas were sufficient to withstand summary judgment motion). Thus, we conclude the District Court erred in not finding defendants were entitled to qualified immunity, and we reverse and remand for entry of an order granting their motion for summary judgment.

Notes and Discussion

1. Qualified Immunity and "Deliberate Indifference" Was the *Barney* district court justified in dismissing the claims against the County, Sheriff Limb, and the Commissioners? Explain. Would it have been unfair to hold the County liable for

Mr. Pulsipher's behavior, given that no one had previously complained about his conduct? Did Ms. Newby establish deliberate indifference on the part of the D.C. Jail? Explain.

Does the deliberate indifference standard, applicable in prison cases, resemble the one applied to schools in Title IX cases? Do you notice any differences in the applicable standards for schools and prisons?

2. Humane Conditions of Confinement The two requirements for finding a violation of an inmate's right to humane conditions of confinement include an "objectively, 'sufficiently serious'" deprivation and a "sufficiently culpable state of mind" by an official. Did the plaintiffs meet the first requirement? Explain. Did plaintiffs establish the subjective state of mind requirement to satisfy the second prong of the test? Should Sheriff Limb and the Commissioners have known of a risk when they allowed only one guard to monitor female prisoners? Is it only gender differences that might explain a risk of sexual assault or might a power disparity highlight the risk? Did the court mistakenly ignore the power disparity?

Why did the *Newby* court find a violation when the *Barney* court did not? What facts distinguish these two cases in an Eighth Amendment analysis? Did the prior case history of the D.C. jail play a role in the outcome of the case?

3. Equal Protection Was it true, as the *Barney* court confirmed, that "no evidence in the record" demonstrated "that jail conditions for female prisoners violated clearly established equal protection rights"? How might the plaintiffs have procured evidence "that women serving two-day sentences . . . received treatment different from men serving similar lengths of time"? Wasn't it enough that these women experienced sexual assault that male prisoners did not endure? Or did the court properly focus on programming?

4. Physical Contact Was the *Howard* court correct that "sexual harassment, absent contact or touching, does not constitute unnecessary or wanton infliction of pain"? Explain.

5. Deference to Prison Administration In footnote 17, the *Barney* court expressed its reluctance to interfere in the day-to-day administration of the prison. Did legitimate penological concerns justify the deference the court displayed? Explain. When, if ever, do the protection of society and the maintenance of inmate control justify the violation of individual civil rights?

6. Relief The *Barney* court reasoned that because the section 1983 claim against Mr. Pulsipher was still pending, the plaintiffs were "not left entirely without relief." Was this conclusion realistic? Why or why not? What might be an appropriate award of damages for the *Barney* and *Newby* plaintiffs?

7. Detained Children Following the Trump administration policy of separating children from their parents at the border, allegations of sexual assault by those detained children rose dramatically. The children are not technically "prison inmates," but they are not free to leave. According to a Department of Health and Human Services (HHS) tally, more than 4,500 allegations of sexual abuse have been reported by minors in the custody of HHS between 2014 and 2018.[12] The Department of Justice received more than 1,000 case reports.[13] In March 2019, Senators Chuck Grassley (R-Iowa) and Dianne Feinstein (D-Calif.) requested that the HHS inspector general "investigate reports of rampant sexual abuse against children in government facilities at the southern border."[14] PREA does not cover immigration detention centers.

8. Female Prison Guards While prison employees can file EEOC claims and Title VII lawsuits, female prison guards face unique problems. According to a *New York Times* report, "Some inmates do not stop at stares. They also grope, threaten and expose themselves. But what is worse, . . . male colleagues can and do encourage such behavior, undermining the authority of female officers and jeopardizing their safety. Other male employees join in the harassment themselves."[15] Despite a damning 2010 EEOC report, and attempted remediation by the Bureau of Prisons ("BOP"), problems continue. "In May 2017, the House Oversight Committee opened an investigation into the agency, writing that despite continuous allegations of sexual misconduct, 'the BOP continued to award bonuses to top administrators.'"[16]

9. Intersectional Aspects of Prison Abuse Reports link transgender and gender nonconforming inmates with increased risk of sexual assault and abuse. For example, Stacy Rojas, a gender nonconforming former inmate, was allegedly abused daily. Rojas filed suit over an attack that also targeted two other cellmates. "[I]n November 2015, guards allegedly stomped on one woman's breast, cut another's clothes off, left them in isolation cells so long they had no choice but to soil themselves, and berated them with graphic sexual insults and suggestions." Rojas believes that there is a reason that #MeToo has not helped the prison population. "Rojas said part of what is most misunderstood about incarcerated women, and especially transgender and gender nonconforming people behind bars, is the sense that they chose to break the law or be different, and so they may not be worthy of the same attention or protection."[17]

---

12. Matthew Haag, *Thousands of Immigrant Children Said They Were Sexually Abused in U.S. Detention Centers, Report Says*, N.Y. TIMES (Feb. 27, 2019).

13. Nathaniel Weixel, *Thousands of Migrant Children Allegedly Sexually Assaulted While in US Custody*, THE HILL (Feb. 26, 2019).

14. Rachel Frazin, *Feinstein, Grassley Call for Investigation into Minor Sexual Abuse at HHS Facilities*, THE HILL (March 6, 2019).

15. Caitlin Dickerson Hazing, *Humiliation, Terror: Working While Female in Federal Prison*, N.Y. TIMES (Nov. 17, 2018).

16. *Id.*

17. Marisa Endicott, *'No Longer Human': Women's Prisons Are a Breeding Ground for Sexual Harassment, Abuse*, THINKPROGRESS (Aug. 29, 2018).

According to *ThinkProgress*, which detailed Rojas's story, the Bureau of Justice reported that between 2009 and 2011, women comprised 13% of the jailed population. However, women were the targets of 67% of all sexual victimization of prisoners by staff. The Vera Institute reports that women in jails disproportionately experience unemployment or underemployment prior to incarceration. A third suffer from mental illness and two-thirds are women of color. Many are survivors of sexual abuse.[18] These characteristics may heighten their vulnerability.[19]

10. Case Law Update Standards described by Robertson and employed in the cases dating back 20 years have not changed significantly. For example, in *Boxer X v. Harris*, 437 F.3d 1107 (11th Cir. 2006), the court found, "We conclude that a female prison guard's solicitation of a male prisoner's manual masturbation, even under the threat of reprisal, does not present more than *de minimis* injury. Accordingly, we affirm the dismissal of Boxer's claim under the Eighth Amendment."[20]

In contrast, cases involving a sexual battery still trigger liability. For example, deciding a procedural issue in *Ortiz v. Jordan*, 562 U.S. 180 (2011), the Supreme Court reviewed the case of a female inmate (Ortiz) who was sexually fondled and digitally penetrated by a male guard. The Court summarized the *Ortiz* history:

> The case proceeded to trial, and a jury returned a verdict of $350,000 in compensatory and punitive damages against Jordan [a prison case manager] and $275,000 against Bright [a prison investigator]. . . . The District Court entered judgment for Ortiz in accordance with the jury's verdict. . . . The Court of Appeals [] had no warrant to upset the jury's decision on the officials' liability.[21]

This case demonstrates the level of deference and protection of prison officials by some judges.

Finally, in *Wood v. Beauclair*, 692 F.3d 1041 (2012), the Ninth Circuit Court found that even a "consensual" relationship between a prison guard and an inmate might invalidate consent to sexual activity. The court stated that "because of the enormous power imbalance between prisoners and prison guards, labeling a prisoner's decision to engage in sexual conduct in prison as 'consent' is a dubious proposition."[22] The court, therefore, reversed summary judgment on the inmate's Eighth Amendment claim.

---

18. Malika Saada Saar et al., *The Sexual Abuse to Prison Pipeline: The Girls' Story* (2015), https://rights4girls.org/wp-content/uploads/r4g/2015/02/2015_COP_sexual-abuse_layout_web-1.pdf.

19. *Id.*; *see also* Matthew Haag, *7 Prison Guards In Pennsylvania Charged with Sexually Abusing Inmates*, N.Y. Times (Feb, 16, 2018).

20. *Boxer X*, 437 F.3d at 1111.

21. *Ortiz*, 562 U.S. at 187, 192.

22. *Wood*, 692 F.3d at 1044.

3. Sexual Harassment in the Military— Introduction[23]

Like prisons, the military has been plagued with accounts of sexual harassment and abuse for decades.[24] For example, in 1992 Navy Lt. Paula Coughlin revealed that she had been groped in a "gauntlet" at the 1991 Tailhook Symposium.[25] In December 2011, Jesse Ellison reported in the *Daily Beast*, "Women in the military are now more likely to be raped by fellow soldiers than they are to be killed in combat."[26] She also noted that "in 2010, there were 3,158 military sexual assaults reported, according to the Department of Defense's Sexual Assault Prevention and Response Office—a number that, by the Pentagon's own admission, represents just 13.5% of the estimated 19,000 assaults that actually occurred last year."[27]

When the #MeToo movement swept the country in late 2017, *Time* magazine featured an essay by a member of SWAN (Service Women's Action Network), Antonieta Rico. She asked why the voices of military women were not being included in the #MeToo movement. She explained:

> Women in the military have been speaking out about sexual harassment and assault for decades, from Tailhook in the early 1990s to Marines United earlier this year. And for decades the American public has ignored our voices, allowing the military brass to pay lip service to eradicating the problem of sexual assault in the ranks, and failing to hold them accountable when, as scandal after scandal shows, sexual predators in the military continue to harass and assault with impunity.[28]

Her question resonates as the military, which does prohibit sexual harassment and abuse of its personnel,[29] annually documents reports of continued abuse.

---

23. Adapted from JENNIFER ANN DROBAC, SEXUAL EXPLOITATION OF TEENAGERS: ADOLESCENT DEVELOPMENT, DISCRIMINATION & CONSENT LAW 27–29 (2016).

24. *See* Danielle Christenson, *Chain of Command: The Barriers of Reporting Sexual Assault in the Military*, VIRTUAL COMMONS-BRIDGEWATER STATE UNIVERSITY, May 13, 2014, http://vc.bridgew .edu/honors_proj/42; THE INVISIBLE WAR (Chain Camera Pictures et al., 2012).

25. Michael Winerip, *Revisiting the Military's Tailhook Scandal*, N.Y. TIMES (May 13, 2013). For further discussion of Tailhook and similar military sexual assault scandals, see Lindsay Rosenthal & Lawrence Korb, Center for American Progress, *Twice Betrayed: Bringing Justice to the U.S. Military's Sexual Assault Problem*, Nov. 2013, https://www.americanprogress.org/wp-content/uploads /2013/11/MilitarySexualAssaultsReport.pdf.

26. Jesse Ellison, *Judge Dismisses 'Epidemic' of Rape in Military Case*, DAILY BEAST (Dec. 13, 2011).

27. *Id.*

28. Antonieta Rico, *Why Military Women Are Missing from the #MeToo Moment*, TIME, Dec. 12, 2017. "Last month, we stood beside Sen. Kirsten Gillibrand as she once again reintroduced the Military Justice Improvement Act, which would take the decision to prosecute felonies, including sexual assaults, away from commanders who are at times the very perpetrators of the assaults, and put it in the hands of military prosecutors." *Id.*

29. *See, e.g.*, 10 U.S.C.A. § 1561 (West 2016) (originally enacted as Pub. L. No. 105-85, Div. A, Title V, § 591(a)(1), 111 Stat. 1760 (1997)) (requiring investigation of sexual harassment by

For example, in May 2018, the Department of Defense released its fiscal year 2017 report that recounted a 10% increase of service member reports of sexual harassment across all four military departments. "The report for fiscal 2017 says the department received 6,769 reports of sexual assault involving service members as either victims or subjects of criminal investigation, a 9.7% increase over the 6,172 reports made in fiscal 2016."[30] These reports suggest that any remedial measures taken have not cured the problem. In fact the problem may have gotten worse. The 2019 report for fiscal year 2018 noted that sexual assaults on women increased by 50%.[31]

However, some changes have occurred. In 2015, 38 U.S.C.A. § 1720D took effect. It requires the Secretary of Defense to provide psychological counseling and other services for personnel who have experienced sexual misconduct and assault.[32] The Secretary also appeared to want change. During Sexual Assault Awareness and Prevention Month 2018,[33] Secretary James Mattis issued a memorandum that said, in part:

> Due to the age at which nearly all recruits enter the military, NCOs and officers must carry this special responsibility for the care of our troops. While casualties on the battlefield are understood to be consistent with our military duties, I accept *no* casualties due to sexual assault within our ranks. Military leaders are to be zealous in carrying out *in loco parentis* responsibilities and ridding our ranks of such illegal, abhorrent behavior.[34]

His emphasis on "no casualties" suggests an intention to eradicate the problem. However, the vague reference to the age of recruits and the parental responsibilities of military leaders might cause some readers a bit of concern. Why the focus on parenting by leaders? Why is criminal sexual assault a parenting issue? And are the perpetrators usually young recruits (who ironically lack power within the military hierarchy)?

These questions are not new in response to declarations by military brass. In 2013, "Air Force Chief of Staff Gen. Mark Welsh suggested . . . that the spike in reports

---

commanding officers); *see also, e.g.,* 10 U.S.C.A § 6980 (West 2013) (originally enacted as Pub. L. No. 109-364, Div. A, Title V, § 532(a)(2), 120 Stat. 2201 (2006)) (establishing a Navy policy on sexual harassment and sexual violence). A Pentagon survey estimated that 26,000 people had been sexually assaulted in the military in 2012. Jennifer Steinhauer, *Joint Chiefs' Answers on Sex Crimes Dismay Senators*, N.Y. TIMES, June 5, 2013, at A12.

30. Lisa Ferdinando, *DoD Releases Annual Report on Sexual Assault in Military*, DoD NEWS (May 1, 2018).

31. DEPARTMENT OF DEFENSE, DEPARTMENT OF DEFENSE ANNUAL REPORT ON SEXUAL ASSAULT IN THE MILITARY FISCAL YEAR 2018 3 (April 9, 2018); Dave Philipps, *'This Is Unacceptable.' Military Reports a Surge of Sexual Assaults in the Ranks*, N.Y. TIMES, May 3, 2019, at A19.

32. 38 U.S.C.A. § 1720D (a)(1) (West 2015).

33. *Sexual Assault Awareness & Prevention 2018*, U.S. DEP'T OF DEFENSE, https://dod.defense .gov/News/Special-Reports/0418_sexual-assault-awareness-and-prevention/.

34. Defense Secretary James N. Mattis, U.S. Dep't of Defense, *Memorandum for All Members of the Department of Defense/Subject: Sexual Assault Awareness and Prevention*, April 18, 2018, https:// dod.defense.gov/portals/1/features/2018/0418_SAPR/SAAP-OSD004331-18-RES.PDF; *see also* Ferdinando, *supra* note 30.

of sexual assaults in the military could be blamed on the 'hook up mentality' of the country's young people."[35] Was Secretary Mattis referencing a similar theme five years later—that sexual assault is a problem of the "ranks" to be addressed by elite military leaders? At the very least, Welsh's assertion indicates confusion. "Hooking up" refers to casual, consensual sex, and that is not the same as assault and rape. The conflation of consensual sexual activity and sexual abuse highlights why military leaders might be having problems eradicating sexual violence. Second, the implication of Welsh's remark is that Army, Navy, Air Force, and Marine leaders cannot control sexual harassment or assault in the military, in part because they are not even able to identify it properly.

All of this discussion begs the question whether the perpetrators are actually young people. Certainly, not all of them are. Lt. Col. Jeffrey Krusinski, who led the Air Force's sexual assault prevention program, was arrested for sexual assault when he was in his forties.[36] Brigadier General Bryan T. Roberts, who faced allegations of adultery and misconduct involving a physical altercation, was in his 50s.[37] Master Sgt. Brad Grimes, who was charged with several sex-related crimes, was an 18-year veteran of the Army.[38] Sgt. First Class Michael McClendon, who was accused of videotaping West Point female cadets undressing and in the showers from July 2009 to May 2012, joined the Army in 1990.[39] In 2011 Tech. Sgt. Jaime Rodriguez was 32 and a recruiter when he sent a 17-year-old recruit "lewd text messages and naked photos of himself." Seventeen other women claim he tried to initiate sexual relationships with them.[40] In sum, these are not young, inexperienced soldiers, but seasoned officers and soldiers who allegedly took advantage of their rank and positions.[41] One wonders whether military leaders understand that sexual harassment is first and foremost an abuse of institutional power—power that most young recruits don't have.

Whether military leaders understand the nature and dynamics of sex-based harassment is an important question because they retain control of sexual

---

35. Liz Halloran, *Stunned By Military Sex Scandals, Advocates Demand Changes*, NPR (May 25, 2013).

36. Jeffrey Krusinski, *Air Force Officer in Charge of Sexual Assault Prevention Program, Arrested for Alleged Sexual Assault*, Huffington Post (May 7, 2013).

37. Thom Shanker, *South Carolina: General Faces Adultery Investigation*, N.Y. Times (May 21, 2013).

38. Chris McGuiness, *Grimes Found Guilty of 2 Charges in Prostitution Court-Martial*, Killeen Daily Herald (Dec. 4, 2013); *see also* FME News Service, *Soldier Pleads Guilty in Prostitution Ring Case*, tdtnews.com (Mar. 12, 2015), http://www.tdtnews.com/news/article_db1f1984-c818-11e4 -9dfe-0f21ece9a93c.html.

39. Shanker, *supra* note 37; Barbara Starr, *Army Sergeant Accused of Videotaping Female Cadets at West Point*, CNN (May 22, 2013).

40. Sig Christiansen, *Court Told Recruiter Became a Predator*, San Antonio Express-News, Jan. 8, 2013.

41. *See* Invisible *supra* note 24 (depicting the military's failure to prevent, investigate, and properly remedy military rape by U.S. soldiers).

harassment and assault claims within the armed forces. These officers usually decide if and how allegations are charged.[42] As one commentator explained:

> If the allegation is founded (or substantiated), the accused's brigade commander has the power to act on the substantiated allegation and may use non-judicial or administrative processes or, normally through the case's referral to a higher-level commander, court-marital. Should the case reach court-martial stage, military prosecutors pursue a conviction under the applicable UCMJ articles.[43]

The 1950 *Feres* doctrine prevents the application of Title VII and tort claims in the context of military employment.[44] Therefore, if superior officers refuse to prosecute or properly discipline offenders, survivor members may find themselves without alternatives, adequate remedies, or worse—facing fierce retaliation. In sum, military criminal prosecution or commander-imposed discipline are the only remedies. The targets cannot collect personal injury damages.[45]

Sen. Kirsten Gillibrand has introduced the Military Justice Improvement Act (MJIA) multiple times.[46] This bill "would take the decision to prosecute felonies, including sexual assaults, away from commanders who are at times the very

---

42. THE UNIFORM CODE OF MILITARY JUSTICE, http://www.au.af.mil/au/awc/awcgate/ucmj.htm.

43. Julie Dickerson, *A Compensation System for Military Victims of Sexual Assault and Harassment*, 222 MIL. L. REV. 211, 216–217 (2014); *see also* Rebecca Huval, *Feres Doctrine and the Obstacles to Justice for Military Rape Victims*, PBS INDEPENDENT LENS BLOG (May 9, 2012) (noting that a military "judge could potentially be their rapist's best friend. He chooses the jury and has the power to "change the charge, reduce the sentence, or even overturn the verdict.").

44. Feres v. U.S., 71 S.Ct. 135, 146 (1950) (holding that "the Government is not liable where the injuries arise out of or are in the course of activity incident to [military] service"); Mackey v. U.S., 226 F.3d 773 (6th Cir. 2000) (finding that the *Feres* doctrine extends to intentional torts including sexual harassment); *see also* Huval, *supra* note 43.

45. Kathleen Gilberd, *Challenging Military Sexual Violence*, MILITARY LAW TASK FORCE OF THE NAT'L LAWYERS GUILD (NLG), July 2017, http://nlgmltf.org/military-law-library/publications /memos/military-sexual-violence/. The NLG advised:

> [Military survivors] may ask for corrective action such as a transfer or a removal of retaliatory actions, but not for money damages for pain and suffering. Courts seldom step in unless a service member has tried all available administrative remedies, such as an EO complaint, and judges generally defer to military discretion about personnel matters. But a court can order the military to enforce its own regulations or order it to do more than the regulations require.

Id.

46. According to a press release on her website:

> Gillibrand, Ranking Member of the Senate Armed Services Personnel Subcommittee, has introduced the *Military Justice Improvement Act* every year since 2013. The bill has been voted on twice on the floor of the Senate, winning a bipartisan majority vote both times but failing to overcome a filibuster threshold of 60 votes. Gillibrand today called for another vote on the *Military Justice Improvement Act* to hold the military accountable for sexual assault against American service members.

Press Release, With Scandal After Scandal In The Military, Gillibrand Stands With Bipartisan Group Of Senators To Demand Congress Finally Address Crisis Of Military Sexual Assault And Protect Service Members (Nov. 16, 2017).

perpetrators of the assaults, and put it in the hands of military prosecutors."[47] Critics of this legislation claim that removal from the chain of command would "undermine military readiness and unit cohesion."[48] However, by leaving these cases with those officers who may have biases or incentives not to discipline their direct reports, military leaders ignore abuses. Lory Manning, a retired Navy captain and fellow at SWAN explained, "These same leaders don't want to pass judgment on each other because they have known each other for decades in which their careers often intersected."[49]

For example, in September 2015, a female civilian reported that her boss, Air Force Col. Ronald S. Jobo, sexually assaulted her on two occasions and engaged in additional offensive conduct. Text messages, including a video of him masturbating, corroborated many of her allegations. Under military law, this type of conduct should have led to a public court-martial. Jobo would have faced "up to seven years in prison and a requirement to register as a sex offender." However, in March 2016, Lt. Gen. John F. Thompson "decided against charging Jobo with abusive sexual contact, or any crime at all. Instead, Thompson imposed what the military calls nonjudicial punishment, or discipline for minor offenses. Jobo was forced to retire and demoted one rank, to lieutenant colonel." This case did not become a matter of public record because military disciplinary actions are confidential.[50]

As with cases prompting the #MeToo movement, we might not know of this military sexual abuse epidemic were it not for stellar investigative journalism. Reporter Craig Whitlock notes, "An examination of the Jobo investigation, based in part on an internal 400-page law enforcement case file obtained by *The Washington Post*, casts doubt on the military's promises to crack down on sexual misconduct and hold commanders accountable for how they administer justice."[51] Was the Jobo case unusual? Probably not. *USA Today* reporter Tom Vanden Brook explained:

> Since 2013, military investigators have documented at least 500 cases of serious misconduct among its generals, admirals and senior civilians, almost half of those instances involving personal or ethical lapses. . . . Many cases involve sex scandals, including a promiscuous Army general who led a swinging lifestyle, another who lived rent-free in the home of a defense contractor after his affair fell apart and another who is under investigation for sending steamy Facebook messages to the wife of an enlisted soldier on his post.[52]

---

47. Rico, *supra* note 28; *see also* Thomas Gibbons-Neff, *Pentagon Misled Congress About Military's Handling of Sexual Assault Cases, Report Says*, Wash. Post (April 4, 2016).

48. Lawrence Korb, Opinion: *Time for America's Military to Face Its Own Problem of Sexual Assault*, The Hill (Nov. 3, 2017).

49. Tom Vanden Brook, *Senior Military Officials Sanctioned for More Than 500 Cases of Serious Misconduct*, USA Today (Oct. 24, 2017, updated Oct. 25, 2017).

50. Craig Whitlock, *How the Military Handles Sexual Assault Cases Behind Closed Doors*, Wash. Post (Sept. 30, 2017).

51. *Id.*

52. Vanden Brook, *supra* note 49.

This description confirms that the military sexual abuse epidemic is not simply a problem of "the 'hook up mentality' of the country's young people."[53]

Many military personnel understand the extent of the problem and that remedies for sexual abuses depend on rank. Members say, "Different spanks for different ranks."[54] According to one former Air Force prosecutor, Don Christensen, "The everyday troop is court-martialed for what a general officer is given a slap on the hand for." Christensen advised that the problems will continue until the military punishes high-ranking officers by stripping them of their retirement pay and barring them from later lucrative work with defense contractors.[55]

In March 2019, Senator Martha McSally (R-Ariz.), the first woman in the Air Force to fly in combat, revealed that she was sexually assaulted multiple times and once raped by a superior officer when serving. She did not report the abuse because she "didn't trust the system at the time."[56] Later, when McSally spoke of the abuse, she was appalled by the military's response and considered quitting the Air Force. "Like many victims, I felt like the system was raping me all over again. . . ."[57] Stacey Thompson, who was sexually assaulted in the Marines and who later founded #MetooMilitary[58] commented, "If they didn't take her [McSally] seriously, and they did not do anything about it at her level, why would we think they would have done anything about it at lower-ranking levels?"[59]

However, McSally does not endorse Gillibrand's initiative to take prosecution of such cases out of the chain of command. McSally explains, "I share the disgust of the failures of the military system and many commanders who failed in their responsibilities . . . . But it is for this very reason that we must allow—we must demand—that commanders stay at the center of the solution and live up to the moral and legal responsibilities that come with being a commander."[60]

Notes and Discussion

1. Prevalence Is the prevalence of sexual harassment in the military surprising? Explain. If there is a problem, what are the possible responses to ameliorate the environment?

2. Chain of Command Should these cases remain in the chain of command? Should military targets have access to Title VII protections? Would a military prosecutor or

53. Halloran, *supra* note 35.

54. Vanden Brook, *supra* note 49.

55. *Id.*

56. Emily Cochrane & Jennifer Steinhauer, *Senator Martha McSally Says Superior Officer in the Air Force Raped Her*, N.Y. Times, (Mar. 6, 2019).

57. *Id.*

58. #MetooMilitary, https://www.metoomilitarymvmt.org/.

59. Jennifer Steinhauer & Richard A. Oppel Jr., *Senator Martha McSally's Revelation of Assault May Reopen Debate*, N.Y. Times (Mar. 7, 2019).

60. *Id.*

even outside oversight undermine military readiness and unit cohesion? Or might such control and oversight bolster military readiness and unit cohesion?

4. Sexual Harassment in the Military — Case Law and Further Comment

Because the *Feres* doctrine disallows personal injury claims against the military, most survivors have little incentive to pursue civil claims related to their injuries. Few cases document the evolution of law regarding military sexual harassment. Some cases concern the Eighth Amendment and others focus on civil rights claims. Consider these typical military court cases. Think about whether sexual harassment case resolution should remain in the chain of command and whether military targets should have access to Title VII protections.

Becker v. Pena

107 F.3d 877 (9th Cir. 1997)

BROWNING, RYMER, and T.G. NELSON, Circuit Judges

I.

Carolyn Becker's Title VII claims were properly dismissed. Title VII protections do not extend to uniformed members of the Coast Guard. *See* Gonzalez v. Department of the Army, 718 F.2d 926, 928–29 (9th Cir. 1983).

II.

The district court lacked subject matter jurisdiction over Becker's claims under the Federal Tort Claims Act because her alleged injuries were incident to her military service. *See Feres v. United States*, 340 U.S. 135, 146 (1950). Her allegation that the defendants negligently failed to supervise the harassers "goes directly to the 'management' of the military; it calls into question basic choices about the discipline, supervision, and control of a service [member]."

While the acts of sexual harassment served no military purpose, they were incident to Becker's military service. Virtually all of the harassing conduct occurred during working hours on the Coast Guard base. Becker's harassers were predominantly superior in rank and were subject to military discipline for harassing her. *See Lutz v. Secretary of the Air Force*, 944 F.2d 1477, 1487 (9th Cir. 1991) (suggesting that an injury that arises on the job is incident to military service).

III.

Becker failed to state a Fifth Amendment claim upon which relief can be granted. She may not sue Gregory Blanford, Daniel Shipman, and James Bankson because "enlisted military personnel may not maintain a suit to recover damages from a superior officer for alleged constitutional violations." She may not sue Admiral Kramek and Secretary Pena for failing to train Coast Guard members to obey the law. *See* [*United States v. Shearer*, 473 U.S. 52, 58 (1985)](*Feres* doctrine bars suits that question the military's decisions about management and supervision). And she may not state a direct constitutional claim against the Coast Guard.

IV.

We do not reach Becker's claims under 42 U.S.C. §§ 1985(3) and 1986 because she failed to exhaust her administrative remedies. Becker admits that she has not followed the procedure for obtaining administrative relief outlined in the Military Civil Rights Manual or in the Uniform Code of Military Justice. She contends she need not exhaust these administrative remedies because her harassing supervisors denied her the opportunity for administrative redress by denying her access to the Chetco River commanding officer from July 1992 through September 1993. The Coast Guard does not dispute the impropriety of the harassing officers' conduct. However, subsequent to this period, Becker received personal counselling [sic] from Military Civil Rights Counselors/Facilitators on how to file both informal and formal discrimination complaints in accordance with the Military Civil Rights Manual. She never pursued these avenues. Nor did Becker utilize 10 U.S.C. § 938, a provision of the Uniform Code of Military Justice that enables a servicemember to complain of unredressed wrongs committed by a commanding officer to "*any* superior commissioned officer who [must] forward the complaint to the officer exercising general court-martial jurisdiction over the officer against whom it is made." (emphasis added).

We reject Becker's argument that she need not pursue her administrative remedies because they do not provide adequate relief. Although monetary damages are not available, she may be eligible for disability benefits, back pay, promotion, reinstatement, and adjustment in seniority level. We also reject Becker's contention that exhausting her administrative remedies would be futile. She has not adduced any evidence that the Coast Guard or the Department of Transportation would not fully and fairly consider her complaints.

United States v. Castillo

59 M.J. 600 (2003)[61]

DORMAN, Chief Judge:

In accordance with her pleas, the appellant was convicted at a special court-martial before military judge alone of an unauthorized absence terminated by apprehension, in violation of Article 86, Uniform Code of Military Justice, 10 U.S.C. § 886. She was awarded a bad-conduct discharge, confinement for 51 days, and reduction to pay grade E-1. The convening authority (CA) approved the sentence as adjudged.

We have examined the record of trial and conclude that the findings and the sentence, as modified herein, are correct in law and fact. Following our corrective

---

61. Sentence Adjudged 27 Feb. 2001. Decided 30 Sept. 2003. Castillo was a Lance Corporal (E-3), U.S. Marine Corps.

action, no errors remain that are materially prejudicial to the substantial rights of the appellant.

This case is now before us for a second time. On 31 July 2001, we granted relief to the appellant's assignment of error alleging that her sentence was inappropriately severe. . . . We also clearly stated that we were remanding the record of trial "to the [CA] for a new action consistent with our *decision*." *Castillo*, slip op. at 10 (emphasis added).

. . . .

Sentence Appropriateness

. . . .

The appellant stands convicted of an unauthorized absence that lasted for 366 days, an absence cut short only by the appellant's apprehension. Such an offense standing alone is a very serious breach of military discipline, and in most instances would warrant a bad-conduct discharge. The offense, however, is but one half of the equation.

The appellant enlisted in September 1997 and had not engaged in any documented misconduct prior to the commencement of her unauthorized absence in January 2001. As we noted in significant detail in our earlier opinion, the appellant's absence was mitigated by the fact that prior to her unauthorized absence she had reported intermittent incidents of sexual harassment over a period of two years. These incidents were investigated by several different investigating officers, one of who [sic] a Marine Major concluded that the appellant's allegation of an indecent assault should have been reported by the command, but was not, to the Provost Marshal's office. Additionally, the command Equal Opportunity Advisor documented the appellant's complaints detailing specific instances of sexual harassment at various times by six different senior enlisted Marines during a 23-month period. This advisor concluded that the appellant was "the victim of some very offensive behaviors." That behavior ranged from verbal harassment to sexual assault. Defense Exhibit A at 43.

As we said in our earlier opinion, "the record shows a young Marine who appeared to be performing well and who most likely would not have committed this offense, but for the depression and helplessness she felt in being periodically victimized by Marine NCOs senior to her." Slip opinion at 10. Upon reconsideration of the third assignment of error, and considering the entire record, we find that this assignment of error also has merit.

Conclusion

The findings are affirmed. With respect to the sentence, only that portion of the approved sentence as extends to confinement for 51 days and a reduction to pay grade E-1 is affirmed.

Notes and Discussion

1. *Feres v. United States* Military personnel cannot sue civilly for injuries suffered incident to military service. Does court deference to military management parallel that given to the administration of prisons? Does the deference to military management justify the denial of civil damages in all cases? More specifically, will our armed forces be less prepared for battle or attack if we allow targets of sexual harassment to sue for their injuries? Can military discipline alone curb sexual harassment in the military or does the civil court system (or Congress) need to intervene? Explain.

2. **Administrative Redress** Why might military women fail to exhaust internal administrative remedies for sexual harassment? Are the damages available to military victims the same as those available under Title VII? If not, explain the differences. Discuss the advantages and disadvantages of allowing the military justice system to impose criminal sanctions on sexual harassers.

Is it more damaging to military management to allow women to sue civilly for sexual harassment or to have them petition the United Nations for relief as one Navy rape survivor did?[62]

3. **Exit** Unlike workers who may leave (but for a variety of reasons choose not to leave or are constrained by economic necessity) the hostile work environment, prisoners and military personnel cannot walk away from an abuser and a hostile environment. Should the rules prohibiting sexual harassment in these settings be tougher given that the target is a captive? Are there other provisions that might be implemented that might address the target's inability to exit an abusive prison or military situation? How should the court have disciplined Lance Corporal Castillo for going AWOL (absent without leave)? Note the irony of subjecting Castillo to penal confinement for her attempt to escape sexual harassment.

4. **Investment and Expertise** A military commander can assess the government's investment in an accused soldier or officer when considering how to respond to a complaint. The commander can also consider how well an accused harasser performs his military duties. Should civil courts consider whether or not an accused harasser is a rainmaker for a corporation? Should they consider whether an accused doctor or professional is an expert in his field? How, if at all, is the military different from a corporate employer in this respect? Which is more important, the military justice system or the military?

5. Gender Panic, Backlash, and Responsibility in Segregated Environments — Common Themes and New Approaches

Many scholars who have examined sexual harassment in the highly regulated, and often sex-segregated, environments of prisons and the military see them as unique environments. However, Professors Martha Chamallas and Diane Mazur

---

62. *See* Amy Herdy & Miles Moffeit, *Betrayal in the Ranks*, Denv. Post, Nov. 18, 2003, at A1.

see the military, for example, as an exaggerated version of the civilian world. In her 1998 article *The New Gender Panic: Reflections on Sex Scandals and the Military*, Professor Chamallas suggests, "[M]y examination of sex regulations within the military leads me to believe that the military is a microcosm of the civilian world. The tensions and contradictions experienced more generally are clearly present in the military context, often in exaggerated form."[63]

Chamallas discusses the military sex scandals of the 1990s and the consideration of the re-segregation of women within the branches of the military. She notes, "[T]he gender panic—particularly the move to resegregate the sexes during basic training—represents a gender backlash. The unfortunate irony is that, rather than being a cure for sexual harassment, sex segregation is likely to foster and perpetuate sexual harassment."[64]

Even though Chamallas references the military sex scandals of the 1990s, one might apply her theories regarding sex-based harassment to current military issues and to civilian dynamics. Consider that Vice President Mike Pence "does not dine privately with other women or attend events with alcohol unless his wife is there."[65] About this protocol, Professor Joanna Grossman commented, "We have a president [Donald Trump] who brags about grabbing women by the pussy—and a vice president [Mike Pence] who won't even have dinner with them. These are two sides of the same coin, both reflecting the fundamentally unequal sphere working women inhabit because of male behavior."[66]

The #MeToo movement, discussed in greater detail in Chapter 10, has also prompted a so-called "backlash." Following Dr. Christine Blasey Ford's sexual assault allegation against then-Judge Brett Kavanaugh, President Trump commented, "It's a very scary time for young men in America when you can be guilty of something you may not be guilty of. This is a very difficult time. . . . In this realm, you're truly guilty until proven innocent."[67] While some people might consider the source and discount this comment, Trump may actually speak for numerous Americans.

In October 2018, *The Economist* reported poll data regarding attitudes concerning sexual harassment a year after the start of #MeToo. It found that "18% of Americans now think that false accusations of sexual assault are a bigger problem than attacks that go unreported or unpunished, compared with 13% in November last year [2017]." It also noted, however, that the National Sexual Violence Resource

---

63. 83 Minn. L. Rev. 305, 307 (1998).

64. *Id.* at 374.

65. Brooke Seipel, *Pence Jokes: My Wife Couldn't Be Here Because She Had 'Dinner Plans,'* The Hill (Mar. 1, 2017); Aaron Blake, *Mike Pence Doesn't Dine Alone with Other Women. And We're All Shocked,* Wash. Post (Mar. 30, 2017).

66. Joanna Grossman, *Vice President Pence's "Never Dine Alone with a Woman" Rule Isn't Honorable. It's Probably Illegal.,* Vox (Dec. 4, 2017).

67. Eugene Scott, *Trump Says Men Don't Feel Safe from False Persecution. That's Not a New Feeling—For Black Men,* Wash. Post (Oct. 3, 2018).

Centre calculates that only 2% to 10% of assault cases are falsely reported, while 60% of sexual assaults are not reported to police.[68] Writer Ephrat Livni suggests, "It seems that the story of #MeToo has turned into yet another opportunity for men to talk about themselves—how they've suffered as a result of accusations, or redeemed themselves and deserve our attention again, or how the world's gone mad and lost its standards, or how they are allies and not bad guys." She adds, "Whatever the response, men retain cultural dominance, so much so that a man like Kavanaugh, accused of attempted rape, can trigger fears that boys won't get to be boys anymore if women keep telling their stories."[69]

A. Gender Panic and Resegregation

Given the current climate in the wake of #MeToo, Professor Chamallas's theories about sexual harassment in the military may shed light on the continuing problems not only within the armed forces, but also in the White House and beyond.

The New Gender Panic:
Reflections on Sex Scandals and the Military
Martha Chamallas[70]

. . . .

III. Three Theoretical Frames: A Feminist Take on the Gender Panic

At its most basic, the gender panic in the military involves the interplay of three critical elements: (military) employment, sexual behavior, and gender. Structuring the topic this way suggests that it is ripe for feminist analysis and that we could learn something useful from the body of social science research on women and organizations. To begin with, there is a rich literature investigating gender dynamics in the workplace, including how the gender composition of a working group and the distribution of power within an organization can affect the incidence of gender bias and sexual harassment. Sociologists and legal academics have explored the special predicament of the "token" woman, an apt characterization of the female soldier who is still likely to find herself far outnumbered by men within an historically male-dominated environment. Additionally, perhaps no topic has generated more interest among feminist scholars than the meaning of "consent" in sexual relationships and the complexity of defining sexual harassment given the differing perspectives and social positions of the parties involved. Allegations that drill sergeants raped female recruits without resorting to actual physical force, for example, closely resemble feminist descriptions of sexual exploitation and abuse of power outside the military context.

---

68. *Measuring the #MeToo Backlash*, Economist (Oct. 10, 2018).

69. Ephrat Livni, *There's a Problem at the Heart of #MeToo—Here's How to Solve It*, Quartz (Oct. 14, 2018).

70. 83 Minn. L. Rev. 305 (1998).

In the last decade there has also been a tremendous growth in the volume and sophistication of writings about the social meaning of gender. The new gaylegal scholarship has generated deeper understandings of masculinity that can help us to dissect those aspects of military culture that operate as formidable barriers to gender integration.

. . . .

A. The Dynamics of Tokenism

Perhaps because of the volume of media attention devoted to women in the military, we may lose sight of the fact that there are still, relatively speaking, not that many women in the armed forces. Currently only about thirteen and a half percent of service personnel are women. Although this represents a dramatic increase from the two percent figure for women who served in 1972, it is still fair to characterize women's presence as "token" in the social science meaning of the term. In the sociological literature "tokenism" is used to describe the situation of a group that is dramatically under-represented in a given organizational setting. Relative numbers are important in this theory because of severe limitations on the extent to which small minority groups can influence the culture of the places where they work. As long as they are still considered oddities and outsiders, members of the token group are likely to be hampered by lack of acceptance for their individual talents. They are often looked upon as symbols of their group and socially constructed in highly predictable ways. Tokens are rarely perceived as leaders or exemplary teammates.

The point at which a group gets beyond token representation to achieve a "critical mass" will differ from context to context. However, the figure of twenty-five percent is most often cited as an indication that a given group has the ability to form alliances and coalitions and to engage in effective strategies to influence the culture of an organization. Before this point is reached, tokens are more vulnerable to gender bias, including various forms of stereotyping and typecasting.

Tokenism theory has slowly been gaining acceptance outside the academy. Most significantly, the case law under Title VII has begun to recognize the connection between tokenism and gender discrimination. In *Price Waterhouse v. Hopkins*, the United States Supreme Court acknowledged the link between tokenism and the prevalence of stereotyping which prevented a talented woman from being made partner in a large accounting firm. In the influential case of *Robinson v. Jacksonville Shipyards, Inc.*, a trial court credited the testimony of a social psychologist who took the position that tokenism fostered a virulent form of sexual harassment of blue collar women. At the shipyards, the very presence of the token women posed a challenge to the hyper-masculine working environment.

As an employer of women, the military is poised to go beyond tokenism, at least in some of the services. What happens in the next decade could thus have a crucial long-term impact on women's status in the military. . . . Even more so than most employers, the military makes deliberate decisions about how many women it intends to recruit. The representation of women thus depends not only on market forces and women's preferences, but on defined military policy. Most importantly, each service has a policy on "accessions" for female and male recruits, setting numerical goals for the sexes in the upcoming year. . . .

. . . .

The low representation of women in the armed forces makes a considerable difference in the everyday life of soldiers. It manifests itself first in basic training. The advisory report was quick to put the issue of gender-integrated training "in perspective" by noting that at the present time, despite public perception, only a minority of male recruits routinely train with women in basic training. . . . Except for the Marines, this is not a result of a restrictive formal policy, but stems solely from the fact that there are not enough women to integrate every unit, particularly if the service decides to cluster women recruits rather than widely disperse them on a random basis.

Social scientists studying civilian workplaces have stressed that the existence and effects of tokenism must also be assessed at the level of the working group, i.e., the group of individuals who have face-to-face daily interaction. Even when the overall representation of women in a large organization increases, it may have little effect on the personal interactions of the workers if the women are so dispersed that their presence has little chance to affect the culture of the working group. The relative number of women in the military is important under tokenism theory, not primarily because it represents the number of "opportunities" available to women, but because it is a proxy for determining the "male" or "gender-integrated" character of the working environment.

Advocates for gender-integrated training have asserted that there is an inverse relationship between the level of gender-integration and the level of sexual harassment. . . .

Tokenism theory thus directly contradicts the traditional view that separating the sexes is a cure for sexual harassment. Because tokenism theory starts from the premise that the character of the working culture affects the way people behave and interact, it posits that changing the demographics of a group may be the surest way to change the culture, and ultimately the behavior of the majority in the group. It also rejects the more biologically-premised view that men will inevitably be tempted to abuse women, unless their access to women is restricted. For feminists, tokenism theory offers the promise of integration and equal access, without having to endure harassment and sexual abuse as the price of admission.

Another aspect of tokenism theory that seems particularly relevant to the current gender panic is its focus on the gender composition of the group that makes decisions. In examining the informal structures of an organization, sociologists have looked to see *who* exercises power, in particular whether any (and how many) of the token group are also located in supervisory or leadership positions. . . . Some women leaders do bring new perspectives into their decisionmaking and may be more likely to detect subtle, but harmful, forms of gender bias. Female leaders can also serve as role models for both males and females under their supervision.

Theorists have also noted that as more women are promoted to leadership roles, their authority seems more "natural."

. . . .

Overall, the most significant insight to import from tokenism theory into the military context is its questioning of the impulse to segregate or exclude women as a long-term strategy to cut down on the incidence of sexual harassment. The research on women and organizations suggests that coercive behavior such as sexual harassment has a structural as well as a moral dimension. Tokenism theory points to the gender demographics and distribution of power within an organization for keys to understanding how an organization is likely to respond to sexual harassment and how a change in relative numbers of men and women can bring about a change in the working environment. . . .

B. Redefinitions of Consent

The conceptual frame that unites the recent scandals in the military is that they all are tied to sex. In one sense, of course, this is unremarkable. Because the conduct that gave rise to the high profile cases most often involved prohibited sexual intercourse, it is not surprising that the furor over the incidents is referred to as a "sex scandal." However, even labeling the controversy in this way is quite telling and presupposes that the problem is really about sex, rather than, for example, about the abuse of power, the military's policies on women, or the social construction of gender. The label of "sex" masks a significant, ongoing debate between traditionalist and feminist cultural forces over where to draw the line between permissible, private sexual conduct on the one hand, and impermissible sexual exploitation on the other.

Currently, the military's prohibitions on sexual conduct are a strange amalgam of traditional and feminist viewpoints. The military's rules against adultery, for example, seem to emanate from an earlier era when marriage was regarded as the sole demarcation line separating legitimate from illicit sex. These traditionalist prohibitions contrast with the military's definition of "constructive force" used in rape prosecutions, that finds philosophical support in contemporary feminist conceptions of "consent" and "coercion." Finally, the various anti-fraternization rules prohibiting consensual sex under a variety of circumstances have differed so greatly among the services that it is impossible yet to link them to any specific viewpoint or to trace a logic — traditionalist, feminist, or otherwise — behind their enforcement.

. . . .

2. Constructive Force

. . . .

The recent court-martial of Staff Sergeant Delmar Simpson has highlighted the contested nature of the concept of consent.[71] Simpson was charged under Article 120

---

71. Chamallas explains:
   The most visible of the perpetrators was Staff Sergeant Delmar Simpson, who was convicted in April 1997 of raping six female recruits under his command. The charges of

of the Uniform Code of Military Justice, the rape provision, which requires proof that the accused committed sexual intercourse "by force and without consent" of the victim. As mentioned earlier, the rape charges against Simpson were based on his use of "constructive force." Simpson's lawyer argued that because he did not use a weapon, exert physical force or specifically threaten to use physical force, the charges should be dismissed. The defense also stressed that some of the trainees who submitted to Simpson's advances offered no physical or verbal resistance to his orders. The trial judge rejected Simpson's restrictive definition of constructive force, however, and sent the case to the jury to decide whether Simpson's conduct constituted coercion.

As the trial judge explained it, the doctrine of "constructive force" was broad enough to cover cases in which a drill sergeant abuses his authority to compel unwilling recruits to give in to sexual demands, even in the absence of specific threats or a showing of force. The judge stressed that "drill sergeants commanded so much authority over trainees—ordering them where to eat and sleep and how to act—that they were like parents" and that recruits were "conditioned to follow drill sergeants' orders."[165] Because of the extraordinary power that drill sergeants had over recruits, the court ruled that they did not need to use a weapon or threaten the trainees with harm to fit the definition of "constructive force." Instead, the jury was to find Simpson guilty if it found that Simpson's actions created "a reasonable belief in the victim's mind that death or physical injury would be inflicted on her and resistance is futile."

The trial judge's definition of "constructive force" followed a line of military cases in which rape convictions have been obtained even though the victims offered no physical resistance and the accused made no specific threats of physical harm. The requisite "force" and "lack of consent" have been found in the victim's passive acquiescence and unwelcoming behavior when ordered to submit to sexual intercourse by a superior officer. In one important case,[168] for example, a sergeant who supervised a female trainee during basic training was convicted of rape when

---

rape were based on Simpson's use of "constructive force" to compel the women to submit to have sex with him. As a drill sergeant, Simpson had the authority to control the daily lives of the trainees and the case against him rested on abuse of that authority. According to the testimony of the recruits, Simpson engaged in such coercive conduct as ordering a recruit to disrobe in front of him, requiring a woman to report to his office wearing no underwear, and forcing a woman to trade sex as payback for Simpson's helping her avoid punishment for a disciplinary infraction. The military jury found Simpson guilty of eighteen rape charges. He was sentenced to twenty-five years imprisonment. Chamallas, *supra* note 70, at 310–11.

165. ... The judge's view of the extraordinary power of drill sergeants was supported by the testimony of a private who explained why she did not resist Simpson: "I just didn't feel like I had a choice. ... He's a drill sergeant. ... He was supposed to know what's best for me." Jackie Spinner, *Three More Soldiers Testify Against Sergeant; Women Say They Had No Choice but to Submit*, WASH. POST (Apr. 18, 1997), at B3.

168. *See* United States v. Clark, 35 M.J. 432 (C.M.A. 1992).

he ordered the trainee to follow him to an isolated shed, grabbed and kissed her and ordered her to take off her clothes. The court found the requisite force in the act of penetration itself, even though the trainee had not expressly said "no," but manifested her lack of consent principally by not returning the kiss and stiffening her body. In deciding that the evidence was sufficient to sustain a conviction, the court underscored "the unique situation of dominance and control presented by appellant's superior rank and position." In such cases, the label of "constructive force" allows the fact finder to take a "totality of the circumstances" approach, permitting consideration of all individual and social factors relevant to a finding of coercion. This approach lessens the danger that the victim's failure to offer physical or verbal resistance will be seized upon as the determinative factor, with the result that sexual aggression may not be labeled rape simply because the victim's passivity gave the accused no reason to use overpowering force to accomplish his objectives.

The interpretation of "constructive force" used in Simpson's court-martial resembles feminist definitions of consent and the standard of unwelcomeness used in sexual harassment cases. The emphasis is on abuse of power, stressing the inequality in the relationship between drill sergeant and recruit. It is also noteworthy that, similar to the plight of workers who are forced to have sex with their boss to keep their job, the recruits in the Simpson case likely feared that their military careers would be jeopardized if they resisted. In this respect, the drill sergeant represents a particularly powerful kind of supervisor, one who has the ability to affect a recruit's personal freedom as well as her job security. The Simpson court-martial also was marked by close consideration of the context in which the sexual conduct took place, permitting the jury to take into account all the circumstances in making its determination of coercion. They presumably were free to take into account the recruit's fear relating to her status in the military as well as her fear of imminent physical harm. Feminists have long advocated such a contextual approach in making determinations of consent, particularly by insisting that the absence of physical or even verbal resistance on the part of the victim should not be used as a litmus test in all cases.

. . . If there is no civilian analogue to the drill sergeant, no employment supervisor who commands the kind of intimidating authority that was wielded by Simpson, it may be pointless to compare the military's application of "constructive force" doctrine to standards used in civilian rape trials. However, I do think it is important to reflect on the fact that Simpson received a long prison term for conduct that might not have produced as readily a conviction in a civilian prosecution. I have little doubt, however, that his conduct constituted sexual harassment and would have subjected him to civil liability if his actions were covered under Title VII. That he faced criminal charges in the military demonstrates the degree to which new definitions of consent have influenced military justice and marks a departure from traditional criminal law.

. . . .

4. The Need for Reconceptualization

. . . .

I endorse the willingness of military judges to recognize that officers are in a position to exercise "constructive force" to pressure those under their command to submit to sex against their will. Victims should not be required to offer resistance in every case. Nor should the offender escape punishment simply because he does not resort to physical force or explicit threats of physical force. The recent gender panic, however, does make me wonder whether the prison term of twenty-five years meted out to Staff Sergeant Delmar Simpson may be too harsh, particularly when we compare his treatment to similarly situated offenders outside the military or to more highly-ranked offenders within the military. Most significantly, because military defendants may not bring civil rights claims for racial discrimination, there is insufficient assurance that the courts-martial of Simpson . . . [was] not tainted by racial bias. The lack of availability of civil rights suits in the military context means that we lose the valuable opportunity of having a jury decide claims of gender and race discrimination under a preponderance of the evidence standard. Such civil rights suits have the advantage of allowing vindication of plaintiffs' rights without sending offenders to jail. Particularly in the highly contested area of the legal regulation of sexual conduct, such a compromise is of great utility.

. . . .

C. The Social Meaning of Gender

There is a widespread belief that the military is quintessentially a "male" institution and that it is unrealistic to expect that changes relating to gender in the larger society will necessarily penetrate this last bastion of male supremacy. Given that women have now secured a presence in the military, at least comparable to their representation in corporate board rooms and other male-dominated sectors, it is time to look more closely at what we mean by the "maleness" of the military and how that might affect the specific policy issues we have been addressing. The recent scholarship on gender and the military has focused on *military culture* as the term that best conveys the complex of attitudes, daily interactions and institutional structures that can give us a clue as to why the military might be so resistant to women and so fearful of feminization.

An eloquent voice in the literature is that of Kenneth Karst, who regards the military as an important site for the construction of masculinity. In his view, the military is "male" not only because it contains eighty-five percent men and has been even more intensely male-dominated for its entire history. The "maleness" of the military also derives importantly from its capacity to function as a symbol of what it means to be a man, that is, to produce and reproduce meanings of masculinity. In his words: "Masculinity is traditionally defined around the idea of power; the armed forces are the nation's preeminent symbol of power; and not incidentally, 'the Marines are looking for a few good men.' The symbolism is not a side effect; it is the main point."

The bad news for women is that many contemporary theorists tell us that masculinity is often defined through opposition — that we can best tell what is masculine by what is not feminine. Simone de Beauvoir developed the concept of the "other" in *The Second Sex*, many feminist theorists have approached gender as a socially constructed concept that tells us more about dominant views of masculinity than about the nature of women. Political theorist Sally Kenney explains that "[m]en are defined and define themselves in opposition to a set of categories assigned to women, usually whatever qualities or characteristics are less valued for the fully human, rational, creative or competent." This point should be distinguished from the more traditional view that regards men and women as different and complementary. The observation made by Karst and others is that masculinity as an identity is often built around the exclusion (and subordination) of women and that "gender, unlike sex, is not found in nature, but created and understood through representation."

This view of the construction of masculinity as an identity constructed in opposition to femininity is very much related to a central theme in recent gaylegal and feminist theory, namely, the theme of gender polarity. Scholars such as Sandra Bem have argued that an important feature of the oppression of women and sexual minorities is the cultural tendency to superimpose a male/female dichotomy onto virtually every aspect of social life, from the clothes we wear, to the products we buy, to the way we express emotions and sexual desire. Masculinity and femininity have been so thoroughly constructed as opposites (as in the "opposite sex") that we often fail to see how individuals fall on a continuum of personal styles, sexual orientations, and behavioral traits and instead expect people to follow "mutually exclusive scripts for being male and female." Perhaps most importantly, people who are seen as deviating from the gender script — notably, gay men and lesbians — are regarded as problematic and disruptive of good order.

. . . .

Oncale is a threshold opinion that challenges the conventional wisdom about sexual harassment, without endorsing a coherent theory about its nature or origin. It is significant that the Court seemed to embrace the feminist position that sexual harassment is not necessarily about sexual desire and may stem from hostility rather than attraction. But not surprisingly given the procedural posture of the case, the Court did not dwell on the power dynamics that might have been at play in the very case before it. There was no discussion of why the men on the oil rig might have singled out Oncale for hostile treatment or what function the harassment performed in that particular all-male culture. Most importantly, the Court did not explain how male-on-male harassment might be regarded as sex-based discrimination when it seemed highly unlikely that a female roustabout would have been welcomed in such an environment. The Court enlarged the image of sexual harassment beyond opposite-sex harassment, but did not speculate on how this expanded concept might change our understanding of what is *sexual* conduct. In other words, *Oncale* provides no theory of sexuality or sexual aggression to supplant traditional notions of sexuality such as sexual desire and attraction.

A cogent statement of such a theory can be found in an amicus brief in *Oncale* authored by Catharine MacKinnon on behalf of groups of male victims of rape and sexual abuse and profeminist men's organizations. In the brief, MacKinnon elaborates on her dominance theory of sexual harassment and gives us new insight into the power dynamics behind sexualized aggression. MacKinnon starts out by observing that men are most often raped by other men when there are no women around, "in prisons, in confined and isolated work sites, in men's schools and colleges, in the military, in athletics, in fraternities." It is important to recognize that MacKinnon would classify these rapes as "sexual" even though the rapists regard themselves as heterosexual and are not motivated by sexual desire. In other words, that the rapes are "power rapes" does not mean that they are not also sexual.

. . . .

Conclusion

. . . .

. . . The three theoretical frameworks I have used to deconstruct the recent gender panic (tokenism, consent, and the social construction of gender) point to organizational structure and culture, rather than to biology, for clues to understanding the heated controversies relating to gender and the military that have absorbed the nation in the past year. If, as I suggest, the military is a microcosm of larger society, it is not surprising that there is a struggle over where to draw the line between permissible and impermissible sexual conduct under military law, given the contest between traditional and feminist viewpoints in the civilian world.

. . . .

Additionally, the recent courts-martial for sexual misconduct and prosecutions for consensual sex demonstrate a need to develop a new conception of sexual ethics in the military. In my view, the guideposts for such a reconceptualization should be principles of consent and gender equality, rather than traditional notions of sexual morality. The refinement of the "constructive force" doctrine to prevent recruits from being pressured to have sex with drill instructors against their will is important because it acknowledges the importance of power differentials, of context, and of the perspective of rape victims. However, particularly with respect to enforcement of its policy against sexual harassment, the military's response is currently limited by the ban against filing anti-discrimination civil suits. The use of criminal sanctions, particularly long prison terms, is too blunt a tool to control all forms of sexual misconduct. It can backfire and deter even-handed enforcement of the law.

. . . .

Notes and Discussion

1. Segregation and the Solution of Exclusion Is sex segregation an appropriate response to sexual harassment? Is it an appropriate response to the fear of a false allegation? Should congressional leaders conclude from the pervasiveness of sexual harassment in the military that the women do not belong in the institution? If we no longer question whether women belong in the workplace, is it inappropriate to question whether women belong in the military? Or is the military distinguishable from the civil workplace?

2. **Gender Panic** Is there a gender panic in today's culture? Explain. What is the appropriate response to this phenomenon when it occurs? How should military personnel deal with this problem?

3. **Intersectionality** Is it possible that race influences the redress of sexual harassment allegations in the military? Explain.

4. **Tokenism** According to Chamallas, how does tokenism affect the position of women in the military? How do the *Price Waterhouse* and *Jacksonville Shipyards* cases help explain the effect of tokenism in the military? What did Chamallas propose as the solution for the problem of tokenism?

Arguably, tokenism is still a problem in military ranks. Today, women comprise 16% of enlisted forces throughout the military and 18% of the officer corps. Women still make up less than 25% of Navy and Air Force enlisted personnel, less than 20% of the Army, and only about 10% of Marines.[72]

Is tokenism a problem in civilian contexts? Explain.

5. **The Combat Exclusion** In 2013, Defense Secretary Leon Panetta ordered the military to allow women to serve in combat positions. The Marine Corps applied for an exemption that then-Defense Secretary Ash Carter denied in late 2015.

However, former Defense Secretary James Mattis gave "a dim view of females serving in infantry jobs, telling Virginia Military Institute students that the jury is out on whether women can succeed in combat." He is reported to have "likened the issue to having someone break into your house and having to decide 'who grabs the baseball bat' to protect the children and 'who reaches for the phone to call 911.' He didn't offer suggestions on what the answer would be."[73] Following Secretary Mattis's criticism of Trump's foreign policy, President Trump forced Mattis's resignation.[74] President Trump has not named a permanent successor so the future of women in combat, and the military more generally, remains unclear. Was the combat exclusion a good idea? Explain.

6. **Consent and "Constructive Force"** Is the concept of "constructive force" useful in sexual harassment cases? Was it an accurate descriptor as used in the Simpson court-martial? In other words, did Simpson use something related to force to gain

---

72. George M. Reynolds & Amanda Shendruk, *Demographics of the U.S. Military*, COUNCIL ON FOREIGN RELATIONS (April 24, 2018), https://www.cfr.org/article/demographics-us-military.

73. Lolita C. Baldor, AP, *Mattis: Jury Is Out on Women Succeeding in Combat Jobs*, MILITARY TIMES (Sept. 25, 2018).

74. Idrees Ali & Steve Holland, *Trump, Annoyed by Resignation Letter, Pushes Out Mattis Early*, REUTERS (Dec. 23, 2018).

sexual access to his trainees or did he simply use his military authority? Why might military officials want to promote the concept of constructive force?

Did Chamallas set military women up for trials of their conduct when she suggested that "[v]ictims should not be required to offer resistance in every case"?

7. Military Penalties Are some military penalties for sexual harassment too harsh? Did Chamallas draw an effective comparison between criminal penalties for rape and military penalties for sexual harassment? Explain.

8. Gender Polarity Does gender polarity pose a problem for military women as Chamallas suggested? Is Chamallas correct that "[by] denying the possibility that men in the unit may have sexual contact, all problematic aspects of managing sexuality get mapped onto women"? Is the sexual abuse of men invisible in our culture and particularly in the military? Might information concerning the sexual abuse of men in prisons explain same-sex sexual harassment more generally?

B. Accepting Not Blame But Responsibility

In contrast to Professor Chamallas, Professor Diane Mazur challenges whether women are served by a conception that their "agency" is only "partial." In her article, *Women, Responsibility, and the Military,* Mazur explores "responsibility" in the context of sexual harassment and assault in the military. Her unique point is that an acknowledgement of responsibility, a context-influenced factor especially important in the military, may empower women. Consider whether, as part of the #MeToo movement, everyone must all share responsibility whenever possible.

Women, Responsibility, and the Military

Diane H. Mazur[75]

. . . .

A number of writers have considered the dilemma that victimization and responsibility create for women, and they have generally relied on the theory of "partial agency" in resolving the conflict.[1] Agency is a broad concept that encompasses an individual's capacity for independent decision-making and ability to choose, to refuse, and to consent—essentially all the personal ingredients required for the exercise of responsibility. For women, however, agency "is necessarily partial or

---

75. 74 NOTRE DAME L. REV. 1 (1998)

1. *See* Kathryn Abrams, *Complex Claimants and Reductive Moral Judgments: New Patterns in the Search for Equality,* 57 U. PITT. L. REV. 337, 348–50, 361 (1996) [hereinafter Abrams, *Complex Claimants*]; Kathryn Abrams, *Sex Wars Redux: Agency and Coercion in Feminist Legal Theory,* 95 COLUM. L. REV. 304, 324–29, 343–46 (1995) [hereinafter Abrams, *Sex Wars Redux*]; . . . Martha R. Mahoney, *Exit: Power and the Idea of Leaving in Love, Work, and the Confirmation Hearings,* 65 S. CAL. L. REV. 1283, 1305–18 (1992). . . . *But see* Sherry Young, *Getting to Yes: The Case Against Banning Consensual Relationships in Higher Education,* 4 AM. U. J. GENDER & L. 269, 292–301 (1996) (criticizing characterization of women as lacking in agency).

constrained" because women "are limited by structures or relationships of oppression." "It is remarkably difficult, in the face of contemporary findings on rape, sexual harassment, and the wage gap or work/family conflict, to conclude that women enjoy, and should be represented by feminists as enjoying, uncompromised powers of self-determination."

. . . .

. . . What kind of responsibility does partial agency give to, or take from, women? Does partial agency only establish that women are not responsible for the behavior of men, or does it also suggest women are unable to take the responsibility necessary to improve their own lives?

There may be no one answer to these questions that applies to all women under all circumstances. Legal scholarship has examined partial agency largely in generalities; little attention has been paid to its application in the context of any specific institution. This Article takes that step and will test the productiveness of describing women as limited agents in the context of the United States military.

. . . If the notion of partial agency could be effective in advancing the status of military women, it would probably also advance the interests of women more generally. If, however, the notion of partial agency would work to the detriment of military women, we should at least reconsider the theory's general utility.

. . . .

I. Women's Agency in the Military

. . . .

. . . Feminist scholars have failed to examine in any specific sense the responsibilities that women accept as part of the military institution. "To the degree that servicewomen are discussed by feminists, they are characterized primarily as victims." But this sole focus on women's victimization necessarily results in a restricted view of women's agency. This view assumes that the only relevant forms of agency are those acts of resistance women take in response to sexually oppressive behavior, ignoring entirely women's agency in relation to their military responsibilities. The full scope of women's agency is far broader than just women's interaction with men, and should also include women's agency as part of the military institution they serve.

. . . [Mazur discusses the responsible role of women in missile launch crews.]

It is probably very fortunate that missile launch crews were integrated to include women twenty years ago [~1978], because I have doubts that it would happen today. The crisis-level of attention currently given to issues of sexual misconduct in the military has created an atmosphere making it less likely, ironically, that women's military responsibilities would be expanded. Feminists have taken positions on behalf of servicewomen that sound very much like partial agency, which, in the context of the military, may be counterproductive in the long-term.

. . . .

These descriptions of limited or partial agency are not at all new; they have been raised before on behalf of civilian women in contending that the law of sexual harassment should reflect the perspective of the reasonable (female) victim, not the offending (male) harasser. What is new is the suggestion in this Article that descriptions of women as partial agents with respect to sexually oppressive behavior may be so fundamentally inconsistent with the agency requirements of a particular occupation that they effectively exclude women from participation.

. . . .

. . . Unlike the stereotypical view of military discipline that many hold—unquestioned obedience achieved through coercion and retaliation—safety in military technology, particularly nuclear weaponry, requires decentralized authority and decision-making. Even the lowest-ranking individual involved has the authority to challenge and overrule superiors in the interests of safety.

Reliance on the judgment of lower-ranking servicemembers plays a necessary role in the concept of "redundancy," one of the most important factors in nuclear safety. Redundancy in either personnel or technology can increase overall safety even if individual components of the system are less than perfectly reliable. . . .

. . . .

Once a [missile] launch procedure begins, the only thing that will prevent an accidental, unauthorized, or mistaken use of nuclear weapons is the independent judgment and agency of an individual crew member. There is no provision for any partial agency on the part of a woman missileer whose partner is a man.[35]

II. Women's Agency and Sexual Misconduct

How close is the comparison between women's agency with respect to military responsibility and women's agency with respect to sexual misconduct? . . . We assume that women have complete capacity to consent in contract, absent extraordinary disparity in power, but question whether women exercise full agency in matters of sexual consent. We recognize that women's equal responsibility for the burdens of military service is a prerequisite for equal citizenship, but question whether women exercise full agency in response to breaches of military law.

Women's agency in response to sexually oppressive behavior is an extremely sensitive issue. To many feminists, agency leads to an assignment of responsibility, and

---

35. . . . In comparison to the Vietnam War era, military women are now more often in a position to commit war crimes. If they are ordered by male superiors to commit war crimes, will we excuse them on the basis of their limited agency with respect to men?

Servicemembers have an obligation to disobey illegal orders from superiors despite the power and authority conferred by higher rank. "They must learn to follow orders yet retain sufficient autonomy to refuse illegal orders. . . ." JAMES H. TONER, TRUE FAITH AND ALLEGIANCE: THE BURDEN OF MILITARY ETHICS 46 (1995). "No one can escape the dilemmas, whether he be a four-star general or a rifleman, a man or a woman." James Glover, *A Soldier and His Conscience, in* THE PARAMETERS OF MILITARY ETHICS 143, 143 (Lloyd J. Matthews & Dale E. Brown eds., 1989).

responsibility then leads to an assignment of blame. As a result, if women are characterized as having anything more than partial agency, they are left open to charges that they are somehow at fault for men's conduct. Agency, however, need not lead inevitably to blame. Servicemembers with nuclear duties, for example, are asked to take responsibility for the misconduct of others and respond in a way that will ultimately improve safety. Taking this responsibility for reducing risk to themselves and others, however, does not mean that they are at fault in any way for the original misconduct.

. . . .

I do not mean to suggest that an emphasis on women's partial agency is never appropriate or that women are never limited by oppressive circumstances in the choices they have available to them. A more specific analysis of women's agency in response to sexual oppression, however, might identify those circumstances in which it is both reasonable and necessary for the law to expect women to exercise greater agency.

A. Avoiding the Extremes of Agency Theory

. . . .

Treating responsibility not as blame but as the ability to respond—that is the key to characterizing the law of sexual harassment in a way that is constructive for women. But the temptation toward the categorical position seems irresistible, arising from an enormous reluctance to evaluate women's behavior at all. Suggesting that women have choices in how they respond to sexual harassment will inevitably lead to judgments of "bad" choices as well as "good" choices. Scholarship on sexual harassment, therefore, tends to minimize agency in an attempt to shield women's behavior from the risk of unfair review.

. . . In the context of sexual harassment, women could potentially take responsibility to confront and object to the behavior, or to report to higher authority the misconduct they are unable to control. Once again, I am not suggesting that women are responsible for, or are at fault for, men's behavior—but they could potentially take responsibility for their own behavior in responding to misconduct in a constructive way. Whether the law of sexual harassment should encourage such constructive responses is a question that has not yet been answered.

Most writers in the field, however, prevent the question from being asked at all. With consensual misconduct, it is easier to eliminate the issue by simply declaring that "there is no such thing" as a consensual relationship under circumstances of inequality.[49] With sexual harassment, a woman acts reasonably even though she does

---

49. *See* Susan Estrich, *Sex at Work*, 43 STAN. L. REV. 813, 831 (1991) ("The more radical response to this argument is that there is no such thing as truly 'welcome' sex between a male boss and a female employee who needs her job.").

not challenge, object to, or complain about misconduct, because it is possible she could lose her job if she refuses to be a compliant victim. Both of these assumptions, although they carry some degree of truth, are "conversation stoppers." They leave no room for rational analysis of factual circumstances and no room for discussion of whether different assumptions might lead to a more effective remedy. Although, for example, there may be a possibility a woman could be fired for confronting harassment, there is almost a certainty the harassment will not end until she does confront it.

. . . .

B. Women's Agency and the Definition of "Welcomeness" in Sexual Harassment Law

. . . .

. . . Interestingly, critiques of women's agency and critiques of the welcomeness requirement echo one another in that both characterize women as diminished or limited in their capacity for responsible choice. If we assume that women are limited in their capacity to respond constructively to sexual oppression, then we never have to consider what a constructive response might be and whether the law should encourage it. If we assume that women are incapable of contributing to an unprofessional atmosphere of sexual interaction in the workplace, then we never have to consider whether their behavior is ever counterproductive for the advancement of women and whether the law should discourage it.

Once again, it all comes back to how one views the concept of responsibility. Critics of the current state of sexual harassment law believe that judicial scrutiny of welcomeness implies that women are ultimately responsible for men's misconduct. "[I]n making the determination of the harassment of women dependent upon the extent of 'sexually provocative' behavior by women, the Court adopts a rule which holds women responsible for their own torment." But this criticism is overstated. Women are responsible for their own conduct, not men's conduct. If sexual harassment law denies some women a remedy, it does not do so because these women are base, undeserving of human decency, or unworthy of respect. It does not do so because some women deserve in any way to be harassed. Properly applied, it should deny a remedy only if women's conduct is counterproductive to the goal of improving the status of women in the workplace.

. . . .

. . . I am suggesting that we must consider whether it is constructive to assume, with respect to the element of welcomeness, that women are incapable of contributing to a sexualized environment. We must similarly consider whether it is constructive to assume, with respect to sexual harassment, that women are incapable of responding to inappropriate conduct in a responsible manner. It is possible that an expectation of diminished capacity ultimately works more to the detriment than to the benefit of all women.

C. The Tentativeness and Timidity of Partial Agency

. . . .

The theory of partial agency confronts strategic assumptions with facts and specificity. It searches out specific "incidents of self-direction"—acts of agency—"highlighting the ways in which many oppressed women express resistance." In identifying particular acts of agency that women choose under oppressive circumstances, the approach of partial agency concedes, even celebrates, that some capacity for choice exists. Women are characterized as "neither wholly empowered, nor wholly incapacitated, in those contexts where they are targets of sexualized conduct." Partial agency therefore runs counter to the impulse of pure dominance theorists to conceal facts demonstrating that agency exists and therefore avoid judgment on whether it was exercised reasonably.

Partial agency's emphasis on factual context rather than generality can only be a positive for women. It opens discussion of what—exactly what—is reasonable to expect from women functioning under oppressive circumstances. It also forces an examination of the relationship between reasonableness and constructiveness, which is another way of describing responsibility. Even if a legal standard accurately measures what is reasonable, or prevalent, or expected in the behavior of women, we should then ask whether what is reasonable is also constructive. "Reasonable" conduct that is counterproductive to the goal of improving the status of women may not be responsible conduct if we treat responsibility not as blame but as the ability to respond.

With sexual harassment, the fundamental agency question is whether it is reasonable to expect women to express unwelcomeness directly by either objecting to offensive conduct or by reporting conduct they cannot control to higher authority. The issue directly affects the outcome of sexual harassment litigation, as courts may require, or at least consider, evidence of verbal confrontation in deciding whether workplace conduct was welcome.

. . . .

Law has the potential to be "a system of incentives for encouraging socially optimal behavior." It can balance short-term expedience with long-term benefit and encourage conduct—even if it is not the easiest, most risk-free choice at the time—that ultimately works to reduce the need for legal intervention. There is a justifiable reluctance to expect more from women under oppressive circumstances, and the suggestion that women should respond more constructively can turn into "blaming the victim" in an instant. But we do women no favors if we are afraid to encourage the behavior necessary to achieve workplace equality.

I strongly disagree with the assumption that individual confrontation of sexual harassment does little to reduce its frequency. It may be easier to assume that women's agency is ineffective than to accept the consequences of its effectiveness. But in the long term, we cannot continue to work at cross-purposes by excusing women from exercising responsibility in response to sexual oppression. Women can, and should, take responsibility—defined not as blame, but as the ability to respond—in controlling inappropriate behavior in the workplace.

III. A New Standard of Responsibility

How should the law measure what is a responsible, rather than a merely reasonable, response to sexually oppressive behavior? The first mistake would be to assume that the answer would be the same for all women, under all circumstances. This was the promise of partial agency; it could have highlighted specific factual circumstances that increased or decreased capacity for agency. Rather than risking judgment of some women, however, partial agency ultimately assigned a similarly limited agency to all women.

. . . .

Feminists have expressed concern that the "reasonable woman" standard may be built on the skewed experiences of white, straight, class-privileged professional women. The worry is that this essentialist picture erases the perspectives of those who fail to fit the mold, but the danger in the agency context may be something greater. If characterizations of diminished agency are written to fit a narrow slice of professional women who see themselves as having a particularly limited capacity to respond constructively to sexual misconduct, then the bulk of women may be disadvantaged as a result. Not only are the specific facts that make their perspectives distinctive eliminated, but the generalities substituted for them are at odds with the agency they are otherwise expected to exercise.

. . . .

B. Reconciling Women's Different Agencies

For the most part, anti-essentialism has failed to move beyond the most superficial assertions of relevant difference. Factual complexity is hidden rather than explored; we concede that "of course, women differ from one another," but then retreat from any analysis of how that difference might make some legal standards counterproductive for some or even most women. A greater attention to the factual complexity of life experience would help to fill out the standard anti-essentialist distinctions of race, class, and sexual orientation.

. . . .

These approaches to limited agency are right in that they maintain a primary focus on men, who are currently the primary source of misconduct in either example. These approaches to limited agency, however, are wrong in that they isolate a limited area of agency for disparate treatment—women's agency with respect to the sexual misconduct of men. This disparate treatment can be seen from two perspectives. First, women are assumed to exercise a generally full and independent agency with respect to public-sphere activities and responsibilities, but not with respect to sexual activities and responsibilities. Second, women are assumed to exercise a generally full and independent agency even under conditions of inequality, but not under conditions of inequality between women and men. Taken together, the central assumption of limited agency is that women have a diminished capacity to advance their own interests in interactions with men when the subject is related to sex.

. . . .

But it would be just as inaccurate to assume that women enjoy unrestricted agency—obviously we have yet to reach the day in which women exercise equal influence and control, particularly in historically male-dominated institutions. The task, then, is to devise a standard that realistically reflects the agency that women do have, without unnecessarily diminishing that agency in a way that is counter-productive to women's advancement. . . . The most productive approach would take into account the surrounding factual context and attempt to make consistent the different agencies that women exercise; it would never validate behavior that con-tributes to women's inequality in the long term.

Recall that responsibility is best viewed not as blame, but as the ability to respond in a constructive manner—with constructiveness measured by benefit to the actor who takes responsibility for her own conduct, not the conduct of others. Ability to respond to workplace misconduct of any variety is usually restricted by one's status or authority in the workplace, and so any fair standard concerning sexual misconduct would take into account that status and authority. To the extent that a legal standard required that a woman's behavior in response to sexual misconduct be in some respect reasonable, reasonableness would be evaluated in the context of a woman's general workplace duty and authority.

Proof of welcomeness issues in sexual harassment cases can serve as an illus-tration. Rather than excusing all women from demonstrating unwelcomeness by direct objection or report because some women may not feel comfortable doing so, a court would inquire into the plaintiff's general workplace duty and authority. Does the plaintiff, for example, have as a part of her duties a particular responsibil-ity to control and educate others concerning inappropriate sexual conduct in the workplace? Does her general authority give her the latitude to confront misconduct and mistakes concerning work-related tasks? If a plaintiff has neither the duty nor the authority to ever confront, for any reason, a particular colleague or superior, then it may be reasonable under the law to expect her to respond to sexual miscon-duct in an indirect or ineffective way.

Returning to the earlier detailed description of the professional responsibilities of Air Force missile launch officers, it would be counterproductive to excuse women missileers from responding constructively—responsibly—to inappropriate sexual conduct in the workplace. The Air Force expects and requires direct confrontation by its missileers when the stakes are much more significant; it would be inconsistent to assume that women lose that capacity to confront when the improper behav-ior is sexual misconduct. Furthermore, military officers (and enlisted supervisors as well) have a duty to control and educate others concerning sexual misconduct, not only for their own benefit but also for the benefit of the women they command and supervise. It would undermine the status of these military women to excuse them from responsible behavior that the military would otherwise expect without question.

. . . .

C. Why the Feminist Accusation of "Acting Like a Man" Is Always Counterproductive

There may be no more counterproductive feminist criticism than the charge that there is something wrong with a woman's behavior that is perfectly feasible, responsible, and constructive, simply because she is "acting like man." The following criticism of the hypothetical woman who responds directly and effectively to sexual harassment is a typical example: "Such a woman complains in a way that effectively stops the harassment. Such a woman does not suffer in silence or confide only in other women. In short, the 'reasonable woman' is very much a man."[123]

What is surprising about much of this commentary is how it seemingly seeks to freeze traditional sex-role behaviors as they are, failing to recognize that not all behavior more typical of women is good and, correspondingly, not all behavior more typical of men is bad. Stereotypical extremes of female-identified and male-identified behaviors are presented as the only options available for women to adopt, setting the stage for criticism of courts who would withhold a remedy for either choice. . . .

. . . .

The choices presented to women, therefore, are only two: behave in an extreme and stereotypically masculine fashion (offensively or unprofessionally) or behave in an extreme and stereotypically feminine fashion (ineffectively or dysfunctionally). Both may tend to result in findings of welcomeness, but they are unrepresentative of the range of choices available. Behaving like a woman, unfortunately, never seems to include behaving constructively, even when constructive behavior may be an option. For a woman to directly express an objection to a man's conduct, for example, is considered a "[Clint] Eastwood-style response" and not "socially plausible." An expectation of "blunt objection" by women is dismissed as "stark" only because the behavior is more characteristic of men.

. . . .

We must get beyond the feminist assumption that anything that is traditionally male is inappropriate for women or that anything traditionally female is worth protecting under the law. Almost twenty-five years ago, the psychological research of Sandra Bem demonstrated that "androgynous" women and men—people with strengths in both feminine and masculine domains—had the greatest range of abilities to respond effectively under changing circumstances. For example, the androgynously gifted might be similarly skilled at standing firm against an opposing group

---

123. Estrich, *supra* note 49, at 846.

or at nurturing children and others in need. "Androgyny provides both a vision of utopia and a model of mental health that does not require the individual to banish from the self whatever attributes and behaviors the culture may have stereotypically defined as inappropriate for his or her sex."[137]

. . . .

This restrictive mindset is particularly counterproductive in any examination of the role of military women. Military service has traditionally embraced characteristics that are also traditionally identified with men. Some of these male-identified traits are dysfunctional in the modern, sex-integrated military, to be sure, but many are functional and, indeed, necessary for effective performance. To suggest that feminine, but dysfunctional, behavioral counterparts should be equated with productive, but masculine, traits in order that gender characteristics be treated alike only guarantees that military women will be second-class servicemembers.

An example helps illustrate the problem. All young officers, men and women alike, are taught the importance of developing what is called "command presence." Command presence is an overall bearing or demeanor that speaks of influence, persuasiveness, trust, knowledge, and responsibility. It is that ability to arrest the attention of subordinates, to have them believe you know what you are doing, and to motivate them to perform their duties in the best way they can. Command presence comes across in voice, in posture, and in word choice, but not necessarily in size or maleness.

. . . .

As with the theory of partial agency, women are best served by analyses that are factually complex and not superficially extreme. We should identify and legally defend substantive, productive strengths that are traditionally female-identified without unnecessarily excusing women from also adopting male-identified productive qualities. Mary Anne Case has described how the Los Angeles Police Department discovered that female officers were disproportionately more likely to have "interpersonal skills, sensitivity, politeness, and the ability to communicate," and that systematic underevaluation of these very effective policing skills resulted in unfairly low performance ratings for women.

It overstates an extremely good point, however, to then question whether "aggressiveness is a useful quality in a police officer" or conclude "how much more effective feminine qualities are than masculine qualities in the work of the police." It is not an either-or proposition. Police officers—or military servicemembers—with the broadest range of productive skills will always be the most valuable, and it is counterproductive to condescendingly shield women from requirements that will encourage them to incorporate those skills—even the skills that are considered traditionally masculine.

---

137. [*See* Sandra Lipsitz Bem, The Lenses of Gender: Transforming the Debate on Sexual Inequality 124 (1993).]

It is much more productive to first determine which traits, behaviors, or strengths should be valued in a given circumstance — regardless of gender association — and then make certain that the law defends individuals — regardless of sex — who have achieved those characteristics. Joan Williams describes this as "sex neutrality" rather than "gender neutrality," an approach that "refus[es] to reinforce the traditional assumption that adherence to gender roles flows 'naturally' from biological sex." It provides room to question whether the norms of certain occupations should be re-examined to remove ineffective, gendered expectations that achieve little but the exclusion of women, but it will not excuse women from expectations simply because they were once associated with men.

Conclusion

Catharine MacKinnon has been the most prominent advocate of the "anti-subordination" approach to equal treatment for women under the law. This approach eliminates the sometimes wasteful legal exercise of determining whether women are truly different from men in some relevant way, or whether that difference justifies different treatment under the law, all in an effort to decide whether a particular legal distinction constitutes sex discrimination. Professor MacKinnon's anti-subordination analysis cuts effectively right to the heart of the matter. No matter how rational, justified, or explainable a policy or practice might be, the only appropriate question to ask is whether it "contributes to the maintenance of an underclass or a deprived position because of gender status." If the law in its effect will contribute to the subordination of women, it should constitute sex discrimination. In other words, the ends are much more important than the means; the result is much more important than the justification.

We should follow the same guidelines in evaluating feminist legal theory. This is where the weakness of partial agency lies, in its disregard for the effect of the theory as applied. Partial agency's justification has become more important than its result; its short-term benefit more important than its long-term consequence. Every time the law reduces its expectations for constructive, responsible behavior from women, we may take small steps forward by winning a few lawsuits but still take large steps back from equality. The only question to be asked, then, is whether intentional descriptions of women as agency-diminished will ultimately contribute to the subordination of women. With respect to military women, it will, and we should reconsider the effect it will have for women in general.

Notes and Discussion

1. Partial Agency According to Mazur, what is partial agency? How does Mazur's notion of female agency differ, if at all, from Professor Mahoney's, *supra* Chapter 2? Does ignorance about military service contribute to a restricted view of female agency in that context? Did Mazur's description of missileer nuclear-weapons duty clarify the issue of female agency in the military? Is partial agency incompatible with military service? Explain.

2. Responsibility and Agency Define the two kinds of responsibility that Professor Mazur discussed. How did she want to see women assume responsibility when confronting sexual harassment? Are responsibility and partial agency incongruent?

3. Welcomeness Did Mazur agree with Professor Estrich's rejection of the unwelcomeness requirement, *supra* Chapter 3? Why or why not? Is it reasonable to expect women to object to sexual harassment in a direct manner? What did Mazur suggest? Did Mazur agree with Professor Abrams on this issue?

4. Anti-Essentialism How did Mazur think women could "confront the enforced generality that tends to limit all women equally"?

5. Reasonableness of a Target's Response What questions would Mazur ask to determine how a target might reasonably have responded to inappropriate conduct? Why did Mazur place such a high value on understanding factual context, associated with a woman's exercise of agency?

6. Application of Law and Ethics
Hypothetical #8

Sandra Smyth, a public defender, represents George, a prisoner at New Columbia Penitentiary. He has been accused of sodomizing another prisoner, Jon, who was treated in the prison hospital for his injuries. George admitted to Sandra that he committed this criminal and civil offense. He described the episode in detail. The details matched those in the prison incident report.

Legal Issue: Can Jon sue George or New Columbia Penitentiary for sexual harassment?

Ethics Issues: Can Sandra ethically represent George? Can she ethically refuse? If George wants to testify at his trial that he did not commit the rape, can Sandra ethically let him take the witness stand?

What if George told Sandra that he threatened to sodomize Jon who had been demanding his cigarettes but that he never touched Jon? George just wanted to scare off Jon and now Jon was retaliating?

Legal Issue: Does George's new revelation change your view of whether Jon can successfully sue George or New Columbia Penitentiary for sexual harassment?

Lt. Sandra Smyth, a Judge Advocate General (JAG) defense attorney in the Navy, meets with her new client Juana, a recent recruit. Juana has been accused of being absent without leave (AWOL). Juana reveals to Sandra that her basic training officer has been finding fault with her performance and requiring that she report to his office where he sexually assaults her. To avoid additional abuse, she left the base to go home and discuss the situation with her parents. She was arrested by military police at home.

Legal Issue: Can Juana sue her training officer or the Navy for sexual harassment? Is the sexual abuse a good defense to the AWOL charge?

Chapter 9

Continuing Controversies and New Developments in Sexual Harassment Law

To this point, this textbook has reviewed the development of sexual harassment law since its creation in the latter half of the twentieth century. In addition, it has explored which laws apply in particular environments and the prima facie cases under those statutory schemes that prohibit sex-based discrimination more generally. This chapter considers other topics relevant to the study of civil, sex-based harassment and assault interdictions and prosecutions. In addition to the more widespread phenomenon of public sexual harassment, it covers special factors that can influence a sexual harassment or civil assault case. Five topics addressed below include harassment in other physical places, online harassment, the First Amendment defense, access to the plaintiff's sexual history, and publicity in commonplace cases.

1. Harassment in Other Physical Settings[1]

In contrast to the power hierarchies of prisons and the military discussed in the last chapter, public settings and private not-for-profit organizations are much less closely regulated by law. For example, neither Title VII, Title VIII, Title IX, nor the Eighth Amendment apply specifically when a priest molests a parishioner.[2] Volumes have been written about the sexual abuse of adherents by priests, pastors, church youth leaders, and other adults affiliated with religious institutions.[3] A recent *NPR News* report details the emergence of a #NunsToo movement. Nuns are speaking

---

1. Adapted from JENNIFER ANN DROBAC, SEXUAL EXPLOITATION OF TEENAGERS: ADOLESCENT DEVELOPMENT, DISCRIMINATION & CONSENT LAW 26–42 (2016).

2. The U.S. Conference of Catholic Bishops commissioned a voluntary survey conducted of the U.S. dioceses, commonly known as the *John Jay Report*. The study indicated that about four percent (4,392) of U.S. Catholic priests were accused of sexual abuse between 1950 and 2002 in 10,992 individual reports of abuse. KAREN T. TERRY ET AL., THE CAUSES AND CONTEXT OF SEXUAL ABUSE OF MINORS BY CATHOLIC PRIESTS IN THE UNITED STATES, 1950–2010 8 (2011).

3. *See, e.g.,* DONALD H. MATTHEWS, SEXUAL ABUSE OF POWER IN THE BLACK CHURCH: SEXUAL MISCONDUCT IN THE AFRICAN AMERICAN CHURCHES (2012); SEXUAL ABUSE IN THE CATHOLIC CHURCH: A DECADE OF CRISIS, 2002–2012 (Thomas G. Plante & Kathleen L. McChesney

511

out and Pope Francis recently acknowledged years of sexual abuse of nuns and others by priests.[4]

This textbook does not review sexual abuse by clergy but notes that religious institutions are often exempt from full state and federal antidiscrimination law application.[5] Religious entities are specifically exempted from Title VII when it comes to hiring co-religionists. Thus, a Catholic Church can permissibly hire only Catholics. In addition, the Supreme Court has recognized a "ministerial exemption" based on the religion clauses of the First Amendment, which prohibits any government inquiry into a religious entity's choice of leader. Thus, this exemption permits the Catholic Church to refuse to allow women to serve as priests.[6] However, these institutions and their personnel are answerable under state personal injury laws. Those laws may include civil claims for assault and battery, intentional infliction of emotional distress, negligent infliction of emotional distress, negligent hiring and supervision, defamation, and other negligence claims.

Religious institutions are not the only organizations that are less than fully accountable under antidiscrimination law, however. For example, many volunteer and membership organizations are not fully accountable under the statutory schemes that we have covered.[7] Such groups include: service organizations, such as the Red Cross; professional groups, such as bar and medical associations; and social clubs, such as the Lions and Kiwanis. Another set consists of youth sports teams, choirs, and bands that may not be affiliated with a school or have paid employees. They also experience problems with sexual predation by adults. The reason these organizations are not fully accountable is because, as noted in prior chapters, Title VII protects only paid employees. Typically, an individual must receive a salary or regular financial compensation in order to qualify as an employee within the meaning of Title VII.[8] Additionally, the employer must control the work of the paid employee.[9] Thus, clients and members are not covered and these service organizations are not liable under Title VII for harassment against such targets.

---

eds., 2011); MARCI A. HAMILTON, JUSTICE DENIED: WHAT AMERICA MUST DO TO PROTECT ITS CHILDREN 67–96, 144–51 (2008).

4. Sylvia Poggioli, *After Years of Abuse by Priests, #NunsToo Are Speaking Out*, NPR (Mar. 18, 2019).

5. *See, e.g.*, Ira C. Lupu & Robert W. Tuttle, *#MeToo Meets the Ministerial Exception: Sexual Harassment Claims by Clergy and the First Amendment's Religion Clauses*, 25 WM. & MARY J. WOMEN & L. 249 (2019).

6. Corporation of Presiding Bishop v. Amos, 483 U.S. 327 (1987); Jennifer A. Drobac & Jill L. Wesley, *Employment, in* RELIGION AND THE STATE 451–503 (Boris I. Bittker, Scott C. Idelman & Frank S. Ravitch, eds., 2015).

7. *See, e.g.*, Keiko Rose, *Volunteer Protection under Title VII: Is Remuneration Required?*, 2014 U. CHI. LEGAL F. 605 (2014).

8. Juino v. Livingston Parish Fire Dist. No. 5, 717 F.3d 431 (5th Cir. 2013).

9. Covington v. International Ass'n of Approved Basketball Officials, 2013, 710 F.3d 114 (3d Cir. 2013).

In other settings, there may be no "responsible" organization. Street harassment occurs by and between individuals or informal groups. Moreover, many commercial transactions may not be covered. For example, a customer in a store might harass another customer. Images displayed in a mall could be considered sexual harassment in an office workplace. Different contexts require different socio-legal approaches to sex-based harassment. This chapter briefly explores three more settings where in-person harassment occurs: youth sports, and USA Gymnastics in particular; street harassment; and commercial discrimination. Consider whether antidiscrimination law should cover these settings.

A. Sexual Harassment in Youth Athletics and Volunteer Organizations

In 2016, an investigation by reporters at *The Indianapolis Star* revealed that USA Gymnastics had been concealing allegations concerning sexual abuse by more than 50 coaches for years.[10] At the time, the gymnastics organization justified its conduct. It argued that its executive policy required the dismissal of complaints as "hearsay" unless the complaint had been signed by the target or the target's parent. Experts suggest that this policy could deter people from reporting abusive conduct. USA Gymnastics could not say who formulated the policy or when.[11]

Assuming the truth of the allegations, these coaches committed not only civil law violations but also sex crimes against their young athletes. One particularly abusive perpetrator was Larry Nassar, a former doctor for USA Gymnastics. In October 2017, Nassar accepted a plea agreement to multiple counts of criminal sexual abuse of his gymnastics patients. In January 2018, a judge sentenced Nassar to 40 to 175 years in prison. At the sentencing hearing, 156 women and girls made statements about their abuse by Nassar.[12] Nassar's successful criminal prosecution certainly enhanced the likelihood of success in all the associated civil cases related to his behavior.

In addition to criminal charges filed by state prosecutors, the athletes (or their parents or guardians) filed personal injury tort claims against not only Nassar but also the coaches and other USA Gymnastics personnel, seeking compensation for the girls' trauma. In 2018, USA Gymnastics filed for bankruptcy to deal with the pending civil claims. USA Gymnastics said that the claims are covered by insurance "and their [settlement] value will not be affected."[13] In other words, USA Gymnastics

10. Christine Hauser & Karen Zraick, *Larry Nassar Sexual Abuse Scandal: Dozens of Officials Have Been Ousted or Charged*, N.Y. TIMES (Oct. 22, 2018).

11. Marisa Kwiatkowski, Mark Alesia & Tim Evans, *A Blind Eye to Sex Abuse: How USA Gymnastics Failed to Report Cases*, INDIANAPOLIS STAR (Aug. 4, 2016).

12. *Who Is Larry Nassar?*, USA TODAY, https://www.usatoday.com/pages/interactives/larry-nassar-timeline/. In addition, officials at USA Gymnastics may have violated state child abuse reporting laws in failing to report what they knew or suspected.

13. *USA Gymnastics Files for Bankruptcy in Order to Support Sexual Abuse Survivors*, BBC SPORT (Dec. 2018).

was assuring the public that it was not seeking bankruptcy protection to avoid paying civil damages to the survivors. USA Gymnastics also committed "to support its athletes, to fully operate and meet its responsibilities to the entire membership and to expeditiously resolve the claims made by the survivors of sexual abuse perpetrated by Larry Nassar."[14]

Note that USA Gymnastics made reference to its "membership." What is not clear is whether these women or their parents sued USA Gymnastics for sexual harassment and sex-based discrimination. As noted, the athletes and their parents are not paid employees of USA Gymnastics so Title VII does not technically apply. USA Gymnastics is not a "school" that receives federal funding so Title IX does not apply. USA Gymnastics is a not-for-profit organization and not a governmental entity so the Eighth Amendment and 42 U.S.C. § 1983 (civil rights action for deprivation of rights) do not apply. USA Gymnastics is a membership organization, like a club. There is no federal law that specifically covers sex-based discrimination against unpaid club and non-profit organization members. Other personal injury claims that survivors undoubtedly filed do not highlight the systemic and discriminatory nature of what USA Gymnastics and its personnel did.

One might think that the USA Gymnastics scandal was a one-off, involving a rogue organization or bizarre circumstances. The sexual exploitation of athletes, however, is not a new phenomenon. In its policy statement, the Women's Sports Foundation declares, "Sexual harassment is a recognized social problem in sport. Sexual harassment in sport deters girls and women from participating and developing as athletes."[15] Before #MeToo, neither the Women's Sports Foundation, nor apparently anyone else, described the prevalence of this problem in youth athletics outside the purview of Title IX. However, even without comprehensive study of the issue, organizations are now making changes. In February 2018, *NBC News* reported, "In a first for any Olympic Games, centers to address incidents of sexual misconduct were opened over the course of the 16-day sporting event as a way for athletes, volunteers, spectators and anyone else to come forward for help."[16]

Sexual harassment is a serious problem for male athletes as well as females. Again, many of the issues arise in volunteer youth organizations. However, one particularly heinous case in 2011 involved a charity program, The Second Mile, started by former assistant football coach Gerald Sandusky and affiliated with Pennsylvania State University.[17] A jury convicted Sandusky of 45 counts of criminal sex charges

---

14. *Id.* (quoting the USA Gymnastics governing body).

15. Women's Sports Foundation, Sexual Harassment and Sexual Relationships between Coaches, Other Athletic Personnel and Athletes: The Foundation Position, www.womenssportsfoundation.org/home/advocate/title-ix-and-issues/title-ix-positions/sexual_harassment (last visited May 5, 2019).

16. Erik Ortiz, *Olympics Opened First-Ever Sexual Assault Centers as at Least 10 Cases Reported,* NBC News (Feb. 24, 2018).

17. Mark Scolforo, *Penn State Reaches Financial Settlement with Jerry Sandusky's Defunct Charity, Second Mile,* Pittsburgh Post-Gazette (Mar. 20, 2019).

involving 10 boys over a period of more than a decade.[18] Allegations of a university cover-up complicated the cases. Weighing witness testimony, the report of the special investigative counsel determined:

> [I]n order to avoid the consequences of bad publicity, the most powerful leaders at the University—[Graham B.] Spanier, [Gary C.] Schultz, [Joseph V.] Paterno and [Timothy M.] Curley—repeatedly concealed critical facts relating to Sandusky's child abuse from the authorities, the University's Board of Trustees, the Penn State community, and the public at large.[19]

Thus, not only did school officials fail to report abuse, they actively concealed it to avoid negative publicity. This chapter explores the phenomenon of publicity at greater length in the last section.

When Sandusky's victims filed civil claims against him and Penn State, the question arose whether Title IX applied. The abused boys were not students at Penn State but Title IX applies generally to all "persons." It also covers conduct by third parties, such as Sandusky, who was not officially a Penn State employee for 15 of the years that he abused the boys. Instead, the question centered on whether the abuse occurred "under" the Penn State program. Joanna Grossman and Deborah Brake suggested, "At a minimum, the sexual assaults that took place in the showers of the Penn State locker room or sauna would fall within the statute's reach."[20]

In 2013, Penn State settled approximately 25 civil law cases by boys abused by Sandusky.[21] One case involved "claims on the grounds of negligence, negligent supervision, premises liability, intentional infliction of emotional distress and a civil conspiracy to endanger children."[22] By November 2015, settlements amounted to almost $93 million. However, strict confidentiality agreements (discussed generally in Chapter 10) and vague news reports make it difficult to know which specific claims those settlement amounts covered.[23] Finally, in March 2019, The Second Mile and Penn State reached an agreement that Penn State would receive the remaining assets of the charity organization. The Pennsylvania Attorney General's office was to oversee the transfer of "$733,000 to Penn State," a fraction of the liability that Penn State experienced as a result of its affiliation with The Second Mile and Sandusky.[24]

---

18. Ian Simpson, *Sandusky Found Guilty on 45 of 48 Sex Abuse Charges*, Reuters (June 22, 2012).

19. Freeh, Sporkin & Sullivan, LLP, Report of the Special Investigative Counsel Regarding the Actions of The Pennsylvania State University Related to the Child Sexual Abuse Committed by Gerald A. Sandusky 16 (July 12, 2012).

20. Joanna L. Grossman & Deborah L. Brake, *The Penn State Scandal: Why Is No One Talking about Title IX?*, Verdict (Nov. 15, 2011).

21. Robert W. Wood, *Penn State's $60M Abuse Settlement Won't Erase Sandusky Name*, Forbes (July 19, 2013).

22. Mike Dawson, *Victim 6 in Jerry Sandusky Case Sues Penn State, Second Mile*, Centre Daily Times (Jan. 23, 2013).

23. AP, *Penn State's Sandusky Settlements Total $93 Million*, USA Today (Nov. 27, 2015).

24. Scolforo, *supra* note 17.

B. Sexual Harassment in Public[25]

Even less regulated than volunteer organizations, public streets, transportation, and meeting places offer some harassers anonymity and escape from liability. By 1994, a number of feminist academics had analyzed sexist conduct, directed primarily at women in public, and some had delved into the legal prohibitions against such conduct.[26] That year Deirdre Davis defined the five characteristics of street harassment:

> First, street harassment occurs in a public place. Second, the remarks are passed among unacquainted members of the opposite sex. . . . Third, the expected response to a compliment—thank you—is unacceptable to the harasser and often leads to escalating hostility. . . . Fourth, the remarks often refer to parts of the body not available for public examination. . . . Finally, the remarks are usually not positive appraisals; in fact, they are often quite derogatory.[27]

Modern definitions of street harassment are broader. In her 2010 book *Stop Street Harassment: Making Public Places Safe and Welcoming for Women*, Holly Kearl discusses street harassment, including whistles, catcalls, obscene comments, and other more threatening behaviors, such as stalking.[28] Kearl's Stop Street Harassment website states, "These are common forms of sexual harassment in public spaces initiated by strangers that millions of people worldwide experience, especially girls and women."[29] Kearl explains that friends, family, and others had told her the calls and whistles were "a compliment." She writes, "I did not see my experiences in the larger context of women's inequality in society or piece together how many of us can't go about our daily lives without men objectifying, insulting, or threatening us."[30]

Until recently, few people had surveyed the prevalence of street harassment. A recent study by NORC at the University of Chicago finds that most female respondents have experienced sexual harassment in a public place. Often the misconduct occurs in "a street, store or restaurant . . . (68% of women and 23% of men)." When researchers "include mass transit and nightlife venues, that statistic for sexual harassment in all public spaces (or, street harassment) rises to 71% women and 28%

---

25. Adapted from Drobac, *supra* note 1, at 30–34.

26. *See, e.g.*, Cynthia Grant Bowman, *Street Harassment and the Informal Ghettoization of Women*, 16 Harv. L. Rev. 517, 519 (1993) (discussing "street harassment"); Carol Brooks Gardner, *Passing By: Street Remarks, Address Rights, and the Urban Female*, 50 Soc. Inquiry 328 (1980) (discussing "street remarks").

27. Deirdre Davis, *The Harm That Has No Name: Street Harassment, Embodiment, and African American Women*, 4 UCLA Women's L.J. 133, 138–40 (1994).

28. Holly Kearl, Stop Street Harassment: Making Public Places Safe and Welcoming for Women 21 (2010).

29. *Street Harassment and the Law: Introduction*, Stop Street Harassment, http://www.stopstreetharassment.org/strategies/sshlaw-intro/ (last visited May 6, 2019).

30. Kearl, *supra* note 28, at 21.

men."[31] The study also notes that "81% of women and 43% of men reported experiencing some form of sexual harassment and/or assault in their lifetime."[32]

Another interesting aspect of this empirical research is that the researchers asked about reporting and accusations. First, very few people confront their harassers or otherwise report the behavior. Second, the evidence suggests that very few people falsely report sexual harassment. "Only 1% of those who self-reported that they have never committed sexual harassment or assault said they were told by an individual that they had done so."[33]

So, why is street harassment per se still prevalent outside the workplace — in public? First, many still may not recognize street harassment for what it is, sex-based oppression. Hollaback! is another organization whose mission it is to educate people about street harassment. Its website explains, "We work together to understand the problem, ignite public conversations, and develop innovative strategies that ensure equal access to public spaces." As part of its Manifesto, Hollaback! announces, "It's time to transform the culture that perpetuates harassment and violence."[34]

Second, despite the pervasiveness of public sexual harassment, women often lack the resources and means to implement effective reform. Whom can one sue for public harassment? What laws can one use? How expensive is it? How can one prove damages? The damage caused by pervasive public harassment is a bit like the damage to the pyramids caused by the polluted winds. This damage is subtle, accumulating over time.

Third, state laws may not adequately address street harassment. If they do, many people may not realize that some forms of street harassment are unlawful.[35] A 2014 guide by Hollaback!, TrustLaw, and DLA Piper now offers "legal definitions and information on all forms of street harassment across 22 countries and in 12 languages."[36] Rather than further outlaw street harassment, however, some feminists would like to see targeted public service announcements and other media campaigns raise consciousness about street harassment.[37] A good way to curb oppressive behavior is to point it out and denounce it. Hollaback! and Stop Street Harassment

---

31. NATIONAL OPINION RESEARCH CENTER, MEASURING #METOO: STREET HARASSMENT FACT SHEET — 2019 (April 30, 2019), http://www.stopstreetharassment.org/wp-content/uploads/2012/08/Street-Harassment-Factsheet-2019-Study.pdf.

32. NATIONAL OPINION RESEARCH CENTER, MEASURING #METOO: EXECUTIVE SUMMARY (April 30, 2019), http://www.stopstreetharassment.org/wp-content/uploads/2012/08/Executive-Summary-2019-MeToo-National-Sexual-Harassment-and-Assault-Report.pdf.

33. *Id.*

34. ABOUT, HOLLABACK!, https://www.ihollaback.org/about/.

35. For a listing of laws that prohibit street harassment of various forms, see TALIA HAGERTY ET AL., KNOW YOUR RIGHTS: STREET HARASSMENT AND THE LAW 15–291 (2013) (state-by-state listing of laws that prohibit some form of street harassment).

36. HOLLABACK! ET AL., STREET HARASSMENT: KNOW YOUR RIGHTS (Sept. 2014), https://www.ihollaback.org/wp-content/uploads/2014/10/Street-Harassment-Know-Your-Rights.pdf.

37. *See, e.g.,* DROBAC, *supra* note 1, at 41–42.

also engage in these extralegal responses. Hollaback!'s website contains links to guides, curricula, and mobilization strategies.[38]

As one considers how far American culture has come in the appreciation of human dignity and cooperative respect since the 1960s, one might further consider how far society could progress in the next 50 years. Are today's public and retail messages holding us back or propelling us forward?

2. Online Harassment

Modern technology has made it possible for sexual harassment to occur outside of the physical world, in cyberspace. The growth—and now ubiquity—of the internet has led to a corresponding onslaught of sexist harassment, illegal threats, invasions of privacy, and other practices that can make online spaces uncomfortable and even dangerous for women. The anonymity of cyberspace allows users to target obscene, misogynistic, and violent comments at female users, with little risk of repercussion. The internet also provides a powerful tool for harassers, stalkers, and scorned lovers to harm women (and men) who reject them in the "real world."

Online conduct does not always stay in cyberspace. As the boundary between our online and our offline lives becomes increasingly blurred, harassment that starts on the internet can have very serious real-world consequences. Targets of particularly severe harassment may suffer extreme anxiety, have to leave their jobs, and move out of their homes.[39] Even less serious harassment can wear down a female internet user, who must always brace for sexist epithets and sexual comments whenever she ventures into the online realm.

A. Terminology and Prevalence

In order to understand the phenomenon of online sexual harassment, one must be familiar with the different terms that describe various forms of online abuse. Many of these terms overlap, and they do not have a single, precise, legal definition. The definitions below come from legal commentary, government data-gathering websites, and state laws.

- *Cyberstalking* is conduct in cyberspace that causes substantial emotional distress in a person and serves no legitimate purpose. It involves repeated communications that have coercive, threatening, intimidating, or sexual overtones.

- *Cyberharassment* covers a variety of disturbing online behaviors. It includes obscene, offensive, or insulting messages directed at an individual. Cyberharassers might also flood the internet with false, obscene statements about a

---

38. RESOURCES, HOLLABACK!, https://www.ihollaback.org/resources/.
39. DANIELLE KEATS CITRON, HATE CRIMES IN CYBERSPACE 3–11 (2014).

target, so that anyone who searches for her online sees the offensive material. They may also send offensive material about the target to her friends, family, classmates, or employer, in order to embarrass and demean her. Online impersonation is another form of harassment, which occurs when a harasser sends or posts offensive messages, or solicitations for sex, that purport to be from the target.

- *Cyberbullying* is the term often used when minors engage in cyberharassment. Because many of the minors who engage in such harassment target their classmates, schools have increasingly attempted to prevent and address the problem. This phenomenon is addressed in greater detail in Chapter 6.

- *Doxing (or doxxing)* occurs when someone posts private, personal information—such as a home or email address, or phone number—on the internet. Often such a posting accompanies encouragement of other users to contact the person with harassing messages.

- *Revenge porn* is the unauthorized distribution of sexually explicit images or videos of an individual. Typically, but not always, the perpetrator is an ex-boyfriend, and the victim is a woman who provided the images as part of a consensual relationship with the understanding that they would remain private. Entire websites exist for the purpose of distributing revenge porn. These sites extort their victims to pay in order to have their photos removed from the site, a solicitation known as sextortion.

The language that describes cyberharassment is evolving as online media and platforms change. These basic terms, however, are useful to targets and their allies who educate others and decry online abuse.

In a powerful 2014 article, journalist Amanda Hess recounts her own experience, and the experiences of many other women, of being targeted by online threats, obscene messages, and abuse:

> The examples are too numerous to recount, but like any good journalist, I keep a running file documenting the most deranged cases. There was the local cable viewer who hunted down my email address after a television appearance to tell me I was "the ugliest woman he had ever seen." And the group of visitors to a "men's rights" site who pored over photographs of me and a prominent feminist activist, then discussed how they'd "spend the night with" us. ("Put em both in a gimp mask and tied to each other 69 so the bitches can't talk or move and go round the world, any old port in a storm, any old hole," one decided.) And the anonymous commenter who weighed in on one of my articles: "Amanda, I'll fucking rape you. How does that feel?"
>
> None of this makes me exceptional. It just makes me a woman with an Internet connection. Here's just a sampling of the noxious online commentary directed at other women in recent years. To Alyssa Royse, a sex and relationships blogger, for saying that she hated *The Dark Knight*: "you are

clearly retarded, i hope someone shoots then rapes you." To Kathy Sierra, a technology writer, for blogging about software, coding, and design: "i hope someone slits your throat and cums down your gob." To Lindy West, a writer at the women's website Jezebel, for critiquing a comedian's rape joke: "I just want to rape her with a traffic cone." To Rebecca Watson, an atheist commentator, for blogging about sexism in the skeptic community: "If I lived in Boston I'd put a bullet in your brain." To Catherine Mayer, a journalist at *Time* magazine, for no particular reason: "A BOMB HAS BEEN PLACED OUTSIDE YOUR HOME. IT WILL GO OFF AT EXACTLY 10:47 PM ON A TIMER AND TRIGGER DESTROYING EVERYTHING.[40]

This recount highlights just how disturbing and extreme some online threats can be. It also explains why some women feel compelled to leave their homes or take other disruptive, responsive safety measures.

To illustrate the problem of online harassment, Professor Danielle Citron provides the example of a software developer and tech blogger named Kathy Sierra:

> In early 2007, a group of anonymous individuals attacked Ms. Sierra on her blog and two other websites, MeanKids.org and unclebobism.com. Posters threatened rape and strangulation. Others revealed her home address and Social Security number. Individuals posted doctored photos of Ms. Sierra. One picture featured Ms. Sierra with a noose beside her neck. The poster wrote: "The only thing Kathy has to offer me is that noose in her neck size." Another photograph depicted her screaming while being suffocated by lingerie.[41]

Given that these were anonymous attackers, Ms. Sierra is left wondering who wishes her dead or injured. Any stranger could be a threat.

Professor Citron discusses another example, a law student who was initially targeted on a discussion board for college and graduate students called AutoAdmit. Someone (possibly a man whom she had refused to date in college) began posting threatening and offensive messages about her. Before long, entire threads were devoted to spreading lies and obscene messages about her. Attackers posted her personal information. They sent offensive emails about her to the faculty of the law school she attended, to law firms at which she was interviewing for jobs, and to her eventual employer (the Department of Justice). Every professional opportunity that the student wished to pursue was potentially sabotaged by the torrent of abusive and offensive online information about her.[42]

Cyberharassment can occur anywhere online. It happens in chat rooms, on message boards, on social media, and anywhere else a person can receive an electronic

---

40. Amanda Hess, *Why Women Aren't Welcome on the Internet*, PACIFIC STANDARD (Jan. 6, 2014).

41. Danielle Keats Citron, *Cyber Civil Rights*, 89 B.U. L. REV. 61, 65 (2009).

42. CITRON, *supra* note 39, at 39–45.

communication. The so-called GamerGate controversy exposed a particularly virulent set of these practices in the arena of online gaming and gaming journalism. Game developer Zoe Quinn became the target of online threats, doxing, and other abuse after she designed a non-traditional game. Harassers falsely accused her of having sex with a member of the gaming press in order to obtain favorable reviews of the game. Cultural critic Anita Sarkeesian became the target of similar abuse after she announced that she was working on a project, which criticized sexism in video games. "Gamergate" was the name given to the phenomenon involving the angry gamers—who appeared to resent female encroachment in the video game space. It became the subject of millions of tweets and countless threads on sites such as Reddit and 4chan.[43]

Researchers estimate that 40% of internet users will experience some form of cyberharassment.[44] Internet users harass each other based on any number of characteristics, from sports team allegiance to race. It is clear, however, that cyberharassment disproportionately affects women. Working to Halt Online Abuse (WHOA) is a nonprofit organization that collects information about cyberharassment. Of the 4,043 people who reported complaints to WHOA between 2000 and 2014, 70% were women.[45] Without My Consent, a nonprofit organization that combats online invasions of privacy, conducted an internet survey about cyberharassment. Eighty-two percent of the respondents who reported experiencing harassment were women.[46] In 2006, researchers from the University of Maryland set up a number of fake online accounts and then dispatched them into chat rooms. Accounts with feminine usernames incurred an average of 100 sexually explicit or threatening messages per day, while masculine names received only 3.7 similar messages.[47]

Notes and Discussion

1. The Prevalence of Cyberharassment Why is online harassment so common? How is cyberharassment different from harassment that occurs face-to-face? Certain characteristics of the internet make it particularly susceptible to abuse. The anonymity afforded by the internet is clearly a factor. People are willing to say things under the cover of anonymity that they might never say with attribution. Professors Lyrissa Lidsky and Thomas Cotter observe that, "technology separates the speaker from the immediate consequences of her speech, perhaps (falsely) lulling

---

43. *See, e.g.,* Nathan Rott, *#Gamergate Controversy Fuels Debate on Women and Video Games,* NPR (Sept. 24, 2014).

44. Maeve Duggan, Pew Research Center, Online Harassment 2017 (July 11, 2017), https://www.pewinternet.org/2017/07/11/online-harassment-2017/.

45. Haltabuse.org, WHOA (Haltabuse.org) Comparison Statistics 2000–2013, http://www.haltabuse.org/resources/stats/Cumulative2000-2013.pdf.

46. Dan Taube et al., Preliminary Report: Without My Consent Survey of Online Stalking, Harassment and Violations of Privacy 2 (Sept. 2014).

47. Robert Meyer & Michel Cukier, *Assessing the Attack Threat Due to IRC Channels, Proceedings of the 2006 International Conference on Dependable Systems and Networks,* Int'l Conference on DSN 467–72 (2006).

her to believe that there will be no consequences. Since the Internet magnifies the number of anonymous speakers, it also magnifies the likelihood of false and abusive speech."[48] Similarly, the internet makes it possible for harassers to target people whom they do not know. Social science research demonstrates that people are more willing to cause harm to others when the others are depersonalized.[49]

The networked nature of the internet also creates a so-called "compounding effect." Users connect with others through discussion forums or followers on social media. Because of this web of connection, thousands of people may view a single harassing comment. Viewers might decide to pile on in what becomes a cybermob. A harasser might use his platform to encourage his fellow internet users to harass a particular target across multiple platforms. Similarly, by providing different forums for like-minded people, the internet can create echo chambers, where users hear only ideas that reinforce their own world view. This can lead to a phenomenon known as group polarization, in which people's views become more entrenched, exaggerated, and extreme. Group polarization has been well-documented, for example, in white supremacist sites.[50]

2. Avoiding Harm? Some commentators have argued that the internet is a "rough and tumble" place and, therefore, women with an online presence should expect a degree of abuse. What steps should a woman have to take to avoid being on the receiving end of cyberharassment? For most women, simply unplugging is not an option. Some women make their living by writing and posting content online. For many others, being online is a necessary aspect of their job. Given the amount of discourse, commerce, and basic daily functions that occur online, simple reversion back to analog is impractical, incompatible with a modern career, and disenfranchising. Moreover, the suggestion that women bring harassment on themselves by engaging in activity online is arguably another form of victim-blaming. Professor Danielle Citron argues:

> Cyber harassment victims are not to blame for their suffering. They cannot walk away from on-line abuse, as the "Turn off your computer" refrain suggests. Rape threats, posts suggesting their interest in sex, damaging lies, and nude photos cannot be ignored. Employers, clients, and friends will see the harassing posts when they search victims' names whether or not the victims shut down their computers, blogs, or social network sites.

> . . . .

> In any event, whether cyber harassment victims could mitigate their injuries is not the issue. No one should be expected to withdraw from on-line

---

48. Lyrissa Barnett Lidsky & Thomas Cotter, *Authorship, Audiences, and Anonymous Speech*, 82 NOTRE DAME L. REV. 1537, 1575 (2007).

49. PATRICIA WALLACE, THE PSYCHOLOGY OF THE INTERNET 126 (2001).

50. Brian Levin, *Cyberhate: A Legal and Historical Analysis of Extremists' Use of Computer Networks in America*, 45 AMER. BEHAV. SCIENTIST 958–88 (2002).

activities to avoid targeted attacks, much as women should not have been told to leave their jobs to avoid supervisors' sexual demands[.][51]

Targets of cyberharassment can pursue legal and extralegal avenues for relief. These avenues will likely undergo significant change as both the law and the technology involved continue to develop.

B. The Legal Response

1. Criminal Law

Three federal criminal statutes address cyberharassment. First, the Interstate Communications Act (ICA) makes it illegal to "transmit[] in interstate or foreign commerce any communication containing any threat to kidnap any person or any threat to injure the person of another."[52] Second, the Federal Interstate Stalking Punishment and Prevention Act (FISPPA) prohibits someone who has the "intent to kill, injure, harass, intimidate, or . . . intimidate another" from using "any interactive computer service or electronic communication service or electronic communication system of interstate commerce" in order to place a person in reasonable fear of death or serious bodily injury or to "cause, attempt to cause, or engage in conduct that would reasonably expect to cause substantial emotional distress."[53] These statutes serve for the most serious cyberstalking cases. They are of less utility on more typical cyberharassment cases, however, because they require proof of intent to harm (FISPPA) or a direct and credible threat (ICA). Congress amended The Telephone Harassment Act in 2006 to include electronic communication. This third law prohibits anyone from using electronic communications "without disclosing his identity and with intent to annoy, abuse, threaten, or harass any person . . . who receives the communications."[54] This Act is more useful than FISPPA in a cyberharassment case because it requires a showing of only an intent to harass, not an intent to harm.

In addition, almost every state has laws that criminalize cyberstalking or cyberharassment, but they differ in their specific requirements.[55] Many states did not enact new laws to prevent these crimes, but rather added a cyberharassment provision to the existing telephone harassment, stalking, or general harassment statutes. Others states have separate statutes that prohibit specific behaviors. For example, California has a separate statute that makes it a crime to electronically distribute

---

51. Citron, *supra* note 36, at 100–01.

52. 18 U.S.C. § 875 (West 2019).

53. 18 U.S.C. § 2661A (West 2019).

54. 18 U.S.C. § 223(a) (West 2019).

55. In 2013, the National Conference of State Legislatures compiled a list of all state laws related to cyberstalking and cyberharassment. The list no longer appears on the NCSL website, but a copy of it appears at https://scornedbutnotbeaten.wordpress.com/tag/cyberstalkingharassment-laws-by-state/.

personal information.[56] Texas has made online impersonation a separate crime.[57] A significant majority of states also have statutes that specifically criminalize revenge porn.[58] If a harasser or domestic abuser continues the online harassment or abuse, the target may be able to obtain an order of protection requiring him to cease and take down harassing messages.

2. Civil Law

Cyberharassment and cyberstalking constitute a number of common law torts, including defamation, intentional infliction of emotional distress, and invasion of privacy. Tort actions have been particularly effective for revenge porn targets. In recent cases, judges have awarded successful revenge porn plaintiffs hundreds of thousands,[59] and even millions[60] of dollars in compensatory and punitive damages.

Revenge porn targets can also use copyright law, in some circumstances, to gain relief.[61] For success with this approach, the target must have created and registered a copyright of the images. Once she obtains a copyright, she must also file a notice-and-take down request with the site. If the site fails to remove the images, she can then sue for a copyright violation.[62]

Schools and employers may be liable under Title IX or Title VII if their students or employees engage in cyberharassment. Harassment on a school or company website would almost certainly constitute the basis for a hostile environment claim. The case is less clear when classmates or co-workers harass one another on sites that are not owned or controlled by the school or employer.

For example, in *Chinery v. American Airlines*,[63] and a companion case, *Medlin v. American Airlines*,[64] the plaintiffs were flight attendants who alleged that they were harassed by fellow flight attendants in a Facebook group for flight attendants called "Wingnuts." The court dismissed both plaintiffs' claims because it found that neither alleged conduct severe or pervasive enough to violate Title VII. The court also

---

56. Cal. Penal Code § 646.9(a) (West 2019). In addition, California makes it a crime to issue a threat through electronic communications, regardless of whether there is actual intent to carry out the threat. Cal. Penal Code § 422(a) (West 2019).

57. Tex. Penal Code Ann. § 33.07(a) (West 2019).

58. Cyber Civil Rights Initiative, 44 States + DC Now Have Revenge Porn Laws, https://www.cybercivilrights.org/revenge-porn-laws/.

59. Kat Stafford, *Oakland County Woman Gets $500K in Revenge Porn Case*, Detroit Free Press (Aug. 25, 2016).

60. Sara Ashley O'Brien, *Woman Awarded $6.45 Million in Revenge Porn Case*, CNN.com (Apr. 9, 2018).

61. For a profile of Carrie Goldberg, a lawyer who has dedicated her practice to combating revenge porn, see Margaret Talbot, *The Attorney Fighting Revenge Porn*, New Yorker (Dec. 5, 2016).

62. Digital Millennium Copyright Act, 17 U.S.C. § 512 (West 2019). One revenge porn target was awarded $450,000 for copyright infringement. *See* O'Brien, *supra* note 60.

63. 2018 WL 4055308 (E.D. PA 2018).

64. 2018 WL 4055307.

noted that "whether the alleged harassment over Facebook . . . actually occurred in a work environment" was a "serious question[]," albeit one that it did not need to address.

In *Feminist Majority Foundation v. Hurley* (discussed in Chapter 6), female students alleged that their university (UMW) failed to address the severe cyberharassment that they experienced after they spoke out about sexual violence on campus. The district court dismissed the plaintiffs' claim, holding that the plaintiffs had failed to impute liability to UMW under Title IX. The district court explained that the sexual harassment endured by members of Feminists United "took place in a context over which UMW had limited, if any, control."[65] The Court of Appeals disagreed:

> Although that harassment was communicated through cyberspace, the Complaint shows that UMW had substantial control over the context of the harassment because it actually transpired on campus. Specifically, due to Yik Yak's location-based feature, the harassing and threatening messages originated on or within the immediate vicinity of the UMW campus. In addition, some of the offending Yaks were posted using the University's wireless network, and the harassers necessarily created those Yaks on campus. Moreover, the harassment concerned events occurring on campus and specifically targeted UMW students.[66]

This decision makes clear that some courts at least will place liability with organizations that control aspects of cyberspace.

Notes and Discussion

1. Existing Laws, New Context As discussed above, some state and federal statutes have simply added online communications to their existing laws against stalking and harassment. Are there any potential problems with this approach? One commenter notes that, despite the fact that many states have laws that address various aspects of the problem, "the laws are inconsistent, inadequately developed, and do not criminalize the many ways a perpetrator can commit cybercrimes."[67] Victim impersonation, for example, is an offense that is unique to the online environment.

One attorney has developed a novel approach to the problem of online impersonation: she is suing the social networking site Grindr under a product liability theory. The plaintiff's identity was impersonated by someone who posted messages stating that he was available for hardcore sex and bondage. Because of Grindr's geolocation features, individuals who wanted to respond to the ad could track the victim's whereabouts. Hundreds of men started showing up at the victim's home and

---

65. Feminist Majority Foundation v. Univ. of Mary Washington, 283 F. Supp. 3d 495, 501 (2017).

66. Feminist Majority Foundation v. Hurley, 911 F.3d 674, 687–88 (4th Cir. 2018).

67. Cassie Cox, *Protecting Victims of Cyberstalking, Cyber Harassment, and Online Impersonation through Prosecutions and Effective Laws*, 54 Jurimetrics J. 277, 286 (2014).

work, aggressively and sometimes violently confronting him for sex. His attorney contends:

> Grindr does not warn its subscribers that its product may be used to target them for purposes of harassment, rape, and physical assault. . . . Grindr does not verify the identity of its subscribers, and takes no precautions to prevent subscribers using proxies and other technical methods to mask their true identity. . . . Grindr does not use even standard, widely available software programs such as key word searching, proxy blocking, and image recognition software, all routinely used by interactive service providers to control their sites and products and to facilitate the safety and security of their users and the public.[68]

As a result, she argues, the web platform itself is inherently dangerous to users and, therefore, defective. The District Court dismissed these claims, not on the merits, but because the defendants claimed a statutory immunity (discussed in the next section).[69]

2. A Civil Rights Remedy? Some experts argue that civil rights laws are the best avenue for dealing with online sexual harassment, because such laws are tailored to address systemic, sexist harms.

> First, civil rights laws recognize the serious injuries that online mobs inflict on victims, their communities, and society as whole. . . . Traditional tort and criminal law fail to respond to such systemic harm and, indeed, may obscure a full view of the damage.

> Second, a civil rights approach would play a valuable normative and expressive role in society. Civil rights prosecutions would communicate society's commitment to "values of equality of treatment and opportunity" and make clear that conduct transgressing those values will not be tolerated. . . .

> Third, viewing the assaults as civil rights violations might provide an incentive for prosecutors to pursue criminal charges. . . . Prosecutors might devote more resources to untangling a case's difficult technological issues if they recognized its civil rights implications.

> Fourth, . . . [t]he awards of attorney's fees possible under many civil rights statutes might make some cases affordable to pursue.

> Fifth, civil rights suits may reach wrongs that would otherwise escape liability. These include victims' rights to be free from economic intimidation and cyber harassment based on race and gender.

---

68. Complaint at 17, Matthew Herrick v. Grindr, LLC et al., No. 00932-VEC (S.D.N.Y. April 12, 2017).

69. Herrick v. Grindr, LLC, 306 F. Supp. 3d 579 (S.D.N.Y. 2018).

Finally, civil rights law has adapted over the years to many of the conditions that exacerbate the extreme behavior of online mobs. It has had to respond to hateful mobs emboldened by anonymity. It also has confronted the objectification of subordinated people. . . .[70]

Do you agree, in light of the cases discussed above?

C. Extralegal Remedies and Their Limits

Even with robust and up-to-date laws, targets who try to combat cyberharassment face many challenges. For example, they encounter major hurdles when they try to get law enforcement to take their criminal complaints seriously. Reasons for underenforcement by police vary. First, some officers and departments may be unaware of the protective laws. Second, they may not understand the harms that cyberharassment creates. Third, they may lack the technical knowledge to effectively investigate complaints. Professor Citron notes:

Some officers do not get enough legal training; because they do not understand the state of the law, they advise their victims to buy a gun and to sue their harassers in civil court. Some officers lack the technical know-how to track down perpetrators. There is a wide-spread lack of literacy about matters related to the Internet, a problem to which officers are not immune. Some officers refuse to do anything because, in their view, the abuse is too personal, too messy, and too difficult to address.[71]

Citron compares the experience of cyberharassment survivors today with the treatment of domestic violence survivors a generation ago.

The nature of the internet itself creates other challenges. Targets may not be able to identify or block perpetrators, particularly when these harassers take steps to conceal their identities or when they operate as a cybermob. Survivors may be understandably reluctant to talk about what has happened to them or to pursue a legal complaint, because doing so could unleash another torrent of abuse. Targets may encounter difficulties in getting slanderous information scrubbed from the internet. Material that is taken down from one site often reappears on another. Websites can close down and reopen under a new name. Search engine algorithms are not easily changed. Reputation repair services — which remove negative content and manipulate search results — exist, but they are not free.

Indeed, the most effective policing of online harassment would come from the websites and platforms themselves. These gatekeepers are in the best position to monitor the content that they host. Professor Jacqueline Lipton notes that "the platforms provide the gateways for online discourse, allow targets of online abuses to

---

70. Citron, *supra* note 39, at 89–91.
71. *Id*. at 20.

easily identify them, possess the financial resources to compensate targets by way of damages, and have the technical capacity to remove abusive postings and block abusive posters."[72]

Self-regulation, however, is purely voluntary. Section 230 of the Communications Decency Act (CDA) of 1996, passed in the early days of the internet, protects service providers. The CDA immunizes providers of "interactive computer services" from tort liability for most torts for material that harassers post to the sites.[73]

> The near-absolute immunity of on-line service providers under [the CDA] has in practice prevented courts from engaging in meaningful discussions about the standard of care that might be expected of these service providers absent the statutory immunity. . . . [A] victim may effectively have no legal remedy in cases where an anonymous poster cannot be found. There will be no action available against the intermediary and no way of bringing an action against the original poster of the abusive content.[74]

Some platforms have strict standards and managers police posted content. For these sites, a target of cyberharassment or revenge porn can notify the site webmasters and demand that they take down the offending material.[75]

Other platforms' creators are less willing to interfere with user-generated content. Some site owners value the free exchange of ideas more than the protection of users from harassment. Other sites exist for the very purpose of encouraging users to post harassing, obscene, and slanderous messages. Professor Brian Leiter refers to these as "cesspool sites," arguing that they deserve neither CDA immunity nor First Amendment protections.[76]

Any time speech is involved, the First Amendment may become relevant to protect not only the speakers and their speech, but also the recipients of speech. The next section addresses how sexual harassment claims intersect with free speech.

3. The First Amendment Defense

Some defendants have attempted to use a free speech defense in workplace sexual harassment cases. The United States Supreme Court addressed this constitutional

---

72. Jacqueline D. Lipton, *Combating Cyber-Victimization*, 26 BERKELEY TECH. L.J. 1103, 1132 (2011).

73. 47 U.S.C. § 230 (West 2019).

74. Lipton, *supra* note 72, at 1132–33. Note that the CDA does *not* exempt websites from copyright law. 47 U.S.C. § 230(e) (West 2019).

75. The Cyber Civil Rights Initiative publishes the *Online Removal Guide* with the major social media and tech platforms' terms of service policies and instructions for reporting offending content. *See* Cyber Civil Rights Initiative, *Online Removal Guide*, cybercivilrights.org/online-removal.

76. Brian Leiter, *Cleaning Cyber-Cesspools: Google and Free Speech*, in THE OFFENSIVE INTERNET: SPEECH, PRIVACY, AND REPUTATION (Saul Levmore & Martha C. Nussbaum, eds., 2010).

defense only in dictum in *R.A.V. v. City of St. Paul*, 505 U.S. 377 (1992). Writing for the majority, Justice Scalia suggested:

> [S]ince words can in some circumstances violate laws directed not against speech but against conduct (a law against treason, for example, is violated by telling the enemy the Nation's defense secrets), a particular content-based subcategory of a proscribable class of speech can be swept up incidentally within the reach of a statute directed at conduct rather than speech. . . . Thus, for example, sexually derogatory "fighting words," among other words, may produce a violation of Title VII's general prohibition against sexual discrimination in employment practices. . . . Where the government does not target conduct on the basis of its expressive content, acts are not shielded from regulation merely because they express a discriminatory idea or philosophy.[77]

This passage suggests that the Court would not permit a First Amendment defense to eviscerate a Title VII claim. Because of the lack of definitive high court precedent regarding the First Amendment's application, however, lawyers have asserted this defense. Courts are split on the First Amendment's application in harassment cases. Contrast how Judge Howell Melton dealt with this issue in 1991 and how Justice Edith Jones addressed the issue four years later.

Robinson v. Jacksonville Shipyards, Inc.
760 F. Supp. 1486 (M.D. Fla. 1991)

MELTON, District Judge:

. . . .

40. The first amendment guarantee of freedom of speech does not impede the remedy of injunctive relief.

(a) First, JSI has disavowed that it seeks to express itself through the sexually-oriented pictures or the verbal harassment by its employees. No first amendment concern arises when the employer has no intention to express itself and JSI's action in limiting the speech options of its employees in the workplace establishes that the company may direct an end to the posting of materials without abridging its employees' free speech rights.

(b) Second, the pictures and verbal harassment are not protected speech because they act as discriminatory conduct in the form of a hostile work environment. *See Roberts v. United States Jaycees*, 468 U.S. 609, 628 (1984) ("[P]otentially expressive activities that produce special harms distinct from their communicative impact . . . are entitled to no constitutional protection.") . . . In this respect, the speech at issue is indistinguishable from the speech that comprises a crime, such as threats of violence or blackmail, of which there can be no doubt of the authority of a state to punish. *E.g., Rankin v. McPherson*, 483 U.S. 378, 386–87 (1987) (threat to kill the

---

77. *R.A.V.*, 505 U.S. at 389.

President is not protected by first amendment); *United States v. Shoulberg*, 895 F.2d 882, 886 (2d Cir. 1990) (threats to intimidate witnesses). . . . This treatment is consistent with the holding of *Pittsburgh Press Co. v. Human Relations Comm'n*, 413 U.S. 376 (1973), that a ban on discriminatory help-wanted advertisements did not offend the first amendment.

(c) Third, the regulation of discriminatory speech in the workplace constitutes nothing more than a time, place, and manner regulation of speech. . . . The standard for this type of regulation requires a legitimate governmental interest unrelated to the suppression of speech, content neutrality, and a tailoring of the means to accomplish this interest. The eradication of workplace discrimination is more than simply a legitimate governmental interest, it is a compelling governmental interest. *See Rotary Int'l v. Rotary Club of Duarte*, 481 U.S. 537, 549 (1987) (eliminating discrimination against women is compelling governmental interest); *Roberts*, 468 U.S. at 626 (compelling governmental interest lies in removing barriers to economic advancement and political and social integration that have historically plagued women). Given the circumstances of the JSI work environment, the method of regulation set forth in this order narrowly tailors the regulation to the minimum necessary to remedy the discrimination problem. To the extent that the regulation here does not seem entirely content neutral, the distinction based on the sexually explicit nature of the pictures and other speech does not offend constitutional principles. *See Renton v. Playtime Theatres, Inc.*, 475 U.S. 41, 48–49 (1986). . . .

(d) Fourth, female workers at JSI are a captive audience in relation to the speech that comprises the hostile work environment. "Few audiences are more captive than the average worker. . . . Certainly, if employer-employee relations involve sufficient coercion that we justify regulation in other contexts, then this coercion does not suddenly vanish when the issue is submission to racist or sexist speech." The free speech guarantee admits great latitude in protecting captive audiences from offensive speech.

(e) Fifth, if the speech at issue is treated as fully protected, and the Court must balance the governmental interest in cleansing the workplace of impediments to the equality of women, the latter is a compelling interest that permits the regulation of the former and the regulation is narrowly drawn to serve this interest. *Cf. United States v. Paradise*, 480 U.S. 149, 171–85 (1987) (performing similar analysis for race-conscious remedy to race discrimination). Other first amendment rights, such as the freedom of association and the free exercise of religion, have bowed to narrowly tailored remedies designed to advance the compelling governmental interest in eradicating employment discrimination.

(f) Sixth, the public employee speech cases lend a supportive analogy. If this Court's decree is conceptualized as a governmental directive concerning workplace rules that an employer must carry out, then the present inquiry is informed by the limits of a governmental employer's power to enforce workplace rules impinging on free speech rights. In the public employee speech cases, the interests of the employee in commenting on protected matters is balanced against the employer's interests in maintaining discipline and order in the workplace. When an employee's exercise of free expression undermines the morale of the workforce, the employer may discipline or discharge the employee without violating the first amendment. Analogously, the Court may, without violating the first amendment, require that a private employer curtail the free expression in the workplace of some employees in order to remedy the demonstrated harm inflicted on other employees.

(g) Finally, defendants' reliance upon *American Booksellers Ass'n v. Hudnut*, 771 F.2d 323 (7th Cir. 1985), *sum. aff'd*, 475 U.S. 1001 (1986), is misplaced. Two concerns dominate that case. One is the broad definition of "pornography" in the Indianapolis ordinance. This issue is not present in this case because the affected speech, if it is speech protected by the first amendment, is reached only after a determination that a harm has been and is continuing to be inflicted on identifiable individuals. The second concern raised in *Hudnut* is the underlying proposition of the Indianapolis ordinance that pornography conveys a message that is always inappropriate and always subject to punishment, regardless of the context in which it appears. In this case, the context of the speech is the heart of the cause of action and the remedy goes no further than to regulate the time, place, and manner of the offensive speech. *Cf. Bryson*, 888 F.2d at 1567 (public employee may be discharged lawfully for uttering on-job speech which would be protected fully if uttered off-duty and in private).

Notes and Discussion

1. Employer Speech Judge Melton noted that the objectionable speech belonged not to Jacksonville Shipyards but to its employees. Thus, Jacksonville had no protected speech interest. When might this reasoning fail?

2. Time, Place, and Manner Restriction Is it true, as Judge Melton determined, that the regulation of discriminatory speech constitutes nothing more than a time, place, and manner restriction? Are the court's comments concerning content neutrality persuasive? Why or why not?

3. Captive Audience Is it true that workers are a captive audience? Aren't they free to leave? Is a worker captive to a *Playboy* magazine on someone's desk in the same way she is captive to posted pin-ups? Does it matter whether the worker experiences offensive speech directed at her or simply overhears offensive speech? Does it make a difference whether the complainant is captive at an assembly line or on a university campus?

4. Quid Pro Quo/Hostile Work Environment Does it matter to a First Amendment defense whether the objectionable speech constitutes quid pro quo or hostile work environment harassment? Explain. Is all discriminating speech "conduct"?

5. The Chilling Effect Professor Eugene Volokh has argued that Title VII harassment law suppresses speech that should be protected under the First Amendment.

He argues that the terms "severe," "pervasive," "hostile," and "abusive" are "mushy" terms that lead to employers violating employees' free speech rights.[78] Professor David Bernstein has criticized even temporary, partial restrictions on free expression to achieve egalitarian goals. He argued that the subordination of the First Amendment to antidiscrimination laws would necessarily produce authoritarianism.[79] Do these views have merit? In response, Professor Deborah Epstein has argued that these critiques fail to adequately weigh the harms of discriminatory speech. She argues that a strict scrutiny analysis proves that Title VII speech regulation fosters a compelling interest in ending employment discrimination.[80]

DeAngelis v. El Paso Municipal Police Officers Assoc.
51 F.3d 591 (5th Cir. 1995)

EDITH H. JONES, Circuit Judge:

. . . .

Background

After six years on duty with the El Paso Police Department as a patrol officer and detective, Sylvia DeAngelis became the first female sergeant in October, 1987. Within a few months of promotion, she was satirized by an anonymous writer in *The Silver Badge*, a newsletter of the El Paso Municipal Police Officers Association (the Association), an organization similar to a police officers' union. The author's *nom de plume* was R.U. Withmi. He wrote as a patrol officer with nearly 20 years' experience "combatin' crime." His monthly column criticized, in an irreverent and colloquial manner, groups including superior officers, "rear echelon" officers ("REMF's"), bureaucrats, and "weenie boys." R.U. Withmi lashed out at changing times in the police department while longing for the good old days. The incursion of females into the department, a quintessential element of modernization, did not escape his sharp pen.

This lawsuit arises from several of his columns, published between November 1987 and February 1990, that derogatorily referred to policewomen. About a thousand copies of *The Silver Badge* were printed monthly and distributed at a minimum to 700 police officer members of the Association.

Publication of the columns angered more than two dozen female police officers, who asked the police chief and officers of the Association to stifle R.U. Withmi. The police chief, despite his discomfiture, had no direct authority over the Association,

---

78. Eugene Volokh, *What Speech Does "Hostile Environment" Harassment Law Restrict?* 5 GEO. L.J. 627 (1997); *see also* Eugene Volokh, *Freedom of Speech and Workplace Harassment*, 39 UCLA L. REV. 1791 (1992).

79. David E. Bernstein, *Defending the First Amendment from Antidiscrimination Laws*, 82 N.C. L. REV. 223, 240–46 (2003).

80. Deborah Epstein, *Free Speech at Work: Verbal Harassment as Discriminatory (Mis)treatment*, 85 GEO. L.J. 649 (1997).

and the Association, after a vote of the membership in early 1990, rejected their leaders' advice to require that R.U. Withmi unmask himself.

Peculiarly, although specifically offered the opportunity, none of the police-women ever chose to write a response to R.U. Withmi for *The Silver Badge*.[2] The record mentions no boycott of the Association or its newsletter, no challenge to the officers' election. Sergeant DeAngelis' Title VII claims are before this court.

Discussion

. . . .

. . . One must infer that because the R.U. Withmi column appeared monthly in *The Silver Badge*, and the challenged articles appeared over a course of 30 months, none of the twenty articles not offered in evidence at the trial court was hostile to women.

1. *December 1987*—Well-low and BE-hold!!, the Holiday Season is here! It seems like just the other day we got a new Chief and them 87 low bid police cars had just arrived. As the new year fast approaches these here parts and we all git just a little older, I has begun to get a lil' nostalgic in my old age a rememberin' when things was a little different. It is my opinion that we here are in a new age of patrolmen, patrolwoman, defectowoman, sergeant dingy woman and now thanks to the appeal process, patrol other! I just think a people are changing and we are getting a new generation of patrolmen in as few as five years! I remember the good ol' days when finding the criminal was more important to the patrolmen then keeping your hair in place! I wonder how far back you remember? I remember these things, let's see if you do . . . Remember when? . . . Do you remember when there were no women workin' the streets? (Ah yes, those were the good days! . . . Sorry gals, truth hurts!) . . .

2. *February 1988*—I never thought I would make the newspaper El Paso Rag, an E-I-E-I-O complaint or be blasted out of my socks by our Presidente himself!

3. *March 1988*— . . . only REAL MEN wear them ole wool pants! You don't see any of the "jefes" with a bottle of hair spray on their Sam Browns! . . . And I don't EVEN want to start up against the "girls" so my Commandante Presidente don't get "scared" again with his poison pen!

4. *August 1988*—I was surprised to think they were also training some good lookin' K-9s up there but I was told those were the female recruits! I swear!, complete with collars! Oh well, my mistake!

5. *October 1988*—I understand I done rustled the feathers of a few Female Recruit Officers and their "Daddys" up there on the "HILL." Well, ole' RU's a so sorry because I sometimes get carried away with tellin' things they way it is. Don't worry, I think I was wrong because the public will treat you with all the "respect"

---

2. Except perhaps a brief anonymous editorial from "I.N. Wifya" which expressed disgust and disagreement with R.U. Withmi on a variety of issues including remarks about the attractiveness of the new female recruits.

you deserve IF you get out there, and they will never call you names other than "officer." And wherever you answer the call, you will always get the cooperation you deserve. And no one will call you names to your face. So, life will be a bowl of cherries on the streets and everythin' you've been told is the truth . . .

6. *January 1989*— . . . now the patrol stations have to pull out a FULL DUTY policeMAN from the field to do the desk work! . . . I just want a car that works, and a supervisor with some sense . . . and a female officer that places her ability before her gender and IA out of my way!

7. *February 1989*— . . . with just one whack of the pluma we had musical supervisors all over the City. . . . Chances are purty darn good that we all probably know who the real problem was. But no names these days because of them EEOC Fed boys!

8. *July 1989*—Anyway, fly that flag, be glad yore American, have a job, are male, and workin' patrol.

9. *February 1990*—We had a hell-uva BS session at shift meeting (a place REMF's know nuthin' about!) regarding women in combat. . . . Physically, the police broads just don't got it! Different standards or not, on the real streets the crooks don't fight women different than men! Why shoot, a guy weighing 140 pounds is just a lil' bird to me, but a fit to fight police broad of 140 pounds ain't just around that often! Someone tell me I'm wrong![4]

10. *April 1990*—My academy Joe weenie partner dun informed me that this here bits o truth I writes each months just plain gots alotta folks supportin' it!

Sergeant DeAngelis acknowledged that only the first column directly referred to her as Sergeant "dingy woman," evidently a shorthand expression for "dingbat." She asserts that the column concerning her "E-I-E-I-O complaint" ridiculed her as well as EEOC. Another column singled her out as one of the few officers to carry a flashlight on her belt in the daytime. And she believes that the reference to musical supervisors in the February 1989 column implied that her troubles caused a shift around the police department. All of the other columns, DeAngelis conceded, refer to women in general, as was brought home to the police department and the Association by the uproar of many female police officers at their appearance.

Whether the four columns that refer to DeAngelis, taken alone or in conjunction with the other six columns appearing at irregular intervals in two and a half years, amounted to severe or pervasive sexually discriminatory intimidation, ridicule or insults depends in part upon their context. The R.U. Withmi column did not represent a boss's demeaning harangue, or a sexually charged invitation, or a campaign of vulgarity perpetrated by co-workers: the column attempted clumsy, earthy humor. R.U. Withmi intended to be a curmudgeon, the police department's Archie Bunker or Homer Simpson, who eyed with suspicion all authority figures,

---

4. This column spawned the class action lawsuit in state court by 22 women police.

academy-trained officers, police dispatchers, newfangled procedures and gear—whatever had changed from the old days. Misogyny naturally came with R.U.'s territory, although, against the backdrop of his other barbs, it can hardly be called an obsession. In any event, much of his humor lacked volatility: his reference to a police officer as a "policeMAN" or his exhortation to "be glad you're male . . .", for instance, hardly rank in the firmament of sexist vilification.

. . . .

We conclude that these columns are the equivalent of the "mere utterance of an . . . epithet which engenders offensive feelings in an employee." *Meritor Savings,* 477 U.S. at 67, 106 S.Ct. at 2405. Consequently, they were not severe or pervasive enough to create an objectively hostile or abusive work environment. *Harris,* [510] U.S. at [23], 114 S.Ct. at 370. Four printed derogatory references to Sergeant DeAngelis at irregular intervals in two and a half years do not evince sufficient hostility toward her as a matter of law.

. . . .

Because we have concluded that insufficient evidence supports DeAngelis' claim of a sexually harassing work environment, we do not reach the difficult question whether Title VII may be violated by expressions of opinion published in the R.U. Withmi columns in the Association's newsletter. Where pure expression is involved, Title VII steers into the territory of the First Amendment. It is no use to deny or minimize this problem because, when Title VII is applied to sexual harassment claims founded solely on verbal insults, pictorial or literary matter, the statute imposes content-based, viewpoint-discriminatory restrictions on speech.[6] *See* Eugene Volokh, *Freedom of Speech and Workplace Harassment,* 39 U.C.L.A. L. Rev. 1791 (1992); Kingsley R. Browne, *Title VII as Censorship: Hostile Environment Harassment and the First Amendment,* 52 Ohio St. L.J. 481 (1991). Whether such applications of Title VII are necessarily unconstitutional has not yet been fully explored. *But see Robinson v. Jacksonville Shipyards,* Inc., 760 F. Supp. 1486 (M.D.Fla. 1991). The Supreme Court's offhand pronouncements are unilluminating.[7]

. . . .

------

6. We do not mean that sexual propositions, quid pro quo overtures, discriminatory employment actions against women or "fighting words" involve the First Amendment.

7. The Court's pronouncement in *R.A.V.,* that "sexually derogatory 'fighting words,' among other words, may produce a violation of Title VII's general prohibition against sexual discrimination in employment practices" does not mean that Title VII trumps First Amendment speech rights. Rather, as the next sentence in *R.A.V.* explains, conduct not targeted on the basis of its expressive content may be regulated. R.A.V. v. City of St. Paul, Minnesota, 505 U.S. 377, 391–393 (1992). Citing *R.A.V.,* the Court in *Wisconsin v. Mitchell,* 508 U.S. 476, 487 (1993) reiterated that conduct not targeted on the basis of its expressive content may be regulated by Title VII. However, application of Title VII to the "conduct" in the case *sub judice* would do precisely that—regulate speech on the basis of its expressive content.

Conclusion

Title VII cannot remedy every tasteless joke or groundless rumor that confronts women in the workplace. For DeAngelis, the price of success as the police department's first woman sergeant included transitory ribbing by R.U. Withmi. The newsletter columns, however, were not so frequent, pervasive or pointedly insulting to DeAngelis as to create an objectively hostile working environment. The totality of circumstances do not prove that her working conditions were disadvantaged because she was mentioned in four R.U. Withmi columns. Likewise, three printed references to her EEOC complaint do not constitute retaliation under Title VII.[8]

The judgment of the district court is therefore *Reversed* and *Rendered* for the Association.

Notes and Discussion

1. The First Amendment The court held that for "claims founded solely on verbal insults, pictorial or literary matter, the statute [Title VII] imposes content-based, viewpoint-discriminatory restrictions on speech." Compare this decision with *Harris*. In *Harris*, the Supreme Court found verbal harassment violative of Title VII and never addressed the First Amendment defense, despite the briefing on the First Amendment proffered by both parties and amici curiae. What are the differences between the two fact situations? In a review of the "totality of the circumstances," should the court exclude evidence of verbal insults, pictorial, and literary matter, as protected by the First Amendment? If so, how might Justice Jones have decided Lois Robinson's case against Jacksonville Shipyards?

The *DeAngelis* court highlighted that "although specifically offered the opportunity, none of the policewomen ever chose to write a response to R.U. Withmi for The Silver Badge." Would more "speech" have cured the problem for DeAngelis? Should courts penalize those targets of offensive speech when they fail to "talk back"? Consider the experience of many cyberharassment survivors (discussed in the previous section), who understandably fear that "fighting back" online will just cause them to experience more abuse. Does *Faragher*, with its creation of the affirmative defense, suggest that survivors must "talk back" by complaining? Or is the accessing of a protective policy different from the speech argument?

2. Content Based Speech If the law permits content-based restrictions only in rare cases when the restrictions are narrowly tailored to further a compelling state interest, is there an aspect to Title VII regulation that provides for such narrow tailoring? Does the limitation on regulation posed by the severity or pervasiveness requirements create a narrow tailoring? Why or why not?

3. Verbal Act John Wirenius argues that "conduct which creates a hostile work environment fits largely within the parameters of what the Supreme Court has long

---

8. Because we reverse the underlying findings of liability, we also vacate the award of punitive damages.

recognized as a 'verbal act[.]'" He explains that such performed, hostile speech "remains outside the boundaries of First Amendment protection, not based upon governmental disapproval of the speech in question but because those words spoken in the particular factual context have the effect of an act, not of a communication."[81] Do you agree?

4. On Appeal The appellate court reversed the district court's decision in *DeAngelis*, not with a ruling on the First Amendment, but because it determined that the offensive conduct failed to meet the severe or pervasive threshold level to constitute actionable harassment. In dicta, however, the court explored the First Amendment defense. It concluded that when conduct consists of "pure expression," antidiscrimination law conflicts with the First Amendment. Relying on the content-based, viewpoint-discriminatory nature of the speech restriction, the court ignored some of the important issues mentioned in *Robinson*, such as the compelling goal of ending employment discrimination that might justify speech restrictions.

5. Expressive Workplaces Should there be a different standard for expressive workplaces, like newspapers, movie studios, or cabarets?[82] What about a boss who claims a First Amendment "creative expression" right to work naked?[83]

6. Public Workplaces Professor Lawrence Rosenthal has argued that governmental power to forbid harassing speech in the workplace is unconstrained by the First Amendment under the law of managerial prerogative, adopted by the Supreme Court in the 2006 case of *Garcetti v. Ceballos*.[84]

7. Speech Protections under the National Labor Relations Act Broad workplace "civility codes" that limit or restrict speech may violate the National Labor Relations Act (NLRA), which guarantees workers' right to freely discuss workplace conditions without fear of reprisal. The National Labor Relations Board has ruled that vulgar language and obscene gestures in some workplace situations are protected by the NLRA. *See, e.g., Fresenius USA Manufacturing, Inc.*, 358 NLRB No. 138 (2012) (referring to female employees as "pussies" and "cat-food lovers" in trying to garner support for the union is protected); *but see, PPG Industries*, 337 NLRB 1247 (2002) (where a male union supporter's comment to a female colleague that employer was "screwing her" and "f***ing her" so she should sign a union card was not protected); *The Boeing Company and Society of Professional Engineering Employees in Aerospace, IFPTE Local 2001*, 365 NLRB No. 164 (2017) (civility rules are generally acceptable

---

81. John F. Wirenium, *Action as Words, Words as Actions: Sexual Harassment Law, The First Amendment and Verbal Acts,* 28 WHITTIER L. REV. 905, 907 (2007).

82. *See* Jonathan Segal, *The Expressive Workplace Doctrine: Protecting the Public Discourse from Hostile Work Environment Actions,* 15 UCLA ENT. L. REV. 1 (2008).

83. *See* Kimberly Phillips, *My Body is a Sacred 'Garment'—Does the First Amendment Creative Expression Protection Shield Clothing Designers Who Work Naked?,* 42 RUTGERS L. REV. 82 (2014–2015).

84. Lawrence Rosenthal, *The Emerging First Amendment Law of Managerial Prerogative,* 77 FORDHAM L. REV. 33 (2008).

under the NLRA). The EEOC and NLRB are reportedly working on joint guidance regarding the line between harassment and protected concerted activity.

8. Public Universities Unlike private educational institutions, sexual harassment policies at public schools and colleges are subject to First Amendment scrutiny. If these policies impact speech, they must be content and viewpoint neutral and narrowly tailored. Offensive speech is protected by the First Amendment, but speech severe enough to cause a discriminatory effect is not. Therefore, public schools must be careful to craft a clear and specific policy that is not overbroad or vague.

The standard for severity, as established in *Davis v. Monroe County Board of Education*, is that the harassment must be "so severe, pervasive, and objectively offensive that it effectively bars the victim's access to an educational opportunity or benefit" (see Chapter 6). Verbal conduct does not rise to this level unless it is repetitive and widespread, which is more likely if disseminated online. In *Corlett v. Oakland University*,[85] a federal district court dismissed a student's First Amendment challenge to punishment under a sexual harassment policy for submitting to his teacher an essay that described his sexual attraction to her and detailed her physical appearance. The court ruled that the essay, written for a course assignment and directed at his professor, was not protected by the First Amendment. The *Corlett* court cited the Sixth Circuit's decision in *Settle v. Dickson County School Board*,[86] which held that "effective education depends not only on controlling boisterous conduct, but also on maintaining the focus of the class on the assignment in question."

4. The Plaintiff's Sexual History

Historically, defense counsel often used a harassment plaintiff's sexual history to impugn her credibility. Evidence that a woman had consented to sex in the past would be used to argue she had a propensity to consent to sex and had acted in conformity with that propensity at the time of the alleged rape. Moreover, the "unwelcomeness" requirement in sexual harassment statutes created an incentive for defendants to point to a plaintiff's sexual history as evidence that she welcomed the harassment. Anti-rape activists in the 1970s pushed for laws to prohibit the use of sexual history in order to counteract cultural stereotypes, victim blaming, and biases against women in rape trials. In 1978, Congress amended the Federal Rules of Evidence to add Rule 412, commonly known as the "rape shield rule." Rule 412 bars evidence of the intimate details of a survivor's prior sexual history with other partners in a criminal rape or sexual abuse trial.

In 1994, Congress expanded the applicability of Rule 412 to civil cases, including Title VII sexual harassment cases. While character evidence is generally admissible under Federal Rule of Evidence 404, Rule 412 created a presumption that a sexual

---

85. 958 F. Supp. 2d 795 (E.D. Mich. 2013).
86. 53 F.3d 152, 155 (6th Cir. 1995).

harassment survivor's sexual history and propensities are inadmissible. The rule states, "evidence offered to prove the sexual behavior or sexual predisposition of any alleged victim is admissible if it is otherwise admissible under these rules and its probative value substantially outweighs the danger of harm to any victim and of unfair prejudice to any party."[87]

Despite this limitation, Federal Rule of Civil Procedure 35 allows for discovery of a party's mental or physical condition when it has been placed at issue. Because *Meritor* condones investigations into the plaintiff's dress, conduct and demeanor, courts often permit discovery regarding these issues. Defense counsel's attempt to discover, or introduce at trial, sensitive information regarding the plaintiff's sexual history with persons other than the accused, however, may subject a plaintiff to emotionally distressing exposure of her intimate sexual history and trauma.[88]

Harris v. Forklift Systems,[89] resolved that a plaintiff need not suffer a nervous breakdown in order to sue. However, *Harris* specified that the plaintiff must demonstrate subjective offense to the alleged conduct. Therefore, defense counsel often attempts to discover or introduce the plaintiff's psychological history and profile to rebut the plaintiff's claims of offense and emotional distress. Defense counsel may also seek information about a plaintiff's personal medical information in order to discredit her. Plaintiff's counsel often objects to attempts to obtain the plaintiff's sexual and medical history.

In the following discovery and evidence decisions, courts balance relevance and the accused's need to support a defense against the plaintiff's privacy interests and the potential for prejudice. Consider whether the holdings seem fair to both parties.

Rodriguez-Hernandez v. Miranda-Velez

132 F.3d 848 (1st Cir. 1998)

LYNCH, Circuit Judge.

. . . The main issues presented by this appeal are whether the jury's verdict in favor of the customer dictates that the verdict against her employer be reversed [and] whether the court's evidentiary and juror peremptory challenge rulings were correct. . . .

I.

. . . .

[Sandra] Rodriguez worked as an office manager for Occidental International, a Florida company with offices in Florida and Puerto Rico. Rodriguez started

---

87. F.R.E. §412 (2019).

88. *See* Katie M. Patton, *Unfolding Discovery Issues that Plague Sexual Harassment Suits*, 57 Hastings L.J. 991 (2006) (discussing the tension between the broad discovery allowed under Federal Rule of Civil Procedure 35 and the limitations on admissibility of sexual history and predisposition evidence in Federal Rule of Evidence 412).

89. 510 U.S. 17 (1993).

working for Occidental in December of 1988 in the Traffic and Claims division of the Puerto Rico office. She was twice promoted, and was put in charge of overseeing the daily operations of her office in February of 1990. While she was never formally evaluated during her employment, Rodriguez received regular praise for her work, and before the suspension and dismissal that led to this lawsuit, she had never been the subject of disciplinary action.

Occidental International sells electrical and industrial equipment. Occidental's most important market was Puerto Rico, and its most important customer was the Puerto Rico Electric Power Authority ("PREPA"). At the time of Rodriguez's dismissal, approximately 80% of Occidental's business in Puerto Rico was with PREPA.

Omar Chavez was the President and sole shareholder of Occidental. Chavez lived in Florida, and would make monthly business trips to Puerto Rico. Chavez pursued a number of strategies which he thought would ensure continued good relations between Occidental and its customers, particularly with PREPA.

Evidence presented at trial showed that Chavez primarily employed young, attractive women, known to customers as "Occidental Gals," and instructed them to be especially cordial to PREPA employees.

Good relations were particularly important with highranking PREPA officials like Edwin Miranda-Velez, the Chief of PREPA's Materials Management Division and the overseer of PREPA's public contracts for the type of goods sold by Occidental. Chavez introduced Rodriguez to Miranda, and told her that Miranda was very important for Occidental's business and that she and the other employees should be nice to him and "keep him satisfied." She was instructed to visit Miranda every time she went to the PREPA offices.

Occidental pursued other strategies.... In December of 1990, Chavez threw a party for PREPA officials at a local hotel. The members of the Occidental Puerto Rico staff, all female, were instructed to attend the event unaccompanied, so they would be available to dance with the PREPA executives. The night's entertainment at that party included a dancing show performed by scantily clad women.

The close relationship with PREPA benefitted Occidental, and Chavez, in several ways. Chavez was able to learn from Miranda in advance what bids would be coming up and how much Occidental's competitors were bidding. Miranda helped to steer business to Occidental through requests for proposals that were handled outside the ordinary bidding process. For example, Miranda helped Occidental to obtain a transportation contract on an "emergency" basis. Miranda signed all pertinent documentation and recommended payments to suppliers. There were also allegations that Miranda was able to help Occidental avoid trouble over tax disclosures.

Miranda began to make unwelcome approaches and suggestive comments to Rodriguez. He invited her out to dinner. He asked her to visit his office after hours and on Friday evenings. He anonymously sent her flowers for her birthday and included a sexually explicit card. Rodriguez complained to Chavez about this behavior; Chavez responded by stressing that Miranda was an important client, but assured her that he would deal with the problem.

The culmination, as it were, of Miranda's advances came on February 28, 1992. Miranda called Rodriguez and told her he would come pick her up to take her to a motel. Rodriguez, upset by Miranda's latest advance, called Chavez to complain about Miranda's call. Chavez responded by defending Miranda, and saying that Rodriguez should respond to Miranda "as a woman." Rodriguez told Chavez that if he would do nothing about the situation, she would take her complaints to the Director of PREPA.

That weekend, Chavez flew to Puerto Rico. On March 9, 1992, Chavez gave Rodriguez a letter informing her that she was suspended from work for thirty days. The letter stated the reasons for her suspension as unauthorized use of company property, contracting for services in the company name without authorization, and absenteeism. On April 6, Rodriguez received a second letter dismissing her from employment at Occidental. The grounds for her dismissal were an unexplained imbalance of $157.00 in petty cash funds and negligence in executing daily functions such as picking up company mail, as well as the problems noted in the March 9 letter. Rodriguez had never been notified of any such deficiencies before.

. . . .

III.

. . . .

C. Evidentiary Rulings

. . . .

1. Rulings under Rule 412

Defendants continually sought to make an issue of plaintiff's sexual history. In the course of this litigation, defendants attempted to paint the plaintiff as sexually insatiable, as engaging in multiple affairs with married men, as a lesbian, and as suffering from a sexually transmitted disease.[2] Defendants claimed that plaintiff had an affair with a married man that caused her to become distracted from work, and led to the lapses for which she was fired.

Fed.R.Evid. 412 was designed to prevent misuse of a complainant's sexual history in cases involving "alleged sexual misconduct." In a civil case, the sole exception to Rule 412's prohibition of evidence offered to prove "that any alleged victim engaged in other sexual behavior" or "any alleged victim's sexual predisposition" is that

> evidence offered to prove the sexual behavior or sexual predisposition of any alleged victim is admissible if it is otherwise admissible under these rules and *its probative value substantially outweighs the danger of harm to*

---

2. During discovery, defendants requested that plaintiff submit to an AIDS test, apparently to substantiate their allegations of promiscuity. The request was denied.

any victim and of unfair prejudice to any party. Evidence of an alleged victim's reputation is admissible only if it has been placed in controversy by the alleged victim.

Fed.R.Evid. 412(b)(2) (emphasis added). Rule 412 thus reverses the usual approach of the Federal Rules of Evidence on admissibility by requiring that the evidence's probative value "substantially outweigh" its prejudicial effect.

Rule 412 mandates procedural safeguards for the introduction of such evidence under the 412(b)(2) exception. A party intending to offer such evidence must file a motion specifically describing the evidence and its purpose at least fourteen days before trial, serve the motion on all parties, and notify the alleged victim. Before admitting the evidence the court must conduct an in camera hearing to afford the victim and parties a right to be heard.

The district court ruled that evidence concerning plaintiff's moral character or promiscuity and the marital status of her boyfriend was inadmissible under Rule 412. But the court allowed defendants to introduce evidence directly relevant to their theory that plaintiff's relationship distracted her from work. The court also held that evidence concerning plaintiff's allegedly flirtatious behavior toward Miranda was admissible to determine whether Miranda's advances were in fact "unwanted."

These evidentiary rulings were well within the district court's discretion. The court struck an acceptable balance between the danger of undue prejudice and the need to present the jury with relevant evidence, particularly in light of Rule 412's special standard of admissibility.

2. Rulings under Rule 403

Nor is there any abuse of discretion in the district court's other evidentiary rulings. Under Fed.R.Evid. 402, all relevant evidence is admissible unless otherwise provided by federal law. Under Fed.R.Evid. 403, relevant evidence may be excluded if its probative value is "substantially outweighed" by the danger of prejudice or confusion.

Defendants challenge the exclusion of certain telephone records, rebuttal evidence by some of plaintiff's coworkers, and an answering machine tape. We agree with the district court that the testimony and phone records would have been, at best, cumulative. The district court conducted lengthy proceedings over the admissibility of an answering machine tape produced by Chavez that purportedly contained several messages from Rodriguez to Chavez that could imply that they had been intimate. The defendants argue that this piece of evidence would have shown that "plaintiff treated Chavez affectionately and could not have been complaining of sexual harassment." An FBI analysis of the voice on the tape was inconclusive. The court ruled that the tape was inadmissible under Fed.R.Evid. 403, and we agree that this dubious evidence had minimal probative value, and had great potential to confuse the jury.

Defendants complain of a "double standard" because the district court allowed information introduced by plaintiff while excluding evidence introduced by defendant. The court allowed evidence concerning the close ties between Occidental and PREPA, including evidence of political donations, Occidental's tax status, the dancing show at the 1990 Christmas party, and a letter regarding Occidental's sales volume. In fact, as to the excluded evidence, Fed.R.Evid. 412 required the district court to apply a stricter standard with regard to admission of evidence of plaintiff's sexual history than to the evidence admitted under the more liberal standard of Fed.R.Evid. 402 & 403. This evidence was directly relevant to the theory of Rodriguez's case—that Chavez and Occidental were willing to fire her when she complained about Miranda in order to maintain their close relationship with Miranda and PREPA.

Having examined each of the district court's evidentiary rulings, we find none that represents an abuse of its discretion. Even if the court's exclusions were error, none of the excluded evidence would have had an impact on the outcome of the trial, as it would have at best been duplicative of evidence that was admitted.

Excel Corp. v. Bosley
165 F.3d 635 (8th Cir. 1999)

SIPPEL, District Judge.

. . . .

I.

. . . [Kristine] Bosley began working at Excel, a meat packing plant, in July 1990. Bosley was married to Johnson at that time. Johnson was also employed at Excel. Bosley separated from Johnson in 1993. Both continued to work at Excel. At trial, Bosley introduced testimony and other evidence that Johnson subjected her to sexual harassment during confrontations at work. There was also evidence that Bosley reported this harassment to Excel's management, but that management personnel did little to investigate or end the harassment.

Bosley was a line worker on the kill floor at Excel. Her position was such that she was not allowed to leave her work station, even to use the restroom, without permission from a supervisor. Johnson was a "floater" at the plant. He worked at different workstations in the plant for absent employees. He circulated regularly on the kill floor where Bosley worked.

The record is replete with evidence of the harassment suffered by Bosley. At various times at the workplace, in the presence of other coworkers, Johnson called Bosley "bitch", "slut" or "whore" [sic]. Johnson also threatened to kill Bosley's friend, now husband, Jeff Bosley. Bosley repeatedly reported the unwelcome harassment to the management at Excel. She also reported fear of Johnson's temper.

Excel's first action was to tell both Bosley and Johnson to keep their disputes at home. Later, following screaming matches on the kill floor, Bosley and Johnson were separated but neither was sanctioned. Johnson continued to harass Bosley even throwing meat and animal organs at her. This was a violation of work rules.

Beginning on May 4, 1994, Bosley took personal time off from work due to the stress of the harassment and other personal problems. She returned to work on May 9, 1994 to find Johnson once again, near her work station on the kill floor. Johnson continued his harassment calling her names such as "fucking bitch." Bosley asked the floor supervisor to relieve her temporarily from her work station. The supervisor refused, despite knowledge of the harassment and Johnson's proximity to Bosley. About fifteen minutes later, Bosley again requested permission to leave her work station. The supervisor denied her request again. Johnson continued to harass Bosley. In frustration, Bosley pushed Johnson once in the chest and told him to get out of the area and go back to his assignment. At that point, the supervisor intervened and escorted Johnson from the area.

After Bosley pushed Johnson, she was sent to a supervisor's office. Physical contact between employees is a work rule violation. Bosley was placed under "indefinite suspension." Bosley was upset. As she was leaving the work floor, Bosley saw Johnson in another room. Bosley believed that Johnson was not being sanctioned as strongly as she was, if at all. Bosley pushed past a supervisor to enter the room to talk to Johnson. This incident was reported as Bosley having struck a supervisor.

The events of May 9, 1994 formed the basis for the decision to terminate Bosley on May 16, 1994. Excel did not sanction Johnson for any of the events of May 9, 1994.

Bosley's claims that Excel fired her in violation of Title VII were tried to a jury. Both Bosley's claim of hostile work environment sexual harassment and disparate treatment based on sex were submitted. The jury returned a verdict for Bosley on her claim of hostile work environment sexual harassment. . . . The jury found for Excel on Bosley's claim of disparate treatment. . . .

II.

. . . .

C. Evidence of Sexual Activity

Excel argues that the district court erroneously ruled that evidence of alleged sexual relations between Bosley and her exhusband outside the work place was inadmissible.

. . . .

At trial Excel sought, pursuant to Federal Rule of Evidence 412, to admit evidence of sexual relations between Bosley and her exhusband. These sexual relations were alleged to have taken place outside of the work place during the same time period as the complained of sexual harassment. Excel made an offer of proof of this evidence. During the offer of proof, Johnson testified that he and Bosley had sexual relations on several occasions during the time of the alleged harassment.

Excel also sought to offer the testimony of Dr. Patrick Barrett, a clinical psychologist who Johnson saw twice during the time of the alleged sexual encounters.

Dr. Barrett testified that he met once with Johnson alone and the second time with Johnson and Bosley. Bosley was in attendance at Dr. Barrett's request. Barrett testified that during the visit with Johnson alone, Johnson told him Bosley was giving him ambiguous signals and that Bosley occasionally slept with him. Dr. Barrett testified that Bosley may have acknowledged sending Johnson mixed signals. Dr. Barrett could not recall whether Bosley acknowledged sleeping with Johnson.

The district court ruled that the testimony of Johnson and Dr. Barrett was inadmissible under Federal Rule of Evidence 412. Rule 412 allows admission of evidence of an alleged victim's past sexual behavior or alleged sexual predisposition in sex offense cases. Specifically Rule 412(b)(2) allows for the admission of such evidence in a civil case if it is otherwise admissible under the Rules of Evidence and its probative value substantially outweighs the danger of harm to any victim and of unfair prejudice to any party. We note that the applicability of Rule 412 to evidence proffered in a lawsuit brought pursuant to Title VII has not been decided by this Court. However, it is not necessary for us to make that determination here. Rule 412 was the only basis for admissibility asserted by Excel. Admissibility of the evidence under any other rule is not before the Court. Assuming, without deciding, that Rule 412 is applicable to the evidence proffered in this case, we cannot find that the district court abused its discretion in refusing to admit into the record, evidence of alleged sexual relations between Bosley and Johnson outside the workplace.

The evidence in the record does not support a finding that the district court manifestly erred in refusing to admit the offered testimony. The alleged sexual activity took place outside the workplace. There was no allegation that Excel was aware of it or that it informed Excel's actions regarding the sexual harassment about which Bosley complained. This was the issue before the jury not Bosley's actions outside the workplace. Further the danger of harm and unfair prejudice to Bosley was great. The district court did not abuse its discretion in refusing to admit the testimony of Johnson and Dr. Barrett. Accordingly, we affirm the actions of the district court.

Sanchez v. Zabihi

166 F.R.D. 500 (D. N.M. 1996)

SMITH, United States Magistrate Judge.

. . . .

Discussion

1. Relevant Facts

On July 21, 1995, Plaintiff filed this Title VII action against Defendants, alleging that by [sic] she was subjected to sexual harassment which resulted in a hostile work environment. Specifically, Plaintiff contends Defendant Mohammad Zabihi made numerous unwanted sexual advances towards Plaintiff at the workplace, and that she was harmed as a result.

. . . .

2. The Motion to Compel

In the instant motion, Defendants seek to compel Plaintiff to respond to Interrogatory No. 1, which states:

1. In the last ten (10) years, have you ever:

a. made any personal, romantic, or sexual advances towards any coworker, or any person with whom you worked at the time, or any person who also worked at your same place of employment; or

b. been the subject of personal, romantic, or sexual advances by a coworker, or by any person with whom you worked at the time, or by any person who also worked at your same place of employment; or

c. had a close personal, romantic, or sexual relationship, however brief, with any coworker, or any person with whom you worked at the time, or any person who also worked at your same place of employment?

If so, for each item above, please identify the person(s) involved, the relevant date(s), the relevant place(s) of employment, the number and/or frequency of any such advance(s), whether such advance(s) were welcome or unwelcome, whether you or the other person(s) involved ever complained in any way regarding any such advance(s), and the length and duration of any such relationship(s).

Plaintiff answered as follows: "Under Rule 412, Federal Rules of Evidence, as amended in 1994, evidence of the victim's prior sexual conduct is not admissible. Thus, this interrogatory is not reasonably calculated to lead to the discovery of relevant evidence."

Although not raised in the pleadings, Defendants now assert a "sexual aggressor" defense. They contend (in the present motion and at the February status conference) that Plaintiff, rather than Defendant Zabihi, was in fact the sexual aggressor making sexual advances towards Zabihi in the workplace. Thus, Defendants essentially defend this action by claiming that Plaintiff cannot show that the sexual harassing behavior was unwelcome. . . .

3. Federal Rule of Evidence 412

. . . .

Although the present motion arises in the context of discovery under Rule 26 of the Federal Rules of Civil Procedure, the Court must remain mindful of Rule 412 and its implications. The Advisory Committee addressed the relationship between the two rules in its notes to the 1994 amendments:

The procedures set forth in subdivision (c) do not apply to discovery of a victim's past sexual conduct or predisposition in civil cases, which will be continued to be governed by Fed.R.Civ.P. 26. In order not to undermine the rationale of Rule 412, however, courts should enter appropriate orders pursuant to Fed.R.Civ.P. 26(c) to protect the victim against unwarranted inquiries and to ensure confidentiality. Courts should presumptively issue protective orders barring discovery unless the party seeking discovery makes a showing that the evidence sought to be discovered would be relevant under the facts and theories of the particular case, and cannot be obtained except through discovery.

FED.R.EVID. 412 advisory committee's note. Therefore, I find that Rule 412 is applicable and has significance in deciding the present discovery motion. Consequently, I find that Defendants' assertion that Plaintiff has waived all objections to answering the interrogatory by asserting Rule 412 to be without merit.

4. Evidence of Habit under Rule 406

One argument advanced by Defendant in their motion to compel is that the evidence sought goes to show habit under Rule 406. On this point, I find the court's reasoning in *Priest v. Rotary*, 98 F.R.D. 755, 75859 (N.D.Cal. 1983)[refusing to allow discovery of plaintiff's sexual history to show "habit"], persuasive and squarely on point. Accordingly, I will deny this basis of Defendants' motion because it is devoid of merit.

5. Evidence Related to the Sexual Aggressor Theory

Rule 26(b) of the Federal Rules of Civil Procedure allows for a broad range of discovery in that "[t]he information sought need not be admissible at the trial if the information sought appears reasonably calculated to lead to the discovery of admissible evidence." Fed.R.Civ.P. 26(b). Hence, the information sought in Defendants' Interrogatory No. 1 is not required to be admissible evidence itself, but it must seem reasonably calculated to lead to the discovery of admissible evidence somewhere down the road.

Therefore, the proper query before this Court is whether the information sought in Interrogatory No. 1 is reasonably calculated to lead to the discovery of admissible evidence in light of the parties' claims and defenses, while remaining mindful of the policy underlying Rule 412 that protects victims of sexual misconduct from undue embarrassment and intrusion into their private affairs. After carefully balancing the various policy considerations and examining the specific claims and theories of this case, I find that the information sought in Interrogatory No. 1 should be narrowly tailored to allow for some discovery while also protecting Plaintiff's privacy interests.

At the outset, it should be noted that at this juncture, the Court is hindered in making a ruling because the Court has not seen the information sought by Defendants. If this were instead a motion to determine the evidentiary admissibility of Plaintiff's sexual conduct, the parties and the Court would proceed in accordance with Rule 412(c), which provides, *inter alia*, that the court conduct an *in camera* hearing and afford the parties a right to be heard. Further, the motion, related papers and record of the hearing would be sealed and remain sealed until further court order. In the present discovery motion, I do not have the information needed to make a final decision on the information sought. Therefore, I will employ several of the procedural safeguards used in a Rule 412(c) proceeding in the context of the present Rule 26 discovery motion. This will serve the purpose of providing the Court with the information sought by Defendant so that I can make a decision based on the competing interests of protecting Plaintiff's private affairs while allowing discovery related to the theories of this case.

I find that Interrogatory No. 1 is required to be answered by Plaintiff, subject to the following limitations. First, I find the interrogatory to be overly broad. It will be limited to inquiring about matters occurring three years before the alleged incidents of sexual harassment by Defendant Zabihi. Second, the word "personal" in subsections (a), (b) and (c) of Interrogatory No. 1 will be stricken for vagueness. Third, Plaintiff is not required to answer about any matter involving the coworker who later became her spouse.

The interrogatory will be answered under oath, sealed and submitted to Mr. Robert Lohbeck, Defendants' attorney, PERSONALLY AND FOR HIS REVIEW ONLY. Mr. Lohbeck is prohibited from divulging any information contained in Plaintiff's answer to anyone, including his clients, without (1) a motion by Defendants; (2) a hearing on the matter; and (3) an order from the Court. I wish to emphasize that this order applies only in the context of the discovery stage of this action and nothing in this order should be construed to pertain to the admissibility of this information at trial under Rule 412.

Notes and Discussion

1. Rule 412 The Congressional Advisory Committee Notes explain Rule 412's purpose:

> Rule 412 has been revised to diminish some of the confusion engendered by the original rule and to expand the protection afforded alleged victims of sexual misconduct. Rule 412 applies to both civil and criminal proceedings. The rule aims to safeguard the alleged victim against the invasion of privacy, potential embarrassment and sexual stereotyping that is associated with public disclosure of intimate sexual details and the infusion of sexual innuendo into the factfinding process. By affording victims protection in most instances, the rule also encourages victims of sexual misconduct to institute and to participate in legal proceedings against alleged offenders.

> . . . .

> Subdivision (b)(2) governs the admissibility of otherwise proscribed evidence in civil cases. It employs a balancing test rather than the specific exceptions stated in subdivision (b)(1) in recognition of the difficulty of foreseeing

future developments in the law. Greater flexibility is needed to accommodate evolving causes of action such as claims for sexual harassment.[90]

Does Rule 412 sufficiently protect a sexual harassment plaintiff from defense efforts to discredit her with her sexual history? Explain. What procedural mechanism facilitates protection?

Professor Jane Aiken concluded in her review of the efficacy of Rule 412 that it did not adequately protect civil plaintiffs. In her article, she recommended changes to the Rule:

> The problems . . . in ensuring a fair and consistent application of Rule 412 are the result of the Rule's reliance on judicial discretion. Courts interpret and apply law through the lens of their own experiences. Given nothing else to work with, it is likely that their lens will be as tainted by cultural biases as any other. If, instead, the civil rule mirrored the criminal rule—which outlines specific times in which evidence of a victim's past could be introduced at trial—we might avoid much of the confusion that Rule 412's civil provision has engendered. Such a rule might look like the following:

> Retain 412(a)'s language indicating that such evidence is generally inadmissible. Strike Rule 412(b)(2) and replace with following:

> (2) In a civil case, the following evidence is admissible, if otherwise admissible under these rules:

>> (A) evidence of specific instances of sexual behavior by the alleged victim with respect to the alleged perpetrator; and

>> (B) evidence of specific instances of sexual behavior by the alleged victim after an in camera showing by a proponent that such sexual conduct was the actual cause of the severe and emotionally devastating harm alleged in plaintiff's complaint.

> Subsection A is designed to indicate what evidence would be admissible to prove the defense of "welcomeness." . . .

> Subsection B recognizes that sexual conduct by the plaintiff may be relevant to determine if the defendant actually caused the injury that plaintiff claims.[91]

Is Professor Aiken correct? In *Fitzpatrick v. QVC, Inc.* the court relied on Rule 412 to exclude evidence of the plaintiff's sexual orientation in a same-sex sexual harassment case. The court found the plaintiff's sexual orientation would have

---

90. Advisory Committee Note adopted by Congressional Conference Report accompanying Pub. L. 103322 [hereinafter Advisory Committee Note]. *See* H.R. Conf. Rep. No. 103711, 103rd Cong., 2nd Sess., 383 (1994).
91. Jane H. Aiken, *Protecting Plaintiffs' Sexual Pasts: Coping with Preconceptions Through Discretion*, 51 Emory L.J. 559, 582, 584 (2002).

no probative value in determining whether he was offended by his supervisor's advances.[92]

2. State Protections Few states offer the type of protection afforded by Rule 412 in civil cases. California is one. Consider the following California statutory provisions. Do they offer greater protection than Rule 412?

West's Annotated California Codes, Code of Civil Procedure
Part 4. Miscellaneous Provisions
Title 3. Of the Production of Evidence
Chapter 3. Manner of Production
Article 3. Discovery

§ 2017. Pending actions; scope of discovery; sanctions

(a) Unless otherwise limited by order of the court in accordance with this article, any party may obtain discovery regarding any matter, not privileged, that is relevant to the subject matter involved in the pending action or to the determination of any motion made in that action, if the matter either is itself admissible in evidence or appears reasonably calculated to lead to the discovery of admissible evidence. Discovery may relate to the claim or defense of the party seeking discovery or of any other party to the action. Discovery may be obtained of the identity and location of persons having knowledge of any discoverable matter, as well as of the existence, description, nature, custody, condition, and location of any document, tangible thing, or land or other property.

. . . .

(d) In any civil action alleging conduct that constitutes sexual harassment, sexual assault, or sexual battery, any party seeking discovery concerning the plaintiff's sexual conduct with individuals other than the alleged perpetrator is required to establish specific facts showing good cause for that discovery, and that the matter sought to be discovered is relevant to the subject matter of the action and reasonably calculated to lead to the discovery of admissible evidence. This showing shall be made by noticed motion and shall not be made or considered by the court at an ex parte hearing. This motion shall be accompanied by a declaration stating facts showing a good faith attempt at an informal resolution of each issue presented by the motion.

The court shall impose a monetary sanction under Section 2023 against any party, person, or attorney who unsuccessfully makes or opposes a motion for discovery, unless it finds that the one subject to the sanction

---

92. Fitzpatrick v. QVC, Inc., 1999 WL 1215577 (E.D. Pa.), at *4.

acted with substantial justification or that other circumstances make the imposition of the sanction unjust.

West's Annotated California Codes, Evidence Code
Division 6. Witnesses
Chapter 6. Credibility of Witnesses
Article 1. Credibility Generally

§ 783. Sexual harassment, sexual assault, or sexual battery cases; admissibility of evidence of plaintiff's sexual conduct; procedure

In any civil action alleging conduct which constitutes sexual harassment, sexual assault, or sexual battery, if evidence of sexual conduct of the plaintiff is offered to attack credibility of the plaintiff under Section 780, the following procedures shall be followed:

(a) A written motion shall be made by the defendant to the court and the plaintiff's attorney stating that the defense has an offer of proof of the relevancy of evidence of the sexual conduct of the plaintiff proposed to be presented.

(b) The written motion shall be accompanied by an affidavit in which the offer of proof shall be stated.

(c) If the court finds that the offer of proof is sufficient, the court shall order a hearing out of the presence of the jury, if any, and at the hearing allow the questioning of the plaintiff regarding the offer of proof made by the defendant.

(d) At the conclusion of the hearing, if the court finds that evidence proposed to be offered by the defendant regarding the sexual conduct of the plaintiff is relevant pursuant to Section 780, and is not inadmissible pursuant to Section 352, the court may make an order stating what evidence may be introduced by the defendant, and the nature of the questions to be permitted. The defendant may then offer evidence pursuant to the order of the court.

West's Annotated California Codes, Evidence Code
Division 9. Evidence Affected or Excluded by Extrinsic Policies
Chapter 1. Evidence of Character, Habit, or Custom

§ 1106. Sexual harassment, sexual assault, or sexual battery cases; opinion or reputation evidence of plaintiff's sexual conduct; inadmissibility; exception; cross-examination

(a) In any civil action alleging conduct which constitutes sexual harassment, sexual assault, or sexual battery, opinion evidence, reputation evidence, and evidence of specific instances of plaintiff's sexual conduct, or any of such evidence, is not admissible by the defendant in order to prove consent by the plaintiff or the absence of injury to the plaintiff, unless the injury alleged by the plaintiff is in the nature of loss of consortium.

(b) Subdivision (a) shall not be applicable to evidence of the plaintiff's sexual conduct with the alleged perpetrator.

. . . .

(d) If the plaintiff introduces evidence, including testimony of a witness, or the plaintiff as a witness gives testimony, and the evidence or testimony relates to the plaintiff's sexual conduct, the defendant may cross-examine the witness who gives the testimony and offer relevant evidence limited specifically to the rebuttal of the evidence introduced by the plaintiff or given by the plaintiff.

(e) Nothing in this section shall be construed to make inadmissible any evidence offered to attack the credibility of the plaintiff as provided in Section 783.

3. The Plaintiff's Sexual Conduct Did the *Rodriguez-Hernandez* court properly exclude evidence of Sandra Rodriguez's sexual conduct with persons other than the alleged perpetrators? Was the court justified in admitting the evidence of her relationship with her boyfriend to prove she was distracted from her work? Should it have excluded the evidence of flirtatious behavior with Miranda? Explain.

Did the *Rodriguez-Hernandez* appellate court express an opinion concerning the defense's attempts to characterize the plaintiff? Might the cultural norms of the geographic locale of *Rodriguez-Hernandez* help explain the defense's tactics? Or might defense counsel have attempted this kind of a defense in any locale in the United States in the mid-1990s? Explain.

Did the *Bosley* court properly exclude the evidence concerning Kristine Bosley's alleged sexual relations with her ex-husband? Why or why not? If the defense had argued for its admission under another evidentiary rule, might the outcome have been different? What rule(s) could the defense have asserted?

Did the *Sanchez* court properly allow discovery of the plaintiff's past sexual behavior? Why or why not? Isn't the "sexual aggressor" theory the same as a "she's slutty" defensive theory?

Courts will occasionally allow admission of sexually related information for the defense to demonstrate that the plaintiff did not find the work environment hostile. *See, e.g., Dufresne v. J.D. Fields and Co., Inc.,* 2001 WL 30671 (E.D. La.) (allowing the introduction of evidence that the plaintiff had downloaded pornographic material from the internet that she sent to a co-worker but disallowing introduction of the contents of the pornography itself); but see *Wolak v. Spucci,* 217 F.3d 157, 160 (2d Cir. 2000) (excluding evidence of plaintiff's private sexually related conduct and holding that "a woman's expectations about her work environment cannot be said to change depending upon her sexual sophistication").

4. Pattern or Practice What is the difference, if any, between a pattern or practice of sexual harassment and a predisposition or propensity to sexually harass? How could defense counsel demonstrate a pattern and practice by the plaintiff, without delving into her sexual history, to discredit her claims against the accused?

5. The AIDS Test In *Rodriguez-Hernandez*, the defense requested that Rodriguez submit to an AIDS test, "apparently to substantiate their allegations of promiscuity." The Advisory Committee Notes of Rule 412 provide guidance on issues like this one:

> As amended, Rule 412 bars evidence offered to prove the victim's sexual behavior and alleged sexual predisposition ... Past sexual behavior connotes all activities that involve actual physical conduct, i.e. sexual intercourse or sexual contact. *See, e.g., United States v. Galloway*, 937 F.2d 542 (10th Cir. 1991), *cert. denied*, 113 S.Ct. 418 (1992) (use of contraceptives inadmissible since use implies sexual activity); *United States v. One Feather*, 702 F.2d 736 (8th Cir. 1983) (birth of an illegitimate child inadmissible); *State v. Carmichael*, 727 P.2d 918, 925 (Kan. 1986) (evidence of venereal disease inadmissible). In addition, the word "behavior" should be construed to include activities of the mind, such as fantasies or dreams. *See* 23 C. Wright and K. Graham, Jr., Federal Practice and Procedure, § 5384 at p. 548 (1980) ("While there may be some doubt under statutes that require 'conduct,' it would seem that the language of Rule 412 is broad enough to encompass the behavior of the mind.").

Note that Rule 412 deems evidence relating to venereal disease inadmissible. Assume defense counsel had read these notes and knew AIDS test results would be excluded. What else might have motivated *Rodriguez* defense counsel to request an AIDS test?

6. Evidence of Dress, Speech, and Lifestyle In *Meritor*, the Court determined that evidence of dress and speech were relevant in a sexual harassment case. The Advisory Notes deal with this type of evidence:

> [R]ule [412] has been amended to also exclude all other evidence relating to an alleged victim of sexual misconduct that is offered to prove a sexual predisposition. This amendment is designed to exclude evidence that does not directly refer to sexual activities or thoughts but that the proponent believes may have a sexual connotation for the factfinder. Admission of such evidence would contravene Rule 412's objectives of shielding the alleged victim from potential embarrassment and safeguarding the victim against stereotypical thinking. Consequently, unless the (b)(2) exception is satisfied, evidence such as that relating to the alleged victim's mode of dress, speech, or life style will not be admissible.

. . . .

The [(b)(2)] balancing test requires the proponent of the evidence, whether plaintiff or defendant, to convince the court that the probative value of the proffered evidence "substantially outweighs the danger of harm to any victim and of unfair prejudice of any party." This test for admitting evidence offered to prove sexual behavior or sexual propensity in civil cases differs in three respects from the general Rule governing admissibility set forth in Rule 403. First, it reverses that usual procedure spelled out in Rule 403 by shifting the burden to the proponent to demonstrate admissibility rather than making the opponent justify exclusion of the evidence. Second, the standard expressed in subdivision (b)(2) is more stringent than in the original rule; it raises the threshold for admission by requiring that the probative value of the evidence substantially outweigh the specified dangers. Finally, the Rule 412 test puts "harm to the victim" on the scale in addition to prejudice to the parties.

Does amended Rule 412 require a motion to the court in all sexual harassment cases in which the defense wants to introduce evidence of the plaintiff's dress and speech? Why or why not?

7. The Accused's Conduct Were the *Rodriguez* defendants correct that the court used a "double standard" in admitting evidence? Why or why not?

Occasionally, the plaintiff will have reason to propound discovery of medical evidence. For example, in *Hargrave v. Brown*,[93] the plaintiff alleged that her supervisor had masturbated on her and moved to compel DNA testing. The court borrowed reasoning from paternity cases to compel the alleged perpetrator's production of a biological sample.[94]

8. Title VII Discrimination Did Johnson really "discriminate" against his ex-wife? Explain. Did his behavior constitute sexual harassment? Was Excel justified in terminating Bosley for violating company policy? Under what specific reasoning was Excel probably found liable? Did Rodriguez have a good retaliation claim? Explain.

9. Disparate Treatment Explain why the *Bosley* jury might have found for Excel on the disparate treatment claim?

10. Customer Liability What common law claims might Rodriguez have brought against Miranda?

11. Discovery Limitations Was it logical for the court to limit discovery in *Sanchez* to the last three years? Was it logical for the court to allow No. 1(b) for the discovery of evidence that plaintiff was a "sexual aggressor"? Why did the court limit discovery concerning any "coworker who later became her spouse"? By limiting discovery as to a future spouse, did the court make a moral judgment about sexual aggression by women? Specifically, did the court imply that sexual aggression by a woman

93. 783 So. 2d 497 (La. App. 2001).
94. *Hargrave*, 783 So. 2d at 499–501.

makes her morally suspect, and therefore an unbelievable plaintiff, unless that woman "redeems" herself by marrying her target? Did the *Sanchez* court adequately protect the plaintiff by ordering her responses placed under seal for only defense counsel's review? Why or why not?

Socksbrunot v. Hirschvogel Inc.

184 F.R.D. 113 (S.D. Ohio 1999)

SARGUS, District Judge.

. . . .

I.

. . . .

. . . In this sexual harassment, hostile work environment case, the defendant presented an abundance of evidence to support its theory that, if a hostile work environment based upon sexual harassment existed, the plaintiff herself either created the environment or welcomed the conduct. Plaintiff argues that all such evidence should have been first sifted through the requirements of Federal Rule of Evidence 412 and then much, if not all, of such evidence ultimately should have been excluded.

. . . .

II.

. . . [T]he plaintiff claims that her supervisor, Charles Benz, Comptroller of Hirschvogel Incorporated ("Hirschvogel"), engaged in sexually explicit speech which was both vulgar and demeaning.

These comments, according to plaintiff, created a hostile work environment which ultimately forced her to resign from her employment. According to the plaintiff's testimony, Bentz made repeated comments as to the size of her breasts; asked her what type of condoms she used; asked her to sit on his lap; told her that he knew she could not go without sex for more than three to four days; remarked that her lipstick made her look like a whore; and told her that a coworker wanted to have sex with her. The plaintiff also testified that Bentz told her, "[y]ou want me . . . why don't you just admit it." Additionally, Bentz asked her to bring in the videotape made of her delivering her son so he could "see another side" of her.

Plaintiff also offered evidence to show that Bentz had sexually harassed another employee, Cindy Lehman, who, together with plaintiff, complained directly to the president of Hirschvogel. Thereafter, the president, while announcing and publicizing a new sexual harassment program, named the alleged harasser, Charles Bentz, as one of the contact persons to whom sexual harassment complaints could be made.

The defendant offered several defenses to plaintiff's claims. Evidence was offered that the defendant corporation took steps to prevent sexual harassment by formulating and implementing a detailed sexual harassment program. In addition, testimony was adduced to the effect that the plaintiff initiated conversations with coworkers, including Bentz, as to topics of a sexual nature. Further, Bentz and other witnesses testified that many of the crude and explicit comments that plaintiff claimed were made by Bentz (and several of which he admitted) followed equally crude and explicit comments by the plaintiff.

III.

. . . .

The issue in this case is whether Rule 412 prohibits or limits testimony offered by the defendant employer that the plaintiff spoke to coemployees about personal, sexual matters, and therefore invited the crude sexual comments from her supervisor. The first matter to be resolved is whether Rule 412 even applies to the question. While the Rule itself provides no direct answer to that question, both the Advisory Committee Notes and subsequent case law aid in the analysis. In the 1994 amendments to Rule 412, Congress also adopted the text and supporting Advisory Committee Note of the Advisory Committee on Criminal Rules of the Judicial Conference. Rule 412 applies to evidence offered to prove that a victim of sexual misconduct in a civil case either (a) engaged in other sexual behavior, or (b) had a sexual predisposition. Neither of the terms "sexual behavior" or "sexual predisposition" is defined.

The Advisory Committee Notes, however, include a further analysis by stating under subdivision (a) ". . . unless the (b)(2) objection is satisfied, evidence such as that relating to the alleged victim's mode of dress, speech, or life style will not be admissible." Further, the Advisory Committee Notes accompanying Rule 412(c) state that, "[i]n an action for sexual harassment, for instance, while some evidence of the alleged victim's sexual behavior and/or predisposition in the work place may perhaps be relevant, nonwork place conduct will usually be irrelevant." Finally, the Advisory Committee Notes make two additional references to the fact that Rule 412 applies to claims of sexual harassment. "Rule 412 will, however, apply in a Title VII action in which the plaintiff has alleged sexual harassment." . . .

. . . .

The limited number of cases interpreting Rule 412 are in accord with this conclusion. In *Sheffield v. Hilltop Sand & Gravel Co.*, 895 F. Supp. 105 (E.D.Va. 1995), the court addressed the question of whether Rule 412 applied in a sexual harassment case. The defendant argued, as does Hirschvogel, that the plaintiff's conduct sought to be explored was relevant to the issue of "welcomeness" and was therefore beyond the scope of Rule 412. According to the defendant therein, such evidence was not offered to show "predisposition" or other "sexual behavior" which, as previously described, is presumptively inadmissible subject to the requirements of the Rule.

The district court rejected the argument. The evidence sought to be offered by the defendant included the plaintiff's description of her sexual relations with her husband, and the plaintiff's use of vulgar language in the workplace. The district court concluded that both categories of evidence "endeavor to establish the plaintiff's sexual behavior and her predisposition to engage in such conduct." Accordingly, the court concluded that Rule 412 must govern the admissibility of such conduct.

Similarly, in *Barta v. City & County of Honolulu*, 169 F.R.D. 132, 136 (D.Haw. 1996), the court found that Rule 412 applied in a case alleging sexual harassment. While the decision involved the relationship of Rule 412 with Federal Rule of Civil Procedure 26, which governs the scope of pre trial discovery, the court refused, on the authority of Rule 412, to permit questioning of the plaintiff as to her offwork conduct.

Finally, in *Howard v. Historic Tours of America*, 177 F.R.D. 48 (D.D.C. 1997), the defendants sought pretrial discovery of any prior sexual partners of the two plaintiffs. The defendants claimed that since the plaintiffs had alleged sexual harassment, they could defend by demonstrating that plaintiffs' prior sexual conduct disproved their claim that the offensive conduct was "unwelcome." Further, defendants claimed that plaintiffs' provocative behavior was also admissible on the issue of "unwelcomeness."

The court had no difficulty in finding that Rule 412 clearly limited the evidence which the defendants sought to elicit. The court first noted that any conduct of the plaintiffs unbeknownst to the alleged harassing employees was thoroughly irrelevant. Further, the court found the fact that a plaintiff may have had consensual sex with one coworker does not in any way justify an assumption by another coworker that his workplace advances would therefore be welcomed. Based upon Rule 412, the court prohibited the defendants from seeking such evidence through discovery.

This Court concludes that Rule 412 clearly applies to a civil case involving sexual harassment and that the admissibility of instances of a prior sexual conduct or speech is limited by the terms of the Rule. While relevant evidence is generally admissible under Federal Rule of Evidence 403, evidence subject to Rule 412 is presumptively inadmissible, even when offered to disprove "unwelcomeness" in a sexual harassment case.

IV.

. . . .

On June 29, 1998, the plaintiff filed a motion *in limine* based upon Rule 412 and sought a pretrial hearing pursuant to subpart (c)(2). The plaintiff sought to limit introduction of any testimony to the effect that she engaged in consensual sexual relationships before marriage, or that she had engaged in relations with a former supervisor while employed by an unrelated and former employer.

Prior to trial, the defendant made no attempt to comply with Federal Rule of Evidence 412(c)(2) and sought no pretrial determination as to whether evidence relating to sexual speech or conduct of the plaintiff was admissible. The defendant opposed the plaintiff's motion *in limine* by asserting the following arguments: (1) Rule 412 was inapplicable because the evidence at issue involved workplace speech or conduct and was not offered to prove "sexual predisposition" or prior "sexual behavior"; (2) the evidence was admissible to show that the conduct complained of by the plaintiff was not "unwelcome"; and (3) the evidence was admissible on the issue of damages.[3]

Neither party submitted in advance of trial any detailed description of the evidence in dispute. The defendant represented that the evidence it intended to offer was not designed to prove "sexual predisposition," but only that the plaintiff initiated and engaged in workplace conversations of a sexual nature. Without a hearing, on July 14, 1998, the Court granted in part the motion of the plaintiff. The Court agreed the testimony proposed by the defendant could lead the jury to draw an impermissible inference upon learning that the plaintiff had a sexual relationship with a former supervisor. The Court prohibited the defendant from eliciting any testimony describing the plaintiff's sexual relationship with a former supervisor. The Court also ordered that the testimony elicited must involve the issue of "welcomeness." The defendant was permitted, however, to offer evidence as to workplace conversations which plaintiff initiated or contributed to regarding sexual matters. The Court expressly held that Federal Rule of Evidence 412 did not govern the admissibility of the evidence in question.

The Court is now convinced that its Order of July 14, 1998 was erroneous. In addition to the analysis set forth above describing the need for and scope of Federal Rule of Evidence 412, the conduct of the six day trial thoroughly convinces this Court that an extensive, detailed review of the evidence should have occurred and limitations should have been imposed to insure that the jury did not consider evidence otherwise prohibited or limited by Rule 412. While neither party violated the Order of July 14, 1998, the Court is convinced, having heard the disputed testimony in much greater detail and with more sharply defined contour, that a great deal of highly prejudicial, personally invasive, and legally irrelevant evidence was heard by the jury in this case.

The first of such evidence involved statements allegedly made by the plaintiff as to a sexual relationship with a Richard Head, a former supervisor at a prior place of employment. The defendant asserted throughout this litigation that it was not attempting to use evidence of the relationship to demean the character or reputation of the plaintiff, nor to show either sexual predisposition or prior sexual behavior. Yet, the defendant certainly knew that by offering to show plaintiff's reference to the prior affair in workplace conversations that the jury would learn of the extramarital relationship.

The defendant elicited testimony concerning the Richard Head affair from a great number of witnesses, including the plaintiff, Michael Wesney, Deborah Cole, Kris Smith, Melanee Mareno and Judy Horn. Yet, the record developed at

---

3. Rule 412 makes no exception for evidence otherwise covered by the Rule but offered as to the issue of damages. The Court is not inclined to create such an exception. The Rule itself would permit the proponent of such evidence to move for its admissibility under Rule 412(b)(2) and (c) if a Court were to find that the probative value substantially outweighed the danger of harm to the victim and of unfair prejudice to any party.

trial contains no evidence that Charles Bentz, the one Hirschvogel supervisor whom the plaintiff claimed was the sole creator of the hostile work environment, ever heard the plaintiff state that she had any type of sexual relationship with Richard Head.

. . . .

A great deal of other evidence subject to Rule 412 was also offered by the defendant without compliance as to both the procedural and substantive requirements of support under subsection (c)(2). The defendant asserts . . . that plaintiff, by failing to depose all of defendant's witnesses, looks to Rule 412 as a remedy for her failure to conduct discovery. This argument is wholly unavailing. The Court first notes that discovery is a right, not an obligation of the plaintiff. Further, the testimony adduced at trial indicated that the plaintiff is now unemployed and may not have had the means to depose all of the potential witnesses identified by the defendant corporation. Finally, the fact a party fails to depose every witness does not dispense with the necessity of adhering to the Rules of Evidence.

More importantly, Federal Rule of Evidence 412 does not permit a defendant to first offer evidence of "sexual predisposition" or prior "sexual behavior" at trial. Subpart (c)(2) requires that such evidence be the subject of a sealed motion filed fourteen (14) days in advance of trial. The Rule places no obligation on the plaintiff to file a motion *in limine* concerning such evidence which may or may not be offered by the defendant.

. . . .

. . . The evidence [presented concerning conversations about oral sex] paints the plaintiff as a person who is both sexually aggressive and verbally descriptive as to matters many, if not most, jurors would find highly personal and offensive. Neither of these characteristics, in the absence of linking such conversations to Bentz, bears on any of the issues in the case.

. . . .

Evidence that a plaintiff in a sexual harassment case may have flirted with the alleged harasser is clearly within the type of conduct described as "sexual behavior" or "sexual predisposition" described in Rule 412. Such evidence should have been considered, weighed, and ruled upon prior to trial. Given the fact that Bentz never described the plaintiff as flirtatious, the Court is convinced that such evidence could not meet the standard set forth in Rule 412(b)(2) in that the probative value is weak and the potential harm or prejudice to the alleged victim is strong. Such testimony could improperly paint the plaintiff as having invited sexual harassment, when even the alleged harasser, the supposed target of the flirtatiousness, failed to support the testimony.

3. Use of profanity by the plaintiff.

The defendant introduced without objection testimony from virtually every witness it presented that the plaintiff frequently used profanity in the workplace, including a four letter word beginning with the letter "f" and a five letter word beginning with the letter "b."[5] While the plaintiff denied such statements, Charles Bentz testified that the plaintiff used such reference during a conversation involving the two of them. Because such alleged statement was, according to Bentz, made to him by plaintiff, and the statement used a word having reference only to the female reproductive anatomy, these statements are excluded from the analysis of the other profanity allegedly used by the plaintiff.

As noted above, Federal Rule of Evidence 412 encompasses an alleged victim's speech when such speech is used to rebut a claim that conduct constituting sexual harassment was "unwelcome." As further support for this proposition, the Court notes, for instance, that the use of profanity by a plaintiff would be thoroughly irrelevant in a personal injury automobile case. Likewise, the evidence presented here that the plaintiff used profanity was clearly offered by the defendant to make at least an inference that the plaintiff could not have found the claimed sexually derogatory and explicit statements of Charles Bentz to be unwelcome.[6]

. . . .

. . . The plaintiff's claims of sexual harassment allegedly perpetrated by Charles Bentz involved specific, explicit sexual speech. The defense was well within legal bounds to offer contextual explanations of such conversations and to show that the plaintiff herself may have initiated explicit sexual speech in her conversations with Bentz. The defense, however, included much more, including (a) highly personal sexual conversations to which Bentz was not a party; (b) allegations of flirting between Bentz and plaintiff, which not even Bentz claimed occurred; and (c) generalized, undifferentiated testimony that plaintiff used profanity in the workplace. All of this evidence was testified to in great length and detail by a series of witnesses.

In addition, the jury was presented with other evidence not objected to by the plaintiff and not within the scope of Rule 412 which should not have been admitted. The defendant elicited testimony from a series of witnesses that the plaintiff described her baby as the "baby from hell." Plaintiff denied making such statements. Also presented from several witnesses was testimony that the plaintiff stated she regretted having a husband who was a "blue collar" employee.

While this evidence should have been objected to and stricken from the record, the Court is not confident that the statements, standing alone, prevented a fair trial. The Court is, however, convinced that the negative inferences accompanying such statements—that the plaintiff disliked her own child and husband—dovetailed with similar negative inferences created by the violation of Federal Rule of

---

5. Testimony was also elicited from several witnesses that the plaintiff referred to Marjorie Hunt with an offensive word which was meant to describe a part of the female anatomy and rhymed with Hunt's last name.

6. In fact, defendant's opening statement to the jury made manifestly clear that this tactic would be its primary defense. Nearly every witness called by defendant was used to develop this precise inference.

Evidence 412. The defense thus presented the picture of a sexually aggressive, foul-mouthed, bad mother and wife, none of which was relevant unless tied to the context of the specific claims made by her against Charles Bentz.

V.

With the benefit of hindsight, this Court concludes that a plethora of evidence was improperly presented to the jury in this case. Such evidence was presented in violation of Federal Rule of Evidence 412. Moreover, much of the evidence should not have been admitted even under the more liberal standard set forth in Federal Rule of Evidence 403. The quantum of such inadmissible evidence combined with the highly prejudicial content of the testimony convinces this Court that the plaintiff was denied a fair trial. This Court cannot say, as required by *Kotteakos v. United States*, 328 U.S. 750, 756 (1946), that the judgment in this case was not "substantially swayed by the error."

The Court notes that the plaintiff seeks a new trial based on only one of two grounds available under Federal Rule of Civil Procedure 59. No claim is made that the verdict was against the manifest weight of the evidence. The trial in this case included admissible evidence upon which a reasonable jury could have found for either the defendant or the plaintiff. The same trial also included a large amount of prejudicial evidence which the jury should not have heard and which denied the plaintiff the right to a fair trial, entitling her to relief under Federal Rule of Civil Procedure 59. . . .

The Motion of the plaintiff for a new trial (Doc. 73) is therefore GRANTED. This case shall be reset for trial and a scheduling order shall issue.

Notes and Discussion

1. Plaintiff's Sexual History In *Rodriguez-Hernandez*, the court allowed evidence of Rodriguez's flirtatious behavior and in *Socks-Brunot*, the court rejected its use. What were (or might have been) the differences in the two courts' reasoning that led to these opposite results? How was the reasoning in *Bosley* similar to that in *Socks-Brunot*? In *Sanchez*, the court allowed discovery of the plaintiff's sexual history in response to the "Sexual Aggressor Theory." If *Socks-Brunot* defense counsel had raised such a theory, might the court have ruled against the plaintiff? Explain. In *Socks-Brunot*, the court relied on *Howard*. In *Howard*, the court disallowed discovery of the plaintiff's prior sexual partners, in part because consensual sex with one co-worker does not support the notion that the plaintiff welcomed the advances of the accused. Compare *Howard* to *Sanchez* and explain which determination is more persuasive.

2. Speech and Dress Will more rulings like *Socks-Brunot* weaken the impact of *Meritor*'s holding that evidence of plaintiff's speech and dress are relevant in sexual harassment cases? What impact, if any, will more *Socks-Brunot*-style decisions have on defense counsel and their litigation tactics? Ethically speaking, should they have an impact? If *Socks-Brunot* had no impact and the bench wanted to curb discovery or litigation abuses, how could it?

3. Discovery and Trial Evidence In *Socks-Brunot*, the court referred to *Barta,* in which the court used Rule 412 to disallow discovery of off-work conduct. Was that denial a proper use of Rule 412? Should courts allow Rule 412 to limit discovery under Federal Rule of Civil Procedure 26? Explain.

4. New Trial Was the granting of a new trial warranted in *Socks-Brunot*? Does a new trial seem like an unfair penalty? Why or why not?

5. Publicity

The prior section highlights the trauma that a plaintiff who brings a sexual harassment case may face when her conduct and sexual history are "on trial." What complicates these cases are that they attract media interest, even when the parties are not famous politicians or celebrities. When a case involves public figures, the media attention increases exponentially, as the Harvey Weinstein allegations demonstrated. Occasionally, counsel has little control over media coverage since some reporters cover the courthouse and investigate new, interesting filings. News of a sexual harassment case can appear in print before the defendants realize they have been sued. Thus, plaintiff's counsel should refrain from filing suit until she and her client prepare for the media attention that may follow.

Plaintiffs often feel conflicted about media attention. They may fear the loss of privacy, scrutiny of their behavior, and public humiliation or shame associated with their charges. They express concerns about getting substitute employment after news of their complaint circulates. Alternately, plaintiffs can feel that bad press will shame the harasser and discredit the employer. They may hope that defense fears over publicity will prompt a pre-filing settlement. Defendants want to avoid embarrassing publicity and business losses that poor press and sympathy boycotts engender. Counsel can minimize press damage by advising their clients how to conduct themselves publicly and how to respond to media inquiries.

As a new lawyer and within months of starting her own law practice, Jennifer Drobac learned the importance of media attention and how to respond to inquiries from reporters. In 1992, just months after the Anita Hill/Clarence Thomas hearing, Drobac received a referral of what looked like a sexual harassment case involving a new software company. Within a day of her filing of the lawsuit, she received a call from *San Jose Mercury News* reporter, Paul Rogers. She offered "No comment" in response to his request for information about the case. Rogers informed Drobac that he would write the story with or without her comment but that he could better report the truth if he could cover all sides of the story. He offered to call her back and take a prepared statement, which she ultimately gave. While Drobac's comments did not make a huge difference in the case, those of others did. The following article excerpts demonstrate how media coverage can impact a sexual harassment case and its parties.

Software Firm Founder Accused of Sexual Harassment

Paul Rogers, *The San Jose Mercury News*[95]

The president of one of Northern California's leading computer software companies has been accused of sexual harassment by three former executive secretaries who charge they were repeatedly groped, propositioned and forcibly kissed by him at work. Lloyd Mitchell, 61, the founder of the Santa Cruz Operation, was named in a civil lawsuit filed this week in Santa Cruz County Superior Court. Administrative assistants Pam Davids, 47, Sharon Peters, 37, and Susan Franks, 44, all Santa Cruz County residents, seek unspecified damages for behavior they classify as "oppressive, demeaning, sexually belittling, intimidating, exploitive and abusive."

The suit claims that since August 1991, Mitchell made a habit of shutting the door to his office and refusing to allow them to leave unless they kissed him on the lips. It also charges Mitchell with caressing the women's buttocks, grabbing Franks's breasts, making them clean up fingernail clippings and soiled handkerchiefs from his desk and pressuring them to go with him during work hours to a remote wooded homesite.

In an interview Friday, Mitchell denied the allegations. "Did it say I raped anybody? Did it say I pinned anybody down?" he said. Asked to reply to accusations of hugging and kissing Davids and Franks against their will during business hours, Mitchell replied, "How serious a crime is that?" ... Mitchell said he decided to fight the charges in open court, rather than settle them privately, because he is certain of his innocence. "Most of what's in there is pure crap," he said. "Some of what's in there is subject to interpretation."

Davids was fired in July. Franks quit in February. Peters, who worked for a senior vice president, was transferred to another department after filing a complaint in August with the state Department of Fair Employment and Housing in San Jose. The suit notes that Mitchell has employed nine personal secretaries during the past five years. "Is that a crime?" he asked.

Several hours later, Mitchell phoned the Mercury News to make additional comments about the lawsuit. "We are taking this suit very seriously," he said. "It is published and established policy of SCO to be very conscious of the rights of everybody." He noted that several women are in senior management positions in his company.

Davids began work at SCO, as the company is known locally, in June. On her first day on the job, Mitchell "hugged her and caressed her buttocks," according to the 50-page lawsuit. Two days later, Mitchell said Davids "had a nice body and advised her not to let herself get a wide bottom," it states. On June 5, he told her, "God, you're good-looking ... I wonder what you look like in a nightie." Three times during

---

95. Paul Rogers, *Software Firm Founder Accused of Harassment*, SAN JOSE MERC. NEWS (Dec. 5, 1992), at 1A. Some names have been changed to protect the privacy of the parties.

the next month, Davids claims, Mitchell pressured her to go with him to a remote wooded property. According to county land records, Mitchell owns a 26-acre home-site east of DeLaveaga Park in Santa Cruz. She refused each time. On July 14, Davids met with Greg Damon, the company's vice president for human relations, to discuss the alleged sexual harassment. . . . Damon told her to work out a plan with Mitchell or to look for another job, according to the suit. She charges that Damon said Mitchell was just kidding, "That's just Lloyd," he said, brushing aside her request for a transfer. On July 17, after Mitchell refused to discuss Davids's concerns, she called in sick, the suit says. The same afternoon, she received a call from Damon's office saying she had been fired.

Peters began working at SCO in September, 1990 as a secretary for Senior Vice President Sam Flora. Her desk was near Mitchell's office. She claims Mitchell called her into his office on July 26, 1991, to criticize her weight. When Peters began to cry, he said, "When was the last time you had a boyfriend? When was the last time you were even with a man?" according to the suit.

The third woman, Franks, worked as Mitchell's personal secretary before Davids was hired. From July 1991 to February 1992, he called her into his office several times a week, according to the suit. "Almost invariably, Mitchell insisted that Franks give him a kiss before she could leave his office," the suit states. "If Franks hesitated, Mitchell placed himself between Franks and the closed office door, insisting on a kiss before she left. Mitchell always moved his head to make sure he kissed Franks on the lips." . . . The suit also charges that Mitchell grabbed Franks around the waist one day and said, "You really have a firm tush." Similar to Davids, Franks was invited up to Mitchell's wooded property, she said. In February, she went. While there, Mitchell grabbed her and "kissed her on the lips and tried to force his tongue into her mouth." She resigned from the company shortly afterward.

None of the three women returned telephone requests for comment. . . . Mitchell, who is divorced, was asked if he had any regrets. "I certainly regret that I hired those three girls," he said.

Another Worker Targets Mitchell
An Ex-Aide Charges Him with Sexual Harassment

Paul Rogers, *The San Jose Mercury News*[96]

Another former executive secretary of computer pioneer Lloyd Mitchell has gone public with sexual harassment charges, alleging Mitchell drove her to his wooded property last May, ordered her to remove her blouse and then exposed himself before she ran away, fearing she was about to be raped. On Tuesday, Jenny Esperanza, 52, of Santa Cruz joined a lawsuit filed Dec. 3 in Santa Cruz County Superior

---

96. Paul Rogers, *Another Worker Targets Mitchell An Ex-Aide Charges Him with Sexual Harassment*, SAN JOSE MERC. NEWS (Dec. 16, 1992), at 1B. Some names have been changed to protect the privacy of the parties.

Court by three former secretaries against Mitchell, the president and founder of Santa Cruz Operation.

She becomes the fifth top administrative assistant to accuse Mitchell, a 61-year-old divorcee, of regularly groping, propositioning and kissing female employees against their will. Her charges are the most serious to date. The company has denied all the charges.

Esperanza also alleges that several days after the Rodney King verdict last spring, Mitchell said to her and a group of other assistants, "When are those niggers going to realize it's a white boys' world?" . . .

Neither Mitchell nor SCO spokesman Dan Hanson has returned calls to the Mercury News since a recent story in which more than 20 former employees accused Mitchell and his son, Executive Vice President Doug Mitchell, of more than a decade of intimidation, harassment and boorish behavior toward female employees. . . . Esperanza was not available for comment Tuesday.

2 Agencies Investigating Ex SCO Chief

Paul Rogers, *The San Jose Mercury News*[97]

Police in Santa Cruz County have begun investigations to determine whether former computer executive Lloyd Mitchell committed sexual battery or other crimes against secretaries who have sued him for sexual harassment.

Mitchell, a 61-year-old software pioneer who founded Santa Cruz Operation Inc. (SCO) and resigned in disgrace six weeks ago, is the target of probes by two agencies, the Santa Cruz Police Department and the Santa Cruz County Sheriff's Department. Law enforcement officials say they are looking into possible battery and sexual battery violations—misdemeanor crimes that carry penalties of up to one year in jail. "We are working on it right now," Deputy Police Chief Jeff Locke said Thursday. "If these allegations are true, we're more than willing to bring them forward for prosecution." Mitchell recently hired Santa Cruz criminal attorney Paul Meltzer to advise him on the police inquiries. "I would be surprised if criminal charges were filed," Meltzer said Thursday. . . .

Meltzer, who has represented such diverse clients as San Jose U.S. District Judge Robert Aguilar on corruption charges and San Jose garbage truck mechanic Stephen Trujillo, who police say dismembered his girlfriend and threw her off the Santa Cruz wharf in September, noted that the standard of proof in criminal court is stricter than in civil. "I'm sure that if Mr. Mitchell were so unfortunate to be charged with these offenses and brought to trial, he should be acquitted," Meltzer said.

Police began looking into criminal charges last week. . . . Locke said Thursday his officers have contacted the women's attorney, Jennifer Drobac, requesting interviews

---

97. Paul Rogers, *2 Agencies Investigating Ex SCO Chief*, SAN JOSE MERC. NEWS (Feb. 12, 1993), at 1B. Some names have been changed to protect the privacy of the parties.

with the women. He said police also will interview other employees at SCO. Mercury News interviews with former employees, combined with complaints filed with the Department of Fair Housing and Employment in San Jose, paint a picture of SCO as a company in which top executives led by Mitchell tolerated groping, hugging, kissing and intimidation of female employees for more than a decade. "More victims could come forward," Locke said. Drobac said she will allow the women to speak with sheriff's detectives or city police investigators. "We will cooperate to the best of our abilities," she said, refusing to discuss specifics.

Drobac and Mitchell's lawyers in San Jose have spent the week taking sworn depositions from the female plaintiffs. That law firm, Jackson, Tufts, Cole & Black, came under criticism last week when it was disclosed the attorneys had hired a private detective to research sexual histories, medical records and credit information of the former secretaries.

. . . "These are not vengeful women," Drobac said. "They have chosen to pursue their individual cases in a manner that the law provides for." Because the statute of limitations for battery expires after one year, only two of women, Esperanza and Peters, have complaints that are recent enough to warrant investigation.

. . . Mitchell has not been available for comment since his Dec. 21 resignation. When he stepped down from the $165 million software manufacturer, he maintained his innocence, calling all the charges "completely false and unfair." In recent weeks, SCO has hired a new president, begun sexual harassment workshops and launched a massive public relations campaign to salvage its image.

Notes and Discussion

1. Defense Comments How badly did Mitchell injure himself by commenting in the first interview? Should those comments to the press be admissible at trial? Does it appear that his lawyer had sufficient client control or briefed him appropriately before he responded to press questions? What could his lawyer have done better?

Why did Mitchell telephone the reporter, Paul Rogers, several hours after the initial interview? Did his later comments counter the damage his prior ones might have done? Should counsel for SCO have directed someone other than Mitchell, the alleged harasser, to make a statement? In the second article, Rogers noted that the company "denied all the charges." He also reported, "Neither Mitchell nor SCO spokesman Dan Hanson has returned calls to the Mercury News since a recent story. . . ." Why might a company spokesperson fail to make a strong statement to the press?

2. Plaintiff Comments Why did none of the plaintiffs respond to Rogers' inquiries for the first article? If that was a conscious choice, was it a wise one? Why or why not?

3. Pleading Quotes Note how often Rogers uses quotes in his stories. Most of these Rogers drew not from the parties or counsel but from the complaint filed. Additionally, because the complaint quoted other workers, Rogers could quote them for the stories without even speaking with them post-filing. These stories demonstrate the utility of a detailed pleading, drafted with an advocate's perspective.

4. Additional Plaintiffs/Witnesses Another consequence of media coverage is the discovery of additional plaintiffs and witnesses. These people can significantly bolster a case with additional information and claims. Shortly after news of the original suit, Jenny Esperanza contacted Drobac (plaintiffs' counsel) who had been searching for her. Counsel amended the original complaint to include Esperanza's claims. Note that the criminal investigation did not commence until after Esperanza came forward with her charges.

5. Counsels' Comments Consider Meltzer's willingness to comment to Rogers and the substance of his remarks. Did Meltzer succeed in minimizing damage? What might his strategy have been? Did news of Meltzer's prior representation of Judge Aguilar help Mitchell? Did mention of Trujillo's dismemberment of his girlfriend injure Mitchell? Do Mitchell's prior statements to Rogers lead one to associate him more with one prior criminal defendant than the other?

Does Drobac's comment that she will allow the women to speak with sheriff's detectives suggest that she did not allow them to speak with Rogers? If so, why not? Do Drobac's comments help her clients' case? Why did she refuse to discuss the specifics of the criminal charges?

6. Consequences The last story reports that Mitchell resigned less than three weeks after the filing of the complaint. Might the negative press coverage have precipitated that departure? Rogers also noted that SCO had "launched a massive public relations campaign." How might such a campaign cure SCO's ills?

Chapter 10 takes a closer look at media coverage of high-profile cases. As social media and reposting enhance news coverage, publicity takes on even greater importance today than it did at the turn of the twenty-first century.

6. Application of Law and Ethics
Hypothetical #9

Plaintiff's counsel, Kay, telephones her contact at the Daily, Walter. She tells him that she is about to file a case against Microsystems and that Walter will want to be the first to cover the story. Kay invites Walter to come to her office and preview a copy of the complaint.

At Kay's office, Walter reads that Microsystems employee, Gus, has accused Vice President Mathews of sexually and physically harassing him. Among numerous charges, Gus alleges that Mathews insisted that Gus accompany him to a recent trade-show in Olympia where Mathews booked a single bedroom to economize.

The first day during the show, Mathews repeatedly slapped Gus' buttocks as was common for the guys to do back at the office. Mathews also referred to Gus as his "boy." Gus alleges that he was quite embarrassed when Mathews suggested they take a break to go to the bathroom and "shake their joy sticks."

That night back at the room Mathews offered Gus a marijuana cigar that Gus refused and insisted that they watch XXX-rated movies on the adult movie channel. When Mathews tried to get into Gus' bed that night, Gus fled the room and Olympia and flew back to San Jose. The next morning Gus found an e-mail on his computer from Mathews, terminating him for insubordination and making sexual advances toward Mathews.

Walter asks Kay whether Gus and Mathews are gay. Kay responds that Gus is not. She suggests that Mathews has been convicted for soliciting a male prostitute but that she is not sure and that Walter should check that fact. She says, "He [Mathews] probably does little boys, too." Walter also asks why Gus waited so long to bring the suit since the actual date of the trade-show was more than a year ago.

Kay answers that she met Gus on the flight back from Olympia. Seeing that he was still quite upset Kay asked him about his troubles and when she heard his story suggested he telephone her. She even gave Gus her business card. He contacted her the day after he was fired but she has been really busy and has not had a chance before now to draft the complaint. "The claim is still good," she assures Walter, because she only got the "right-to-sue" letters a few months ago.

The next morning the front page of the Daily carries the following headline and story, "PARENTS OF YOUNG BOYS BEWARE, EX-CON AND MICROSYSTEMS V.P. ACCUSED OF SEXUAL HARASSMENT."

Ethical Issues:

1. Can Kay ethically invite Walter to her office to preview the complaint?

2. If she had just filed the complaint, could she invite Walter to her office to discuss it?

3. Could she simply alert Walter to the fact she had just filed a complaint?

4. Can Kay ethically discuss Mathews' alleged criminal conviction with Walter?

5. Can Kay ethically discuss her opinion that Mathews "does boys"?

6. Was it an ethical violation for Kay to give Gus her business card and suggest that he call her while on the flight from Olympia?

7. Was it an ethical violation for her to ask what was upsetting him?

8. Has Kay committed an ethical violation by waiting more than a year to file Gus' complaint?

Legal Issue: Might Kay face any other problems because of this delay?

Chapter 10

The Future: #MeToo and Legal Reform

1. Introduction

A Google search of "#MeToo" in early January 2019 produced more than 220 million results.[1] This hashtag—a measure of online discussions about sexual harassment and assault—first went viral in the fall of 2017. On October 5, *The New York Times* broke a story about how Hollywood producer Harvey Weinstein had paid off sexual harassment accusers for decades.[2] Jodi Kantor and Megan Twohey reported "previously undisclosed allegations against Mr. Weinstein stretching over nearly three decades. . . ."[3] Weinstein allegedly abused many women, including Ashley Judd, Ambra Battilana, and Emily Nestor, to name just three discussed in Kantor and Twohey's article.[4] Then, on October 10, *The New Yorker* magazine published an in-depth investigation by Ronan Farrow revealing the extent of Weinstein's sexual harassment and assault of women seeking employment at his company.[5] Continuing media reports regarding egregious sexual assault and misconduct by Weinstein outraged the public.[6]

This news of Weinstein's transgressions became the tinder that ignited on October 15 with a tweet by Hollywood celebrity Alyssa Milano. The tweet read, "If you've been sexually harassed or assaulted write 'me too' as a reply to this tweet." With her tweet, Milano wanted to highlight the pervasiveness of systemic discrimination, assault, and harassment.[7] The #MeToo campaign exploded, with more than 500,000 uses on Twitter by October 16 and 12 million Facebook posts during the first 24 hours.[8]

---

1. #MeToo, Google (Jan. 8, 2019).

2. Jodi Kantor & Megan Twohey, *Harvey Weinstein Paid Off Sexual Harassment Accusers for Decades*, N.Y. Times (Oct. 5, 2017).

3. *Id.*

4. *Id.*

5. Ronan Farrow, *From Aggressive Overtures to Sexual Assault: Harvey Weinstein's Accusers Tell Their Stories*, New Yorker (Oct. 10, 2017).

6. Tom Ashbrook, *Harvey Weinstein and Sexual Harassment in the Workplace*, WBUR On Point (Oct. 11, 2017).

7. Nadja Sayej, *Alyssa Milano on the #MeToo Movement: "We're Not Going to Stand for it Any More,"* Guardian (Dec. 1, 2017).

8. Nicole Smartt, *Sexual Harassment in the Workplace in a #MeToo World*, Forbes (Dec. 20, 2017).

Ten years earlier, Tarana Burke had created the "Me Too" campaign when she founded Just Be Inc., a nonprofit organization to help survivors of sexual harassment and assault and build self-worth among girls of color.[9] While working with African-American youth, Burke had frequently heard girls speak about their experiences of sexual violence. When one of her favorite girls had confided in her about sexual harassment from her mother's boyfriend, Burke had wanted to share her own experiences of similar abuse. According to Burke, when she was a girl, "I needed empathy. I needed someone who heard me and saw me and believed me and put me on a road to healing. That's how #MeToo was born, out of this necessity."[10] *Time* magazine named Burke and other women speaking out about sexual harassment and assault the 2017 Person of the Year, dubbing them "the silence breakers."[11]

Milano's tweet unleashed a storm of responses, with women across the country and around the world sharing their personal stories of sexual harassment and assault. In the following weeks, many more celebrities stepped forward, such as Lady Gaga and Viola Davis, but the women telling their stories were from all walks of life, young and old, nurses and engineers, teachers and farmworkers, and others.

Many attribute the eruption of the #MeToo movement to the election of President Donald Trump, whom at least 24 women have accused of inappropriate sexual conduct. Milano said:

> This man in office is an admitter of "grabbing pussy." It not only horrified sexual assault survivors, but all women, as he's trying to roll back our rights. . . . I don't know if this movement would have turned into what it has if this president wasn't in office.[12]

Many women were appalled by Trump's victory on November 7, 2016. They had enough of exploitation, sexual assault, and harassment, and were speaking out about it. The #MeToo campaign became part of a national discussion of workplace and campus sexual misconduct and exploitation that continued into 2019.[13] Revelations demonstrated the prevalence and magnitude of this problem.[14]

In the months that followed the October explosion of #MeToo, men fell from power in astonishing numbers. One of the first dramatic impacts of the "me too" uprising was the election for the Alabama Senate seat vacated by Jeff Sessions, whom President Trump appointed to be U.S. Attorney General. In December 2017, Democrat Doug Jones defeated Republican Roy Moore, who had been accused by several

---

9. *Purpose*, JUST BE INC., https://justbeinc.wixsite.com/justbeinc/purpose-mission-and-vision.

10. Waverly Colville, *#MeToo Movement Founder Speaks to Capacity University of Missouri Crowd*, COLUMBIA DAILY TRIBUNE (Feb. 21, 2018).

11. Stephanie Zacharek, Eliana Dockterman, & Haley Sweetland Edwards, *The Silence Breakers: The Voices that Launched the Movement*, TIME (Dec. 18, 2017).

12. Sayej, *supra* note 7 (quoting Milano).

13. *Id.*

14. Michael Levenson & Cristela Guerra, *Sexual Harassment Allegations Lead Millions of Women to Say #MeToo*, BOSTON GLOBE (Oct. 16, 2017).

women of sexual abuse decades before, when they were teenagers.[15] The #MeToo reckoning took down male leaders across industries, across the country, and around the world.[16] Nine members of Congress, including Senator Al Franken (D-MN),[17] lost their jobs in response to sexual harassment allegations. Archconservative Representative Trent Franks (R-AZ) resigned after news broke that he had offered a female employee $5 million to carry his child.[18] While serving on the House Ethics Committee, which investigates sexual harassment, Representative Patrick Meehan (R-PA) settled a sexual harassment lawsuit with a staffer. In late April, he announced he was not running for re-election.

Dozens of state legislators resigned or were removed from office, and many more were reprimanded, disciplined, and placed on probation or on unpaid leave while under investigation.[19] New York Attorney General Eric Schneiderman stepped down just hours after news broke of his repeated abuse of women.[20] The public radio host Tom Ashbrook, former "Today" host Matt Lauer,[21] and chef Mario Batali were all taken down by #MeToo accusations. By February 2018, more than 70 men accused of sexual misconduct had left their positions of power.[22] By October 2018, more than 200 powerful men had lost their jobs, and more than half of those were replaced by women.[23]

Women and girls spoke up and were believed in courts as well. In mid-April 2018, a jury convicted Bill Cosby of sexual assault after the female judge in the case admitted the testimony of some of his 60-plus accusers. He was later sentenced to three to ten years in prison. Olympic athlete physician Dr. Larry Nassar was convicted and sentenced to between 40 and 175 years in prison after scores of young women testified in excruciating detail about the lasting harm of his sexually abusive behavior when they were children. In another doctor sex abuse case, the University of Southern California agreed in October 2018 to pay $215 million to settle the sexual abuse

---

15. Associated Press, *Republican Roy Moore, Comedian Louis CK Accused of Sexual Misconduct* TRT WORLD (Nov. 11, 2017).

16. *See, e.g.*, Stephanie Akin, *Congress Took Three Decades to Come This Far, Sexual Harassment Victim Says*, ROLL CALL (Nov. 11, 2017); Erica Werner, *Female Lawmakers Allege Harassment by Colleagues in House*, AP NEWS (Nov. 3, 2017).

17. *See, e.g.*, Sheryl Gay Stolberg, Yamiche Alcindor & Nicholas Fandos, *Franken to Resign from Senate Amid Harassment Allegations*, N.Y. TIMES (Dec. 7, 2017).

18. Amber Phillips, *Nine Members of Congress Have Lost Their Jobs Over Sex in Six Months*, WASH. POST (Apr. 28, 2018).

19. Associated Press, *Sexual Misconduct Claims Adding up in State Legislatures*, US NEWS & WORLD REPORT (Apr. 11, 2018).

20. Jane Mayer & Ronan Farrow, *Four Women Accuse New York's Attorney General of Physical Abuse*, NEW YORKER (May 7, 2018).

21. *See, e.g.*, Jason Schwartz & Michael Calderone, *NBC's Shifting Statements on Lauer Draw Scrutiny*, POLITICO (Nov. 30, 2017).

22. Sarah Almukhtar, Michael Gold & Larry Buchanan, *After Weinstein: 71 Men Accused of Sexual Misconduct and Their Fall from Power*, N.Y. TIMES (Feb. 8, 2018).

23. Audrey Carlsen et al., *#MeToo Brought Down 201 Powerful Men. Nearly Half of Their Replacements Are Women*, N.Y. TIMES (Oct. 29, 2018).

claims of more than 500 current and former students against Dr. George Tyndall, who was the USC staff gynecologist from 1988 to 2016.[24]

While some criticized the movement for ignoring women of color,[25] cross-class, cross-race, and cross-sector coalition building became a key strategy of the movement. Hollywood celebrities teamed up with farmworkers to launch the Time's Up Legal Defense Fund. That organization raised more than $22 million to support thousands of women who reported sexual harassment in more than 60 employment sectors, including agriculture, home care, the restaurant industry, retail, manufacturing, policing, and state and local government. The Time's Up Legal Defense Fund, administered by the National Women's Law Center, created a network of more than 780 attorneys to help people reporting sexual harassment and assault in the workplace. These lawyers provide free legal consultation to callers, inform them of their rights, and help them file cases if they are eligible and desire to do so.[26]

In this chapter, you will learn about some of the foundational documents of the #MeToo movement and the emergence of Time's Up. You will also learn about how the women's movement is leveraging increased awareness and anger about sexual harassment and assault to change law and policy.

2. #MeToo and Cross-Sector Organizing

On November 10, 2017, Monica Ramirez — the President of Alianza Nacional de Campesinas (the National Farmworker Women's Alliance) — wrote a letter of support and solidarity to the Hollywood celebrities accusing Harvey Weinstein and other men in Hollywood of sexual harassment and assault. Alianza Nacional de Campesinas is an organization comprised of current and former farmworker women, and women from farmworker families. In her letter, Ramirez highlighted parallels between the experiences of female farmworkers and the Hollywood celebrities, calling for them to work together to combat sexual harassment and assault in the workplace. The letter was published in *Time* magazine at www.time.com /5018813/farmworkers-solidarity-hollywood-sexual-assault/. In response, Hollywood celebrities responded with their own letter, published in *The New York Times* on January 1, 2018, which you can find at www.timesupnow.com/history. Read these letters and consider the questions below.

---

24. Amanda Lee Myers, *USC Agrees to Pay $215M to Settle Doctor Sex Abuse Claims*, AP NEWS (Oct. 19, 2018).

25. Angela Onwuachi-Willig, *What About #UsToo?: The Invisibility of Race in the #MeToo Movement*, 128 YALE L.J.F. 105 (2018).

26. NATIONAL WOMEN'S LAW CENTER, TIME'S UP LEGAL DEFENSE FUND STATS AND NUMBERS, https://nwlc.org/resources/times-up-legal-defense-fund-stats-numbers/.

Notes and Discussion

1. Cross-Sector Solidarity How does the farmworker women's letter connect their own experiences with that of Hollywood actresses? Do they "share a common experience"? What purpose does highlighting their commonalities serve? Are there common legal strategies that might be useful to both farmworkers and Hollywood actresses? Are there distinctions between sexual harassment in the fields and in filmmaking that might warrant different legal approaches?

2. Privilege and Intersectionality How does the Time's Up letter draw distinctions between the experiences of Hollywood actresses and that of farmworkers and other low-income workers such as housekeepers, waitresses, and factory workers? The Time's Up letter notes the privileges that Hollywood actresses have that farmworkers do not have. What are these privileges and what are their significance? How do they affect the abilities of women to respond to sexual harassment and to hold men accountable for sexual harassment and abuse? Think back to Chapter 2 on intersectionality. Has anything changed since 1991 when Anita Hill testified concerning Clarence Thomas's behavior?

3. Power and Sexual Abuse The Time's Up letter states that "systemic gender-inequality and imbalance of power fosters an environment that is ripe for abuse and harassment against women." How do gendered power imbalances lead to sexual harassment? How do racial disparities, immigration status, and sexuality contribute to abuse? What solutions do the letter writers suggest?

4. Open Letters as a Strategy for Social Change Why did farmworker women write an open letter to Hollywood celebrities? Other groups of women, such as women working in the national security sector, have written open letters describing sexual harassment and assault.[27] Are open letters a useful tool for social change?

In the following article, the feminist magazine, *Ms.*, traces the #MeToo uprising and how women organized to create change. Consider the various groups of women it discusses, and the parallels between and differences in their experiences.

The Weinstein Effect

Linda Burstyn, *Ms.*[28]

How the downfall of one sexual predator can usher in an era of change for women everywhere.

Like any good movie, the story of the downfall of Harvey Weinstein resonates because it's more than a story about one man and the women who accused him of harassment, rape and assault. It's the story of *many* men in power and *many* women

---

27. Open Letter from Ambassador Gina Abercrombie-Winstanely et al., to the National Security Community (Nov. 28, 2017).

28. Linda Burstyn, *The Weinstein Effect*, Ms., Spring 2018, at 21–25.

victimized. And it's the story of not just Hollywood, but also of Silicon Valley and Capitol Hill. Newsrooms and sports teams. Big business and small. Hotels and restaurants, and farms and assembly lines.

It's the story of the many industries and companies where supervisors and bosses have, at least until now, turned a blind eye — or even given a wink and a nod — toward allegations of harassment and assault. It's the story of a country that likes to think of itself as a leader in gender equality, but in fact has a long way to go.

For the moment, there's been some reckoning. Powerful men have been brought down by women who've accused them of sexual harassment or assault and the torrent of accusations shows no indication of abating.

In the weeks since the Harvey Weinstein article appeared in *The New York Times*, more than 100 women have come forward with allegations of sexual harassment or assault or rape by the movie mogul. Comedian Louis C.K. saw the release of his latest movie canceled and ties to media companies FX Networks and FX Productions severed after five women accused him of sexual harassment. Gal Gadot — aka Wonder Woman — refused to sign on for a superhero movie sequel unless director and producer Brett Ratner, accused of sexual harassment by six women, is cut from the franchise.

MSNBC commentator Mark Halperin was fired after a dozen women accused him of sexual harassment. Roy Price, Amazon Studios chief; Leon Wieseltier of *The New Republic* and *The Atlantic* magazines; Michael Oreskes, NPR chief editor — all gone after women came forward to expose them.

Women senators and congresswomen have recounted their own stories of sexual harassment. Allegations have surfaced in legislatures in Minnesota, Kentucky, Illinois, Oregon and Rhode Island, while in Sacramento, Calif., nearly 200 women added their names to a letter detailing an environment of pervasive sexual wrongdoing in the statehouse. Women farmworkers joined the "Take Back the Workplace March" in Los Angeles to demand an end to decades of abuse by foremen, and women hotel workers are insisting on protections that shield them from hotel guests who harass and assault them.

At press time, nearly 2 million women and men had come forward using the hashtag #MeToo to recount their own experiences with sexual harassment and assault. The hashtag has gone viral globally, trending in 85 countries, according to news accounts. A local variant in France, #BalanceTonPorc (roughly translated as "squeal on your pig"), urged users to name their alleged abusers.

There is no doubt that as the numbers of women speaking out increase, others feel comfortable coming forward as well. Still, it will pass, as all moments do, and what will be left behind? Will the shrugging culture of "boys will be boys" give way to a new culture that allows women to be women — as equals — in the workplace? What can be done to ensure that when the waters recede from this watershed moment, the land that's revealed underneath is forever changed?

Banding Together

There is power in numbers—and the numbers of women coming forward with allegations of sexual harassment are reaching a tipping point.

"We speak on behalf of the approximately 700,000 women who work in the agricultural fields and packing sheds across the United States," said a spokesperson from the Alianza Nacional de Campesinas, a group of current and former farmworker women and women who come from farmworker families. They had joined the Nov. 12 "Take Back the Workplace" march in Los Angeles, organized by women in the entertainment industry.

"Even though we work in very different environments, we share a common experience of being preyed upon by individuals who have the power to hire, fire, blacklist and otherwise threaten our economic, physical and emotional security," the spokesperson continued. "[R]eporting any kind of harm or injustice committed against us doesn't seem like a viable option. Complaining about anything—even sexual harassment—seems unthinkable because too much is at risk, including the ability to feed our families and preserve our reputations."

A survey of complaints filed with the Equal Employment Opportunity Commission (EEOC) shows that women of color are disproportionately impacted by sexual harassment, as are women working in industries with a high proportion of low-wage jobs—at hotels, in food service and agriculture—where they are harassed by not only supervisors, but also by co-workers and customers.

"Hotel workers have long been on the front lines of the #MeToo movement," says Maria Elena Durazo of the hotel employees and restaurant workers' union Unite Here. A study by Unite Here Local 1 in Chicago found that more than 45 percent of women hotel housekeepers in the city have opened a guest's room and found a naked man at the door, and more than 10 percent of women hotel workers reported being pressured for sex.

"Studies like the one in Chicago . . . have confirmed what housekeepers have known for years . . . they work alone in areas that have no access to surveillance cameras or security guards," Durazo says. "When incidents do occur, housekeepers are often unwilling to report them out of fear that they won't be believed or that the hotel managers will avoid confronting the offending guest."

Unite Here is pushing for local laws to require greater protections. Chicago and Seattle were two of the first cities to enact ordinances that require hotels to provide panic buttons workers can use to summon security and to refuse future reservations to men who have a history of sexual harassment or assault. Hotel workers in Long Beach, Calif., are demanding a similar ordinance.

In Silicon Valley, a place where "bro culture" has been warmly embraced (at least by too many men there), top male executives have been brought down this year after women's collective complaints of sexual harassment.

Despite its forward-looking mandate, Silicon Valley has been one of the hardest places for women to get a foothold. In 2012 Ellen Pao became one of the first tech women to file a gender-discrimination case. She lost the lawsuit against her former employer, Kleiner Perkins Caulfield Byers, but her example propelled others to come forward—through what has come to be called "the Pao Effect." Gender-discrimination lawsuits have since been filed against Twitter, Facebook, Microsoft, Uber and a major venture capital firm.

Niniane Wang, a founder of the Silicon Valley company Evertoon, is among the recent Silicon Valley complainants. Wang says she was harassed by venture capitalist Justin Caldbeck while he was a financial backer for her previous startup, Sunfire. Caldbeck is a man who can, and often does, make or break a fledgling tech business. His company, Binary Capital, is responsible for financing many start-ups just like Wang's.

"He actually pressured me to have sex with him," Wang told *Ms.* "It was uncomfortable because I knew I had to continue having a professional relationship with him."

Wang spoke with some female friends in Silicon Valley and discovered there were other women who had similar experiences with Caldbeck. She made a decision. "My goal was to get a predator out of power," Wang says.

She and two other women—Susan Ho and Leiti Hsu—carefully spent as many as 100 hours compiling evidence they needed to expose Caldbeck. And their careful strategy paid off. Within a week of taking their accusations to a local tech-industry publication, Caldbeck was forced to step down from the firm he co-founded, despite initially denying the accusations.

"Even just four years ago, women in Silicon Valley wouldn't talk about the difficulty of being a woman in this environment; not even to other women!" Sarah Lacy, owner of the tech-world publication Pando, told *Ms.* "Back then it was all about 'How can I get ahead in a patriarchy?' Now it's 'How can I overthrow it?'"

Lacy used the loud voice of her web publication to research and then publicize sexual harassment complaints against Uber founder and chair Travis Kalanick, in particular the charges brought by ex-Uber employee Susan Fowler. Partly because of Lacy's spotlight, Kalanick and business chief Emil Michael were both forced to step down from the company.

Lacy has embraced the idea of women joining forces against sexual harassers and taken it one step further. She's created a way for women to find support from each other through monthly dinner parties for top women in tech. The ground rules are simple: It's all off the record. They eat and vent around one big table.

"It's a slightly different group every time," Lacy explained. "Female CEOs and investors and tech workers. One woman who came, a very powerful woman, ended up reporting someone for harassment after our first dinner. She later told me that she had never felt like she'd had that kind of emotional support she needed to do that before."

Social media, including invitation only Facebook groups and anonymous apps, are also dramatically increasing the likelihood victims will find one another. "If men in the Valley knew about these groups and the conversations that are happening, they'd be terrified," Lacy added.

Untying the Legal Gag

Just a few weeks after the Harvey Weinstein story broke, Liz Manne, a former movie exec, wrote powerfully on indiewire.com about the sexual harassment and assault she experienced while working at New Line Cinema in the 1990s. The trauma happened decades ago, yet it haunts her still. But what bothers her the most over time, she says, is the legal device that worked against her.

> I'm not naming my perp because he's long gone from his post, and fuck that guy, anyway. . . . It's not about him. It's not about me. . . . It's about the NDAs [nondisclosure agreements], these nefarious and ubiquitous clauses that persecute and gag women in perpetuity. It's about these draconian legal devices that force us women to negate parts of our life and pretend that sexual violence is on par with patent violation, multiplying our pain many times over.

Manne is one of scores of women in various industries who didn't formally file a complaint about workplace wrongdoing because she didn't want to lose her job—or get painted with that career-ending brush of "difficult woman." Eventually her contract was not renewed anyway, and when that happened, she had to sign an NDA in order to receive the severance package that was offered to her. The "perp" could not be publicly identified, was never made to pay for his offenses and Manne was left with a paycheck, but no justice.

"In my case, the sexual assault was terrible and traumatizing," Manne told *Ms.* "But the worst part—the very worst part of it, the enduring part of it—is the gag order. This 20 years of legally imposed silence."

Nondisclosure agreements, what Manne was required to sign for her severance package, are common. The agreements—formulated, in theory, to give companies protection from employees leaking industry secrets or taking personal grievances into the public square—are harmful in cases of sexual harassment.

"Employers should have a broad disclaimer saying that nothing in this NDA should be construed as precluding the employee from reporting sexual harassment or other personal violations to the appropriate authorities, including the EEOC or law enforcement," says Debra Katz, a civil rights lawyer specializing in sexual harassment law for more than 30 years. "Employees often don't realize that you can never preclude someone from talking to law enforcement or testifying against someone because of illegal behavior. You always have that right, no matter what the wording of the NDA."

The National Labor Relations Act forbids employers from trying to stop employees from discussing sexual harassment. However, when employees report such wrongdoing to their firm's HR department, all too often they find that HR is more interested in protecting the bosses than in following the law. This apparently happened in the Weinstein Company and was one of the reasons the list of victims there is so long. There was nowhere for the women to turn. As Manne says, "The NDAs create protection for harassment to continue unabated."

So do mandatory arbitration clauses that require confidentiality—and they're a standard feature in employment contracts.

In the case of Gretchen Carlson, Fox News required her to submit any discrimination claims to arbitration, legally preventing her from pursuing those claims publicly in court. After Fox News didn't renew her contract, she found a way around the forced arbitration gag, suing former boss Roger Ailes in his personal capacity under state law. "Carlson's savvy choice brought her claim outside the terms of her employment contract, but many harassment victims are not able to use this workaround," Katz explained.

"Mandatory arbitration harms individual victims, who lose access to jury trials and the leverage of public exposure that can incentivize employers to settle strong claims," Katz continued. "It also denies the public information about the practices of our corporate citizens."

Since Carlson's suit was filed, more than 20 women have come forward about misconduct they'd suffered at the hands of Ailes. Wanting to avoid an embarrassing trial, Fox paid Carlson $20 million and offered a public apology. Last fall Carlson published a book, *Be Fierce: Stop Harassment and Take Your Power Back*, that includes a 12-step guide for people experiencing sexual harassment.

Meanwhile, Ailes was forced out of Fox News in 2016, receiving a $40 million severance package. (Ailes has since died.) It's recently been revealed that before Bill O'Reilly was forced to leave Fox News, several multimillion-dollar sexual harassment settlements were paid out by Fox News' parent company, 21st Century Fox, or by O'Reilly himself, including one for $32 million. Just before Thanksgiving, 21st Century Fox reached a $90 million settlement with shareholders over claims for harms to the company as a result of the sexual harassment scandals. And the Manhattan U.S. Attorney's office is investigating Fox News to determine whether it misled investors by failing to disclose the magnitude of such payouts.

Lawmakers, recognizing the damages of forced secrecy, are starting to respond. California state Sen. Connie Leyva will introduce legislation in January to ban secret settlements in sexual assault, sexual harassment and sex discrimination cases.

Fatima Goss Graves, president of the National Women's Law Center (NWLC), also says it's critical that Congress lift a cap it put in place 25 years ago limiting the amount of punitive damages that can be assessed in individual sex discrimination lawsuits to $300,000. "The cap sends a message to employers that addressing discrimination is just the cost of doing business, instead of a strong message of deterrence. To them, $300,000 is basically a rounding error."

"Tackling institutional structures and laws and policies that allow low levels of accountability [is] extremely important," Graves continues. NWLC has announced the creation of a nationwide legal network for gender equity. "When we first launched the network, we did so with 70 attorneys participating," Graves says. "And now, a month later, we have over 250."

Seizing the Moment

Feminists had been working since the 1970s to have sexual harassment in the workplace defined as illegal discrimination, but it wasn't until 1986 that the Supreme Court, in the case *Meritor Savings Bank v. Vinson*, ruled that sexual harassment was a violation of Title VII of the Civil Rights Act of 1964.

Five years later when Anita Hill came forward to speak out against Supreme Court nominee Clarence Thomas, the country—especially women—got a three-day lesson about what sexual harassment looked like and how the law prohibits it. At the time of her testimony, 60 percent of Americans didn't believe Hill. Perhaps more people would have believed her if the other women who had worked with Thomas and were prepared to testify about his inappropriate behavior had been allowed to testify before the Senate Judiciary Committee. Thomas, who denied all allegations, was confirmed as a Supreme Court justice by a vote of 52 to 48.

Many predicted the treatment of Hill by the Judiciary Committee would discourage women coming forward, but in the aftermath of her testimony, the EEOC saw a more than twofold rise in sexual harassment claims by women. Moreover, Hill's testimony contributed to the passage of the Civil Rights Act of 1991, which expanded the remedies available to victims of workplace discrimination. The law provided, for the first time, that women could sue for punitive damages in cases of sex discrimination, though the damages were capped at $300,000 per individual plaintiff.

And then there was the presidential election of 2016 featuring Donald Trump's "grab them by the pussy" remarks. Trump's victory in the election—despite losing the popular vote by nearly 3 million votes—radicalized women throughout the country. Some 5.9 million marched the day after his inauguration; a tsunami of women wore pink "pussy hats" in repudiation of Trump and his misogynistic agenda.

Millions more have marched and protested since the massive Women's Marches. Thousands of women have stepped forward to run for political office, winning big in November. And millions of women have joined the #MeToo movement, speaking out against sexual harassment when they see it.

The anger is real and the backlash to Trump is helping fuel a shift in the way women are believed and the way they're treated in the workplace. "This moment feels like a new opportunity to finally get at the cultural pieces that have allowed harassment and workplace violence to persist," NWLC's Graves observes.

Perhaps it's true. Perhaps this is "the moment" so many women have been waiting for. Perhaps, as unlikely as it may seem, the election of Trump, putting a harasser in the White House, will usher in an era of positive change in America. Two things are for sure: This is only the tip of the iceberg. And Pandora's box has been opened.

Notes and Discussion

1. Reporting Sexual Harassment to Employers Burstyn argues that often "HR is more interested in protecting the bosses than in following the law." What conflicts of interest do HR personnel experience when investigating sexual harassment? How might this serve as a barrier to justice? Recall *Faragher*'s requirement that employees report sexual harassment to their employers. What was the purpose of this requirement? Does this requirement open employees up to manipulation and abuse if the priority of HR is to protect the boss rather than uncover and remedy sexual harassment and abuse?

2. Gag Rules How do broad nondisclosure clauses and mandatory arbitration agreements perpetuate sexual harassment in the workplace? How might these legal maneuvers favor employers? Might banning nondisclosure clauses in settlement agreements harm some employees?

3. Women Mobilizing Burstyn describes how the Anita Hill/Clarence Thomas hearings inspired women to report sexual harassment in increasing numbers and contributed to the passage of the Civil Rights Act of 1991. She suggests that the election of a president accused of sexual harassment and assault has mobilized women once again. And then the Senate hearings with Christine Blasey Ford and Brett Kavanaugh opened old wounds and again generated mass protests of women speaking out against sexual harassment and assault. EEOC reports of sexual harassment have increased sharply since Trump took office and women ran for elective office in record numbers in the 2018 mid-term elections. What legal reforms might result from these developments?

4. Cultural Change? Has "the shrugging culture of 'boys will be boys'" given way to a new culture? What has been the impact of the #MeToo Movement?

5. #HimToo Shortly after #MeToo went viral, some people began using #HimToo to raise awareness about male survivors of sexual assault and harassment. Later, others began using it to refer to male perpetrators. In the fall of 2018, during the Senate hearings on sexual assault allegations against Supreme Court nominee Brett Kavanaugh (discussed below), #HimToo morphed into a reference to men claiming to be victims of false accusations. In the wake of #MeToo, some men threatened to refuse to work with women for fear of being accused of sexual harassment. A Pew Research Center survey in April 2018 found that most people were more concerned that men would get away with sexual harassment than they were worried that men might be fired prematurely. Democrats, however, were far more likely than Republicans to perceive men getting away with sexual harassment, and women not being believed, as major problems.[29]

---

29. Nikki Graf, Pew Research Ctr., Sexual Harassment at Work in the Era of #MeToo (Sept. 15, 2019).

3. Legal Reform

The #MeToo uprising has created an opportunity for women's rights advocates to make renewed demands for legal reforms they have long sought. The National Women's Law Center (NWLC), which runs the Time's Up Legal Defense Fund, is calling on state and federal lawmakers to revise laws to create more accountability for sexual harassment and assault. In the following NWLC report, Maya Raghu and Joanna Suriani describe in detail their proposals for legal reforms to strengthen sexual harassment law.

#MeTooWhatNext:
Strengthening Workplace Sexual Harassment Protections and Accountability

Maya Raghu & Joanna Suriani[30]

. . . In Federal Fiscal Year 2016, nearly 30,000 harassment charges were filed with the U.S. Equal Employment Opportunity Commission (EEOC); nearly one-quarter of those charges alleged sexual harassment, and 83.4 percent of sexual harassment charges were brought by women. But the charge statistics do not even begin to represent the extent of sexual harassment in the workplace, given that a survey found that 70 percent of workers who experience sexual harassment say they have never reported it. Whether suffering harassment from supervisors, coworkers, or third parties, such as customers, most victims of harassment are suffering in silence.

Sexual harassment is an expression of power. It is used to reinforce cultural norms about appropriate roles, behavior, and work for women and men, and to exert control over people with less power and status in society, and in the workplace—particularly women, women of color, immigrants, and LGBTQ people. Indeed, women are the majority of those who are sexually harassed; at least 25 percent, and as many as 85 percent, of women surveyed report having experienced sexual harassment at work. The sexual or sex-based element of the workplace harassment these individuals experience, including demands for sexual favors, or denigrating and humiliating comments, is a way of enforcing and perpetuating gender inequality at work.

No occupation is immune from sexual harassment, but the incidence of harassment appears to be higher in workplaces with stark power imbalances between workers and employers, and is exacerbated by the devaluation of work performed by women. Women, and particularly women of color and immigrant women, are over-represented in low-wage jobs, which often lack legal protections and critical supports like higher wages, fair and predictable schedules, access to health insurance,

---

30. Maya Raghu & Joanna Suriani, Nat'l Women's Law Ctr. Report, #MeTooWhatNext: Strengthening Workplace Sexual Harassment Protections and Accountability (Dec. 2017) (notes deleted).

and paid time off, leaving workers vulnerable to exploitation. Accordingly, industries with a high proportion of low-wage jobs, such as food service, hospitality, and agriculture, have high incidences of sexual harassment. High rates of sexual harassment are also present in workplaces that have traditionally excluded women, including both blue collar jobs like construction, and white collar ones like medicine and science.

In recent months, ever-increasing numbers of women, and some men, who have experienced sexual harassment at work have come forward to disclose their experiences. Many of these individuals remained silent for years because the risks of speaking out were too high. Victims were reluctant to make allegations of sexual harassment for a number of reasons, including fear of losing their jobs or otherwise hurting their careers, fear of not being believed, and the belief that nothing would be done about the harassment.

. . . .

This is a critical moment to advance key policy initiatives to better protect workers, promote accountability, and prevent harassment. These initiatives, which many states have already implemented or begun to explore, would expand protections to greater numbers and types of workers, improve victims' ability to hold employers and individual harassers accountable, redress victims' harm by improving recovery of monetary damages, restrict employers' efforts to impose secrecy regarding harassment, and emphasize prevention strategies.

Extending Protections to More Employees

Title VII and state antidiscrimination laws provide important protections against workplace sexual harassment—but only for some employees. Individuals deserve to be protected from sexual harassment on the job regardless of the size of the establishment where they work or their employment classification.

Protecting Employees of Small Businesses

Title VII's protections only apply to employers with fifteen or more employees. For those employees working for a business with less than fifteen employees, there is no federal remedy for workplace sexual harassment. Reducing the employer size threshold for harassment laws and other antidiscrimination laws, as several states have already done, would ensure that employees working for small businesses will no longer be left without recourse when they are harassed. Antidiscrimination laws in Alaska, Colorado, the District of Columbia, Hawaii, Maine, Michigan, Minnesota, Montana, New Jersey, North Dakota, Oklahoma, Oregon, South Dakota, Vermont, and Wisconsin cover employers with one or more employees, ensuring that employees working for employers of all sizes have a legal remedy if they experience harassment.

Protecting Independent Contractors

Title VII and most state antidiscrimination laws by their terms only protect "employees" from sexual harassment on the job. This leaves the growing segment of workers classified as "independent contractors" without protection from workplace harassment. Freelancers and individuals who work in the gig economy, for example, have no legal protection against workplace sexual harassment in most of the country. Employers' misclassification of people as independent contractors in an attempt to limit their liability under labor and employment laws also threatens many individuals' ability to avail themselves of sexual harassment protections.

Some of the country's most vulnerable workers—like home healthcare workers and domestic workers—are often classified as independent contractors. Amending antidiscrimination laws to apply to independent contractors would extend protection from workplace harassment to many women of color and immigrants, who make up the vast majority of individuals in these jobs. A few states and localities have taken action to ensure that all workers, regardless of employment classification, are protected from workplace sexual harassment.

California's workplace antidiscrimination statute prohibits "harassment" of employees, job applicants, unpaid interns, volunteers, and any person "providing service pursuant to a contract," including independent contractors. In 1996, the Supreme Court of **Washington** held that independent contractors are protected under Washington's law against discrimination, which includes a prohibition on sexual harassment in the workplace. Lower courts in Washington have found that independent contractors are protected under the law against discrimination's sexual harassment provisions in particular. **New York City**'s Human Rights Law specifies that "natural persons employed as independent contractors to carry out work in furtherance of an employer's business enterprise who are not themselves employers" are considered employees under the law's protection. However, New York State's Human Rights Law does not protect independent contractors.

Strengthening Employees' Ability to Hold Employers and Individual Harassers Accountable

Title VII imposes a legal obligation on employers to protect their employees from sexual harassment. Accordingly, employers can be legally responsible for sexual harassment against their employees and liable to them for damages.

When an employer is liable for harassment depends on the type of harassment, and who committed it. The Supreme Court has made clear that employers have a heightened legal obligation to guard against supervisor harassment because of the potential for supervisors to exploit their authority over their subordinates by harassing them. Therefore, if the harassment by a supervisor results in a tangible employment action against the victim (such as firing, demotion, or a pay cut), the employer is automatically responsible. If the harassment does not result in a tangible employment action, then the employer will be automatically liable unless it can show that (1) the employer exercised reasonable care to prevent and promptly correct any harassment, and (2) the employee unreasonably failed to take advantage of the company's preventive or corrective measures or to otherwise avoid harm, like a system for reporting and investigating harassment.

The employer may also be liable for harassment by a low-level supervisor, coworker, or customer if the employer was negligent in allowing the harassment to occur—meaning that the employer knew or should have known about the harassment and failed to take immediate and appropriate corrective action.

However, individual harassers may not be held personally liable for workplace sexual harassment under federal law.

While judicial interpretations have made it more difficult to hold employers accountable under federal law, some state courts and legislatures have made it easier for workers who have been harassed to bring those responsible to justice. Strengthening accountability for both employers and individual workplace harassers helps ensure that meaningful remedies are available for those who are victims of sexual harassment.

Holding employers accountable for harassment by a low-level supervisor

Recent interpretations of Title VII have limited victims' ability to obtain legal redress when they experience sexual harassment by low-level supervisors. In 2013 in *Vance v. Ball State University*, the Supreme Court significantly undercut protections against supervisor harassment by essentially reclassifying as coworkers those lower-level supervisors who direct an employee's daily work activities, but do not have the power to take concrete employment actions like hiring and firing employees. This means that when employees with the authority to direct daily work activities—but not the authority to hire, fire, and take other tangible employment action—harass their subordinates, their employers are no longer vicariously liable for that harassment. Instead, lower-level supervisors without the power to take tangible employment actions are now treated as coworkers, and in order to succeed in her sexual harassment case, the victim of harassment must make the much tougher showing that the employer was "negligent" in allowing the harassment to occur.

The *Vance* decision is grossly out of touch with the realities of the workplace, as supervisors with the authority to direct daily work activities can wield a significant amount of power over their subordinates. This is a particular problem for many workers in low-wage jobs, the majority of whom are women. For too many workers seeking justice against workplace harassers in positions of power, important administrative and legal remedies are out of reach due to the Supreme Court's misguided decision. Since *Vance* limited vicarious liability for supervisor harassment, victims have had their claims thrown out by courts and have been prevented from bringing claims at all.

The Fair Employment Protection Act would restore strong protections for employees from supervisor harassment, but it has not advanced in Congress. At the state level, the **New Jersey** Supreme Court rejected Vance's restrictive definition of "supervisor" for employees bringing sexual harassment claims under the state law against discrimination. Instead, the court adopted the more expansive definition that existed before *Vance*—that a supervisor is an employee with the power to direct a victim's daily work activities.

Holding a workplace harasser individually accountable for harassment

Under Title VII, it is an "employer's" legal duty to protect employees from sexual harassment. Federal courts have interpreted this to mean that only businesses or organizations, and not individuals, may be held liable for sexual harassment pursuant to Title VII. While an employer may take action to discipline, fire, or otherwise penalize the harasser, federal law does not permit victims to hold individual harassers—whether a supervisor, coworker, client, or customer—directly and personally accountable for sexual harassment. As a result, if an employer chooses not to take action against a harasser, the harasser may suffer no consequences for his or her behavior.

While this is an evolving area of law, several states currently permit victims to sue their individual harassers under state antidiscrimination laws. Through both state court decisions interpreting state antidiscrimination laws, and through legislation specifically addressing liability for sexual harassment, states have allowed harassers to be held personally accountable for harassment in particular circumstances. In the **District of Columbia**, **Massachusetts**, **Michigan**, **Missouri**, **Montana**, **New Mexico**, and **Washington**, a harasser who is a supervisor can be held individually liable for sexual harassment. In **California**, **Iowa**, and **Vermont**, any employee can be held individually liable for harassing another employee, regardless of whether the harassed employee is a subordinate or a coworker.

Redressing the Harm to Victims of Harassment

If an employee wins a sexual harassment lawsuit, the employee can obtain several forms of relief, including monetary damages. Title VII provides for the recovery of compensatory and punitive damages. Compensatory damages compensate victims for out-of-pocket expenses caused by the harassment and for any emotional harm. Punitive damages may be awarded to punish an employer who acted maliciously or recklessly in engaging in harassment.

However, a plaintiff's recovery of compensatory and punitive damages is capped under federal law depending on the size of the employer. For a plaintiff succeeding in a harassment case against an employer with 15–100 employees, for example, damages are capped at $50,000, no matter how severe the harassment or how culpable the employer. Even for employers with more than 500 employees, damages are capped at $300,000.40 This means that in the most egregious cases of employer-sanctioned sexual harassment, up to and including sexual assault, if a jury awarded a plaintiff millions of dollars in compensatory and punitive damages, the most she could recover from a large employer is $300,000, which could be insufficient to compensate her for the injuries she suffered. Such limited remedies also reduce employer incentives to prevent harassment before it happens; $300,000 is a small amount to a large and profitable corporation. Damages caps mean that employers can come out ahead by gambling that it costs less to discriminate than to create a workplace free of discrimination and harassment.

Some state antidiscrimination laws prohibiting harassment provide for the recovery of compensatory and punitive damages, but often without caps, or with higher limits than those under federal law. **California, Hawaii, Massachusetts, New Jersey, Ohio, Oregon, Vermont**, and **West Virginia** do not limit plaintiffs' compensatory and punitive damages, ensuring that victims of harassment can be fully compensated for the harm they suffered. In other states, however, no such compensation is available.

Restricting Employer-Imposed Secrecy and Restoring Victims' Voices

Individuals may accept employment with a company without knowing if discrimination and harassment are particular problems at that workplace. Once employed, harassers and employers use a variety of legal tools in order to limit how, when, why, and to whom an employee can disclose details about harassment. Through employment agreements—entered into upon hiring at a new job, and settlement terms—agreed to when resolving a sexual harassment complaint—employees can be forbidden by contractual terms from speaking out about sexual harassment and assault. Such circumstances operate to isolate victims, shield serial predators from accountability, and allow harassment to persist at a company. Policy efforts to increase transparency regarding the incidence of harassment at a company would redress the power imbalance exacerbated by employer-imposed secrecy provisions, and restore victims' voices.

Limiting Employer-Imposed Secrecy in Employment Agreements

Employers sometimes use employment agreements to forbid employees from speaking out about sexual harassment and assault. Other provisions in such agreements also often prohibit employees from going to court to enforce their rights, instead forcing employees to litigate sexual harassment and assault claims in a private arbitration, which is frequently designed, chosen, and paid for by the employer or corporation, and conducted and resolved in secret.

Federal laws, like the National Labor Relations Act (NLRA) and Title VII, limit an employer's ability to enforce contracts that restrict employees' ability to discuss employment conditions or situations. An employer cannot, for example, forbid employees covered by the NLRA from discussing employment conditions with each other, including sexual harassment. Employers also cannot require an employee to waive their right to report violations of federal law to civil rights enforcement agencies like the Equal Employment Opportunity Commission, or require employees to waive in advance the ability to report a crime to authorities.

Despite these protections, employers continue to use contractual provisions to prevent employees, including victims, from publicly disclosing the details of sexual harassment or assault, allowing serial harassers to act without accountability, and preventing employees from joining together to counter a predator. Other provisions in employment agreements, such as confidentiality clauses prohibiting employees from publicly disparaging the employer, and forced arbitration clauses requiring all employment-related disputes to be settled in private arbitration proceedings, are standard provisions in some industries, imposed on new hires as a condition of their employment. These contractual provisions can mislead employees as to their legal rights and prohibit employees from publicly telling their story, which in turn makes it less likely that other victims of harassment will speak out and hold their employers accountable.

Prohibiting contractual provisions that restrict employees' ability to speak out about harassment as a condition of employment—especially contractual language that makes a victim question whether they can report harassment to federal and state antidiscrimination agencies, and force employees to give up their day in court—would help lift the veil of secrecy that enables predatory behavior, and protect employees' right to speak with enforcement agencies and act collectively to challenge harassment. Because the Federal Arbitration Act likely preempts any state attempts to limit mandatory arbitration clauses, a federal remedy such as the Arbitration Fairness Act or the Ending Forced Arbitration of Sexual Harassment Act is necessary.

Restoring Victims' Power in Settlement Agreements

Nondisclosure clauses in settlement agreements also often operate to prevent harassment victims from speaking out publicly about the harassment they experienced, the fact of settlement, the settlement terms, or the identity of the parties as a condition of their settlement with a harasser or employer. Here too secrecy can help hide the true extent of sexual harassment at a workplace, shield a serial harasser from accountability, and prevent other victims from coming forward.

On the other hand, victims sometimes want to ensure confidentiality as to these matters in order to protect themselves from retaliation or damage to their professional reputations and job prospects. Moreover, the promise of mutual nondisclosure as to some or all aspects of the settlement can provide victims with useful leverage in settlement negotiations. A policy banning all nondisclosure agreements in sexual harassment settlement agreements could make employers less likely to settle claims of harassment, forcing victims of harassment to take up the difficult, expensive, and time consuming task of pursuing legal claims in court in order to obtain any restitution. Accordingly, regulation of nondisclosure clauses in settlements must be carefully calibrated to balance these competing interests, restoring power to a victim to decide what should be confidential.

A few states have limited when employers can impose contractual conditions in settlements that silence employees. In 2006, **California** passed a law prohibiting the use of nondisclosure agreements in any settlement of felony sex offenses. The statute was amended in 2016 to also prohibit nondisclosure agreements in settlements for other non-felony sexual crimes, including childhood sexual abuse, sexual exploitation of a minor, and sexual assault against an elder or dependent adult. In 1990, **Florida** became the first state to pass a "Sunshine in Litigation" law, which prohibits court orders and settlements that would have the purpose or effect of "concealing a public hazard." By the terms of the statute, a "public hazard" is a "device, instrument, person, procedure or product[] that has caused and is likely to cause injury," which to date has been primarily applied in cases of products liability and sexual abuse of minors. Several other states, including **Delaware, Indiana, New York, North Carolina, Oregon,** and **Washington** have adopted similar Sunshine in Litigation statutes.

Requiring Disclosure or Reporting of Harassment Claims, Charges, and Lawsuits

Greater transparency regarding discrimination complaints, formal charges, and lawsuits filed against an employer, and the resolution of those claims, would help alleviate the secrecy around harassment, thereby empowering victims and encouraging employers to implement prevention efforts proactively. For instance, civil rights agencies could make publicly available the type and number of discrimination charges filed against a business or organization, whether the charges were dismissed or resolved, and general information about the nature of the resolution (for instance, whether the charge was resolved through a monetary settlement). Such information could be made available on the agency's website, so that members of the public could conduct searches by company name, while at the same time protecting the identity of individuals who filed charges.

Another transparency initiative could require contractors, as a condition of submitting a bid or keeping an awarded contract, to report regularly to the relevant agency the type and number of discrimination complaints or lawsuits filed against the company within a particular time period, and the nature of the resolution of claims or lawsuits. Making even some portion of the reported information publicly available would provide job applicants and employees with valuable information about discrimination and harassment at a particular workplace. Such reporting also would encourage employers to implement practices to effectively address complaints and prevent sexual harassment.

Requiring Sexual Harassment Prevention Strategies

Prevention should be a primary goal for employers in addressing sexual harassment. While Title VII has been interpreted to provide employers with an incentive to adopt sexual harassment policies and training, such practices are not mandatory, and often fail to effectively prevent harassment. Harassment prevention ultimately requires changes in attitude and behavior, for which there is no short-term solution. Yet for businesses, investing in sexual harassment prevention is not only the right thing to do, it is the financially advantageous thing to do. Preventing sexual harassment in the first instance helps employers avoid costly litigation, settlements, and higher insurance premiums, as well as attendant negative publicity and lower productivity.

Implementing a Comprehensive Prevention Program

Harassment prevention involves changing workplace culture and practices, and that change starts at the top. The organization's highest leadership must make clear that sexual harassment is taken seriously, and commit appropriate time and resources to implement strong prevention and response strategies. Many companies have a written policy prohibiting sexual harassment, but such a policy is only the first step in prevention. An employer must also have policies and procedures regarding how to report harassment (with multiple avenues for making a report), how harassment complaints will be promptly and thoroughly investigated and addressed, and ensuring that harassment perpetrators will be held accountable. Employers also should have strong and appropriately enforced policies against retaliation.

An effective prevention program should also include an anonymous climate survey of employees, which will help management understand the true nature and scope of harassment and discrimination in the workplace. The survey can help inform important issues to be included in training, and help identify problematic behavior that may be addressed before it leads to formal complaints or lawsuits.

All of these policies and procedures are essential elements for prevention, and must be implemented through training for all employees, including managers and supervisors. Although many companies provide sexual harassment training, it often falls short of the mark. Effective training must go beyond mere compliance, or simply telling employees what the law requires. Training is more likely to be effective if it helps employees and supervisors recognize sexual harassment in the context of their specific workplace, and understand their rights and responsibilities. Training should explain how to report harassment as a victim or a witness, as well as the reporting and investigation process, the consequences for engaging in harassment, and identify internal and external resources that are available to an employee who feels they have been harassed. The most effective training is live, rather than video training or self-administered online training; mandatory; frequent (upon hire and at least annually thereafter); interactive; relevant to the particular workplace context; and requires employees to problem solve common scenarios, including by utilizing bystander intervention techniques.

Mandating Workplace Training

To varying degrees, states have imposed requirements on public and private sector employers to train employees on preventing, recognizing, and reporting sexual harassment. Existing state requirements vary by which employers must provide training, which employees must participate, whether trainings must be repeated over time, and whether the content of the training must conform to a state standard. The most effective harassment training mandate would apply to all employers in both the public and private sectors, and require all employees to participate, with possible additional training for supervisors. The training mandate should further require that trainings be given with regularity, both upon an employee's hire and at reoccurring intervals thereafter, and specify the content that must be included in the training.

Twenty-seven states require at least some form of statutorily mandated sexual harassment training. Only three of these states—**California**, **Connecticut**, and

Maine—require employers in the private sector to provide workplace sexual harassment training. The training requirements for private sector employers in California and Maine include important provisions such as the number of training hours required, whether employees as well as supervisors must be trained, and how often regular retraining must occur. Both California and Maine also include some information on the content of the required training, which is critical in guiding employers to implement effective trainings.

South Dakota and **Washington** impose a training requirement on businesses contracting with the state, although South Dakota's requirement only applies to a limited group of contractors.

An additional twenty-two states require only public sector supervisors and employees to participate in mandatory training; ten states require all public employees to participate, while twelve states require only some public employees in certain departments or positions to participate. An additional eight states have explicit statutory or regulatory guidance merely encouraging, but not mandating, private sector employers to implement sexual harassment training, or any form of training.

Existing state efforts' narrow scope, and failure to provide detailed requirements for training or for broader prevention strategies, likely undermines their effectiveness. The most powerful policy efforts would mandate instituting and implementing a variety of prevention strategies beyond training, including a broader array of harassment policies and procedures explaining how to report harassment, providing multiple points for reporting, conducting prompt investigations and responding to harassment complaints, strong and consistently enforced policies against retaliation, and disciplinary consequences for harassers.

Eliminating the Tipped Minimum Wage

The federal minimum cash wage for tipped workers has been frozen at $2.13 per hour for 25 years, and now represents less than a third of the federal minimum wage ($7.25 per hour). Women, who represent two-thirds of tipped workers nationally, are hit especially hard by this poverty level wage.

Although employers are legally required to make up the difference between the regular minimum wage and the lower wage they pay their tipped workers if the tips they receive fall short of this amount, this requirement is difficult to enforce and employers often fail to comply. As a result, tipped workers frequently struggle to make ends meet on unpredictable tips with virtually no dependable income from a paycheck.

Tipped workers also are particularly vulnerable to sexual harassment and sexual assault at work, because of their typically limited power within the workplace, because of the economic vulnerability that leaves them without a financial cushion if they lose their job, and because of the need to please the customer in order to bring home anything approaching an adequate wage. Tipped workers' reliance on tips to supplement a sub-minimum wage forces them to tolerate sexual harassment and other inappropriate behavior from customers just to make a living, which in turn perpetuates a culture of harassment in tipped industries.

Equal treatment for tipped workers—that is, requiring that tipped workers are paid the regular minimum wage before tips—can help alleviate tipped workers' vulnerability to sexual harassment. Some states now require employers to pay their tipped employees the regular minimum wage regardless of tips. **Alaska, California, Minnesota, Montana, Nevada, Oregon,** and **Washington** are "equal treatment" states. And as of 2016, **Hawaii** has a maximum tip credit of 75 cents, meaning that tipped employees can be paid no less than 75 cents below the regular minimum wage, and only if the total wages paid by her employer plus tips equal at least $7.00 more than the regular minimum wage. Adopting one fair wage helps ensure that tipped workers in service industries no longer have to endure sexual harassment in order to support themselves and their families.

As the movement ignited by #MeToo shows, for too long, many women, and some men, have suffered workplace sexual harassment in silence, with little or no accountability for harassers. Now more than ever, corporate leaders and policymakers must step forward to go beyond simply responding to harassment, to refashioning systems, laws, and culture ensuring victims can obtain justice, predators are held accountable, and sexual harassment is eradicated.

Notes and Discussion

1. Reforming Laws Women are challenging the statutory limitations of Titles VII and IX, as well as court decisions limiting these laws' reach and impact. Are the suggested improvements likely to be effective? For a discussion of how the #MeToo movement is shaping the law, see Rebecca Hanner White, *Title VII and the #MeToo Movement*, 68 EMORY L.J. 1014 (2018); Elizabeth Chika Tippett, *The Legal Implications of the MeToo Movement*, 123 MINN. L. REV. 129 (2018); and Ramit Mizrahi, *Sexual Harassment Law After #MeToo: Looking to California as a Model*, 128 YALE L.J.F. 121 (2018).

2. Covering Small Businesses and Independent Contractors Why aren't all workers protected by sexual harassment laws? What are arguments for and against extending sexual harassment protections to smaller employers? Some employers circumvent sexual harassment laws by characterizing their employees as independent contractors. Is this an argument to extend the law to cover independent contractors? If so, how would that work?

Many of Weinstein's accusers were not employees of the Weinstein Company. They were independent actresses or temporary employees, who may have received their paychecks from contract worker agencies. Title VII does not cover many of these workers in relation to the companies that contract for temporary workers and independent agents.[31] In 2018, New York City adopted the Stop Sexual Harassment in

---

31. Julia Horowitz & Sara Ashley O'Brien, *How Do You Report Sexual Harassment When There's No HR?*, CNN MONEY (Oct. 16, 2017).

NYC Act that expanded coverage of gender-based harassment claims under the New York City Human Rights Law to all employees, including independent contractors. (The law also extends the statute of limitations for claims alleging gender-based harassment from one to three years.) California's Fair Employment and Housing Act covers independent contractors, unpaid interns, and volunteers.

3. Employer Liability NWLC suggests expanding employer liability for sexual harassment. What changes would be effective? How would employer liability for the actions of low-level supervisors help? See Chapter 4 on Employer Liability.

4. Individual Liability Under Title VII Recall the discussion of individual versus employer liability in Chapter 4. In *Robinson v. Jacksonville Shipyards, Inc.*, 760 F. Supp. 1486 (M.D. Fla. 1991), the court concluded that an individual could be held liable for sexual harassment and discrimination under Title VII. *See also, Ruich v. Ruff, Weidenaar & Reidy, Ltd.*, 837 F. Supp. 881 (N.D. Ill. 1993) (defining "employer" to include a partner of a law firm). Since 1991, however, almost every court that has considered the question of individual liability under Title VII has rejected it. Some legal scholars have argued that Title VII should hold individual harassers liable.[32] Is it appropriate to hold individuals liable for sexual harassment? Why or why not? For plaintiffs, what are the tactical and practical advantages and disadvantages of naming individual defendants? Does individual immunity diminish Title VII's effectiveness or enhance it?

In *Meritor Savings Bank FSB v. Vinson*, the Supreme Court recognized that Congress intended for courts to "look to agency principles for guidance" in determining liability for sexual harassment under Title VII. The RESTATEMENT (SECOND) OF AGENCY states that "Principal and agent can be joined in one action for a wrong resulting from the tortious conduct of an agent . . . and a judgment can be rendered against each." Rest. (2d) Agency, § 359c(1) (1957). Thus, the law of agency recognizes personal liability for agents. *Griffith v. Keystone Steel & Wire*, 858 F. Supp. 802, 806 (C.D. Ill. 1994). Does the RESTATEMENT OF AGENCY lend support for the imposition of individual liability under Title VII?

5. Individual Liability Under State Law Many state statutes prohibit discrimination by any "person" and thereby avoid the problems courts have encountered in interpreting Title VII. Many state statutes also prohibit aiding and abetting discrimination by individuals. *See, e.g.,* Cal. Gov. Code § 12940 *et seq.* Some targets of sexual harassment have pursued state-law tort claims against individual harassers. Claims that may be used include tortious interference with contractual

---

32. *See, e.g.,* Miller v. Maxwell's International Inc., 991 F.2d 583 (9th Cir. 1993) (ruling that individuals are not liable under Title VII). *But see* Anthony D. Pignotti, *If You Grab the Honey, You Better Have the Money: An In-Depth Analysis of Individual Supervisor Liability for Workplace Sexual Harassment*, 5 AVE MARIA L. REV. 207 (2007) (arguing for individual liability under Title VII); Tracy L. Gonos, *A Policy Analysis of Individual Liability — The Case for Amending Title VII to Hold Individuals Personally Liable for Their Illegal Discriminatory Actions*, 2 NYU J. LEGIS. & PUB. POL'Y 265 (1999) (same).

relations, loss of consortium, intentional and negligent infliction of emotional distress, assault and battery, false imprisonment, invasion of privacy, defamation, and misrepresentation. Common law tort remedies allow for the recovery of punitive damages. Another option is criminal charges such as rape, forcible sodomy, sexual assault and battery, obscene telephone calls, solicitation, lewd conduct, pandering, false imprisonment, aiding and abetting, conspiracy, compounding, concealing, and obstructing.

6. Compensatory and Punitive Damages Recall the discussion of damage caps in Chapter 5. Should Title VII have caps on damages? What is the impact of the damages cap? Note that there are not caps on damages for race discrimination in employment, including racial harassment, under 42 U.S.C. § 1981a. For a critique of the damages cap, see Lynn Ridgeway Zehrt, *Twenty Years of Compromise: How the Caps on Damages in the Civil Rights Act of 1991 Codified Sex Discrimination*, 25 YALE J. L.& FEMINISM 249 (2014).

7. Mandatory Arbitration In November 2018, after employee protests and walkouts, Google and Facebook ended forced arbitration for sexual harassment claims.[33] Several states have passed or are considering laws restricting mandatory arbitration clauses in employment contracts. In 2018, New York State passed a law prohibiting mandatory arbitration. N.Y. C.P.L.R. § 7515. The same year, Washington State enacted a law prohibiting employment contract provisions or agreements that require employees to resolve "claims of discrimination in a dispute resolution process that is confidential." S. Bill 6313 (Wash. 2018). In October 2018, California Governor Jerry Brown vetoed a law banning mandatory arbitration in that state. Are mandatory arbitration clauses in employment contracts fair?

8. Nondisclosure Agreements and Employer Secrecy Employers use nondisclosure and mandatory arbitration clauses in employment contracts, as well as nondisclosure clauses in settlement agreements, to avoid public exposure of sexual harassment in their organizations. Is there a public interest argument for prohibiting employers from hiding illegal conduct within their organizations? Harvey Weinstein used nondisclosure provisions in sexual harassment settlement agreements to prevent exposure of his decades-long abuse of women. How would mandatory reporting of sexual harassment have impacted the Weinstein Company? In the 2018 case of *Epic Systems Corp. v. Lewis*, 138 S. Ct. 1612 (2018), the Supreme Court ruled that employers could require mandatory arbitration in employment contracts. Is this fair? See Symposium on the Court's Ruling in *Epic Systems Corp. v. Lewis*, SCO-TUSBLOG (May 24, 2018), https://perma.cc/D4Q5-ZAEC.

In 2017, Congress passed a law disallowing tax deductions for sexual harassment settlements subject to nondisclosure agreements.[34] Some states are restricting

---

33. Jena McGregor, *Google and Facebook Ended Forced Arbitration for Sexual Harassment Claims. Why More Companies Could Follow*, WASH. POST (Nov. 12, 2018).

34. *See* Internal Revenue Code § 162(q) (Supp. V 2017); Margaret Ryznar, *#MeToo & Tax*, 75 WASH. & LEE L. REV. 53 (2018).

nondisclosure agreements in settlement agreements. New York now prohibits non-disclosure provisions in sexual harassment settlement agreements unless the complainant prefers to include such a provision. N.Y. C.P.L.R. § 7515.

9. Eliminating the Subminimum Wage Suing an employer under Title VII is time-consuming, expensive, and unrealistic for many employees. Some worker advocates are promoting preventative strategies that address structural factors in the workplace that make employees vulnerable to sexual harassment. How does tipping make workers vulnerable to sexual harassment? Organizations such as the Restaurant Opportunities Centers United are organizing "one fair wage" campaigns across the country to eliminate the subminimum wage. See Chapter 2. What other structural changes to the workplace might reduce sexual harassment?

10. Sexual Harassment in Congress Why is there a separate, private procedure for adjudicating sexual harassment complaints against members of Congress? Is this procedure justified? In December 2018, Congress passed an amendment to the Congressional Accountability Act. It bars the use of taxpayer funds to settle sexual harassment cases against members of Congress. It also speeds up resolution of cases and protects interns and fellows. Additionally, the amendment increases transparency around sexual harassment settlements. The final law did not include several provisions advocated by the bill's sponsor, Senator Jackie Speier (D-CA). Excluded were a guarantee of employer-backed legal counsel for all survivors, expansion of the protections to all forms of discrimination, and independent investigations at the start of the review process. In addition, on the Senate side, reimbursement for settlement payments would not be automatic but would be determined by the Senate Ethics Committee.

11. Violence Against Women Act Since 1994, VAWA has provided funding for domestic violence shelters, rape crisis centers, and campus sexual assault programs. Periodic reauthorizations of the bill were bipartisan until 2013, when Republican opposition became significant. The bill was due for reauthorization in the fall of 2018, but Congress failed to act, endangering programs that provide critical services to survivors of gendered violence. Temporary spending bills have kept some of the funding in place, but the government shutdown in late 2018 led to the suspension of funding for many programs. The #MeToo mobilization and concern about violence against women contributed to Democrats' winning the House in November 2018, with pledges to reauthorize VAWA funding. Nevertheless, VAWA funding ran out in February 2019.

In 2016, the EEOC Select Task Force on the Study of Harassment in the Workplace issued a comprehensive report on best practices for eliminating workplace sexual harassment. The report was based on research and testimony from more than 30 witnesses, including sociologists, industrial-organizational psychologists, investigators, trainers, lawyers, employers, and advocates. The key finding was that leadership is critical to changing workplace cultures to prevent sexual harassment. Consider excerpts from the report.

EEOC Select Task Force on the Study of Harassment in the Workplace Report of Co-Chairs Chai R. Feldblum & Victoria A. Lipnic[35]

Moving Forward: Preventing Harassment in the Workplace

Harassment in the workplace can sometimes feel like an intractable problem. The question is whether there is anything we can do to prevent harassment to a significant degree. We believe the answer to that is "yes." We also believe that it will not be easy to achieve this goal. If it were easy, it would have happened a long time ago. The following sections lay out our analysis, based on what we have learned over the past year, for achieving what some may see as a quixotic goal, but which we see as a moral and legal imperative.

A. It Starts at The Top

Over and over again, during the course of our study, we heard that workplace culture has the greatest impact on allowing harassment to flourish, or conversely, in preventing harassment. We heard this from academics who testified to the Select Task Force; we heard it from trainers and organizational psychologists on the ground; and we read about it during the course of our literature review.

Two things—perhaps two faces of the same coin—became clear to us. First, across the board, we heard that leadership and commitment to a diverse, inclusive, and respectful workplace in which harassment is simply not acceptable is paramount. And we heard that this leadership must come from the very top of the organization.

Second, we heard that a commitment (even from the top) for a diverse, inclusive, and respectful workplace is not enough. Rather, at all levels, across all positions, an organization must have systems in place that hold employees accountable for this expectation. These accountability systems must ensure that those who engage in harassment are held responsible in a meaningful, appropriate, and proportional manner, and that those whose job it is to prevent or respond to harassment, directly or indirectly, are rewarded for doing that job well, or penalized for failing to do so.

These two sides of the coin—leadership and accountability—create an organization's culture. An organization's culture is set by the values of an organization. To achieve a workplace without harassment, the values of the organization must put a premium on diversity and inclusion, must include a belief that all employees in a workplace deserve to be respected, regardless of their race, religion, national origin, sex (including pregnancy, sexual orientation, or gender identity), age, disability, or genetic information, and must make clear that part of respect means not harassing an individual on any of those bases. In short, an organization's commitment to a

---

35. CHAI R. FELDBLUM & VICTORIA A. LIPNIC, U.S. EQUAL EMP. OPPORTUNITY COMM'N, SELECT TASK FORCE ON THE STUDY OF HARASSMENT IN THE WORKPLACE: REPORT OF CO-CHAIRS 8 (June 2016) (notes deleted).

harassment-free workplace must not be based on a compliance mindset, and instead must be part of an overall diversity and inclusion strategy.

Organizational culture manifests itself in the specific behaviors that are expected and formally and informally rewarded in the workplace. As one of our witnesses explained, "[O]rganizational climate is an important driver of harassment because it is the norms of the workplace; it basically guides employees . . . to know what to do when no one is watching."

Organizational cultures that tolerate harassment have more of it, and workplaces that are not tolerant of harassment have less of it. This common-sense assumption has been demonstrated repeatedly in research studies. If leadership values a workplace free of harassment, then it will ensure that harassing behavior against employees is prohibited as a matter of policy; that swift, effective, and proportionate responses are taken when harassment occurs; and that everyone in the workplace feels safe in reporting harassing behavior. Conversely, leaders who do not model respectful behavior, who are tolerant of demeaning conduct or remarks by others, or who fail to support anti-harassment policies with necessary resources, may foster a culture conducive to harassment.

Leadership

What steps can an organization's leadership take to ensure that its organizational culture reflects the leadership's values of not tolerating harassment and promoting civility and respect?

First, leadership must establish a sense of urgency about preventing harassment. That means taking a visible role in stating the importance of having a diverse and inclusive workplace that is free of harassment, articulating clearly the specific behaviors that will not be acceptable in the workplace, setting the foundation for employees throughout the organization to make change (if change is needed), and, once an organizational culture is achieved that reflects the values of the leadership, commit to ensuring that the culture is maintained.

One way to effectuate and convey a sense of urgency and commitment is to assess whether the workplace has one or more of the risk factors we describe above and take proactive steps to address those. For example, if employees tend to work in isolated workspaces, an employer may want to explore whether it is possible for the work to get done as effectively if individuals worked in teams. In a workplace where an employee's compensation is directly tied to customer satisfaction or client service, the employer may wish to emphasize that harassing conduct should be brought immediately to a manager's attention and that the worker will be protected from retaliation. In workplaces with many teenagers and young adults entering the workforce, the employer may wish to have an orientation in which conduct that is not acceptable is clearly described and workers are encouraged to come forward quickly with any concerns.

Another way to communicate a sense of urgency is to conduct a climate survey of employees to determine whether employees feel that harassment exists in the workplace and is tolerated. Several researchers have developed such climate surveys, and the military has adopted them on a widespread scale in recent years. After a holistic approach to prevention has been put into place (as described in the remainder of this section), such climate surveys can be repeated to ensure that change has occurred and is being maintained.

Second, an organization must have effective policies and procedures and must conduct effective trainings on those policies and procedures. Anti-harassment policies must be communicated and adhered to, and reporting systems must be implemented consistently, safely, and in a timely fashion. Trainings must ensure that employees are aware of, and understand, the employer's policy and reporting systems. Such systems must be periodically tested to ensure that they are effective. Our detailed recommendations concerning these policies and trainings are discussed in the following sections.

Third, leadership must back up its statement of urgency about preventing harassment with two of the most important commodities in a workplace: money and time. Employees must believe that their leaders are authentic in demanding a workplace free of harassment. Nothing speaks to that credibility more than what gets paid for in a budget and what gets scheduled on a calendar. For example, complaint procedures must be adequately funded in the organization's budget and sufficient time must be allocated from employee schedules to ensure appropriate investigations. Similarly, sufficient resources must be allotted to procure training, trainings must be provided frequently, and sufficient time must be allocated from employee schedules so that all employees can attend these trainings. Moreover, if an organization has a budget for diversity and inclusion efforts, harassment prevention should be part of that budget.

Finally, in working to create change, the leadership must ensure that any team or coalition leading the effort to create a workplace free of harassment is vested with enough power and authority to make such change happen.

Accountability

Because organizational culture is manifested by what behaviors are formally and informally rewarded, it all comes down to accountability—and accountability must be demonstrated. An employer that has an effective anti-harassment program, including an effective and safe reporting system, a thorough workplace investigation system, and proportionate corrective actions, communicates to employees by those measures that the employer takes harassment seriously. This in turn means that more employees will be likely to complain if they experience harassment or report harassment they observe, such that the employer may deal with such incidents more effectively. This creates a positive cycle that can ultimately reduce the amount of harassment that occurs in a workplace.

With regard to individuals who engage in harassment, accountability means being held responsible for those actions. We heard from investigators on the ground, and we read in the academic literature, that sanctions are often not proportionate to the inappropriate conduct that had been substantiated. If weak sanctions are imposed for bad behavior, employees learn that harassment is tolerated, regardless of the messages, money, time, and resources spent to the contrary. Similarly, if high-ranking and/or highly-valued employees are not dealt with severely if they engage in harassment, that sends the wrong message loud and clear.

With regard to mid-level managers and front-line supervisors, accountability means that such individuals are held responsible for monitoring and stopping harassment by those they supervise and manage.

For example, if a supervisor fails to respond to a report of harassment in a prompt and appropriate fashion, or if a supervisor fails to protect from retaliation the individual who reports harassment, that supervisor must be held accountable for those actions. Similarly, if those responsible for investigations and corrective actions do not commence or conclude an investigation promptly, do not engage in a thorough or fair investigation, or do not take appropriate action when offending conduct is found, that person must be held accountable.

Accountability also includes reward systems. If leadership incentivizes and rewards responsiveness to anti-harassment efforts by managers, that speaks volumes. When the right behaviors (e.g., creating civil and respectful workplaces, promptly reporting and investigating harassment claims, aggressively managing employees involved in or not adequately responding to harassment) are rewarded, that sends a message about what an organization's leadership cares about. For example, a number of witnesses noted that companies who were successful in creating a culture of non-harassment were those that acknowledged and "owned" its well-handled complaints, instead of burying the fact that there had been a complaint and that discipline had been taken.

Perhaps counter-intuitively, rewards can also be given to managers when—at least initially—there is an increase in complaints in their division. We heard that using the metric of the number of complaints lodged within a particular division, with rewards given to those with the fewest number of complaints, might have the counterproductive effect of managers suppressing the filing of complaints through formal and informal pressure. In contrast, if employees are filing complaints of harassment, that means the employees have faith in the system. Thus, using the metric of the number of complaints must be nuanced. Positive organizational change can be reflected in an initial increase of complaints, followed by a decrease in complaints and information about the lack of harassment derived from climate surveys.

Before moving on to detailed recommendations, we pause to highlight a radically different accountability mechanism that we find intriguing, and solicited testimony regarding at one of our public meetings. A number of large companies, such as McDonald's and Wal-Mart, have begun to hold their tomato growers accountable by buying tomatoes only from those growers who abide by a human rights based Code of Conduct, which, among other elements, prohibits sexual harassment and sexual assault of farmworkers. This effort, called the Fair Food Program, was developed and is led by the Coalition of Imokalee Workers (CIW), a farmworker-based human rights organization in Florida. The companies agreed to the program because of consumer-driven market pressures, and most of the agricultural companies that entered the program did so because of the resulting financial pressures.

As part of the program, the CIW conducts worker-to-worker education programs. There is also a worker-triggered complaint resolution mechanism, which can result in investigations, corrective action plans, and if necessary, suspension of a farm's "participating grower" status, which means the farm could lose its ability to sell to participating buyers. There are currently 14 businesses and 17 growers participating in the program.

The most important lesson we learned from our study is that employers must have a holistic approach for creating an organizational culture that will prevent harassment. If employers put a metric in a manager's performance plan about responding appropriately to harassment complaints, but then do nothing else to create an environment in which employees know the employer cares about stopping harassment and punishing those who engage in it — it is doubtful that the metric on its own will have much effect. If an employer has a policy clearly prohibiting harassment that is mentioned consistently at every possible employee gathering, but does not have a system that protects those who complain about harassment from retaliation, the policy itself will do little good. It is not that policies and metrics are not important. To the contrary, they are essential components of a harassment prevention effort. But holistic refers to the whole system. Every activity must come together in an integrated manner to create an organizational culture that will prevent harassment.

B. Policies and Procedures

Policies, reporting procedures, investigations, and corrective actions are essential components of the holistic effort that employers must engage in to prevent harassment. In this section, we set forth what we have learned about how to make each of these components as successful as possible.

Anti-Harassment Policies

An organization needs a stated policy against harassment that sets forth the behaviors that will not be accepted in the workplace and the procedures to follow in reporting and responding to harassment. Employees in workplaces without policies report the highest levels of harassment.

EEOC's position, which after our study we believe remains sound, is that employers should adopt a robust anti-harassment policy, regularly train each employee on its contents, and vigorously follow and enforce the policy. EEOC recommends that a policy generally include:

- A clear explanation of prohibited conduct, including examples;

- Clear assurance that employees who make complaints or provide information related to complaints, witnesses, and others who participate in the investigation will be protected against retaliation;

- A clearly described complaint process that provides multiple, accessible avenues of complaint;
- Assurance that the employer will protect the confidentiality of harassment complaints to the extent possible;
- A complaint process that provides a prompt, thorough, and impartial investigation; and
- Assurance that the employer will take immediate and proportionate corrective action when it determines that harassment has occurred, and respond appropriately to behavior which may not be legally-actionable "harassment" but which, left unchecked, may lead to same.

An employer's policy should be written in clear, simple words, in all the languages used in the workplace. The points we note above describe the content of an effective policy, but the words of the policy itself should be simple and easy to understand. Similarly, an effective policy should make clear that harassment on the basis of any protected characteristic will not be tolerated.

It is also not sufficient simply to have a written policy, even one written in the most user-friendly fashion. The policy must be communicated on a regular basis to employees, particularly information about how to file a complaint or how to report harassment that one observes, and how an employee who files a complaint or an employee who reports harassment or participates in an investigation of alleged harassment will be protected from retaliation.

Finally, we urge employers who may read this and conclude that their policies are currently effective and in line with EEOC's recommendations to consider this report as an opportunity to take a fresh and critical look at their current processes and consider whether a "reboot" is necessary or valuable. Appendix B includes a checklist for an effective harassment prevention policy.[36]

Social Media

An additional wrinkle for employers to consider, as they write and update anti-harassment policies, is the proliferation of employees' social media use. The Pew Research Center recently found that 65% of all adults—90% of those 18–29 year olds, 77% of those 30–49—use social media. Safe to say, employers can expect a time when virtually the entirety of their workforce is using social media.

Arguably, the use of social media among employees in a workplace can be a net positive. As noted by a witness at the Commission's 2014 meeting on social media, social media use in the workplace can create a space for "less formal and more frequent communications." Via social media, employees can share information about themselves, learn about and understand better their colleagues, and engage each

---

36. Appendix B is not included here but is available in the original document.

others' personal experiences through photos, comments, and the like. If this leads to improved work relationships and collegiality, social media can benefit a workplace.

Unfortunately, social media can also foster toxic interactions. Nearly daily, news reports reflect that, for whatever reasons, many use social media to attack and harass others.

During the Commission meeting on social media, witnesses talked about social media as a possible means of workplace harassment. For that reason, harassment should be in employers' minds as they draft social media policies and, conversely, social media issues should be in employers' minds as they draft anti-harassment policies.

For example, an anti-harassment policy should make clear that mistreatment on social media carries the weight of any other workplace interaction. Supervisors and others with anti-harassment responsibilities should be wary of their social media connections with employees. And, procedures for investigating harassment should carefully delineate how to access an employee's social media content when warranted.

In context, social media — specifically its use in the workplace — is relatively new. Plus, it seemingly changes at an exponential pace. For now, however, the constant for employers is that social media platforms are potential vehicles for workplace-related interactions. And wherever that exists, employers must be aware that harassment may occur.

"Zero Tolerance" Policies

Finally, we have a caution to offer with regard to use of the phrase "a 'zero tolerance' anti-harassment policy." We heard from several witnesses that use of the term "zero tolerance" is misleading and potentially counterproductive. Accountability requires that discipline for harassment be proportionate to the offensiveness of the conduct. For example, sexual assault or a demand for sexual favors in return for a promotion should presumably result in termination of an employee; the continued use of derogatory gender-based language after an initial warning might result in a suspension; and the first instance of telling a sexist joke may warrant a warning. Although not intended as such, the use of the term "zero tolerance" may inappropriately convey a one-size-fits-all approach, in which every instance of harassment brings the same level of discipline. This, in turn, may contribute to employee underreporting of harassment, particularly where they do not want a colleague or coworker to lose their job over relatively minor harassing behavior — they simply want the harassment to stop. Thus, while it is important for employers to communicate that absolutely no harassment will be permitted in the workplace, we do not endorse the term "zero tolerance" to convey that message.

Reporting Systems for Harassment; Investigations; Corrective Actions

Effective reporting systems for allegations of harassment are among the most critical elements of a holistic anti-harassment effort. A reporting system includes a means by which individuals who have experienced harassment can report the harassment and file a complaint, as well as a means by which employees who have observed harassment can report that to the employer.

Ultimately, how an employee who reports harassment (either directly experienced or observed) fares under the employer's process will depend on how management and its representatives act during the process. If the process does not work well, it can make the overall situation in the workplace worse. If one employee reports harassment and has a bad experience using the system, one can presume that the next employee who experiences harassment will think twice before doing the same. Finally, ensuring that the process that commences following a report is fair to an individual accused of harassment contributes to all employees' faith in the system.

For employers that have a unionized workplace, the role of the union in the employer's reporting system is significant. If union representatives take reports of harassment seriously, and support complainants and witnesses during the process, that will make a difference in how employees who are union members view the system. Similarly, because unions have obligations towards all union members, the union must work with the employer to have a system that works in a fair manner for any individual accused of harassment.

There is a significant body of research establishing the many concerns that employees have with current reporting systems in their workplaces. In response to some of those concerns, we heard broad support for reporting systems that are multifaceted, including a choice of procedures, and choices among multiple "complaint handlers." Such a robust reporting system might include options to file complaints with managers and human resource departments, via multi-lingual complaint hotlines, and via web-based complaint processing. In addition, a multi-faceted system might offer an employee who complains about harassment various mechanisms for addressing the situation, depending on the type of conduct and workplace situation. For example, an employee may simply need someone in authority to talk to the harasser in order to stop the behavior. In other situations, the employer may need to do an immediate intervention and begin a thorough investigation.

Of course, the operational needs and resources of small businesses, start-up ventures, and the like, will differ significantly from large, established employers with dedicated human capital systems or "C Suites" of senior leadership. But the principle of offering an accessible and well-running reporting system remains the same.

As noted in the previous section, a safe and timely reporting system that operates well also communicates to employees the leadership's commitment to the words it has set forth in its anti-harassment policy. We heard some innovative ideas for making that commitment clear. One witness described a company that established a small internal group of key "C-Suite" personnel who were informed immediately regarding any harassment complaint (unless a conflict of interest existed). The small group of senior leaders was then regularly updated regarding investigation outcomes and prevention analysis. In a smaller business, this "group of senior leaders" may be the business's owner or the highest-ranking members of management.

We heard strong support for the proposition that workplace investigations should be kept as confidential as is possible, consistent with conducting a thorough and effective investigation. We heard also, however, that an employer's ability to maintain confidentiality—specifically, to request that witnesses and others involved in a harassment investigation keep all information confidential—has been limited in some instances by decisions of the National Labor Relations Board ("NLRB") relating to the rights of employees to engage in concerted, protected activity under the National Labor Relations Act ("NLRA"). In light of the concerns we have heard, we recommend that EEOC and NLRB confer and consult in a good faith effort to determine what conflicts may exist, and as necessary, work together to harmonize the interplay of federal EEO laws and the NLRA.

Based on what we have learned over the last year, we believe there are several elements that will make reporting systems work well and will provide employees with faith in the system. These are largely consistent with the recommendations made above regarding the content of an effective anti-harassment policy:

- Employees who receive harassment complaints must take the complaints seriously.

- The reporting system must provide timely responses and investigations.

- The system must provide a supportive environment where employees feel safe to express their views and do not experience retribution.

- The system must ensure that investigators are well-trained, objective, and neutral, especially where investigators are internal company employees.

- The privacy of both the accuser and the accused should be protected to the greatest extent possible, consistent with legal obligations and conducting a thorough, effective investigation.

- Investigators should document all steps taken from the point of first contact, prepare a written report using guidelines to weigh credibility, and communicate the determination to all relevant parties.

The bottom line, however, is that we need better empirical evidence on what type of reporting systems are effective. Many witnesses told us it would be extraordinarily valuable for employers to allow researchers into their workplaces to conduct empirical studies to determine what makes a reporting system effective. We agree with that suggestion, although we are cognizant of the concerns that employers may have in welcoming researchers into their domains. For example, we recognize that employers will want to have control over how data derived from its workplace will be used, and equally important, not used.

In light of what we have learned in this area, we offer the following recommendations:

- Employers should adopt and maintain a comprehensive anti-harassment policy (which prohibits harassment based on any protected characteristic, and which includes social media considerations) and should establish procedures consistent with the principles discussed in this report.

- Employers should ensure that the anti-harassment policy, and in particular details about how to complain of harassment and how to report observed harassment, are communicated frequently to employees, in a variety of forms and methods.

- Employers should offer reporting procedures that are multi-faceted, offering a range of methods, multiple points-of-contact, and geographic and organizational diversity where possible, for an employee to report harassment.

- Employers should be alert for any possibility of retaliation against an employee who reports harassment and should take steps to ensure that such retaliation does not occur.

- Employers should periodically "test" their reporting system to determine how well the system is working.

- Employers should devote sufficient resources so that workplace investigations are prompt, objective, and thorough. Investigations should be kept as confidential as possible, recognizing that complete confidentiality or anonymity will not always be attainable.

- EEOC and the National Labor Relations Board should confer, consult, and attempt to jointly clarify and harmonize the interplay of the National Labor Relations Act and federal EEO statutes with regard to the permissible confidentiality of workplace investigations, and the permissible scope of policies regulating workplace social media usage.

- Employers should ensure that where harassment is found to have occurred, discipline is prompt and proportionate to the behavior(s) at issue and the severity of the infraction. Employers should ensure that discipline is consistent, and does not give (or create the appearance of) undue favor to any particular employee.

- In unionized workplaces, the labor union should ensure that its own policy and reporting system meet the principles outlined in this section.

- EEOC should, as a best practice in cases alleging harassment, seek as a term of its settlement agreements, conciliation agreements, and consent decrees, that any policy and any complaint or investigative procedures implemented to resolve an EEOC charge or lawsuit satisfy the elements of the policy, reporting system, investigative procedures, and corrective actions outlined above.

- EEOC should, as a best practice in cases alleging harassment, seek as part of its settlement agreements, conciliation agreements, and consent decrees, an agreement that researchers will be allowed to work with the employer in assessing the impact and efficacy of the policies, reporting systems, investigative procedures, and corrective actions put into place by that employer. While we encourage EEOC to seek such an agreement when appropriate, we do not suggest that the agency must do so in all instances, or that failure to obtain such an agreement should derail otherwise acceptable settlement proposals.

- Groups of employers should consider coming together to offer researchers access to their workplaces to research the effectiveness of their policies, reporting systems, investigative procedures, and corrective actions put into place by those employers, in a manner that would allow research data to be aggregated in a manner that would not identify individual employers.

C. Anti-Harassment Compliance Training

There are many reasons why employers offer anti-harassment trainings. Employers who care deeply about stopping harassment use training as a mechanism to do so. After EEOC's 1980 guidelines suggested methods for preventing sexual harassment, many employers started to offer training as one of those methods. Trainings got a boost after the Supreme Court's decisions in *Ellerth* and *Faragher* provided employers an incentive to demonstrate they had taken appropriate steps to prevent harassment. Finally, requiring employers to put training into place is a staple of the conciliation agreements and consent decrees that EEOC and private plaintiff attorneys negotiate every year. California and Connecticut have mandated such training for employers with 50 or more supervisors, and Maine has mandated such training for employers with 15 or more supervisors.

Given the amount of resources employers devote to training, and the fact that training is one of the primary mechanisms used to prevent harassment, we explored whether training is effective in preventing harassment, and if so, whether there are some forms of training that have better outcomes than others.

We came to two overarching conclusions:

- There are deficiencies in almost all the empirical studies done to date on the effectiveness of training standing alone. Hence, empirical data does not permit us to make declarative statements about whether training, standing alone, is or is not an effective tool in preventing harassment.

- The deficiencies notwithstanding, based on the practical and anecdotal evidence we heard from employers and trainers, we conclude that training is an essential component of an anti-harassment effort. However, to be effective in stopping harassment, such training cannot stand alone but rather must be part of a holistic effort undertaken by the employer to prevent harassment that includes the elements of leadership and accountability described above. In addition, the training must have specific goals and must contain certain components to achieve those goals.

Research on the Effectiveness of Training

Witnesses who provided testimony to the Select Task Force, and our own reading of the literature, exposed the problems of the empirical evidence to date regarding the effectiveness of training programs standing alone.

First, most of the studies use researcher-designed training, and each of those trainings has different content, lengths, and leaders. It is hard to know if something works when the "what" that you are studying is not the same.

Second, our research (which was thorough, if admittedly not an exhaustive review of all literature over the past three decades) discovered only two studies based on large-scale evaluations of anti-harassment training designed by employers (not researchers) that were given to a significant number of employees who were taking the trainings in their actual workplaces. A set of studies, conducted in the late 1990s by Professor Magley and her colleagues, evaluated trainings at two large employers—a large regulated utility with one location and a large agribusiness with several worksites. Another study, published in 2001 by Professors Bingham and Scherer, evaluated an anti-sexual harassment program provided to employees at a medium-sized university.

Third, because it is difficult for researchers to gain access to workplaces to study (which is why there are so few research studies of this kind), many researchers design experiments using student-volunteer samples or other small volunteer samples in organizational settings. In many studies, the researchers survey participants pre- and post-training and evaluate the effectiveness of the training based on self-reported answers immediately following the training. These studies are not to be discounted, but their limitations must be acknowledged.

Finally, all of the evidence regarding the effectiveness of training is based on studies of sexual harassment training, not general harassment training.

What can we learn from these studies, limited as they are?

First, it appears that training can increase the ability of attendees to understand the type of conduct that is considered harassment and hence unacceptable in the workplace. The most interesting study in this regard was of federal employees. Rather than conducting a large-scale evaluation of a particular training, researchers compared results from the three surveys done by the Merit Systems Protection Board of federal employees over the course of a decade and a half—in 1980, 1987, and 1994. Their analysis found that participation in training was associated with an increased probability, particularly for men, of considering unwanted sexual gestures, remarks, touching, and pressure for dates to be a form of sexual harassment. The training seemed particularly successful in clarifying for men that unwanted sexual behavior from co-workers, and not just from supervisors, can be a form of sexual harassment.

Ensuring that employees know what an employer considers to be harassment is obviously an essential element for effective implementation of an employer's anti-harassment policy. In the 2001 study by Professors Bingham and Scherer of a 30-minute training, participants demonstrated more knowledge about sexual harassment than those who had not participated in the training. In the 1997 study by Professor Magley and her colleagues, some attendees of the trainings (but not all) evidenced increased knowledge of sexual harassment. Given that Hispanic employees in that study did not evidence increased knowledge, the researchers observed that culturally-appropriate training might have made a difference. Other studies also suggest that trainings have a positive impact on knowledge acquisition.

Second, it is less probable that training programs, on their own, will have a significant impact on changing employees' attitudes, and they may sometimes have the opposite effect. The 2001 study by Professors Bingham and Scherer evaluated a 30-minute training focused on sensitizing attendees to sexual harassment. Men who completed the training were more likely to say that sexual behavior at work was wrong, but they were also more likely to believe that both parties contribute to inappropriate sexual behavior. Other experiments indicate that participants who come into the training with more of a tendency to harass or with gender role conflicts (based on questionnaires completed prior to the training) are more likely to have a negative reaction to the training.

In the 1997 study conducted by Professor Magley and her colleagues, there was no evidence of any backlash to the trainings. However, the personal attitudes of participants toward sexual harassment were minimally changed or completely unchanged. Finally, a few lab-based experiments have shown some positive effects on attitudes or behaviors following training.

Third, in the study by Professor Magley and her colleagues (the only study to test for this result), there was no evidence that the training affected the frequency of sexual harassment experienced by the women in the workplace or the perception by women that certain sexual conduct was sexual harassment. However, on the positive side, complaints to the human resources department did increase after the training. The researchers postulated that the increase was the result of a multi-faceted approach taken by the employer and not the result of the training alone. For example, prior to the training, the employer had provided employees with a number of additional resources to lodge complaints (including hotlines) and had begun improving its procedures for complaint follow-up.

As Professor Magley and her colleagues have pointed out, a common theme among the research studies is that effective training does not occur within a vacuum. Researchers have suggested a range of ideas for creating harassment-free and supportive work environments in which non-training factors are included together with training.

In sum, the existing empirical evidence is conflicting and sometimes surprising. It leaves us with a few conclusions:

- Many anti-harassment trainings offered today seek to achieve two goals — give employees information about the employer's anti-harassment policy (including how to file complaints) and change employees' attitudes about what type of behaviors in the workplace are wrong.

- The limited empirical data we have to date indicates that training can increase knowledge about what conduct the employer considers unacceptable in the workplace. In particular, training may help men understand that certain forms of sexual conduct are unwelcome and offensive to women.

- The limited empirical data we have to date indicates that sensitivity training (as currently done) in some instances might be mildly positive, often is neutral, and in some circumstances actually may be counterproductive.

- It is possible that individuals who receive training may be more likely to file a complaint, if the training does not stand alone and the employer has taken other steps to convince employees that the employer will be intolerant of sexual harassment.

We cautioned above, and we caution again, that the results of these studies implicate only the effectiveness of the specific trainings that were evaluated. The data cannot be extrapolated to support general conclusions about the effectiveness of training.

. . . .

Experience on the Ground

Regardless of the empirical data from research studies, we heard from practitioners with decades of experience that training — especially compliance training — is a key component of any harassment prevention effort. We also heard that training must have certain components to be successful. We provide below the insights we learned from these practitioners.

Compliance Training for All Employees

Compliance training is training that helps employers comply with the legal requirements of employment non-discrimination laws by educating employees about what forms of conduct are not acceptable in the workplace and about which they have the right to complain. We do not believe that such trainings should be limited to the legal definition of harassment. Rather the trainings should also describe conduct that, if left unchecked, might rise to the level of illegal harassment. For example, some instances of gender-based harassment or sexually-motivated harassment will be legally actionable only if they are sufficiently pervasive to create a hostile work environment, as defined by the law. But compliance training should focus on the unacceptable behaviors themselves, rather than trying to teach participants the specific legal standards that will make such conduct "illegal." In addition, compliance training should explain the consequences of engaging in conduct that is unacceptable in the workplace, including that corrective action will be proportionate to the severity of the conduct.

Compliance training that teaches employees what conduct is not acceptable in the workplace should not be a canned, "one-size-fits-all" training. Effective compliance trainings are those that are tailored to the specific realities of different workplaces. Using examples and scenarios that realistically involve situations from the specific worksite, organization, and/or industry makes the compliance training work much better than if the examples are foreign to the workforce. In addition, depending on the makeup of the workforce, employers may wish to consider conducting training in multiple languages, or providing for different learning styles and levels of education.

Compliance training should also clarify what conduct is not harassment and is therefore acceptable in the workplace. For example, it is not harassment for a supervisor to tell an employee that he or she is not performing a job adequately. Of course, the supervisor may not treat employees who are similar in their work performance differently because of an employee's protected characteristic. But telling an employee that she must arrive to work on time, or telling an employee that he must submit his work in a timely fashion, is not harassment. Nor do we suggest that occasional and innocuous compliments—"I like your jacket"—constitute workplace harassment, but rather reflect the reality of human experience and common courtesy.

Compliance training should also educate employees about their rights and responsibilities if they experience conduct that the employer has stated is not acceptable in the workplace. Again, the training need not focus on legal issues regarding notice and liability. Rather, the training should make clear to employees the (hopefully) multiple avenues offered by the employer to report unwelcome conduct based on a protected characteristic, regardless of whether the individual might or might not describe that conduct as "harassment." Compliance training should also describe, in simple terms, how an employee who witnesses harassment can report that information.

Finally, compliance training should describe, in simple terms, how the formal complaint process will proceed. This includes information on how an investigation will take place and what confidentiality a complainant can expect. The training should make clear that the employer will take all reports seriously, investigate them in a timely fashion, and ensure that complainants or those who report observing harassment will not experience retaliation for using the reporting system. (Of course, for participants to believe this, the employer's reporting system must indeed operate in this fashion).

Compliance Training for Middle-Management and First-Line Supervisors

All employees need the compliance training described above. But managers and supervisors need additional training if the employer wants to address conduct before it rises to the level of illegal harassment and wants to ensure compliance with employment non-discrimination laws.

As noted previously, to create an organizational culture in which employees believe that the organization will not tolerate harassment, managers, and supervisors must receive clear messages of accountability. Compliance training translates those expectations into concrete actions that managers and supervisors are expected to take—either to prevent harassment or to stop and remedy harassment once it occurs.

Compliance training provides managers and supervisors with easy-to-understand and realistic methods for dealing with harassment that they observe, that is reported to them, or of which they have knowledge or information. This includes practical suggestions on how to respond to different levels and types of offensive behavior, and clear instructions on how to report harassing behavior up the chain of command. It should also stress the affirmative duties of supervisors to respond to harassing behavior, even in the absence of a complaint. Again, this training should be tailored to the specific worksite, organization, and/or industry, so that the examples used are helpful to managers and supervisors.

Managers and supervisors are the heart of an employer's prevention system. As one witness with decades of experience in the practice of workplace training and investigation noted succinctly:

> If I had limited assets to improve the climate of any organization, I would invest ninety-five percent of them in middle managers. These are the people who make all of the difference in the day-to-day lives of organizations and people. When we train middle managers, we don't just train them about how to spot and address problem behavior—we teach them empirically sound things to do and say when an employee seeks them out to discuss a problem.

What we set forth above concerns the content of effective compliance training. There are also principles for the structure of successful compliance trainings.

- *Training should be supported at the highest levels.* As noted previously, employees must believe that the leadership is serious about preventing harassment in the workplace. Training alone is not sufficient to establish the credibility of the leadership in this regard—but compliance training provides a moment at which the focus is on achieving this goal and thus, leadership should take advantage of that moment. The strongest expression of support is for a senior leader to open the training session and attend the entire training session. At a minimum, a video of a senior leader might be shown at the beginning of the training and a memo from leadership to all employees sent prior to the training can underscore the importance and purpose of the training. Similarly, if all employees at every level of the organization are trained, that both increases the effectiveness of the training and communicates the employer's commitment of time and resources to the training effort.

- *Training should be conducted and reinforced on a regular basis for all employees.* Again, as we noted earlier, employees understand that an organization's devotion of time and resources to any effort reflects the organization's commitment to that effort. Training is no different. If anti-harassment trainings are held once a year (or once every other year), employees will not believe that preventing harassment is a high priority for the employer. Conversely, if anti-harassment trainings are regularly scheduled events in which key information is reinforced, that will send the message that the goal of the training is important. While this is one area where, in general, repetition is a good thing, we caution against simply repeating the same training over and over, which risks becoming a rote exercise. Rather, we urge employers to consider training that is varied and dynamic in style, form, and content.

- *Training should be conducted by qualified, live, and interactive trainers.* Live trainers who are dynamic, engaging, and have full command of the subject matter are the most likely to deliver effective training. Since one of the goals of compliance training is to provide employees information about the type of conduct the employer finds unacceptable in the workplace, it is important for a trainer to provide examples of such conduct, or have individuals portray scenarios of such conduct, and then be able to answer questions. In addition, compliance training teaches supervisors and managers how to respond to a report or observance of harassment. These can be difficult situations and a live trainer is most suited to work through questions with the participants. For some employers, however, providing live trainers will not be feasible because they are cost prohibitive or because employees are physically dispersed. In such cases, online or video-based trainings should still be tailored to specific workplaces and workforces and should be designed to include active engagement by participants.

- *Training should be routinely evaluated.* Employers should obviously not keep doing something that does not work. Trainers should not only do the training, but should evaluate the results of the training, as well. By this, we mean more than handing a questionnaire to participants immediately after the training asking if they found the training to be helpful. Evaluations are most effective if they are done some time after the training and participants are asked questions such as whether the training changed their own behaviors or behaviors they have observed in the workplace. The evaluation should occur on a regular basis so that the training can be modified, if need be. Similarly, training evaluation should incorporate feedback from all levels of an organization, most notably, the rank-and-file employees who are being trained, lest "evaluation" becomes a senior leadership "echo chamber."

Based on our year of examination—and cognizant of the limitations of empirical, academic data—we still conclude that effective compliance training is a necessary tool to prevent harassment in the workplace. Every employer should have in place, at a minimum, compliance training that includes the content and structure described above. However, since compliance training only goes so far, the following section presents additional ideas for training that may help the holistic effort of preventing harassment in a workplace.

In light of what we have learned in this area, we make the following recommendations:

- Employers should offer, on a regular basis and in a universal manner, compliance trainings that include the content and follow the structural principles described in this report, and which are offered on a dynamic and repeated basis to all employees.

- Employers should dedicate sufficient resources to train middle-management and first-line supervisors on how to respond effectively to harassment that they observe, that is reported to them, or of which they have knowledge or information — even before such harassment reaches a legally-actionable level.

- EEOC should, as a best practice in cases alleging harassment, seek as a term of its settlement agreements, conciliation agreements, and consent decrees, that employers adopt and maintain compliance training that comports with the content and follows the structural principles described in this report.

- EEOC should, as a best practice in cases alleging harassment, seek as a condition of its settlement agreements, conciliation agreements, and consent decrees, an agreement that researchers will be allowed to work with the employer to assess the climate and level of harassment in respondent workplaces pre- and post-implementation of compliance trainings, and to study the impact and efficacy of specific training components. Where possible, this research should focus not only on the efficacy of training in large organizations, but also smaller employers and newer or "start up" firms. While we encourage EEOC to seek such an agreement when appropriate, we do not suggest that the agency must do so in all instances, or that failure to obtain such an agreement should derail otherwise acceptable settlement proposals.

- Groups of employers should consider coming together to offer researchers access to their workplaces to research the effectiveness of trainings, particularly in the context of holistic harassment prevention efforts, in a manner that would allow research data to be aggregated and not identify individual employers.

- EEOC should compile a resource guide for employers that contains checklists and training modules for compliance trainings.

- EEOC should review and update, consistent with the recommendations contained in this report, its anti-harassment compliance training modules used for Technical Assistance Seminars, Customer Specific Trainings, trainings for Federal agencies, and other outreach and education programs.

D. Workplace Civility and Bystander Intervention Training

Employees need to know what conduct is unacceptable in the workplace (whether or not they might describe such conduct as harassment), and managers and supervisors need effective tools to respond to observation or reports of harassment. But regardless of the level of knowledge in a workplace, we know from the research that organizational culture is one of the key drivers of harassment. We therefore explored trainings that might have an impact on shaping organizational cultures in a way that would prevent harassment in a workplace.

Among the trainings we explored, two stood out for us as showing significant promise for preventing harassment in the workplace: (1) workplace civility training; and (2) bystander intervention training.

Workplace civility training is not new to the workplace. Many employers have put such trainings into place, often in response to concerns about bullying or conflict in the workplace. Bystander intervention training, by contrast, is not prevalent in workplaces. Such training has proliferated in recent years in colleges and high schools as a means of stopping sexual assault. We hope the information presented in this report will encourage employers to consider implementing these trainings as a means of preventing workplace harassment.

Workplace Civility Training

Employers have offered workplace civility training as a means of reducing bullying or conflict in the workplace. Thus, such training does not focus on eliminating unwelcome behavior based on characteristics protected under employment non-discrimination laws, but rather on promoting respect and civility in the workplace generally.

According to researchers, incivility is often an antecedent to workplace harassment, as it creates a climate of "general derision and disrespect" in which harassing behaviors are tolerated. For example, in studies of attorneys and court employees, researchers found significant correlations between incivility and gender harassment. Researchers also have found that uncivil behaviors can often "spiral" into harassing behaviors.

Incivility can also sometimes represent covert manifestations of gender and racial bias on the job. In other words, facially neutral, uncivil behaviors may actually be rooted in animus against members of a protected class and may subtly contribute to a hostile work environment. We fully recognize that Title VII was not meant, and should not be read, to be "a general civility code for the American workplace."[37] But promoting civility and respect in a workplace may be a means of preventing conduct from rising to the level of unlawful harassment.

Workplace civility trainings focus on establishing expectations of civility and respect in the workplace, and on providing management and employees the tools they need to meet such expectations. The training usually includes an exploration of workplace norms, including a discussion of what constitutes appropriate and inappropriate behaviors in the workplace. The training also includes a heavily skills-based component, including interpersonal skills training, conflict resolution training, and training on effective supervisory techniques.

---

37. Oncale v. Sundowner Offshore Services, 523 U.S. 75 (1998).

The beauty of workplace civility training is that it is focused on the positive—what employees and managers should do, rather than on what they should not do. In addition, by appealing to all individuals in the workplace, regardless of social identity or perceived proclivity to harass, civility training might avoid some of the resistance met by interventions exclusively targeting harassment.

We heard some concern that a focus on workplace civility might reinforce stereotypes (e.g., that women need to be treated with special care and concern). Empirical data to support this concern appears lacking. In contrast, there is some empirical data (and many anecdotes) to support the effectiveness of civility training in enhancing workplace cultures of respect that are subsequently incompatible with harassment.

Workplace civility training has not been rigorously evaluated as a harassment prevention tool per se, but we believe that such training could provide an important complement to the compliance training described in the previous section. Moreover, it would be helpful to have additional research on the possible effects of workplace civility training in reducing the level of workplace harassment based on EEO protected characteristics.

Finally, we recognize that broad workplace "civility codes" which may be read to limit or restrict certain forms of speech may raise issues under the NLRA, which is outside of the jurisdiction of EEOC. In light of that potential tension, we recommend that EEOC and NLRB confer and consult, and attempt to jointly clarify and harmonize the interplay of the NLRA and the federal EEO statutes.

Bystander Intervention Training

Bystander intervention training has long been used as a violence prevention strategy, and it has become increasingly utilized by colleges and high schools to prevent sexual assault. The training has been shown to change social norms and empower students to intervene with peers to prevent assaults from occurring. Most bystander intervention trainings employ at least four strategies:

- Create awareness—enable bystanders to recognize potentially problematic behaviors.
- Create a sense of collective responsibility—motivate bystanders to step in and take action when they observe problematic behaviors.
- Create a sense of empowerment—conduct skills-building exercises to provide bystanders with the skills and confidence to intervene as appropriate.
- Provide resources—provide bystanders with resources they can call upon and that support their intervention.

One organization that provides training on campuses, Green Dot, creates a sense of empowerment by focusing its training on "three D's:" (1) confront the potential perpetrator of sexual assault in a direct manner, and ask the person to cease the behavior; (2) distract the potential perpetrator of sexual assault, and remove the potential victim; or (3) delegate the problem to someone who has the authority to intervene.

We believe that bystander intervention training might be effective in the workplace. Such training could help employees identify unwelcome and offensive behavior that is based on a co-workers' protected characteristic under employment non-discrimination laws; could create a sense of responsibility on the part of employees to "do something" and not simply stand by; could give employees the skills and confidence to intervene in some manner to stop harassment; and finally, could demonstrate the employer's commitment to empowering employees to act in this manner. Bystander training also affords employers an opportunity to underscore their commitment to non-retaliation by making clear that any employee who "steps up" to combat harassment will be protected from negative repercussions.

The founder of Green Dot told us that, although the training was originally applied to the reduction of sexual assault, domestic violence, and stalking, she believed the training framework could be successfully applied to harassment in the workplace. Similarly, a few researchers have explored the potential of using bystander intervention training in the workplace, and they are encouraged by the possibilities. The studies caution, however, that suggested bystander responses must be crafted for use in the typical situations in which workplace harassment takes place. In addition, the organizational culture must encourage and support bystander intervention and reporting, and provide a safe system in which bystanders may do so.

As with workplace civility training, more research is needed to determine the effectiveness of bystander intervention training as a workplace harassment prevention measure. But we believe such training has real potential to positively impact organizational culture. We know that most co-workers are not comfortable when harassment occurs around them, even when they are not the direct victims of the harassment. Bystander training could teach co-workers how to recognize potentially problematic behaviors; motivate and empower employees to step in and take action; teach employees skills to intervene appropriately; and give them resources to support their intervention.

Organizational culture starts from the top. But reinforcing that culture can and must come from the bottom, middle, and everywhere else in between. Bystander intervention training provides that reinforcement in a particularly concrete manner.

Case Study: Green Dot in Anchorage, Alaska

"Green Dot" is a violence prevention program focused on providing bystanders with the strategies and techniques they need to: (1) identify situations that can lead to acts of violence (represented on incident maps by a red dot); and (2) intervene safely and effectively. A "green dot" represents "any behavior, choice, word, or attitude that promotes safety . . . and communicates utter intolerance for violence." The goal is to have sufficient positive interventions such that the green dots totally overwhelm the red dots.

The city of Anchorage, Alaska received a grant to implement the Green Dot program at the community level, including at bars and restaurants. When discussing early warning signs of violence, bar and restaurant groups often shared examples where violent or potentially violent behaviors were happening to staff. Examples ranged from intoxicated patrons violating physical boundaries of servers to discussions of bar cultures that accepted or even encouraged some levels of harassment of staff by customers—all in the spirit of keeping the party atmosphere going and the drinks and tips flowing.

As a result of the Green Dot training, bar and restaurant owners in Anchorage began to develop new cultural norms. They hosted trainings, developed policies, included relevant messaging in their signs and bulletins, and engaged in a host of creative ideas such as Green Dot trivia, contests, and competitions. Both staff and patrons acquired new skills to respond to potential harassment or violence.

Based on what we have learned in this area, we offer the following recommendations:

- Employers should consider including workplace civility training and bystander intervention training as part of a holistic harassment prevention program.

- EEOC and the National Labor Relations Board should confer, consult, and attempt to jointly clarify and harmonize the interplay of the National Labor Relations Act and federal EEO statutes with regard to the permissible content of workplace "civility codes."

- Researchers should assess the impact of workplace civility training on reducing the level of harassment in the workplace.

- EEOC should convene a panel of experts on sexual assault bystander intervention training to develop and evaluate a bystander intervention training module for reducing harassment in the workplace.

- EEOC should, as a best practice in cases alleging harassment, seek as part of its settlement agreements, conciliation agreements, and consent decrees, an agreement that researchers will be allowed to work with the employer in assessing the efficacy of workplace civility training and/or bystander intervention training on reducing the level of harassment in the workplace. While we encourage EEOC to seek such an agreement when appropriate, we do not suggest that the agency must do so in all instances, or that failure to obtain such an agreement should derail otherwise acceptable settlement proposals.

- Groups of employers should consider coming together to offer researchers access to their workplaces to research the effectiveness of workplace civility and bystander intervention trainings in a manner that would allow research data to be aggregated and not identify individual employers.

E. Getting The Word Out

We spent a significant amount of time discussing outreach and education with the Select Task Force members and witnesses. Outreach is needed for workers, employers, and the general public. On-the-job, employer-sponsored training is one form of outreach and education for employees. In this section, we highlight a number of other approaches worthy of consideration.

Getting the Word Out: Providing Simple and Easy-to-Access Information

There is a significant amount of information regarding workplace harassment available on the web. But information on the web can be overwhelming and is not always correct. This is a problem for both employers (especially small business employers with limited resources) and employees.

As Jess Kutch, the co-founder and co-director of Coworker.org told us: "[Internet search results] either give very basic advice (sometimes even wrong advice) or they give you dozens of links to deep legalese that wouldn't be helpful for most people." She also noted that very few search results lead to mobile friendly websites, which is problematic because many workers—low-wage workers, in particular—rely on their mobile phones to access information on the internet. Of course, some workers cannot get their information from the internet at all—either because they do not have access to the internet, cannot find sufficient information in their own language if they do not read English, or are not literate.

We also heard a fair amount about the utility of EEOC's resources on the web. Some Select Task Force members felt that EEOC's guidance on harassment was overly legalistic, and with regard to some issues, outdated. In addition, they noted that EEOC's website is neither mobile-friendly nor fully accessible to non-English speakers. One Select Task Force member sought more information on prevention strategies and noted a dearth of user-friendly tools (such as model harassment policies, effective investigation outlines, and promising practices) that could help employers in their efforts to prevent harassment. One witness suggested that EEOC's information on how to file a complaint is difficult to understand, and that the actual process of filing a complaint can be difficult and cumbersome for potential charging parties.

We took all suggestions to heart about what EEOC could do in terms of outreach and education, and a number of our recommendations at the end of this section reflect ideas that we heard. We also recognize the many successful outreach efforts EEOC has done in the past and continues to be engaged in, including the extensive (and highly regarded) outreach training EEOC conducts through its field offices and personnel. EEOC has also made outreach and education for small businesses a priority through its Small Business Task Force, which in 2016 issued a simplified, one-page fact sheet designed to help small business owners better understand their responsibilities under the federal employment anti-discrimination laws.

But we wanted to expand our ideas beyond what EEOC might do. To reach all the people who need to be reached, we need more than just one (or even several) government agencies involved in the effort.

The good news is that many non-profit organizations are using innovative mechanisms to get the word out. For example, as we described above, the Fair Food

618 · 10 · THE FUTURE: #METOO AND LEGAL REFORM

Program, run by the Coalition of Imokalee Workers in Florida, has developed educational materials created by farmworkers themselves. With these materials, the Coalition of Imokalee Workers provides in-person worker-to-worker education on worker rights at all farms that participate in the Fair Food Program.

Similarly, ROC-LA, a restaurant worker center in Los Angeles, California, provides "know your rights" trainings both individually and to groups. The trainings focus on real-life application of employee rights, including protection from retaliation and the importance of gathering evidence in cases of harassment. ROC-LA also provides a free, weekly legal clinic for its members and has posted a simple "know your rights" brochure on its website that it is available in English, Spanish, and Chinese.

On the employer side, membership organizations like the Society for Human Resource Management maintain libraries of resources on their websites, and provide webinars and conferences for their members that address a number of employment issues, including prevention of harassment. And of course, there are many conferences, webinars, training programs, and written materials on legal issues concerning harassment.

The Commission is in the process of updating its Enforcement Guidance on Harassment, and we believe it will be a useful guide for employers and employees. Similarly, EEOC's Communications and Outreach Plan proposes upgrading the technology and user experience of EEOC's website, including making its website mobile-friendly and accessible in a number of languages.

There is, however, much more to be done to reach various audiences that would benefit from learning about how to prevent harassment, and how to complain about it or report it when necessary.

Based on what we have learned in this area, we offer the following recommendations:

- EEOC should develop additional resources for its website, including user-friendly guides on workplace harassment for employers and employees, that can be used with mobile devices.

- Non-profit organizations should conduct targeted outreach to employers to explain the business case for strong harassment prevention cultures, policies, and procedures.

- Non-profit organizations (including employee advocacy organizations, business membership associations, and labor unions) should develop easy-to-understand written resources and other creative materials (such as videos, posters, etc.) that will help workers and employers understand their rights and responsibilities.

- EEOC should partner with internet search engines to ensure that a range of EEOC resources appear high on the list of results returned by search engines.

Getting the Word Out to Youth

We heard from a number of Select Task Force members and witnesses that there needs to be explicit and focused outreach to youth, even before they enter the workforce. As one witness explained:

> Students who are about to be in their first-ever work situations need to be informed about (a) their rights to work in an environment free from harassment, intimidation, and /or discrimination, based on race, color, national origin, sex (including sexual orientation and transgender status), disability, and age . . . (b) what conduct is not permitted in the workplace (which may differ somewhat from what is acceptable at school); and (c) what they should do when they see or are subjected to any conduct they believe may be prohibited discrimination or harassment.

Another witness explained that some teenagers and young adults "either are unaware of what constitutes harassment or, given their youth, simply don't care." Select Task Force members and other witnesses stressed the importance of reaching youth before they enter the workforce, so that they understand workplace norms and how they differ from classroom or social norms. We also heard that traditional outreach mechanisms (materials posted on a website, worker centers, conferences, etc.) may not be the most effective in reaching youth, and that more creative approaches are necessary.

We commend the work EEOC has already done, and is continuing to do, in outreach to youth through its Youth@Work initiative. Youth@Work is EEOC's national outreach and education campaign targeted to young workers, which was launched in 2004. Since that launch, EEOC has maintained and periodically updated the campaign. Most recently, in 2016, the agency redesigned the Youth@Work website, made it mobile-friendly, expanded the campaign's social media strategy, and expanded its substantive treatment of a number of developing areas of employment non-discrimination law. We encourage EEOC to continue to make this program current, meaningful, and accessible to youth.

In light of what we have learned in this area, we offer the following recommendations:

- EEOC should continue to update its Youth@Work initiative (including its website) to include more information about harassment.

- Colleges and high schools should incorporate a component on workplace harassment in their school-based anti-bullying and anti-sexual assault efforts.

- EEOC should partner with web-based educational websites, such as Khan Academy or YouTube channels that have a large youth following, to develop content around workplace harassment.

- EEOC should establish a contest in which youth are invited to design their own videos or apps to educate their peers about workplace harassment.

F. It's On Us

Harassment in the workplace will not stop on its own. The ideas noted above are helpful, but ultimately, may not be sufficient. It is on all of us to be part of the fight to stop workplace harassment. We cannot be complacent bystanders and expect our workplace cultures to change on their own.

For this reason, we suggest exploring an It's On Us campaign for the workplace. The It's On Us campaign for colleges and high school campuses is an outgrowth of the White House Task Force to Protect Students from Sexual Assault that recognized the need to change the cultures of educational institutions. The campaign is housed at Civic Nation, a non-profit organization focused on engaging millennials. The It's On Us campaign is premised on the idea that sexual assault is not just about a victim and a perpetrator. It calls upon everyone to do his or her part to be a part of the solution.

As the former leader of the It's On Us campaign explained to us, if students, faculty, and campus staff are passive observers when they see the possibility of sexual assault, they reinforce a culture that tolerates such behavior. But if students, faculty, and campus staff are empowered to be part of the solution to preventing sexual assault, and are given the tools and resources to do so, their role as engaged bystanders will make a significant difference in changing the educational culture.

It would be an audacious goal to launch a similar It's On Us campaign in workplaces across our country—in large and small workplaces, in urban and rural areas. But doing so would transform the problem of workplace harassment from being about targets, harassers, and legal compliance, and make it one in which co-workers, supervisors, clients, and customers all have roles to play in stopping harassment.

The campaign focuses on three core pillars: increasing bystander intervention, defining consent, and creating an environment to support survivors. These pillars can be adjusted to better fit the scope of anti-harassment efforts in the workplace—particularly when it comes to bystander intervention and creating an environment where targets feel comfortable coming forward to report.

We have no illusions that such a campaign would be easy to launch. But witnesses who testified before the Select Task Force believed it was possible to transfer to the workplace the principles of the It's On Us campaign, and the skills that bystanders would need. We agree. If successful, such an effort could pay high dividends in the workplace well beyond the impact of any policy, procedure or compliance training.

An It's On Us campaign for the workplace would require the active engagement of business partners, employee advocacy partners, and ordinary people across the country. But we have a blueprint from the existing It's On Us campaign in the educational setting. The campaign was successful due in large part to its multi-faceted approach of using a wide-scale awareness campaign with a robust local organizing model to engage people both online and offline.

We are not starting from scratch with this idea. But someone has to bring the campaign to the workplace. Why not all of us?

In light of what we have learned in this area, we offer the following one, very big, recommendation:

- EEOC assists in launching an "It's on Us" campaign to end harassment in the workplace.

Notes and Discussion

1. Changing Workplace Culture The EEOC report argues that changing workplace culture is key to ending sexual harassment and emphasizes the importance of leadership and accountability to making these changes. Is this enough? How likely is workplace culture to change in the context of a broader society that sexually objectifies women in the media and that tolerates high rates of sexual assault and street harassment?

2. Compliance versus Diversity and Inclusion The report argues that creating a harassment-free workplace "must not be based on a compliance mindset, and instead must be part of an overall diversity and inclusion strategy." What is a "compliance mindset"? How is a "diversity and inclusion strategy" different?

3. Motivating Employers to Address Sexual Harassment The report argues that real change requires money and time. What factors have persuaded employers to make these investments? What motivated employers to adopt the Fair Food Program protecting farmworkers from sexual harassment?

4. Schools and Title IX Are any of the suggestions in the EEOC report applicable to educational environments? Why or why not?

4. Conclusion

A year after the initial #MeToo revelations, after the fall of hundreds of powerful men in Hollywood, the media, politics, and corporate America,[38] everything had seemingly changed. Women were not only more likely to report abuse, but they were more likely to file lawsuits, and to challenge this behavior and the status quo. EEOC sexual harassment charges increased significantly in fiscal year 2018, up more than 12% from the previous year. The EEOC saw 50% more sexual harassment lawsuits filed in fiscal year 2018 than in the previous year.[39]

In February 2018, one of the architects of sexual harassment law, Catharine MacKinnon, published *The New York Times* op-ed titled "#MeToo Has Done What

---

38. *262 Celebrities, Politicians, CEOs, and Others Who Have Been Accused of Sexual Misconduct Since April 2017*, Vox (Jan. 9, 2019).

39. Press Release, U.S. Equal Emp. Opportunity Comm'n, EEOC Releases Preliminary FY 2018 Sexual Harassment Data (Oct. 4, 2018).

the Law Could Not." MacKinnon argues that decades of sexual harassment litigation has not created real social change. She concludes the op-ed with these words: "But it is #MeToo, this uprising of the formerly disregarded, that has made untenable the assumption that the one who reports sexual abuse is a lying slut, and that is changing everything already. Sexual harassment law prepared the ground, but it is today's movement that is shifting gender hierarchy's tectonic plates."[40]

Shortly after MacKinnon published this op-ed, President Donald Trump nominated Judge Brett Kavanaugh to the United States Supreme Court. When multiple sexual assault allegations surfaced in the days after Kavanaugh's initial hearings, members of Congress and the public demanded public hearings on the allegations. Republican leaders on the Senate Judiciary Committee resisted at first, but eventually allowed just one of Kavanaugh's accusers to testify — Professor Christine Blasey Ford. Having learned from the bad publicity resulting from the Senators' harsh questioning of Anita Hill years before, the 10 white male Republican Senators on the Judiciary Committee (two of whom had been on the committee years before during the Clarence Thomas hearings) hired Arizona sex crimes prosecutor Rachel Mitchell to question Blasey Ford.

Blasey Ford delivered a devastating account of an incident years before when she and Kavanaugh were at a high school party. She testified that he and a friend had pushed her into a bedroom and assaulted her. Kavanaugh denied this and other accusations, describing them as a partisan attack on his character. The Senators, especially Lindsey Graham, expressed extreme indignation on Kavanaugh's behalf that the accusations had been made. After the hearings, mass protests and public pressure led to a limited FBI investigation, but the Senate nevertheless confirmed Kavanaugh to a lifetime position on the U.S. Supreme Court. Clearly, MacKinnon had underestimated the resilience of gender hierarchy in American society.

Just weeks after the hearings, however, women made a historical showing in the mid-term elections, with record-breaking numbers of women winning seats in Congress, state legislatures, and statewide offices. But shortly after the elections, and despite the #MeToo movement, the Department of Education issued Title IX regulations that restricted sexual assault investigations on college campuses.[41]

In the spring of 2019, members of Congress introduced the Bringing an End to Harassment by Enhancing Accountability and Rejecting Discrimination (BE HEARD) in the Workplace Act. The Act would extend federal antidiscrimination law to all employers, no matter the size, as well as to independent contractors and LGBT people. The Act would ban mandatory arbitration clauses and nondisclosure agreements. It would also eliminate the sub-minimum wage for tipped workers and authorize grants for low-income workers to obtain legal resources if they

---

40. Catharine A. MacKinnon, *#MeToo Has Done What the Law Could Not*, N.Y. TIMES (Feb. 4, 2018).

41. Dep't of Educ. Proposed Regulations on Title IX, 34 C.F.R. Part 106, RIN 1870-AA14 (2018).

are harassed. Additionally, the Act would expand the definition of supervisor and clarify what constitutes sexual harassment (now determined under the exceedingly high "severe or pervasive" standard).[42] While this Act has little chance of passage in the near term, it serves as a symbol that some, mostly new members of Congress, recognize that legal reform is critical.

Social change is slow. More than 40 years after feminists gave sexual harassment a name, women still struggle to eradicate sex-based abuse and discrimination. Employers have devised ways around the law. These detours and others, however, are all the more reason to continue the fight for fair and safe workplaces, schools, homes, and streets for all people.

---

42. Vania Leveille & Lenora M. Lapidus, *The BE HEARD Act Will Overhaul Workplace Harassment Laws*, SPEAK FREELY (April 10, 2019).

Table of Names

Index